HUMOR AND THE GOOD LIFE
IN MODERN PHILOSOPHY

HUMOR AND THE GOOD LIFE IN MODERN PHILOSOPHY

SHAFTESBURY, HAMANN, KIERKEGAARD

Lydia B. Amir

Cover: Jan Steen. *The dancing lesson*. 1660–1679. oil on panel. 68.5 × 59 cm (27 × 23.2 in). Amsterdam, Rijksmuseum Amsterdam.

Published by State University of New York Press, Albany

For information, contact State University of New York Press, Albany, NY
www.sunypress.edu

Production by Eileen Nizer
Marketing by Fran Keneston

Library of Congress Cataloging-in-Publication Data

Amir, Lydia.
    Humor and the good life in modern philosophy : Shaftesbury, Hamann, Kierkegaard / Lydia Amir.
        pages cm
    Includes bibliographical references (pages) and index.
    ISBN 978-1-4384-4937-1 (hardcover : alk. paper)
    1. Life. 2. Wit and humor. 3. Shaftesbury, Anthony Ashley Cooper, Earl of, 1671–1713. 4. Hamann, Johann Georg, 1730–1788. 5. Kierkegaard, Søren, 1813–1855. I. Title.

BD435.A58 2014
128—dc23   2013003304

10 9 8 7 6 5 4 3 2 1

CONTENTS

LIST OF ABBREVIATIONS

The following abbreviations are used in the text, followed by page numbers indicated by Arabic numerals. Roman capital letters indicate parts, books or volumes, and Roman lower-case letters indicate chapters.

WORKS BY ANTHONY ASHLEY COOPER SHAFTESBURY

CR: *Characteristics of Men, Manners, Opinions, Times, etc.*, ed. John M. Robertson, in two volumes, 1963

CR3: *Characteristics of Men, Manners, Opinions, Times, etc.*, 6th edition, corrected, in three volumes, 1737

Inquiry: *Inquiry Concerning Virtue or Merit*

Letter: *Letter Concerning Enthusiasm*

Life: *The Life, Unpublished Letters, and Philosophical Regimen of Anthony, Earl of Shaftesbury*

Misc.: *Miscellaneous Reflections on the Preceding Treatises, and other Critical Subjects*

Moralists: *The Moralists, a Philosophical Rhapsody*

P.R.O.: The Shaftesbury Papers in the Public Record Office in at Kew, Surrey.

Essay: *Sensus Communis, an Essay on the Freedom of Wit and Humour*

Soliloquy: *Soliloquy, or Advice to an Author*

WORKS BY SØREN KIERKEGAARD

AC: *Attack upon "Christendom"*

CA: *The Concept of Anxiety*

CD: *Christian Discourses*

CI: *The Concept of Irony with Constant Reference to Socrates*

COR: *The Corsair Affair*

CUP: *Concluding Unscientific Postscript*, edit. and trans. by Howard V. Hong and Edna H. Hong.

CUPL: *Concluding Unscientific Postscript*, trans. by David F. Swenson and Walter Lowrie.

ED: *Edifying Discourses*

EO: *Either/Or*

FSE: *For Self-Examination. Judge For Yourself!*

FT: *Fear and Trembling*

JC: *Johannes Climacus, or De omnibus dubitandum est*

JP: *Journals and Papers*

PA: *The Present Age*

Pap.: *Papirer*

PC: *Practice in Christianity*

PF: *Philosophical Fragments*

PV: *The Point of View for My Work as an Author*

R: *Repetition*

SLW: *Stages on Life's Way*

SUD: *The Sickness unto Death*

SV: *Samlede Værker*

TC: *Training in Christianity*

WL: *Works of Love*

ACKNOWLEDGMENTS

I am deeply indebted to Erin Kelly, Lionel McPherson, and Yehuda Shavit—wonderful philosophers and dear friends—for their practical help, commendable patience, and unflinching support. The initial research for the book was facilitated by the help of Sarah Blatcher Cohen and Gary Cohen, who promised to change my life, and did.

I am indebted to Simon Critchley for alerting me to the importance of Shaftesbury and to the Kierkegaard Research Center in Copenhagen for hosting me. I express my heartfelt gratitude to Larry Ventis and Larry Mintz, who hosted me as a visiting scholar respectively at the College of William and Mary, Williamsburg, Virginia, and at the University of Maryland, Maryland. In Williamsburg, I enjoyed the college's updated library on humor as well as the support and interest of John Morreall, who, at the time, had written all the major books on philosophy and humor. I am deeply grateful to him.

I am truly obliged to the philosophers who commented on previous drafts of the monograph: Erin Kelly, Yehuda Shavit, Noa Shein, Alicia Tessler, Yair Shlein, and Eli Benzaquen. I am grateful to David Segal and Itay Ehre for their advice on subjects pertaining to their respective areas of expertise.

I owe much to the patience of various English editors: Judi Felber, Kate Neptune, David Kelly-Hedrick, and especially Linda Landau, who managed to guide the work to completion.

I wish to express my gratitude to my colleagues and friends at the International Society for Humor Studies, the International Society for Value Inquiry, and the various associations of Practical Philosophy for their sustained interest in and support of my work.

I owe particular thanks to my faithful assistants, the staff and academics of my department, especially Simi Sarig, Hillel Nossek and Eva Berger, who supported my research. The extraordiany help of the librarians at the

College of Management, Rishon LeZion, Israel, and the College of William and Mary, Williamsburg, Virginia, is greatly appreciated.

I am especially grateful to my parents and my loyal friends for their patience, support, and love.

Last but not least, I wish to express my gratitude for the financial support provided for this research, first, by the chairs of the School of Media Studies (Arnon Zuckerman) and the Department of Behavioral Sciences (Amichai Zilberman) at the College of Management, Rishon LeZion, Israel; and, later, by the Research Fund of the Research Authority (Hillel Nossek, Zvi Safra, Seev Neumann) of the College of Management Academic Studies, Rishon LeZion, Israel. The former enabled me to start the research, and the latter, to bring it to completion.

INTRODUCTION

The aim of this study is to investigate the role of humor in the good life. Various disciplines, such as medicine, psychology, and the social sciences, have praised humor for its individual and social benefits.[1] However, the question of the good life is fundamentally a philosophical question; it is important to inquire into whether philosophers have given humor any role in the good life.

Although philosophers have always been interested in laughter, the accepted view is that they have rarely approved of it as a practice or as a subject worth exploring. Still, I suggest that a thorough study of ancient philosophy reveals a variety of relations between philosophy and the comic that have been epitomized in legendary figures such as the ridiculous philosopher (Thales), the laughing philosopher (Democritus), and the comical philosopher (Socrates). This relationship is also seen in the conceptions and practices of philosophy as comedic (Plato, the Cynics) and in views that associate the comic with the ideal of the gentleman—wit as a virtue (Aristotle)—or with human nature in general—laughter as the mark of the human (Aristotle). These relations between philosophy and the comic developed into traditions in Antiquity that have survived throughout the Middle Ages and flourished in the Renaissance before being rediscovered in the Modern era.[2] Before the eighteenth century, however, *pace* some laughing philosophers of the Renaissance, philosophers seldom gave humor or any other form of the comic a prominent role in the good life. This study seeks to redress the neglect of such an important topic by concentrating on the small number of modern philosophers who have explicitly entrusted humor with a role in the good life as they conceive it.

Only two answer this description: the eighteenth-century British philosopher, the third Earl of Shaftesbury, and the nineteenth-century Danish philosopher, Søren Kierkegaard. Although Kierkegaard refers to Shaftesbury when introducing his interest in the legitimacy of comic, their thought on this subject is related mainly through the work of the eighteenth-century theologian and critic, Johann Georg Hamann.[3] One more philosopher has given humor a prominent role within the good life, the French contemporary philosopher, Gilles Deleuze; as he is a postmodern philosopher, I address his thought elsewhere.[4] Frederich Nietzsche and George Santayana have prioritized instead *laughter*'s role in the good life, and their thoughts on the subject are examined in a separate study.[5] This study focuses, then, on the respective views of the good life of Shaftesbury, Hamann, and Kierkegaard, and the role they assign in it to humor and other related forms of the comic. The latter include, first, the comic in general as well as in its relation to the tragic; good humor, ridicule and wit for Shaftesbury; and finally, irony, for both Hamann and Kierkegaard. This investigation concludes with my contribution to the discussion of humor in the good life. Drawing on recent research on humor, the tragic, the comic, and ridicule, I propose a prominent role for humor in the good life, which is accessible and perhaps even useful to contemporary readers.

When I mentioned to a colleague that I was writing a book on humor and philosophy, he laughed and said it would be a very short book. He was mistaken, unfortunately, yet he voiced the accepted view according to which philosophy has little in common with humor. Humor, it is thought, is frivolous, whereas philosophy is grave; humor is irrational, whereas philosophy is the epitome of rationality; humor is ambiguous and equivocal, whereas philosophy aims for clarity; and humor is indirect, whereas philosophy is explicit. Moreover, humor is spontaneous and leads to a bodily reaction—laughter—whereas philosophy is systematic and addresses the mind. Thus, humor has no place in philosophy's lofty enterprise. Many introductory works on humor in other disciplines succinctly sum up philosophy's negative attitude toward humor, emphasizing the tradition of Pythagoras, the laughterless (*agelastos*) philosopher, and comparing it with religion's, especially Christianity's, hostility toward humor and laughter.[6]

Yet almost all philosophers have been interested in humor. Some have attempted to understand its nature (Plato, Aristotle, Descartes, Hobbes, Kant, Schopenhauer, Spencer, Bergson, Kierkegaard, and Santayana). Concerned for its ethical and political implications, various philosophers have refined it and laid out rules for its use (Plato, Aristotle, Cicero, Aquinas, Spinoza, and Kierkegaard). Others furthered our appreciation of its rhetorical power (Gorgias, Aristotle, Cicero, and Quintilian). Philosophers have used humor mainly as a tool for moral criticism: of ignorance (Plato); of the tragic view of life (Plato, the Stoics); of morality and religion (the pre-Socratic Xenophanes, the Cynics, the Peripatetic Theophrastus, the Pyrrhonian skeptical philosopher Timon of Phlius, the Platonic philosopher Lucius Apuleius, the Renaissance philosophers Erasmus and Thomas More, and the Modern philosophers Pascal and Voltaire); and of "academic" philosophy (the Cynics, Nietzsche, and Kierkegaard). Philosophers have rarely considered laughter essential to the good life. The few exceptions are Democritus, deemed the "laughing philosopher"; Aristotle, who saw in "wit" (*eutrapelia*) one of the social virtues constitutive of the good life; the Stoic Seneca, who proposed laughter as an alternative to anger and sadness, thus making laughter constitutive of the good, that is, peaceful life; Montaigne, who preferred the "laughing philosopher," Democritus, to the "weeping philosopher," Heraclitus, and deemed us the laughable as well as the laughing species; Erasmus, who saw wisdom in folly; and Spinoza, who considered laughter the "pure joy" that enables us to partake in God's nature.

Since the eighteenth century, however, a new form of laughter—humor—has fulfilled a new and important role in philosophy. In the present study of Shaftesbury, Hamann, and Kierkegaard, I trace the emergence of humor's importance to modern philosophy, as well as the debts these philosophers owe to the views of various ancient philosophers (such as Democritus, Heraclitus, Gorgias, Socrates, Xenophon, Plato, Aristotle, the Cynics, Cicero, Epicurus, the Pyrrhonian Skeptic Timon, the Stoics Epictetus, Sotion, Seneca, Marcus Aurelius; and Plutarch). I also consider medieval, Renaissance, and other modern philosophers' views of humor (such as Aquinas, Erasmus, Montaigne, Hobbes, Descartes, Spinoza, Leibniz, Locke, Berkeley, Mandeville, Beattie, Hutcheson, Collins, Ramsay, Kames, Reid, Adam Smith, Campbell, Tucker; Pascal, Voltaire; Kant, Hegel, Schopenhauer, Herder, Lessing, Shlegel, Jean Paul, Solger, Feuerbach, Carlyle, Emerson, Bergson, Santayana, Sartre, and Camus), as well as the views of lesser philosophers, psychologists, literary figures, divines, and theologians. The outcome of this study is the insight that humor, when used to further the philosophic ideals of self-knowledge, truth, rationality, freedom, virtue, happiness, and wisdom, can be one of the most useful tools available to a philosopher.

This is not a study in aesthetics. My interest lies in explicit arguments for the role humor should play in the good life, rather than style or definitions of humor. I have respected, accordingly, the philosophers' use of terms and definitions if provided and Kierkegaard's use of pseudonyms to utter different views on the comic, irony, and humor. I have added biographical information and historically contextualized the discussion when necessary, because I believe that a philosopher's view of self-referential humor is rarely dissociated from his use of humor, and humor and related terms are better studied in context since their meaning and use change according to places and epochs.

Last but not least, the three thinkers addressed here propose alternatives to organized religion, yet remain deeply religious: Shaftesbury's philosophy is ultimately a religious faith, Hamann converted early in life to the religion of his youth, Lutheran Protestantism, and Kierkegaard is profoundly Christian. To understand their views, the discussion necessarily refers to the relationship of humor to religion, especially Christianity.

In the first chapter, I introduce the third Earl of Shaftesbury's view of the good life and the role of humor in it. Shaftesbury's originality lies in his unprecedented and unparalleled defense of humor, wit, ridicule, and good humor as important epistemological tools that promote truth and rationality. Shaftesbury considers ridicule a test of truth, humor a tool for reason, properly educated laughter a form of critical reflection, and good humor or cheerfulness the disposition in which philosophical and religious truth are most effectively comprehended.

The theory that ridicule is a test of truth has been interpreted as meaning that whatever cannot withstand free and humorous examination cannot be well grounded in reason, and that ridicule's chief value may lie in its use as a test of demeanor to unmask imposture. Both interpretations are true and compatible with a more literal interpretation of Shaftesbury's view that relates the idea that ridicule is a test of truth to Shaftesbury's theory of truth. According to the latter interpretation, truth and virtue are ultimately congruous and harmonious, whereas error and vice are incongruous and inharmonious. Because the essence of the comic for Shaftesbury is incongruity and inconsistency, he sees error and vice as inherently ridiculous. On the other hand, truth and virtue do not lend themselves properly to comic treatment, as their mark is congruence and consistency. This reading is truer to Shaftesbury's intention, I believe, but it makes the relation between ridicule and truth dependent on a view of truth that most of us may find difficult to endorse.

Shaftesbury uses ridicule to criticize enthusiasm, a popular term at the time denoting religious fanaticism. He suggests that individuals must search inward to discover the principle of mastering enthusiasm for beneficial use. Humor can be potently associated with enthusiasm because at the root of enthusiasm lies melancholy. By curing melancholy, humor helps achieve good humor. This unique combination of enthusiasm and humor is both original and effective in that it diagnoses enthusiasm as essentially melancholic; and drawing on a centuries-old belief, offers humor as melancholy's cure.

A necessary tool for self-education and moral advice, humor serves as a test of truth through the sociability of dialogue in the philosopher's inner dialogue, conversation, and writing. Humor counters overwhelming enthusiasm, deflates emotional excess, discloses intellectual and moral obtuseness, and enables the development of a sense of proportion necessary for a philosophical character. In conversation, wit and humor—more efficacious than earnest criticism for the distance they create between passion and argument—promote the philosophic goal of rationality as free critical debate. The use of humor and wit in philosophic writing annuls the writer's authority, thereby promoting the autonomy of the reader, a necessary condition for developing independent thought and moral self-education.

By challenging the melancholy of solitary reason, humor exchanges life-denying solitude for life-promoting good humor, a necessary condition for understanding the world's harmony, human goodness, God's good humor and Christianity's cheerfulness, and for appropriately creating in oneself the virtuous and good-humored character that constitutes the good life. As a liberating, life-giving, and life-forming power of the soul, humor is constitutive of the Shaftesburean good life, for without humor, the good life cannot be attained nor maintained.

Shaftesbury has assigned humor an unparalleled role within philosophy, in stating that ridicule is a test of truth, that humor and good humor have a habilitating function with regard to truth, that to be effective, criticism must be humorous, and that humor is the mark of rationality. The view that criticism must be humorous in order to be effective has antecedents in moral exoteric philosophy. The rest of Shaftesbury's views are extremely original. The view that ridicule is a test of truth gained followers in the eighteenth century after having been at the heart of a raging controversy about ridicule's relation with truth and reason. The idea that humor has a habilitating function with regard to truth influenced Hamann, and through Hamann, the young Kierkegaard. Yet the view that humor is the mark of rationality is unprecedented and without followers.

The chapters on Shaftesbury and Kierkegaard are separated by an intermezzo that presents the role humor plays in the German philosopher Johann Georg Hamann's view of the good life. Hamann is an important link between Shaftesbury and Kierkegaard, I suggest, as Hamann develops Shaftesbury's view of humor and passes it on to Kierkegaard, Hamann's only disciple: Kierkegaard found in Hamann his view of humor and a model for using irony and humor as indirect communication in the service of Christianity.

Hamann adopted Shaftesbury's view of the habilitating role of humor with regard to truth. He agrees with Shaftesbury on the correspondence of true humor to reality and therefore on the view that humor represents the state of mind in which truth is best apprehended. However, truth, for Hamann, is the reality of Christ that can only be apprehended by faith.

Hamann follows Shaftesbury in holding that humor (and Hamann adds irony) is epistemologically necessary for grasping the truth, but differs from Shaftesbury about the contents of the truth. Contrary to the usual philosophical categories, humor and irony are the only appropriate modes of thought for grasping the truth, that is, the "Word that has become flesh." Participation in humor, Hamann claims, is analogous to repentance, which in itself is closely connected with faith. The person who cannot understand the humor cannot see the truth, as it is defined by Hamann's conception of faith.

Faith is the existence of the whole person in the mode of humility. It has the further correlates of offence at God's condescension and the concealment of His revelation, faith as characterized by the sign of contradiction, and finally, metaschematism, which for Hamann refers to the assumption of another cause as if it were his own in order to expose its weaknesses and contradictions. Hamann uses irony to express the latter idea and humor to express the first three ideas—contrasts, or mixing the high and low for expressing God's condescension; contradiction for expressing the concealment of God's revelation, or the theological theory of *Kneschtsgestalt Christi* that emphasizes the contradiction of Christ himself appearing in the "form of a servant"; and paradox for expressing the incarnated coincidence of opposites that is our road to salvation. Hamann's originality lies in his application of the Biblical doctrine of *Knechtsgestalt Christi* to Aesthetics, which makes humor the best expression of Christian theological doctrines and the key for understanding them.

Hamann also uses irony, albeit negatively, to point to human finitude. Irony is necessity's iron law of negation, canceling all human striving and aspirations till they amount to nothing. Irony is the grim fate that inevitably triumphs over human finitude, ensuring that all human projects end in death. Humor to Hamann is divine freedom, disjunctive with irony's grim necessity. Humor affirms that God is wholly other and that Divine reason is fundamentally disjunctive with human reason and consequently bound to appear absurd to humans. For Hamann, humor is the appropriate human attitude toward Divine folly because only in the absurd does the possibility of seeing God arise. The significance of humor, then, is not only to expose the impoverished state of finite reason, but also to laugh at all human attempts to scale the heavens with unassisted understanding. Humor's positive function is higher than irony's negative function: It opens a person to the acceptance of the reality of paradoxical truth and ultimately to the acceptance of the highest paradox of all—the incarnation. Thus, for Hamann, humor is the road to salvation.

In the second chapter, I introduce the Danish philosopher Søren Kierkegaard's views on the roles played by humor, irony, and the comic in the good life. Early in his career, Kierkegaard adheres to Hamann's view of humor and accordingly considers Christianity the most humorous form of life. Eventually disengaging himself from Hamann, he rejects this view, arguing that Christianity is inaccessible to humor. Humor, however, is a way of life for Kierkegaard, a phase that can help the intellectual accede to faith, and a mask of the truly religious person. As a way of life, humor is a worldview in which the tragic and the comic are held in balance and the fundamental paradox of life and the contradictions of individual existence are given full expression. This is the worldview that represents philosophy as lived thought as epitomized by Socrates. Kierkegaard criticizes organized religion, proposing instead a tragic faith characterized by resignation, guilt, suffering and dread, which from the vantage point of humor can be cho-sen as a worldview, for the latter is the closest to a religious life. At the highest level of existence, which is Christian faith, humor is still possible, but only as an incognito, as a mask to hide the profound religiousness of the true Christian.

By equating humor with philosophy, Kierkegaard attributes to humor the highest possible role within philosophy as he conceives it. The main problem with his view of humor results from its dependence on his view of religion. This accounts for the subordinate role he gives humor with regard to religion and for his view of humor as tied up with God, guilt, and suffering.

The comic has an original role to play within Kierkegaard's philoso-phy as well. The comic is not the highest category for Kierkegaard, as it is subsumable under the tragic not only in the hierarchy of life's stages, but within each stage as well. Within these limitations, however, the comic fulfills a crucial role in the Kierkegaardian good life: It is an instrument of truth, the primary tool of philosophy once it steps into the new existen-tial role Kierkegaard designs for it, which is to lead the individual toward worshiping the true God. The comic is the main criterion of advancement one has on the negative Kierkegaardian theological ladder and the major positive indicator of one's relation to the truth. Kierkegaard maintains, I suggest, that by examining the content of our laughter we can know the sort of person we are. Kierkegaard thus views the comic as both sword and shield whose mastery is crucial for inner progress from lower to higher stages of existence. For lack of an external criterion for inward advancement, which is the sole progress Kierkegaard recognizes, the comic is the main tool of examination, correction, and evaluation an individual possesses for reflecting on himself, his life, and his personal experiences, and for communicating this to others.

In order to fulfill its role in promoting truth, the comic becomes for Kierkegaard an ethical-religious category. Nothing is further from Kierkegaard than the freedom of wit and humor advocated by Shaftesbury. Kierkegaard's ethics of the comic, devised on the basis of his hierarchy of existential spheres, prescribes a correct use of the comic, which will lead to the good life. The ethics of the comic justifies laughter when an individual's existential position in life is higher than the position at which one is laughing. Through this device, I suggest, Kierkegaard makes certain that his edifying lessons on the comic bear on his lessons on the good life, because laughing well is living well for Kierkegaard. And, as Kierkegaard forbids himself from teaching the latter, yet indulges, albeit through pseudonyms, in teaching the former, the comic attains additional power as Kierkegaard's main tool for teaching the good life.

Yet Kierkegaard's notion of the comic is contingent on a certain philosophical anthropology that involves infinity as constitutive of the self and assumes the incapacity of the self to become whole without God. This makes the comic much more dependent on Kierkegaard's controversial view of religion than common use allows. Kierkegaard's tendentious view of the comic as well as his Christianized notion of humor may be at odds with nonreligious persons. For a view of the comic that is independent of metaphysical assumptions, and a view of humor free of God and guilt, we must turn to the last chapter.

To fill the gap between the nineteenth and twenty-first centuries, I begin the last chapter by reviewing the observations on humor, and if necessary for its understanding, on the comic, of Schopenhauer, Hegel, Hegel's followers, Carlyle, Jean Paul, Santayana, Bergson, and Freud before introducing my view of the role of humor in the good life.

The tragic sense of life is a vision that wanders wild without the cathexis provided by the aesthetic form in which it originated. The tragic sense of life requires the therapy that humor is able to provide. Tragic intrapsychic conflicts can be construed as comical incongruities as evidenced by the history of the genres of tragedy and comedy, certain theories of humor, and the affinity of humor with sadness and suffering. A conflict that is sensed as tragic and perceived as comical leads to a humorous mood that reflects the ambiguity of life and the ambivalence of humankind. A humorous mood is helpful for becoming aware of conflicts, for deliberating over them, and for leaving unresolved the basic human conflict between one's desires and one's capacity for fulfilling them on the instinctual, emotional, and intellectual level. It is important not to resolve this conflict, I suggest in contradistinction to redemptive theories both religious and otherwise and to philosophical theories aiming at peace of mind, because such resolutions come at a price: They either renounce one's desires, or one's reason, or both. Although living with unresolved conflict is difficult, humor can play an important role in relieving the tension it creates.

Nevertheless, the humorous mood is transitory, and when it dissolves, there emerges the ridicule of repeatedly transmuting tragic oppositions into comical incongruities with an increasing capacity for suffering the former and no steady results from the latter. The resultant awareness is the view of human beings as ridiculous or *Homo risibilis*.

Ridicule dissolves, however, if we adhere to the view that we are ridiculous only to the extent that we ignore ourselves. The resolution that obtains mirrors both the resolution of the comedy plot, where the true identity of the hero changes everything, and the process of two-staged theories of humor, which require a higher level of resolution of the initial incongruity in order for a situation to be humorous.

Through a multistage process involving a systematic use of humor that disciplines our taste to find pleasure in incongruities that are not immediately funny to us, a ladder of perfection can be climbed that leads to a state rivaling the highest philosophic and religious ideals. This achievement is gradual and is based on changing visions according to one's capacity to transmute suffering into joy through the alchemy of humor. The lucidity we gain frees us from the comic as well as the tragic, at least from that part of the tragic that has been transmuted into the comic and has thus become constitutive of the tragic-comic protagonist that describes each of us. The freedom that results from the newfound harmony with oneself, others, and the world is characterized by joy and serenity.

Philosophers have been much more interested in tragedy than in the comic. At best, they have studied irony. It may come as a surprise that philosophy entertains important relations with the comic that go back to the ancient Greek and Hellenistic philosophers. Renaissance, modern, and postmodern philosophers have revived and innovated as the notions of humor, laughter, and the comic change over the centuries. Yet Philosophy's relations with the comic have been understudied. This book fills a void, then, by investigating the relationship of humor with truth, reason, self-knowledge, and the good life. This is uncharted territory for philosophers, as well as humor theorists and academics of other disciplines.

CHAPTER 1

SHAFTESBURY

RIDICULE AS THE TEST OF TRUTH

How happy would it be, therefore, to exchange this vulgar, sordid, profuse, horrid laughter for that more reserved, gentle kind, which hardly is to be called laughter, or which at least is of another species?

—Shaftesbury (*The Life, Unpublished Letters, and Philosophical Regimen of Anthony, Earl of Shaftesbury*)

Modern philosophy's study of humor in the good life begins with a British philosopher of the Enlightenment, the third Earl of Shaftesbury. Shaftesbury's search for a form of humor "suitable with one who understands himself" (*Life*, 226) places humor at the core of the philosophic ideal of self-knowledge.[1] As he revives the ancient philosophical practices that emphasize the importance of humor in the active philosophical life, he recalls the irony of the Xenophonic Socrates, the Aristotelian virtue of wit (*eutrapelia*), the Cynic's ideal of free speech, and the Stoic's use of humor to advance moral education, and assigns to each an important role in modern philosophy.

Shaftesbury's originality lies in his unprecedented and unparalleled defense of humor, wit, ridicule, and good humor as important epistemological tools that promote truth and rationality. Shaftesbury considers ridicule a test of truth, humor a tool for reason, properly educated laughter a form of critical reflection, and good humor or cheerfulness the disposition in which philosophical and religious truth are most effectively comprehended. He views humor as a necessary tool for self-education and moral advice in the philosopher's inner dialogue, conversation, and writing. Humor counters overwhelming enthusiasm, deflates emotional excess, discloses intellectual and moral obtuseness, and enables a sense of proportion necessary for a philosophical character. In philosophical conversation, wit and humor—more efficacious than earnest criticism for the distance they create between passion and argument—promote the philosophic goal of rationality as free critical debate. Finally, the use of humor and wit in philosophic writing annuls the writer's authority, thereby promoting the autonomy of the reader, a necessary condition for developing independent thought and moral self-education. Critics and commentators have addressed many of these interconnected themes, but their treatment of Shaftesbury's discussion is random. In contrast, I emphasize in this chapter the richness of Shaftesbury's treatment of humor and its centrality to his understanding of the good life.

Shaftesbury was raised and educated in the first Earl's household by John Locke, thus giving rise to the latter's *Some Thoughts Concerning Education*.[2] The third Earl had received under Locke's tutelage a thorough education in Greek and Latin, which made him remarkably knowledgeable in ancient philosophy. Reviving the ancient ideal of the active philosophical life, Shaftesbury attempted to harmonize a political life with a philosophical one, alternating between intense public service and periods of philosophical retreats, until he abandoned London for health reasons (1711). His grandfather founded the Whig party, which the third Earl generally supported although not unconditionally so. Following Locke's advice he began his adult life by extensive travels through the continent, living twice in Holland where he befriended French Protestants and skeptics, and most probably became acquainted with Spinoza's philosophy.[3]

Shaftesbury founded the "moral sense" school of ethics, according to which natural affection for virtue predisposes human beings to act virtuously.[4] Although much of Shaftesbury's work differed from the dominant style of philosophical discourse of his era and the philosophical tradition since then,[5] his philosophy was very much in vogue during the first half of the eighteenth century, so much so that Oliver Goldsmith was prompted to write that Shaftesbury had "more imitators in Britain than any other writer I know" (Goldsmith 1759, 15). Indeed, Francis Hutcheson, the most important English-speaking philosopher between Berkeley and Hume, championed his thought, and Mandeville, Berkeley, and Butler testified to Shaftesbury's importance by criticizing his work.[6] Shaftesbury also enjoyed an equally high status abroad. Leibniz praised him.[7] Montesquieu referred to him as one of "the four great poets" of the Western world along with Plato, Malebranche, and Montaigne (Montesquieu 1979, VII, 171), and his eulogy of Shaftesbury was paraphrased by a multitude of learned men in France, Germany, and England. Shaftesbury's influence could be traced in the work of the French philosophers LeClerc, Voltaire, and especially

Diderot, and through the efforts of Robert Molesworth, Shaftesbury's writings influenced the Dublin scene as well as numerous writers of the Scottish enlightenment. Herder labeled Shaftesbury the "beloved Plato of Europe" and the "virtuoso of humanity," who "has had a marked influence on the best minds of our century, on those who have striven with determination and sincerity for the true, the beautiful, and the good."[8]

Shaftesbury provided the philosophical basis for the eighteenth century's change of attitude toward laughter, which propelled humor into British social, economic, and political significance:

> First had come the Puritan, enthusiastic, morose, and austere, then the rake, cynical, gay and debauched: two extremes in agreement of the natural depravity of human nature, and either intensively holy or intensely profane. What good-natured men wanted was a more equable way of life, in which the archetype was neither the saint nor the wit but the benevolent and good-humoured gentleman, cheerful in his religion, sober in his wit: his theologians were the latitudinarian divines, his journalists were Addison and Steele, his philosopher Shaftesbury . . . (Tave 1960, 3)[9]

The typical English moralist of the Enlightenment, Shaftesbury was representative of the widely prevailing way of thought sweeping Europe throughout the eighteenth century,[10] during which amiable humor replaced Hobbes' laughter of superiority.[11] The new view of humor as incongruity, which Shaftesbury helped to promote, elevated it to an unprecedented moral and intellectual height, creating thus an appreciation of humor that continues to this day.

Shaftesbury's original views on humor not only influenced his contemporaries, but also had an enormous subsequent effect on aesthetics. Despite his extreme criticism of contemporary satire, especially the work of Swift, Shaftesbury justified satiric attempts to establish moral and social truths. Moreover, his views on the relation of humor to truth, reason, virtue, and religion launched an ongoing debate among philosophers, characterized by Richard Brett as "an interminable philosophic controversy over the subject of ridicule, which rose to a special prominence and roused peculiarly strong emotions" (Brett 1951, 168). In particular, Shaftesbury unmistakably influenced subsequent philosophers who defended humor, notably Hamann and, either directly or not, Kierkegaard. Shaftesbury's innovative views and widespread influence require that we begin with the Enlightenment philosopher to formulate the main issues of the role of humor in modern philosophy.

Significant as Shaftesbury's views are, it is not an easy task to extract from his work an explicit theory of the role of humor in the good life. First, he purposefully avoids a systematic exposition of his thought. Although he delineates his own project with various references to ancient philosophy, it is Socrates who is his pre-eminent philosophical model. Accordingly, Shaftesbury maintains that the aim of the philosopher is to edify by furthering the other's autonomy. By contrast, the magisterial approach, which induces passivity before authority, is not suitable to philosophy's aim and capacity. Philosophy aims at producing moral agents, and the form of Shaftesbury's collected writings, *Characteristics of Men, Manners, Opinions, Times* (1711), is meant to meet this challenge by transforming readers into philosophers who are morally intelligent agents. Moreover, the magisterial approach violates the limits of human knowledge, promising more than philosophy can provide. Endorsing the skeptical methodology of various Greek philosophers and such moderns as Pierre Bayle, Shaftesbury urges his readers to embark on an open-ended quest for truth. With the exception of one early systematic work published without his consent,[12] he writes letters, dialogues, and miscellanies, which he considers more suitable to his educational goals. This style of philosophizing, however, presents an obstacle in the way of a clear-cut understanding of his views on humor.

Second, Shaftesbury makes extensive use of wit, humor and irony, and on occasion assumes an external perspective ostensibly not his own, which occasionally obscures the meaning of his writings. His *The Adept Ladys* (1702), a short satire on some representatives of the Quakers, *A Letter Concerning Enthusiasm* (1708), and *Sensus Communis: An Essay on the Freedom of Wit and Humour* (1709), establish Shaftesbury as a wit and bring him notoriety as a champion of raillery in discussions of such serious subjects as religion; but they also ambiguate his views on the tools he uses to convey his message. Edward Fowler, the hostile author of *Reflections upon A Letter Concerning Enthusiasm* (1709), while finding the letter has "sparkling Air, nice Turns, and clever sorts of Fancy, or lively Allusions," has conceded its wit to be "full of Wind, and much Froth" (Fowler 1709, 24; quoted in Wolf 1993, 565). Moreover, in the five highly discursive essays, *Miscellaneous Reflections on the Preceding Treatises, and other Critical Subjects*, Shaftesbury added to the *Characteristics*, he assumes the voice of a commentator on the contents of the latter. He presents himself in the *Miscellaneous* as a "critic or interpreter of this new writer" who comments on "some late pieces of a British author." The "author of the preceding treatises," he qualifies as "being by profession a nice inspector into the ridicule of things" (*Misc.*, I, ii; CR II, 163), and deems the author of the

Miscellanies a "mere comic humorist in respect of those inferior subjects," which, after the manner of his "familiar prose satire," he presumes to criticize (*Misc.*, V, i; CR II, 446). Editor Lawrence Klein justly remarks, then, that Shaftesbury takes great care in giving the *Characteristics* play, both in the sense of humor and playfulness, and in the sense of variety and open-endedness (Klein 1999, xiii). The humor and playfulness that characterize Shaftesbury's work, while fitting his purpose, hinder a clear understanding of his views on humor.

Third, the nature and purpose of Shaftesbury's humor is not entirely clear on the basis of his writing style and the available biographical evidence. The biographical details about Shaftesbury's humor are scarce. We know that he could appreciate ridicule's bite because in his early teens he probably had to endure it from his classmates, and throughout his life he must have continued to encounter the scorn his grandfather's name provoked.[13] Raised by the latter, he may have been influenced by the remark his grandfather used to repeat, as Locke recorded: "There were in every one, two men, the wise and the foolish, and that each of them must be allowed his turn. If you would have the wise, the grave, the serious, always to rule and have the sway, the fool would grow so peevish and troublesome, that he would put the wise man out of order and make him fit for nothing."[14] Moreover, Shaftesbury's style generates disagreement among commentators as to the quality, naturalness, and purpose of his humor. Stanley Grean notes Shaftesbury's "heavy use of irony and satire, particularly when dealing with religious issues" (Grean 1967, xvii). In contrast, Richard Wolf (1993) finds Shaftesbury's works humorous and devoid of the biting wit of his contemporaries, such as Jonathan Swift's. Wolf adds that both Shaftesbury's reservations about raillery and his manner of harnessing wit and humor in the service of philosophy were strongly influenced by his devotion to certain strands of classical thought and to classical models, especially those of Socrates, Xenophon, and Horace (Wolf 1933). Similarly, John Toland suggests that Shaftesbury's innate disposition is toward "*Socratic* Irony and innocent Raillery" (Toland 1721, viii). John Robertson, in contrast, finds Shaftesbury melancholic in his private notebooks, not written for publication and published posthumously as *Exercises* (*Askêmata*). Robertson concludes that humor, ridicule, and banter are not natural to Shaftesbury, but the outcome of self-discipline (Robertson 1963, xxi–ii).[15]

Fourth, Shaftesbury holds strong reservations about his advocacy and use of satiric wit that are clearly seen in his *Exercises* and his reply to Leibniz's critique of the *Characteristics* (1711). Referring to himself in the third person, he writes:

Particularly in what relates to the two great concessions of that author in favour of raillery and the way of humour. Does not the author himself secretly confess as much in his work? And does he not seem to despise himself . . . when, after having passed his principal and main philosophical work . . . he returns again to his mixed satirical ways of raillery and irony, so fashionable in our nation, which can be hardly brought to attend to any writing, or consider anything as witty, able, or ingenious which has not strongly this turn?[16]

More than any other work he wrote, *The Adept Ladys* illustrates the sort of jester's performance for which Shaftesbury castigated himself. His biographer, Robert Voitle, labels it a "hasty *jeu d'esprit* and not a very witty one" (Voitle 1984, 199). The challenge Shaftesbury set for himself for the first time in *the Letter Concerning Enthusiasm* was to manage his dangerous talents as a writer of raillery in order to encourage thought and virtue in his reader. Wolf suggests that in Shaftesbury's subsequent works "it is the concept of a fair, decorous, and proportionally appropriate raillery that makes his approach very different from that found in *The Adept Ladys* and in such works as Swift's *Tale of a Tub*" (Wolf 1993, 7).[17] Similarly, John Hayman aligns Shaftesbury with Augustan satiric reformers, such as Addison and Steele, who are intent on curbing the malice of contemporary raillery and providing a proper model of good humored mental disposition (Hayman 1968, 1970). Given the expectations that an author's wit exemplifies his views on wit and humor, assessing Shaftesbury's reservations about his use of wit is relevant to understanding his views.

A fifth difficulty for a study of Shaftesbury's view of the role of humor in the good life is his inconsistent use of relevant terms. Shaftesbury uses *raillery, ridicule, banter, buffoonery, laughter, comic, satire, wit, humor,* and *good humor.* Moreover, he confesses to lacking an appropriate term for designating the kind of laughter he advocates, that "more reserved, gentle kind, which hardly is to be called laughter, or which at least is of another species" (*Life,* 226). Stuart Tave remarks:

If we look closely at what he means by "ridicule," we find something far more benevolent than satiric, something very like the familiar figure of "good humour," heightened by an airy, gentlemanly ease. We can do no better than go directly to his opponents, who saw this quite clearly, though to them it was clearly evidence of Shaftesbury's confusion or dishonesty. (Tave 1960, 35)[18]

Leibniz, for example, notices as well that Shaftesbury is an inconsistent advocate of raillery or ridicule. He maintains that when Shaftesbury
introduces the concept of "good humor," he partly retracts from his position on ridicule. Shaftesbury seeks no quarrel with his critic but rather is
honored and satisfied by "the candor and justness of his censure."[19] Laurent
Jaffro, a contemporary scholar sympathetic to Shaftesbury's endeavor, similarly remarks on Shaftesbury's inconsistent use of terms:

> . . . in the same discourse, Shaftesbury confounds laughter (in
> its different forms), smile, mockery and amiable pleasantry; he
> moves from passions to styles and literary genres; he substitutes
> to laughter the general problem of ridicule and the question
> of the art of ridiculing. At the end of these metamorphoses,
> laughter is nothing else than reflection" (Jaffro 1996, 43; my
> translation).

Although this is an apt description of Shaftesbury's confusion of terms,
I suggest that there is a certain degree of consistency in their use.

A sixth and final obstacle to a systematic exposition of Shaftesbury's
view on humor is voiced in his reply to Leibniz's criticism of his thesis
on ridicule. Shaftesbury's response is to admit that his views on "the way
of humour" are continuously evolving.[20] Françoise Badelon justly remarks,
then, that "the place of laughter is the object of a permanent discussion
in Shaftesbury's work" (Badelon 2000, 29; my translation).

The question I address in this chapter is: What is the role of humor
in the Shaftesburean good life? Keeping in mind the problems involved
in attempting a systematic account of humor within the Shaftesburean
good life, I first introduce Shaftesbury's view of the good life. I then differentiate between good humor, ridicule, humor, and wit in subsequent
sections that center on Shaftesbury's views of the comic, ridicule, humor,
and wit. I suggest that Shaftesbury refers to ridicule as humor when used in
inner dialogue and as wit or humor when used in conversation. Following
eighteenth-century custom, wit and humor are not clearly differentiated
although Shaftesbury does on occasion suggest that the former is a means
to the latter. Ridicule and raillery are not discarded in favor of good humor,
as some commentators have argued (i.e., Leibniz, Tave): good humor cannot
fulfill a critical function, whereas ridicule can and Shaftesbury is definitely
interested in the corrective and critical role of laughter no less than in
the open and cheerful disposition that goes by the name of good humor.

A study of Shaftesbury's views of the tragic and the comic as they
apply to life is important for determining the appropriate attitude toward

it, whether life should be approached in earnest or jest. I suggest that Shaftesbury's attitude is encapsulated in his notion of good humor, which is nonetheless not clearly differentiated from humor. I address ridicule subsequently as the principal term for which Shaftesbury is renowned, clarifying its relation to truth and reason, and introducing Shaftesbury's application of ridicule in fighting fanaticism, curbing enthusiasm, and criticizing organized religion. An elaboration on ridicule's application as humor within inner dialogue or soliloquy, and as humor and wit within philosophical conversation and writing follows. In the concluding remarks, I assess the originality and feasibility of using humor within the good life as recommended by Shaftesbury.

A comprehensive study of the comic and related notions such as ridicule, humor and wit, and good humor within Shaftesbury's thought has not been undertaken. Although all comprehensive studies of Shaftesbury address some of his views on ridicule, wit, humor, and good humor, they tend to focus on a limited aspect of one or two views in isolation: the political aspect of the freedom of ridicule (Grean 1967); the cultural aspect of humor and politeness (Klein 1994); Shaftesbury's view on ridicule as a test of truth and its influence on satire (Brett 1951) or the controversy it generated (Aldridge 1948); the relationship of enthusiasm and humor (Larthomas 1985, 1986); and the role of humor and wit in writing (Benda 1982), in conversation (Malherbe 2000), in communication in general (Jaffro 1998), and in sociability (Brugère 1999). Moreover, these studies do not explicitly connect humor and related notions to the Shaftesburean good life because the question of their role in such a life has not been asked. This chapter fills a lack, then, by providing a comprehensive study of all the notions related to the comic that are relevant to an understanding of Shaftesbury's view of the good life, and in explaining their necessary role in attaining to such a life. I argue that without the use of ridicule, humor and good humor, the Shaftesburean good life cannot be attained.

THE GOOD LIFE

"The most ingenious way of becoming foolish is by a system," Shaftesbury asserts (*Soliloquy*, iii, 1; CR I, 189). He attests thus to his main inspiration, the open-ended teachings of Socrates, not only as interpreted in its more orthodox form by Plato, but also as expressed more popularly by Xenophon. Despite the Greek and Roman sources of Shaftesbury's thought, in particular Platonism and Roman Stoicism, Shaftesbury's main purpose is to address contemporary needs. More interested in reforming the morals, manners and taste of his day than in discursive reasoning, he aims to promote liberty by devising a cultural program for a post-courtly European culture. To this end, he criticizes the court, ridicules the Church, and rebukes contemporary philosophy for its aloofness from practical affairs and neglect of its role as moral and political educator.

Shaftesbury tells us that his "design is to advance something new, or at least something different from what is commonly current in philosophy and morals" (*Misc.*, III, i; CR II, 251–2). Hardly distinguishable from good education, philosophy for Shaftesbury is a practical endeavor. He intends to bring philosophy back to the everyday world, an aspiration that explains the themes, design and style of his work. Like Hobbes and Locke, who strengthened their influence by writing in plain language, Shaftesbury aims to reach a lay audience unfamiliar with philosophical terminology. Shaftesbury endeavors to rescue the philosophical tradition of the Cambridge Platonists from their dull and pedantic folio volumes, in order to make them available to individuals of culture and sensibility. Bemoaning philosophy's fate in the modern world, Shaftesbury complains, "she is no longer active in the world nor can hardly, with any advantage, be brought on the public stage. We have immured her, poor lady, in colleges and cells, and have set her servilely to such works as those in the mines. Empirics and pedantic sophists are her chief pupils" (*Moralists*, I, 1; CR II, 4–5). It appears he convinced his contemporaries of the importance of his project, for Addison, the editor of the *Spectator*, is a close reader of Shaftesbury's *Characteristics*, and subscribers are duly informed of the paper's policy to bring "philosophy out of closets and libraries, schools and colleges, to dwell in clubs and assemblies, at tea-tables and in coffee-houses" (quoted in Brett 1951, 41).

To justify his approach, Shaftesbury depicts the English gentleman bored and bullied by clerics and academics. He regularly denigrates the clerical and the homiletic, the academic and the pedantic. He considers sermons and lectures unsuitable vehicles for edification, and often dismisses or ridicules their formal, systematic, consistent, methodical, and abstract character. He blames these traits for the sterility of most philosophical writing. He condemns the style of the pulpit and the classroom as authoritarian or "magisterial," a word that, in light of its Latin origin—*magister*—combines a reference to the schoolteacher and to the magistrate. Indeed, as Laurence Klein notes, Shaftesbury's *Characteristics* is a collection of "rhetorical gambits aiming to represent a discursive practice distinct from that of the lecture or the sermon" (Klein 1999, xiii).

Shaftesbury maintains that a more polite approach than the lecture or the sermon is required for a more effective philosophy. For Shaftesbury, *politeness*, a term referring to the conventions of both good manners and refined conversation, fulfills the fundamental rhetorical necessity of making concessions to the knowledge, interests, and attention span of an audience. In this respect, Klein explains, Shaftesbury aims to regulate "style or language by the standard of good company and people of the better sort"—members of the English upper orders, wealthy although not necessarily landed gentlemen, educated and literate although not necessarily learned, men of the world who could naturally be reached through humor, playfulness, variety, and open-endedness (Klein 1994, 75; 1999, xiii). Shaftesbury replaces the magisterial manner with a polite form of writing that is more informal, miscellaneous, conversational, open-ended, and skeptical.

Philosophy, insists Shaftesbury, should make people effective participants in the world. Neither an intellectual discipline for specialists nor a profession, it is rather wisdom accessible to every thoughtful individual: "If philosophy be, as we take it, the study of happiness, must not everyone, in some manner or other, either skillfully or unskillfully philosophize?" (Moralists, iii, 3; CR II, 150; see 153). Given the profusion of human weaknesses, however, it is a therapeutic enterprise as well. In order to understand how philosophy succeeds as a practical activity in pursuit of moral self-knowledge and moral transformation, Shaftesbury's views of virtue, enthusiasm, and beauty should be explored: Virtue is a noble enthusiasm that forms an inward harmonious beauty, unattainable, however, without the use of humor.

VIRTUE

Shaftesbury's philosophy reflects the change in attitude toward nature and evil in the transition from the seventeenth to the eighteenth century, when, as Basil Willey explains, "the Fall is no longer a haunting obsession, and whatever may be true of man, Nature is now to be contemplated as the finished and unimprovable product of divine wisdom, omnipotence, and benevolence" (Willey 1986, 35).[21] Shaftesbury parts company with theologians who postulate a personal Devil, as well as with philosophers like Bayle who propose a Manichean approach to evil. His optimistic philosophy plays a major role in transforming nature from a fallen world into a revelation of divine goodness and beauty. Nature in this view is God's good creation designed for human use and enjoyment.

The world is providentially ruled by a Supreme Mind that may be alternatively conceived as the Soul of the universe or as a personality that transcends the world.[22] The Supreme Mind's rule is absolutely beneficent: Nothing in the universe is "ill" relative to the whole, and everything is as it must be.[23] In this perfect universe the goodness or evil of each system is judged in terms of the functioning of the system as a whole: "Pleasure and pain, beauty and deformity, good and ill, seemed to me everywhere inter-woven," declares Philocles, the protagonist of *The Moralists*, "and yet, this tapestry made of many contrasting colors produces a harmonious over-all effect" (*Moralists*, i, 2; CR II, 14). That which we consider "evil" is compa-rable to some of the details of this tapestry, the shading in a picture, or the dissonances in a symphony. Nature, the Sovereign Artist, creates harmony out of contrasting elements. According to this view "seeming blemishes" are the results of limited perspectives. Nature does not err, and "when she seems most ignorant or perverse in her productions, I assert her even then as wise and provident as in her godliest works" (*Moralists*, i, 3; CR II, 22).

Shaftesbury views Nature as an arena of conflicting forces and inter-ests in which the lower species must always yield to the higher, the lesser to the greater. In this ecologically ordered world of mutual interdependence among living organisms in their natural setting, terrestrial forms are main-tained by mutual sacrifice and surrender, as one species preys on another. If in the hierarchy of organisms the sacrifice of one species is considered appropriate at the lower levels, it must be so at all levels, including the human. Each system of organisms is contained in some larger system to which its own interest or good is subordinated. Ultimately, all species are subject to "the superior nature of the world" (*Moralists*, i, 3; CR II, 22). According to this view, we must not expect exceptions to be made to pre-serve individual creatures or even species that are necessarily transient. Not only is it justifiable for one species to prey on another, but also disasters such as earthquakes or floods, which harm individual creatures or destroy whole species, are justified on the grounds that all lesser systems of beings must submit to the necessary order of nature as a whole.

The absolute "benevolence" of the ruling Mind, according to Shaftes-bury, serves as a model for the proper frame of mind of the human being. People are so constituted as to find happiness in all benevolent affections and actions, and misery in the contrary.[24] For Shaftesbury, continuously changing Nature manifests a perfect adjustment of matter to form, and form to environment, as in Stoic doctrine. Shaftesbury finds the same perfection in the harmony of the human affections, as in the harmony and proportion manifested in the greater world.[25] Delight in evil, he acknowledges, exists but it is "unnatural" (*Inquiry*, II, ii, 3; CR I, 331).

This being so, all cajolery and terrorism used by religion are vicious and fallacious. God, he claims, is to be loved without hope of reward or fear of punishment.[26] In Shaftesbury's view true religion should be based on nature rather than on revelation. Religion is an enemy of virtue in so far as it deprecates human good nature and relies on future rewards and punishments: "Little were you aware," Theocles exclaims in *The Moralists*, "that the cruel enemy opposed to Virtue should be religion itself!" Theocles concludes that "by building a future state on the ruins of virtue, religion in general, and the cause of a deity is betrayed; and by making rewards and punishments the principal motives to duty, the Christian religion in particular is overthrown, and its greatest principle, that of Love, rejected and exposed" (*Moralists*, ii, 2; CR II, 256).

Orthodoxy is also the enemy of true or natural religion because it establishes faith not on the beautiful and harmonious order of things (the best and only genuine external evidence), but on miracles, that is, on violations of this order.[27]

Immortality is likely enough, Shaftesbury holds, yet future happiness is not a reward for right living, because virtue and happiness are the same.[28] Similarly, future punishment should not be an incentive for acting morally because such considerations weaken natural moral interests and because there is no merit in moral acts prompted by fear of punishment. Nonetheless, he concedes that a strong hope of future reward and fear of future punishment may lead men into habits conducive to true virtue, whereas a weak belief in future rewards and punishments is entirely detrimental to morality.[29]

Virtue is natural to humankind, but is nevertheless subject to refinement. Perfect virtue in this view amounts to a perfected taste in morals. To be good-humored and cultured is to be religious and moral, and thus happy. Conversely, malevolence and malfeasance lead to misery.[30]

Shaftesbury advocates this view of virtue as early as his first publication, a laudatory preface to an edition of sermons by the Cambridge Latitudinarian, Benjamin Whichcote (1698). Whimsically apologizing for publishing yet more sermons when so great a number have already been preached and printed with so little apparent effect, he asks, why it is that men who profess to be Christians live the lives they do. This is not, he suggests, on account of any radical depravity to be found in mankind, but rather because exhortation is misdirected when religion is perverted to serve political ends. In response to the view that natural sociability and goodness are not innate human characteristics, which is accepted by atheists and defenders of religion alike, Shaftesbury affirms the divine perfection of nature and the "good nature" of the human being against atheists, who see the universe as a chaos of atoms, and against the orthodox, who hold that we live in a world that has been permanently ruined by the fall of Adam.[31]

Like Nature, Shaftesbury claims, human beings are essentially "good," and, in contradistinction to Hobbes' view, naturally sociable.[32] Human virtue consists, he says, in "following Nature," in the sense that it is a reproduction within the individual microcosm of the harmony and proportion manifest in the greater world. In the *Inquiry* (1699), Shaftesbury proposes to differentiate the "good and natural" affections, which are directed toward the general welfare of a group, from the "ill and unnatural," which are directed neither toward private nor public good.[33] We possess by nature a faculty he calls the "moral sense," which enables us to both distinguish between right and wrong and prefer the right (*Inquiry*, I, iii, 2; CR I, 262). This faculty is closely akin to the aesthetic sense, by which we recognize and approve the harmonious and proportionate. The virtue of a rational creature consists in a "rational affection" toward what is right, that is, a "just sentiment" or a "proper disposition" (*Inquiry*, I, iii, 2; CR I, 262).

Shaftesbury follows the Stoics in holding that the conditions for our happiness are internal and subject to our own power, that "opinion" is important in attaining the good life, and that the highest good is not the "tumultuous joy" of unregulated passions, but a "constant, fixed, and regular joy, which carries tranquility along with it, and which has no rejolt" (*Life*, 116). Heavily influenced by Greek thought, Shaftesbury's philosophy is nonetheless crucially shaped by a modern way of thinking, as is also evidenced in his theory of enthusiasm.

ENTHUSIASM

Shaftesbury's theory of enthusiasm, which accounts for the importance he attributes to humor, is another modern twist of an ancient view, in this case the important role Plato assigns to enthusiasm in his philosophy (*Phaedrus* 241e, 249e, 253a, 263d; *Ion*; *Symposium*). For Shaftesbury, enthusiasm is the inner movement of the human spirit, carrying it beyond itself toward the vision of the good. Only the mind so "taken up in vision" is capable of the affection that is the essence of the moral life—the life in harmony with Nature and God.

Shaftesbury's theory of enthusiasm thus resolves an epistemological problem. Knowing with certainty that all things work for the best presupposes a comprehension of the universe as a whole that is impossible for the finite mind to grasp (*Moralists*, iii, 1; CR II, 108). Because it is impossible to know that everything "demonstrates order and perfection," we must rely on enthusiasm or ultimate commitment to show us the way (*Moralists*, ii, 4; CR II, 67). Human beings are able to surmount the limitations of finitude, and, at least at moments, to intuit the harmony of the whole universe, through ecstatic moments of faith or enthusiasm in which the mind is "caught up in vision." Shaftesbury's final epistemological appeal is not to evidence or logic alone, but to enthusiasm. He considers enthusiasm a rational process that does not contradict logic or evidence, but rather affords a higher vantage point from which logic and evidence derive their meaning. This is the only standpoint from which one can be reconciled to a view of the paradoxical relationship of universal and particular providence, and to the concept of particular evils embedded in the universal Good.

Enthusiasm arose within Protestant discourse as a way to characterize and disparage the excesses of Protestant fervor. The term first appeared in the early seventeenth century, meaning "divine possession," and by 1656 the word "enthusiast" first appeared in an English dictionary, where it referred to Reformation Anabaptists as "a sect of people that thought themselves inspired with a Divine spirit, and to have a clear sight of all things which they believed."[34] "Enthusiasm" may have been transformed into a general slur against Nonconformists because it attacked religious positions in terms of the believer's psychology and "transferred religious argument from issues of doctrine to estimations of social personality" (Klein 1994, 162). In the Restoration period, the valence of "enthusiasm" was entirely negative, but, by the 1690s, the term came under transvaluative pressure.[35] Shaftesbury made a twofold contribution to the transformation of "enthusiasm." First, he joined in the transvaluation, establishing a positive meaning for it. Second, he continued the polemical and denigrating uses of "enthusiasm," but found new objects for them.

Shaftesbury's rehabilitation of the affections as foundations of moral agency sanctioned a re-estimation of passionate phenomena such as enthusiasm. Shaftesbury embraces enthusiasm as an important expression of natural affection, as he explains referring to himself in the *Miscellany*: "So far is he from degrading enthusiasm or disclaiming it in himself; that he looks on this passion, simply considered, as the most natural, and its object as the justest in the world" (*Misc.*, II, i; CR II, 176). Although enthusiasm at best is Platonic divine love inspiring in the individual an understanding of the order of the world and a respect for ultimate beauty, the notion can be applied to lesser states of inspiration as well. At all levels of intensity, however, enthusiasm lifts the individual beyond his ordinary capacities into a higher level of cognition enabling the intuition of matters beyond the self. In this respect, enthusiasm is an essential feature of humanity, closely related to the sociability first described by Shaftesbury in the *Inquiry Concerning Virtue*.

Unless refined, enthusiasm is vulgar and conducive to vice, delusion, and self-deception. In his *Letter Concerning Enthusiasm* (1708), motivated by the appearance in London of a group of prophetically inspired Christians, Shaftesbury sets the "prophets" aside and, applying his notion of enthusiasm, proceeds to attack the Church. Zealots can be found inside the established Church as well as at its borders. Because enthusiasm is a pervasive feature of human life, enthusiastic prophets are all too likely to pass it on to the reigning clerics and magistrates, thereby giving rise to fanaticism. Thus, Shaftesbury takes a stock element of Anglican polemic and turns it against the Anglican Church, or at least its High Church functionaries.

In keeping with the Protestant tradition he inherited, Shaftesbury defines religious enthusiasm as "uncontrolled passion." He portrays "every worshipper of the zealot-kind" as affectively unhinged, "no longer self-governed, but set adrift to the wide sea of passion" (Misc., V, iii; CR II, 353–69). He makes clear that enthusiasm in general is a condition in which sound affections escape the mind's control and grow to excess—a classic instance of the loss of autonomy, as depicted in the Inquiry. Moreover, as the Inquiry leads one to predict, enthusiasm is highly conducive to vice. In addition to affections that are inherently vicious, affections can become vicious if not harmoniously balanced or moderated by reason: "Above all other enslaving vices, and restrainers of reason and just thought, the most evidently ruinous and fatal to the understanding is that of superstition, bigotry, and vulgar enthusiasm" (Misc., II, i; CR II, 180; see also Misc., V, iii; CR II, 345).

Shaftesbury describes "virtue itself" as "no other than a noble enthusiasm justly directed and regulated" (Misc., II, i; CR II, 176). Enthusiasm is not only the culmination of Shaftesbury's philosophy, but also the dynamic element that enlivens it and sets his thought apart from that of the Deists and rationalists of the Augustan age. Although his allegiance lies with reason, Shaftesbury insists that reason must continually strive to transcend itself. The processes of discursive reason are not, and can never be, sufficient for achieving a complete understanding of the harmonious universal order.

BEAUTY

Shaftesbury's view of the ultimate harmony of nature necessarily leads him to assert the substantial unity of the true, the beautiful, and the good. Nature is a teleological continuum in which all things contribute (when viewed in the largest sense) to the good and the beautiful. Thus, he writes, "the most natural beauty in the world is honesty and moral truth. For all beauty is truth" (Essay, iv, 3; CR I, 94). Harmony and proportion are the classic attributes that link this triad of values: ". . . what is beautiful is harmonious and proportionable; what is harmonious and proportionable is true; and what is at once both beautiful and true is, of consequence, agreeable and good" (Misc., III, ii; CR II, 268–9).

The harmonious and the proportionate are also the fruitful or the useful in the highest sense (*Misc.*, II, ii; CR II, 207). The physical harmony of the body, Shaftesbury notes, is linked with attractiveness and health, just as emotional harmony is a prerequisite for virtue. However, *utility*, as Shaftesbury uses the term, does not have merely a material or economic connotation, but is broadly conceived as comprehending all that is useful in achieving the larger ends of human life. Therefore, it is not merely the appearance of beauty that counts but the beauty that lies within. External beauty's purpose is to lead us to the inner beauties that are "the most real and essential," and that not only afford the greatest pleasure but also are of the highest benefit.

The taste for the aesthetic in Shaftesbury's thought is nowhere more clear than in his emphasis on harmony and proportion that is a ground-motif of his metaphysical and ethical theory, as well as of his aesthetics. "The study and love of symmetry and order" is not only the basis of our appreciation of beauty; it is also the source of philosophical and scientific inquiry (*Misc.*, III, ii; CR II, 267). He finds in it the basis for the disinterested pleasure that the study of mathematics affords. The mind delights in those "inward numbers" that designate the ultimately proportionate relationships of all that participates in Being itself: "There is a power in numbers, harmony, proportion and beauty of every kind, which naturally captivates the heart and raises the imagination to an opinion or conceit of something majestic and divine" (*Misc.*, II, 1; CR II, 174). There is "a natural joy in the contemplation of those numbers. That harmony, proportion and concord, which supports the universal nature and is essential in the constitution and form of every particular species or order of beings. . . ." There is a "beautiful, proportioned and becoming action" (*Inquiry*, II, ii, 1; CR I, 296), which is "improving to the temper, advantageous to social affection, and highly assistant to virtue, which is itself no other than the love of order and beauty in society" (*Inquiry*, I, iii, 3; CR I, 279).

Shaftesbury refers again and again to music, architecture, and painting analogies when defending his theory against the Hobbes-Locke thesis of natural indifference toward the good. According to the latter view, nothing is intrinsically good or bad, admirable or contemptible, except in relation to some law or rule under which it is made to fall, and backed by penalties: "That all actions are naturally indifferent; that they have no note or character of good or ill in themselves; but are distinguished by mere fashion, law, or arbitrary decree."[36] In contradistinction to this view, Shaftesbury maintains that right and wrong are just as fixed to standards in nature as are harmony and dissonance in music. Something akin to harmony or proportion of numbers is to be found in all these fields. In *Soliloquy*, the true artist is said to be one who is not "at loss in those numbers which make the harmony of a mind. For knavery is mere dissonance and disproportion" (*Soliloquy*, i, 3; CR I, 136). The genuine artist must have an eye or ear for these "inward numbers" (*Soliloquy*, iii, 3; CR I, 217), and "the real honest man . . . instead of outward forms of symmetries, is struck with that of inward character, the harmony and numbers of the heart and beauties of the affections . . ." (*Misc.*, II, i; CR II, 177).

The meaning of "inward numbers" as a key to the virtuous character is obscure: It is not clarified in Shaftesbury's writings and perhaps was not fully clear to him. There may be some Platonic-Pythagorean background to it, which presumably he inherited from Ficino and the Cambridge Platonists. Does he find a basic resemblance between a moral and a mathematical insight? This line of thought has been developed by a number of thinkers of this period, including Samuel Clarke, Sir Isaac Newton's collaborator, and William Wollaston.[37] Charles Taylor suggests that these thinkers are wrong, however, because

> the key analogy behind his numbers and proportions seems to be not so much mathematical necessity as the requirements of orderly wholes. The good life, the good character, was one in which everything took its right place and proportions, no more, no less. The key concept was therefore something like the original Platonic or Stoic one of a whole of things, ordered for the good. One finds the standards by which to live, the firm criteria in nature of the right, through a grasp of the whole order in which one is set. The good person loves the whole order of things. (Taylor 1989, 254)

Shaftesbury does not limit the "natural joy" he describes to the contemplation of harmony and proportion in the fine arts, but finds this joy in the whole range of human activities and pleasures. For Shaftesbury, harmony is not merely a mechanical symmetry of parts in a whole, but rather an organization manifesting an inner creative power. Far from viewing harmony as a static balance of forces, he thinks of it dialectically as the product of a complex interplay of tensions. This is clearly evidenced in his views of the inner harmony of the affections and of the ultimate harmony of Nature. Although he praises symmetry, he does not view harmony as a simple balance of uniform elements. This is evident in his description of the beauties of the natural world, which reveals a genuine appreciation for irregular or asymmetrical design (*Moralists*, iii, 2; CR II, 125).

For this reason Shaftesbury maintains that "the science of virtuosi and that of virtue itself become, in a manner, one and the same" (*Soliloquy*, iii, 3; CR I, 217). The virtuoso appreciates or creates aesthetic form. Because for Shaftesbury aesthetic and moral forms are continuous, to be a virtuoso is one of the best preparations for the moral life; better, he remarks, than mere pedantry or empty scholarship. The true virtuoso understands the principles of harmony that underlie both good art and genuine character. "The moral artist who . . . is thus knowing in the inward form and structure of his fellow-creature, will hardly, I presume, be found unknowing in himself, or at a loss in those numbers which make the harmony of a mind" (*Soliloquy*, i, 3; CR I, 136). Shaftesbury explains that this does not apply to the artist who merely copies external forms, but to the one who represents "the graces and perfections of minds," that is, the moral artist who knows the laws of internal form (135).

Beauty is one of Shaftesbury's "innate" ideas, one of those "ideas" that humans are "really born to and could hardly by any means avoid" (*Misc.*, I, i; CR II, 178). Beauty depends upon the sense of harmony and proportion that Shaftesbury considers "con-natural" and one of the strongest capacities of the mind. Indeed, in addition to explicitly equating the quest for goodness with the quest for beauty, Shaftesbury contends that becoming moral involves becoming a kind of "self-improving artist." The term *self-improving artist* is particularly apt, as it captures Shaftesbury's idea that living well involves taking oneself to be a work of art that one should strive to make as beautiful as possible. Or, as Shaftesbury put it, the "wise and able Man" is he who "having righter models in his eye, becomes in truth the architect of his own life and fortune" (*Moralists*, iii, 2; CR II, 144). Thus, Shaftesbury's moral theory culminates in an aesthetic of creative "inward form," and his legacy is none other than the Greek idea of the beauty of morals. This renewed connection between morality and beauty is one of Shaftesbury's major contributions to the history of ideas.[38]

The moral or good life should never degenerate into moralism, ossified virtue, or mechanical conformity to external or too abstractly applied laws. The good life requires the spontaneity rediscovered after reflection, invention, and creativity; it requires a certain genius. Shaftesbury invites moralists to see in morality one of the fine arts, maybe the finest, given that morality is the art of living.

Shaftesbury insists that humor is indispensable for the practice of the art of living. The good life lies in the cheerfulness, the happiness, and the quietude that result from the exercise of a virtuous character. The harmony of the virtuous character is an effect of proportion, moral tact, and the spontaneity, art, or genius required for its continuous creation. Humor is essential for attaining this character because it teaches proportion, it has the flexibility necessary to promote tact and the art needed to work with one's character in a creative and spontaneous manner.

Yet Shaftesbury does not clearly differentiate between good humor and humor, and between ridicule and humor. Thus, both the following discussion of the comic, which introduces the notion of good humor, and the subsequent discussion of ridicule are relevant to an understanding of the role of humor within the Shaftesburean good life.

THE COMIC

The question of whether life is tragic or comic may be important in its own right. In a study of humor in the good life, it gains added significance because whether we perceive life as tragic or comic may determine whether it should be approached in earnest or jest. For Shaftesbury life is neither tragedy nor comedy, thus neither gravity nor jest is the proper attitude toward it: It is rather a mixture of earnestness and jest. For want of a better term, Shaftesbury deems this mixture, "another species of laughter," which he identifies sometimes as good humor and sometimes as humor (*hilaritas*). Good humor and humor are not clearly differentiated, but Shaftesbury occasionally suggests the latter is a means to the former. Humor is a remedy for the melancholy he diagnoses as the source of both a tragic view of life and certain forms of the comic. Shaftesbury's reasons for assessing life as neither tragedy nor mere comedy, as outlined later, shed light on his views of good humor and humor, and on his difficulty of differentiating the two.

THE TRAGIC AND THE COMIC

Shaftesbury rejects the idea that existence is ultimately tragic on the grounds that the cosmic system excludes all real ill, the world is ruled by both universal and personal providence, human nature is good, death is natural, and virtue secures happiness.

Evil is relegated to the status of appearance and is denied thereby ultimate reality. Nothing that is wholly evil can exist because it would be entirely self-negating (*Moralists*, ii, 3; CR II, 57). Evil, for Shaftesbury, is not an absolute entity; it can only be understood as part of the structure of our experience. The common error human beings make is to evaluate the natural order in relation to the satisfaction of their individual needs and desires. It is the species as a whole, however, and ultimately the universal scheme of things that must be given primary consideration. Nature is "not for man, but man for Nature," and it is man who must "submit to the elements of Nature, and not the elements to him. Few of these are at all fitted to him, and none perfectly" (*Moralists*, ii, 4; CR II, 73).

Nonetheless, Shaftesbury maintains that providence works in and through all events, even the smallest. That is, no part of the universe is logically exempt from the purposive control of the Supreme Mind. Although Shaftesbury holds that "Providence is in all,"[39] that it is both universal and particular, it is only when we see it as universal can we understand it as particular. This line of reasoning leads Shaftesbury to the extreme statements found in his *Exercises*, the private notebooks published after his death: "Persuade them that to be affronted, to be despised, to be poor or to smart, is not to suffer; that the sack or ruin of cities and destruction of mankind are not in themselves ill; and that with respect to the whole, these things are orderly, good, beautiful." One should learn not only to accept whatever happens in the course of events, but also love it, whether it is "hardship, poverty, sickness, death." God kills "kindly, fatherly; for the good of everything, and as the preserver of the whole" (*Life*, 30, 43). Shaftesbury uses more carefully guarded language in the *Characteristics*, though the underlying sentiment is the same.

This is the kind of optimism that Voltaire mercilessly lampoons in *Candide* (1759).[40] For Shaftesbury, however, the notion of evil is significant for designating the existence of unfortunate events in relation to individuals or nations. Shaftesbury does not deny that evil is an actual part of our experience; it is absolute, not proximate, evil that he rejects, and he does so on the grounds that it has no ontological status. His treatment of proximate evils is rigorous and his optimism is by no means naïve and unrealistic. He does not gloss over or deny the depth or the extent of moral and social evils, and he is keenly aware of the power of irrational impulses, the "unnatural affections," in human nature. His letters reveal more clearly than the *Characteristics* that he views life as a continuous struggle against evil forces and corrupted interests. He never advocates the inevitability of progress, and he negates the moral perfectibility of humanity. In *The Moralists*, Palemon cries out: "Oh! What treacheries! What disorders! And how corrupt is all!" (*Moralists*, i, 2; CR II, 13).

Shaftesbury does not ignore the reality of suffering nor seeks to blind us to the tragic facts of our finite experience. Finite tragedies, those from which we suffer in experience, should be properly interpreted, however, as an integral part of a rationally governed whole. To this purpose, we need a right view of God. In contrast, melancholy is at the origin of an erroneous view of religion that yields a tragic view of life: "The melancholy way of treating religion is that which, according to my apprehension, renders it so tragical, and is the occasion of its acting in reality such dismal tragedies in the world" (*Letter*, 4; CR I, 24). It is imperative for Shaftesbury to dissociate religion from melancholic and tragic moods. Otherwise, instead of knowing God, in whom there is no darkness, we risk ascribing our morose attitude and vindictiveness to Him. Melancholy distorts our vision of the world and dread prevents a true understanding of God. Projecting our ill-temper unto God impedes us from approaching Him freely and joyfully. Only ill-humor fails to recognize that God is "the best-natured" mind in the word: "I very much question whether anything besides ill-humor can be the cause of atheism; and certainly nothing else can make us think the Supreme manager sullen, sour, or morose" (*Letter*, 5, 3; CR I, 29, 17–18).

In this passage as well as in others, Shaftesbury's view of melancholy as "ill-humor" is expressed in the terms of the ancient theory of "humors" still in vogue in the eighteenth century. Originally referring to bodily liquids whose balance or imbalance results in health or illness, humoralism is a variant of Empedocles' theory of the four "roots" (earth, air, fire, water), later named the four "elements," the four qualities (hot, cold, moist, dry), and the four temperaments. The four humors and four qualities are phlegm (water, or a watery substance), which is cold and moist; blood, which is hot and moist; black bile or gall, secreted from the kidneys and spleen, cold and dry; and yellow bile or choler, secreted from the liver, hot and dry. Theophrastus (Aristotle's follower and the playwright Menander's teacher) and others developed a set of characters based on the humors to which Shaftesbury is referring. Those with too much blood were sanguine, with too much phlegm phlegmatic, with too much yellow bile choleric, and with too much black bile melancholic. The idea of human personality based on humors contributed to the character comedies of Menander and, later, Plautus. For many centuries, humoralism was accepted culturally as well as medically.[41] Although the theory of humoral types was quite fashionable in England at the end of the seventeenth century, by the eighteenth century the meaning of the English term *humor* became progressively disengaged from the theory of liquids. *Humor* was employed more frequently to designate a disposition of character and to refer to the disequilibrium of humor that reinforces certain psychological traits.

We know of humor's power against melancholy since antiquity as well as through the Renaissance school of medicine of Montpellier, where the French doctor Louis Joubert published treatises on the therapeutic value of humor.[42] Humor, Shaftesbury suggests, "is a kind of specific against superstition and melancholy delusion" (*Essay*, iv, 1; CR I, 85). Arising from the fear of chaos and arbitrariness in nature, melancholy yields disorders such as atheism, fanaticism or superstition—another form of depraved religion. By undermining melancholy or ill-humor, humor helps in attaining the contrary disposition of character—good humor. Shaftesbury maintains that emotional states determine our outlook on life. Thus good humor acquires an epistemological value for him as the only disposition that enables us to perceive the truth about God, nature, human nature, and virtue.

Shaftesbury's argument for good humor can be found in the second miscellany section commenting on his defense of raillery in *Sensus Communis*. Some of the issues about humor, good humor and religion are broached here, although not rigorously pursued. Adopting a formal pose, Shaftesbury announces:

1st. That wit and humor are corroborative of religion, and promotive of true faith.

2nd. That they are used as proper means of this kind by the holy founders of religion.

3rd. That notwithstanding the dark complexion and sour humour of some religious teachers, we may be justly said to have in the main a witty and good-humored religion. (*Misc.*, II, iii; CR II, 217)

The apparently rigorous form of exposition quickly dissolves into loose argument, interspersed with anecdote and stylistic digression before it is abandoned entirely (217–37). Shaftesbury toys here with the relation between seriousness and formal method. Failing to provide a formal exposition of his thoughts, he begs the "methodical reader" to forgive a "writing which is governed less by form than humour" (236).

Shaftesbury's third point is the most substantive. Unfortunately, he abandons his experiment in "formalism" before attending to it. Nevertheless, it is clear that the proposition is intended to praise concepts of divinity as beneficent, interpretations of Jesus as morally exemplary, and the ethic taught by Christianity as benevolent. Shaftesbury devotes considerable attention to the second point, maintaining that the chief "voices" in the Judeo-Christian tradition speak in a good-humored way. Shaftesbury classifies as good-humored writers the authors of the Old Testament, Jesus, the Apostles, and God (227–31). Christ's miracles "carry with them a certain festivity, alacrity, and good humour," and God's good-humored attitude toward Jonah, and even Satan, is for Shaftesbury a model to be emulated. Since the evidence of God's cheerful and good-natured ways are everywhere, he concludes that we have "in the main a witty and good-humoured religion" (217; 229–31). Acknowledging religion as witty and good-humored, as Shaftesbury proposes, would counter the sourness of enthusiastic intolerance: "All I contend for is to think of [religion] in the right humour . . . Good humour," he writes. Insofar as the *Characteristics* constitute a "plea for complacency, sociableness, and good humour in religion," it seeks to submit religion to the discipline of politeness (224).

Perceiving human nature as irremediably flawed may provide an additional argument for viewing life as tragic, but Shaftesbury's bitter view of humanity expressed in certain passages of his precocious *Inquiry Concerning Virtue* is attenuated in his later work, *The Moralists*. Palemon delivers an angry harangue against humanity in the first few pages of the book, yet Palemon's attitude reflects the very idea that the dialogue as a whole seeks to refute.

Shaftesbury's optimism regarding humanity is based on his belief in innate social feelings and a natural capacity for correcting imperfections. Shaftesbury maintains that each particular organism in Nature "certainly and constantly produces what is good to itself, unless something foreign disturbs or hinders it, either by overpowering and corrupting it within, or by violence from without. . . . All weaknesses, distortions, sicknesses, imperfect births, and the seeming contradictions and perversities of nature" result from the influence of some alien element (*Soliloquy*, i, 1; CR I, 106). There exists a built-in tendency in all organisms to correct their own ailments or flaws. Although his argument seems particularly weak at this point,[43] he seems to see in humor and wit the remedy for human ailments: ". . . nature has given us [humor] as a more lenitive remedy against vice, and a kind of specific against superstition and melancholy delusion" (*Essay*, iv, 1; CR I, 85); "for against serious extravagances and splenetic humours there is no other remedy than this [wit]" (*Letter*, 2; CR I, 15). Indeed, melancholy is manifested in isolation and an indifference to social duties and affections for our fellow humans. An excessive love of self, which breeds melancholy, interferes with our duty to an undifferentiated friendship for humanity. To cure melancholy is to put an end to isolation by enabling the social affections necessary for virtue. Humor as a natural cure for melancholy helps bring about the happiness that virtue secures. The role of humor in Shaftesbury's view nuances his earlier bitter view of humanity.

Finally, death, seen by the vulgar as tragic, is for Shaftesbury a natural and harmonious process: "It is a consummation. All the numbers are full; the measures perfect; the harmony complete" (*Life*, 266). The virtuous man has nothing to fear from death, because "by virtue all is made well; for now, if for now only; for hereafter, if for hereafter" (258–66). Death is not to be feared and virtue is sufficient both for this life and an afterlife.

Shaftesbury's rejection of the tragic view of life is firmly grounded, then, in his denial of the ultimate existence of evil, his affirmation of innate goodness and the human ability for self-correction, his confident belief in a benevolent and humorous God, and his conviction that wit and good humor play an important role in religion. Because life is not a tragedy, melancholic and grave attitudes toward life should be eradicated through the remedies with which nature has provided us, namely, wit and humor.

GOOD HUMOR

Life is not tragic for Shaftesbury. This does not mean that he sees it as comedy. He records his thoughts on the matter in his notebooks:

> The buffoon on the stage. We are all but spans and candle-ends. But this is a jest. Is it so? Bring me a Caligula; 'twill be quickly earnest. The comedy of the Gallo-Greeks. Excellent play. Admirable comedian. Nothing more instructive. Who could better make this out? Who ever saw this ridicule better and showed it more perfect? But this was horrid! Was it so? When the jest is turned, it seems it is in earnest and not to be laughed at . . . For what jest with one who considers vicissitudes, periods, the immediate change and incessant eternal conversions, revolutions of world? (*Life*, 66, 193–4)

Shaftesbury admired Epictetus and may have been influenced by the Roman Stoic philosopher's views on laughter. For Epictetus the worst vices are lack of endurance (*intolerantia*), which is a developed form of grief, and lack of restraint (*incontinentia*), which is a persistent inclination toward hilarity. Epictetus finds fault with hilarity (*elatio animi*) because it expresses excessive joy in all that appeals to our appetite. He recommends shunning hilarity and practicing soberness: "Laughter should not be much, nor frequent, nor unrestrained," he advises, and recommends that the philosopher "avoid provoking laughter" as well: "It is a habit from which one easily slides into the ways of the foolish, and apt to diminish the respect which your neighbours feel for you" (Epictetus 1937, CLXV, CLXXI).[44] Shaftesbury develops these views in his *Exercises*:

> No comedy (mere comedy). . . . In the things within is earnest. In the things *without*, what is all but jest? . . . see then if the greatest seriousness be not a very jest. Therefore, be it jest or earnest with others, it can be neither to thyself. Their jest, their earnest: both in a manner a jest. But the use of this jest, a serious matter and far from jest. So then use it right within; and for without remember the medium and find the balance as become thee. (*Life*, 193–4)

Shaftesbury's internalization of jest may be a response to the Epictetan rejection of laughter. Moreover, by distinguishing between the vulgar and the philosophical use of jest, Shaftesbury lends philosophical value to internal laughter.

Another ancient philosopher Shaftesbury seeks to emulate in the matter of jest is the Xenophonic Socrates. Contrary to the doxology of ancient philosophy, Shaftesbury describes a genealogy according to which Socrates "containing within himself the several genius's of philosophy, gave rise to all those several manners in which that Science was delivered."[45] The manners to which Shaftesbury refers are the sublime, the comic, the methodical, and the simple, each associated with one of Socrates' disciples. Plato, "of noble birth and lofty genius, who aspired to poetry and rhetoric," according to Shaftesbury, followed the sublime route. Antisthenes, "of mean birth, and poorest circumstances, whose constitution as well as condition inclined him most to the way we call satiric, took the reproving part, which in his better-humoured and more agreeable successor [Diogenes] turned into the comic kind." Aristotle is the progenitor of the methodical (or scholastic) manner of philosophizing. The fourth is Xenophon the polite, "another noble disciple, whose genius was towards action, and who proved afterwards the greatest hero of his time" (*Soliloquy*, II, ii; CR I, 254–6).

Shaftesbury finds in Xenophon an author who "was as distant, on the one hand, from the sonorous, high, and pompous starin; as, on the other hand, from the ludicrous, mimical, or satiric" (*Soliloquy*, II, ii; CR I, 254–6). In his notes for a projected book on the life of Socrates ("Design of a Socratick History"), Shaftesbury complains that Plato's version of his master was sometimes too buffooning. Xenophon "took the genteeler part, and softer manner. He joined what was deepest and most solid in philosophy, with what was easiest and most refined in breeding, and in the character and manner of a gentleman."[46]

The most frequently cited author in the *Characteristics* is not Xenophon, however, but the first century BC satirist and popularizer of Stoicism—Horace. Shaftesbury sees in Horace a fellow aspirant of Stoic wisdom, who succeeded in using his comic gifts in the service of philosophy when addressing an audience predisposed to wit and humor rather than severe virtue. In writing for men such as the corrupt Maecenas, the Roman poet is forced to conceal his Stoicism "artfully" with "an Air of Raillery." Shaftesbury notes, however, that Horace at his best employs a refined form of humor, observing a "just measure" of irony that can be distinguished from the scurrility of his Epicurean period. Shaftesbury associates this superior form of irony with the Socratic way, and commends it as "not offensive, Injourouse, Hypocritical, Bitter, and contrary to all true simplicity, Honesty or good Manners."[47]

Shaftesbury's view of the right use of jest leads to a criticism of the satirists and the unrestrained comics of both antiquity and his era. Contrary to Horace, who used wit to promote philosophic truth, Shaftesbury condemns Lucian of Samasota, the second century AD satirist, for being dissolute in style and manners, denouncing him as a wretch, profane, "horridly Vicious and Licentious."[48] The Greek playwright Menander is moral and polite, as is his Roman counterpart, Terence, but the remaining playwrights are condemned by Shaftesbury: "As for Aristophanes, a Plautus, a modern play, modern wit, raillery, humour, away!"[49] Shaftesbury also finds fault with ridicule as practiced in his day: So excessively and extensively this distasteful wit is used, that the ablest men in affairs of state are the most notable buffoons, the most celebrated men of letters, the greatest masters of burlesque (*Essay*, i, 2; CR I, 44–45). "Buffoonery, satire and the common wit" are examples of contemptible human pursuits (*Life*, 53); contemporary satire is "scurrilous, buffooning, and without morals or instruction" (*Soliloquy*, ii, 3; CR I, 173), and Swift is detestable, obscene and profane—a false wit.[50] Satire is the necessary outcome of melancholy:

> All splenetic people, whether naturally such or made so by ill usage, have a necessary propensity to criticism or satire. The spirit of satire rises with the ill mood, and the chief passion of men thus diseased and thrown out of good humour is to find fault, censure, unravel, confound and leave nothing without exception and controversy. (*Misc.*, II, 3; CR II, 384–5)

Shaftesbury's view of life as no mere comedy is reflected in his criticism of comedies and satires that attempt to raise a laugh with no regard for morality.

Following the Stoics, Shaftesbury maintains that there is a correlation between the way we view reality and our attitude toward it. However, the vulgar attitude is not indicative of the true state of things: "The same rash opinion creates the evil as the good, where in reality there is neither. . . . Why tragedy? Why a stage? Why witnesses?" (*Life*, 203). In contradistinction to the vulgar view of reality, he resolves that "no more of these parts to act, no tragedy. No comedy (mere comedy)" (*Life*, 193–4). Violent alternations from earnestness to jest should be particularly avoided: "Ridiculous! In humour; out of humour. Now no jest; now no earnest. Now play, odious; now seriousness, more odious. All joy (good news!). All sorrow (bad news again!)" (*Life*, 193). He portrays accordingly his ideal as a balance:

This middle genius, partaking neither of hearty mirth nor seriousness . . . If on the one hand thou strenuously resist what offers from the vulgar side and that facetious comic kind, whatever it be of wit, jest, story, and the like; and if, on the other hand, thou as strenuously resist and abstain from that as ridiculous seriousness and solemnity in these affairs, eager contention and striving in the concerns of others, and for the reformation and conviction of others. (*Life*, 194–5)

Elsewhere he describes "a mirth not out of the reach of wit is gravest. A gravity not abhorrent from the use of that other mirth. In this balance seek a character" (*Life*, 362). The mixture of "jest" and "earnest" that Shaftesbury calls "soft irony" characterizes the social self at its best, that is, a social self that corresponds with the philosophical self: "Such a tenour as this, such a key, tone, voice, [is] constituent with true gravity and simplicity, though accompanied with humor and a mind of raillery" (*Life*, 362–6). While the Shaftesburean ideal self maintains gravity and simplicity, it mitigates seriousness with humor and raillery.

Because Shaftesbury believes that the appropriate attitude toward life that is neither tragic nor comic is a middle way characterized by neither hearty mirth nor seriousness, he is not interested in the satirical method but rather in a "sober kind of cheerfulness." He admires the method of the magistrate who uses no "caustics, incisions, and amputations," all satirical methods, but "softest balms," and "with a kind of sympathy" soothes, satisfies, and endeavors "by cheerful ways, to divert and heal" (*Letter*, 2–3; CR I, 17, 12, 14). Good humor is his explicit remedy for the melancholy of satire (*Misc.*, II, iii; CR II, 223).

Both in the *Exercises* and in an unpublished text in Latin, "Pathologia sive Explicatio Affectum Humanorum," Shaftesbury portrays his ideal by differentiating between hearty laughter and a gentler kind of laughter. In the *Exercises*, he writes:

How happy would it be, therefore, to exchange this vulgar, sordid, profuse, horrid laughter for that more reserved, gentle kind, which hardly is to be called laughter, or which at least is of another species? How happy to exchange this mischievous, insulting, petulant species for that benign, courteous, and kind? This rustic, barbarous, inane, for that civil, polite, humane? The noisy, boisterous, turbulent, loud, for the still peaceful, serene, mild? (*Life*, 226)

He advises himself to use this kind of laughter only: "Remember what a happiness, improvement, enjoyment, to reserve all that is humorous and pleasant in the temper for such geniuses as those, and for that divine facetiousness (if so I may call it) of the divine man [Epictetus]" (*Life*, 82).[51] The geniuses whose laughter he seeks to emulate are, as we have seen, Socrates and his follower Xenophon, the playwright of the new comedy Menander, but also the cynics Demonax and Diogenes,[52] because cynicism was praised by Epictetus. This philosophic laughter, the Epictetean "divine facetiousness," Shaftesbury calls good humor, or simply humor—the term by which we know it today.

A telling description of Shaftesbury's favored kind of laughter can be found in the unpublished Latin text that antedates *A Letter Concerning Enthusiasm*—"Pathologia sive Explicatio Affectum Humanorum."[53] His general argument in this work is that Horace, while laughing, provides a complete description of Stoic epistemology in the third satire of his second book. It is all a matter of judging Horace's irony, and his laughter, aright. Shaftesbury's treatise finishes with a long discussion on the nature of laughter, whose end he reiterates in *A Letter Concerning Enthusiasm*. As his later prose in English tends to avoid the pedagogic style that characterizes "Pathologia," nothing he subsequently writes on the subject of laughter is as precise as its description in "Pathologia." In this work, Shaftesbury distinguishes between two different kinds of laughter, *jocositas* or mockery, which is a form of evil, and *hilaritas*, the Latin term for humor, which is a form of admiration:

> For *hilaritas* [humor] and *jocositas* [mockery] are not the same thing. Indeed, *hilaritas*, this sort of moderate laughter which can be mastered is a form of admiration, a certain joy which is born of the spectacle or the examining of an exterior object that we judge beautiful. For if we consider this object as pertaining to ourselves, either naturally or at the end of the effort which allowed us to make it ours, immediately such joy deteriorates into boastfulness or pride, if it is about very high qualities. *Jocositas* is a sort of hearty laughter, which does not let itself be managed, for it is the joy that a shameful hideousness in another causes us, which is foreign to us but as if it represented a good for us. Pleasure and joy can come from a good and beautiful object, either such or one which we take it for such. Since such a laughter is no desire nor aversion nor pain, but pleasure and joy, it follows necessarily that its object, that is, this ridicule or this evil, is held as good and beautiful from our point of view. It is therefore from malevolence

and hatred that this laughter stems, it is therefore a species of evil (malevolence), a pleasure derived from the misfortune of another. (P.R.O 30/24/26/7, I, my translation)

The remainder of the text makes Shaftesbury's case clear—because *jocositas* or hearty laughter cannot be tamed, it must be eradicated. As Shaftesbury explains in his notebooks, until this kind of laughter is completely eliminated, laughter cannot be controlled. Only when hearty laughter has entirely vanished, can the other kind of laughter—"this sort of moderate laughter which can be mastered"—be used without fear of losing control. The second kind of laughter, *hilaritas*, derives from admiration and laughs with beauty rather than at ugliness. Admiration should be directed only outwards, for when directed inward it turns into pride or boastfulness. As in the *Exercises*, Shaftesbury calls *hilaritas* good humor or simply humor.

Through his notion of humor, Shaftesbury revives an ancient philosophic ideal that furthers the eighteenth-century view of humor as amiable. The notion of amiable humor is promoted by, and in turn helps to promote, close interrelations between jest, on the one hand, and earnestness, tragedy, tears, melancholy, sympathy, and pathos, on the other.[54] The ideal of amiable humor underlies Shaftesbury's disapproval of other forms of the comic whose aim is not moral criticism and also presupposes the taming of any other kind of laughter.

Shaftesbury is part of the Cambridge Latitudinarian tradition, which holds a similar view on the importance of good humor. According to the Latitudinarians, nature and reason as the first manifestations of divine light are not wholly corrupted by the fall. Claiming an affinity with John Tillotson, the archbishop of Canterbury, as well as to the Cambridge divines, the Latitudinarians insist on the necessity of a good disposition because faith lies not in sermons but in practice, and true practice cannot be motivated by fear. Shaftesbury's first venture into literature is a laudatory preface to an edition of sermons by the Latitudinarian Benjamin Whichcote (1698).[55] For Whichcote humor is the appropriate disposition of the Christian. He argues that Christian life is not based on fear of sanctions, whether civil (as he thought Hobbes held) or divinely decreed (as in radical Calvinism, which he perceives as melancholic). On the contrary, he claims, Christian life presupposes the development of a good nature, the cultivation of a good temperament, and the prayer of joy.

The Latitudinarians consider (good) humor in this sense to be identical with the religious attitude, but they oppose raillery and wit. Tillotson distinguishes between joy that facilitates the reception of Revelation, and ridicule and wit that erroneously attack the most sacred subjects. Stuart

Tave suggests that "the subsuming category of ill-natured wit, of which rail-lery was the social form and satire the literary, was ridicule, and against this, the root of evil, the severest attack was made" (Tave 1960, 27). Shaftesbury is not only part of the Latitudinarian tradition, but also more generally, of the seventeenth-century movement that attempted to bring joy back to religion.[56] He deviates considerably, however, from the Latitudinarian tradi-tion: In equating wit and humor, he transforms Whichcote and Tillotson's views on humor from a disposition toward religion into a judgment of reli-gion.[57] Moreover, whereas both consider good humor an attitude that opens the mind to faith, the Latitudinarians reject ill-intentioned wit or raillery. Shaftesbury, in contrast, defends wit and raillery unconditionally, allowing its use in matters of religion as well. For this reason, Shaftesbury's views of ridicule, humor, and wit cannot be reduced to his ideal of good humor.

RIDICULE

Shaftesbury ascribes epistemological value to good humor as the attitude through which truth is most likely to be grasped. Important as good humor is to the Shaftesburean good life, Shaftesbury is best remembered by both defenders and adversaries as the proponent of a doctrine compressed into the phrase "ridicule, the test of truth." *Ridicule* is an important term in an investigation of Shaftesbury's view of humor in the good life, not only because the term has been closely associated with him, but also because it is the key to understanding Shaftesbury's views of humor and wit. Determin-ing the meaning of "ridicule, the test of truth," requires, first, examining Shaftesbury's explanations of the relations of ridicule with truth and reason; and, second, understanding how Shaftesbury uses the notion of ridicule in his writings.

RIDICULE AND TRUTH

The phrase "ridicule, the test of truth" never appears in exactly this form in the *Characteristics*, although Shaftesbury comes close to it in several places. There are four passages that seem to refer to ridicule as the test of truth. The first passage associates reasoning with the test of ridicule: "How comes it to pass, then, that we appear such cowards in reasoning, and are so afraid to stand the test of ridicule?" (*Letter*, 2; CR I, 10). The second suggests that justified raillery is a principal proof of truth: "Truth, 'tis supposed, may bear all lights; and one of those principal lights, or natural mediums by which things are to be viewed, in order to a thorough recognition, is ridicule itself, or that manner of proof by which we discern whatever is liable to just raillery in any subject" (*Essay*, i, 2; CR I, 44). The third substitutes wit and humor to ridicule: "Without wit and humour, reason can hardly have its proof or be distinguished" (*Essay*, i, 5; CR I, 52). Finally, the fourth passage suggests that humor and gravity test each other: " 'Twas the saying of an ancient sage . . . that humour was the only test of gravity, and gravity of humour. For a subject which should not bear raillery was suspicious; and a jest which would not bear serious examination was certainly false wit" (*Essay*, i, 5; CR I, 52). A closer approximation to "ridicule, the test of truth" is found in some of the index entries Shaftesbury listed in the 1712 edition of the *Characteristics*:

> Ridicule, its Rule, Measure, Test.
> Test of Ridicule.
> Truth bears all Lights. —Ridicule a Light, Criterion to Truth.
>   (CR3 III)

The controversy surrounding Shaftesbury's view of ridicule and its relation with truth and reason has generated a heated debate in the eighteenth century, which is addressed at the end of this chapter. To this day, commentators are divided in their understanding of the meaning of Shaftesbury's views of ridicule.[58] The majority of contemporary scholars, however, agree that the phrase "ridicule, the test of truth" does not adequately represent Shaftesbury's views because, they point out, he is advocating "the test of ridicule" and not a "test of truth."-

Shaftesbury never implies that "Ridicule is the only infallible test of truth," as one of his contemporaries claims,[59] nor does he ever contend, as another charges, that ridicule "may be successfully applied to the investigation of unknown Truth" (Brown 1751a, 6). For Shaftesbury, ridicule is not a means to discovering new truth, nor is it a logical proof of the truth or falsity of a proposition. It is doubtful that Shaftesbury ever thinks of ridicule as a mode of cognition. Ridicule is an instrument of reason, and it is reason ultimately that must distinguish between truth and falsehood. Nonetheless, there are four major ways of understanding what Shaftesbury means by ridicule as the test of truth.

1. One way of understanding "ridicule, the test of truth" is to take the phrase at face value and to assess it in light of Shaftesbury's theory of truth. Shaftesbury holds that reality is an organic, harmonious, and perfectly congruous whole. Any statement that is true, or any statement that is descriptive of this reality, cannot but refer to these features, and although these characteristics may not give us a definition of truth, they

do provide us with a criterion of truth. On the contrary, anything that lacks the characteristics of organic harmony and congruity is unreal. Any statement, therefore, that is incongruous, any statement that reveals an internal disharmony, is untrue. Falsehood is characterized by a quality that can only be described as ridiculous.

To assess Shaftesbury's view of ridicule, his view of truth should be further clarified. Shaftesbury never doubts that a genuinely free interplay of ideas ensures that the best will prevail; only bad ideas suffer when subjected to free and humorous treatment:

> I can very well suppose men may be frightened out of their wits, but I have no apprehension they should be laughed out of them. I can hardly imagine that in a pleasant way they should ever be talked out of their love for society, or reasoned out of human-ity and common sense. A mannerly wit can hurt no cause or interest for which I am in the least concerned; and philosophical speculations, politely managed, can never surely render mankind more unsociable or uncivilized. (*Essay*, ii, 3; CR I, 65)

Shaftesbury's defense of freedom of thought is based on the assumption that truth is more powerful than error: "Truth is the most powerful thing in the world, since even fiction itself must be governed by it, and can only please by its resemblance" (*Letter*, 1; CR I, 6). Falsity mimics truth, exists only as its parasite, and lies paradoxically reaffirm it. Thus, Shaftesbury is overwhelmingly confident that, where men are allowed free trial and experience, truth will prevail: "Let but the search go freely on, and the right measure of everything will soon be found" (*Letter*, 2; CR I, 10). In accordance with Shaftesbury's belief that free trade in goods is indicative of a healthy economy, free trade in ideas indicates a healthy culture. Free exchange of ideas is important for the religious sphere as well. As expected from an advocate of rational religion, reason for Shaftesbury presents no threat to religious truth. True theism can only benefit from the establish-ment of an entire philosophical liberty (*Life*, 353), by which he means rational discussion in contradistinction to an appeal to emotions.

Shaftesbury's confidence in the power of truth to maintain its own in free discussion may seem optimistic, but it is not naïve. He recognizes that human beings may err as well as be misled by others, and that liberty can be abused, but he believes that generally extremes balance each other and are tempered by good manners; atheists in his own time, he notes, are using "modester and more polite" language (*Life*, 353). It is important to remember, finally, that his optimism about the predominance of truth is conditional on the degree to which human beings attain self-mastery and harmony of the affections, which are the prerequisites of sound reasoning and true freedom.

In a world where truth predominates and reason always benefits by free discussion, ridicule can pose no threat. In *A Letter Concerning Enthusiasm* Shaftesbury asks: "What ridicule can lie against reason?" (*Letter*, 2; CR I, 10). Indeed, he suggests that virtue has less to fear from its "witty antagonists" than from some of its ardent defenders. Yet, one cannot help asking, what about wit that is not "mannerly" and philosophy that is not "politely managed?" Like others in the eighteenth century, Leibniz believes that the widespread use of ridicule might hurt truth itself because "men love less to reason than to laugh." Though he approves the use of wit against fanaticism, Leibniz fears the consequences of its application to the "truly good and sacred," for anything, regardless of its merit, can be made to appear ridiculous.[60] Moreover, Leibniz thinks that since laughter escapes reason and thus tends toward excess, the distinction between vulgar and moderate laughter is aleatory. The vulgar is more extensive than generally assumed: a great number of educated persons are vulgar with regard to reason, Leibniz believes. To count on reason to regulate laughter is illusory. Shaftesbury is particularly open to this criticism, Leibniz suggests, for at times he seems to forget the questionable ends to which humor may be put.

Two answers to these objections can be found in the *Characteristics*. The first is that humor should be controlled and regulated; the second is that truth is congruous and harmonious. Acknowledging the excesses to which wit may be carried, Shaftesbury's first answer insists primarily on the auto-regulation of humor:

> 'T'is in reality a serious study to learn to temper and regulate that humor which nature has given us as a more lenitive remedy against vice, and a kind of specific against superstition and melancholy delusion. There is a great difference between seeking how to raise a laugh from everything, and seeking in everything what justly may be laughed at. (*Essay*, iv, 1; CR I, 85)

There is a difference between "genteel wit" or "true raillery," on the one hand, and mere "buffoonery" or "banter," on the other. For Shaftesbury, the former is an instrument of reason; it presupposes self-control and the regulation of the passions. The latter form of laughter, "banter," is a passion, as are "extravagant mirth, airiness, humour, fantasticalness, buffoonery, drollery," whose control is as difficult as it is necessary and might come at the social cost of appearing uncouth:

There is nothing more unsafe, or more difficult of management. . . . It is enough to say that it is wholly unmanageable
whilst any of that impotent sort remains, or whilst anything
of this kind is in the least degree involuntary in the temper,
and not perfectly under command. But what strength of mind,
constancy, and firmness this implies is easy to understand. (*Life*,
152–3)

Moreover, laughter is "malignity hid under humanity" (160). It should
be rejected since it runs counter to sympathy:

Consider the thing itself; in the bottom, what? [malevolence]. . . .
Gall, venom; but of a different kind, and more hidden. That anger;
this contempt. That reproof; this reproach. . . . See it in excess,
see it when given way to and soundly followed. The characters it
forms, the tempers, humors, morals of such as these. . . . The well-
bred people . . . and the mere vulgar—porters, carmen, clowns;
and to which of these most belongs the hearty laugh? . . .
    Caligula, whose whole character was of this sort: a play,
sport, a mockery of mankind; . . . and all this with humour,
raillery, wit, a comedy. . . . Go to prison and see things there.
Who merrier (as they say) than those jail-birds? See . . . the
character of the galley-slaves and common rogues. The humour
of the soldiery when most of all cruel and in the very actions
of cruelty. . . . Who merrier? Where is drollery, buffoonery, jest
more perfect or more thorough? Where is the laugh heartier,
sounder? Who have more of it? Deeper of it? Who have it in
more perfection, more *bona-fide*, and (as they say) from the very
heart? Poor, mad people and naturals, how treated? . . . The
diversion of seeing Bedlam. The usual entertainments of princes
and such as those: the court fool, the dwarf, man-monkey, or
any such mockery of human kind . . . yet what is better received
than these jests? What a better laugh? See the malignity of this,
and by this judge of all other laugh. (*Life*, 225–6)[61]

This amounts to a rejection of laughter. It is surprising coming from the
advocate of the freedom of ridicule, but not from "the friend of man," as
Herder called Shaftesbury.[62]
    As with any other passion, laughter can be tamed by Stoic techniques
of self-mastery: "The best practice and exercise is to go by contraries, just in
the teeth of temper, just opposite to humour" (*Life*, 195). Another exercise

is to "laugh alone and even at serious times, or rather then most at all." Choosing laughter "at contrary times, and excite to it rather than be carried to it by temper," helps control it. More advice includes avoiding "drollery and obscenity," which are of "the ill sort" that pertain to "that wrong and involuntary kind." The general guiding maxim is Epictetean: "Let not your laughter be excessive" (82). Shaftesbury uses the Stoic techniques of inversion and reduction: Inversion is defined as "the wrestling [of fancies] from their natural and vulgar sense into a meaning truly natural and free of delusion and imposture"; reduction, to use a medical metaphor, is to purge a representation artificially inflated, and as though it were purulent, in order to reduce it to its true principle (P.R.O. 30/24/27/10, 112, 354). With inversion and reduction, humor (*hilaritas*) takes the place of mockery (*jocositas*), as the goal of the soliloquy is to tame impotent laughter in order to make room for laughter as an instrument of reason. Moreover, the eradication of hearty laughter is necessary in order to find a balance between gravity and mirth: "A mirth not out of the reach of wit is gravest . . . a gravity not abhorrent from the use of that other mirth . . ." (362). This is Shaftesbury's ideal of good humor.[63]

In addition to the private taming of laughter, Shaftesbury maintains that wit and humor tend to correct and refine themselves in company. "Freedom of wit," thus, is the best protection against false wit or "scurrilous buffoonery":

> . . . wit will mend upon our hands, and humour will refine itself, if we take care not to tamper with it, and bring it under constraint, by severe usage and rigorous prescriptions. All politeness is owing to liberty. We polish one another, and rub off our corners and rough sides by a sort of amicable collision. (*Essay*, i, 1; CR I, 46)

Even if wit exceeds its proper limits, which Shaftesbury concedes it may, an appeal to the magistrate for repression by force is not a good policy. If persons do not have the good sense to correct erroneous impressions in their own minds, governmental interference is not likely to help; rather it may make the situation worse, for political repression tends to encourage the "bantering" spirit.

Although thought cannot be forcibly controlled, the public expression of opinion can and should be regulated to some degree. In public gatherings certain conventional limitations should be accepted willingly out of respect for common feeling and as a matter of good taste: "The lovers of mankind respect and honor conventions and societies of men" (*Essay*, i, 1; CR I,

46). In general, Shaftesbury's views on tolerance are in accord with those of John Locke and Matthew Tindal, whom he expressly praises.[64] Thus, the liberty he defends amounts to "the liberty of the club," or the complete liberty of private conversation (*Essay*, i, 5; CR I, 53).

Shaftesbury's claim that humor should be both autoregulated and refined through private conversation is his first response to those who criticize his view of ridicule as a test of truth. The second and more fundamental answer Shaftesbury offers is based upon the conviction that truth and virtue are ultimately congruous and harmonious, whereas error and vice are incongruous and inharmonious. Because the essence of the comic for Shaftesbury is incongruity and inconsistency, he sees error and vice as inherently ridiculous. On the other hand, truth and virtue do not lend themselves properly to comic treatment, as their mark is congruence and consistency:

> Nothing is ridiculous except what is deformed; nor is anything proof against raillery except what is handsome and just. . . . A man must be soundly ridiculous who, with all the wit imaginable, would go about to ridicule wisdom, or laugh at honesty, or good manners. (*Essay*, iv, 1; CR I, 85f)

Shaftesbury concedes that humor may be directed against good causes and against truth itself. He is willing to take this risk, however, because of his conviction that in a free society truth in the long run triumphs. Truth prevails because he believes true wit picks the right objects to ridicule, whereas false wit does not.

The theory that ridicule is a test of truth may be seen as a logical development of Shaftesbury's optimistic philosophy. Philosophical optimism of the kind advocated in the *Characteristics* considers evil illusory. Much of what we regard as evil is not evil at all, according to this view, only part of a larger good; but in so far as evil does manifest itself, it conflicts with what is real. It can be laughed at as, strictly speaking, pure nonsense. Intrinsic evil is self-contradictory because ultimately it does not exist. Evil, which is tantamount to ugliness for Shaftesbury, is ridiculous, not only in the sense that it is capable of being ridiculed, but also in the sense that it is silly. This is the belief at the core of Shaftesbury's remarks on ridicule. One can safely laugh at evil, for good will always stands the test of ridicule, whereas evil will be seen in its true light as foolish. Thus, Shaftesbury maintains "it is the hardest thing in the world to deny fair honesty the use of this weapon, which can never bear an edge against herself" (*Essay*, iv, 1; CR I, 85).

The idea that ridicule is a test of truth should be understood in light of Shaftesbury's theory of truth is Richard Brett's reading. He bases it on his conviction that the idea that ridicule is a test of truth is not something Shaftesbury thought out in passing. More than an aphorism, it is something he consistently maintained, firmly believed, and that moreover makes sense in relation to his view of truth as congruence and falsehood as incongruity (Brett 1951, 171).[65] The problem with this reading is that it makes the relation between ridicule and truth dependent on a view of truth that most of us may find difficult to endorse. Konrad Lorenz's recent views on humor may shed light on the meaning of Shaftesbury's view of ridicule as a test of truth without encountering this obstacle.

2. Konrad Lorenz makes humor a detector of insincerity rather than falsehood. Repeating almost *verbatim* the usual arguments in favor of the idea that ridicule or humor are allies of reason, Lorenz writes that Humanistic ideals "have for their ally a heaven-sent gift of man . . . a faculty as specifically human as speech or moral responsibility: humour. In its highest forms, it appears to be specially evolved to give us the power of sifting the true for the false" (Lorenz 1966, 252). According to this view, humor is not a detector of error, but of lies and insincerity, and may function as the best test of truth in that sense:

> Humour is the best of lie-detectors and it discovers, with an uncanny flair, the speciousness of contrived ideals and the insincerity of simulated enthusiasm. When pompousness is abruptly debunked, when the balloon of puffed-up arrogance is pricked by humour and bursts with a loud report, we can indulge in uninhibited refreshing laughter which is liberated by this special kind of sudden relief of tension. It is one of the few absolutely uncontrolled discharges of an instinctive motor pattern in man of which responsible morality wholly approves. Responsible morality not only approves of the effects of humour but finds a strong support in it . . . satire is the right sort of sermon for today. In any case, there is no doubt that humour is rapidly becoming more effective, more searching and more subtle in detecting dishonesty. (252–3)

According to Lorenz and Shaftesbury before him, humor, inasmuch as it ridicules insincere ideals, is a powerful ally of morality, and even more so when used as self-ridicule.[66]

3. Like Lorenz, Alfred Aldridge, Ernst Cassirer and Jean-Paul Larthomas translate Shaftesbury's doctrine of ridicule as the test of truth into

a statement about insincerity (Aldridge 1945, 154; Cassirer 1953; Lartho-mas 1986). Ridicule should be used against a mistaken seriousness and an arrogated dignity, against pedantry and bigotry (Cassirer 1953, 183). Shaftesbury believes that whoever fears the liberty of wit and humor hides his pretensions under false gravity. This is the very essence of imposture (Larthomas 1986, 359). Gravity, seriousness, and formalism are indicative of imposture, and should be eradicated in us first (*Letter*, 2; CR I, 10–11). But Larthomas adds the following argument: If the relation to truth is false, if the conviction is inauthentic, virtue is only "mechanical." This is a consistent theme in Shaftesbury, inspired even in the terminology used by one of the Cambridge Platonists, John Smith. In *Excellency and Noble-ness of True Religion* (1660), Smith writes: "There are a sort of *mechanical* Christians in the world, that not finding Religion acting like a *living form* within them, satisfy themselves only to make an Art of it. . . . But true Religion indeed is not Art, but an *inward* Nature that contains all the laws and *measures* of its motion within it self" (Smith 1660, chap. 3, sec. 1).

Larthomas' reading of Shaftesbury elucidates the role of ridicule not as a test establishing truth, but rather as a test of the authenticity of a subjective appropriation of truth. The tact appropriate to the moral sense maintains the mobility of the relation of the finite to the infinite, of the internal form to the Idea, of reason and enthusiasm. Through its relation to the infinite, enthusiasm exalts value; on the other hand, through their relation to the finite, wit and humor minimize and relativize value. The tact required for moral sense presupposes a shift in emphasis from ridicule to the urbanity of wit and humor, and from the other as the target to oneself. This will be explained further in the section on wit and humor.

4. Finally, one more reading of ridicule as a test of truth should be mentioned. For Stanley Grean, the phrase "ridicule, the test of truth" denotes the free and objective state of mind with which we approach a subject and evaluate it (Grean 1967, 123–4). Nothing should be exempt from raillery as a means—whether by satire, irony, farce, or simply asking "is it not ridiculous?"—to examine the various aspects of a subject. Grean suggests that the logical terminology "test" and "criterion," although mis-leading, have at least a figurative application: Ridicule has a kind "of *proving* power in that what cannot stand up under free and humorous examina-tion, in Shaftesbury's opinion, is not well-grounded in reason and Nature" (Grean 1967, 124).

Stuart Tave, however, dismisses ridicule altogether: not only "Shaft-esbury nowhere clearly says that it is a test," but "his true path was the middle way of good humour" (Tave 1960, 35, 39). Shaftesbury's true path is indeed good humor, as Tave argues, but I believe he is mistaken in dismissing ridicule, which is the Shaftesburean way of attaining good humor.

With the exception of Tave's view, the above interpretations are not mutually exclusive. If ridicule is the test of truth for Shaftesbury, as I believe, with Brett, that it is, it follows that whatever cannot withstand free and humorous examination cannot be well-grounded in reason either, as Grean holds, and that ridicule's chief value may lie in its use as a test of demeanor to unmask imposture, as Aldridge, Cassirer and Larthomas maintain. Examining Shaftesbury's use of ridicule to restrict enthusiasm—a necessary condition for achieving a harmonious and virtuous character— may help determine the meaning of ridicule as a test of truth.

APPLYING RIDICULE

Shaftesbury uses ridicule to criticize enthusiasm, a popular term at the time denoting religious fanaticism. He suggests that individuals must search inward to discover the principle of mastering enthusiasm for beneficial use. This is accomplished through humor and the rhetorical device of ridicule, whose desired effect is to encourage dialogue and the open testing of ideas.

Two instances of ridicule aimed against religious enthusiasm include a satire and an open letter. In the short satire *The Adept Ladys* (1702), Shaftesbury mocks representatives of the Quaker sect accused of "enthusiasm," a state that poses a threat to the enthusiast as well as society because he lacks the self-awareness required for limiting delirium. In *A Letter Concerning Enthusiasm* (1708), a response to the London appearance of a group of prophetically inspired Christians, Shaftesbury anonymously ridicules religious delusion. He proposes good humor as a more efficient means than shrill polemics and publicly orchestrated persecutions to disarm what are considered dangerously deluded people. Shaftesbury introduces humor into the discussion of religion because he believes that there is no better test for the truth of a claim than its ability to withstand ridicule. Good humor not only fosters tolerance, but by permitting wit and ridicule to examine religious doctrine, also furthers freedom of thought.

Not surprisingly, *A Letter Concerning Enthusiasm* was greeted with a storm of abuse, its opponents rushing to publish against what they considered an assault on religion itself. In response to several pamphlets attacking the *Letter*,[67] Shaftesbury wrote *Sensus Communis: An Essay on the Freedom of Wit and Humour* (1709), where he elaborated his views on humor and did nothing to remove the impression given in his *Letter*. Shaftesbury's *Miscellaneous Reflections* unmistakably ridicules the integrity of priestcraft, the authenticity of the Scriptures, the credibility of miracles, and the High Church's dangerous pretensions (Misc., II, ii; CR II, 212–4).[68]

Shaftesbury maintains that religion must be subjected to the test of ridicule, a view that disturbed many of his ecclesiastical contemporaries. This idea, however, is not new. John Dryden, for example, considers the "satirical poet . . . the check of the laymen on bad priests" (Dryden 1926, II, 260; quoted in Grean 1967, 122), and poking fun at clerics a practice at least as old as Chaucer. Shaftesbury, however, gives it a sharper expression. Not only enthusiasm, but also all religious practices and beliefs should be able to vindicate themselves when put to humor's test. He commends the "reverend authors" who make use of humor to answer heresy and doubt, suggesting that they may laugh some men into religion who had previously been laughed out of it. Shaftesbury finds a deep underlying connection between true religion and "good humor"; in light of the fact that mental attitudes associated with humor open rather than close the mind to true faith, only false religion has reason to fear humorous treatment.

Shaftesbury caricatures the zealot as a figure of unsociability (Moralists, I, iii; CR I, 24–25). The enthusiast attempts to impose his will on others and coerce them into accepting his opinion; Shaftesbury sees him as the opposite of the person whose social interactions foster in others a sense of their autonomy. It is against this antisocial figure that Shaftesbury mounts his defense of raillery as a servant of reason: "freedom of raillery" is "a liberty in decent language to question every thing, and an allowance of unraveling or refuting any argument, without offence to the arguer" (Essay, ii, 4; CR I, 49). The assertion that certain subjects are too grave to be ridiculed should be discarded because "gravity is of the very essence of imposture." The substance and tone of public discourse has to be as free as possible of unwarranted claims to authority. It is necessary to distinguish true gravity from false gravity, and only the former can withstand ridicule. Moreover, a public discourse that is not grave but "light" is quite probably the most serious discourse of all (Essay, i, 6; CR I, 54).

Because for Shaftesbury enthusiasm is the product of "ill-humor" and fear, persecution is bound to promote not discourage such fanaticism (Misc., II, iii; CR II, 221). The state should thus exercise good humor and seek to allay fears rather than raise them when dealing with socially dangerous fanaticism. This is the only hope, according to Shaftesbury, for inducing an attitude of acceptance toward new or different ideas. The view that fanaticism or enthusiasm is the product of ill-humor or melancholy can be found in Locke's An Essay Concerning Human Understanding: Fanaticism is melancholy mixed with devotion (Locke, 1964 [1690], Bk. IV, chap. 19, sec. 7). Humor can be potently associated with enthusiasm because at the root of enthusiasm lies melancholy:

> There is a melancholy that accompanies all enthusiasm. Be it love or religion (for there are enthusiasms in both) nothing can put a stop to the growing mischief of either, till the melancholy be removed and the mind at liberty to hear what can be said against the ridiculousness of an extreme in either way. (*Letter*, 2; CR I, 12)

By curing melancholy, humor helps achieve good humor. This unique combination of enthusiasm and humor is both original and effective in that it diagnoses enthusiasm as essentially melancholic; and drawing on a centuries-old belief, offers humor as melancholy's cure.

Shaftesbury's *Letter* opens a debate on the relationship between laughter, reason and fanaticism that continues into the eighteenth century. The *Letter* inaugurates the modern notion of humor and prefigures the romantic understanding of enthusiasm. Historical circumstances account for the writing of *A Letter Concerning Enthusiasm*, but it is Plato's philosophy that explains its meaning. Shaftesbury's aim is not to condemn or scorn enthusiasts, but to educate them. They should look inward for the principle that will check their delirium. To this end, Shaftesbury proposes a new combination of enthusiasm and humor, which he develops in the treatise, first entitled *The Sociable Enthusiast* (1705) and published later as *The Moralists* (1709). The plural in the title signals the existence of two main approaches to morality: a skeptical, critical approach inherited from Locke and Bayle, and a poetic, inspired approach inherited from the platonic Eros and renewed in the Italian renaissance. These two approaches must unite for Shaftesbury in a new "mixture" that offers a new perspective of enthusiasm.[69]

Enthusiasm is the capacity to be exalted by great ideas and, like laughter, is characteristic of human nature. Shaftesbury's view of enthusiasm derives from two Platonic sources: Plato's comparison in the *Ion* between poetic inspiration, on the one hand, and Corybantic dancers and Bacchic frenzy, on the other (533e–534a); and his detailed description, categorization, and etymology of madness in the *Phaedrus* as prophetic, telestic, poetic, and erotic madness (244–245c3). In the dialogue between Ion and Socrates, Plato first ties the term enthusiasm to the way a poet and a person reciting poetry can become enthralled by the divine. God-given madness, like motivational love discussed in the *Symposium*, is a good phenomenon. Divine inspiration figures in the greatest of achievements: poetry, medicine, rescue from disaster, and philosophical insight. In the precursor to the term *enthusiastic*, Plato suggests that when the agent is in *enthousiazôn*, a god is "in" the agent (*Phaedrus* 241e, 249e, 253a, 263d). Alternatively, when the agent is inspired—a "spirit" (*daimon*) is "in" her. In the *Ion*, it is not a failure of rationality to be divinely possessed and, in this sense, out of one's mind. But it is a failure of rationality not to be able to distinguish between the divine influence and one's own cognitive activities.

Plato's distinction in the *Phaedrus* between different kinds of "madness"—rational madness, god-given madness, and disordered desiderative states or mental illness—indicates for Shaftesbury the possibility of reasonable enthusiasm. Both in the *Symposium* and the *Phaedrus*, love and happiness cannot be pursued in an attitude of thorough soberness: Love is madness and philosophers are in love with wisdom; thus, rational madness is an essential part of the good life.[70]

Shaftesbury draws on Plato's intimation of rational madness to promote a sociable and philosophical enthusiasm that walks a narrow path between delirium and reason. Shaftesbury defines reasonable enthusiasm as that which expresses the sublime in human passions. Enthusiasm is a passion in which philosophers partake as well, granted they know, as Theocles in *The Moralists* knows, how to use inner transport without lapsing into melancholy.

For both Plato and Shaftesbury human rationality requires enthusiasm. Whereas for Plato rationality includes a motivational force so strong that it is plausibly associated with a god, for Shaftesbury reasonable enthusiasm is initially directed toward the harmony of nature, and only later, toward God. He advances a natural religion, that is, a theistic (or deistic) enthusiasm aimed at replacing disorder with an orderly, harmonious, and proportionate nature created by a benevolent God. The quality of Shaftesbury's nature worship is best illustrated in the concluding sections of *The Moralists*. Through Theocles, he indulges in an astonishing outburst on the wonders and perfections of nature, disclosing a degree of enthusiasm unparalleled in any of his writings. Gravity, seriousness, and formalism should be eradicated in order to open the way to well balanced judgment. It is this inward balance achieved through humor that prompts Shaftesbury to abandon "raillery" in favor of "wit and humor." What began as a ridicule of enthusiasts has been transformed into an inner check on enthusiasm through humor—the term Shaftesbury uses for inner ridicule.

Shaftesbury's originality lies in the new meaning of enthusiasm he proposes:

> . . . all sound love and admiration is enthusiasm. The transports of poets, the sublime of orators, the rapture of musicians,

the high strains of the virtuosi—all this is mere enthusiasm! Even learning itself, the love of arts and curiosities, the spirit of travelers and adventurers, gallantry, war, heroism—all, all is enthusiasm! It is enough; I am content to be this new enthusiast in a way unknown to me before. (*Moralists*, iii, 2; CR, II, 129)

In contrast to the mysticism cultivated by positive religions, enthusiasm has become a passionate interest for the things of this world without idolizing them. Jean-Paul Larthomas finds in Shaftesbury's view on wit and humor the English version of the critical spirit of Protestantism that rejects the idol of the tribe. Shaftesbury's originality lies in creating a new alliance between these two human characteristics—humor and enthusiasm.

HUMOR AND WIT

Shaftesbury maintains that ridicule or raillery should be applied to the inner philosophic life's soliloquy, as well as to philosophic conversation and writing. In the soliloquy of the inner life, ridicule's specific aim is to help form a balanced and harmonious character by deflating the passions and curing the melancholy that gives rise to unchecked enthusiasm. When referring to ridicule as a tool used in inner dialogue, Shaftesbury sometimes uses the word "humor." The character formed through soliloquy is both mirrored and further educated through philosophic conversation and writing by using ridicule, now referred to as "wit and humor." In accordance with eighteenth-century thought and practice, Shaftesbury does not clearly differentiate between wit and humor.[71] Humor, however, as distinguished from good humor, acquires for Shaftesbury the modern meaning of sympathetic yet critical laughter.

Humor serves as a test of truth through the sociability of dialogue, whether as soliloquy, philosophic conversation or philosophic writing. Humor's role in soliloquy is to restrain enthusiasm's excesses, thereby opening the way to achieving a balanced character—the goal of the Shaftesburean good life. Together with wit, humor's role in philosophic conversation and writing is to further moral education through the combination of sociability and rationality. By challenging the melancholy of solitary reason, humor exchanges life-denying solitude for life-promoting good humor. To understand the role of wit and humor within the Shaftesburean good life, I suggest clarifying the relation between humor and enthusiasm, the role of humor in soliloquy, and the roles of wit and humor within philosophic conversation and writing.

HUMOR AND ENTHUSIASM

Shaftesbury's uniqueness lies in establishing a significant new alliance between two human characteristics—humor and enthusiasm. He does not consider them essential attributes of human nature nor mere "accidents." Rather, he refers to them as characteristics, that is, distinctive signs of the human species. Shaftesbury does not write a treatise of human nature, however, because the definition of this "nature" varies within civilizations and throughout history.

Human nature contains the principle of its change, and is thus defined differently in various ancient civilizations, such as "Athens and Persia," as well as in modern cultures. A movement enabling a dynamic alliance between enthusiasm and humor characterizes human nature. The moralist, according to Shaftesbury, is sensible of the rhythm of subjectivity that spreads and checks itself, switching from exaltation to self-criticism "like a diastole and a systole of the soul," to use Jean-Paul Larthomas' analogy (Larthomas 1986, 38; my translation). Within this rhythm, laughter is a sudden degradation, a sudden reduction of value to nothing or almost nothing. Because the soul aspires to heights, this reduction is followed by a new height of emotion. This rhythm should be controlled by defining its limits, that is, its "inward numbers and proportions" (Misc., III, ii; CR II, 270), and by taking into consideration the characteristics of the culture in which one lives.

Shaftesbury's greatest innovation, according to Larthomas, lies in the form (the determining and limiting principle) of the character each of us creates. Monitoring the self becomes a critical principle for creativity, a "limit" for the genesis of the form in the platonic sense of "limit" found in the Philebus. There Plato introduces the finite element that mingles with and regulates the infinite as that which measures all things, assigns to them their limit, preserves them in their natural state, and brings them within the sphere of human cognition. Plato describes this as harmony, health, order, and perfection.

According to Shaftesbury, each person must create the form of his or her own humanity out of pre-existing matter. Pico de la Mirandola eloquently describes human creativity in similar terms in On Human Dignity:

> I have placed thee at the center of the world, that from there
> thou mayest more conveniently look around and see whatsoever
> is in the world. Neither heavenly nor mortal have I made thee.
> Thou, like a judge appointed for being honorable, art the molder

and maker of thyself; thou mayest sculpt thyself into whatever shape thou dost prefer. (Pico de la Mirandola 1965, 5)

Shaftesbury's ideal is the virtuoso, a metamorphosis of the gentleman into an artist of his own humanity. A new sensibility is born, an awareness of the "moral sense" as a creative discernment of the self-forming self. Enthusiasm, he believes, is thus a force inspiring creativity. Voltaire concurred with this idea of enthusiasm. The rarest thing, he writes in the "enthusiasm" entry of his *Philosophical Dictionary*, is the combination of enthusiasm with reason, as reasonable enthusiasm is the patrimony of great poets (Voltaire 1901a [1764]).

Shaftesbury's concept of enthusiasm is related to another concept of equal importance for him, the *sensus communis*. Enthusiasm aspires to communicate itself: In its savage form it communicates by contagion, and in its educated form through persuasion. Laughter too, he claims, is a form of communication because we seldom laugh alone; and when we do, given that laughter is sharing, we presuppose at least a kind of connivance, a tacit form of common sense. For Shaftesbury, laughter also can be the spontaneous censure of the community. Independently of Shaftesbury but along these same lines, Konrad Lorenz has remarked that human laughter resembles the victory ceremony of geese, and that both censure and victory resemble militant enthusiasm (Lorenz 1966, 253). Laughter and enthusiasm are two forms of communication that unite easily, according to Shaftesbury. They transcend themselves in poetic inspiration because we relate to the infinite through enthusiasm and to the finite through wit and humor.

Shaftesbury suggests that the false sublime, or excessive gravity, is easily degradable in enthusiasm: The residue of self-love leads to vanity and imposture. Laughter, on the other hand, corrects the lack of proportion characteristic of enthusiasm's elevated passion. Laughter limits the excesses of enthusiasm and educates it, provided laughter has already been tamed. Indeed, Shaftesbury insists in his *Exercises* on the necessity of dominating the *hubris* of laughter, which leads rapidly to the dissolution or at least to the degradation of the self. A just inward proportion finds an optimum between the two opposed excesses, derisive destruction, on the one hand, and visionary exaltation, on the other, reminding us of the Aristotelian mean between extremes (*Nicomachean Ethics* 1108a).

Only enthusiasm educated by appropriate wit and humor can liberate the secret genius of each person. Shaftesbury refers to this genius as one's "inward form" informed by its characteristic or inward proportions: "Where then is this beauty or harmony to be found? How is this symmetry to be discovered and applied? Is it any other art than that of philosophy or the study of inward numbers and proportions, which can exhibit this in life?" (*Misc.*, III, ii; CR II, 270). It remains to be seen how humor works to this end in the inner life.

HUMOR IN INNER DIALOGUE

Humor is a tool in the service of reason whose purpose is to help the individual develop the appropriate character. Through humor, the self apostrophizes itself, that is, holds a counter-discourse with itself, thereby enabling the division required for dialogue in the inner philosophic life. As for Shaftesbury, the essence of philosophy lies in self-creation and self-transformation, the role he allots to humor in the inner life makes it indispensable for philosophy as he understands it. Indeed, he reads the Roman Stoics as guides to the practice of self-formation, and both in his notebooks and in his published works he describes a therapeutic role for philosophy.[71] In *Soliloquy*, for example, philosophy aims to "teach us our-selves, keep us the self-same persons, and so regulate our governing fancies, passions, and humours, as to make it comprehensible to our-selves, and knowable by other features than those of a bare countenance" (*Soliloquy*, III, i; CR I, 184). Similarly, in *Miscellaneous Reflections*, philosophy is defined as "mastership in life and manners" (*Misc.*, III, i; CR II, 254), a discursive interpretation of philosophy that shaped Shaftesbury's notion of philosophy as public discourse. Since the aim of all moral reflection is to form the moral self, ethical insight without experiential implementation is sterile. Forming the moral self involves prying the autonomous self from its adhesion to society. This is the goal of Shaftesbury's *Characteristics* as a whole.

Michael Prince suggests that in the process of describing dialogue as a mimetic genre, Shaftesbury subtly shifts the scene of the dialogue's enactment from society and the stage to the theater of the mind. Dialogue becomes a dramatic method for self-inspection. The external drama between hero and under-characters both provokes and is provoked by an inner struggle to unite an identity similarly divided between a higher or better self, on the one hand, and lower drives and interests, on the other (Prince 1996, 62).

Shaftesbury's aim is to discover how we may form that which in the polite world is recognized as good taste: "For who would not rejoice to be always equal and consonant to himself . . . ?" (*Misc.*, III, ii; CR II, 266–72). Philosophy as "the study of inward numbers and proportions" leads the mind to freedom and independence:

> By knowing itself and its own proper powers and virtues . . . it
> sees its hindrances and obstructions, and finds they are wholly

from itself, and from opinions wrong conceived. The more it conquers in this respect . . . the more it is its own master, feels its own natural liberty, and congratulates with itself on its own advancement and prosperity. (*Misc.*, IV, i; CR II, 282)

This is the meaning of inward proportion and regularity of affection (*Misc.*, IV, ii; CR II, 290), for "'tis we ourselves create and form our taste. If we resolve to have it just, 'tis in our power. We may esteem and resolve, approve and disapprove, as we wish" (*Misc.*, III, ii; CR II, 271–2).

To form one's taste demands courage and the will to undertake a radical inward transformation:

But who dares search opinion to the bottom, or call in question his early and prepossessing taste? Who is so just to himself as to recall his fancy from the power of fashion and education to that of reason? Could we, however, be thus courageous, we should soon settle in ourselves such an opinion of good as would secure to us an invariable, agreeable, and just taste in life and manners. (*Misc.*, IV, i; CR II, 282)

"The narrowest of all conversations," soliloquy, or self-discourse, is the means for this end. Nonetheless it is "wholly impracticable without a previous commerce with the world; and the larger this commerce is, the more practical and improving the other . . . is likely to prove" (*Misc.*, III, i; CR II, 252). Given that the relation to fellow human beings cannot be dissociated from the relation to oneself, the dialogue as defined by Shaftesbury corresponds to the soliloquy or conversation with oneself in the following sense: the soliloquy is possible only if it is conceived as a dialogue, that is, only if the self divides in two (Malherbe 2000, 130). Humor enables such division because humor is a doubling of and a distancing from oneself. It is not only a critical disposition towards others, but also toward oneself. Laughter is simply the social expression of the development of the critical spirit. Because there is no separation between external social criticism and internal criticism with respect to humor for Shaftesbury, laughter is seen as an exchange with others as well as with oneself.

Shaftesbury compares criticism to surgery, suggesting that a person practice on himself this type of operation, for he has "the highest tenderness and regard" for the patient and yet can "act with the greatest resolution and boldness." By virtue of this soliloquy, he becomes two distinct persons. Surgeon and patient become preceptor and pupil, who teach and learn respectively (*Soliloquy*, i, 1; CR I, 103–12). The ancient doctrine of "the daemon, genius, angel or guardian-spirit" to whom we are strictly "joined and committed from our earliest dawn of reason or moment of our birth," Shaftesbury redescribes as the doctrine whereby "we had each of us a patient on ourselves," that "we were properly our own subject of practice" and that "we then became due practitioners when, by virtue of an intimate recess, we could discover a certain duplicity of soul and divide ourselves into two parties" (*Soliloquy*, i, 2; CR I, 112). Rather than a dialogue of equals, the discussion resembles a Socratic dialogue, in which one voice is persuasively interrogatory and the other is passively indicative.

David Marshall explains that Shaftesbury conceives the inner world as a realm in which the conditions and capacities of discourse are applicable (Marshall 1986, 9–73). Indeed, Shaftesbury re-describes the Delphic inscription "Know thyself" as an exhortation to soliloquy:

> This was, among the ancients, that celebrated Delphic inscription, "Recognize yourself!," which was as much as to say, "Divide yourself!" or "Be two!" For if the division were rightly made, all within would, of course, they thought, be rightly understood and prudently managed. Such confidence they had in this home-dialectic of soliloquy! (*Soliloquy*, i, 2; CR I, 113)

Furthermore, Shaftesbury maintains that human beings naturally feel a division within themselves between a better self—the "true and natural self"—and a worst self (*Soliloquy*, iii, 1; CR I, 183). Laughter serves as a criticism of the worst self. This is the basis of Shaftesbury's method of inward dialogue or "soliloquy," which he regards as an essential means of self-knowledge and self-mastery:

> "Mere quibble!," you will say, "for who can thus multiply himself into two persons and be his own subject? Who can properly laugh at himself or find in his heart to be either merry or severe on such an occasion?" (*Soliloquy*, i, 1; CR I, 105)

By imagining themselves as "two distinct persons," individuals can examine themselves and their conduct with the hope of achieving self-understanding and self-improvement (*Soliloquy*, i, 1; CR I, 105). This method is another aspect of Shaftesbury's concept of rational self-reflection or "conscience." Imperfect persons cannot be virtuous without self-denial, that is, without subduing the false self and controlling their passions. Yet the truly evil person cannot engage in this inward colloquy because he cannot face himself.

In *Soliloquy*, Shaftesbury writes, "dialogue is at an end. The ancients could see their own faces, but we cannot" (*Soliloquy*, i, 3; CR I, 134). Dialogue nonetheless plays a key role in Shaftesbury's thought, for dialogue also provides a way to come to terms with the self. Dialogue provides not only the medium but also the structure for philosophical thinking. It offers a private "looking glass" in which we "might discover ourselves, and see our minutest features nicely delineated, and suited to our own apprehension and cognizance." The form of writing used by poets and philosophers is advocated as a form of thinking, a "pocket-mirror" of the mind in which we should "by virtue of the double reflection, distinguish ourselves into two different parties." This work of self-inspection is what Shaftesbury calls the "dramatic method" of philosophy. The reflection provided by this dramatic method is double because "two faces . . . present themselves to our view" (*Soliloquy*, i, 3; CR I, 128–9): we face ourselves divided into two parts, playing or impersonating two different interlocutors. However, in order to become a spectator of this double reflection of ourselves in dialogue, we must first divide ourselves. The division into two parts by the dialogic method is itself doubled: One is divided to face an image of oneself divided in two; one becomes an audience to oneself playing two different parts. This double and doubling reflection is the image and enactment of the message which, according to Shaftesbury, comes to us from the Greeks, "that celebrated Delphic inscription," which Shaftesbury renders as "recognize yourself: which was as much as to say, divide yourself, or be two" (*Soliloquy*, i, 2; CR I, 113).

The "lover, author, mystic," and "conjuror" cannot be left to themselves the way "the man of sense, the sage, or the philosopher" can (*Soliloquy*, i, 3; CR I, 126). For the former "the world is ever of the party" (*Soliloquy*, i, 1; CR I, 109). The philosopher, however, should not need to address his thoughts to a real or imaginary partner. Philosophers who are "able to hold themselves in talk are never less alone than when by themselves" (*Soliloquy*, i, 2; CR I, 113). Shaftesbury's "home-dialect of soliloquy," based on a dialectical "doctrine of two persons in one individual self" establishes an "inspector or auditor . . . within us" (*Soliloquy*, i, 2; CR I, 113, 121–2). Thus, the dialogist is independent of the other because he internalizes the other within himself, or externalizes a part of himself to play the role of inspector (from *spectare*: to look) or auditor. As David Marshall explains, "the act of soliloquy allows one to be by oneself because it sets up a scene of theatre within the self" (Marshall 1986, 38).

This is a "dramatic method" by which a "person of profound parts" (*Soliloquy*, i, 1; CR I, 105), acting as if he were alone, divides himself into actor and audience and gives his thoughts "voice and accent" (*Soliloquy*, i, 2; CR I, 113). The philosopher plays the part of actor, playwright, and director in the play which, according to Shaftesbury, has only "one character or principal part" and "is almost one continued moral: a series of deep reflections drawn from one mouth, upon the subject of one single accident" (*Soliloquy*, ii, 3; CR I, 180). The Shaftesburean philosopher talks to himself "in different persons, and under different characters" (*Soliloquy*, iii, 2; CR I, 207). In addition to being by himself, Shaftesbury's philosopher is also besides himself when in the "method of soliloquy":

> By a certain powerful figure of inward rhetoric, the mind apostrophizes its own fancies, raises them in their proper shapes and personages, and addresses them familiarly, without the least ceremony and respect. By this means it will soon happen that two formed parties will erect themselves within. For the imaginations or fancies being thus roundly treated are forced to declare themselves and take party. (*Soliloquy*, i, 2; CR I, 123)

Philosophy, in these terms, turns the mind into a sort of play: into a dramatization of itself. An individual gives rise to different persons who act out points of view and represent their interactions. In this manner, writes Shaftesbury, we are instructed "to personate ourselves" (*Soliloquy*, i, 2; CR I, 114). To personate, from the Latin *perso-na-re* (to represent, bear the character of) and originally from *perso-na* (mask), means to act or play a part, presumably the part of a character in a drama. That is, to learn to act, play, represent, or exhibit dramatically is to assume a character for ourselves. The dramatic method of soliloquy in its dialogic mode teaches us to dramatize our own characters.

Michael Prince suggests that Shaftesbury sees "the mind as capable of sustaining a dramatic interplay of diverse voices" (Prince 1996, 53n). The goal of the inward dialogue is to educate the passions through reason in order to change habits. The practice the Stoics use is to "set a contrary habit to counteract this habit." Echoing Epictetus, Shaftesbury asserts that "the best Practice and Exercise is to go by contraryes, just in the teeth of Temper, just opposite of Humour."[73] As the human temper is suspended between poles of expectation and dejection, the solution of such pendular movements is an object of training. Moreover, the very polarity of the emotions is the basis of a dialectical method. The principle of Shaftesbury's philosophical regimen as described in his *Exercises* is a deliberate self-contrariness. Lawrence Klein explains that "the over-florid emotional palette had to be countered by the self-conscious pursuit of pallor and grayness, and vice versa" (Klein 1994, 86). In this respect, Shaftesburean self-directed humor functions by apostrophizing fancies with inward exclamations of "Ridiculous!" Shaftesbury's originality lies in his use of humor as a means of deliberate self-contrariness with the purpose of deflating the emotions, especially the passion of enthusiasm.

HUMOR AND WIT IN PHILOSOPHIC CONVERSATION

Shaftesbury insists that soliloquy presupposes conversation and a previous commerce with the world: "The larger this commerce is, the more practicable and improving the other [soliloquy or self-discourse] . . . is likely to prove" (*Misc.*, III, 1; CR II, 252). Philosophic conversation, which mirrors the character that is formed inwardly, presupposes the inner dialogue of the philosophic life.

Quoting Horace to the effect that "a jest often decides weighty matters better and more forcibly than can asperity" (Horace, *Satires*, I, x, 14, 15.11), Shaftesbury suggests that reason is well served by a lighter conversation:

> If rational discourses (especially those of a deeper speculation) have lost their credit, and are in disgrace because of their formality; there is reason for more allowance in the way of humour and gaiety. An easier method of treating these subjects will make them more agreeable and familiar. (*Essay*, i, 6; CR I, 54)

By being critical, a humorous conversation undermines unwarranted assertion; by being open-ended, it illuminates various aspects of the subject at hand; and by being amiable, it encourages further discussion. Such a conversation has other virtues as well. For one thing, it is free:

> It is the habit alone of reasoning, which can make a reasoner. And men can never be better invited to the habit, than when they find pleasure in it. A freedom of raillery, a liberty in decent language to question every thing, and an allowance or unraveling or refuting any argument, without offence to the arguer, are the only terms which can render such speculative conversations any way agreeable. (*Essay*, i, 4; CR I, 49)

Ideal conversation is a moral framework for public interchange, according to Shaftesbury, because conversation of this sort embodies the norms of freedom, equality, activity, and pleasure. In allowing individuals to become more rational and more autonomous, it fits into an emancipatory program. At the same time it is a model of intellectually productive discourse because it provides the best conditions for the advancement of reason.

Imposing silence on an audience by making them unwilling listeners is an undesired alternative to ideal conversation, according to Shaftesbury. In an oratorical situation one participant appropriates the discourse to himself. In this case, an unequal relationship between orator and auditor takes the place of a shared exchange of words among participants in a conversation. When one person monopolizes the conversation, dominance replaces equality, gravity replaces lightness, discomfort replaces pleasure, and dogmatism replaces skepticism. Reason is less efficiently served in the oratorical situation not only because criticism is silenced but also because auditors are more likely to be repelled than convinced (*Essay*, i, 4; CR I, 49–50).

The orator that is characterized in *Sensus Communis* is the same figure as the reformer against whom Shaftesbury warned in his notebooks: The "reformer" sanctimoniously brings his self-seriousness to bear on others in a way that tends toward offensiveness and affectation. Yet substituting conversation for oratory is not enough, Shaftesbury claims, because there is plenty of conversation in society already. However, it is trivial. Because conversation is usually composed of acts of mutual flattery among hyper-sociable beings, the discussion is bound to degenerate into inanity. Because such conversations generally constitute the English elite's social and intellectual environment, Shaftesbury sees their degeneration as a grave problem. According to Philocles in *The Moralists*, conversation requires reason and learning as well as playfulness and dalliance.[74] Instead of the prevalent forms of elite life, Philocles envisions other forms inspired by antiquity, where:

> Reason and wit had their Academy, and underwent this trial;
> not in a formal way, apart from the world; but openly, among
> the better sort, and as an exercise of the genteeler kind. The
> greatest men were not ashamed to practice this, in the intervals
> of public affairs, in the highest stations and employments, and
> at the latest hour of their lives. (*Moralists*, i, 1; CR II, 9)

The *sensus communis*, according to Shaftesbury, develops the sort of wit and humor that ridicules justly and without offence: "For without wit and humor, reason can hardly have its proof or be distinguished." Shaftesbury recalls the formula of the sophist Gorgias Leontinus: "It was the saying of an ancient sage that 'humour was the only test of gravity, and gravity, of humour.'" He adds that one should suspect a truth that cannot stand against raillery, and humor that is not tempered with gravity: "For a subject which would not bear raillery was suspicious, and a jest which would not bear a serious examination was certainly false wit" (*Essay*, i, 5; CR I, 52).

The more accurate translation of the passage from Aristotle's *Rhetoric* reads: "Gorgias said it was necessary to spoil the seriousness of opponents by jest and their jest by seriousness" (*Rhetoric* 3.18.7). Shaftesbury transforms the sophist's rhetorical advice into a statement with philosophic import. This accords with his belief that eloquence and philosophy should converge. As we recall, "truth, it is supposed, may bear all lights, and one of those principal lights, or natural mediums, by which things are to be viewed, in order to a thorough recognition, is ridicule itself, or that manner of proof by which we discern whatever is liable to just raillery in any subject" (*Essay*, i, 1; CR I, 44). For Shaftesbury then, the object of conversation should lose its seriousness so that the wits may approach it freely, discuss it and evaluate its truth. Humor, thus, is policed and is therefore neither derision nor buffoonery. Liberty of tone, he claims, is nothing but the expression of the liberty of thought that is indispensable when approaching truth.

Because no subject, whether moral, political, or religious, is important in itself, it is the enunciator's seriousness that is at stake and not that of the conversation. Laughter may appear to some as a sign of violence, but for Shaftesbury it is an indication of tolerance (*Misc.*, III; CR II, 238–73). The amiable nature of humor does not follow from a principle of charity or external sociability, but is intrinsic to its operation. Railing against the declared importance of a truth changes the relation to the other. In attacking a principle, one is in danger of threatening the other's liberty of thought, and the discussion may degenerate into a battle of dogmas and, ultimately, of passions. Raillery, however, detaches truth from its passionate origin: Both the other and oneself find or regain the capacity for free examination and thereby a possibility of concord, or at least a possibility of entering into an accord that is indispensable to conversation.

As Shaftesbury consistently repeats, the practice of humor presupposes mutuality (*Essay*, i, 1; CR I, 44; iv, 3; CR I, 97). The distance from oneself that humor creates opens a space for the examination of truth and enables conversation to unfold without any of the speakers appropriating or claiming authority. Therein lies humor's merit. Conversation is a social form in which liberties are tried and truths are proposed, corrected, and established through discussion. To prefer good humor over rigid formalism is to socialize the discourse, that is, to place oneself in the true condition of discourse. This is a rational task; it is the opposite of melancholic reasoning, which is the mark of a temperament that tends toward isolation.

From this exchange arises a sense common to all the interlocutors. Shared notions emerge from the discussion and are corrected by it. This common sense reflects the conversation, for everyone refers to it as that which can regulate the discussion and decide the question at hand. Agreement regarding content is not reached spontaneously, however. Common sense proceeds, initially, from a sort of good will, from a love of the public *res*: "A public spirit can come only from a social feeling and sense of partnership with humankind" (*Essay*, iii, 1; CR I, 72). The controversy is tempered by a natural social affection, that is, by benevolence toward all human beings. Common sense is then generated in the conversation without losing this relational quality—each tests his own sense with respect to the other. Because common sense is shared truth, it cannot impose itself as a corpus of more or less shared prior principles. Rather, it emerges slowly. Both its determined content and its regulative power are established in accordance with liberties that do not conflict with each other. This is the same process we use for appreciating a work of art. According to Shaftesbury, the acknowledged truth of a work emerges from a dynamic relationship between points of view and the harmony of various kinds of appreciation for the work. In this way, conversation gives an aesthetic turn to philosophy.

Following the eighteenth-century tendency to view humor and wit as more or less synonymous, Shaftesbury does not clearly differentiate between humor and wit. Wit is the exercise of the mind that practices humor. It is a judgment that points to the inability of pure speculative reason to govern the lives of human beings and their ideas.[73] Wit contributes to the art of conversation, which, by grounding philosophy in human activity, turns it into a lively practice. The judgment inherent in wit draws attention to a more flexible and refined reason that takes into consideration the power of primitive human nature. By enabling a purification of sensibility, wit bears witness to the affective power of judgment. Wit points to the entertaining power of the mind when the mind is seen not only as an intellectual operation, but also as a creator of a philosophic style that privileges pleasantness in the text or in conversation over the dry gravity of treatises and systems. In the necessary passage from the natural to the policed state, wit furthers philosophic speculation through a sociability characterized by polite behavior, ideas and sentiments (*Essay*, ii, 3; CR I, 65–66). To make use of humor is to exercise wit—a wit constituting the operation of the mind when it works in singular turns—that is, to exert the keen observation of the philosopher through benevolent criticism of earnest reason.

Philosophic conversation plays a major role in Shaftesbury's project to make the good life accessible to all. By playing a crucial role in philosophic conversation, humor and wit help to attain the virtue and happiness of the good life. Philosophy, then, is knowledge acquired through conversation, a discourse governed by the rules of tolerance and the conventions it selects, and an inquiry that criticizes itself through wit and humor and that delights in the beauties and pleasures of the truths it discovers. Inasmuch as philosophic conversation does not require relinquishing freedom of thought, it strengthens our freedom to question everything by enabling us to adopt both the tone and the form of the discourse. This project is described and exemplified in the *Characteristics of Men, Manners, Times, Opinions*, and in the notebooks as well, where Shaftesbury defines the ideal of social behavior as a middle position between frivolous sociability and rigid gravity. For both the individual and society at large, he aspires to a synthesis of sociability and philosophical seriousness that also parallels his goal in philosophic writing.

HUMOR AND WIT IN PHILOSOPHIC WRITING

Shaftesbury's intellectual project can be cast as a search for an adequate form of philosophy both as an introspective endeavor and a social activity. This search affects the manner of writing philosophy as well:

> In reality, however able or willing a man be to advise, it is no easy matter to make advice a free gift. For, to make a free gift indeed, there must be nothing in it which takes from another to add to ourselves. In all other respects, to give and to dispense is generosity and goodwill, but to bestow wisdom is to gain a mastery which cannot so easily be allowed us. Men willingly learn whatever else is taught them. They can bear a master in mathematics, in music or in any other science, but not in understanding and good sense. It is the hardest thing imaginable for an author not to appear assuming in this respect. (*Soliloquy*, i, 1; CR I, 103)[76]

For advice to be accepted it should be proffered lightly: "I have taken it strongly into my head that there is a certain knack or legerdemain in argument, by which we may safely proceed to the dangerous part of advising and make sure of the good fortune to have our advice accepted if it be anything worth" (*Soliloquy*, i, 1; CR I, 104). Humor and wit provide the lightness and agility necessary for philosophy as moral education:

> As grave however as morals are presumed in their own nature, I look upon it as an essential matter in their delivery to take now and then the natural air of pleasantry. The first morals which

were ever delivered in the world were in parables, tales, or fables. And the latter and most consummate distributers of morals, in the very politest times, were great taletellers and retainers to honest Aesop. (*Misc.*, IV, i; CR II, 283)

Humor frees both the reader and the author—the author becomes unassuming while the reader is free to appropriate the moral truth as she wishes.

The aim of using humor in philosophic writing is twofold: First, to reach a larger public as did ancient philosophers in their exoteric writings in antiquity; and second, to encourage independent reflection in the reader. The writer's use of humor is self-effacing, thereby enabling the reader to engage in the inner work necessary for moral improvement.

The views of the Cynics and Roman Stoics on the role of humor within moral teaching are relevant to Shaftesbury's own view. The mixture of humor and popular philosophy was characteristic of Cynic literature. By the middle of the third century BC., Cynicism had evolved a type of literature, the serio-comic (*to spoudaiogeloion*), that offered definite genres for the popular exposition of philosophy. By that time, both the Epicureans and the Stoics were prepared to popularize their teachings. The Stoics always used Cynic literary genres for their exoteric teachings. By "speaking the truth, laughingly" (*Ridendo dicere verum*), the Stoics promoted the importance of taking oneself less seriously than is the custom. To that end, they recommended a style based on a mixture of humor and seriousness that proposed laughter as a means to assuming a more balanced perspective of serious matters.

Shaftesbury recommends wit and humor in philosophic writing for the benefit of the author as well. The full title of his work *Advice to an Author* is preceded by *Soliloquy*, thereby drawing attention to the melancholy of the solitary creative writer (*Soliloquy*, iii, 2; CR I, 197–212). To fight melancholy the author must transcend his solitude. The very act of writing should be an exercise in sociability: Wit is assigned a primary role, accompanied by humor whose aim is to erode all that is life-denying.

The priority Shaftesbury assigns to criticism, ridicule, tolerance, and a more egalitarian pedagogy leads also to a defense of mixed and low genres (Prince 1996, 29–35). The doctrine of ridicule, for instance, accompanies a defense of satire, parody, and comedy. Shaftesbury maintains that "the only manner left in which criticism can have its just force amongst us, is the ancient comic; of which kind were the first Roman miscellanies or satiric pieces" (*Soliloquy*, ii, 2; CR I, 169). In this passage he elevates the miscellany and satire. Elsewhere, however, he seems to prefer the burlesque and the parodic novel. These forms are valued for their active agency in the world. They effect change by parodying outdated values. Parody enables an easier and more familiar dissemination of cultural knowledge, and provides a model of inclusiveness that replicates and encourages new patterns of social transformation. The exemplary artist in this case is not the virtuoso who has "in a manner" set himself above the world. Instead the exemplary artist is the "counter-pedagogue" who, of necessity, violates order and proportion for the sake of criticizing society's false values. Shaftesbury likens himself to Cervantes in order to explain why his own writings ("these my miscellaneous works") are mixed genres, why the champion of classical unity is himself a "mere comic humorist" and a compositor of "prose satire" (Misc., V, i; CR II, 314; Prince 1996, 36–37).

Shaftesbury draws political analogies between genres and institutions, equating mixed genres with a desirable solution to political absolutism. Moreover, he establishes theological analogies between magisterial modes and schismatic debate, prescribing comic forms as a cure for textual absolutism.[77] He advocates a range of dialogic and comic genres that preserve the freedom of the reader. The genres that serve his ideal of writing as conversation include the essay, the miscellany (Misc., I, iii; CR II, 94), the letter, and the dialogue (Soliloquy, ii, 3; CR I, 198–9). Regardless of genre, Shaftesbury strives to write in "the way of Chat," that is, according to the discourse of easy and accessible conversation (Misc., II, iii; CR II, 216–7).[78]

Shaftesbury assigns central significance to the letter as a polite genre because letters are a form of writing one level removed from public conversation.[79] A defining feature of the essay as a form of writing is the recognizable and self-explanatory voice. The essay appears to be spontaneous, uncertain, and free of formal constraints. Miscellany, like satire and parody, is valued for its active agency in the world. Its formal inclusiveness captures the undirected energy of the society at the time, which was becoming increasingly mobile, mixed, and impervious to received structures of subordination. Shaftesbury sees in the essay "a more familiar style," appropriate to "pleasanter reflections," and offers a clear definition of the essay style, namely as the "way of Chat" combined with such discursive qualities as informality, raillery, liberty, grace, and, quite explicitly, pleasure (Misc., II, iii; CR II, 216–7).[80]

Shaftesbury assigns the highest value to dialogue as the perfect vehicle for philosophical training. He makes a case for the formal as well as the intellectual value of dialogue. Dialogue, he claims, elides prose and poetry, the philosophic and the literary; yet its essential value lies in its effectiveness in leading the reader to self-knowledge.[81]

Although the Characteristics is Shaftesbury's grand endeavor in discursive philosophy, another unrealized project reveals much about his ambitions for philosophical writing. This is his "Socratick History," a series of translations from the chief ancient sources on the life of Socrates, set among introductions, explanatory essays, and notes by the Third Earl. Although he did not complete the project, Shaftesbury filled a notebook with reflections that indicate not only his moral and civic concerns, but also his formal criteria for philosophy and his view of the role of the comic in philosophy.[82]

From the notebook for the "Socratick History," we learn that Shaftesbury sees in the Xenophonic Socrates a vindication of the active ideal of philosophy as opposed to the contemplative ideal embodied by Plato. He writes on the projected book's role in edification, on the inclusive intended audience of the book, and on the role of humor in it. He would use humor "if possible or as much as possible," endeavor to be "entertaining and eloquent," imitate Plato's *Apology* as an instance of "that air of negligence and good humour," and quote Horace frequently "because he is now so much in esteem, and by this there would appear an Air of Gallantry and Humour" to the book (P.R.O. 30/21/27/14, 50, 52, 75). Adopting a somewhat distanced stance toward the matter, he would maintain a laughing irony about it.

This projected work is meant to be both moral, that is, philosophical, and polite. Its politeness, intended to make it a pleasurably attractive piece of reading, would be a function of the author's politeness. He would preserve moral scale, eschewing at one end of the spectrum excess detail and elaboration and on the other mysterious depth and abstraction. He would consistently avoid the temptations of didacticism, dogmatism, and authority. Rather, he would be diffident and unassuming. Such an authorial stance amounts to an imitation of the ancient sources as Shaftesbury perceives them. Socrates is the original not only for the picture of the moral philosopher, but also for the dialogic and ironic authorial manners of the texts written by Plato and Xenophon.

The composite form of the *Characteristics* supports Shaftesbury's project of increasing the autonomy of the reader by reducing the authoritative character of the author. Although it contains pieces labeled "miscellanies," the *Characteristics* is itself precisely such a miscellany, and Shaftesbury's remarks in favor of miscellanies are applicable to the entire work. The miscellaneous character is not simply a matter of genre, but also of voice as well, because by virtue of its composite character, the *Characteristics* is not a monologic discourse.

Humor plays a crucial role throughout Shaftesbury's discussion of philosophy in all its varied forms, whether soliloquy, conversation, or writing. A method for challenging all forms of irrationality, humor denotes a fundamental capacity for the apprehension of the true, the beautiful, and the good. Humor is a liberating tool freeing us from patterns of action and thought that are ultimately life-destroying. Humor is an essential element of the tact requisite to moral sense and the sociability necessary to common sense. Without humor the virtue and happiness constituting the Shaftesburean good life are unattainable.[83]

CONCLUDING REMARKS: HUMOR, GOOD HUMOR, RIDICULE, AND THE SHAFTESBUREAN GOOD LIFE

Shaftesbury had an immense influence on aesthetics in Britain and abroad. His *Characteristics* went through eleven English publications by the year 1790, and his work became classics in England. Numerous writers of the Scottish enlightenment adopted Shaftesbury's doctrine of enthusiasm, and through the efforts of Robert Molesworth, his writings influenced the Dublin scene, especially Francis Hutcheson's early work.[84] Shaftesbury enjoyed an equally high status in Europe.[85] Germany proved to be particularly receptive to Shaftesbury's philosophy, and his aesthetic theory contributed significantly to the rise of Romanticism there. Even as his star was waning in England, his concepts were helping to shape the ideas of Kant as well as Lessing, Mendelssohn, Wieland, Goethe, Herder, and Schiller. Richard Brett notes that "German scholars have often shown a greater appreciation for Shaftesbury's importance and the distinctive character of his thought than Anglo-American scholars" (Brett 1951, 206). In Germany and Scandinavia, Shaftesbury was considered a romantic figure. His influence on the eighteenth-century Danish writer, Ludwig Holberg—Søren Kierkegaard's unacknowledged mentor[86]—and the Swedish critic, Thomas Thorild, led to the romanticism of these northern thinkers.

Shaftesbury has assigned humor an unparalleled role within philosophy, which may be encapsulated in the following tenets: (1) ridicule is the test of truth; (2) humor and good humor have a habilitating function with regard to truth; (3) to be effective, criticism must be humorous; and (4) humor is the mark of rationality. I assess the originality and feasibility of Shaftesbury's views by addressing these four tenets.

RIDICULE AS THE TEST OF TRUTH

The view that ridicule is the test of truth, which has been synonymous with Shaftesbury's name, is undeniably original, as no one before has ever proposed something similar. This view makes sense, however, mainly within the context of Shaftesbury's metaphysics and epistemology. Shaftesbury holds that reality is an organic, harmonious, and perfectly congruous whole. Any statement that is descriptive of this reality cannot but refer to these features, and although these characteristics may not give us a definition of truth, they do provide us with a criterion of truth. On the contrary, anything that lacks the characteristics of organic harmony and congruity is unreal. Any statement, therefore, that is incongruous, any statement revealing an internal disharmony, is untrue. Falsehood is characterized by a quality that can only be described as ridiculous.

To maintain the view that ridicule is the test of truth, then, requires embracing the religious faith that Shaftesbury's metaphysics represents. Shaftesbury argues for his optimistic metaphysics in two ways: On the one hand, he contends that the evidence of benevolent design to be found in the natural world establishes the existence of a ruling Mind that is benevolent and all powerful; on the other hand, he reasons that given such a directing Intelligence, it necessarily follows that the cosmic order is good. However, he admits that to know with certainty that all things work for the best would require that we comprehend the universe as a whole, an impossible task for a finite mind (*Moralists*, iii, 1; CR II, 108). It is at this point that the doctrine of enthusiasm becomes relevant. The human being is able to surmount the limitations of his finitude and, at least at moments, to intuit the harmony of the Whole in the ecstatic moments of faith or enthusiasm in which the mind is caught up in vision. Enthusiasm is the fulfillment of our highest potentialities as rational beings—the extension of the powers of reason in its highest limits. However, "reason" is understood here in its broadest sense: it includes and is more than the processes of discursive intellect. It comprehends the whole realm of common concepts that arise from the shared life and experience of the human community.

One of Shaftesbury's basic arguments is that no one can believe in God and his goodness without first having a clear conception of God and goodness. By goodness alone trust is created (*Moralists*, ii, 5; CR II, 92). Thus, reason precedes faith and ethics precede theology. True religion depends on philosophy, but philosophy in turn depends on religion. Philosophy and reason for Shaftesbury are broadly conceived. Not a narrow empiricism or a strict rationalism, philosophy is a discipline so comprehensive that it can take in the realm of enthusiasm as well. Reason and faith are neither inconsistent nor opposed. Faith is a commitment of the whole person, intellectually, emotionally, and volitionally. But it is philosophy rather than theology that is made the final judge of all sciences and all knowledge, for by philosophy "religion itself is judged, spirits are searched, prophecies proved, miracles distinguished" (*Soliloquy*, iii, 1; CR I, 193).

Judged as a purely rational system that attempts to justify God's ways to humankind, Shaftesbury's philosophy fails. The evidence he presents can be matched by an equal amount of counterevidence. Stanley Grean suggests that much of what Shaftesbury thought clearly implied a designing Mind, we see today as a product of natural mechanisms of adjustment operating according to the patterns of statistical probability. Yet as a religious faith, his philosophy finally stands or falls to the extent that it makes "the tragic and the absurd endurable by including them in an ultimately meaningful universe" (Grean 1967, 87–88). As a philosophy of life, it falls short for many in the contemporary world because, despite his realism, Shaftesbury's effort to see the necessity of all things prevents him from doing full justice to the inexplicably tragic dimensions of human experience.

Without taking into account Shaftesbury's metaphysics, the view that ridicule is the test of truth is controversial. The controversy over whether ridicule is a test of truth—whether ridicule is the proof of truth, or one of its tests, or not at all indicative of truth—and the ensuing controversy of its relation with reason—whether ridicule is a faculty that operates independently of reason or in conjunction with it—occupies an important place of concern for philosophers of the eighteenth century. Never before has the relation between ridicule and truth been put on the agenda, or the definition of ridicule as a faculty been entertained; and never before has the way it works with reason been explored. The view that ridicule is a test of truth, then, generated a heated controversy in the eighteenth century, which deserves a thorough examination.

Although Shaftesbury's theory of ridicule brought him scorn from various quarters, there were those who supported it and not only from the ranks of the Deists and the Free Thinkers.[87] Francis Hutcheson, who was a devout Presbyterian minister, saw nothing in it to upset the beliefs of true religion. His early work, *Reflections upon Laughter* (1750), is an elaboration and defense of Shaftesbury's views.[88] His thesis is the same as Shaftesbury's: One can ridicule religion and morality, but ridicule will not prevail against truth. It is precisely this that allows ridicule to be a criterion of truth. Anthony Collins, who supported Shaftesbury's theory in his *Discourse Concerning Ridicule and Irony* (1729), followed Hutcheson.

In his *The Pleasures of Imagination* (1744), the English poet and physician Mark Akenside (1721–1770) apodictically declared that ridicule is a test of truth and that it functions as an independent sense or faculty. He was astonished that divines like William Warburton, who attacked Shaftesbury, should imagine they were serving religion by vilifying ridicule as the favorite weapon of the Free Thinkers: ". . . it is beyond all contradiction evident that we have a natural sense of feeling of the ridiculous," Akenside writes, and a good reason may be assigned "to justify the Supreme Being for bestowing it" (Akenside 1744, 105–6). It is a valid faculty, he argues, for practical rather than theoretical matters. Just as the faculty of reason examines a metaphysical proposition and rejects it for being false when its content, which was said to be equal to another, is then shown to be unequal, "so in objects offered to the mind for its esteem or applause, the faculty of ridicule feeling an incongruity in the claim, urges the mind to reject it with laughter and contempt" (7). Akenside's sense of ridicule is the converse of the moral sense; the moral sense is the instinctive recognition of whatever is beautiful, true, and good. The sense of ridicule, on the other hand, is the recognition of whatever is deformed, false, and evil. The final cause of the sense of ridicule, the good reason justifying the Supreme Being for bestowing this sense on humans, is the aid it affords reason in depressing the giddy aims of folly. Unlike reason, the sense of ridicule acts "at once/ By . . . prompt impulse." Thus,

> . . . benignant Heaven,
> Conscious of how dim the dawn of truth appears
> To thousands; conscious what a scanty pause
> From labours and from care, the wiser lot
> Of humble life affords for studious thought
> To scan the maze of nature; therefore stam'd
> The glaring scenes with characters of scorn,
> As broad, as obvious to passing clown,
> As to the letter'd sage's curious eye. (Akenside, III, 269–77)[87]

Unlike Hutcheson, although similar to Shaftesbury, Akenside does not make a distinction between laughter and ridicule. Laughter for Akenside is synonymous with ridicule, "gay contempt," or "gay derision." His primary interest is in ridicule as a weapon. Akenside is important because where Hutcheson, with his thoughts on burlesque, had spoken only of a contrast of dignity and meanness, Akenside generalizes this principle to "some incongruous form,/ some stubborn dissonance of things combin'd," and he seems to be the first to provide a well-known analysis of laughter in which the words "incongruous" and "incongruity" appear. Incongruity in itself, however, is of little significance for him, "for the sensation of ridicule is not a bare perception of the agreement or disagreement of ideas; but a passion or emotion of the mind consequential to that perception" (Akenside 7). The passion or emotion he is referring to is scorn. In the 1744 version of the *The Pleasures of Imagination*, most of the passage on ridicule and laughter was devoted to a satiric cataloguing of the various levels of contemptible behavior.

Support for ridicule as a test of truth is also offered by Lord Kames. Following Akenside in regarding ridicule as an independent faculty, Kames maintains that in addition to our sense of beauty and grandeur (sublimity), we have a sense of ridicule equally competent in its sphere and necessary for detecting improprieties. Kames takes it for granted "that ridicule is not a subject of reasoning, but of sense or taste" (Kames 1762, II, 183). He rephrases the question of ridicule as a test of truth, stating it "in accurate terms" as "whether the sense of ridicule is the proper test for distinguishing ridiculous objects from what are not so." He comes to the conclusion that it is the only true test, for the subject "comes not, more than beauty or grandeur, under the province of reason" (184). The person who has taste applies the test of ridicule to any subject that has acquired an unnatural degree of veneration, separating it from its artificial connections and exposing its native improprieties. Kames follows Shaftesbury and Akenside in asserting that intrinsically grave and serious matters are not vulnerable to attacks from ridicule and that ridicule should not be condemned because it is subject to abuse. "Were we destitute of this test of truth," he concludes, "I know not what might be the consequences: I see not what rule would be left us to prevent splendid trifles passing for matters of importance, show and form for substance, and superstition or enthusiasm for pure religion." Though those who have a talent for ridicule are quick-sighted in improprieties, Kames finds that the talent "is seldom united with a taste for delicate and refined beauties" (184).

Thomas Reid, one of the Scotch Common Sense philosophers, also developed Akenside's account of the sense of ridicule later in the eighteenth century. In determining first principles, Reid argues in 1785, we find great difference of opinion among philosophers, but fortunately Nature has given to the candid and honest part of mankind a way of arriving at unanimity—common sense. It is due to common sense that "every man is a competent judge . . . the learned and the unlearned, the Philosophers and the day-labourer are upon a level, and will pass the same judgment, when they are not misled by some bias." Opinions that contradict first principles are not only false, like all errors, but literally absurd. To discountenance absurdity, Nature has given us, he claims, a particular emotion—ridicule—which seems to be intended for this very purpose of putting out of countenance what is absurd, either in opinion or practice. Ridicule includes both a feeling and a particular act of judgment based on the principles of common sense. According to Reid, ridicule is a weapon that cuts with as keen an edge as argument. In the same way that argument refutes error, ridicule exposes absurdity. If no blinding prejudices interfered, he says, no absurdity could withstand the pencil of a Lucian, a Swift, or a Voltaire (Reid 1863 [1785], essay VI, chap. IV, 438–9).

In his *Essay on Ridicule* (1753), Allan Ramsay maintains that ridicule is a test of truth and, in contrast to Akenside, Lord Kames, and later Reid, that it is part of the reasoning process. Ramsey intimates that he has "long thought that those advocates for ridicule, who set it in opposition to reason, did its cause very little honour or service" (Ramsay 1753, 7). Ramsay admits the weaknesses in Shaftesbury's system: Shaftesbury had confused ridicule with cheerfulness, pleasantry and good humor, none of which may be classed as a test of truth. Yet, Ramsey attempts to prove that ridicule is "one of the tests of truth (by its detection of falsehood) and, as such, to be indulged without any limitation" (4–5). Examining examples of ridicule in the works of authors of acknowledged wit, Ramsey comes to the conclusion that there are two sorts of ridicule. One, which may be styled simple, direct or unreflected ridicule, "consists of the bare representation of what is improper in manners or actions." The other, argumentative ridicule, is employed in discussing propositions, or matters of enquiry, and is "the art of showing that to be ridiculous which is imagined to be so" (79; 7). Only this sort of ridicule pretends to be a test of truth, based on the principle only vaguely implied by Shaftesbury that ridicule is part of the reasoning process. Argumentative ridicule, according to Ramsay, is a type of analogical reasoning used to oppose false opinions (41; 53).

Ramsey admits that ridicule is a mode of eloquence—the art of convincing and persuading—but because persuasion is based on reason, eloquence must not be separated from argument. Ridicule as a species of persuasion belongs to the mixed kind of eloquence, and because ridicule is argumentative, it is one of the methods of reasoning (17). The only difference between ridicule and serious reasoning, according to Ramsey, is that ridicule excites laughter in the hearers, but serious argument does not (30). In support of Shaftesbury, he maintains "that gravity is the proper test of ridicule, and ridicule the proper test of gravity." Ridicule pretends to destroy only falsely serious arguments and only they shun and disclaim its test (33). Ridicule should be employed upon objects both "false and important," that is, false opinions held in great solemnity and seriousness. Thus, the use of ridicule justified when dealing with religious subjects (47). Finally, ridicule in public instruction is more than a sugar coated pill used to render the discussion palatable; it is rather an essential part of the argument: "In speculative, as well as in active life, the ways of wisdom are really ways of pleasantness" (82).

On the other side of the controversy, champions of religious orthodoxy in particular were quick to concentrate their attacks on Shaftesbury's
theory of ridicule. The third dialogue of George Berkeley's *Alciphron, or
the Minute Philosopher* (1732) is devoted to an examination of Shaftesbury's
philosophy. Alciphron, who in this dialogue represents Shaftesbury, is led to
admit that five and six centuries before his day anyone who had believed
the Copernican system, or that blood circulates, would have been laughed
at and scorned. Yet any of Alciphron's contemporaries who did not believe
these theories would now be equally ridiculed. If truth has any permanence,
Berkeley concludes, ridicule is no criterion of truth and falsehood (Berkeley
1901, II, 149).

In reply to both Shaftesbury and Akenside, the clergyman William
Warburton clarifies the controversy by insisting that it should be stated
whether ridicule as a test of truth refers to the recognition of an error
already known or the means to detecting a new error. Warburton flatly
denies that ridicule is a test of truth if it means the detection of error
(Warburton 1811). He does not state, however, whether he regards ridicule
as part of reason, but his friend, the clergyman John Brown, made a great
effort to establish that it is a passion operating independently of reason
and, as such, incapable of serving as a test of truth. Brown's most significant
contribution is the trend of thought, later developed by William Preston,
which reveals the variable and subjective nature of ridicule (Preston 1788).
He claims that because of its variable nature, ridicule is really a measure
of esteem or valuation, and not of truth (Brown 1751a). This is the most
telling argument against ridicule's capacity to be a test of truth.

Brown clearly regards ridicule as a passion and takes Shaftesbury to
task for exempting it from the rule of reason, particularly since Shaftesbury
is careful to stress the role of reason in the good life in all his writings.
This is the real issue and the point of contention between Brown and
Shaftesbury. Brown and Shaftesbury hold reason to be the highest faculty
of mankind, but unfortunately neither of them clearly articulates its relation
to ridicule. Shaftesbury merely implies that it is associated with ridicule,
while Brown fails to prove that it is a separate faculty. In his treatment in
verse of the same subject, *An Essay on Satire Occasioned by the Death of Mr.
Pope* (1751b), Brown assumes that Shaftesbury regards ridicule as a rational
faculty: "Lo Shaftesbury rears her high on reason's throne,/And loads the
slave with honors not her own" (quoted in Aldridge 1945, 148, n. 65).

The most convincing arguments of the debate are Ramsay's on the
one hand—that ridicule is part of the reasoning process and as such a test
of truth, and Brown's on the other—that because of its variable nature,

ridicule is really a measure of esteem or valuation, and not of truth (Ramsay 1753, 70, n. 12; Brown 1751a). Alfred Aldridge sums up the issue thus:

> The entire controversy, including the cogency of Shaftesbury's original treatises, depends upon whether ridicule is or is not regarded as a rational faculty. If it is, as in Ramsay's essay, it is a test of truth; otherwise, it is not. Thus the whole controversy, like many others, really resolved itself into a matter of proper definition. (Aldridge 1945, 155–6)

Shaftesbury merely implies, I suggest, that reason is associated with ridicule, but does not clearly articulate reason's relation to ridicule.

The discussion about ridicule's relation to truth and reason subsided at the end of the nineteenth century and has not been resumed since. Yet the controversy over ridicule's relation to reason promoted the endorsement among Shaftesbury's followers of a theory of humor as incongruity, a theory that emphasizes the cognitive nature of humor. The view of humor as incongruity is an alternative to Hobbes' definition of laughter as an expression of one's sense of superiority. Hobbes arrives at the conclusion that laughter is a manifestation of pride, vanity, and scorn after having examined laughter from psychological, moral and social perspectives. He defines laughter in *Human Nature* (1640) as a "sudden glory arising from some sudden conception of some eminency in ourselves, by comparison with the infirmity of others, or with our own formerly" (Hobbes 1839–45, IV, chap 9, sec.13). In a parallel passage in *Leviathan* (1651), he criticizes facile self-congratulating laughter:

> Sudden glory is the passion which makes those grimaces called laughter, and is caused either by some sudden act of their own, that pleases them; or by the apprehension of some deformed thing in another, by comparison whereof they suddenly applaud themselves. And it is incident most to them, that are conscious of the fewest abilities in themselves; who are forced to keep themselves in their own favour, by observing the imperfections of other men. And therefore much laughter at the defects of others, is a sign of Pusillanimity. For the great minds, one of the proper works is, to help and free others from scorn; and compare themselves only with the most able. (*Leviathan*, vol. 3, part I, chap. 6, sec. 27)

Great persons do not scorn others; Hobbes explains elsewhere that great persons do not need to compare themselves with their inferiors in order to attain a correct measure of their worth:

Great persons, that have their minds employed on great designs, have not leisure enough to laugh, and are not pleased with the contemplation of their own power and virtues, so as they need not the infirmities and vices of other men to recommend themselves to their own favour by comparison, as all men do when they laugh.[89]

Hobbes' definition of laughter explicitly refers to laughter at one's own past foibles. This does not mean that Hobbes interprets laughter as a sympathetic act. Rather, self-referential laughter is still a form of superiority that "put[s] the rest into jealousy and examination of themselves" (Hobbes 1839–45, IV, chap. 9, sec. 13, 45–47). However, he also insists that "laughter *without offence* must be at the *absurdities* and infirmities *abstracted* from persons, and when the company may laugh together" (46–47). One can argue that, for Hobbes, laughter that rises from incongruity, not from a sense of superiority, is really the only legitimate kind. Stuart Tave emphasizes, however, that this view is certainly not the eighteenth-century reading of Hobbes (Tave 1960, 69).[90]

HUMOR AND GOOD HUMOR AS HABILITATING TRUTH

The relation of ridicule to truth—whether it is or is not the test of truth—does not exhaust Shaftesbury's views on the epistemological value of humor and good humor. In maintaining that humor and good humor enable us to grasp the truth, he imparts to these notions a habilitating role.[91]

Shaftesbury means by truth, first, the right view of God, the world, and human nature, which for him are God's benevolence, nature's harmony, and innate human goodness. Good humor as the predisposition to gaiety is a necessary condition for understanding goodness: "We must not only be in ordinary good-humour, but in the best of humours, and in the sweetness, kindest disposition of our lives, to understand well what true goodness is . . ." (*Letter*, 4; CR I, 24–25). Thus good humor acquires an epistemological value for Shaftesbury as the only disposition that enables the perception of the truth about God, nature, human nature, and virtue. *Strictu sensu*, then, good humor promotes truth if the world is indeed good and harmonious. If the world is not such a place, Shaftesbury's recommendation of good humor is prudential advice, based on his view that emotional states determine our outlook on life.

Good humor has a habilitating function with regard to truth in another sense as well. It provides the openness necessary for the pursuit of truth, that is, through pleasant, free and well-intentioned conversation. It is through conversation that the truth of human matters is pursued, if not reached, and there is no conversation without social pleasure. Good humor establishes an atmosphere of tolerance that invites the other's opinion.

For Shaftesbury, "humors" evolve from a prelogical state as fluids to a logical state as "good humor." Good humor symbolizes the passage from the natural state to the policed state. The development of good humor is a logical, reflexive use of "humor," which makes gaiety a figure of social truth illuminating the entire community's need to control its future. The movement from "humor" to good humor culminates in an intellectual act of judgment according to the equation: Reason equals taste and taste equals cheerfulness. The recourse to good humor inaugurates, then, the truly cultured era of humanity, when truth can be pursued through reasoning. Cheerfulness and laughter are used to achieve a serious aim: the eradication of a community built exclusively on the prelogical stage of the emotive communication of "humor" as temper.

If *good humor* has a habilitating function with regard to truth, it remains to be seen whether *humor* also promotes truth. The answer is hindered by the fact that in Shaftesbury's writings humor is not clearly differentiated from either good humor or ridicule. In the unpublished "Pathologia," for example, Shaftesbury portrays a new kind of laughter, *hilaritas*, or humor, which delights in the beautiful rather than in the ugly. This form of humor is not easily differentiated from good humor. Nevertheless, an assessment of its value and originality is in order.

If we take *hilaritas* to mean good-natured humor, I do not know how much Shaftesbury should be credited for innovating on this subject. There are important antecedents to Shaftesbury's *hilaritas*, and he appeared to have been familiar with a number of them. In contradistinction to the accepted view, as stated, for example, by Max Eastman in *The Sense of Humor*, Louis Cazamien, Henri Haury, and earlier, Mary Grant, maintain that the discovery of benign humor is not an eighteenth-century phenomenon (Eastman 1972 [1922], 167; Cazamien 1952; Haury 1955; Grant 1924, 148). Ancient Greek and Hellenistic philosophers differentiated between kinds of laughter and favored the mild and good-natured laughter, as exemplified by Xenophon, Aristotle, Cicero, and the Stoics' preferred choice of irony or humor.

Socratic irony, as understood by Xenophon, is Shaftesbury's ultimate model in the *Exercises*, but Aristotle also serves as a model for good-natured laughter. The Aristotelian virtue of *eutrapelia*, the social virtue of cheerfulness, or wit, is the antecedent of Shaftesbury's notion of good humor. Employing his usual tripartite division, Aristotle maintains in the *Nicomachean Ethics* that the excess of laughter is buffoonery and its deficiency is boorishness. Nonetheless, there exists a "true wittiness" characteristic of an honorable and free person:

But those who joke in a tasteful way are called ready-witted, which implies a sort of readiness to turn this way and that; for such sallies are thought to be movements of the character, and as bodies are discriminated by their movements, so too are characters. (Aristotle, *Nicomachean Ethics*, 4.8. 1127b ff; see *Rhetoric*, 2.12 1389 11–12)

The ready-witted (*eutrapelos*), being a tactful person, does not utter injurious or offensive comments, whereas the buffoon says and does anything in order to raise a laugh. Only the ready-witted, being a refined person, can decide what is appropriate and what is inappropriate regarding laughter and what is suitable for a free man to say and hear.

Aristotle's view of humor is reprised by Cicero, who clearly shows a theoretical preference for good-natured humor: his "*hilaritas*" as well as "*festivitas*" imply a kindly spirit of jesting (Grant 1924, 107). It is the Stoic Panaetius (c. 185–109 BC), however, whose views are best preserved in the adaptation of his work *On the appropriate* by Cicero in the latter's *De Officiis*, who incorporates Aristotle's views into Stoicism to make the school palatable to the Romans. Panaetius takes virtue to be a mean between two vices, and this doctrine, alien to true Stoic principles, forms the basis of the treatment of laughter in Cicero's *De Officiis*. Moreover, Socrates becomes for Panaetius the ideal embodiment of Aristotle's *eutrapelos*, or Cicero's liberal joker (his coining for Aristotle's free man). This kind of humor Panaetius found to be the most appropriate for the plain style his teacher Diogenes of Babylon developed. Panaetius assailed the aesthetic and moral coarseness of Cynic speech with its vulgar and frank humor as a sin against social propriety, favoring instead Aristotle's definition of the liberal jest.

George Converse Fiske traces the development of the theory of diction and humor appropriate to the *sermo* or conversational discourse in plain style—the type of oral and written expression favored by the truth-loving Stoics—formulated for the Romans by Diogenes of Babylon and Panaetius, and employed as a result of their influence in nearly all the literature emanating from the Scipionic circle. This was a society of the noblest and most intelligent men of Rome that gathered around Scipio Aemilianus and his Greek friends, the historian Polybius and the philosopher Panaetius (Fiske 1920, 17; 1919). Fiske maintains that the Socratic theory of irony—the type of liberal humor pervading the conversations of Socrates and the Platonic dialogues—that was widely prevalent in the Scipionic circle accords with the rhetorical theory appropriate to the conversational discourse in plain style. We know that through Roman philosophers, the Hellenistic schools of philosophy influenced later generations in the Renaissance, Early Modern times and the Enlightenment, and we also know that Shaftesbury was steeped in Roman philosophy. Thus, if we take Shaftesbury's *hilaritas* to mean good-natured humor, we cannot credit him with much originality.

However, the good humor of *hilaritas* stems from the admiration of (external) beauty. There are no views of laughter in ancient philosophy that come close to Shaftesbury's admiration for beauty. Nevertheless, the seventeenth-century philosopher Baruch Spinoza, an important forerunner of Shaftesbury (Robertson 1963, xxxi), uses *hilaritas* to define a new form of laughter, which has been translated into English as "cheerfulness" or gaiety (*Ethics*, III, P11Schol.).[92] According to Spinoza, cheerfulness cannot be excessive and is always good while its opposite, melancholy, is always evil (*Ethics*, IV, P42, and Dem.; P44Schol.). Spinoza differentiates in most of his writings between scorn and mockery, which he rejects, and laughter, which he embraces. In the *Political Treatise*, he warns us not to scorn or mock, urging us, rather, to understand humankind (1951, I, 4). In the *Ethics*, mockery is defined as a form of hatred, and thus a kind of sadness, which can never be converted into joy. Laughter and joking, when not excessive, in contrast, are characterized as pure joy, partaking thus in Spinoza's pantheistic God-Nature (*Ethics*, IV, P45 Cor. 2, and Schol.).[93] Similarly, in the *Short Treatise on God, Man, and his Well-Being*, he differentiates between mockery and ridicule, on the one hand, and laughter, on the other: "Mockery and ridicule rest on a false opinion and indicate an imperfection in he who mocks and ridicules," he writes. "They indicate an imperfection in him who mocks because either what is mocked is ridiculous or it is not." If it is not, it should not be mocked. If it is, it should be amended by other means than mockery. In contradistinction, "laughter is not related to another, but only to the man that notices something good in himself; and because it is a kind of joy, there is nothing to say about it which has not already been said about joy," that is, it is always good (1985b, II, chap. 11, 115–6).

Spinoza's *hilaritas* or cheerfulness may be an antecedent to Shaftesbury's good humor. Editor John Robertson has maintained that Shaftesbury's philosophy is none other than Spinoza's.[94] However, there are important differences between the *hilaritas* of each philosopher. Although for Shaftesbury the source of *hilaritas* is always external, an admiration of external beauty and never of oneself, the source of Spinoza's *hilaritas* is internal, a delight in oneself. It is Spinoza that innovates radically. Shaftesbury's *hilaritas* innovates in the admiration of beauty it involves, given that Shaftesbury has adopted the ancient philosophers' association of ridicule with ugliness or disharmony, but Shaftesbury limits the range of *hilaritas* by excluding one's character from being a source of admiration.

There are also differences between Spinoza's attitude toward mockery and Shaftesbury's attitude toward ridicule. Although Spinoza does not mock even when the object is ridiculous, but suggests improving it by other means, Shaftesbury considers humor a tool for improving oneself as well as others. Thus, Shaftesbury's view of humor is more akin to Descartes' view of mockery: A moderate use of mockery could correct vices by making them appear ridiculous (Descartes 1955, II, sec. 124–7). The comparison between Shaftesburean humor and Cartesian ridicule can be made because Shaftesbury conflated humor, not only with good humor, but also with ridicule. Regardless of its role as the test of truth, ridicule, in the form of humor, may have a habilitating role with regard to truth in inward dialogue, in conversation, and in writing.[95] This is the subject of the next section.

HUMOR AS EFFECTIVE CRITICISM

Shaftesbury holds the view that criticism, to be effective, should be humorous. Independent of the view of "ridicule, the test of truth," this view is still premised on the lesser assumption that truth cannot be hurt by humor. Because truth can withstand "all lights," including that of ridicule, Shaftesbury asserts that humorous criticism should not to be feared.

Moreover, to be effective, criticism should be humorous, first, because criticism is most effective when specific and humor is always specific. Brand Blanshard reminds us that "most of us are incapable of moving freely in the world of pure universals . . . we must touch ground again pretty often to renew our strength and courage . . . most men's minds are so constituted that they have to think by means of examples" (Blanshard 1980, 140). Second, humor reduces anxiety, alerts the mind, and enhances creativity as well as liberty of thought—all processes that ameliorate reasoning and open-mindedness. Finally, humor itself enables cognitive change. Because in humor our perception becomes more attentive, the sensible world takes on a new value, and its image becomes clearer under the humorist's gaze. His gaze acquires the acuity of a new vision; and as all the senses participate in this change, it is the whole of our perception that is modified (Cazamien 1952, 107). John Lippitt has recently explained how these characteristics of humor and similar characteristics of irony are helpful in moral transformation (Lippitt 2000b, 159).

The view that effective criticism must be humorous has been in practice since the exoteric moral teachings of the ancient philosophers and revived by Renaissance and modern philosophers.[96] Hub Zwart reminds us that moral criticism is a comic genre: "Since time immemorial, moral criticism used to be intimately connected with comedy and laughter" (Zwart

1996, 17). Although the value of laughter for purposes of reform was not recognized by Aristotle, nor included in his theory of the liberal jest, Aristophanes was conscious that a serious moral purpose could be served by laughter (*Frogs*, 339), and Plato in one passage seems to admit as much (*Republic*, fifth book, 452 D). But it is with the later Cynics that there is a formal alliance of laughter to moral teaching.

One important Cynic trait was the use of laughter to help convey paradoxical thinking in order to attract and influence a wide audience. The common people, unlike the eager young companions of Socrates, had neither the leisure nor the inclination to "follow the argument wherever it might lead, not caring how many digressions were made, provided that truth was attained in the end" (Plato, *Theaetetus*, 172 D). They wanted the lessons of philosophy presented ready digested and in an easily remembered form. Primarily to cater to their needs, there evolved the literary forms that comprise the genus of the serio-comic, the prose forms of which were mainly the adaptation and popularization of "Socratic" literature, while in verse the influence of the old gnomic poetry, the Mime, and Comedy are all discernible. The serio-comic (*To spoudaiogeloion*) was the distinguishing mark of Cynic literature (Strabo, xvi. 759). According to Demetrius, "the moralists often employ humorous forms of composition on suitable occasions, as at festivals and banquets, and in attacks on luxury . . . such is the manner of Cynic literature" (Demetrius, 1932, 170). The aim of these philosophers was to combine the *dulce* (the pleasurable) and *utile* (the useful), or rather to enforce the *utile* by means of the *dulce*. The proponents of this device explained its logic in the following simile: They were like physicians who smear the edge of the cup with honey that the draught may not prove so bitter.

The evolution of the serio-comic is in the main an attempt to adapt the "Socratic" forms of popular philosophical propaganda to the requirements of the Hellenistic age. The conversation and character of Socrates had given rise to the Socratic dialogue that in the hands of Plato became perhaps the supreme achievement in prose form. The spirit of Socrates' irony and Plato's brilliant fancy had introduced into the Socractic dialogue an element of the *geloion* (laughable) in the form of parody and myth. A less serious form of composition was the Symposium; and the *Memorabilia* of Xenophon was the first work in a genre that was to gain great popularity in the third century BC and later. Finally, Plato, Isocrates, and Aristotle had used the epistle for philosophical exposition. For the Cynic teachings, verse also was employed. These were the traditional forms of philosophical propaganda available by the end of the fourth century BC.

The Cynics developed a powerful and many-sided instrument for popular philosophical propaganda from the "Socratic" literary forms and the old gnomic poetry, and the serio-comic was a fertile influence successively on Hellenistic, Roman, and later Greek literature. Cynicism influenced all the Hellenistic schools of philosophy (Long 1996). The Stoics always used Cynic literary genres for their exoteric teachings. The vehicle for Stoic popular propaganda or preaching was the diatribe, the chief genre of the serio-comic in literature; but the Cynics' devices also influenced the remaining Hellenistic schools, Epicurianism, and Pyrrhonian Skepticism. Rhetorical strategies depending on intricate comic structures, particularly those of parody, were a conscious technique of exoteric philosophical literature, as well as of dramatic comedy; thus it was recognized in practice, if not in theory, that the power of humor to alter our perceptions by exposing latent incongruities was a means of generating critical thought from a new perspective. This recognition provided the aesthetic justification for the varied forms of literary jesting produced in the late classical and early Hellenistic periods. In fact, an observation voiced by Caesar Strabo in the discussion of wit in Cicero's *De Oratore* suggests that the serious ramifications of humor had come to be widely appreciated: "There is no type of joke from which serious inferences may not be drawn" (2.250; cf. 2.262–3.52). And Horace adds: "A jest often decides weighty matters better and more forcibly than can asperity" (Horace, *Satires*, I, x, 14, 15.11).

For Shaftesbury, all philosophy is exoteric moral teaching. Hence, he revitalizes the ancient philosophers' device for exoteric moral teaching and defends the necessity of its use for all the forms of his philosophical expression, from inner dialogue to philosophic conversation and writing. As Huston Smith reminds us, most people are exoteric, which means that feeling or experience counts for them more than thought (Smith 2000, 259). Brand Blanshard urges the philosopher to be careful with the beliefs he is attacking, because they are intertwined with hopes and fears:

> On the great issues of philosophy many of men's hopes and fears do hang. . . . It is true that the philosopher must live in a drier climate than most men would find habitable . . . but . . . If the philosopher is a good human being, he knows that many of the beliefs he is attacking are intertwined inextricably with the hopes and feelings of those who hold them, and his controversial manner will take note of these involvements. (Blanshard 1980, 127–32)

When philosophy is not conceived as an esoteric activity, humor can be helpful in furthering philosophy's critical aims.

While not original in itself, the view that effective criticism must be humorous innovates when it is implemented in inner dialogue and the reciprocity of conversation, rather than in the one-sidedness of philosophic writing or teaching. In inner dialogue, the role of humor is disciplinarian: It forms and corrects one's judgment by reducing the arrogant seriousness and false grandeur of the self. It is a negative instruction that aims at self-knowledge and self-formation through awareness of the limits of self-expansion. In conversation, the inter-subjective condition of the comic presupposes a commonality of both feeling and judging (implicitly) things, situations, and ideas. We have to temper this spontaneous judgment by another form of reflexive consciousness of common sense, which is called taste or tact. But when this is done, judgment equals good sense, and laughing, as judging, is reason working to diminish the excesses of sensibility. Laughter produces a derisory awareness of the subjective when the subjective is confronted by an authentic rational judgment. "The things themselves," explains Ernst Cassirer, "upon seeing their images as mirrored by this elemental power of the intellect, recognize, so to speak, their true inner proportion and return to it. In so doing they regain their appointed place in reality" (Cassirer 1953, 179).

We must introduce judgment in the initial affective dynamic of laughter by confronting laughter with sense. With humor, the notion of sense takes root in the exchange between persons, revealing in the process of communication the moment when sense vacillates. The philosophic value of humor lies in its being a privileged instrument of sense, because humor is a vacillation of sense that confirms or refutes within the coherence of the whole that which one believes. Laughter can be a criterion of sense because it incorporates a theory of sense that enables the interrogation of human practices. Conversation is the *par excellence* locus of humorous expression because through a succession of questions and answers conversation enables humor to exert a tight criticism of sense in the name of a pre-existing common sense. This is why humor—the criticism of sense by laughter—provides a foundation for philosophical criticism. In the *Essay on the Freedom of Wit and Humour*, laughter as humor is an instrument of reason, making the exercise of humor a social art that is both sensible and intelligent. As a measured and measuring laughter, humor, thus, is an expression of the philosophical orientation of the art of conversation.

Shaftesbury also innovates in singling out enthusiasm as the main human characteristic humor should criticize. The aim of the association between humor and enthusiasm is to make enthusiasm creative rather than visionary. The Enlightenment and the *Aufklärung* begin with a fundamental conflicting attitude towards enthusiasm, one that seeks to eliminate the irrationality of superstition without drying up the fountain of its fervor. Following Shaftesbury, Kant entrust English humor with the important mission of resolving this conflict.[97]

The association of humor with enthusiasm did not strongly influence continental philosophers (Larthomas 1986), but Voltaire used the connection when plagiarizing Shaftesbury's *Letter* in his *Treatise on Toleration*.[98] Laurent Jaffro remarks that Voltaire implicitly presupposes that reason used in earnest is not satisfying as a corrector of enthusiasm. He implies that reason without laughter is more dangerous than laughter without reason (Jaffro 1996, 230). Moreover, the poet Christoph Martin Wieland and the playwright, aesthetician, and theologian Gotthold Ephraim Lessing were the first, but not the last, German authors who have understood humor's significance. Wieland holds that wit and humor are immanent methods that enlighten inspiration, and Lessing exemplifies the association of humor with enthusiasm in his notion of "creative critique."[99]

In the German sensibility of the epoch, both aesthetic and religious, the most appropriate word to translate Shaftesbury's new enthusiasm was "*Freude*" (joy). Larthomas maintains that this accounts for "a lyrical fervor in the theme of joy, in poetry as well as in music, which explains, perhaps, a certain romantic rejection of humor" (Larthomas 1986, 368; my translation). There is a difference between Romantic irony and Shaftesburean humor. The Romantic spirit (*Witz*) translates the finite's inadequacy to express the infinite, perceived by the "absolute liberty of the self," as Johann Gottlieb Fichte would say. Irony manifests the refusal, but also the incapacity, of the incessant play of the imagination to satisfy itself in finite determinations. Irony becomes, then, the spur of the creative process; according to Frederick Shlegel's definition, it is "a continuous succession of self-creation and self-destruction." It is the ego that creates (or destroys) itself in the work, since it is the ego that feels itself infinite when confronting nature, and later the whole of reality, where the ego sees only the play of its imagination. This explains the yearning that saddens the romantic spirit (*Witz*), and makes it an aspiration that is always unsatisfied.[100]

Shaftesburean wit and humor proceed from an inverse sentiment. Caught in the manifestation of an infinity of profusion and plenitude (*The Moralists*, iii, 1; CR II, 110f.), the self becomes aware of its limits without suffering melancholy: "Wit is the critical awareness that sheds light on the distance separating the infinite demand of the Idea from the finite forms with which we work" (Larthomas 1986, 369; my translation). The difference between the enthusiasm of *The Moralists* and this aspiration, this romantic *Sehnsucht* in which Werther indulges so unhappily, lies in a lucid mistrust of the indeterminate and its languishing charms. According to Larthomas, Romantics "lose themselves readily in the evocation of the unlimited, a projection of the cherished Self's power whose fundament is nostalgia or the 'desire of desire'" (Larthomas 1986, 369; my translation).

Shaftesbury would have undoubtedly considered with some irony this delectable *Sehnsucht*, especially since he always connotes the adjective "*romantic*" with nuances of chimerical "melancholy," or of extravagant exaltation epitomized in Cervantes' *Don Quijote*. He would have been suspicious of a *Schwärarmerei*, an extravagant enthusiast defined by excessive sentimentality, a dreamer in his relationship to the infinite. One should distance oneself from this dangerous type through the love of the limit in the Greek sense, that is, the love of form. The "beautiful soul" is the Greek soul, who loves form. Shaftesbury would have recognized it in Goethe's classicism, but not in Jean Paul, Tieck, or even Novalis' romanticism.

Shaftesburean humor is the sign of the awareness of finitude. Humor is the acceptance of an inward measure, of an equilibrium that welcomes the inward truth of every situation, even if and maybe because, understanding does not always comprehend the why and how. Humor, for Shaftesbury, is thus the positive expression of the awareness of our limits, both as intelligent and sensible beings.

HUMOR AS THE MARK OF RATIONALITY

Shaftesbury's view that humor is the mark of rationality complements his view of effective criticism as humorous. First, Shaftesbury equates rationality with critical dialogue; by further equating criticism with humor, however, Shaftesbury makes humor the mark of rationality.

Reason, for Shaftesbury, is dialogical and rhetorical. Knowledge is part of social life and, thus, reason depends on laying down the conditions for reasonable social conduct. Truth about human matters is not discovered through abstract philosophy, but through the rigors of conversation. Reason is directly sociable, a factor of morality and community. Society is more important than the individual because it enables a vaster and more fecund reflection. Conversation establishes communication, which is necessarily grounded in community. Conversation is the model of communication of all philosophic truth and the ability to converse is one of the most defining characteristics of the person who uses his reason. The dialogical polyphonic model of conversation inspires all discourse that aims at rationality or truth. Thought exists only when it puts passion into movement; it is best advanced through conversation, whose characteristics are mobility, unpredictability, and dramatization. Conversation must be aporetic, free, and open-minded to fulfill its critical function. Reason does not reason, but converses, for Shaftesbury, and free conversation is aporetic.

In this matter, as in other matters, Shaftesbury draws his inspiration from the ancient Greek and Roman philosophers who used dialogue to discuss philosophic questions. The characters of Plato's dialogues, and especially Xenophon's, test each other's positions with wit and humor, Shaftesbury believes, seeking to arrive at ideas that can withstand the criticism of ridicule. This is the means by which reason should operate, because "without wit and humour, reason can hardly have its proof or be distinguished" (*Essay*, i, 5; CR I, 52). Shaftesbury equates criticism with humor, as humor is a vacillation of sense that confirms or refutes that which one believes within the coherence of the whole. Humor is a criticism of sense by laughter, which constitutes the premises of philosophical criticism, as we have seen in the previous discussion of humor as effective criticism.

By equating criticism with rational thought, and further equating humor with criticism, Shaftesbury makes humor the mark of rationality. In his equation of criticism with rational thought, Shaftesbury anticipates Karl Popper's critical rationalism.[101] By taking the additional step of equating humor with criticism thereby making humor the mark of rationality, Shaftesbury advances a view that is entirely original, without precedent or followers. This view can be accepted as a better version of Karl Popper's thesis that critical thinking is the very essence of rationality because it takes into consideration the psychological resistance to criticism that Popper acknowledges but refuses to address.

Rarely has there been a thinker who has invested humor and ridicule with such a mighty task as represented by Shaftesbury's four tenets, namely, that ridicule is the test of truth, that humor and good humor have a habilitating function with regard to truth, that criticism must be humorous in order to be effective, and that humor is the mark of rationality. Shaftesbury is the first to attribute an important role to humor, ridicule and good humor within philosophy. Because the practice of reason is a practice on oneself, and because true knowledge lies in self-knowledge and self-formation, the creation of a harmonious and virtuous character is the goal of the philosophical life—the good life as Shaftesbury conceives it. Humor has never been given a higher place within the good life: As a liberating, life-giving, and life-forming power of the soul, humor is constitutive of the Shaftesburean good life, for without humor, the good life cannot be attained nor maintained.

Shaftesbury's views on humor and good humor as the state of mind in which truth is best apprehended influenced his translator, the German philosopher Johann Georg Hamann (1730–1788). Hamann follows Shaftesbury in holding that humor (and Hamann adds irony) are epistemologically necessary for apprehending God, although his view of God differs from that of Shaftesbury. Shaftesbury's influence on Hamann is important in itself, but for an enquiry into the role of humor in the good life, it is Hamann's, as well as his follower, Johann G. von Herder's, influence on Søren Kierkegaard that is significant. Accordingly, Hamann's views are introduced in an intermediary chapter before addressing Kierkegaard's views on the role of humor in the good life.

HAMANN—HUMOR AND IRONY AS CATEGORIES OF UNDERSTANDING

I am the most Christian Eulenspiegel.

—Hamann (1949–57, II, 117)

The eighteenth-century German philosopher and theologian, Johann Georg Hamann, converted in his 20s to Lutheran Protestantism, the religion of his youth, and has been widely known by the singular epithet "Magus in Norden" ever since. The epithet, which refers to the star of Bethlehem and the Magi in Matthew 2:2, ascribes great religious fervor to Hamann, and it is Hamann's defense of religion in the midst of the Enlightenment that gives him historical importance. Isaiah Berlin describes him as the one man who "struck the most violent blow against the Enlightenment and began the whole romantic process" (Berlin 1999, 40): "Half hidden by the fame of his disciples: F. H. Jacobi, Schelling, Niebuhr, Jean Paul, Friedrich Carl von Moser, and by the admiration of Herder, Goethe, and Kierkegaard," Hamann is "the forgotten source of a movement that in the end engulfed the whole of European culture" (Berlin 1994, 4–5). Immanuel Kant, his neighbor and friend, with whom he quarreled all his life, financially supported this "pioneer of anti-rationalism in every sphere."

Hamann wrote under many pseudonyms and in a style that has proved to this day to be unreadable. The obscurity of his writings has contributed to his disputable status as a philosopher. Renowned for his humor and irony, Hamann dubbed himself the "most Christian Eulenspiegel" (Hamann 1949–57, II, 117; O'Flaherty 1967, 36).[1] He is introduced here as an important link on the subject of humor between Shaftesbury and Kierkegaard. The influence of this obscure thinker on Kierkegaard has led commentators to deem Kierkegaard Hamann's sole "authentic disciple" (Jørgensen 1968, 164), and Kierkegaard himself viewed his own work as a development of

Hamann's (*JP* 2, 1559). On the subject of humor, Hamann's influence on Kierkegaard is unmistakable: Kierkegaard found in Hamann his view of humor and a model for using irony and humor as indirect communication in the service of Christianity.

Hamann was influenced by Shaftesbury. He translated Shaftesbury's essays into German and referred to him often in his writings.[2] He carried on Shaftesbury's intent to write a Socratic history, by writing his *Socratic Memorabilia, Compiled for the Boredom of the Public by a Lover of Boredom, With a Double Dedication to Nobody and to Two.*[3] More than the memoirs, Hamann's search for a new understanding of what it means to be human in *Aesthetics in a Nutshell* bears the mark of Shaftesbury's influence.[4] Moreover, despite their different approaches to truth, Hamann adopts Shaftesbury's view of the habilitating role of humor with regard to truth.

Hamann is deeply religious; God, for him, is certainly not the abstract unity and harmony that serves Shaftesbury and other deists, but is rather creative and passionate—above all He is to be loved and worshipped. More importantly, although for Shaftesbury Christ plays no role in religion, for Hamann religion is inconceivable without Him. Hamann opposes Shaftesbury's dismissal of the supernatural foundation of religion, and rejects the idea that philosophy is a rival to theology. He objects to natural religion because it is not connected to tradition, sense experience, or history. Hamann accepts, however, Shaftesbury's positive view of enthusiasm, his criticism of abstractions in philosophy, his identification of theory with practice, and his emphasis on practical morality, self-knowledge as the goal of all knowledge, and human communication as mutual mirroring, as well as Shaftesbury's views on creativity. He agrees with Shaftesbury on the correspondence of true humor to reality and therefore on the view that humor represents the state of mind in which truth is best apprehended. However, truth, for Hamann, is the reality of Christ that can only be apprehended by faith. Participation in humor is analogous to repentance, which in itself is closely connected with faith. Humor and irony are omnipresent in Hamann's style because they represent for him categories of understanding. The person who cannot see the humor or the irony literally "cannot see the point."

During the greater part of the nineteenth century, when naturalism and positivism prevailed, Hamann is generally neglected by leading scholars. Already in 1960, however, Ronald Gregor Smith refers to a "Hamann renaissance" (Smith 1960b, 17; 1960a), which Berlin attributes to Hamann's originality: Hamann was "a man of original opinions, the importance of which has become apparent only in our time" (Berlin 1962, 272). This includes his view of humor and irony and the crucial role he ascribes to them in the good life.

THE GOOD LIFE

Hamann holds that there exists a prerational reality, and the way we arrange it is ultimately arbitrary (Hamann 1949–57, III, 191). He denies that there is an objective order, a *rerum natura*, whether factual or normative, from which all knowledge and all values stem and by which all action can be tested. Reason is given to the heathen, he insists, and the Law to the Jews, so that they can see their ignorance and their sins. The worship of reason that characterizes prominent figures of the Enlightenment, such as Frederick the Great and Voltaire, is not only mistaken, but tyrannical, leading to the suppression of individuality, as well as of the individual's irrational and unconscious forces. Systems and epistemologies are philosophy's idols, and few, such as Socrates and Hume in their ignorance of the truth, are able to see through them. God works in ironic ways to advance his purpose. Faith, not knowledge is the answer to ignorance. Hamann sees himself as the Socrates of Christianity, with his wooden arm showing the way, the role that Kierkegaard later adopts for himself.

According to biographer Oswald Bayer, Hamann converts in his 20s to Lutheran Protestantism, the religion of his youth (Bayer 2011). His religious conversion is to a doctrine known to those familiar with the writings of the German Protestant mystics and their followers in Scandinavia and England. They view the sacred history of the Jews as not merely an account of that nation's guidance from darkness to light by God's almighty hand, but a timeless allegory of the inner history of the soul of each person. The sins of individuals are like the sins of nations, and the story of the wanderings of the Israelites, Hamann declares, is the story of his life. This is the inner sense of the biblical words, and he who understands them understands himself because all understanding is self-understanding. The spirit alone can be understood, and to find it the human being needs only, and must only, look within himself. God's word is the ladder between heaven and earth sent to aid weak and foolish children—it alone will vouchsafe them a glimpse of what they are and why they are as they are, and what their place is, and what they must do, and what they must avoid. The Bible is a great universal allegory, a similitude of that which occurs everywhere and at every moment. So indeed is human history and nature properly understood with the eyes not of analytical reason but of faith, trust in God, and self-examination, for all these are one.

To be human is to understand oneself, which can only be accomplished through that kind of exchange in which persons mirror one another, as humans are social by nature. Hamann does not glorify the emotions nor does he prize the power of volition. Rather, the gospel engages an existent being, a unity; faith points to a certain mode of existence of the whole being. Hamann's individual is the historical, authentic being, as opposed to the abstract "pure" mind inhabiting a body. He is flesh and blood, rational yet emotional, intellectual but also sexual. In his autobiography, Goethe expresses Hamann's central principle thus: "Whatever a man wants to accomplish—by deed or word—must have as its source his united powers in their totality, since all that is divided is worthless" (Goethe 1848, 446–7). Goethe sees Hamann as a great awakener, the first champion of the unity of the human being involving all faculties—mental, emotional, physical, and creative—as well as the response to the misunderstanding, misrepresentation, and harm created by lifeless French criticism's dissection of his activity.[5]

Self-knowledge is a descent into hell, yet the human being is described not only in terms of depths, but also of heights (Hamann 1949–57, III, 199). It is the inherent human contradiction that provides the most striking content of self-knowledge. Hamann's concern is the significance of the "infinite incongruity between man and God" and the "similar incongruity between man and man" (312–13). It is this infinite incongruity that makes all imperatives, no matter how categorical, witnesses to human damnation. Moreover, the greater the approximation to this imperative, the stronger the threat; the more sensitive an individual becomes to this "incongruity," the less he wishes to ground his personal being in his sense of accomplishment.

Authority must be one and not many. Residing not in reason, but in paradox and absurdity, it is "foolishness to the Greeks" (III, 410; IV 462; see I Cor. I: 23). Hamann's principal emphasis is on the humility of God and the corresponding humility of the human being. God is humble in condescending to be the Father in creation, the Son in incarnation, and the Holy Spirit that communicates the message of life through human history, human language, and a human book. The corresponding humility of the human being is the *sine qua non* condition for understanding the Bible. If the condescension of God is God's humility, the response of the individual's life that "answers to" this humility is faith or humility. Faith is the mode of existence of the whole human being—head, heart, and bowels—which corresponds to God's condescension, receives God's gifts under the conditions in which they are given, and therefore sees the exalted in the lowly, the majestic in the humble, the Lord of glory in the Crucified, the Christ in the bread and wine, the Presence of God in all His creation, and the Spirit in human language. This humility is similar to the concern, the single-mindedness, the tenderness, the warmth, and the sensitivity to the Other found in friends and particularly in lovers (II, 171).

For Hamann, faith is not irrational or even "super-rational." It is not a leap across an abyss, but a stooping down. It is not discontinuous with our experience as creatures of God, but only discontinuous with the ways we conduct ourselves. Although "crisis" and "decision" are part of the whole cloth of human existence, these phenomena are carefully guarded from overemphasis. Hamann expresses his own "conversion" as a meditation over a considerable period of time ("The Diary of a Christian," 1949–57, I). Yet faith is a miracle, the miracle par excellence: It is a gift of the Spirit. "Miracle" points to the fact that one cannot engineer this event of faith in another person, as faith is "not communicable as a type of goods . . ." (To Jacobi, 27–30 Apr. 1787). Miracle does not mean the irrational and the "supernatural" because if all is of God, then all is natural. For Hamann, miracle is not an erratic disturbance in the external order of things. Miracle is an event in the inner being of the individual; it is the mover from pride to humility, from independence to dependence: "All the miracles of the holy scriptures happen in our souls" (Hamann 1955–79, I, 78).

The opposite of faith as humility is the human predicament of the separation from God, which is maintained by pride and an unwillingness to relinquish the human drive for autonomy and passion for self-dependence. This is sin. In its intellectual form this predicament is illustrated by the philosophy of Hamann's day. The criteria for faith as humility are derived from the Object of faith, the Truth itself: Genuine God in condescension and genuine man in humility (i.e., Jesus Christ). The criteria for faith are given by the appearance of truth, and the truth is marked off by these criteria.

This view of condescension in Hamann has several correlates. First, the revelation of God comes in concealed form, as the lowly and the offensive. God's means of reaching the individual or God's revelation are concrete, even foolish. The Holy Spirit has become a history writer of foolish, indeed sinful human actions (First Hellenistic Letter, 1955–79, II, 171). The only appropriate mode for the incredible condescension of God in telling us about the creation is the simple, the lowly and the foolish. In fact, Hamann's life and authorship are a commentary on the first four chapters of First Corinthians from which his grave inscription was taken: "The one becomes all; the Word becomes flesh; the Spirit becomes letter; to the Jews an offense, to the Greeks foolishness . . ." Hamann declares that "the *foolishness of Christianity*" is entirely to his taste and the desire of his heart, suitable to his "sound reason and human feelings . . ." (To Jacobi, 1–2 March 1786; To Jacobi, 1–5 December 1784).

A second correlate of Hamann's view of condescension is that truth is tied to the sensual and the physical. His concern is a concept of truth that implicates faith. If truth is flesh (John I: 14), then Christianity is incompatible with, or at least cannot allow itself to be dominated by, certain concepts of truth. Under the conditions of existence pure truth, abstracted from the sensual and material, is inaccessible. A third correlate is that the natural and the concrete take primacy over the artificial and the abstract. A fourth and final correlate is that God takes seriously the human situation of existence in the flesh as well as human history. That which has occurred in the Incarnation is not an isolated truth, but has pregnant suggestions for understanding Hamann's view of his task as a thinker and his existence as a Christian. This is the significance of his program of metaschematism—taking up his opponent's position as if it were his own in order to expose its weaknesses and contradictions. It is also the significance of his style and method, exemplified in his use of humor and irony.

HUMOR AND IRONY

Hamann's style is his soul, a deliberate mimicry of the Incarnation to which it is a witness. Referring to the *Memorabilia*, James O'Flaherty notes, "all the elements which characterize the outward form of the work are designed so as to transcend themselves, to point beyond themselves to a greater reality" (O'Flaherty 1967, 84). Years later, Hamann emphasizes this principle as characteristic of his writings in general: "The inner or invisible part of my few writings may indeed even remain the most excellent part. . . ." (Letter to J. G. Herder, 20 March, 1773; Hamann 1955–79, III, 40). Such a practice was for him symbolic of God's dealing with the human being, and, hence, was more veridical than classical art with its rationalistic implication of being an adequate and exhaustive surrogate for that which it represents.

In an attempt to understand Hamann's view of his own method, we can do no better than to consider the lines he wrote in 1773 to Friedrich Carl von Moser:

> Your Excellency has had the grace to sympathize most cordially with the invisible aspect of my writings. . . . Socrates' vocation of transplanting morality from Olympus to the earth and of rendering it visible in a practical way coincides with my own in that I have sought to profane a higher sanctuary and, to the proper umbrage of our lying, sham, and boastful prophets, to make it commonplace in an analogous way. In short, all my *opuscula* taken together comprise an Alcibiadean shell. Everyone has found fault with the form of the satyr or Pan, and no one has taken notice of the old relic of the smaller Luther catechism . . . (December 1; Hamann 1955–79, III, 66)

In Plato's *Symposium*, Alcibiades compares Socrates to Silenus, ugly outside and beautiful inside. In his writings, Hamann seeks to emulate the Alcibiadean shell, hiding the Christian message the same way Socrates has hidden Pagan ethics.

One form of Hamann's style, which is used as a variant form of concealment, is his humor. Hamann applies the same categories of understanding that are central to his theological epistemology. Contrary to the usual philosophical categories, they are the only appropriate modes of thought for grasping the truth, that is, the "Word that has become flesh." Because he considers humor and irony categories of understanding he uses them abundantly in his writings. Participation in humor, he claims, is analogous to repentance, which in itself is closely connected with faith, and the person who cannot understand the humor cannot see the truth.

Faith is the existence of the whole person in the mode of humility. It has the further correlates of, (1) offense at God's condescension, (2) the concealment of God's revelation, (3) a characterizing sign of contradiction, and (4) metaschematism. Hamann uses humor to express the first three ideas and irony for the fourth.

1. To express God's condescension, Hamann uses the device of *Stillbruch or* contrasts. Hamann's style of writing attempts to conform deliberately to the truth in Christ (i.e., to the condescension of God in Incarnation and in the Spirit). Truth is always embodied for Hamann. The more elevated the concept, the more he seems delighted in juxtaposing it to what is lowly, eccentric, or even trivial.[6] The contrasts involved in *Stillbruch* stem from his notion of the brokenness and incompleteness of human nature and the world, and thus form the profoundest depths of his religious faith. The effect of mixing the farcical with the sublime is always to raise a question in the reader's mind as to the author's real intention, a question that can only be resolved by further reflection beyond the self-contradictory appearance.

2. Conformity to the Incarnation means conformity to the "truth which lies in concealment" (Hamann 1949–57, II, 77). This is the theological theory of *Kneschtsgestalt Christi*, which emphasizes the contradiction of Christ himself appearing in the "form of a servant," as the Apostle Paul says in his letter to the Philippians (2:7), and the idea that divinity most often appears in lowly form and is thus often unrecognized. Hamann insists on a variant of this theory as the inescapable precondition for a valid aesthetic, ethical, and religious knowledge. For Hamann, the genuinely moral person is always better than he appears to be—the "hypocrite reverse" (Hamann 1949–57, III, 410; IV, 462). Authentic knowledge is not a product of overweening reason, he claims, but of ordinary language, which is lower in the hierarchy of things than the *ratio* (see O'Flaherty 1966). In

theological matters he ascertains that divinity appears most redemptive in lowly, despised, or foolish form, that is, in *forma servi*.

3. Most important for understanding Hamann's view of humor is Giordano Bruno's metaphysical "celebrated principle of the coincidence of opposites," which Hamann opposes to "the principles of contradiction and sufficient reason." He declares: "I have not been able to endure the latter from my academic youth on, and without Manichaeism have found contradictions elsewhere in the elements of the material and intellectual world" (To Jacobi, 16 Jan. 1785; Hamann 1955–79, III, 107). Everywhere Hamann sees "one note of immeasurable height and depth." Nonetheless, it is in the Incarnation—where God and man are one—that differences, opposites, and contradictions are most clearly confirmed and made visible. Our very salvation, therefore, is based on this incarnated "coincidence of opposites": the forgiveness and judgment of God—two opposing concepts that seem to destroy one another. For this reason he relates spiritual beauty to the unlovely, the eccentric, or the grotesque. This is how we arrive at a paradoxical view of reality and Christ as the embodiment of this reality. O'Flaherty explains the centrality of this view in Hamann:

> [N]o thinker understood the vital importance of the paradox in religion more clearly than did the Magus. Although Hamann's conviction that religious truth must be expressed in paradoxi-cal form derived principally from the New Testament, he was also convinced that the early Greek religion had anticipated this insight and that the "rationalist" Sophists had emasculated it. He also calls attention to the contradictions in Socrates. (O'Flaherty 1967, 79)

The contradictions O'Flaherty mentions are Socrates' homosexuality, which Hamann sees as a moral flaw, and Socrates' ignorance defined by the god as wisdom (n. 42). Hamann thought his manner of writing more profoundly corresponded to the ambiguity and the raggedness of reality than the writing styles reflecting the prevailing spirit of the age. "Beautiful nature," "sound nature," and "good taste," all Shaftesburean concepts, are lumped together by Hamann, who describes them as "chimeras and as three of the most pernicious prejudices of the 'century of good taste'" (Hamann 1949–57, II, 356). His faith compelled him to speak the one veridical language, namely, the language of paradox and obscure allusion in order to be the wooden arm signpost that points the way (76).

Stillbruch, or contrasts, is associated with the theological doctrine of *Knechtsgestalt Christi* and the metaphysical doctrine of *coincidentia opposito-*

rum. Hamann's theology determines his aesthetics, which is characterized by mixing the high and the low, concealing, and using contradiction—aims that are well served by humor. What is original with Hamann is the application of the Biblical doctrine of *Knechtsgestalt Christi* to Aesthetics, making of humor the best expression of Christian theological doctrines.

4. Hamann's principle of "Metaschematismus" partially explains his use of irony. In order to understand what Hamann meant by this term, it is necessary to turn to the passage of the New Testament in which Paul exhorts the members of the Church at Corinth to lay aside their dissensions and their tendency to form cliques. Instead of referring directly to the various disputants at Corinth, he writes about his own relationship to Apollos and about the relationships of those who would follow him and those who would follow Apollos. He does this in order to lead them by an indirect method to an understanding of their own general predicament: "And these things, brethren, I have in a figure transferred to myself and to Apollos for your sakes that ye might learn in us not to think of men above that which is written, that none of you should be puffed up for one against the other" (I Cor. 4:6). Employing Paul's Greek word, meaning to "transfer in a figure," Hamann calls the process "metaschmatisieren" and extends its meaning.[7]

For Hamann, to metaschematize means to substitute a set of objective relationships for an analogous set of personal or existential relationships, or the reverse, in order to determine through the insight born of faith their common meaning.[8] In Hamann, it refers to the taking up of his opponent's position—the assumption of another cause as if it were his own in order to expose its weaknesses and contradictions. On January 28, 1776, he wrote to Herder: "You know that this unknown figure is one of my cherished advantages in writing, especially in regard to that which I call the economy of the plan and which is called in poetry the fable" (Hamann 1955–79, III, 215). Thus, Hamann's literary method requires direct personal involvement and indirect communication. The fables of an Aesop or a La Fontaine, for example, are a method of indirect communication; but they are not metaschematic, for they do not relate in any way to objective facts, and they do not bespeak the personal involvement of their authors. They share, however, one important feature with Hamann's method: their real meaning is to be sought beneath the surface appearance. "Genuine insight into any spiritual reality does not, according to the Magus, spring directly from either the objective or the subjective facts of a given situation alone, but from the interpretation made possible by transferred or metaschematized relationships illuminated by faith" (O'Flaherty 1967, 90). What Hamann does, however, is to recognize that the base elements of life may, if transformed, serve as more effective symbols of the spirit than those elements that are by nature noble. This conception does not originate with Hamann, but is derived from the Biblical revelation and Christian theology. The Greek myths before the ancient rationalists succeeded in emasculating them are an anticipation of the Christian point of view.

It is the principle of metaschematism that determines the inner form of Hamann's writings, "the unitary principle of organization which lends inner form to what seems at first glance to be the chaotic tangle of ideas in his writings" (Unger 1991, I, 502): "Genuine insight into any spiritual reality does not, according to the Magus, spring directly from either the objective or the subjective facts of a given situation alone, but from the interpretation made possible by transferred or metaschematized relationships illuminated by faith" (O'Flaherty 1967, 90). The Magus writes in the *Socratic Year* to J. G. Lindner: "I have had to write a great deal and about difficult things; therefore I have exerted myself to be brief and I have not been able to make my thoughts clearer otherwise than by expressing their main features as strongly as possible and by transferring them to foreign objects" (Hamann 1955–79, I, 324).

Hamann uses the very language of his opponent, or employs sarcasm or irony, often without warning, or any indication of its presence. He expresses himself "in many tongues" and speaks the language of the "Cretan, Arabian, white man, Moor, and Creole" (To J. G. Lindner, 18 Aug. 1759). The prophets are models of ironic style, in contrast to the "children of unbelief," who show a weak aptitude for irony (To his brother, 21 May 1760). Hamann's identification with Socrates for the purpose of wrestling with two intellectuals of the Enlightenment, Kant and Christoph Berens, for whom Socrates meant so much, is an example of his "metaschematism." When he writes that there is "no better sword than Goliath's" (To J. G. Lindner, 5 June 1759), Hamann may have been thinking of the Incarnation, whereby God identifies Himself with the human being and in effect seizes the weapons of those who have become his enemies, and in this form of irony, "catches the conscience" of humankind, turning His enemies into His own people. Hamann wishes to emulate this method despite the dangers of falling into sophistry, on the one hand, or into an autonomous, secularist enterprise on the other, two dangers he did not succeed in avoiding at times.[9]

In addition to using irony to expose the weaknesses and contradictions of his opponent's position, Hamann also uses irony, albeit negatively, to point to human finitude. Irony, for Hamann, is lower than humor, which also has a positive function: Humor opens the individual to paradoxical truth, thereby preparing the way to the truth of the Incarnation. Irony is necessity's iron law of negation, canceling all human striving and aspirations, so that they amount to nothing. Whereas irony is the grim fate that inevitably triumphs over human finitude, ensuring that all human projects end in death, humor to Hamann is divine freedom, disjunctive with irony's grim necessity. Humor, in this view, is positive in that it affirms that God is wholly other. Thus, if truth ever penetrates the sphere of human endeavor, it will surely appear very different from our finite understanding of what it ought to look like. In other words, divine reason is fundamentally disjunctive with human reason and consequently bound to appear absurd to humans. For Hamann, humor is the appropriate human attitude toward Divine folly because only in the absurd does the possibility of seeing God arise. The significance of humor, then, is not only to expose the impoverished state of finite reason, but also to laugh at all human attempts to scale the heavens with unassisted understanding. Humor's positive function is higher than irony's negative function: It opens a person to the acceptance of the reality of paradoxical truth, and ultimately to the acceptance of the highest paradox of all—the incarnation. Thus, humor is the road to salvation.[10]

The habilitating function of humor, which Hamann inherited from Shaftesbury and made his own, influenced Kierkegaard. The latter continues Hamann's use of irony and humor as devices of indirect communication in the service of Christianity, adopts Hamann's view of humor's superiority to irony, and most importantly, embraces humor as the means for opening the human being to paradoxical truth. In the next chapter, we see the extent of the influence of "the greatest humorist in Christianity" (*Pap.* II A 75), as Kierkegaard labels Hamann, on the Danish philosopher's view of the role of humor in the good life.

CHAPTER 2

KIERKEGAARD

HUMOR AS PHILOSOPHY AT ITS BEST

As soon as I am outside my religious understanding, I feel as an insect with which children are playing must feel, because life seems to have dealt with me so unmercifully; as soon as I am inside my religious understanding, I understand that precisely this has absolute meaning for me. Hence, that which in one case is a dreadful jest is in another sense the most profound earnestness.

—Kierkegaard (*Stages on Life's Way*)

Nineteenth-century Danish philosopher, Søren Kierkegaard, refers to Shaftesbury, as well as to Hegel, to introduce his interest in the legitimacy of the comic:

> In the previous century, a thesis propounded by Lord Shaftesbury that makes laughter the test of truth engendered several little research projects to find out whether it is so.[1] In our day, Hegelian philosophy has wanted to give predominance to the comic. The question of the legitimacy of the comic, of its relation to the religious . . . is of essential importance for a religious existence in our time, in which the comic runs off with the victory everywhere. (*CUP1*, 512–3)[2]

The comic has become "the tempter in our time," but if we understand it correctly we will lose our laughter. Kierkegaard intends to provide us with the necessary understanding: One of his pseudonym affirms that "if there is anything I have studied thoroughly, from A to Z, it is the comic," and "the more competently a person exists, the more he will discover the comic" (*CUP1*, 483; 462; 281).

101

In teaching us how to laugh, Kierkegaard provides a theory of the comic with the intent of demonstrating that Christianity is out of the comic's reach (CA, 128; CUP1, 483). If he did only this, however, he would not be different from many critics of Shaftesbury. Kierkegaard's singularity is that in the process of explaining the comic and its legitimate use, he gives to the comic, together with irony and especially humor, the most important place a philosopher has ever attributed to them. Humor for Kierkegaard is philosophy at its best, which, together with the comic, the tragic, and irony, is elevated to the level of existential categories that are essential for the good life. Furthermore, Kierkegaard sees in the comic an instrument of truth, the primary tool of philosophy once it steps into the new existential role Kierkegaard designed for it—to lead the individual toward worshiping the true God.

Other readings of Kierkegaard have failed to appreciate the essential relation of the comic with truth as well as its consequence: In order to further truth, the comic becomes for Kierkegaard an ethical-religious category, making it much more dependent on Kierkegaard's controversial view of religion than common use allows. This is true as well of the various forms of the comic Kierkegaard uses, such as irony and especially humor, which becomes a Christianized notion serving Kierkegaard's ladder of perfection toward Christ. By elaborating the roles of the comic, irony, and especially humor as essential to the Kierkegaardian good life, this chapter reveals both Kierkegaard's radical contribution to the history of philosophical thinking about humor, and the singularity of his religious thought disclosed through his ethical-religious notion of the comic and Christianized notion of humor.

For a long time, Kierkegaard harbored thoughts on irony, humor, the comic, and its relation to the tragic. Although he never wrote the doctoral dissertation on Greek and Roman satire he intended to write, he learned much from his study of the subject (Lowrie 1968a, xiv). Four years before writing his dissertation on a related subject, irony (1841), Kierkegaard conjectured that "it would be interesting to follow the development of human nature . . . by showing what one laughs at on the different age levels."[3] He intended this study to reveal the development of one's response to comedy and tragedy at different ages, as well as the relationship between the two. The study was also to contribute to the work he believed ought to be written, namely, "the history of the human soul" (JP 4, 280). It is this story, the history of the soul through its relationship with the comic that Kierkegaard's pseudonymous authorship tells. This explains why most of the major themes of Kierkegaard's authorship can be studied through the window of humor, as Thomas Oden has noted (Oden 2004, 8).

That the "melancholy Dane" had an interest in the comic is explained by his observation that "the melancholy have the best sense of the comic."[4]

Kierkegaard described himself, accordingly, as a two-faced Janus, laughing with one face and crying with the other,[5] and associated in his writings the comic with suffering, and jest with earnestness. "The person who with extreme effort and much self-sacrifice discovers the comic," he complained, "really has no opportunity to laugh himself out; he is too tense and concerned for that" (JP 2, 272). He confessed at the end of his life to having "a secret and happy understanding" with laughter, and to being "rightly understood" as a friend and lover of laughter (PV, 123). He saw himself as a genius and characterized the genius as humorous (PV, 107, 108),[6] and for a large part of his life he fulfilled the role of the humorist, an "intensely religious humorist," to use Walter Kauffman's apt description of him (Kaufmann 1962, 26).

Notorious for teasing when young, Kierkegaard continued this schoolboy habit by incessantly "teasing" prominent figures in Danish cultural life, such as Johan Ludvig Heiberg, Hans Lassen Martensen, and Bishop J. P. Mynster.[7] His public life was quiet, except for two occasions that are relevant to a study of the comic in Kierkegaard's thought. One occasion was his conflict with the satirical paper the Corsair in the 1840s, the second was his attack on Christendom in the 1850s. Kierkegaard attacked the Corsair because he thought the journal did not respect the ethics of the comic. The journal's retaliative sustained mockery of Kierkegaard drove him to despair.[8] With the Corsair affair, Kierkegaard's relationship with the comic took a dramatic turn. In 1849 he wrote, "I am a martyr of laughter and my life has been designed for that; I understand myself so completely as such that it is as if I now understand myself for the first time. To be able to become just that, I am the wittiest of all, possessing a superlative sense of comedy" (JP 6, 119). He redefined the ideal of Imitatio Dei to shed light on this new vision of himself:

> It is frequently said that if Christ came to the world now he would once again be crucified. This is not entirely true. . . . Christ would be ridiculed, treated as a mad man, but a mad man at whom one laughs . . . I now understand better and better the original and profound relationship I have with the comic, and this will be useful to me in illuminating Christianity. (Pap. X A 187)

After the Corsair affair, Kierkegaard consciously adopts the Orthodox Church's ideal of the holy fool or the fool in Christ's name, and thereby redescribes his relationship with the comic.[9]

The second public affair of his otherwise uneventful life was Kierkegaard's open attack on institutionalized Christianity for not preaching what, in his view, the Christian life really demanded. Under his own name, Kierkegaard mounted toward the end of his life an attack on the Danish Church in the newspaper *The Fatherland* (*Faedrelandet*) and in his periodical *The Moment* (*Oiblekket*). This attack has been viewed in various ways, ranging from the claim that Kierkegaard had gone crazy to the view that Kierkegaard was making a pseudonym of his own name, putting on the garb of a gutter-press journalist writing for a *Corsair*-style paper. Kierkegaard deemed Bishop Mynster and the whole order of the clergy comical and accused them of making Christianity "a laughingstock" and a "comedy," of ridiculing the king and the state and of treating God as a fool.[10]

Roger Poole suggests that the major problem in the twentieth-century reception of Kierkegaard is hermeneutic: In what way can one adequately read Kierkegaard? Poole believes that the reason that so little satisfaction has been obtained is because of the refusal to take seriously the nature of "indirect communication." By indirect communication, Poole refers to both the various pseudonymous writers and editors Kierkegaard created and to his use of irony and humor as devices of indirect discourse. Poole complains that even "the existential, humorous, continuously self-referring nature of Kierkegaard's syntax" is expunged from Howard and Edna Hong's translation of Kierkegaard's writings (Poole 1998, 62, 61). Thomas Oden rightly remarks that some commentators may have read Kierkegaard intensively without having ever really noticed his comic side (Oden 2004, 3). One knows various things about Kierkegaard, but not Kierkegaard's "mordant humor, nor the fantastic comedy he played out with his pseudonyms" (Kaufmann 1962, 15). With his marionette show of characters, to use George McFadden's expression, Kierkegaard created out of his own life a drama in Copenhagen, which has been more difficult to discern than Kierkegaard's irony.[11] Kierkegaard himself "envied" his reader, "who in peace and quiet will be able to sit and purely intellectually enjoy the immensely comic drama" he performed "just by living" in Copenhagen (JP 6, 79). Indeed, Richard Simon deems Kierkegaard "the most elaborate comic of the nineteenth century," a reflective comedian, a Christian humorist, a master of irony, a martyr of laughter, a clown." He notes that his writing, especially his pseudonymous authorship, is a clown's work, within which is "a complex and extensive meditation on the meanings of laughter, humor, irony, ridicule, and the comic. It is the most elaborate study of the subject in modern European intellectual history, and for the most part it has been ignored or downplayed by Kierkegaard's critics, for they have been after serious content" (Simon 1985, 85).

Interestingly, Kierkegaard anticipates this attitude to his writings. In *Concluding Unscientific Postscript*, he has one of his pseudonyms, Johannes

Climacus, assess another pseudonym's work, *Stages on Life's Way*. Climacus explains that if the latter has any meaning or significance, it will consist

> in the existence-inwardness of the different stages variously elu-
> cidated in passion, irony, pathos, humor, dialectic. Such things,
> of course, do not occupy assistant professors . . . passion, pathos,
> irony, dialectic, humor, enthusiasm, etc. are considered by assis-
> tant professors to be something subordinate that everyone pos-
> sesses. (*CUP1*, 299)

Kierkegaard believes the erudite are most prone to ignore or misinterpret the comic. Lacking a sense of humor, the assistant professor is the least likely to grasp his or her own comic contradictions (*CUP1*, 281), and the least likely to read Kierkegaard correctly.

Recently, however, postmodern commentators have emphasized the aesthetic use of the comic in Kierkegaard's writings. Walter Kaufmann right-ly remarks, however, "a writer who so persistently distinguished between what he called an aesthetic approach and what we might call an existential approach should not be approached and discussed on the aesthetic plane, as he usually is." Kierkegaard's "central aspirations are almost invariably ignored, and even those who notice them often give reasons why the things that mattered to him may be dismissed as really of no account" (Kaufmann 1962, 18, 11). Indeed, many of Kierkegaard's works are parodic or satiric,[12] but he does not use comical devises for the sole amusement of the reader. As Hugh Pyper suggests, "*Concluding Unscientific Postscript* presents itself as a joke and it is only by taking its character as such entirely seriously that we can deal in earnest with its message" (Pyper 1997, 149). Kierkegaard explains this issue thus:

> The reason why *Concluding Unscientific Postscript* is made to
> appear comical is precisely because it is serious—and people
> think they can better the cause by separating these and trans-
> lating them into pieces of dogma, the whole thing no doubt
> ending in a new confusion where I myself am treated as a cause,
> everything being translated into the objective, so that what is
> new is that here we have a new doctrine, and not that here we
> have personality. (*Pap.* X^2 A 130)

This comment should be appreciated in light of Kierkegaard's assertion that true earnestness is necessarily jestful (*SLW*, 365). Comprehending the comic is thus essential for understanding Kierkegaard's thought.

Kierkegaard's theory stands up well against the great theories of the comic in the history of ideas. Not only does Kierkegaard explore comic perception to its depths, but he also practices the art of comedy as astutely as any writer of his time.[13] His theory of comedy is integrated into his practice of comic perception and, as Thomas Oden notes, "both are integral into his entire authorship" (Oden 2004, 1).[14] Most of Kierkegaard's pseudonyms are fascinated by the meanings of the comic, irony, humor, mockery, ridicule, laughter, and there are extensive commentaries on these meanings and arguments between the pseudonyms throughout the authorship. What simplifies or complicates the reading of these passages, however, is that there are very similar statements in Kierkegaard's journals and autobiographical essays, and, as Richard Simon observes, many of these suggest that Kierkegaard understands himself as a comic figure (Simon 1985, 92).

Kierkegaard is indeed a humorist: Not only do his most important theses appear in a book written by a pseudonym Kierkegaard qualifies as a humorist (Johannes Climacus in *Concluding Unscientific Postscript*), but, through pseudonymous personalities such as Climacus, Quidam, and Frater Taciturnus, Kierkegaard defines the humorist in such a way that it becomes apparent that much of his own life was a concrete actualization of this perspective (Taylor 1980a, 228). However, Walter Kaufmann is right in qualifying Kierkegaard's sort of humor, deeming him an "intensively religious humorist" (Kaufmann 1962, 26).

There are a few commentators who appreciate the philosophic importance, rather than the aesthetic use, of the comic and humor in Kierkegaard's authorship. Merold Westphal suggests that the pseudonym of *Concluding Unscientific Postscript* "portrays the existing thinker as having what we might call a metaphysical sense of humor, an appreciation of the inherent incongruities of being human" (Westphal 1996, 69–70). In his remarkable *Humor and Irony in Kierkegaard's Thought*, John Lippitt notes, "Kierkegaard is one thinker who brings both a philosophical and a religious dimension to the topic of the comic and humor" (Lippitt 2000b, 2). Sylvia Walsh deems humor, irony, the comic, and the tragic, existential categories that are essential to the Kierkegaardian art of existing (Walsh 1994). And Adi Shmüeli asserts that Kierkegaard's thoughts on humor and irony constitute "the most important part of his philosophy, and only by studying them can one understand Kierkegaard's philosophy and his ideas on Christianity" (Shmüeli 1971, 69).[15]

I consider the comic much more important in Kierkegaard's philosophy than the above-mentioned interpreters, however, because I believe Kierkegaard maintains that by examining the content of our laughter we know the sort of person we are. As ethical and religious edification is all that matters for Kierkegaard, this makes the comic the main criterion of advancement one has in the Kierkegaardian negative theology's ladder, that is, the major positive indicator of one's relation to the truth. I suggest that, for Kierkegaard, the comic power is both sword and shield whose mastery is crucial for inner progress from lower to higher stages of existence. For lack of an external criterion for inward advancement, which is the sole progress Kierkegaard recognizes, the comic is the main tool of examination, correction, and evaluation an individual possesses for reflecting on himself, his life, and his personal experiences, and for communicating this to others. Hence, the comic becomes the main tool of philosophy, once philosophy steps into the new existential role Kierkegaard has designed for it, which is to lead the individual toward worshiping the true God.

It is the relation to the comic that defines the existential spheres that have made Kierkegaard's reputation as a philosopher (*CUP1*, 462) and that constitute the stages that lead to the good life. The ethics of the comic based on Kierkegaard's hierarchy of existential spheres prescribes a right use of the comic that leads one to the good life. The ethics of the comic justifies laughter when a person's existential position in life is higher than the position one is laughing at. Through this device, I suggest, Kierkegaard makes certain that his edifying lessons on the comic bear on his lessons on the good life, because laughing well is living well for Kierkegaard. Only the religious person laughs last and well, whereas the rest of us are forbidden to laugh at higher existential spheres lest we appear ridiculous. In this war of laughter, which is a trade of virtues and vices, religion comes out victorious in relation to philosophy as well as in relation to all other life-views, which Kierkegaard's teleological ladder describes as stages of existence.

Still, Kierkegaard assigns humor the highest comic power with the highest possible role within thought: He characterizes the humorist's life as the best existence a thinker can attain, topped only by the supra-rational religious life-view. Humor plays an essential role in religion as well, although the kind of role humor fulfills in Christianity changes as Kierkegaard's view of Christianity evolves. For the young Kierkegaard, humor is intrinsic to the good life defined as the highest life-view, Christianity. For the mature Kierkegaard, however, the existential sphere of humor gains independence from Christianity as a life-view. Lower than Christianity, humor functions also as a border zone from which the leap to a Christian existence may be contemplated, and as a necessary mask of the religious person. The roles humor fulfills in relation to religion and Christianity echo the roles irony fulfills on a lower level in relation to the ethical life. This study investigates the various roles Kierkegaard attributes to humor at different phases of his life and the reasons that account for the changes in his view of the relations between Christianity and humor.

Understanding the comic is essential for understanding the Kierkegaardian good life; without the comic, also in the guise of irony and especially humor, the Kierkegaardian good life is unattainable for many of us. There is only one life-view that can be deemed the Kierkegaardian good life. Kierkegaard sees the remaining life-views, however, not only as "spheres" of existence, but also as stages that may lead to the Christian life. To answer the question of the role of the comic in the Kierkegaardian good life, it is important to understand, then, not only the role of the comic in the Christian life, but also the role of irony and humor as stages along life's way, as well as the role of the comic within the lower stages, such as the aesthetic and the ethical stages.

Many factors make this endeavor difficult. First, various schools of interpretation have differing interests in the comic: on the one hand, postmodern commentators concentrate on the "how" of the comic instead of the "what," thereby overstating irony and often using it to dismiss the very subjects most important to Kierkegaard; on the other hand, the theologians' commentaries relevant to an understanding of Kierkegaard's views on religion, and therefore, on humor, usually ignore the comic. Second, the wealth of opinions about the comic, mockery, laughter, ridicule, irony, and humor, voiced through the pseudonyms' different if not contrary perspectives, stand in the way of a systematic exposition of Kierkegaard's views. Relating opinions to pseudonyms simplifies the task but burdens the reading. Third, the difficulty lies also in the nature of Kierkegaard's writings, which, as Louis Mackey has noted, "resist the intelligence almost successfully" (Mackey 1986, xxiii). The purpose of these writings is to effectuate a change in the reader, certainly not to enable a successful summary of them. All these make Kierkegaard's wish of finding a reader that would enter his books and get lost in them a tangible danger.

Yet I believe that in order to understand the role of the comic in the good life, it is important to address Kierkegaard's views on the comic, irony, and humor in the totality of his writings, both in his journals and authorship, and to respect his wish to relate the views in the voices of the pseudonyms that express them (*CUP1*, 28). Both devices are uncommon in Kierkegaard's commentaries, which either homogenize Kierkegaard's thought on the comic or humor, or narrow the discussion to one work or one pseudonym's view. To understand the role of the comic, irony, and humor in the life-views described in Kierkegaard's authorship, I introduce, first, Kierkegaard's view of the good life, followed by detailed discussions of his view of the comic, irony, and humor. The comic is explained as contradiction, as unified with the tragic, as necessary in communication, and finally, as legitimate and illegitimate. As irony and humor are forms of the comic, I introduce the various roles Kierkegaard finds for them, beginning with irony, which he considers lower than humor. Irony is depicted as a life-view, as a mask of the ethical person, as a tool, as different from humor, and as a defining characteristic of Kierkegaard. Since for Kierkegaard, "the comic power is essentially humor" (*CUP1*, 282), a thorough discussion of the role of humor in Kierkegaard's thought follows. Humor is presented, first, as intrinsic to Christianity—the view the young Kierkegaard held—followed by the view of humor in his mature thought, as an existential stage, as a border zone to the religious from which the leap to a Christian existence may be contemplated, and as a mask of the religious person. I conclude the chapter with a discussion of the role in the good life Kierkegaard allots to the comic and to its highest form, humor, and with an evaluation of the feasibility—mainly for nonreligious persons, but also for religious persons who do not share Kierkegaard's view of religion—of implementing Kierkegaard's views of the comic and humor.

THE GOOD LIFE

Kierkegaard is a philosopher and psychologist, an important literary author, and, as he states in *The Point of View of My Life as an Author*, a religious writer:

> But I do maintain that I know with uncommon clarity and definiteness what Christianity is, what can be required of the Christian, what it means to be a Christian. To an unusual degree I have, I think, the qualifications to be able to present this. I also think it is my duty to do this. ("Armed Neutrality," *PV*, 138)

Despite adhering to a Christian view of existence, Kierkegaard does his best to distance his views from the reader in the bulk of his writing. Instead of explaining in his works how he understands the world, he explores the psychological and intellectual perspectives of a number of views of life. Common to all the views is the notion of goals in life and their effect on the human personality, as well as on the community and human society in general. Kierkegaard uses a series of pseudonyms for that purpose, each inviting the reader to consider whether his description and assessment of the various possible goals, and the path to them, is correct.[16]

Kierkegaard admires Socrates' maieutic method of teaching through discussion. He aims to follow this ideal of the teacher who causes truth to be born in another but who does not have any claim to truth. For Kierkegaard, that truth is the religious life. Although he attempts to hide his personal viewpoint behind his pseudonyms,[17] it is clear from his writings that he regards Christianity as the highest religion to which the Greek world, as representative of paganism, and Judaism, as the forerunner of Christianity, point. In contradistinction to Hegelianism, in which religion and Christianity are made to take a subordinate place to philosophy, Kierkegaard emphasizes the Christian life as the highest worldview. He makes a sharp distinction between Christianity (*Christendommen*) and Christendom (*Chritenheden*). He urges the believer to look for the content of Christianity in the New Testament rather than in the institution of the Church. The individual is encouraged to measure the Christianity of the Church establishment by considering whether it measures up to what is called for by strict New Testament ideality. Christendom is Christianity expressed as a historical sociopolitical institution. Kierkegaard, especially in his later writings, is extremely hostile to the historical spread of Christianity as "Christendom," in which thousands have been, and still are, bound to the Church as an institution without proper reference to the Christian ideal life portrayed in the New Testament.

Kierkegaard is part of a long tradition in the West that sees human life, including the philosophical and religious understanding of life, in terms of illness and health, the diagnosis of disease and deliverance from it. As David Gouwens notes, the diagnosis might be relatively mild (a person lives in misunderstanding or error) or it may be of a deeper spiritual malady (sin) (Gouwens 1996, 27). In either case, this tradition postulates that the condition of ill health includes, as Kierkegaard puts it, diseases of reflection. *Reflection* is a broad term for Kierkegaard. It indicates not only thought and intellectual activity, but also the character or tone of one's imaginative and affective life. For this tradition, salvation as a search for truth becomes a search for wholeness and unity over time.[18] It involves self-analysis and self-examination as a necessary part of "coming to the truth," and recognizes that this kind of thinking is both a clarification of intellectual confusion and a passion desiring a better way of life. In the task of cleansing the glass of vision, philosophy is a way of wisdom and even spiritual rebirth. For this reason, David Gouwens rightly emphasizes that Kierkegaard sees philosophy, especially in its Greek origins, not as a subject, but as a "way" (Gouwens 1996, 28). Philosophical and religious reflection in this tradition are not specialties of some arcane realms of knowledge or matters of technical expertise alone, but are exercises in a discipline aimed at coming to wisdom, a spiritual self as well as at an intellectual *via disciplinae*. At the culmination of modernity, this tradition of philosophy and religious reflection as a spiritual discipline, which derives from Socrates and continues in Christianity, is in danger of being undermined.

The personal and human element in philosophical reflection and in ethico-religious existence is necessarily sacrificed.[19] Two factors undermine the human quest for authentic existence, Hegelianism and "Christendom." Both are expressions of a tendency to conceive existence and existential problems in terms of knowledge. Hegel attempts to understand existence in objective terms, whereas Christendom views Christianity as a doctrine requiring mental assent or dissent on the part of the existing individual. In Kierkegaard's opinion, both Hegelianism and Christendom rob the human being of self-understanding, development as a self, and ultimately a relationship with God. Hegel and Danish Hegelianism,[20] which epitomize the speculative thinkers pertaining to the platonic movement, present a twofold problem: First, the dangers inherent in thinking, and second, the particular institutionalization and professionalization of philosophy and theology in the modern age. Thus, Kierkegaard's diagnosis of the diseases of philosophical and theological reflection is not only a general critique of the dangers of reflection, but also a social critique of how philosophy and theology are practiced in the modern age.

Kierkegaard's own endeavor in countering the diseases of reflection he diagnoses in his contemporaries is to present the reader with a program for attaining an authentic existence. To this end, embracing another form of thinking, subjective thinking, is required as well as arriving at a correct understanding of the human *telos* and how one attains to it, that is, how one becomes a self.

SUBJECTIVE THINKING

Drawing heavily on Hegelian categories and dialectical methods, Kierkegaard turns Hegel "outside-in," as Alastair Hannay succinctly puts it (Hannay 1982, 19–53).[21] The Hegelian dialectic is transposed from the sphere of essence to that of the individual human existence. Kierkegaard concedes that Hegel's speculative construction of the realm of essence and the nature of the categories within it may well be correct. In existence or in "existential dialectics," however, it is the principle of contradiction and not that of identity between thought and being that is valid (*CUP1*, 270–1). The difficulty with the Hegelian system is that one cannot reach reality by thinking because as soon as thought begins to control the real, it translates it into the sphere of the possible. Kierkegaard shows how this reality becomes a problem for thought by concerning himself with the further question as to how far the thinking ego is interested in the reality of its own existence. It cannot simply take cognizance of its own specific and characteristic existence. As soon as the thinking ego performs this act of self-awareness, it automatically differentiates itself from its empirical reality. It does not make this differentiation without keen interest; rather, in making it, it measures the empirical subject against a conceptual ideal subject. By this act, the ego becomes conscious of itself as an existing ego. It neither becomes the ideal nor does it remain the empirical ego. Instead, the ego, which is interested in its own existence, becomes a mediator between the two. But it is precisely in this middle term that reality lies—in this "interesse" as a mediating activity, in the literal sense of the Latin "inter-esse," or "being between."

As soon as the immediately existing ego attains consciousness of itself, this immediacy is suspended by the new awareness of a contradiction between the ideal and the real.[22] This happens because consciousness makes clear its concern about the decisive contradiction and in so doing affirms itself. Hermann Diem rightly maintains, therefore:

> Kierkegaard's whole existential dialectic circles around this attainment of self-consciousness by the ego, by which it becomes aware of itself as existent and so wins reality. This is fundamentally its sole and ever recurrent theme, every implicit aspect of which is unfolded. With relentless persistence, the ego is pinned down to this position with no possibility of escape into the bypaths of speculation. (Diem 1959, 22)

According to one of Kierkegaard's pseudonyms, Johannes Climacus, "existing is a prodigious contradiction from which the subjective thinker is not to abstract . . . but in which he is to remain" (CUP1, 350).

As soon as Kierkegaard's pseudonyms begin characterizing this essential contradiction between the ideal and the real, his philosophical anthropology emerges. There is a contradiction between "the infinite and the finite, the eternal and the becoming" (CUP1, 89). "Psyche and body," which is another wording for the "temporal and eternal" (CA, 85), results in a contradiction between the inner and the outer (CUP1, 89). To "finitude/infinite," the pseudonym Anti-Climacus adds "possibility/necessity, and consciousness/unconsciousness" (SUD, 29). This essential contradiction has far reaching consequences for any attempt to comprehend existence. Thought no longer corresponds to reality and therefore there is no guarantee of knowing whether that which is thought is an actual expression of existence.

Thought is penetrated by a radical uncertainty, and any replacement for Hegelian philosophy must take this uncertainty as its starting point.

In contrast to Hegelian dialectic, existential dialectics places a strict limitation on the activity and competence of thought. It functions very much like a border guard, allowing thought to press forward to its legitimate boundaries, but stopping it from encroaching on existence itself. That is, thought may be legitimately used in the clarification of existential issues but must stop short of absorbing these issues unto itself and reducing them to its categories. Existential dialectics, then, does not explain existence but helps the human being to become aware of crucial existential issues. Furthermore, existential dialectics entails the reduction of the status of thought. In existence, thought finds that it exists alongside categories such as will, feeling, and imagination. Consequently, although thought plays an important role on the human being's existence, it does so only in conjunction with these nonintellectual elements.

Abstract thought is nevertheless important if one uses it correctly to clarify intellectual confusion and to serve the passion of desiring a better way of life. Existential dialectics is also concerned with bringing about reconciliation between thought and being. It does so, however, within existence and the strictures that existence places on the human being. Kierkegaard describes the means by which this is carried out as "subjective reflection." Subjective reflection, unlike its objective counterpart, proceeds not away from but toward existence, namely the existence of the individual human being. It is called "subjective" because it turns toward "subjectivity," that is, the innermost personal being, of the single individual. It is not concerned with establishing a speculative system, but rather with applying the categories of abstract thought to the concrete existence of the individual human being. Johannes Climacus explains the difference between abstract thought and subjective thinking:

> While abstract thought seeks to understand the concrete abstractly, the subjective thinker has conversely to understand the abstract concretely. Abstract thought turns from concrete men to consider man in general; the subjective thinker seeks to understand the abstract determination of being human in terms of this particular human being. (*CUP1*, 315)

Thus, whereas objective reflection only moves in one direction, namely, away from existence to the abstract and essential, subjective thought moves in two directions. First, it makes the movement of objective reflection. That is, abstract thought is used to obtain a conception of existence and of the categories that make it up. Second, it bends objective reflection back on itself and applies it to existence. A circular movement is created in which thought first moves away from existence but is then turned back and applied to its point of origin. A dialectical movement is thus established between existence, the abstract conception of existence, and the existential application of this conception.

The significance of this dialectical movement is twofold. First, subjective reflection provides the existing individual with the means with which to understand personal existence. By means of the first movement, namely that of abstract thought, the individual acquires the concepts with which to understand the self. Thus, in the case of the previous quote, abstract thought provides the existing individual with a concept of humanity. The individual can then use this concept to interpret and comprehend his own individual humanity. By making the second movement of subjective reflection, that is, by applying the abstract concept of humanity to self, the individual achieves an understanding of the individual humanity. In this sense, then, subjective reflection is a reformulation of the Socratic dictum, "Know thyself." It is the process by which the individual comes to achieve a greater understanding of self (*CUP1*, 314–6).

Second, subjective reflection has an ethical function. That is, it provides the individual not only with the wherewithal with which to interpret existence, but also with the means with which to develop and improve this existence. For Kierkegaard, the categories of objective reflection are not only forms of thought but also possibilities. Kierkegaard holds that the process of abstraction used by abstract thought results in an object or aspect of reality being transferred *ab esse ad posse*.[23] If the individual discovers that his existence does not correspond to the abstract conception of what existence ideally is, he is compelled to act to restructure his existence so that it corresponds to this conception.

The question now arises as to how this dialectical process of subjective reflection results in overcoming the contradiction between thought and existence. This division is overcome when the existing individual posits an identity between thought and personal existence. That is, through the application of the categories of objective reflection (thought) to an individual existence (being), an identity can be created. By attempting to live according to the conception of the true nature of existence, the existing individual brings about an identity between thought and being. This identity is short-lived, for living is characterized by striving and not by reaching a result. Nonetheless, it is worth striving for the identity between thought and being, which is reached in moments of passion.

For Kierkegaard, Christianity requires the human being to struggle constantly against the immediate or the phenomenal world. Only the total renunciation of the finite prepares an individual for the religious leap that reveals the existence of the Absolute. Kierkegaard, as a master of indirect communication, attempts to help people free themselves of the immediate. Therefore, he does not teach Christianity directly, nor does he ask the reader to renounce immediate life and believe in God. Quite the contrary, as he declares in the journals:

> my idea, the basis of my life . . . one of the most original ideas in many centuries, and the most original ever expressed in Danish, is that Christianity needed an expert in maieutics, and that I was the one. . . . The category for deploying Christianity does not suit Christendom. Here it is maieutics which is suitable, for it takes as its point of departure the notion that people have the highest good, but wishes to help them realize what they have. (*Pap.* VIII A 42)[24]

Kierkegaard's discussion with others takes place through the authorship, which becomes his version of Socrates' Athenian marketplace. Alongside the nonreligious pseudonymous works, which mainly point to his religious themes, Kierkegaard publishes religious discourses under his own name. There he makes it clear that he is one "without authority," and that although the discourse is directed at the reader, it is equally directed at himself. Moreover, although he writes a number of larger religious works toward the end of his life, he also publishes nonreligious or "aesthetic" pieces to ameliorate the impression of being a religious author. Kierkegaard's authorship thus presents a multifaceted mode of question-and-answer that resembles Socrates' method and the Platonic Socrates' ultimate goal of the good, the true, and the beautiful.

The maieutic relationship is an important aspect of Kierkegaard's philosophy. In his journals, he sees it enabling the reader "to stand alone—by another's help" (*JP* 1, 650, sec. 15). Kierkegaardian maieutics is better understood in the light of his theory of indirect communication. Kierkegaard believes that the truth, which is inwardness, cannot be taught directly. In an indirect communication, the recipient of the communication must decipher the message alone. Only the person whose inwardness corresponds to the communicator's subjectivity can understand the content of the communication.

In *The Point of View for My Work as an Author*, Kierkegaard testifies that his authorship is the product of a religious writer. Some scholars suggest that his testimony cannot be trusted and should thus be considered ironic. They argue that a direct commentary on authorship is really just another form of indirect communication. That is, just as one cannot take the previous pseudonymous works as direct expressions of what the author thinks, so too, one cannot trust the commentary on the authorship as a genuine expression of the author's own views and aims. This problem, and perhaps also the problem of the indirect pseudonymous authorship as a whole, is greatly ameliorated by a thorough study of the entire authorship, and especially of the pseudonymous material. Careful study of the authorship reveals a number of underlying ideas Kierkegaard wants the reader to grasp.[25]

First, although different pseudonyms have different perspectives on life, they all work together to illustrate that the aesthetic life, the life lived for the gratification of the senses, cannot ultimately work because it is against nature, against the fundamental structure of the human psyche. The right path is clearly that of the ethical-religious existence.[26] Second, important aspects of human existence, notably the nature and structure of the human psyche, are expounded on by all pseudonyms. But, instead of forming a contradictory picture, their views form a clear presentation of Kierkegaard's view of the nature and purpose of human life.[27]

Nevertheless, modern scholars have devised a variety of ways to read Kierkegaard's work. This endeavor is due not only to the prolixity and inventiveness of scholars, but also to the fact that Kierkegaard himself is multifaceted as a thinker. Adding his self-proclaimed irony[28] and the pseudonymity of much of his authorship, Kierkegaard's writings appear to be a vast field awaiting the tools of competing schools of thought.[29] "My wish, my prayer," writes Kierkegaard in his own name at the end of *Postscript*, "is that if it might occur to anyone to quote a particular saying from the books, he would do me the favor to cite the name of the respective pseudonymous author" (*CUP1*, 28). I suggest that Kierkegaard's authorship can be read as a whole as long as the reader is sensitive to the ways in which the various characters and pseudonyms speak for themselves alone and does not try to homogenize them.

THE HUMAN TELOS

To understand the basic aim of Kierkegaard's writings, however, it is important to explain his own private assumptions about the world, especially when his life-view is embedded in an authorship of such complexity. Kierkegaard is not only a committed Christian, but also one trained for the ministry. He believes that the Christian view of the world is the factually correct one, although he emphasizes that one must hold the truth of Christianity by faith. Faith in the rightness of the Christian way of life is required because one cannot be objectively certain that God exists.

Moreover, faith is understood to be "against the understanding," for particular religious propositions seem opposed to that which the human mind conceives as possible. Kierkegaard has a very definite understanding of the way things are. This is something that can be too easily overlooked, given that he expounds on the psychology of a wide range of views of life in his authorship.

Kierkegaard is a dualist. He believes the realm of existence to consist of the world of temporality (i.e., space-time as we experience it in daily life) and the realm of eternity. Eternity is the realm of actual transcendence, the dwelling place of God, the goal of humans who can relate to God both in this world and after death. Kierkegaard also speaks of the possibility of damnation in his authorship. Hell, however, is not a separate realm but the state of isolated personal despair of the person who willfully rejects God. Each human being is born into the world with the potentiality of becoming an authentic person. Humans are biologically part of the animal kingdom, but unlike animals, they have a God-created potentiality for spiritual eternal life. Kierkegaard describes the condition of the human self as a synthesis or combination of body (physical biology) and psyche or soul, which has, in addition, the potential for eternal life. To the extent that a choice is made to actualize the potential, there can, and should, arise an already implicit second synthesis between the temporal and the eternal elements in a person's nature, between necessity (the factors of heredity and environment over which one has no control) and freedom (to act). This second synthesis develops through the exercise of moral choice with the aid of self-awareness and self-knowledge. Because the individual is located in this bipolar situation with a foot in temporality and at least a potential foot in the eternal realm, humans can experience anxiety and despair. The phenomenon of despair is a feature of human misrelation to the eternal.

The balanced human being is the one who centers life on the eternal, on eternal values, on eternity, and on God. The immature person is the one who makes the realm of temporality the goal of life. A person can do this by making temporal pleasures the most important thing in life. A person may defiantly try to alter, and thus be master of, these elements of the environment as well as heredity, which ultimately cannot be changed. Self-centeredness lies at the heart of what Kierkegaard labels the "aesthetic" way of life. The movement toward spiritual life occurs only through choosing to live a moral existence. There can be no relationship with the eternal, or God, outside ethics, even if the person concerned is seemingly practicing some form of religiosity.

Kierkegaard presents a number of aesthetes or pleasure seekers, from the amoral person, who has never reflected about the rightness of following instinct, to the one who has deliberately chosen this way of life despite ethics. He describes various forms of morality in his writings. *Saedelighed* (morality) is his term for any code of behavior based solely on temporal values. He does not regard "morality" as genuinely moral because personal egocentricity is replaced merely by purely materialistic codes of self-preservation of the society in question. For Kierkegaard, real morality must be based on some form of eternal value that transcends the community.

Kierkegaard's main ethicist is Judge Williams, a man who espouses a mild form of Christian altruism, in which a person lives a godly life in society, a life that builds up individual and community existence in terms of both temporal and spiritual goods. Although a Christian, the judge is not allowed to represent a religious position because (although he mentions the possibility of ethical dilemma and religious renunciation) he espouses a world-affirming religiosity, as opposed to a strict totally altruistic religious life of "dying to the world." Kierkegaard explores the difficulties surrounding life according to the demands of strict religiousness through other characters. Johannes Climacus and Anti-Climacus are examples of fictional figures that fathom the intellectual and psychological depths of religious and Christian religious life. Whereas Judge Williams explores ethical-religiosity in terms of fighting personal self-centeredness, the two Climacus pseudonyms explore an ethical religiosity that, for the sake of the eternal, give up even the morally good things of the world such as marriage and prospering in the community.

Kierkegaard's doctrine of the "stages on life's way" embodies this religious theology. As accounts of human emotional life with a religious teleology, the stages also envision a particular goal for human existence, which Kierkegaard terms *Salighed*, a supple term that for him embraces "happiness," "eternal happiness," and "blessedness." The goal is anything but hedonistic; rather, it carries strong overtones of "task" and "striving." Concerned not only with "feelings," it aims at the transformation of a person, including emotional transformation, as one who is earnestly oriented toward the task and gift of relating to God.

The various goals embedded in views of life are described as "stages" or "spheres" (*stadier*) of existence. Exactly how many stages there are is not altogether resolved in Kierkegaard's writings.[30] The main stages are the aesthetic, ethical, religious, and, within the religious sphere, "natural" religiosity (Religiousness A) and Christianity (sometimes called Religiousness B). The aesthetic has its goal or *telos* in immediate enjoyment through the satisfaction and refinement of natural drives, passions, moods, talents, mental capacities, and inclinations; the ethical has as its goal victory over the struggle to fulfill universal ethical requirements in the personal life of the existing individual; and the religious has its *telos* in eternal happiness, a fulfillment that is only anticipated in existence through a relationship with God characterized by persistent inner suffering due to consciousness of guilt and sin.[31]

Between the stages, Climacus adds to his analysis two boundary zones or transition spheres: Irony is placed between the aesthetic and the ethical, and humor is positioned between the ethical and the religious (*CUP1*, 501–2). Irony and humor also function within the ethical and religious spheres as the disguise or incognito, through which the ethical and immanent religiousness are given expression. Closely connected to irony and humor are the comic and the tragic. The four concepts are existential categories that are essential, not accidental, to the art of living.

Kierkegaard is convinced that the distance between spheres of existence is bridged, not by any gradual merging or by a necessary transformation of one into another, but only by a "leap" or free decision on the part of the individual. He recognizes certain states of soul, nevertheless, which indicate that a person has plumbed one of the inferior stages to its depths and has reached the extreme limit of that mode of life. A cynical and despairing irony marks the person who has lived an aesthetic life through to its bitter end, and is consequently placed at the borderline, where a leap into the ethical sphere is possible. Humor characterizes the person who has reached the borderline of the ethical sphere. At first, Kierkegaard regards humor as the proper attitude of the Christian with regard to the things of time, a kind of protective covering or incognito, useful in dealing with worldly fortunes and with individuals who do not see the world through the eyes of faith. But by 1845, he feels that humor is not so much a religious as an ethical passion—indeed, that it signifies that a person has reached the borderline of ethical life and is faced with the choice of becoming religious in a plenary way or of thwarting the natural inclination of ethical existence to surmount itself.[32]

During the same year that marked the composition of *Postscript*, the distinctive nature of Christianity is so strongly impressed on Kierkegaard that he ceases to speak of the religious sphere in an unqualified way, and thereafter sharply distinguishes between all natural modes of the religious and the unique Christian religious spirit. This distinction between Religiousness A and Religiousness B is equivalent to designating four stages in the dialectic of life. The immanent modes of religious existence do not exhaust or naturally blend with the transcendent kind of religiousness, which comes only with the gift of Christian faith.

The importance that Kierkegaard attributes to his characterizations of the stages cannot be overestimated. They constitute his "abiding merit to literature" (*Pap.* VII A 127). He thinks he has "nailed down the category relations with regard to Christianity so well that no dialectician would be able to loose them" (*Pap.* IX A 413). The stages are not equally viable options that are equal in value, none having more warrant than the other, as Josiah Thompson and others have claimed (1973). Rather, they are progressive plateaus on a mountainside that Climacus must ascend if he is to attain the highest point and experience the *summun bonum*. Louis Pojman rightly maintains, then, that for Kierkegaard the human being has "an essence, a *telos* [a purpose], and authentic selfhood in realizing that *telos*" (Pojman 1999, 35).

The concept of stages is best seen within the context of Kierkegaard's larger purpose of providing an account of human moods and emotions and the quest for continuity and unity in one's existence. Kierkegaard refers to this as "the eternal" and grounds it in the relationship to God as the source and goal of one's existence. For Kierkegaard, the task of human existence is in large part that of sorting out the complex chaos of moods in one's emotional life into a life that is characterized by the consistency and stability of emotions. In this transition from moods to emotions, a dominant theme is that of attaining a unity in one's life. But, for Kierkegaard, this goal of continuity, integration, and stability is also teleogically oriented, as his doctrine of the "stages on life's way" clearly indicates.

Finally, Kierkegaard's construction of a Christian epistemology involves two more interesting features. He consciously develops Christian ideas out of the rudiments of secular concepts. His treatment of "anxiety" and "despair" in *The Concept of Anxiety* and *The Sickness unto Death* are good examples of this strategy. The process of Christianizing ordinary secular concepts, infusing them with a potency they do not appear to have at first glance, is interrelated with the second important feature of Kierkegaard's philosophy: The strategy of constructing a framework in which the move into Christian faith is shown (albeit indirectly) to be eminently reasonable.

BECOMING A SELF

The hierarchy of the spheres points to a teleology that assists the individual in fulfilling the task that faces him. It is the ethical task of each individual to become a whole person. There are no two ways of doing it, as Kierkegaard emphatically affirms the religious dimension of the self: The false self is the self that the individual has conceived (*SUD*, 30); whereas, the true self is the self grounded in God. The relationship with God is an ontological quality of the self apart from which the self cannot be fully actualized or know itself as the infinite self. "The formula that describes the state of the self when despair is completely rooted out is this: in relating itself to itself and in willing to be itself, the self rests transparently in the power that established it" (*SUD*, 14). This state is faith (*SUD*, 82).

An existing individual does not need to "form existence out of the finite and the infinite [by putting them together], but, composed of the finite and the infinite, he, existing, is supposed to *become* one of the parts [namely, infinite] . . ." (*CUP1*, 420). The individual's decision to risk everything to fulfill his *telos* of eternal happiness is one by which he does "become infinitized" (*CUP1*, 423). It is a choice in which he accepts an identity apart from and superordinate to the finite, even though to avoid another main form of despair—to "will to be oneself" (*SUD*, 14), the individual must accept that possession of the infinite that takes the form of dependence on God.[33]

It is for the acting individual to subordinate finite ends to an absolute end, at least to try to reach that "maximum," which is to maintain simultaneously a relationship to the absolute *telos* and to relative ends, not by mediating them, but by making the relationship to the absolute *telos* absolute and the relationship to the relative ends relative. If, for any individual, says Climacus, "an eternal happiness is his highest good, this means that in his acting, the finite elements are once and for all reduced to what must be surrendered in relation to the eternal happiness" (*CUP1*, 391). Climacus does not mean that by giving up the finite the individual ceases to be human. The point is rather that the individual consciously subjects the finite goals that confront him to an overordinate, nonfinite end, genuinely conceived as nonfinite. Living in the category of spirit requires the individual to be a stranger in the world of the finite. The reason why so few have attempted the life of spirit is because most persons have still not descended deeply enough into despair.

Thus, Climacus defines the task confronting an individual as "simultaneously to relate oneself absolutely to the absolute *telos* (end, goal) and relatively to relative ends" (*CUP1*, 525; see 431–2). The absolute *telos* is eternal happiness, that is, immortality or eternal life (*CUP1*, 559). Relative ends are those that pertain to spheres lower than the religious, that is, to the finite realm. The ethical optimism that initiated the existential task of self-transformation into a state conforming with the ethical ideal, flows progressively into a recognition of impotence found in the existential pathos of immanent religiousness or Religiousness A. Climacus talks of "resignation" (*CUP1*, 400) and of "renunciation of everything" (*CUP1*, 404), the latter being the first true expression of a person's relationship to the absolute *telos*. There are later expressions, first suffering, which is the "essential" expression, then guilt, which is the "decisive" expression of a person's relation to the absolute *telos*. Suffering as dying to immediacy is the essential expression of the existential pathos, the distinctive mark of an existing person's relation to the absolute *telos*:

> The essential existential pathos related itself to existing essentially, and existing essentially is inwardness, and the action of inwardness is suffering, because the individual is unable to transform himself. It becomes, as it were, a feigning of self-transformation, and that is why the highest action in the inner world is to suffer. (*CUP1*, 433)

Later, as the individual accepts the requirements of ethics but also understands that the human being cannot abide by them, he discovers guilt. Guilt is made the decisive expression for the existential pathos, and the distance from the task becomes even greater (*CUP1*, 526).

The individual's task is simultaneously to relate absolutely to the absolute *telos* and relatively to relative ends. However, one cannot have an absolute relationship with the absolute for it is fraught with incertitude. As soon as there is certitude or understanding, paganism or an aesthetic view of religion is the result. One consequence of the dialectic of existence, then, is the uncertainty of thought.

Another consequence of the dialectic of existence is the limitation of thought. Reason is useless and inappropriate for overcoming ultimate despair because sin and self-deception distort the nature of things. However, reason can play the role of servant, pointing to the place where the leap of faith must be made—to Christian faith. Whereas Kierkegaard was confident that dialecticians could not make someone a Christian, dialectic leads "the individual to it, and says: Here it must be, that I can vouch for; if you worship here, you worship God" (*CUP1*, 491):

> Dialectic in its truth is a kindly disposed, ministering power that discovers and helps to find where the absolute object of faith and worship is, where the absolute is—namely, there where in unknowing the difference between knowledge and nonknowledge collapses in absolute worship, there where the objective uncertainty resists in order to force out the passionate certitude of faith, there where in absolute subjection the conflict about right and wrong collapses in absolute worship. Dialectic itself does not see the absolute, but it leads . . . to it. (*CUP1*, 490–1)

The role of reflective reason for Kierkegaard is thus largely negative. By helping us see what a concept is *not*, we may be better able to appreciate what it is. Louis Pojman notes that one of Kierkegaard's favorite epigrams is Spinoza's dictum, "All determination is negation" (Pojman 1984, 145). Kierkegaard sees negative concepts at the heart of human reasoning because they highlight the limits of reason: "Above all, it is a fundamental fallacy to think there are no negative concepts. The highest principle for all thinking, or the proof for it, is negative. Human reason has its limits. There lie the negative concepts" (*Pap.* X² A 354). Irony, paradox, the unknown, the limit, dread, and guilt can all be considered negative concepts. The absurd is also a category, "the negative category of the divine or of the relationship to the divine" (*Pap.* X⁶ B 79). Hegel undoubtedly influences Kierkegaard's use of negativity because for both men, the "negative" is an instrument for reaching the truth, albeit in different ways.[34]

Existential dialectics also expresses the negativity of existence or, as Climacus explains, "the negativity that is in existence or rather, the negativity of the existing subject (which his thinking must render essentially in an adequate form) . . ." (*CUP1*, 82). This is achieved by "always keep[ing] open the wound of negativity" (*CUP1*, 85). That is, existential dialectics does not proceed by negating the negative but by holding the positive in conjunction with the negative. As Climacus puts it:

> When this is the case, when he [the subjective existing thinker], actually existing, renders the form of existence in his own existence, he, existing, is continually just as negative as positive; for his positiveness consists in the continuous inward deepening in which he is cognizant of the negative. (*CUP1*, 84)

If the negative is eliminated, the positiveness that results is "untrue" and "illusory" (*CUP1*, 81). Only in this way can thought do justice to existence and the division between thought and being to which it is subjected. Thus, because the subjective thinker is always equally negative and positive, this thinker is always striving (*CUP1*, 80). The theme that "the positive is recognizable by the negative" is familiar to an existing individual, who is always in the process of striving to realize an ideal that can never be perfectly realized. In the religious sphere, the positive is distinguished by the negative; the relationship with an eternal happiness is distinguished by suffering (*CUP1*, 532). "The negative is not once and for all and then the positive, but the positive is continually in the negative, and the negative is the distinctive mark" (*CUP1*, 524). "The reader will recall," says Climacus, "that revelation is marked by mystery, eternal happiness by suffering, the certitude of faith by uncertainty, easiness by difficulty, truth by absurdity; if this is not maintained, then the esthetic and the religious merge in common confusion" (*CUP1*, 432n). David Law rightly describes Kierkegaard as a negative theologian (Law 1993).

The task Kierkegaard describes does not begin by attempting an absolute relation to the absolute *telos*. Rather, it is done by "taking power away from immediacy" (*CUP1*, 431). The individual is in immediacy and to that extent is actually in the relative ends absolutely. He begins by practicing the absolute relation through renunciation of the relative ends. Moreover, "the task is ideal and perhaps is never accomplished by anyone" (*CUP1*, 431). Furthermore, when one has surmounted immediacy, one is nevertheless in existence and thereby again hindered from absolutely expressing the absolute relation to the absolute *telos*.

Existential dialectics, however, is not only concerned with doing justice to the negativity of existence but also with overcoming this negativity by bringing about reconciliation between thought and being. Truth is the conformity of thought and being. But, if the being involved is empirical, conformity of thought and being is possible only as an ideal toward which one strives, for the empirical being is unfinished and the existing cognitive spirit is itself in the process of becoming. For the existing individual, thought and being can never fully coincide. The unity of thought and being is a task that is posed to the existing individual and is not an accomplished fact. Thus, truth becomes an approximation, an ideal that is asymptomatically approximated, as long as the individual lives in time (*CUP1*, 189, 196).

Kierkegaard identifies subjectivity—the process of appropriating what one has conceived—with truth for an existing individual (*CUP1*, 242) and continues one step further by explaining that to say "truth is subjectivity" is to say that "truth is the subject's transformation in himself." The truth consists not in knowing the truth but in being the truth (*TC*, 202, 201). The truth is the quality of an individual's life, Mark Taylor explains: "to be true to," "to be faithful to" are expressions that exemplify the way Kierkegaard understands religious truth (Taylor 2002, 255). There are two important consequences of the view of religious truth as subjectivity. First, "to subjective reflection, truth becomes appropriation, inwardness, subjectivity, and the point is to immerse oneself, existing, in subjectivity" (*CUP1*, 192). Second, Kierkegaard gives more importance to the quality of the relationship to one's goal or to its possibility than to the nature of that goal and possibility. The person who prays in truth prays to God even if he believes he is praying to an idol, while praying untruthfully to God is much the same as worshipping an idol (*CUP1*, 201).

To reduplicate is to exist in what one understands (*TC*, 133). It refers to the process by which an individual appropriates what has been conceived as a possibility. In so doing, the individual becomes true and "truth is for the particular individual only as he himself produces it in action" (*CA*, 139). By holding that religious truth is subjectivity, Kierkegaard believes that he is fully in line with what he regards as the two most authoritative sources of Christian tradition: the Bible and Luther. *The Letter of James* is Kierkegaard's favorite biblical text (especially 1:22–25; see *ED*, II 84–85); and in Luther's theme of *pro me* or *pro nobis*, Kierkegaard finds the issue of personal appropriation (*CUP1*, 366; Taylor 2002, 257).

Alastair Hannay maintains that Climacus' negative epistemology is not far from positivism, leaving the truth out of our grasp. Climacus' unthinkable hypothesis is that in Christianity the eternal has taken on the form of time, and the example of Christ is revelatory only on the vanishing chance that against all reason it is so. It is up to the individual whether one takes the chance or not. In any event, all one can do is take a step in the right direction (Hannay 2003, 120).

Because Kierkegaard identifies religious truth with subjectivity, religious truth refers to the processive or dynamic life of the individual. For this reason, Kierkegaard refers to subjective truth as "edifying" or upbuilding; that is, the personality of the individual is built up insofar as he appropriates the truth with which he is concerned, or as he strives to achieve his ideals (*WL*, 199–212). The concept of truth is a complex mirror image of Kierkegaard's concept of upbuilding. Hannay explains that to "edify" is to get people to "see their personal and interpersonal situations from another perspective, one from which goals previously aimed at and appraisals previously made can be seen as inadequate. The 'how' here is the medium of moral change; it is only by acquiring a new and more embracing situational understanding that a person can transcend a narrow or egocentric, less moral, point of view" (Hannay 2003, 119). Morality is a matter of personal growth in which a better self is revealed, a self that can be shunned as well as appropriated, and a prospect that exposes whatever may count as a will to strategies of self-deception and to what Kierkegaard calls despair.

Robert Perkins argues that Kierkegaard is a "moral epistemologist" because of the importance of the concept of upbuilding or the edifying in Kierkegaard's dialectic (Perkins 2002, 224). Upbuilding is an essential "predicate of all religiousness" (*CUP1*, 560n). There is a distinction, however, between two levels of upbuilding in Kierkegaard. There is a Christian upbuilding (Religiousness B) and also an upbuilding at the level of human religiousness exemplified by Socrates (Religiousness A). In the latter, the upbuilding element is "the annihilation in which the individual sets himself in order to find God, since it is the individual himself who is the hindrance . . . in the ethico-religious sphere the individual himself is the place [of edification] if the individual has annihilated himself" (*CUP1*, 561n). In the former, the individual does not find the upbuilding by finding the relationship with God within himself, but rather relates himself to something outside himself to find the upbuilding. In Religiousness A (Kierkegaard's category of humane religion, the religion of immanence, of subjectivity, and finally of guilt-consciousness), the individual is the central figure and finds God within himself. In Religiousness B, the individual relates to God as someone external.

Suffering is always the mark of religiousness, but not all suffering is religious. Although Kierkegaard writes much about adversity and the spiritual attitude toward it, adversity is not religious suffering.[35] Religious suffering is based on the inability of the religious person to express the eternal in the temporal. Religious suffering is distinguished by being solely in inwardness: It is partially about not being able to convert pain into perfect joy and partially about uncertainty over the relationship with God (*CUP1*, 451–5). The individual that diminishes the eternal to the size of the temporal, reducing the infinite to the dimensions of the finite, will never know this religious suffering. Socrates' irony is an expression of an inaptitude for comprehending the infinite in philosophy. In Religiousness A, suffering is expressed as guilt-consciousness, and in Religiousness B, it is expressed as sin-consciousness. Kierkegaard requires religious suffering to be hidden in one's inwardness in such a way that it cannot be suspected outwardly. True religiousness resembles God's invisible omnipresence in that it cannot be seen. The god to whom one can point is an idol, and the religiousness one can indicate is imperfect (*CUP1*, 475). Renouncing the world should not be noticeable; hence, the requirement to join the world externally and hide the relationship to the absolute. In other words, the truly religious person should go to an amusement park and enjoy himself.

As Richard Perkins suggests, "Kierkegaard gives up a rich contextual environment for upbuilding that transforms this term into a truth test": Subjectivity and edification are the truth tests for truth (Perkins 2001, 235).[36] Kierkegaard's position looks anarchistic or subjectivistic when we substitute a concern for objectively correct truth for the truth that builds up, but truth is always human truth for Kierkegaard.

The question I address in this chapter is: What is the role of the comic, also in the guise of irony and especially humor, in the Kierkegaardian good life? There is only one life that can be deemed the Kierkegaardian good life. McCarthy rightly points out that for Kierkegaard only the Christian religious life merits the predicate "life-view" because it alone represents true mastery of the moods (McCarthy 1978, chap. 7). Kierkegaard sees the remaining life-views, however, not only as "spheres" of existence, but also as stages (*Stadier*) that may lead to the Christian life. To answer the question of the role of the comic in the Kierkegaardian good life, it is important to understand, then, not only the role of the comic in the Christian life, but also the role of irony and humor as stages on life's way, as well as the role of the comic within the lower stages such as the aesthetic and the ethical stages. I continue, therefore, with an introduction of the role the comic fulfills in the lives Kierkegaard describes, followed by an examination of the role of irony, and finally, of humor.

THE COMIC

The comic is a dominant theme throughout Kierkegaard's writings because the comic is pervasive in life: "On the whole," his pseudonym asserts, "the comic is everywhere" (*CUP1*, 462). The comic is moreover essential in the subjective thinker's thought because "thought must correspond to the form of existence" (*CUP1*, 80). It is furthermore necessary in the subjective thinker's communication, which reflects thought and thereby existence. Because the comic is pervasive in life, thought, and communication, Kierkegaard considers the comic an essential category. He refers to it in his journals as early as 1842 (*JP* 2, 1737), finds for it new applications in his writings, and continually refines it.

In order to understand the role of the comic in the Kierkegaardian good life, I suggest examining the recurrent themes associated with it in Kierkegaard's writings. These are the comic as contradiction, the unity of the comic with the tragic, the role of the comic in communication, and the legitimacy of the comic.[37]

THE COMIC AS CONTRADICTION

One of the characteristics of the comic throughout the entirety of Kierkegaard's writings is that the comic involves an incongruity or contradiction. The comic is "a relation, the misrelation of contradiction" (*CUP1*, 514n). In his journals, Kierkegaard describes human existence as a synthesis of extreme opposites that make for comic awareness because "the category of the comic is essentially contradiction" (*JP* 2, 266). Additionally, several of Kierkegaard's pseudonyms, including Johannes Climacus, Vigilius Haufniensis, and Anti-Climacus, speak of human existence as a synthesis of contrasting or opposing elements, which can never be reduced to one another. These include body and soul, temporality and eternity, possibility and necessity, finitude and freedom, which Kierkegaard parses out as the properties of temporality, finitude, and necessity, on the one hand, and infinitude and freedom, on the other. The self is seen as an attempt to unify them by producing an entity—the spirit—which is greater than the sum of its parts.

Despair, Anti-Climacus concludes in *The Sickness unto Death*, is a symptom of the tension between these two disparate aspects. Considered in this way, a human being is still not a self: "A human being is spirit. But what is spirit? Spirit is the self. But what is the self? The self is a relation that relates itself to itself or is the relation's relating itself to itself in the relation; the self is not the relation but is the relation's relating itself to itself" (*SUD*, 13f).

In existence, the synthesis is uncompleted, ensuring the perpetual presence of the incongruity between the opposing elements. Our identity is found, then, in the movement between reality and ideality. The human situation is by these very polarities enmeshed in ongoing contradictions of the most extreme opposites, caught up in persistent discrepancies, and hence fraught with pathos and existential suffering, characterized by the uneasiness of freedom with itself. In *The Sickness unto Death* and *The Concept of Anxiety* Kierkegaard takes our incapacity to cure ourselves of despair or anxiety by our own powers as a sign of our heteronomy.

The very arena in which the comic appears is a juxtaposition of these opposites—internally conflicted passion—which is the most basic feature of being human. It is in this unremitting interplay of finitude and freedom, temporality and ability that human beings live daily. But incommensurability, polarity, and contradiction are the always-available makings of comedy. Melrod Westphal rightly observes, "Climacus portrays the existing thinker as having what we might call a metaphysical sense of humor, an appreciation of the inherent incongruities of being human" (Westphal 1996, 69–70).

Kierkegaard shares Aristotle's view of the comic as "essentially contradiction" (*Pap*. III A 205, 81). Climacus narrows the scope of comic contradiction by emphasizing that "the comic is painless contradiction" (*CUP1*, 514). Climacus' characterization is in harmony with Aristotle's definition of comedy, which states that "the Ridiculous may be defined as a mistake or deformity not productive of pain or harm to others: the mask [*propopon*], for instance, is something ugly and distorted without causing pain" (*Poetics*, 5:1449a 32–37). Yet Climacus criticizes Aristotle's definition as insufficient for leaving out "whole families of the comic" and for being insensitive to pain: "Even if the distorted face does not cause pain, it is indeed still painful to be so fated as to prompt laughter merely by showing one's face" (*CUP1*, 514n). Through a pseudonym, Kierkegaard expresses here, as he does in most of his works, his sensitivity toward suffering and his aversion to laughing at suffering. The comic can be painless because "the comic interpretation produces the contradiction or allows it to become apparent by having *in mente* [in mind] the way out" (*CUP1*, 516).

Both Kierkegaard and Climacus maintain that the comic emerges as soon as one is aware of instances of existential contradictions: "Where there is life, there is contradiction, and wherever there is contradiction, the comic is present" (*CUP1*, 513–4). By "contradiction" Climacus does not mean formal or logical contradiction. Rather, his view is taken as representative of the theoretical tradition in which the comic is explained in terms of incongruity. The idea that the comic is essentially based on incongruity or "contradiction" is a view on which both Kierkegaard and the various pseudonyms who discuss the comic are united. Kierkegaard seems to adhere to one form of the "incongruity theory" of the comic, which states that the contradiction is sufficient to give rise to the comic.[38]

But Kierkegaard also holds another version of the incongruity theory, which demands that an additional condition be met, namely, that the incongruity be resolved. A "legitimate comic apprehension" cancels the contradiction by having in mind a way out of it. For the comic to be legitimate, a laugher should not only know more than that which he laughs at, but with that extra knowledge, he should rise above the contradiction at which he laughs. Kierkegaard's view of the comic, and that of his pseudonym Climacus, is clearly a version of the incongruity theory. The comic is a result of sensitivity to contradiction, incongruity, and incommensurability. Everyone who has "a sense for the comic" can grasp exactly wherein the contradiction is found.[39]

John Lippitt rightly considers that Kierkegaard's view of the comic as incongruity is his starting point, rather than his only or major contribution to the subject (Lippitt 2000b, 11). Other commentators find in Kierkegaard's thought significant elements of two other theories that explain the comic—the superiority theory and the relief theory.[40] The notion of superiority is significant in relation to the comic because it is the possession of a superior position that enables an individual, according to Kierkegaard, to experience an incongruity as pleasant rather than painful. Someone who apprehends a contradiction as comic does not feel that he himself is governed by the contradiction; the person believes that no one could laugh at him for the same reason he is laughing. Also implicit in Kierkegaard's view is the notion that the comic provides a relief from the vexations of life. The person who sees something comically has found "a way out." Temporarily, at least, he has escaped the pain of life.[41]

It is an important axiom for Climacus that a person in his immediate pathos is always in contradiction with himself. It is therefore necessary to bring the contradictory relationship to consciousness, and this happens only when one is oriented toward a higher ideality. Only here does one see the contradiction and only here can reflection receive its legitimacy as a higher ideality through a reconciliation of contradiction. It is in this context that Climacus develops his theory of the different stages of inwardness, ordered according to how much consciousness of contradiction individual existence has assimilated.

In *Stages on Life's Way*, the comic is viewed in relation to a distinct sequence of modes of existence: Immediacy, immediacy with reflection, aesthetic existence, irony, ethical existence, humor, suffering and guilt, immanent forms of religious consciousness, and Christianity. Understanding the comic requires understanding human nature in its three existential stages: It is fairly easy to locate the stage in which one is currently operating if comic sensibilities are understood. It is also easy to see where another stands in the "stages on life's way" by looking at how that person experiences and understands the comic. To run short of a comic sense is to lack an essential aspect of matured self-awareness. The more one enters into a relationship with oneself and actively recognizes oneself as body/soul, temporal/eternal incongruity, the more one becomes a self, develops a sense of personhood and personal freedom, and is welcomed into comic consciousness.

For the early Kierkegaard, the comic appears at each stage along life's way (aesthetic, ethical, and religious), but has an essential relation with the religious, and especially with Christianity, where the self is understood decisively in relation to the Incarnation and the Atonement. The comic is always based on an experienced contradiction or incongruity, and Christianity is blessed with many such incongruities: God in time, joy amid suffering, sin forgiven. For the young Kierkegaard, thus, Christianity is the most humorous of all forms of religion, an opinion he abandons later in life.[42]

It is the comic that defines the spheres of existence and thereby Kierkegaard's teleology. "On the whole," Climacus claims, "the comic is present everywhere, and every existence can at once be defined and assigned to its particular sphere by knowing how it is related to the comic" (*CUP1*, 462; cf. 513, 520). The importance Kierkegaard attributes to his theory of spheres, singling it out as his "abiding merit to literature" (*Pap.* VII A 127), reflects on the crucial role he attributes to the comic. The various stages of existence may be ranked and legitimated according to whether they have the comic within or outside themselves, that is, by whether the contradiction is understood as the consequence of internal or external conditions. The immediate consciousness has the comic outside itself and ranks at the lowest level; both irony and humor have the comic within themselves and consequently rank higher. Religiousness, with humor as its incognito, ranks still higher. However, here the comic is a relative factor and the individual is legitimated by the passion with which the God-relation is sustained. At the apex is the hidden inwardness of religiousness, which in Climacus' view is inaccessible to comic apprehension precisely because it is hidden and cannot come into contradiction with anything outside itself (*CUP1*, 522). Thus, Climacus asserts, "the matter is very simple. The comic is present in every stage of life . . . because where there is life there is contradiction, and wherever there is contradiction, the comic is present" (*CUP1*, 513–4).

THE COMIC AND THE TRAGIC

The relation between the comic and the tragic is a pervasive theme within Kierkegaard's writings. "The misrelation, the contradiction between the infinite and the finite, the eternal and the becoming" lies at the root of the comic as well as at the root of the tragic (*CUP1*, 89). The difference between the two is that whereas a "legitimate comic apprehension" cancels or knows a way out of the contradiction, the tragic does not (*CUP1*, 516; 523).[43] The tragic is thus the "suffering contradiction" (*CUP1*, 514) that "sees the contradiction and despairs over the way out" (*CUP1*, 516).

There is something inherently tragic about the character of human striving, oriented toward presence and certainty, but never able to overcome its origin in absence and uncertainty.[44] Kierkegaard's originality lies in Climacus' insistence that for exactly the same reason human life is comical. The notion that the subjective existing thinker is the intersection of certainty and uncertainty, of knowledge and ignorance, and thus of positive and negative "can also be expressed by saying that he has just as much of the comic as of pathos" (*CUP1*, 87). The pathetic here refers to the pitiful, or that which properly evokes pity, in other words, the tragic, or the "pathos-filled."[45] Thus, Kierkegaard regards the tragic and the comic as integral features of the subjective thinker's existence; in this capacity they function as expressions of his awareness of the discrepancy between the inner and the outer, the finite and the infinite, and the temporal and eternal in existence.

Insofar as both the tragic and the comic are based on existential contradiction, they are the same. The difference lies in the basis of the contradiction, whether it is based in the real comparing itself to the ideal, or if it is based in the ideal comparing itself to the real. The first magnifies and is thus tragic; the second belittles and is therefore comic:

> The interpretation of the misrelation, viewed with the idea ahead, is pathos; the interpretation of the misrelation, viewed with the idea behind, is the comic. When the subjective thinker turns his face toward the idea, his interpretation of the mis-relation is pathos-filled; when he turns his back to the idea, allowing it to shine from behind into the same misrelation, his interpretation is comic. (CUP1, 90)

If both the comic and the tragic are grounded in contradiction and if human existence is at its very heart a "contradiction," then it is clear why the capacity to sense the tragic and the comic is basic to human life. "Existence itself, existing, is a striving, and just as pathos-filled as it is comic; pathos-filled because the striving is infinite, that is, directed toward the infinite, is a process of infinitizing, which is the highest pathos; comic because the striving is a self-contradiction" (CUP1, 92). The subjective thinker strives to come into the presence of the eternal truth and to exist in the light of this truth. But this striving is also comical because the attempt to embody the infinite and eternal within one's finite and time-bound existence is self-contradictory. This ambiguity in human life may be analyzed in distant objectivity or be defined by its relation to the comic as in Postscript: "The tragic is the suffering contradiction, the comic, the pain-less contradiction" (CUP1, 514) or as in Stages, where unlike the comic, which is "metaphysical disinterestedness," the tragic has a clear affinity to the historical and "has the interest of actuality" (SLW, 446).

Despite their differences, the tragic and the comic are united. John Glenn maintains that in Kierkegaard's thought "the unity of the comic and the tragic has meaning—although a somewhat different meaning—at every stage of human existence" (Glenn 1970, 52). A constant theme in Kierkegaard's writings is that the comic and the tragic, and in later writings, the comic and pathos, or jest and earnestness, are in some sense, one.

Kierkegaard's first variations on this theme seem to be primarily expressions of the disparity between his own inner melancholy and his outward appearance. "I have also united the tragic with the comic. I crack jokes and people laugh—I cry," he writes in his journal in 1837 (JP 1, 5247). In his published works, he gives this theme a subtler literary and philosophical expression. In The Concept of Irony the romantic philosopher unites laughter and tears in romantic irony:

His grief conceals itself in the exclusive incognito of the jest, his joy is enveloped in lament . . . now something is advanced seriously but immediately twisted inside out—and the unity in laughter shall reconcile all oppositions, yet this laughter is in turn accompanied by the distant flute tones of a deep sadness . . . (CI, 301, 320)

Either/Or is the first of Kierkegaard's books in which this theme figures significantly. The nature of this unity is not so much stated as it is instantiated in the existence of A, the pseudonymous author of the first volume. The "Diapsalmata," the collection of lyrical and aphoristic paragraphs, which constitute the overture to the first volume of Either/Or, is an artistic elaboration of the concept of romantic irony, which Kierkegaard presented in his dissertation, The Concept of Irony. A's laughter is hollow and despairing: "What if laughter were really tears?" he asks (EO1, 21). This remark is the first clear intimation in Either/Or of the unity of the comic and the tragic. It indicates, moreover, that this unity is a unity in the direction of the tragic. The same idea can be found in a sketch to Either/Or found in the journals:

Modern tragedy has taken the comic into itself; the more one thinks about it, the more one is tempted to cancel the difference between the tragic and the comic in the unity of the tragic. Both obviously depend upon a misrelation between idea and actuality, and the two ways people have always sought to allay it have been either by laughing or by crying. But the misrelation itself is obviously the tragic, which thus becomes the unity of the tragic and the comic. (Pap. III B 180)

Thus, the comic is subsumable under the tragic, rather than the converse, also within each stage of existence: "The different existence-stages rank according to their relation to the comic in proportion to their having the comic inside or outside themselves, yet not in the sense that the comic should be the highest" (CUP1, 524). The unity of the tragic and the comic within the spheres is a unity in the direction of the tragic.

Kierkegaard's early description of the unity of the comic and the tragic is a prolegomenon to his later reflections in Postscript, which bear on the unity of the comic and the pathos-filled or suffering:

What lies at the root of both the comic and the pathos-filled is the misrelation, the contradiction between the infinite and the

finite, the eternal and the becoming. A pathos that excludes the
comic is therefore a misunderstanding, is not pathos at all . . . If
I have not exhausted the comic to its entirety, I do not have
the pathos of the infinite; if I have the pathos of the infinite, I
immediately have the comic also. (*CUP1*, 89–90)

The role of the comic in both *Stages* and *Postscript* is to purify the
pathos-filled by amending its immaturity (*SLW*, 366; *CUP1*, 87). David
Gouwens perceptfully notes that Kierkegaard stands in a philosophical and
theological tradition more concerned with "self-purification" than with self-
fulfillment (Gouwens 1996, 29, n. 5). The task of human existence is in
large part that of sorting out the complex chaos of one's emotional life
into a life that is characterized by the consistency and stability of emotions. The chaotic emotional life can be described as the problematic of
moods, and a dominant theme in this transition from mood to emotion is
the attainment of unity in one's life.

Vincent McCarthy has carefully studied the moods and their connection to life-views or stages in *The Phenomenology of Moods in Kierkegaard*
(1978). Kierkegaard takes moods and the emotional life with the utmost
seriousness, walking the fine line between the romantics who unduly celebrate them and the intellectuals who shun them. He sees a function of
moods in the life of the whole person and sets out to describe, probe,
explore, and analyze them. He considers the move from the aesthetic to the
religious an intensely rational project from beginning to end, completed by
the pathos of Christian seriousness and intimately linked to the idea of a
life-view pervading Kierkegaard's authorship. McCarthy rightly points out
that for Kierkegaard, only the Christian religious existence toward which
the moods naturally direct the soul of the human being, merits the predicate
"life-view" and represents true mastery of the moods (McCarthy 1978, chap.
7). The dialectic of moods and Kierkegaard's concern with an authentic
philosophy of life converge in his thoughts. Mastering the moods is the
preparation required for articulating the new life-view. In this capacity, the
moods represent the rite of passage from childish illusions about the self to
mature understanding of a proper life-view, representing a radical change
from victim to master of moods.

The movement begins with the unmasking of an illusory life-view,
the aesthetic, and the gradual preparation for the formation of an authentic view of life. This new life-view is formed by means of the spiritual
growth reflected in the sequence of moods, which rise to prominence in the
emotional life of the individual. The aesthete represents the human being

under the illusion of having a life-view and attempting to live according to such a view. It is thus in existence, rather than in detached contemplation, that a life-view is tested and a new life-view is formed. The starting point is the collapse of the aesthetic life-view represented by the mood of irony. McCarthy explains that irony, as a mood, "represents the first conscious breakthrough in the illusion of aesthetic (or nonreligious) existence. A sequence of moods follows naturally one upon the other, viz., anxiety, melancholy, and despair in a series of crisis of the personality" (3).[46] The dialectic of moods represents a purgation, which allows philosophy to take up, once again, its role of service to human existence. By the call to self-understanding in mastering the moods, Kierkegaard seeks to destroy the seduction of the poetic and the false seriousness of academic philosophy, to ground both poetry and philosophy in the depth of existence, and to restore them to authentic articulation of the realities of the individual's being, rather than merely to the fancies of imagination.

In the end, McCarthy notes, "the new understanding gathered from experience is thoroughly consonant with the Christian revelation about the meaning and the destiny of human existence" (McCarthy 1978, 161). The moods individually and in their dialectic first work to destroy the illusory life-view that the aesthetic represents and then lead to the threshold of positivity and to deepened self-understanding, which are essential to an authentic life-view. Authentic Christianity represents the religious solution provided by the grace of a historical event and personal forgiveness; resolving the moods and positing the fullest understanding of the human being.[47] Kierkegaard combines a very contemporary understanding of human spiritual development with an ancient notion of Christianity as a decisive force in one's life.

The pseudonymous author of *The Concept of Anxiety* explains the unique role the comic plays in correcting the moods. When a concept is not treated in the right category,

> the concept is altered, and thereby the mood that properly corresponds to the correct concept is also disturbed, and instead of the endurance of the true mood there is a fleeting phantom of false moods. An error in the modulation is just as disturbing as an error in the development of thought. . . . Yet every error gives birth to its own enemy. Outside of itself, the error of thought has dialectics as its enemy, and outside of itself, the absence or falsification of mood has the comical as its enemy. (CA, 14, 14n)[48]

This is so because, as stated in *Stages*, "the comic purifies the pathos-filled emotions" (*SLW*, 366), that is, the moods. A sense of humor is needed to control one's earnestness, and "he who does not constantly dare to submit his earnestness to the test of jest is stupid and comical" (*JP 2*, 1743). Climacus adds that it is "precisely just as questionable to be pathos-filled and earnest in the wrong place as it is to laugh in the wrong place" (*CUP1*, 525).

But the converse is also true, because "the pathos-filled emotions give substance to the comic." The example given in *Stages* is that "the most devastating comic perception would be one in which indignation is latent—yet no one detects it because of the laughter." Thus, the comic and the pathos-filled are mutually related and fortified by freedom (*SLW*, 366). Like Quidam, Climacus stresses the need for the comic and pathos to be in balance, because "the pathos that is not safeguarded by the comic is an illusion; the comic that is not safeguarded by pathos is immaturity" (*CUP1*, 87).

The subjective thinker is therefore just as "bifrontal as the existence-situation itself," that is, both negative and positive, or both comic and pathos-filled in his existence-relation to the truth (*CUP1*, 89; 80). A comic-tragic apprehension of existence is integral to his makeup because existence itself is both pathetic and comic, being directed toward the actualization of infinitude in the pathos of infinite striving, yet never being able to finish (the tragic) or to give adequate expression to it in external form (the comic).

Ordinarily, these aesthetic elements are divided so as to appear separately in different persons, but the subjective thinker possesses both in equal proportions: He is just as sensitive to the comic as to the pathetic or tragic character of life (*CUP1*, 87). In *Stages*, Quidam suggests that this unity inheres not in a new form of literature, but in the person of Socrates (*SLW*, 365–6). Quidam compares the comic and the tragic to two legs or necessary extremities of movement for the person "who wishes to exist by virtue of spirit and after having abandoned immediacy" (*SLW*, 422). Just as the condition of proper equilibrium lies in the balance between the comic and the tragic, becoming a master of the comic is an infallible mark of one's position in life: "But what does it mean to have actually reflected oneself out of the immediate without having become a master in the comic—what does it mean? Well, it means that one is lying" (*CUP1*, 281).

This particular synthesis of the comic and the tragic Kierkegaard deems the comic-tragic, which should not be confused with the Hegelian concept of the tragic-comic.[49] Kierkegaard considers the latter trivial, resulting in "the many situations over which one does not know whether to laugh or to cry . . . no essential passion is posited; neither the comic nor the tragic is essentially present" (*SLW*, 420). In contradistinction to the Hegelian concept of the tragic-comic, the comic-tragic, or the "truly comic" is the essential nature of human existence: "In the comic-tragic both [the comic and the tragic] are posited and the dialectically infinitized spirit simultaneously sees both elements in the same situation" (*SLW*, 420). Both paganism and the philosophical life that unites thought and deed culminate in the mental fortitude that enables one to see the comic and the tragic simultaneously in the same thing (*SLW*, 422).

Yet the unity of comedy and tragedy represented by the comic-tragic is only penultimate truth. Seeing the comic "with his understanding" (*SLW*, 327) and fortifying himself with the comic for the tragic (*SLW*, 422), the religious person chooses "the tragic higher passion out of the comic and the tragic"; in the higher passion, which chooses the tragic part of the unity, religiousness begins (*SLW* 422):

> Religious earnestness, like the religious, is the higher passion *proceeding* from the unity of the comic and the tragic. This I know precisely because I myself am not religious and have reached this standpoint (of unity) without skipping anything in advance and without finding the religious within myself. (*SLW*, 440)

Religious passion stands out, then, as the decisive category. In *Postscript*, too, Climacus says that to be in passion emerges from the unity of the comic and the tragic: it is "after that" (*CUP1*, 291).[50]

Another level of the unity of the tragic and the comic, and of the pathos-filled and the comic, is found in Kierkegaard's claim that jest and earnestness are united: The presence of the comic ensures the presence of the tragic, so that jest is not merely jest but becomes the expression for the highest earnestness in a person. If one wonders how the comic is generated, the answer is that "true earnestness itself invents the comic," because in spiritual existence "the point is to endure contradiction, but also to keep it at arm's length in freedom" (*SLW*, 366). The comic enables us to endure the contradiction and feel free in it. Kierkegaard maintains that earnestness can detect the comic because it excludes it: "What earnestness wills in earnest it does not regard as comic insofar as it itself wills it, but for that reason it can readily see the comic therein." But he insists that earnestness does not mediate between the comic and earnestness; rather, it "sees through the comic" (*SLW*, 367).

Jest and earnestness may simultaneously be conveyed by the same remark. Socrates is set before us as an example of this sort of bifrontal contradiction: He was a jester indulging in all sorts of frivolity at the same time that he was deeply concerned about the divine. He was disciplining himself throughout life for the divine test (*CUP1*, 89; 90n).[51] What the example of Socrates teaches is that remarks that sound like jests "may also be the highest earnestness, and the speaker, while jesting with someone, may be in the presence of the god" (*CUP1*, 88). Socrates' earnestness was the unity of the comic and the tragic to which Plato refers at the end of the *Symposium* when he has Socrates forcing his companions "to admit that the same man was capable of writing both comedy and tragedy—that the tragic poet might be a comedian as well" (223 c–d). Through the example of the "most earnest man in Greece," Kierkegaard's pseudonym in *Stages* reaches the general conclusion that "earnestness is basically not something simple, a simplex, but is a compositum [compound], for true earnestness is the unity of jest and earnestness" (*SLW*, 365):

> [Socrates'] sense of the comic was just as great as his ethical pathos—therefore he was secured against becoming ridiculous in his pathos; his earnestness was concealed in jest—therefore he was free in it and needed no external support whatsoever in order to be earnest, which is always an indication of a lack of the specific worth of earnestness. (*SLW*, 366)

A "sense of the comic," and the capacity to express it "*in concreto*" (*CUP1*, 524) so as to camouflage one's earnestness in jest, secure autonomy from exteriority and protection from ridicule.

THE COMIC IN COMMUNICATION

The comic has an important role to play in indirect communication—the indirect discourse that uses such modes as parable, metaphor, irony, humor, and poetic style. This communication is expressed as a combination of jest and earnestness, which intends to be illusive. Indirect communication may be defined as a communication that always contains an inner contradiction on one or more levels. Communication involves four components—the object, the communicator, the recipient, and the communication—and the contradiction can be between two or more of these parts. It also can consist of an internal contradiction in one or more of these parts. Kierkegaard grounds this form of communication ultimately in Christianity insofar as he points to analogies between irony and Christian love, between humor and Jesus, and between Jesus as a sign of contradiction and indirect communication. Later in life, Kierkegaard gives up indirect communication and reverts to a direct–indirect form of communication, which he considers a more appropriate communication for Christianity.

Inwardness cannot be communicated directly because expressing it directly is externality, and expressing inwardness directly is no proof at all that it is there. The required communication between individuals should be a "double reflection"; Climacus explains fully although not clearly what is meant by double reflection: "So to compose jest and earnest that the composition is a dialectical knot—and with this to be nobody. If anyone is to profit by this sort of communication, he must himself undo the knot for himself." Climacus stresses the importance of reducing to nil the personality of the communicator, thereby suggesting one of Kierkegaard's reasons for writing pseudonymously: "If what is said is earnestness to the writer, he keeps the earnestness essentially to himself. If the recipient interprets it as earnestness, he does it essentially by himself, and precisely this is the earnestness" (*CUP1*, 264).[52] In *The Point of View*, Kierkegaard explains how one can understand such a communication:

> The true explanation is available to the person who is honestly seeking. . . . Only the requisite earnestness takes hold, it can also solve it, but always only in such a way that the earnestness itself vouches for the correctness . . . a dialectical redoubling relates to true earnestness. Therefore the explanation cannot be communicated to a less earnest person, since the elasticity of the dialectical doubleness is too great for him to manage; it takes the explanation away from him again and makes it dubious for him whether is it indeed the explanation. (*PV*, 34)

As "the religious is earnestness" (*PV*, 10), Kierkegaard assumes that the meaning can be found only by a religious person. Indeed, religious persons "suspect each other because of the consonance of the humorous" (*CUP1*, 511). Kierkegaard conveys, through his pseudonym Climacus, that there is a definite meaning to be found in his writings. He discloses this meaning as well as the appropriate attitude toward jest (whether irony or humor) in his writings. This description is accomplished through Climacus' reaction to an interpretation of the very first review of *Philosophical Fragments*, which appeared in a German journal a year after the publication of *Fragments*.[53] Climacus appreciates the brevity of the review, which consists primarily of an abstract of the book, and thereby represents it as didactic direct communication. "His report is accurate and on the whole dialectically reliable," he writes, "but now comes the hitch: although the report is accurate, anyone who reads only that will receive an utterly wrong impression of the book . . ." However, he takes offence with the reporter's last sentence: "We leave it to each person to consider whether he wants to look for earnestness or possibly for irony in this apologetical dialectic." Climacus explains:

> When the reporter leaves it up to each one whether he will look for earnestness or irony in the pamphlet [*Philosophical Fragments*], this is misleading . . . it is only a matter of *finding* what is there . . . the concluding comment of the report . . . is foolish. Suppose that someone had been present at one of Socrates' ironic conversations; suppose that he later gives a report of it to someone but leaves out the irony and says: God knows whether talk like this is irony or earnestness—then he is satirizing himself. But the presence of irony does not necessarily mean that the earnestness is excluded. Only assistant professors assume that. That is, while they otherwise do away with the disjunctive *aut* [or] and fear neither God not the devil, since they mediate everything—they make an exception of irony; they are unable to mediate that. (*CUP1*, 276–7, n. 422)

Climacus explains that it is only a matter of finding what is there. It will be found by the person who understands the comic, and this can happen only if the reader possesses the same earnestness as the writer: "Only he who himself produces this [the comic out of pathos] will understand it, otherwise not" (*CUP1*, 87), and that the mixture of jest and earnestness "makes it impossible for a third person to know definitely which is which—unless the third person knows it by himself" (*CUP1*, 69).[54]

The main reason for the use of indirect discourse lies in the nature of the message Kierkegaard wants to convey. In 1847, shortly after he has finished his pseudonymous works, he sets about writing lectures on the use and significance of indirect discourse (*Pap.* VII B 81–89). Three tenets underlie Kierkegaard's thought on the communication of the ethical-religious.

The first tenet is that there are ethical facts and that values are facts. There is a hierarchy of values in human existence in which the ethical-religious modalities rank higher than the scientific or the cultural. It is a classical view of the nature of the human being having a *telos*, that is, becoming a certain kind of being capable of fulfillment and happiness. The true human being is a good person, and one who has realized his innate potential in a specific way. That is, he has special or peculiar abilities that must be realized if he is to be fulfilled, but he must realize these abilities in such an ethical-religious way as to realize the "universal human." The good carpenter must become not only a skilled craftsman but, more importantly, a good person.

The second tenet is that one knows the ethical-religious truth:

> The ethical presupposes that every person knows what the ethi-cal is. Why? Because the ethical requires that each person realize it in every instant, but if it is the case, he must know it. The ethical does not begin with ignorance which is to be trans-formed into knowledge, but it begins rather with a knowledge and requires a realization. (*Pap.* VIII B 81, sec. 10)

The ethical is a capacity, a "knowing how" more than a "knowing that." Kierkegaard often uses "ethical" to refer to the whole ethical-religious domain, that which has to do with the human being's essential being or *telos*. Hence, in the previous quote, he seems to refer not only to our moral duty but to knowledge of religious and metaphysical truth as well. He believes that we can know that God exists, that we are immortal, and that we are free beings (*Pap.* V B 40; VI B 45). It is the Christian God that must be believed: "I do not believe that God exists. I know it, but I believe that God existed [the historical]" (*Pap.* VI B 45).[55]

The third tenet is that we have the ability to do our duty in the ethical-religious domain. We have free will and can choose the good. Kierkegaard here—with his version of original sin, which states that it affects the totality of our lives, our reason, as well as our ability to choose the good—simply follows Luther. The main effect of original sin, however, is to prevent or hinder us from wanting to do what we know is our duty. Presumably, if we are not sinful, we can do our duty more easily and will have more immediate access to God's will.

If these three propositions are true, it is of the utmost importance to do everything possible to enable people to choose the good, to become ethical and religious beings who fulfill their *telos*. But how does one get others to choose the good? What sort of communication is appropriate to the task? One of Kierkegaard's most persistent defenses of the use of indirect communication is to point out the inadequacies of direct communication in relation to ethics and religion.

Contrary to the paradigm of objective knowledge, which requires the speaker (teacher), the listener (pupil), and the object (that which would be communicated) (*Pap.* VIII B 81), subjective knowledge or ethical-religious knowledge is altogether different. First, we all know the ethical, thus we need not communicate. Moreover, there is something inappropriate even in attempting to communicate it. "To desire to attempt to communicate the ethical in this matter is precisely the unethical" (*Pap.* VIII B 81). You cannot teach what is already known, so the communicator is canceled-out as is the receiver, for without the communicator or the communicated message, it makes no sense to speak of a receiver. The conclusion is that there is only one communicator, God, and that "ethically every man must stand alone in his God-relationship." Louis Pojman adds another reason, which he infers from Kierkegaard's texts, that like Plato's "Good," the ethical is ineffable, it cannot be said but only seen with the mind's eye (Pojman 1984, 148).

In the realm of the ethical, God is the master-teacher and we are the apprentices. We must learn by doing, by obeying the teacher, which consists in knowing *how* rather than knowing *that*. Ethics must be communicated as an art, not as a science. The error of modern philosophy, according to Kierkegaard, is to presume that ethics is a science that can be taught as any other science.

What sort of communication is appropriate if our aim is to draw the individual away from his false loves and to the place where he can hear his conscience speaking with eternal authority? How do you communicate to someone that he is living an unworthy life, has inappropriate values, and is missing his *telos*? God uses midwives of the spirit to induce labor until we give birth to a new person, until we are forced inward and, if we choose rightly, become new creations. We know how to do the good, and by doing it we become virtuous beings. Kierkegaard tells us that his motivation is to force people inward, where, he hopes, they will gain self-understanding and make better choices pertaining to ethical and religious matters. He identifies this exercise with the Socratic maieutic stimulation. However, whereas Socrates uses the method to produce objective knowledge (cf. *Meno*), Kierkegaard uses it to produce character and action.

One communicates indirectly through hints, symbols, signs, and suggestions and by telling parables and stories that direct the listener inward. At this point irony serves as an appropriate speech act that, if unraveled, points to something hidden. Likewise for Kierkegaard, humor has its essence in paradox, in the juxtaposition of opposites, and so points to what cannot be spoken. Thus, humor is the mode of discourse that uniquely points to the irreducible duality between temporality and eternity.

Kierkegaard grounds this form of communication in Christianity insofar as he points to analogies between irony and Christian love, between humor and Jesus, and between Jesus as a sign of contradiction and indirect communication. In *Works of Love*, Kierkegaard compares Christian love to Socratic irony. Speaking of Socrates and also of the Christian lover, he writes:

> That noble rogue [Socrates] had profoundly understood that the
> highest that one human being can do for another is to make
> him free, to help him stand alone—and he had also understood
> himself in understanding this, that is, he had understood that if
> this is to be accomplished, the helper must be able to conceal
> himself in magnanimously willing his own destruction. He was,
> as he himself called himself, a midwife in a spiritual sense, and
> with every sacrifice he worked disinterestedly in this service—for
> the disinterestedness consisted simply in keeping hidden from
> the one helped how and that he was helped. . . . In such an
> understanding of help to another person there is agreement
> between the true lover and that noble rogue. (WL, 154–5)

Christian love and irony aim at freeing the other person, that is,
making him renounce the immediate. That the Christian loves his neighbor despite everything has an effect on the latter and makes him, in turn,
renounce his attachment to the immanent world. Irony also provokes
renunciation in the other person, although in its own fashion. There is,
however, a difference between irony and Christian love. Irony still trades on
prideful superiority; whereas, Christian love is a complete self-abnegation.
The ironist likes to see himself as an aristocrat. He is proud of being able to
free people and thus shows himself to be superior. That is why the ironist,
Kierkegaard writes, sustains "an indescribable smile." The humorist is also
attached to his capacities although he constantly renounces the immediate.
Laughing and smiling are a form of auto-satisfaction that can be completely
foreign to Christian love.

Kierkegaard also points to analogies between humor and Jesus, and
between indirect communication and Jesus as a sign of contradiction.
Kierkegaard's philosophical production, aside from being a maieutic communication, aims to show that the teachings of Christianity are indirect
because of the nature of its teacher. Anti-Climacus recalls that the God-
man is called a sign of contradiction in the scriptures (Luke 2: 34) and
notes that the unity of jest and earnestness is also an example of a sign
of contradiction. Jesus is not a simple phenomenon, but a contradictory
unity, a synthesis of incommensurables, the lowly and the sublime, godliness
and manliness (PC, 150–2). Just as in the case of humor, Jesus is a sign
disguising contrarieties in its composition. In fact, the two signs, Jesus and
humor, resemble each other even though they are also different.[56]

Later in life, disillusioned with the failure of his pseudonymous
works to allure his readers into an ethical and religious life, Kierkegaard
gives up indirect communication and reverts to a direct–indirect form of

communication, which he considers more appropriate for Christianity. The maieutic cannot be the final form because the truth does not lie in the subject, but in a revelation that must be proclaimed (*JP* 2, 1957). Kierkegaard comes to see his task as one of cultivating a relationship between his readers and God. Even though a strictly religious discourse includes a communication of knowledge, it must be communicated indirectly, because it is still a communication of capability (*JP* 1, 657; 651; 653).

The originality and distinctiveness of Kierkegaard's approach to communication is not entirely without precedent. A model for such an authorship is that of Johann Georg Hamann, for Kierkegaard the humorist par excellence. Another possible model may be found in Friedrich Schleiermacher's *Vertraute briefe uber die Lucinde* ("Confidential letters on Lucinde") (*JP* 1, 3846/Pap. I C 68).[57] Although Hamann is certainly significant, Kierkegaard also refers to Gotthold Ephraim Lessing as a model for communication (*CUP1*, 69), as well as to ancient philosophers as the originators of the interrelatedness of jest and earnestness: ". . . it would be impossible to understand earnestness if one does not understand jest, something (according to Plutarch's *Moralia*) that the earnest Cato Uticensis is supposed to have pointed out long ago by pointing to the dialectical reciprocity between jest and earnestness" (*CUP1*, 70–71). Indeed, Plutarch tells us that Cato the Elder "used to say that those who are serious in ridiculous matters will be ridiculous in serious matters."[58]

Kierkegaard, who considered writing a dissertation on "the concept of satire with the ancients" and "the relation of the various Roman satirists to each other,"[59] was knowledgeable about the serio-comic, the genre the Stoics and the Roman satirists inherited from the Cynics. He may also have known of Shaftesbury's use of it. The serio-comic or "seriousness combined with laughter" (*spoudaiogeloion*) was the singular characteristic of Cynic moralizing often credited as their unique invention. The serio-comic style became a rhetorical mainstay of the Cynics, associated particularly with Crates (third and fourth centuries BC) and his followers. The second century AD satirist Lucian of Samosata was a sort of Cynic, who used humor to provoke the audience to consider the subject simultaneously from divergent, conflicting perspectives. Even more significant for Roman satire was Menippus of Gadara, another Cynic writer of the third century BC. Diogenes Laertius tells us that he completely lacked "seriousness" (*Lives of Eminent Philosophers*, 6.99), but he was generally regarded as an exponent of *spoudaiogeloion* (Strabo, *Geography* 16.2.29). The Romans gave the serio-comic its own genre in the form of satire, notably by the poets Horace and Juvenal, the former explicitly arguing that the best ethical instruction (the *utile*) is mixed with pleasure (the *dulce*) (Horace, *Ars poetica*, 343).

Although late antiquity and the Middle Ages were fond of the antithesis between jest and earnestness, they had somehow lost their ability to conceive of the two in synthesis. Erasmus retrieved Lucian's capacity of using humor to provoke the audience into considering a subject simultaneously from divergent points of view, and, because his books were translated and read all over Europe, he is considered largely responsible for "the ironic smile that curled so many sixteenth-century lips" (Kaiser 1963, 9).[60] Pascal anticipates Kierkegaard in stating that eloquence "requires the pleasant and the real" but the pleasant must "itself be drawn from the true" (Pascal 1941, *Pensées*, Fragment 562).

Indirect communication encompasses more than the use of verbal humor for Kierkegaard. Roger Poole maintains that there were four types of indirect communication until early 1846, and five after the *Corsair* affair. Kierkegaard's indirection took the form of pseudonymity for many of his works; an unremitting irony that did not allow readers to "place" him as author within his own thought process; a stream of "edifying discourses" to "accompany" the works that he called "esthetic"; and a "lived presence" in Copenhagen that would "counteract," or "work against," or in some way dialectically inflect or subvert the expectations about his personality that had been set up by his works, both edifying and aesthetic.[61] This latter kind of nonverbal indirect communication is also a comic devise. It is referred to as a farce in *Repetition* (R, 159–67), as an "immensely comic drama" in the journals (JP 6, 79), and, discernibly, as a harlequin's, clown's, or fool's performance by Richard Simon (Simon 1985, 78–116).[62]

THE COMIC'S LEGITIMACY

Kierkegaard's concern about the ethical dimension of the comic prompts him to differentiate between legitimate and illegitimate uses of the comical. The comical may gain legitimacy in either of two ways: One is based on the relation between the comic and the tragic, and the other is closely associated with the theory of the spheres of existence, which many of Kierkegaard's pseudonymous writings advance. In the theory of the spheres of existence, the hierarchy between the spheres and interspheres establishes the legitimacy of comic apprehension. It is legitimate when the comic apprehension cancels the contradiction by knowing a way out, that is, if the comic apprehension is based on a higher point of view rooted in a higher sphere of existence. "The law for the comic" is very simple, according to Climacus: The comic is wherever there is contradiction and where the contradiction is painless by being "canceled and set right in a higher stage" (CUP1, 520), "since the comic certainly does not cancel the contradiction (on the contrary, it makes it apparent)" (*CUP1*, 519). The legitimate comic is able to cancel the contradiction while the illegitimate cannot.

The test of the comic is to examine the relations among the spheres the comic statement contains. If the relation is not correct, the comic is illegitimate and "the comic that belongs nowhere is *eo ipso* illegitimate" (*CUP1*, 524). Thus, the conditions that make the comic legitimate by canceling the contradiction are, first, that the comic be rooted in a particular existence-sphere (so that anyone who thinks he can "hover" outside existence to laugh at the world thereby makes himself comical), and second, that the existence-sphere in which the comic is rooted be higher than the existence-sphere in which the phenomenon the person is laughing at is rooted:

> The comic interpretation produces the contradiction or allows it to become apparent by having *in mente* [in mind] the way out; therefore the contradiction is painless . . . It follows that this must be understood in such a way that the different nuances in turn obey the qualitative dialectic of the spheres, which denounces subjective arbitrariness. If someone, for example, wanted to make everything comic without any basis, one would see at once that his comic effect is irrelevant, that it lacks a basis in a sphere, and the inventor himself would be made comic from the viewpoint of the ethical sphere, because he himself as an existing person must have his basis in existence in one way or another. (*CUP1*, 516–7)

The illegitimate comic apprehension consists of holding to an illusory way out, either a fantastic resolution of the contradiction, or a failure to appreciate the nature of the contradiction. To laugh at a higher sphere from a lower existence-sphere is illegitimate. A lower existence does not have the power to make a higher one comical, but the lower, by being joined to the higher, can make the relation ludicrous. Thus, "a horse can be the occasion for a man to look ludicrous, but the horse does not have the power to make him ludicrous" (*CUP1*, 518–9).

The sanction for an illegitimate comic apprehension is ridicule. The person who makes fun of what he should not make fun of is ridiculous; that is, the person is wounded by the weapon he uses in something of a boomerang effect: As a consequence of his comment, he is ridiculed rather than ridiculing the object of his laughter. There is no subjective arbitrariness in the comic for Kierkegaard. The same idea about the self-castigating power of ridicule is found in Shaftesbury: "And if I have either laughed wrong, or been impertinently serious, I can be content to be laughed at in my turn. . . . For he who laughs and is himself ridiculous, bears a double share of ridicule . . . we become more ridiculous than the people we ridicule" (*Essay*, iv, 3; CR I, 98; ii, 1; CR I, 57, 59). Because human beings fear ridicule, Kierkegaard assumes that this sanction is strong enough to demolish the attack and disarm the attacker (*PV*, 65, 68):

> One must see how no attack is so feared as that of laughter, how even the person who courageously risked his life for a stranger would not be far from betraying his father and mother if the danger was laughter, because more than any other this attack isolates the one attacked and at no point does it offer the support of pathos . . . (*PV*, 68)

For Kierkegaard, mockery, laughter, and ridicule are deemed "spiritual pains" because "it is terrible for the sensate human being to stand here on earth laughed to scorn" (*PV*, 140, 65).

Another way the comic may gain legitimacy is through its relation to the tragic. In this case, the contradiction that defines both the comic and the tragic need not be canceled, but the comic should be counterbalanced by the pathos-filled. Masuru Otani maintains that for Kierkegaard, a legitimate comic apprehension cancels contradiction, but "the true comic does not" (Otani 1980, 231). Indeed, Climacus holds that "the truly comic," which is humor, "is legitimized in its tragic side" (*CUP1*, 520). In this case, the contradiction is not abolished, there is no way out; rather, humor "reconciles itself with the pain from which despair wants to withdraw, although it knows no way out." This is not a down-side of the legitimate comic, because "despair ought to interpret the contradiction as tragic, which is precisely the way to its healing" (*CUP1*, 520).

The comic may be legitimized in one of the two ways: Either the legitimate comic is rooted in a sphere wherein it can abolish the contradiction, that is, the comic originates in a higher sphere than the sphere at which it laughs; or, in the case of the truly comic or humor, it does not abolish the contradiction, but gains legitimacy by its tragic side (*CUP1*, 520). The latter possibility is important for Kierkegaard also because it diverges from Hegel and the Hegelians' view of the comic. Wherever Hegelians refer to contradiction in the comic, they assume that the contradiction can be canceled. For Kierkegaard, the truly comic does not cancel contradiction.[63]

The ethics of the comic is also voiced in Kierkegaard and his pseudonyms' views on comic writing. In *Stages*, Quidam insists that a kind of pathos is required for true comic writing. This does not mean a narrow-minded earnestness, but a "true earnestness" that unifies jest and earnestness (SLW, 365). This is a demanding standard that makes the comic not merely a category of aesthetics, but a decisively ethical and religious one as well. Johannes Climacus, the author of *Postscript*, reaffirms the message of *Stages* when he stresses the ethical side of comic writing. Continuing the same metaphor as in *Stages*, Climacus maintains that "the power to wield the weapon of the comic is the policeman's shield, the badge of authority, which every agent who in our time really is an agent must carry," a mark of maturity, "an indispensable legitimization for everyone who in our age is to have any authority in the world of the spirit" (CUP1, 250–1, 291). In a powerful passage, he begins a new metaphor, comparing the comic to a harvester's scythe that has a cradle (wooden rods running parallel with the blade) (CUP1, 251).[64]

In *Postscript* Climacus maintains that in his authorship he has "never applied the comic interpretation of anything or anyone without first seeing by comparing the categories from which sphere the comic came and how it is related to the same thing or the same person interpreted with pathos" (CUP1, 519n). In a journal entry, Kierkegaard claims to be unable to bring himself to "present as comic, or in an actual situation to laugh at that under which a man suffers" (JP 2, 1763). In a genuinely comic situation, the comic character must be oblivious to the import of the contradiction and preferably should be happy in his delusion. To avoid being a writer who is "just as sordid as the world he depicts" (JP 2, 1761), there needs to be a concern, rooted in ethical and religious earnestness, about the nevertheless comical absurdity of how often human beings fall into confusion (see also COR, 178–9).

Not only does Kierkegaard insist that he apply the ethics of the comic in his writings, but he also uses it as the basis of his criticism of contemporary comic writing[65] and philosophical and theological speculation.

The criticism of philosophical and theological speculation is *Postscript*'s major target for an inadequate concept of the comic. The ethics of the comic is thus also the basis of Kierkegaard's condemnation of the Hegelian attitude toward Christianity as ridiculous. Kierkegaard's criticism of Hegelianism is directed in particular toward the Danish Hegelians, Hans Lassen Martensen and Baron Holberg.[66] In "Illusion and Satire in Kierkegaard's *Postscript*," John Lippitt explains that Climacus sees any objective or disinterested approach to Christianity as fundamentally misguided: "Objective indifference cannot come to know anything whatever" about Christianity (CUP1, 52); a "passionate" inward relation (of either faith or offense) is essential. The speculative thinker renders himself comical by ignoring this inward relation, or the subjective dimension. If the speculative thinker "says that he builds his eternal happiness [*Salighed*] on speculative thought, he contradicts himself comically, because speculative thought, in its objectivity, is indeed totally indifferent to his and my and your eternal happiness" (*CUP1*, 55). The speculative thinker is comical in his attempt to gain eternal happiness through objective thought because speculative thought cannot provide what the existing individual needs in relation to his desire for an eternal happiness. The comical is rooted in a "misrelation of the objective" (*CUP1*, 55; Lippitt 1999b).

Lippitt believes the Hegelian embodies one form of the "fantastic" Anti-Climacus has introduced in *The Sickness unto Death*. Lippitt explains that knowing becomes fantastic when an increase in knowledge is not matched by an increase in self-knowledge (*SUD*, 31; *CUP1*, 518; Lippitt 1999b). The view that self-ignorance is comical, deemed "unconscious comedy" by Alastair Hannay, may be compared with Henri Bergson's observation that a comic character "is generally comic in proportion of his ignorance of himself" (Hannay 2003, 20; Bergson 1999, 71), and with Plato's identification of "the true character of the comic" as self-ignorance or the opposite of the inscription at Delphi, "Know thyself" (*Philebus* 48–50).

The Hegelian position involves a fundamental confusion between the philosopher as an existing human being who philosophizes and the philosopher as philosophy ("speculative thought") itself:

> There are two ways for an existing individual: either he can do everything to forget that he is existing and thereby manage to become comic (the comic contradiction of wanting to be what one is not . . .) because existence possesses the remarkable quality that an existing person exists whether he wants to or not; or he can direct all his attention to his existing. (*CUP1*, 120)

Hence, as Lippitt explains in *Humor and Irony in Kierkegaard's Thought*, Climacus says that we may object to modern speculative thought for having a comic presupposition, occasioned by its having forgotten "in a kind of world-historical absentmindedness" what it means to be a human being. This is different from what it means "to be human in general, for even speculators might be swayed to consider that sort of thing, but what it means that we, you and I and he, are human beings, each one on his own" (*CUP1*, 120). Any system must be written by an existing human being. This has been forgotten, for "to be a human being has been abolished, and every speculative thinker confuses himself with human kind" (*CUP1*, 124). The highest form of the comic arises precisely when the individual comes directly under the infinite abstraction of "pure humanity," without any of the "intermediary qualifications which temper the humor of man's position and strengthen its pathos, without any of the concrete particulars of organization which the leveling process destroys" (PA, 56; Lippitt 2000b, chap. 2).[67]

Kierkegaard calls us to deliver ourselves from Hegelianism by laughter. Because of Hegelianism's relation to the principle of contradiction, it falsifies the real image of the human being, which is the irresolvable contradiction between the objective and the subjective, between eternity and time. The truth of the subjective individual is the passion for the absolute, but when it is sought where in principle it cannot be found, it gives rise to the comical, for misapplied objectivity is comic.[68]

The role of the comic within the Kierkegaardian good life is better assessed when its workings, under the guise of irony and humor, are understood. Humor and irony take many forms, not the least as interspheres that represent life-views that are located at the lower border of the ethical and the religious lives respectively. From these interspheres, higher spheres can be contemplated and chosen as possible ways of life.

Are irony and humor as interspheres necessary steps in becoming ethical and religious respectively, that is, essential steps toward the Kierkegaardian good life? Opinions on this matter differ. For example, Sylvia Walsh answers positively, and Stephen Evans answers negatively (Walsh 1994; Evans 1983, 190–1), because, as Evans emphasizes, one of the characteristics of irony and humor is their assumption of a certain level of intellectual development on the part of the individual (CUP1, 503, 179; PV, 540). The difficulty that this opinion raises appears when irony and humor are brought into connection with the spheres of existence. If the spheres of existence are universally achievable (CUP1, 160), why are irony and humor, which are not universally achievable, regarded as boundary zones of the spheres? The answer is that there are two ways of realizing oneself: First, the ethical and religious passion that makes a human being a self is achievable by the simple person in a direct or straightforward way; second, irony and humor form transition zones in the existential development of individuals who, because of talent and education become intellectually reflective about life to a special degree. Because Climacus is writing for this group, it is natural for him to include irony and humor in his account of the spheres, without making them spheres in their own right. Yet the distinction between these two classes of people is not a sharp one, at least in economically advanced countries, where universal education is the norm.

An understanding of irony and humor is useful, then, for understanding how one ascends toward the Kierkegaardian good life. The comic power is essentially humor for Kierkegaard, rather than irony. In order to understand the role of humor in the Kierkegaardian good life, I introduce irony first, because, although lower than humor, it is a life-view that is a necessary step before humor.

IRONY

Irony ranks high among Kierkegaard's enduring philosophical preoccupations, and is thus often mentioned in his writings. His career begins with a sustained and explicit treatment of the subject, his university thesis *On the Concept of Irony with Continual Reference to Socrates* (1841). Although he never again essays into a comprehensive theoretical account of irony, the subject recurs as a topic of discussion throughout his authorship. Even more pervasive than his remarks on irony are his varied uses of the trope and other varieties of verbal indirectness.

In *Postscript* there are comic and tragic aspects to both irony and humor (*CUP1*, 520–1), but the relationship between irony and the comic is absent or unclear in earlier works such as *The Concept of Irony* and *Either/ Or I*. At one point in *The Concept of Irony*, it is decisively stated that irony "does not have the redeeming feature of the comic" (*CI*, 256–7).

Several individuals in Kierkegaard's writings are ironic: Johannes, the author of *Either/Or*, is ironic[69]; Constantine Constantius, author of *Repetition*, is called an ironist; other aesthetic characters in Kierkegaard's works are not wanting in ironic skills; nor, for that matter, is Kierkegaard, either "as puppeteer in his aesthetic theatre" or as author in his own right (McCarthy 1978, 31).

To understand irony's complex role within the Kierkegaardian good life, I introduce irony as a life-view or an existential sphere, as a mask or incognito of the ethical person, as a tool, as inferior to humor, and as the characteristic most fitting Kierkegaard according to recent interpretations. I conclude by proposing a way to incorporate irony within Kierkegaard's authorship without labeling him an ironist.

IRONY AS A LIFE-VIEW

Vincent McCarthy explains that irony is a quality little understood and a word often misused: "One tends to label as ironic any sharp comment with a negative twist; and when real irony appears, one as often as not labels it sarcasm, due to the negativity sensed, which is an aspect of the ironic existence-stance" (McCarthy 1978, 17). Andrew Cross proposes to differentiate between "existential, as distinct from merely verbal, irony" in concordance with Kierkegaard's view that "irony is an existential determination, and nothing is more ridiculous than to suppose that it consists in the use of a certain phraseology. . . . Whoever has essential irony has it all day long, not bound to any specific form, because it is the infinite within him" (Cross 1998, 126; *CUP1*, 504). For Kierkegaard, as for his contemporaries and near-contemporaries, irony is not primarily a particular kind of speech act. Rather, it indicates a particular way of engaging in public activity in general. Kierkegaard examines what it is to speak ironically in order to determine what it is to live ironically—to manifest in one's life, unqualifiedly, the attitudes and type of orientation toward the world that constitutes irony.

In *The Concept of Irony*, Kierkegaard addresses the question of what it is to be an ironist. And although he nowhere again lavishes the same degree of attention on this way of life, this is not because his early interest in it is a mere youthful passion. Rather, existential irony comes to occupy a crucial place in the spheres of existence. The conception of existential irony as an important stage in self-understanding, which in *The Concept of Irony* is expressed in saying that irony is "the awakening of subjectivity," remains largely intact in the later writings. And it returns, as an explicit theme in *Postscript*, where it is identified as a transitional stage between the aesthetic and the ethical.[70]

In *Postscript*, the proper place of irony as an existence-qualification is "the *confinium* [border-territory] between the esthetic and the ethical" (*CUP1*, 501–2). An ironic view of life stands between the aesthetic sphere, where there are no distinct ethical commitments, and the ethical sphere, where one commits oneself to eternal, universal values. The ironist has realized the limitations of living aesthetically. The aesthete plays endlessly with various existential possibilities, defers the call existence makes on him by various forms of self-deception, including "the most subtle of all deceptions . . . thinking" (*CUP1*, 253), but postpones vital decisions concerning his own existence. This prevents him from becoming a self, being "an existence-possibility that cannot attain existence," such as A in *Either/ Or* or the "Hegelian"-fantastic thinker. Such a fantasy-existence is no existence at all for Climacus, but runs "aground on time. At its maximum, it is despair" (*CUP1*, 253). The ironist, however, not prepared to make the concrete commitment to "the eternal" characteristic of the ethical, has nothing positive to offer in place of aesthetic existence, which culminates in nihilism. Thus as early as his dissertation, Kierkegaard attacks Socratic irony—more than two-thirds of *The Concept of Irony, With Constant Reference to Socrates* is devoted to the ancient philosopher and his commentators—and especially Romantic irony.

Kierkegaard's view is that Socrates, the archetypal ironist, is an astonishing embodiment of negative freedom, to use Hegel's phrase, of "infinite

absolute negativity." Kierkegaard's text is replete with instructive Hegelian allusions, though Kierkegaard objects to several of Hegel's positions
on irony and Socrates. In *Fear and Trembling*, the narrator declares that
Hegel "strangely enough had not much understanding [of irony], and bore
a grudge against it" (FT, 36).[71] Through his "infinitely exuberant freedom
of subjectivity" (CI, 233), Socrates not only undermines and humiliates
mental blindness, he disaffirms "the whole of actuality" (CI, 97). His irony
is therefore an "infinite nothingness" (CI, 63–64), an endless emptying
or hollowing out. Socratic irony relishes "the whole magic of annihilation" (CI, 92), including the self-annihilation of skeptical estrangement
from existence. Yet we are meant to understand, although Kierkegaard
seems to evince some measure of ambivalence toward Socratic nihilism,
that such irony is a divinely healthy, emancipatory, light-hearted destructiveness. Nevertheless, whatever "positive fullness" (CI, 89) lies within
Socrates remains concealed. And though the content of his life, however
polemically busy, adds up to a void because it never transcends possibility,
Socrates' heroic negativity "is actually an incitement to ideality," to "the
Idea of the good, the beautiful, and the true" (CI, 221).[72]

    The ironist is estranged from existence. The presence of irony in the
personality indicates that there has been a rift in the everydayness in which
human beings are usually caught up. Something has happened that breaks
the flow and, as a result, a new consciousness emerges. For Kierkegaard
this "something" is the stirring that is still unconscious. The ironic subject
has broken with his age; he points toward a vague future and absolutely
denies the present age with a divine madness that leaves no stone standing (CI, 278). As a consciousness thoroughly pervading one's being, irony
is a mood in which one regards oneself, the individual elements of the
actual world, the entirety of the actual, and all future possible actuals in
an attitude of passionate rejection because they do not comprise the ideal.
He is free from the deception of the present actuality, but he is left empty.
Albeit he has reached a higher stage of consciousness, it has provided him
no support to bear the terrible realization of the absence of content and
meaning in his existence. Vincent McCarthy explains that irony as a mood
"represents the first conscious breakthrough in the illusion of aesthetic (or
nonreligious) existence. A sequence of moods follows naturally one upon
the other, viz., anxiety, melancholy, and despair in a series of crisis of the
personality" (McCarthy 1978, 3).

    Irony is a determination of subjectivity. The ironist is free in a nega-
tive sense in that he is freed from the illusion that actuality has validity.
It is also a prophecy of completed personality. The ironist is already the
singular one, the one who has broken with the crowd. He is still not a
complete personality, but he is a subject and exists in the direction of a

higher subjectivity, even if its form is vague and unknown to him. Irony is an existence stance with various possible phases and degrees, and thus a measurement for development of personality in the direction of the religious. There is no insurance that the ironist will reach his destiny. However, insofar as he has begun and is moving in the proper direction and traces the outline of a higher subjectivity, one may say that " . . . the ironist is a prophecy of or abbreviation for a complete personality" (CI, 177).

An "existing ironist" is higher than both immediacy and finite common sense in that he lives his irony: "He himself, existing, expresses it . . . keeps his life in it" (CUP1, 521). Climacus repeats Aristotle's remark that "the ironical man jokes to amuse himself, the buffoon to amuse other people" and adds, "the ironist himself enjoys the comic, in contrast to the joker, who is at the service of others in making something ludicrous" (Aristotle, Rhetoric, III, 18, 7; CUP1, 521). Irony, then, has the comic "within itself" (CUP1, 521). John Lippitt explains that the ironist sees how "the irony of the human situation rebounds upon himself. . . . He views his entire situation and the human condition as being essentially contradictory and therefore comical . . . irony has the comic 'within itself' in the sense that there is a natural 'fit' between the comic and the ironist's own existence" (Lippitt 2000b, 98).

There are negative aspects of irony, however. These are twofold: The ironist lives in possibilities, that is, poetically, and he is non-moral. Irony is thus a stage that one must supersede.

No pure model of irony exists even as an idea. The Romantics represent one possibility of ironic existence. Socrates' stance is viewed differently although termed essential irony. Indeed, Climacus rebukes Magister Kierkegaard for being "an Hegelian fool" in neglecting the ethical side of Socrates as well as the ethical passion of irony (JP 1, 1679/ Pap. II A 37). We turn now to the ethical function of irony.

IRONY AS A MASK

Irony has a double role in Postscript. It is an existential determinant between the aesthetic and ethical existence spheres, but it also functions as an incognito within the ethical. Climacus describes such irony as "the unity of ethical passion, which in inwardness infinitely accentuates one's own I in relation to the ethical requirement—and culture, which in externality infinitely abstracts from the personal I as a finite included among all other finitudes and particulars" (CUP1, 503). In view of his absolute and "infinite" commitment to the requirements of the ethical and in order not to be distracted by the finite or the relativities of the world, "the ethicist places the comic between himself and the world and thereby makes sure that he himself does not become comic through a naïve misunderstanding of his ethical passion" (*CUP1*, 504). That which engages the ethicist absolutely does not engage the others absolutely. He himself then "grasps this misrelation and places the comic in between in order to be able more inwardly to hold fast the ethical within himself (*CUP1*, 505).

Irony is a shield by which the ethicist protects the integrity of his self by creating a private space for the continual renewal of his commitment to the demands of the ethical. It is also an indirect communication of what it is to live ethically. The ethicist has a duty to communicate the ethical to others; this is highlighted in the need to openness in the *Either/Or* account of the ethical, but the ethical cannot be communicated directly. This kind of ethicist might seem like someone for whom "nothing is important" (*CUP1*, 505). But this is the only way in which those progressing toward the ethical and, therefore sufficiently tuned to it, would pick up his cues. The ethicist who uses irony as his mask "is able in turn to see the comic in irony, but he has legitimation to see it only by continually keeping himself in the ethical and thus sees it only as continually disappearing" (*CUP1*, 501).[73]

To be ethical, for Kierkegaard, involves absolutely committing oneself to one's projects (primarily social roles, such as parent, judge or teacher). By such commitment, the individual transcends the aimlessness of living aesthetically. Kierkegaard's ethical individual holds a narrative conception of the self, whereby one's life is given meaning and value—indeed whereby one *becomes* a self—through this commitment to and acting on the responsibilities of such projects. To fail in such a project is, at least partially, to fail as a person. But such a mode of living has limitations arising from two connected problems. First, when commitments arising from two conflicting projects clash (e.g., family duties versus duties to one's country), how do we decide which to prioritize? The problem is the lack of one overriding grounding project. Without such a project, there will always be the threat of conflict between the demands of different projects within the ethical life. Second, how does one choose the projects to commit oneself to in the first place? Despair can arise here too, stemming from a realization of the ultimate arbitrariness of one's selection of projects. After all, of any given project, it could be asked: What gives it its meaning? Why *that* project, and not some other?

Here Kierkegaard thinks the religious individual is at an advantage. For the individual who has made the extra-rational "leap of faith," there is an absolute *telos*—eternal happiness that God may grant—that grounds all other projects. The fully religious individual maintains, along with "a

relative concern for the relative" (commitment to various temporal projects), "an absolute concern for the absolute" (commitment to God). No
temporal goal can warrant such absolute commitment, only the eternal
God.

IRONY AS A TOOL

The irony of any subject is perceived in its most common form as a tool of
discourse. Individuals who are higher than an existing ironist can use irony
as a tool. It has various uses, most of which are exemplified by Socrates.
Irony may be used to emphasize the ignorance of others. Socrates perceives
his mission to be the quest for knowledge; this includes challenging those
who think they know (*Protagoras*). Irony may also push its victim a few steps
in a positive direction although in itself, it posits nothing by encouraging
thought, "quickening it when drowsy, disciplining it when dissipated." This
can be joined to a form of dialectic of which Socrates is the master. The
combination of dialectic and irony represents "irony in its total striving,
and dialectic in its negative, emancipating activity" (CI, 152).

Furthermore, irony as a tool can also lead to a heightened awareness
of finitude (*Phaedo*). Irony drives men from all corners of safety but leaves
them entirely dependent on their own resources to extricate themselves from
the precarious situations in which they always find themselves. Kierkegaard
remarks that irony frees, but also subjugates. It is irony that he considers
responsible for the binding love incited in Alcibiades for Socrates as well
as for his seductive power over the youth of Athens (CI, 85). Kierkegaard
compares Christian love to Socratic irony in *Works of Love* (WL, 154–5)
and finds that the difference between the two is that irony trades on prideful
superiority while Christian love is complete self-abnegation.

Irony is most effective as a tool when it proceeds from a state of
"mastered irony," that is, when irony proceeds from philosophic depth in
one's existence. In the section entitled, "Irony as a mastered moment. The
truth of irony," Kierkegaard offers us the presumably climactic section of
The Concept of Irony. This is a six-page treatment of an inner metamorphosis in which ironic negation is enigmatically negated, thus preparing
the way for an existence of genuine self-mastery. Somehow irony in its
mastered rather than tempestuous condition undergoes an extraordinary
mutation; somewhat magically it now "yields truth, actuality . . . stability
and consistency" (CI, 338–9). It becomes a guide to the authentic life
rather than a seducer; even more so, irony becomes a "cleansing baptism,"
a surgically regenerative power of living boldly, healthily, and truthfully—
even ideally—in finitude.[74]

The result is a balanced attitude toward actuality that properly values it, neither spurning it nor overvaluing it as reflection of the Idea. In achieving balance and serving as a constant check upon one's personal life, the real significance of irony emerges. Irony serves as a disciplinarian, still negative, still positing nothing, but coaxing one in the right direction: "Irony now limits, renders finite, defines, and thereby yields truth, actuality, and content; it chastens and punishes and thereby impairs stability, character and consistence (*CI*, 339). "Mastered irony" reflects an existence which has personally appropriated, and thus mastered, the "essence" of irony. Irony usually serves to drive one to a sense of finitude, to leave one in mid-air. Mastered irony, however, functioning with a deepened perspective of existence, serves as a check on one's personal life. This raises the question of the relationship between mastered irony and humor.

IRONY AS LOWER THAN HUMOR

As early as *The Concept of Irony*, Kierkegaard points cryptically to humor:

Finally, insofar as there can be any question of the "eternal validity" of irony, then this question can only find its answer through an investigation of the domain of humor. Humor contains a far deeper skepticism than irony; for here it is not finitude, but sinfulness, that everything turns upon; the skepticism [of humor] is related to [the skepticism] of irony as ignorance to the old thesis: *credo quia absurdum* ["I believe because it is absurd," attributed to Tertullian]; but it also contains a far deeper positivity [than irony]; for it does not occupy itself with the human, but with theoantropic determinations, it does not find rest in making man human, but by making man God-man. But all this lies beyond the confines of this investigation, and insofar as one should wish matter for afterthought, then I shall refer to Prof. Martensen's review of Heiberg's New Poems. (*CI*, 341–2)[75]

Humor contains a much deeper skepticism and positivity than irony because humor does not find rest in making man human, but in making man God-man. In the journals Kierkegaard first compares humor to irony as a total perspective on the world, but then contrasts it in ways that link humor specifically with Christianity. Both perspectives involve roughly a perception of the world of manners and practices devoid of meanings traditionally presumed attached to them. But where irony, as Kierkegaard writes in one entry, says merely "*nil admirari*" (admire nothing), humor's "diameter" is the greater for embracing the ironist as well. Once the individual sees *himself* in irony's light, there is no longer room for irony's "egoism." In the same entry Kierkegaard states that "humor is lyrical . . . it is the most profound seriousness of life—deep poesy that cannot form itself as such and therefore crystallizes in the most baroque forms" (*JP* 1, 1690/ *Pap.* II A 102).

The irony of Christianity lies in its claim to speak for the whole world when its message is that the world as a whole, or the world simply as such, is not to be spoken for: Its value is not in itself. The humor of Christianity lies in its treatment of the whole world as devoid of value except in relation to a "supposed single truth." The whole world of "princes, power and glory, philosophy, artists, foes and persecutors, etc." becomes valueless and meaningless in the light of this truth (*JP* 1, 1674/ *Pap.* I A 207).

Irony and humor often are described by Kierkegaard as two aspects of what is essentially the same existential situation, with irony as the objective and humor the subjective pole of the dissociation between ideality and reality, between self and world (*JP* 1, 1690/*Pap.* II A 102; *JP* 1, 1711/ *Pap.* II A 608). "Humor," Kierkegaard writes, "is irony carried through its most powerful vibrancy" (*JP* 1, 1699/*Pap.* II A 136). They are like the two ends of a seesaw with irony lying below and humor lifted above the point of balance (*JP* 1, 1671/*Pap.* I A 154). This is to say that the ironic individual suffers under his separation from reality, whereas the humorist rises above it. In this respect irony remains untrammeled in the dialectical phase of existence (i.e., it corresponds to romanticism), whereas humor is closer to the concept of character in its transcendence of the ambiguities and contradictions of dialectics (*JP* 1, 1676/*Pap.* I A 239).

Unlike irony, humor is not founded on the self-projective dynamism or the Idea (or the "I"), but on Christian revelation, presupposing as it does the Christian negation of the world in its entirety. Humor understands that "everything which hitherto had asserted itself in the world and continued to do so was placed in relation to the presumably single truth of the Christians, and therefore to the Christians the kings and the princes, enemies and persecutors, etc., etc., appeared to be nothing and to be laughable because of their opinions of their own greatness" (*JP* 1, 1674/*Pap.* I A 207).

Whereas irony simply plays off one aspect of the world against the other, humor relativizes the world in its entirety. Thus Kierkegaard pictures "a traveling humorist who is making preliminary studies, preparatory work for a theodicy—he travels about seeking as far as possible to experience everything in order to prove that everything is a disappointment" (*JP* 1,1736/*Pap.* III A 98). In this respect, the humorist bears a certain resemblance to Ahasverus, the Wandering Jew. He is entirely solitary, like a beast of prey (*JP* 1, 1719/*Pap.* III A 694), or like Robinson Crusoe on his desert island, for humor is "absolutely isolated, independently personal" (*JP* 1, 1699/*Pap.* II A 136). The humorist has a clear insight into the essential agony of the human situation, a vision the ironist (or poet) cannot achieve:

> When an ironist laughs at the whimsicalities and witticisms of a humorist, he is like the vulture tearing away at Prometheus' liver, for the humorist's whimsicalities are not *capricious little darlings* but the *sons of pain,* and with every one of them goes a little piece of his innermost entrails, and it is the emaciated ironist who needs the humorist's desperate depth. His laughter is often the grin of death . . . (Like the dead man's grin which is explained as the muscle twitch of rigor mortis, the eternally humorous smile over human wretchedness). (*JP* 1, 1706/*Pap.* II A 179)

The humorist's "desperate depth" not only puts him on a different level than the Romantic ironist, it also puts him altogether outside or above the merely aesthetic standpoint, for "humor is not an esthetic concept, but life" (*JP* 1, 1699/*Pap.* II A 136). It follows that it can only achieve an ambiguous and (aesthetically) unsatisfying expression in literature: That aesthetic harmony of idea and form, which is gained at the cost of severance from the actuality of life, eludes the humorist.

Climacus too aims at distinguishing between irony and humor (*CUP1,* 271–2; 448; 551–3). Irony is proud and tends to divide one person from another. It is teasing and self-asserting (*CUP1,* 551):

> Irony is self-assertion, and its sympathy is therefore an altogether indirect sympathizing, not with any one person, but with the idea of self-assertion as every human being's possibility. There-fore, one often finds humor in women, but never irony. Any attempt at it on her part is unbecoming, and a purely feminine nature will consider irony to be a kind of cruelty. (*CUP1,* 553)

Humor is "sympathetic" (*CUP1,* 582) and "profound" (*CUP1,* 552n). The profundity of humor lies in the humorist's comprehension of suffering and guilt, or of "what it means to exist" (*CUP1,* 272), an understanding far superior to that of the ironist. A humorous retort "must always have something profound, although hidden in the jest, and must therefore say more" (*CUP1,* 552n). Being more distanced and disengaged from suffering, the ironist tends to "teasingly" reply "with the aid of abstract dialectic" (*CUP1,* 448n). Lacking in profundity and sympathy, the ironist cannot replace the humorist.[76]

Irony is an important stage in self-understanding as well as a transitional stage between the aesthetic and the ethical. Irony emerges by continually joining the particulars of the finite together with the ethical infinite requirement, thereby allowing the contradiction to come into existence. Irony is a shield by which the ethicist protects the integrity of the self by creating a private space for the continual renewal of his commitment to the demands of the ethical. It is also an indirect communication of what it means to live ethically. Irony is a prophecy of completed personality, but it offers no more than that: It frees while bringing one under its power, and it lacks the qualities of sympathy, profundity, and scope of humor. This raises the following question: Is Kierkegaard as thoroughly ironic as postmodern commentators have portrayed him?

IRONY AS A DEFINING CHARACTERISTIC OF KIERKEGAARD

Irony has been put to use as an interpretative tool for Kierkegaard's writings. In this context, "irony" is understood as a device implying non-serious, or false content, or no content at all. Yet it is important to recall that Kierkegaard warns us through Climacus that irony does not exclude earnestness: If someone says "God knows whether talk like this is irony or earnestness—then he is satirizing himself. But the presence of irony does not necessarily mean that the earnestness is excluded" (*CUP1*, 276–7, n. 422). Therefore, according to Kierkegaard or at least to Climacus' view of irony, Kierkegaard's irony does not imply false or non-serious content.

To be sure, Kierkegaard frequently employs irony in his writings, and given the use of pseudonyms to detach himself from the positions represented, it is not always easy to discern when he is being ironic toward the contents of these positions even if, as Stephen Dunning has pointed out, "irony always tips his hand, as it certainly must if it is to be understood as irony" (Dunning 1985, 5). But the fact that Kierkegaard uses irony does not justify an encompassing interpretation of him as an ironist, especially in the works issued under his own name.

If, however, one is inclined to trust Kierkegaard's direct communication and to regard the irony in his writings as an aesthetic device, or "controlled element," employed for the purpose of indirect communication as well as the protection of the privacy of his own religious inwardness, then one may use the viewpoints to which he explicitly subscribes as guideposts for comparing the views of the pseudonymous authors to his own viewpoints.[77]

I suggest the issues raised by viewing Kierkegaard as thoroughly ironic can be settled by paying attention to Kierkegaard's differentiation between being ironic and creating ironic situations and by differentiating between self-deception and irony. In the long note that addresses the difference between humor and irony, the humorist is described as particularly apt at creating ironic effects and situations:

> If the retort was intended as irony, the speaker would have been a mediocre ironist, because there was in a remark a tone of pain, which from the point of view of irony is entirely incorrect. The remark was humorous and therefore made the situation ironic through the misunderstanding. This in turn is quite right, because an ironic remark cannot make the situation ironic; at most it can create awareness that the situation is ironic, whereas a humorous remark can make the situation ironic. The ironist asserts himself and prevents the situation, but the humorist's hidden pain contains a sympathy whereby he himself cooperates in shaping the situation and thus makes an ironic situation possible. But very frequently what is said ironically is confused with that which, when said, can have an ironic effect in the situation. (*CUP1*, 551–3 n803)

And the contrary is also true: A remark that "is proper irony" can have "a ring of humor, although it is not humorous" (*CUP1*, 551–3 n803).

I suggest that Kierkegaard is not an ironist, but a humorist who creates ironic effects and situations. That Kierkegaard was a humorist can be inferred from his view of the genius as a humorist (*PV*, 107, 108) and of himself as a genius (*Pap.* XI A 266; *PV*, 94, 95), but of a certain kind, that is, "a poetic-dialectical genius, personally and religiously a penitent . . ." (*JP* 4, 6317/*Pap.* XI A 56). In *The Point of View for My Work as an Author*, moreover, Kierkegaard explains, "while the poet-production was being written, the author was living in decisive religious categories." In a note, he adds: "Here one will see the significance of the pseudonyms, why I had to be pseudonymous in connection with the esthetic production, because I had my own life in altogether different categories and from the very beginning understood this writing as something temporary, a deception, a necessary emptying out" (*PV*, 86). Just before that, he writes:

> I had really leaped over, humanly speaking childhood and youth. . . . Instead of having been young, I became a poet, which is youth a second time. I became a poet, but with my religiously oriented background, indeed, with my definite religiousness, the same fact became for me a religious awakening

also. So in the most decisive sense I came to understand myself in the religious, in the religiousness to which I had, however, related myself as to a possibility. (PV, 84)

To relate oneself to the religious as a possibility is to be a humorist, according to Climacus. The live in religious categories while writing poetically is to use humor as an incognito. The deception to which Kierkegaard refers above can apply to the humorist using humor as an incognito, who is a deceiver as well.[78] As Kierkegaard explains, however, the humorist can create an ironic situation (CUP1, 551–3 n803). The situation may be ironic, but the humorist is not, at least not according to Kierkegaard's definition of irony.

Several scholars have commented on Kierkegaard's alleged dishonesty. Joakim Garff's reaction to Kierkegaard's confessions in The Point of View is that "the man has never been honest with himself" (Garff 2002, 94). A recent biographer refers to the "penchant for secrecy and deceptiveness" that runs "as a constant thread through [Kierkegaard's] life and work" and to a lifelong "urge to bait, seduce, and offend his public" (Thompson 1973, 9–10). I tend to agree, but I suggest that these characterizing features should not to be confused with irony. Living in deception does not make a person an ironist, but rather someone in need of irony, according to Kierkegaard's own prescription.

HUMOR

Humor is Kierkegaard's most important category of the comic. Climacus states, "the comic power is essentially humor" and "the contradiction that humor dominates [is] the highest range of the comic" (CUP1, 282, 522). Yet properly speaking, humor is not a subcategory of the comic; rather, it is a mixture of the pathetic and the comic (CUP1, 292).

Kierkegaard's most extensive discussions of humor are in his pseudonymous works. Three figures stand out as paradigms of the humorous stance within these works, Johannes Climacus, Quidam, and Frater Taciturnus. Each one has moved beyond the ethical life-view and has comprehended major dimensions of the religious stance, but none of them has actually become a religious person. Stages on Life's Way is the main arena of Quidam and Frater Taciturnus, and Johannes Climacus discusses humor at length in Concluding Unscientific Postscript.[79]

Kierkegaard offers a theory of humor and two interesting theses about it. The first thesis is that there is an essential connection between humor

and human existence. Humor is no ephemeral or accidental human characteristic, but is grounded in something deeper within our nature or our
condition. The reason humor is basic to human life is that contradiction
is basic to human life, and contradiction is both comic and tragic; hence,
it is humorous. This idea that humor touches something deep is one that
Kierkegaard shares with many other theorists. The second thesis is more
unusual, however, and consequently more controversial. Kierkegaard also
claims that there is an essential connection between humor and the religious life. Quite contrary to the stereotype of the religious life as dour and
somber, completely opposed to the carefree wit of the humorist, Kierkegaard
holds that the highest and deepest kind of humor is rooted in a life-view,
which is recognizably religious, and that, as Stephen Evans puts it, "all
humor is at bottom made possible by those very features of human life
which make the religious life possible" (Evans 1987, 176).

Understanding Kierkegaard's theory of humor is hindered for the following reasons: First, Kierkegaard does not discuss humor for its own sake,
but rather uses it to illuminate his theory of stages of existence; second,
the significance he attributes to humor can be grasped only in light of the
role it plays in the dialectic of the stages of existence; and third, the role
of humor in the dialectic of stages keeps evolving in Kierkegaard's thought.
At first, Kierkegaard considers humor as the proper attitude of the Christian
with regard to the things of time, a kind of protective covering or incognito, useful in dealing with worldly fortunes and with individuals who do
not see the world through the eyes of faith. But by 1845, humor is not so
much a religious as an ethical passion, signifying that one has reached the
borderline of ethical life and is faced with the choice of becoming religious
in a plenary way, or of thwarting the natural inclination of ethical existence
to surmount itself. During the same year, which marked the composition
of *Postscript*, the distinctive nature of Christianity is so strongly impressed
on him that he ceases to speak of the religious sphere in an unqualified
way, and thereafter distinguishes sharply between all natural modes of the
religious and the unique Christian religious spirit. This distinction between
"Religiousness A" (immanent religiousness) and "Religiousness B" (Christianity) is equivalent to designating four stages in the dialectic of life. The
immanent modes of religious existence do not exhaust or naturally blend
with the transcendent kind of religiousness, which comes only with the
gift of Christian faith. Kierkegaard's final position on the relationship of
humor and Christianity is that not only are humor and Christianity not
to be confused, but that Christianity is inaccessible to humor.

To explain humor's multifarious roles within the Kierkegaardian good
life, namely, Christianity, I begin with the young Kierkegaard's view that

humor is intrinsic to Christianity and then introduce the mature Kierkegaard's view of humor as a life-view or existence-sphere, which is higher than any other except the Christian life. This is followed by a discussion of humor as the boundary-zone of religiousness, and finally, by humor as an incognito or mask for the religious person.

HUMOR AS INTRINSIC TO CHRISTIANITY

Kierkegaard begins his lifelong preoccupation with the relation of humor to Christianity by adopting the view that humor is intrinsic to Christianity, which he later renounces. The early view can be traced to Johann Georg Hamann's influence on Kierkegaard, who later abandons the view when he disengages himself from Hamann's influence. Hamann fulfills such an important role in Kierkegaard's thoughts on the role of humor within Christianity that he is rightly depicted as Kierkegaard's "constant paradigm of the standpoint of humor" (Hannay 2001, 72). Kierkegaard's views of irony and humor can be properly understood only in relation to the views of Hamann, who elevates irony and humor to the rank of categories of understanding that are especially apt for comprehending Christianity. Hamann's *Socratic Memorabilia* is useful to Kierkegaard in crafting his dissertation on irony; more significantly, however, it is through Hamann that Kierkegaard discovers the category of humor which replaces the category of irony as the deepest attitude toward existence.

The influence of this obscure thinker on Kierkegaard has led commentators to deem Kierkegaard Hamann's sole "authentic disciple" (Jørgensen 1968, 164). Indeed, Georges Pattison maintains that Kierkegaard takes Hamann's literary method of indirect communication and direct personal involvement as a model for his own authorship, and Kierkegaard himself views his own work as a development of Hamann's (*JP* 2, 1559; Pattison 1992, 66–67). In his recent biography of Kierkegaard, moreover, Alastair Hannay emphasizes the themes in Hamann that Kierkegaard appreciates, such as contextualizing reason, saving Lutheranism from the Enlightenment, and insisting on the inappropriateness of rational criticism and proofs in questions of faith (Hannay 2001, 72). But it is first and foremost Hamann's humor that Kierkegaard admires.[80]

In the journals, Kierkegaard acknowledges that Hamann "could be a good representative of the humor inherent in Christianity." He ends the entry by crowning Hamann "the greatest humorist in Christianity, [which is to say] by virtue of being the greatest within the life-view that, in world-historical terms, is itself the most humorous life-view, [he is] the greatest humorist in the world" (*Pap.* II A 75). What makes Hamann a good representative of the humor inherent in Christianity is his self-induced Socratic ignorance, "forcing oneself down to the lowest position and looking up (i.e., down) at the common view, yet in such a way that behind this self-degradation lies a high degree of self-elevation" (SV vol. 17, Journal DD 3, 6; quoted in Hannay 2003, 21). In other words, Christianity makes nonsense of common sense, which judges Christianity's claims as incongruous. In *Postscript*, Climacus testifies to his admiration of Hamann (*CUP1*, 250).

The evolution of Kierkegaard's thought on the place of humor within Christianity is attested to in the difference between the early entries in his journals and Climacus' mature thought on humor in *Postscript*. Early on, the humorist is depicted as far removed from the systematizing ambitions of the philosopher who "believes that he can say everything," because the humorist "lives in the abundance and is therefore sensitive to how much is always left over" (*JP* 1, 1702/*Pap*. II A 140). Like the Christian revelation itself, its truth is always concealed, even in the very act of communication (*JP* 1, 1682/*Pap*. II A 78). Indeed, "Humor [is] intrinsic to Christianity" (*JP* 2, 251). It is "even present through Christianity" because "truth is hidden in . . . mystery . . . no matter how much Christian knowledge increases; it will still always remember its origin and there know everything. . . ." (Corinthians 1.26; *JP* 2, 252).

The incarnation of God in time is the prototypical event of divine humor. Here the contradiction inherent to humor reaches its highest form and the paradox is absolute, as cross and resurrection constitute an absolute reversal of all human expectations. In Christianity, contradiction becomes normative and paradigmatic. Contradiction is the perspective through which all else is interpreted: It is easier for a camel to go through the eye of a needle than for a rich man to enter the kingdom of heaven (Mt. 19:24); it is the blind who recognize the Messiah (Mt. 9:27); it is the children that know more than the wise; the lilies of the field exceed the finery of Solomon's clothing. All this refracts and pictures the humor of the incarnation. Kierkegaard considers that "humor appears in Christ's own utterance" constantly (*JP* 2, 254).

Just as Socrates pleads ignorance in seeking to reveal the truth, so Christianity seeks the lowliest position (slave, servant) to point to that which is infinitely high. It is precisely from the cave in Bethlehem that Christianity points to the Incarnation of God in a particular person, and from the cross, it points to the atonement. God uses the lowliest things to soar and transcend: Water is changed into wine; the Messiah comes in the form of a child; the thief is admitted immediately into paradise; the ass is transformed into a prophet. In the Kingdom of God, everything is comically upside down. Christianity is nowhere more intensely comic to

Kierkegaard than in the Christmas story. This is where the Absolute Para-dox, the Incarnation itself, the decisive expression of the comic can be found. God comes to humanity in the least expected way, with the greatest depth of contradiction. The nativity demonstrates God's own unexpected and seemingly incongruent way of breaking into time. Only God would have thought of us this way; it is as if the miracle is performed "only to disconcert the professors of physics" (*JP* 2, 253). Here biblical comedy reaches its apex.

Humor has also an intense relationship with suffering. After the apostles were flogged by the Jerusalem authorities and warned not to wit-ness anymore, they left the jail "thanking God that it was granted them to suffer something for the sake of Christ" (*CUP1*, 452). The humor rooted in Christianity stands bravely against the world. At the heart of the view of humor in the New Testament lies gladness for the privilege of suffer-ing. Suffering is transmuted into joy by its relation with eternal happiness. Thus, "the essential relation to an eternal happiness is not suffering but joy . . . joy in the consciousness that the suffering signifies the [redeemed God-human] relation" (*CUP1*, 452). Hence, in the case of martyrdom, the martyr experiences suffering along with more profound experiences of "joy over the significance of this suffering as [redeemed] relationship" (*CUP1*, 453). "All humor [is] developed from Christianity itself" (*JP* 2, 229); and the Christian nature of humor is testified historically as a characteristic of the medieval Church (*JP* 1, 1698/*Pap.* II A 114), manifesting itself in objectified and institutionalized ways (*JP* 1, 1687/*Pap.* II A 85). Yet, when it is most truly itself, humor is intensively individual and personal.

In the early entries of Kierkegaard's journals, humor is considered intrin-sic to Christianity, Christianity is seen as the most humorous view of life, and Hamann is deemed accordingly the greatest humorist (*JP* 2, 1681; see 2, 1682, 1686, 1687, 1690).[81] In *Postscript* (published 1846), however, humor is thought to be inferior to Christianity. Climacus holds that humor, backed by the ideality of Christianity, is the final pathos that still has an external expression. Highest in the hierarchy, though, is hidden religious inwardness, which is raised above all immanent dialectic (*CUP1*, 508; cf. *CUP1*, 554f). In the section entitled "The Dialectical" (*CUP1*, 561–86), the consciousness of sin replaces the consciousness of guilt, and the truth of Christianity is changed "paradoxically-dialectically" to the absurd, the absolutely unintel-ligible, which can only be grasped by another intensification of subjectivity until it reaches the passion of true faith. This is what Climacus, using Hege-lian terminology, calls the crucifixion of the understanding (*CUP1*, 561f). Because there is nothing to understand, there is no place for humor.

It is against a contemporary speculative conception of humor that Climacus in *Postscript* presents the existing humorist, who is not Christian but has Christianity and authentic faith in mind, as the highest possibility for subjectivity (see *CUP1*, 451). Indeed, for Kierkegaard's contemporary Hans Lassen Martensen, who builds upon the reflections of his time, humor is a designation for the culmination of Christianity in Protestantism. From this highest of all possible perspectives, which has incorporated the entire world in its recollection, all human contradictions appear comical.[82] Kierkegaard sees Martensen's humor as objective humor, as a pure perspective of consciousness with no affinity to existence. Therefore, it also lacks a double reflection and the truth of Christianity can thus never emerge as the paradoxical-religious. Without subjectivity there is no faith. Without faith, human beings cannot be reconciled to that which offends the understanding, the absolute paradox.

Kierkegaard rejects the view that identifies Christianity with humor, the view he adopted in his youth and expressed in the early entries of his journals, because he rejects the theological theory of *Kneschtsgestalt Christi*. This theory emphasizes the contradiction of Christ appearing in the "form of a servant," as the Apostle Paul says in his letter to the Philippians (2:7); because divinity most often appears in lowly form, one may fail to recognize it. Hamann insists on some variety of this theory as the inescapable precondition of valid aesthetic, ethical and religious knowledge. Kierkegaard now sees this theory as the kernel of the view, shared with Hamann, which makes Christianity the highest humor:

If it is given and assumed that it is easy to understand that God becomes a particular human being, then the difficulty is only in the next—that he becomes a lowly and despised human being—then in *summa summarum* Christianity is humor. Humor diverts a little of the attention away from the first, the qualification "God," and now stresses that the greatest . . . became the lowliest of all . . . But if Christianity is humor, then everything is confused. (*CUP1*, 596–7)

At this point Kierkegaard considers the view that emphasizes the low aspect of Christ "a childlike orthodoxy." To dwell on Christ's appearance hides the true paradox, that God has become man (*CUP1*, 596). A childish orthodoxy misleadingly emphasizes Christ's suffering and sees as a paradox that Christ entered the world to suffer. But "the fact that the innocent may suffer in this world . . . is by no means absolutely paradoxical, but humorous" (*CUP1*, 597). A childish orthodoxy takes the "terror" away, "the fact which was an offence to the Jews and foolishness to the Greeks" (*CUP1*, 598). Kierkegaard's final position on the relationship of humor and Christianity as absolutely paradoxical and therefore terrifying is that not only are humor and Christianity not to be confused, but Christianity is inaccessible to humor.

Humor is nevertheless far from being a monolithic notion in Kierkegaard's thought. The descriptions Kierkegaard provides range from "immature humor" to "holy jest." Immature humor lags behind what Kierkegaard properly calls humor. Unlike humor, which is an equilibrium between the comic and the tragic, immature humor is nothing more than "a kind of flippancy" or "esthetic subtlety" that "skips past the ethical"; and far from being true religiousness, it is instead a parody of the religious (*CUP1*, 292). In contrast, holy jest is expressed in humor that is the incognito of the religious individual. Whereas jest is an expression for the humorist's revocation of the decisive significance of existence, holy jesting serves as a sign of the utmost earnestness toward existence (*CUP1*, 462, 471–2).

Between immature humor and holy jest (used by those who appear to be humorists but are in fact genuinely religious people hiding behind humor as an incognito) there exists an existential category of humor wherein the "mere" humorist Climacus claims to dwell (*CUP1*, 501). But humor is also a boundary-zone between the ethical and Religiousness A or immanent religiousness; and, as Religiousness A is "not the *specifically* Christian religiousness" (*CUP1*, 555), but an essential prerequisite to it, humor is also the boundary between Religiousness A and Religiousness B or Christianity.

With this in mind, Stephen Evans rightly suggests that humor is not a slot in a lock step of existential positions, but an existential possibility within a "range" (Evans 1983, 201). Indeed, Climacus asserts, "the humorous, precisely at the *confinium* [boundary-zone] of the religious, is very comprehensive" (*CUP1*, 451). This comment, together with humor's apparent "mobility," suggests that it might be able to act as the incognito for both Religiousness A and B. Thus, humor sometimes appears on the boundary of the ethical and "full-blown" Religiousness A and at other times on the boundary of Religiousness A and Religiousness B. Humor can be used as a mask for either forms of religiousness.

In what follows, each of humor's roles is examined separately, beginning with humor as an existence-sphere or life-view, followed by humor as the boundary-zone of the religious, and concluding with humor as an incognito or a mask for the religious.

HUMOR AS A LIFE-VIEW

Humor is an existence-qualification. Climacus speaks of existential humor with personal authority because he identifies himself as a humorist.[83] A humorist is a person who has mastered the comical, who "has the comic *within himself*" (*CUP1*, 521). That is, he perceives the contradiction to be essential rather than accidental in human life. Because humor is not an aesthetic category but "life" (*JP* 1, 1699/*Pap*. II A 136), the humorist is the person who lives his life in humor. Kierkegaard typically speaks of the humorist as someone who, compared with the systematizing philosopher, is particularly aware of how to live:

> The humorist can't really ever become a systematizer, for he regards every system as a renewed attempt . . . to burst the world open with one single syllogism . . . whereas [the humorist] has precisely come alive to the incommensurable which the phi- losopher can never account for and must therefore despise. He lives in the fullness of things and is therefore sensitive to how much is always left over, even if he has expressed himself with all felicity . . . therefore this disinclination to write . . . (*Pap*. II A 140)

For the humorist, what cannot be said is true and primary, whereas the systematizer believes that he can say everything and that whatever cannot be said is erroneous and secondary. As the humorist exists, so also does he express himself (*CUP1*, 449).

The humorous is the consciousness of the failure of the ethical, which recedes before Christianity. This hesitation before Christianity, as a radical cure that one postpones as long as possible, is the distinctive mark of the humorist (*Pap*. I A 89). Kierkegaard, however, emphasizes the life devel- opment necessary for embracing Christianity by pointing to the richness and meaningfulness of the humorist's life: "It is possible both to enjoy life and to give it meaning and substance outside Christianity, just as the most renowned poets and artists, the most eminent thinkers, even pious men, have lived outside Christianity" (*CUP1*, 292–3).

The definition of humor refers to the idea of God: Humor comes about when a totality-category (*CUP1*, 553n) is joined with the God-idea (*CUP1*, 505). A totality-category is a concept that applies to the whole of a person's life. The statement "all in life is disappointing" is an example of a determinant of totality. When a remark does not reflect upon any totality-category, even if it hints at it, it is not humorous. The idea of God is given in immanence since knowledge of the ethical-religious truth and religious and metaphysical truth is given to all in recollection (*Pap*. VIII B 81, sec. 10). We can know that God exists, that we are immortal, and that we are free beings (*Pap*. V B 40). "I do not believe that God exists," writes Kierkegaard, "I know it, but I believe that God existed [the historical]" (*Pap.* VI B 45).[84]

Thus, humor has much in common with Religiousness A or immanent religiousness, not least the view of eternity. Religiousness A, which is in continuation with the ethical, does not express itself in the form of a determinate religion, and thus can exist in paganism as well as Christianity (*CUP1*, 557). It is a natural religiousness, which presupposes only human nature in general. Kierkegaard ascribes it to Socrates; from Socrates' point of view all knowledge is recollection. Because spirit is missing, eternity for the Greeks becomes the intemporality of the past. Recollection is the backward movement discovering eternity as that which was already there before one turned back to it. "Humor is always a revocation . . . is the backward perspective" (*CUP1*, 602). The absolute is present in every human being who discovers himself in recollection and inwardness. Both the humorist and the person in Religiousness A believe with Socrates and Plato that all humans already possess the eternal.

It follows that both the humorist and the person in Religiousness A believe that all attain eternal happiness (*CUP1*, 581, 450). There does not exist an important distinction between religious and nonreligious persons for the humorist, but "a humorous difference: that whereas the religious person utilizes his entire life in becoming aware of the relation to an eternal happiness and the other does not concern himself with it . . . they both, viewed eternally, go equally far" (*CUP1*, 581–2).

Moreover, "the existing humorist is the closest approximation to the religious person" (*CUP1*, 447), because, like the latter, the humorist perceives suffering as essential to human existence. The religious person of Religiousness A and the humorist apply suffering and guilt to the whole of his life: Each of us is totally guilty in relation to God. In this sense suffering and guilt are totality-categories. The "eternal recollection of guilt" of which the humorist is aware (even if he has not decisively appropriated it) makes his comment profound (*CUP1*, 552n). Nevertheless, the humorist "makes the deceptive turn and revokes the suffering in the form of jest" (*CUP1*, 447).[85]

Whereas humor is a revocation of existence into the eternal by recollection backward from adulthood to childhood, Christianity constitutes the movement forward toward becoming a Christian. The humorist's view is sentimental or feminine (*CUP1*, 553, 271n), and it entertains a particular relation with childhood: "The sadness in legitimate humor consists in its reflecting purely humanly, honestly and without deception, on what it is to be a child (literally understood), and it then becomes forever certain and true that this cannot be done over again" (*CUP1*, 602). The humorist has eternity behind it, whereas Christianity has no room for sadness because "to look back . . . is perdition" (*CUP1*, 603).

Humor is said to be on the boundary (*confinium* or border territory) of religiousness (*CUP1*, 500). This means that only against religiosity humor is not justified (*CUP1*, 521). The difference between a humorist and a religious person is that the religious person is related to God (*CUP1*, 505). The humorist admits that he is not related to God, but, on the other hand, he is not like other people below him, for he is not related to what they are related. These other people are related to things in such a way that when one puts them (as a whole) into conjunction with the God-idea, there is a contradiction. The thing to be related to—God—is not among these things: "The humorist levels everything on the abstract relationship with God" (*CUP1*, 448n). A thing given more importance than others is seen to be as unimportant as everything else that is less than God. Thus the humorist "removes the distinction in which the unfortunate one has his life" (*CUP1*, 448).

In order to be justified, the humorist must not be like the person of "finite common sense" who is guilty of the same sort of contradiction he contemplates. The humorist has a thought that takes in the totality of the predicament of the people below him. It is the contradiction between the determinant of totality and the God-idea to which the humorist is related. "The humorist gains legitimization by having his life in it [humor]" (*CUP1*, 521). If he is to be justified, he must find his life in his humor in a way that is essentially different from the way those beneath him find their lives in the objects to which they are related.

"Humor is legitimized in its tragic side . . . it reconciles itself to the pain from which despair wants to withdraw, although it [humor] knows no way out" (*CUP1*, 520). Humor is evidently not comic, for it does not know how to escape pain. Nor is it tragic, for the following considerations: The difference between the tragic and the comic is that whereas the comic apprehension has in mind a way out, the tragic apprehension despairs of a way out (*CUP1*, 516); humor differs from despair in that despair seeks to depart from the pain to which humor attempts to reconcile itself. Thus humor is not tragic, although it has a tragic side. Rather, it can be identified by its ambiguous nature, as being the comic-tragic.

If humor were fully tragic it would despair, and this means it would seek to escape the pain. In despairing over the fact that all those things are less than God and that one should not be related to them, one moves from the pain that all those things are less than God and that of desiring to escape from the pain. In so doing, the despairing person desires an imaginary (and therefore abstract) state, the state of escaping from his plight. He would be like all the others, seeking to find happiness in something that is less than God. But the humorist does not make this move. He feels the pain—he knows no way out—and then he reconciles himself to the pain. He conceals the pain in a jest that dwells on the fact that this is the way things are (that there is a contradiction between the fact that all the things we find before us are possible objects of desire and the God-idea): "There is always a hidden pain in humor" (*CUP1*, 553). The humorist differs from others in that he renounces the pursuit of happiness among temporal things, and therein lies his justification. It is the recognition that he has no worthy object of desire that can make him happy and that would free him from the temporal. Instead of desiring God, the humorist rests in the contemplation of the way things are.

It is a misunderstanding to laugh at humor (*CUP1*, 551n). Whereas the comic is the painless contradiction (*CUP1*, 514), humor is always a concealed pain. The jest is due to the fact that it constantly seems as if humor is aware of something else (*CUP1*, 532n). T. Morris explains that the humorist "presents us with a contradiction and conceals the fact of the contradiction's pain; thus we have the suggestion that there is no pain, that the humorist knows a way out. Thus we can mistakenly take his statement as comic, as a jest" (Morris 1988, 304). The humorist

> comprehends the meaning of suffering in relation to existing, but he does not comprehend the meaning of suffering. He comprehends that it belongs together with existing, but he does not comprehend its meaning otherwise than that suffering belongs together with it. The first is the pain in the humorous; the second is the jest—and this is why one both weeps and laughs when he speaks. (*CUP1*, 447)

The humorist is, opposite the believer, a thinker. It perhaps sounds odd to attribute philosophical significance to humor, but the high evaluation of humor that one finds in Climacus is inherited from a distinct tradition, which holds that humor entered the world with Christianity. Tonny Olesen describes this tradition thus:

> It claims that humor gains its strength by bringing with it a category of totality, that humor is not a designation of the first immediacy but includes reflection, that humor designates the unity of tragedy and comedy, that humor designates a culminat-

ing standpoint, and that humor is melancholic [*vermodig*]. The literature contemporaneous with the writings of Kierkegaard is replete with discussions of humor as the counterpart to Greek irony. (Olesen 2003, 220)[86]

Kierkegaard assigns the humorist the highest reflective place and the ultimate understanding without faith. The humorist understands that which he has deemed existence, but he also knows that with regard to faith, he must give up understanding in order to relate to the truth of Christianity in the medium of existence and in the passion of faith. Socrates was the wisest man of his time in that he knew that he knew nothing. Climacus reaches a similar insight: He understands that he understands nothing in relation to faith and the paradox, except perhaps that Christian faith is the highest form of subjectivity or inwardness. Whereas humor as a life-view is not "essentially different" from irony (*CUP1*, 271), it is essentially different from Christianity. The humorist is a lower form of existence than the Christian, according to Kierkegaard, for the humorist does not relate himself to the God in time, that is, he has not appropriated the absolute paradox into his life (*CUP1*, 272).

HUMOR AT THE BOUNDARY OF RELIGION

At this point, humor tends to become either "religious or demonic" (*JP* 2, 263). Either humor is directed toward the truth of its own subjectivity, which will lead to the religious, or toward a madness like Don Quixote's, which consists in having an absolute relation to the relative: "Don Quixote is the prototype of a subjective lunacy," which is comic in its extreme contradiction (*CUP1*, 195).

Humor seems to play a double role in *Postscript*.[87] On the one hand, humor is said to lie on the boundary between the ethical and the religious, where the humorist evokes a contradiction by setting the God-idea into conjunction with other things, but does not personally have a passionate relation to God (*CUP1*, 505). On the other hand, humor is described as "the final *terminus a quo* in relation to the Christian-religious," which "terminates immanence within immanence" and as "the last stage in existence-inwardness before faith" (*CUP1*, 291). It seems, then, that humor may function as a boundary category at two levels, between the ethical and the religious (the religious here being conceived in the widest sense as including Christianity, but understood mainly in terms of immanent religiousness or Religiousness A), and between Religiousness A and Religiousness B or Christianity[88]:

Thus humor is advanced as the final *terminus a quo* in relation to the Christian-religious. In modern scholarship, humor has become the highest after faith. That is, faith is the immediate, and through speculative thought, which goes beyond faith, humor is reached. This is a general confusion in all systematic speculative thought insofar as it wants to take Christianity under its wing. No, humor terminates immanence within immanence, still consists essentially in recollection's withdrawal out of existence into the eternal, and only then do faith and the paradoxes begin. *Humor is the last stage in existence-inwardness before faith.* . . . Humor is not faith but is before faith, is not after faith or a development of faith. In other words, Christianly understood there is no going beyond faith, because faith is the highest—for an existing person—which has been adequately developed above. Even when humor wants to try its hands at the paradoxes, it is not faith. Humor does not take in the suffering aspect of the paradox or the ethical aspect of faith but only the amusing aspect. It is, namely, a suffering, faith's martyrdom even in times of peace, to have the eternal happiness of one's soul related to something over which the understanding despairs. (*CUP1*, 291–2)

The religious individual is absolutely engaged in his relationship with God (*CUP1*, 508). In order to reach this state the individual must cut off "every teleological relation to what is directed outward" (*CUP1*, 506). If he still desires to accomplish some *telos* in the world, he cannot be absolutely engaged with his relationship with God. The individual achieves this severing through reflection. "In an absolute passion, the passionate person is at the peak of his concrete subjectivity by having reflected himself out of every external relativity" (*CUP1*, 509). Individual teleological relationships can be severed by thinking about the limitation of an object of desire. But to sever every such relationship requires reflecting on a determinant of totality, something that comprehends the limitation of all the objects a person might find desirable. If one must reach the point of realizing that all outward teleological relations are unworthy because they are less than God, then the desire to have an object one could desire would be a desire for God (or else despair).

The humorist is not as such related to God. Thus he is said to reflect with sad longing (*CUP1*, 552n), for melancholy is the state of not finding possibilities that one can desire. In this way melancholy longing brings the individual into a relationship with God; God becomes the object of desire.

Initially the individual desires various unworthy objects. To look for one's happiness through a relationship with something that is less than God is idolatry. To be totally caught up with idols is to be totally guilty. The humorist is thus totally guilty before God. Another way to look at humor is to see it as a reflection on "the totality of guilt-consciousness in the single individual before God in relation to an eternal happiness" (*CUP1*, 554). Humor and religiousness reflect on the same things, but religiousness applies subjective seriousness to the thought. Humor, on the other hand, reflects on the totality of guilt, "but in turn revokes it" (554). This revocation lies in placing oneself under the category of the species: The humorist does not see himself as a guilty individual, but as one of a group of individuals (a species), all of whom are in the same plight. As the religious individual passionately desires God, he recognizes that he is in relationship with God. He moves from a consciousness of sin to a consciousness of forgiveness, and knows he is no longer in the state he is leaving behind. Thus "the consciousness of sin definitely belongs to the consciousness of the forgiveness of sin" (*CUP1*, 524).

Humor on the boundary of the religious comes close to the religious and is often confused with it inasmuch as the humorist, like the religious individual, perceives suffering and its persistence as belonging essentially to existence rather than being something accidental, such as misfortune, which one seeks aesthetically to overcome. "In our day, people have frequently enough been inclined to mistake the humorous for the religious, even for the Christian-religious, and this is why I try to return to it everywhere" (*CUP1*, 451). But in Climacus' opinion the humorist on this level does not comprehend the significance of suffering beyond this bare apprehension of its relevance to existence (*CUP1*, 447). Instead of seeking an explanation of suffering, the humorist takes the opposite course of revoking its significance in jest by making light of the existential plight. Although the humorist, in perceiving the essentiality of suffering in existence, gives more significance to existence than the ironist, existence for the humorist nevertheless lacks the significance it has for the religious individual. This is because the humorist, like the ironist, essentially opts for a retirement out of existence and into the eternal by way of recollection (*CUP1*, 242).

The self-transformation necessary for religious (and ethical) transitions involves describing oneself in two perspectives simultaneously: Sliding between the two perspectives and holding the elements in tension. M. Jamie Ferreira illuminates the former with Gestalt shifts and the latter with metaphor (Ferreira 1991). John Lippitt argues convincingly that the two forms of the comic that Climacus places as boundary zones, irony and humor, fulfill this role in relation to the ethical and the religious, respectively. Antti Mattila explains that one of the best ways to cultivate one's ability to reframe is humor, as reframing plays an important role in humor (Lippitt 2000b, chap. 6; Mattila 2001, 92–94).

In the boundary-zones of humor (and irony), one does not embrace the higher position, but makes some attempt to identify with it imaginatively. Ferreira maintains that leaps are not sudden, but rather the realization that a particular vision has taken hold, such that it has become "so real that it seems to be the only way to see it" (Ferreira 1991, 110, 166). But I think this view blurs the importance of the choice of a higher suffering, which constitutes the higher level on which Kierkegaard repeatedly insists. A better explanation is provided by one of Kierkegaard's pseudonyms:

> As soon as I am outside my religious understanding, I feel as an insect with which children are playing must feel, because life seems to have dealt with me so unmercifully; as soon as I am inside my religious understanding, I understand that precisely this has absolute meaning for me. Hence, that which in one case is a dreadful jest is in another sense the most profound earnestness. (SWL, 365)

It is the humorist's sensitivity to both jest and suffering that allows him realize, once he is ready to think of himself as guilty instead of subsuming guilt under the species, that his life is "a dreadful jest." Quidam makes sense of his suffering by reinterpreting along religious lines the dreadful jest that represents his life.

HUMOR AS A MASK

Humor can also function as the mask or incognito of a religious person, for the religious person does not want to secularize religion by expressing it outward. The attitude of religiousness to the humorous is the following: Religiousness can see the humorous as comic because it knows a way out (CUP1, 521). But if religiousness allows itself to dwell on the fact that it knows a way out, then that fact becomes the thing that makes the religious person happy, rather than his relationship with God. Because religiousness turns away from this particular possible object of desire as it passionately turns toward God, it perceives "the humorous as comic" only as "continuously disappearing" (CUP1, 521–2).

The comic makes itself felt in opposition to the religious "in the same degree as the negative . . . is allowed to be once and for all and thereby sufficient" (CUP1, 524–5). To the extent that someone who has made the religious move desires to rest on his laurels as someone who has succeeded in realizing the totality of guilt (thus treating the past realization of guilt as good for the present and future, once and for all), he now implicitly sees himself as someone who has escaped the plight depicted by humor. Thus, to that extent, he relates to the contradiction of humor as a person who knows the way out, that is, he sees it as comical.

We are told that the person defined by hidden inwardness *must* discover the comic (*CUP1*, 555). This requires a twofold explanation: First, why he must discover the contradiction (which is necessary for there to be the comic); and second, why he must discover the point of view which makes the contradiction painless (why he must have in mind a way out, why he must see the realization of guilt as something that has presented itself once and for all). The thing that makes certain that the religious individual will discover the contradiction is that "he does not dare to express it [his religiousness] in the outer world, because it is thereby secularized" (*CUP1*, 508). The problem is that in expressing what is inward, one is not able to preserve that inwardness. The danger pertains to the way one appears to other people: In order to safeguard and ensure the inwardness of his suffering and his relationship with God, the religious individual sets up a veil between himself and others (*CUP1*, 506).

Yet, "as long as the struggle and the suffering in inwardness continue he will not succeed in hiding his inwardness completely" (*CUP1*, 550-1). One does not simply switch from caring about the opinion of some party to caring about God. What one can do is switch from wanting to express one's inwardness directly to expressing it indirectly. The way this is done is to employ the assistance of the humorous (550-1). The religious sufferer puts a veil between others and himself by employing humor: "Humor becomes his incognito" (*CUP1*, 508). Instead of expressing his relationship with God before other persons, he simply brings to mind the other aspect of what he feels makes him different from other people—that they are all looking for happiness through a relationship with something less than God. He thus makes a remark whose point is that people are stuck here in this world with nothing to desire but things that are less than God. He still feels that he has something different, his inwardness, which he expresses but indirectly (*CUP1*, 501).

The religious sufferer hides his inwardness and "thereby discovers the comic" (*CUP1*, 508). Once he has brought to mind the contradiction that people are looking for happiness among things that are incapable of making them happy, he has the opportunity to relate to that contradiction comically, for he believes that he has a way out, that he has this relationship with God. We are told: "The comic emerges through the relation of hidden inwardness to the surrounding world as the religious person hears and sees what produces a comic effect when it is joined together with his inward passion" (*CUP1*, 511). Part of this quotation does not seem to be in accord with what we have been saying, but the trick is that the religious person *qua* humorist "cooperates in shaping the situation" (*CUP1*, 551n). What the religious individual comes to hear and see is his own remark; the remark is in his environment because he put it there. But the religious individual does not take the time to comprehend the comic (*CUP1*, 508). If he would take the time, he would be seeking his happiness in the fact that he is unlike others, and he would no longer be related to God.

How does the individual move from the position of feeling different from other people (for the humor here is an indirect expression of his relationship with God) to being passionately concerned with maintaining a relationship with God? How does he come to realize that relating to humor comically is a temptation? It is through the recognition that he too is drawn toward finding his happiness in the world about him, rather than in relationship with God; he is like the people to whom he feels superior. "Hidden inwardness must also discover the comic, which is present not because the religious man is different from others but because . . . he is just like everyone else" (*CUP1*, 555). He is like others not merely because he is tempted to relate to the humor as if he knows a way out; he has actually been thinking that he knows a way out all along. It is his desire to express this way out, to express his God-relationship, which started the whole process. Humor as such only pertains to the species, but the religious individual makes the move of realizing that he, a member of this species, is at this very moment doing the same thing as all the other members. It is not simply a matter of algebra, but of introspection. Humor prompts him to look at his own reality, and he then finds that he is as guilty as others for seeking his happiness through a relationship with something less than God (i.e., through the fact that he has a God-relationship). Once again he is in a position to use humor as the starting point for turning to God.

For Climacus, "the highest earnestness of the religious life is distinguishable by jest" (*CUP1*, 235). Whereas jest is the expression of the humorist's revocation of the decisive significance of existence, there is yet another form of jesting that serves as a sign of the utmost earnestness toward existence, which Climacus calls "holy jest" (*CUP1*, 462, 471–2). This form of jest comes to expression in humor that is the incognito of the religious individual. Characteristic of the religious personality, as Climacus understands it, is a consciousness of impotence or the inability to do anything by oneself to transform one's existence into conformity with the ideal (*CUP1*,

461, 484). In the world, however, it may appear that one has the power to do many things. This contradictory state of affairs occasions the discovery of the comic by the religious individual, for that person is able to enjoy the amusement of apparently having the power of accomplishing everything while inwardly understanding this to be an illusion (*CUP1*, 462). This comic discrepancy between the religious individual's outward appearance and actual inner condition makes itself felt in a variety of ways, since the art of the religious individual is precisely to live so that "no one will detect anything in him." As Climacus sees it, true religiousness consists in secret inwardness and has its criterion in invisibility (*CUP1*, 475).[89]

Like the knight of faith in *Fear and Trembling*, the religious individual looks and acts like others, but this is an incognito whereby inwardness is humorously concealed in order to protect it from direct expression and the taint of worldliness (*CUP1*, 500).[90] Like the knight of faith, the religious individual remains in the world rather than withdrawing from it, but this apparent worldliness on his part becomes an incognito, or "veil," behind which the inward suffering and God-relation of true religiousness are ensured and safeguarded. The religious individual is also active in the world, but this outward activity is likewise transformed into an inward matter in the admission before God that one can do nothing by oneself (*CUP1*, 506).

Using humor as an indirect mode of expression, the religious individual appears outwardly to be a humorist, but inwardly is not. On the contrary, Climacus claims that the religious individual is "infinitely higher than" and "qualitatively different from" the humorist (*CUP1*, 501). One crucial difference between the two is that the religious individual is earnest, that is, existentially committed to the religious ideal, whereas the humorist is not. Here again a characteristic noted earlier with respect to the subjective thinker comes into play, namely, that jest functions as the sign of earnestness and, in this instance, that humor functions as a sign of religiousness in the religious individual with humor as an incognito. For the humorist, jest and humor signify nothing but themselves, or more precisely, they signify the opposite of humor in the religious individual, namely, that the humorist does not maintain a decisive relation to God in jesting, but, on the contrary, uses it as a way of distancing herself from such a relation. Thus, the humorist may reflectively comprehend the various movements of the religious sphere, such as resignation, suffering, and the consciousness of guilt, but in an impatient, childlike manner revokes them in the non-serious form of jest. By contrast, the religious individual with humor as an incognito uses humor or holy jest precisely as a means to preserve and give indirect expression to the forms of pathos in his life.

Humor therefore may function in several different ways and on more than one level as an existential art. It should be noted, however, that Climacus restricts the expression of humor as an incognito of the religious to Religiousness A or immanent religiousness, which serves as the *terminus a quo*, or presupposition, for defining Religiousness B or the Christian paradoxical religiousness: "Religiousness with humor as its incognito is still not Christian religiousness" (*CUP1*, 532n; see 534–5, 556). In Climacus' opinion, humor is incapable of dealing with the "decisive Christian category of becoming a Christian," that is, the consciousness of sin, because humor falls essentially under the category of recollection: It is "always a revocation" of existence "into the eternal by recollection backward," whereas Christianity is "the direction forward" that continually moves toward becoming and being a Christian (*CUP*, 602). Here Climacus is in essential agreement with another pseudonym, the humorist Constantin Constantius, who associates humor with recollection rather than the forward movement of repetition. Climacus' point is that humor assumes an essential relation to the eternal that is denied in Christianity on the basis of original sin, and thus it is an inappropriate category for the expression of Christian inwardness.

"Now we are standing at the boundary," says Climacus. "The religiousness that is hidden inwardness is *eo ipso* inaccessible for comic interpretation. It cannot have the comic outside itself because it is *hidden* inwardness and consequently cannot come into contradiction with anything." Hidden inwardness contains the contradiction that humor dominates as something lower than itself. "In this way it is absolutely armed against the comic or is protected by the comic against the comic" (*CUP1*, 522). In the conclusion of *Postscript*, humor is said to be justified regarding Christianity only when the latter becomes aesthetic, that is when it is confused with outward expressions, or when it is confused with paganism: "The existence-sphere of paganism is essentially the aesthetic" (*CUP1*, 432n), says Climacus, and direct recognizability is paganism as well (*CUP1*, 600). Authentic religiousness is not to be laughed at:

> If anyone wants to laugh at this, let him do so, but I would still like to see the esthetician or the dialectician who is able to show the slightest trace of the comic in the suffering of religiousness. If there is anything I have studied thoroughly, from A to Z, it is the comic. It is just for this reason that I know that the comic is excluded in religious suffering, that it is inaccessible to the comic. (*CUP1*, 483)

This implies that the attitude of the religious person to suffering is such that he construes suffering as more tragic than comic. In other words, incongruities can be seen as tragic or comic, and the religious person is ultimately compelled to the former interpretation: "Suffering is precisely the consciousness of contradiction, which therefore is tragically assimilated with pathos into the religious person's consciousness, and thereby the comic is excluded" (*CUP1*, 483). Also in *Stages on Life's Way*, Quidam "sees the comic, but with passion, so that of that he chooses the tragic": "This is the religious," Frater Taciturnus adds, something that the Frater, a humorist who sees the tragic and the comic in equilibrium, cannot understand (*SLW*, 434). Choosing the tragic means reflecting on suffering rather than on the way out of it, that is, viewing one's life in terms of suffering and guilt as totality-categories. Hence, a truly religious person "does not consider the comic as the highest" level (*CUP1*, 462).

We are now in a position to understand the role of humor in the good life as the mature Kierkegaard sees it. The comic power is essentially humor because the contradiction that humor dominates is the highest range of the comic. Humor is thus Kierkegaard's most important category of the comic, although humor is, properly speaking, an ideal balance of the pathetic and the comic. The humorist moves beyond the ethical life-view and comprehends major dimensions of the religious stance, but he does not become a religious person. Nevertheless, all humor is at bottom made possible by the very features of human life that make the religious life possible. The categories of guilt, suffering, and God are essential for the humorist. This is why humor as a life-view constitutes a lower existence bordering on religion or Christianity, a steppingstone for the leap toward faith, and a mask for the religious person. Humor as a life-view is the highest life-view attained by thought, solely through human effort: It is the highest philosophy as lived thought exemplified by Socrates. But it is lower than Christianity, which for Kierkegaard is the sole viable life-view after God's revelation, and which, according to his final view of the matter, is inaccessible to humor. Hence, humor has no place in the good life, according to Kierkegaard, but living in humor is the second-best life, which, moreover, could be helpful in attaining to the best life.

CONCLUDING REMARKS: THE COMIC AND HUMOR IN THE KIERKEGAARDIAN GOOD LIFE

The comic is not Kierkegaard's last word in life or beyond. The comic belongs only to the temporal because all contradictions are canceled in eternity (*Pap*. V B 60, 137; *CA*, 154).[91] Not only is the comic limited *to* life, it is limited *in* life (*EO1*, 41–42).[92] First, the comic, or one of its forms, is not the highest stage in the teleology: Ridiculing Hegelian philosophy for giving "predominance to the comic," Kierkegaard seeks to relegate the comic to the religious (*CUP1*, 512); "in regard to earnestness," Vigilius Haufniensis asserts, "he will know how not to tolerate any joking" (*CA*, 128), a view that is echoed by Climacus (*CUP1*, 483). Second, the comic is subsumable under the tragic not only in the hierarchy of life's stages, but within each stage as well. Within these limitations, however, the comic, and its highest power, humor, fulfill a crucial role in the Kierkegaardian good life, which I purport, first, to explain, and, second, to assess according to both originality and feasibility.

THE COMIC'S ROLE IN INWARDNESS

The ethical task Kierkegaard assigns to each individual is to become a self. But as the self is defined in religious terms, it cannot be brought about by human means alone. Becoming a self requires faith. Once faith enters the picture, the task becomes "simultaneously to relate oneself absolutely to the absolute *telos* (end, goal) and relatively to relative ends" (*CUP1*, 525; see 431). The absolute *telos* is eternal life or "eternal happiness." The religious life is defined as deepening one's inwardness without exterior signs. Subjectivity and upbuilding are the truth-tests of truth, in the sense that living in the truth is living the religious life.

The general movement of progress from the aesthetic life to the religious is through suffering, which creates as its counter-force the comic. The comic corrects the mood, thus enabling the choice of a higher level of suffering or a new pathos, which again is corrected by the comic. This movement culminates with the choice of the tragic over the comic in the balance between the two, which defines the inwardness of the humorist. This choice is faith, which concludes the role of the dialectic or philosophy in its new role, leading the individual to the place where he can worship God rather than idols. To understand the role of the comic in the deepening of inwardness that leads to Christianity, the following points about the comic should be clarified:

1. *The comic reflects and expresses the relative attitude toward relative ends.* As these ends change when one advances, the comic is the main indicator of one and another's situation in Kierkegaard's hierarchical stages. Relating absolutely to relative ends is comical because it involves the self-contradiction of inconsistency. Relative ends should be conquered as jests, that is, they should create in the individual a comical reaction as the appropriate attitude to something lower. According to the sort of comical reaction an individual has or discerns in another's communication, he can

infer the place he and the other person occupy in the teleology as described by the stages of life.

As a higher viewpoint enters into an individual's existence, his former evaluation loses its significance and everything is seen in a new light. The content of the individual's previous experience is fully retained when a new factor enters or when a new stage begins. However, each time this occurs, the total content is seen in a new perspective. This movement from lower to higher viewpoints is the law of repetition directed against Hegel who, according to Kierkegaard's interpretation of his work, maintains that each new, opposing element eliminates the preceding one (*JP* 3, 2858/*Pap.* II A 49).

The individual in the new existential stage maintains a relation with the previous stage by perceiving it, its *telos* and the suffering it entails, as comical. This is important for Kierkegaard, because the task of living includes not only an absolute relation to the absolute, but also a relative relation toward the relative. The relative relation is secured by the comical, which reflects the inferior position of that which has been superseded as a former *telos*. If severing the relation to the finite is blasphemous for Kierkegaard, the comical, under the guise of humor, acquires a theological importance: "Being earnest about anything else than oneself—realizing one's spirit—is comical. On the other hand, whoever has become earnest at the right place will prove the soundness of his spirit precisely by his ability to treat all other things sentimentally as well as jokingly" (*CA*, 150).

2. *The contrast between the inward and the outward creates the comic.* This makes it the sign of a deepened inwardness, which is tantamount to religiosity. Religious suffering stems from the inability of the religious person to express the eternal in the temporal. Religious suffering can be discerned by being solely in inwardness, part of it is created because one is not able to convert pain into perfect joy, and part of it is created because of the uncertainty over the relationship with God (*CUP1*, 451–5). Kierkegaard's first requirement of the religious person is to renounce the world. Renouncing the world should not be noticeable; hence, the requirement to join the world externally and hide the relationship to the absolute. But the contrast between inwardness and outwardness creates the comic, and "the most perfect the contrast of form, the greatest the inwardness . . ." (*SV* 9, 202; quoted in Pattison 1992, 66). The comic that is created by the contrast is the indication of the depth of one's inwardness (*SLW*, 246).

3. *The comic is reflective: It creates a distance from the self that is necessary for progressing.* A situation that contains a contradiction creates suffering, but when the individual reflects on the situation, he sees it with disinterestness, and can thus notice that the situation is also comical: "Reflection

is disinterested: all knowledge is therefore disinterested (mathematical, aesthetic, metaphysical knowledge)" (*Pap.* IV B 1 147), and the comic has "the disinterestedness of metaphysics" (*SLW*, 446). In the comic situation, "reflection is in motion within" (*EO1*, 263). The way out envisioned by the comic is kept *in mente*, that is, confined to the level of thought (*CUP1*, 516). For example, the comic takes no account of the difficulties in actually adopting the way out from suffering offered by religion.

Recall that the difference between the tragic and the comic lies in the interpretation of the misrelation, whether it is seen as the real comparing itself with the ideal or as the ideal comparing itself with the real: "When the subjective thinker turns his face toward the idea, his interpretation of the misrelation is pathos-filled; when he turns his back to the idea, allowing it to shine from behind into the same misrelation, his interpretation is comic" (*CUP1*, 90). The first magnifies the finite and therefore sees it as tragic, whereas the second belittles it and therefore sees it as comical. To step out of the impotence of suffering, one needs perspective. Tragedy confronts the situation as an actual challenge, it "has the interest of actuality" (*SLW*, 446), but at the same time, it sees no way of meeting it. There is no (human) resolution to the contradiction. Alternatively, perspective is gained through a distance from the self, which is the outcome of reflecting on the situation. Reflection discloses the contradiction in the situation and reveals the discrepancy between the real and the ideal to be also comical.

4. *The comic is imaginative: It enables us to "envision" a new situation, which is a necessary preliminary stage to change.* The comic provides a glimpse of a higher view that ultimately lightens the predicament in which the individual is caught. Kierkegaard rejects the notion of the supremacy of thought, and emphasizes the harmony of thought, fantasy, and feeling. To be able to see a way out at all, imaginative reflection has to envisage it. John Lippitt shows how important the role of the comic is, in the guise of irony and humor, in viewing or imagining the situation differently (Lippitt 2000b, 104–20). One has to imagine or envision something, and be able to shift perspectives between the current situation and the imagined situation as a precondition of such a willed change as the "leap" to the ethical or the religious.

5. *The comic, born from suffering, also mitigates it: It allows one to remain in the suffering, which is the precondition of choosing a higher suffering.* "The more one suffers, the more . . . has one a sense for the comic" (*SLW*, 231). Because the comic envisions pain in relation to eternity, Thomas Oden explains, it changes the perspective we have of the suffering contradiction:

Comic consciousness looks from the outside to turn the internal suffering itself into a new configuration by contradiction. Comedy thus becomes the reverse side of suffering. It objectifies and transmutes inward discord by a reversal of perspective. It views pain in relation to eternity. (Oden 2004, 31)

The ironic individual suffers from his separation from reality, whereas the humorist is directly attuned to the pathos of pain. Hence, wherever suffering exists, the seeds of comedy are planted. The parry of jest always springs from pain. With every quip goes a little piece of the humorist's guts (JP 2, 260). Religiously speaking, comic perception is freed from idolatry to see beyond it toward eternity and eternal happiness. The comic detaches itself from absolute seriousness about human incongruities. It maintains distance through the perspective of eternity. Humor provides a greater detachment than the ethical because it can grasp the relativity of human values in relation to eternity. Comic perception frees one to transcend tragic seriousness by beholding it finite, hence, not absolute: "Finite common sense wants to interpret immediacy as comic but in doing that becomes comic itself, because what presumably is supposed to justify its comic effects is that it easily knows the way out, but the way out that it knows is even more comic" (CUP1, 520). In uncovering the seriousness of finitude, comic awareness points beyond finitude.

The absence or falsification of mood has the comical as its enemy (CA, 14n). The comic purifies the pathos-filled emotions so that one's pathos is not vehement and one is not blind in it (SLW, 366), like the "revivalist," who should be differentiated from the "knight of hidden inwardness" (CUP1, 512). This is reminiscent of Shaftesbury's criticism of the "enthusiast," whose enthusiasm should be corrected by ridicule. The comic also is substantiated by "the pathos-filled emotions" (SLW, 367). Climacus stresses the need for the comic and pathos to be in balance because "the pathos that is not safeguarded by the comic is an illusion; the comic that is not safeguarded by pathos is immaturity," and "a pathos that excludes the comic is therefore a misunderstanding, is not pathos at all" (CUP1, 87, 89). The comic balances the tragic and purifies suffering by differentiating between suffering created by external sources and religious suffering, so that one is stable and strong enough to choose a higher level of suffering.

6. *The comic is brought about by fear and dismay, which are important steps in upbuilding.* Whereas another, and perhaps more important step in upbuilding, is love, dismay is the first step to the upbuilding (WL, 199–212): "Where there is nothing at all dismaying and no dismay, there is nothing at all edifying and no edification" (CD, 102). Dismay is facing up to the unpleasant truth that not all is quite right in life. It shows that self-knowledge, a moral knowledge that can make a distinction between good and evil, is involved in upbuilding.

Terror is also important in the Kierkegaardian progress. In *Postscript*, Climacus describes the transition into higher existence-spheres in terms of terror, "otherwise, the upbuilding is make-believe" (*CUP1*, 258). Irony and humor, as forms of life, also are intermediary stages between the aesthetical and the ethical and between the ethical and the religious, respectively. The comic as irony and humor plays an important role in the leap between the stages, which is not incompatible with its description as terror, as "one of the paradoxes that life requires us to hold in tension" (Lippitt 2000b, 168; see 164–8). Additionally, contemporary research has shown that terror itself creates the comic as a necessary relief (Roeckelein 2002, 135–6, 177ff), and we know, at least since Herbert Spencer and Sigmund Freud formulated the release and relief theory of humor, that the comic releases tension and thereby fear (Spencer 1860; Freud 1905).

Kierkegaard envisions another way to overcome fears. In the introduction to *The Sickness unto Death*, Anti-Climacus deems "jest" to be that which the "natural man" catalogs as appalling. To regard something as "nothing" is "jest":

> The Christian has gained a courage that the natural man does not know, and he gained this courage by learning to fear something even more horrifying. This is the way a person always gains courage, when he fears a greater danger, he always has the courage to face a lesser one; when he is exceedingly afraid of one danger, it is as if the others did not exist at all. (*SUD*, 8–9)

One smiles at that which has been conquered as a jest. The comic taints the attitude toward previous fears for the individual who has climbed the teleology.

7. *The comic is the negative in Kierkegaard's negative epistemology and theology.* The role of reflective reason, which uses the comic as a tool, is largely negative for Kierkegaard. When introducing his negative theology, Kierkegaard refers to suffering, guilt, and sin as the negative, and to happiness and joy as the positive. Nevertheless, at the beginning of *Postscript*, the comic is the negative and pathos is the positive: "In his existence-relation to the truth, the existing subjective thinker is just as negative as positive, has just as much of the comic as he essentially has of pathos" (*CUP1*, 80). Elsewhere in *Postscript*, Climacus refers to humor too as the negative (*CUP1*, 501).

One can approach the absolute only negatively, by renouncing the world. Just as resignation determines the individual's absolute orientation toward the absolute *telos*, the continuance of suffering is the guarantee that the individual is in position and keeps himself in position (*CUP1*, 443). However, not all suffering is religious suffering. As there is nothing comical in religious suffering, according to Climacus, perhaps the way to know that the suffering is religious is to realize that it has nothing to do with the relative (*CUP1*, 483). Suffering created by an outward relation (the relative) yields a different kind of comic than religious suffering, which is entirely internal. The main indication one has of advancing toward the religious, given Kierkegaard's criterion of truth and the solitude of the individual, is the quality of the comic he experiences. Thus, the comic plays a unique role in Kierkegaard's epistemology and theology.

8. *A sense of the comic is the opposite of despair, and despair is that which impedes one from becoming a self.* The tension between the poles of the duality, which constitutes every human existence, is the postulated presupposition for the authentic realization of existence and the condition of possibility for despair. Kierkegaard's view is that this tension must be maintained. Ambiguity as the possibility of despair must unceasingly be present, but its actuality, despair itself, must unceasingly be rejected. Kierkegaard insists that despair is precisely the attempt to ignore the "possibility of despair," that is, to repress the tension. However, this attempt does not succeed because the repression does not conquer or abolish the antitheses, but merely removes them from consciousness.

At the end of a long discussion of humor in *Postscript*, Climacus says, "all despair is a kind of ill temper" (*CUP1*, 554). In his essay "Humour and the Irascible Soul," Alastair Hannay suggests that Climacus could have used ill-humor, for "surely all that is intended is some sort of contrast between a sense of the comic and despair as two distinct and opposed attitudes to it all" (Hannay 2003, 148). The idea that the comic is the opposite of both despair and ill-temper is as old as Sotion, Seneca's teacher (first century AD), who contrasted the attitudes of the laughing and the weeping philosophers, Democritus and Heraclitus, with anger (*ira*) at the world.[93] Recall also that Shaftesbury views atheism, which represents the sin of *acedia* or disgust with God—Kierkegaardian ultimate despair—as, nothing but ill-humor: "I very much question," Shaftesbury writes, "whether anything besides ill-humor can be the cause of atheism" (*Letter*, 3). Shaftesbury maintains that melancholy and ill-humor distort our vision of God, for in a state of dread and anxiety we cannot have a true conception of Him.

For Kierkegaard, it is despair that construes contradiction as tragic because despair concentrates on the finite: ". . . the tragic interpretation sees the contradiction and despairs over the way out" (*CUP1*, 516). Despair in its despairing "knows no way out, does not know the contradiction canceled" (*CUP1*, 520), and interprets thus the contradiction as tragic.

In contradistinction, imagination is always infinitizing. The comic, which involves both imagination and reflection, is brought about by looking at the finite from infinity's point of view, as is evident also from the definitions of irony and humor (*CUP1*, 502, 291). Because the comic involves the infinite, it is the antidote to despair, which is brought about by finitude's shortsightedness.

9. *Kierkegaard teaches the nature of the comic and its correct use explicitly and at length*. His is an edifying discourse on the comic. Alastair Hannay remarks on *Postscript* that the work says so much about humor that it might be read as much as a disquisition on humor as a humorous disquisition (Hannay 2003, 17). The edifying discourse discloses an ethic of the comic and a guide for using it, which leads one to the true *telos*: "If you worship here, you worship God," instead of an idol (*CUP1*, 491).

10. *Kierkegaard teaches how to laugh by its opposite, by using one's fear of being ridiculous*. The concern with the legitimacy of the comic brings Kierkegaard to devise an ethics of the comic, whose purpose is to secure an edifying role for the comic. The edifying roles the comic plays differ according to the kinds of legitimacy opened to the comic. If the legitimacy lies in the hierarchy of the stages—the higher being justified in making the lower ridiculous—the comic is edifying in its siding with the higher stage. If the legitimacy lies in the comic being tied up with the tragic or pathos-filled, and in the jest with earnestness, the comic is edifying in serving the tragic. The evasion from suffering the comic provides fortifies the person without sabotaging the choice of suffering, which is the way to its healing. By keeping the pathos in check and avoiding the ridicule of sentimentality or enthusiasm, the comic allows for choosing a higher level of suffering from the right reasons. The former edifying role of the comic corresponds to Plato's idea, according to which the ridiculous person does not know himself (*Philebus* 48–50), and the latter is Shaftesbury's view, according to which the comic keeps enthusiasm in check. In both cases, the comic is edifying, and thus legitimate, when it amends ridicule.

The sanction for an illegitimate comic apprehension is ridicule. There is no subjective arbitrariness in the comic. If a person thinks something said is comical when it is not legitimately so, he is being ridiculed instead of the target of his laughter. Because all human beings fear ridicule (*PV*, 65, 68), Kierkegaard implies that this sanction is strong enough to demolish the attack and disarm the attacker.

In most of the cases where ridicule is advanced as a sanction for using the comic illegitimately, it is inferred that only the jester is aware of the ridicule, for the comic in these cases has no outward expression. "Ridicule" here is synonymous with being in the wrong, of being mistaken about an important issue, of making a fool of oneself in one's own eyes, as in the following examples: "He who does not constantly dare to submit his earnestness to the test of jest is stupid and comical" (*JP* 2, 1743); "[Socrates'] sense of the comic was just as great as his ethical pathos—therefore he was secured against becoming ridiculous in his pathos" (*SLW*, 366). In the imaginary construction of *Stages*, Quidam suggests that the hold "the comic from the outside" can have on a person is an indication that the person's suffering is not religious because it is related to the outside instead of being confined solely to inwardness. If pathos originates in another's actions, one can become comical by another's actions or by a reverse of the situation; whereas, if the comical originates in oneself as a reaction to inward suffering, a person is inadvertently protected from being comical: "I have not established my life on her word and gown. That is why I have perceived the comic from the very beginning, and precisely for that reason I can never in all eternity become comic" (*SLW*, 367). To be secured against the comic in that way is a characteristic of the legitimate comic: "The religious person must discover the comic, if he actually is religious, because otherwise he himself becomes comic" (*CUP1*, 463). This device applies till the very end of the comic power, when the religiosity of hidden inwardness (Religiousness A) is "protected by the comic against the comic" (*CUP1*, 522).

LAUGHING WELL IS LIVING WELL

Together, the 10 points about the comic just mentioned lead to the following considerations.

1. The comic emerges from a retrospective view that presupposes a higher point of view. Only a superior life-view can legitimately laugh at an inferior one. It is ultimately from the Christian point of view that Kierkegaard laughs. "Life can be interpreted only after it has been experienced," he writes in the journals; "it is true what [Hegel's] philosophy says that life can only be understood backward, but it must be lived forward" (*JP* 1, 1025, 1030). The legitimate comic implies looking backward from higher spheres to lower ones. The more one looks backward, comprehends, and conquers in jest, the more comic consciousness one has gained, the more inwardness one has, and the more one has advanced in existence.

2. The comic corrective is the major corrective available for Kierkegaard's negative theology and negative epistemology. The comic (all that has been conquered in jest, all that is beneath one) is the main indication an individual has of advancing, which is described as choosing pathos, stabilizing it with the comic, and choosing a new pathos. This movement is

reminiscent of the Shaftesburean moralist, who is sensible of this rhythm of subjectivity, which takes off and checks itself, switching from exaltation to self-criticism.

3. The comic seems to be Kierkegaard's most effective reflective tool. After one suffers the tragic, one sees and understands the comic. The tragic is felt, the comic is thought. The individual suffers the tragic and sees the comic "with his understanding" (SWL, 327). The first entry in category A of the Papers (April 15, 1834) reads:

> In order to see one light determinately we always need another light. For if we imagined ourselves in total darkness and then a single spot of light appeared, we would be unable to determine what it is, since we cannot determine spatial proportions in darkness. Only when there is another light is it possible to determine what it is, since we cannot determine spatial proportions in darkness. Only when there is another light is it possible to determine the position of the first in relation to the other. (JP 2, 2240/Pap. I A 1)

This entry can be interpreted to mean that Kierkegaard has perceived that no position or point of view can ever be determined solely by itself; it can be more explicitly determined only in relation to another position or another point of view. I suggest that the comic plays the role of the second point of view for Kierkegaard, without which one would be devoid of any sense of proportion and capacity for orientation.

4. The comic entertains an essential relation with the truth, which is at the root of both Kierkegaard's ethics of the comic and his later view, following the Corsair affair,[94] that whoever is in the truth will be ridiculed. The latter is an inversion of Shaftesbury's formula that whatever is true can withstand ridicule. Kierkegaard differs from Shaftesbury in that he prefers to restrict the comic to its legitimate use as secured by his ethics of the comic. As was shown in the last chapter, Shaftesbury opposes the idea that the comic be regulated, either ethically or politically. Unlike Shaftesbury, who allows religion to be ridiculed, Kierkegaard and his pseudonyms forbid it. For example, Vigilius says that "in regard to earnestness he [the religious man] will know how not to tolerate any joking" (CA, 128), a view which is echoed in Climacus (CUP1, 483).

Yet Kierkegaard's view is similar to Shaftesbury in that the latter thinks that truth cannot be ridiculed: One can attempt to ridicule it, but truth will not withstand ridicule. This seems to be Kierkegaard's view as well, as he states that if something is (ethically, religiously) true, it is protected from the comic. Although Shaftesbury grounds this view in a vision of the universe as harmoniously beautiful and of the comic as false because it portrays the beautiful as ugly, Kierkegaard grounds his view in a vision of the human being as a synthesis of contradictions, and truth as the domination of the highest contradiction: If something is true, it has conquered the comical as lower, and in that sense, truth is protected from the comic. "Ridicule as the test of truth," in the sense that truth is immune from ridicule and whoever does not see that is ridiculous, also applies in Kierkegaard's case as the key to his ethics of the comic.

Following Kierkegaard's dispute with the satirical journal the *Corsair*, ridicule becomes the test of truth for Kierkegaard in yet another way. The mark of truth is ridicule, he believes, for "if Christ came to the world now . . . [he] would be ridiculed, treated as a mad man, but a mad man at whom one laughs . . ." Kierkegaard draws personal conclusions about this realization and considers himself from now on a martyr of laughter, whose life has been designed for illuminating Christianity (*JP* 6, 119/ *Pap.* X A 187).

5. In summarizing the role of the comic in inwardness, we turn to the problem facing Kierkegaard—how to advance inwardly when there are no external criteria one can use to measure one's progress: "That subjectivity, inwardness, is truth, is my thesis; that the pseudonymous authors relate themselves to it is easy to see, if in no other way, then in their eye for the comic" (*CUP1*, 282). The comic succeeds through three devices in fulfilling the crucial role it plays in the deepening of inwardness, which is Kierkegaard's sole criterion for advancing.

First, the comic deters. It calls on us to immunize ourselves from laughter by adopting a superior life, so that the wish voiced by Kierkegaard's pseudonym "to have the laugh always on my side" could be fulfilled (*EO1*, 41–42). Human beings can bear many things, but not ridicule, and the strategies one uses to immunize oneself from it constitute a code of conduct Francis Buckley calls "the morality of laughter" (Buckley 2003, x). I find Buckley's views on laughter highly relevant to understanding Kierkegaard's views on the comic. By highlighting comic vices, laughter teaches us a superior lifespan that is immune from ridicule. In the morality of laughter, one cannot help admiring those who have risen above laughter. Self-development is the goal of comic virtues. Laughter always sanctions a butt's comic vice and reveals a correlative comic virtue that immunizes us from laughter. Laughter offers valuable lessons on how to live, for few emotions are stronger than the fear of being a butt. In the war of laughter, contestants trade off laughter in an effort to show that comic virtue is on their side and that their opponents are ridiculous. Moral and comic virtues would be unitary if there were one highest good. A teleological account of laughter is necessarily a superiority explanation because nonsuperiority theories are agnostic about what constitutes the good life.[95]

Kierkegaard's account of laughter is unmistakably teleological, for it assumes, first, that the human being has a natural end (*telos*) through which to realize personal potential, and second, that laughter's message of superiority assists in reaching this end. It therefore fits Buckley's description of the morality of laughter, which is teleological and which presupposes universal standards in which butts are naturally visible. Moreover, like supererogatory virtue, comic laughter is unsatisfied with adherence to the negative injunctions of simple commandments. It seeks something more. It calls on us to immunize ourselves from laughter by adopting a superior life. Comic norms are capable of analysis, and we may usefully search for insights about how we should live by deliberating over what makes us laugh (81, 75–76).

Second, the legitimate comic protects from ridicule. In order to be protected from ridicule, one adheres strictly to the legitimate comic. Kierkegaard refers to this as "being protected from the comic by the comic" (*CUP1*, 522). Being protected from ridicule is important for the following reasons. First, it secures independence from public opinion. This is important as Kierkegaard assumes that to be perceived as comical by others weakens: "The public's eye cannot make him comical in all eternity." Second, being secured against becoming ridiculous in pathos, one "is free in it and needs no external support whatsoever in order to be earnest" (*SLW*, 366). One "places the comic in between in order to be able more inwardly to hold fast the ethical within himself" (*CUP1*, 505). One places the comic between himself and the world, and thereby makes sure that he himself does not become comic "through a naïve misunderstanding of his ethical passion" (*CUP1*, 506), in contradistinction to "an immediate enthusiast." The religious person, however, does not put the comic between himself and other people to laugh at them (*CUP1*, 508), but rather to protect himself.

Third, the comic gives a clear indication of an individual's inward progress. Because the individual has conquered as a jest everything that is lower, Kierkegaard's teleology of the comic warrants that he laughs at it. The comic is both sword and shield that distances the individual from himself: As a counter-force to the tragic, the comic enables reflection, purifies the emotional pathos, shields from ridicule, and stabilizes the inner equilibrium, thus helping to create the conditions for choosing the leap towards a higher level of tragic.

Buckley differentiates between the positive and the normative superiority thesis, a distinction that is helpful in clarifying Kierkegaard's view of the legitimacy of the comic and its role in the dialectic. According to the positive superiority thesis, "laughter announces and enforces a code of behavior through the jester's signal of superiority over a butt. There is not laughter without a butt, and no butt without a message about a risible inferiority." The normative superiority thesis makes the stronger claim that "our laughter communicates a true superiority and that the butt is truly an inferior person." Although the two theses tend to run together, it is important to distinguish them. Buckley considers the former far more plausible than the latter. Those who laugh are sometimes "inferior brutes, and even evil ones as well," and in such cases we should disregard the message (Buckley 2003, xi).

In *Laughter*, Henri Bergson defends both the positive and the normative superiority thesis (Bergson 1999); whereas, Thomas Hobbes subscribes to the former and rejects the latter.[96] I suggest that Kierkegaard adopts both theses, as the normative superiority thesis is the Kierkegaardian concept of the legitimate comic. Kierkegaard, I suggest, would have agreed with Buckley's assertion that "the wit might be a very inferior fellow. What he cannot do, however, is laugh if he thinks himself inferior" (Buckley 2003, xi). Kierkegaard objects to misplaced feelings of superiority, even if their origin lies in self-ignorance. His adherence to the normative superiority thesis is the basis for his denouncing illegitimate uses of the comic.

Kierkegaard's position on the comic may be summed up as the following principles. First, the comic has an objective basis in reality. As Climacus implies, there are ludicrous and non-ludicrous things; "unable to make ludicrous what is not ludicrous," he has an inordinate capacity in "making ludicrous what is ludicrous" (*CUP1*, 622). Second, when one laughs, one feels superior to the object of laughter (the positive thesis of superiority), whether the butt is or is not objectively ludicrous or inferior. Third, one should not feel superior when one is not actually superior, and it is the teleology of the spheres that determines who is inferior to whom. One must learn what to laugh at and what not to laugh at, and how to distinguish between the genuinely superior and the inferior in order to laugh well (the normative thesis of superiority). Fourth, laughing well is living well, for laughing well is being earnest about the right things, having conquered as a jest everything that is lower and maintained a relationship with it as something comical. By learning how to laugh, one upbuilds personal inwardness, and by teaching how to laugh, one helps to edify another's inwardness.

For lack of an external criterion for inner advancement, which is the only sort of progress Kierkegaard recognizes, the comic reveals itself as the main instrument of examination, correction, and evaluation the individual has recourse to when reflecting on himself, his life and experiences.

Hence, the comic becomes the primary tool of philosophy once it steps into the new existential role Kierkegaard designed for it. And humor, as the highest form of the comical, becomes the necessary corrector of pre-Kierkegaardian philosophy because from this point on reflection should incorporate the irrational in the form of doubt about its own certainty. Paraphrasing Shakespeare's melancholic Dane Prince, who claims, "there are more things in heaven and earth, / Horatio, / than are dreamt of in your philosophy" (*Hamlet*, Act II, Sc. V, 160), the philosopher known as "the melancholy Dane" writes:

> Danish Philosophy—if there ever comes to be such a thing—will be different from German philosophy in that it definitely will not begin with nothing or without any presuppositions whatso-ever or explain everything by mediating, because, on the con-trary, it begins with the proposition that there are many things between heaven and earth that no philosophy has explained. By being incorporated in philosophy, this proposition will provide the necessary corrective and will also cast a humorous-defying warmth over the whole (*JP* 3, 3299).

From now on, the philosopher should learn to laugh, as well as keep silent when the knight of faith laughs at him: According to Kierkegaard's ethics of the comic, the most earnest has the last laugh. Accepting this hierarchy involves accepting Kierkegaardian Christianity as the highest life view and the only good life for all individuals.

In conclusion, Kierkegaard's thought focuses on how the individual exists and ought to exist in the world rather than on trying to describe the world in objective terms. Laughter helps to answer the question Plato believes to be the most fundamental problem of philosophy: How ought one to live (*Republic* 352d; see Buckley 2003, 71). I suggest that Kierkegaard's position is that in teaching how to laugh, one is teaching how to live. Because one cannot teach effectively how to live, Kierkegaard forbids him-self the latter task, while indulging through pseudonyms in the former. His is an edifying discourse on the comic, which is the key to his teleological philosophy of the stages of existence: "Every existence can at once be defined and assigned to its particular sphere by knowing how it is related to the comical" (*CUP1*, 462; see 513, 520). This is why Climacus insists that "a sense for the comic" is a vital part of our humanity (*CUP1*, 304)—an assertion that is contingent on a definite view of that which makes us human.

KIERKEGAARD'S CONTRIBUTION

Every human life is religiously designed (CA, 105). With this simple statement, Vigilius and with him, Kierkegaard, closes the doors of his philosophy to all those who do not believe this is so. In the last analysis,
Kierkegaard's thought is unapologetically Christian and relies on Revelation
to provide the final perspective toward which the meaning of experience
points. Kierkegaard attacks modern Pelagian attitudes, and those familiar
with his work readily see the parallels with Augustine. Like Augustine,
Kierkegaard denies that the natural man left on his own can save himself.
This is the basis of his polemic against Romanticism and the hubris of
academic philosophy.

As Vincent McCarthy explains, the psychology that Kierkegaard
describes begins with natural man and moves through a process of self-
discovery (1978). But, for Kierkegaard only the supernatural can, and does,
overcome the disharmony in the human being and reconcile him with
himself after the natural process has been completed. Kierkegaard knows
this as a Christian, on the basis of Revelation, which he accepts, and the
grace of reconciliation, which he claims to have experienced personally.
The super-natural, however, will not be introduced into the human drama
as *deus ex machina*. Rather, for Kierkegaard, it will be portrayed as a continuation that fulfills a natural development and takes one across the threshold.
Revelation will be the grace that moves one forward after having reached
a natural terminus; it will be the understanding of that final step and a
retrospective upon one's development. Revelation, then, provides the final
perspective in which Kierkegaard's religious psychology and philosophical
anthropology operate. From within this perspective, Kierkegaard raises a
challenge to all those who seek to understand humankind—to the poets
and Romantics, to the philosophers, to the theologians and also to the
psychologists, but most of all to the individual.

I propose to assess the contribution made by Kierkegaard's views on
humor and the comic, first, by singling out the Christianization of these
notions in his thought; second, inserting his views within the history of
Christianity's attitude toward laughter; and third, situating them within
the history of philosophy by comparing them with the views of his predecessor—the other modern philosopher who entrusted humor with an
important role within the good life—the Earl of Shaftesbury.

1. Kierkegaard proposes a nonphilosophical notion of the unified personality in which the unifying factor is faith in the inherent (although God-
given) value of what we are and have. Alastair Hannay emphasizes that

Kierkegaard's concept of self belongs to a tradition that is unlikely to afford insights to students of selfhood used to a new and more secular climate of thought (Hannay 2003, 199). Kierkegaard is a dualist who believes that the realm of existence consists of the world of temporality (i.e., space-time as we experience it in our daily life) and the realm of eternity. Eternity is the realm of actual transcendence, the dwelling place of God, the goal of humans who can relate to God both in this world and after death. Because the individual is located in this bipolar situation with a foot in temporality and at least a potential foot in eternity, humans can experience anxiety and despair. Kierkegaard's view of the self grounded in his view of reality is especially relevant to the comic, for the comic is based on a contradiction which is defined in terms of the finite and the infinite.

Kierkegaard's construction of a Christian philosophy or, as he puts it, "a Christian epistemology," involves two interesting features. First, he self-consciously develops Christian ideas out of the rudiments of secular concepts. His treatment of anxiety and despair in *The Concept of Anxiety* and *The Sickness unto Death* are good examples of this strategy: The sickness unto death is a sickness that already assumes the framework of the cure. It is a sickness whose cure is faith, a sickness whose symptoms are described as forms of sin, that is, in terms that already presuppose the religious framework. The Christianization of ordinary secular concepts includes humor, as its definition involves guilt, eternity, and God. In this, Kierkegaard departs from his contemporaries' views of humor, on which he draws for other aspects of humor (Olesen 2003, 225–6, nn. 27–32; see note 86).

The process of Christianizing ordinary secular concepts, infusing them with a potency they do not appear to have at first glance, is interrelated with the second important feature of Kierkegaard's philosophy: The strategy of constructing a framework in which the move from the aesthetic to the religious is shown (albeit indirectly) to be eminently reasonable. This strategy dominates the stages. As the stages are defined also according to their relationship with the comic, this reading illuminates the comic, as well as its relation to the tragic. Sylvia Walsh has convincingly argued that the comic, the tragic, irony, and humor are essential existential categories in Kierkegaard's thought (1994). One should add that Kierkegaard's existential categories are permeated by his Christian philosophy. His is an ethical-religious view of the comic, based on a specific metaphysics and philosophical anthropology. In the same way that the phenomenon of despair has been defined as a feature of human misrelation to the eternal (in religious terms), the opposite of despair, the comic as defined by Kierkegaard, is understandable only when one adopts his philosophical anthropology.[97]

This means that, regardless of the potency of some of Kierkegaard's views (i.e., the necessary contradiction in life and therefore the necessary role the comic plays in it, the importance of the comic, irony, and humor for developing one's personality, the different life views embodied in the stages and the ways in which they contradict each other, the tendency we all have for the aesthetic and for self-deception), those who do not share Kierkegaard's metaphysics and philosophical anthropology cannot implement the comic category Kierkegaard painstakingly expounds. They may experience the comic in their lives, if it is true that suffering generates the comic, but without the religious meaning Kierkegaard attributes to suffering, the comic experienced is different from the ethical-religious category Kierkegaard advances.

2. Both Kierkegaardian views on religion—that Christianity is humorous and that Christianity is not humorous—have precursors as well as contemporary followers, as rekindled discussion about the humor in Christianity has recently shown. The young Kierkegaard's view that humor is identical with Christianity is anticipated by Hamann, Shaftesbury, and ultimately, by the religious Renaissance humanist, Desiderius Erasmus.[98] Young Kierkegaard's main influence on the theme of religion and humor, and Shaftesbury's translator and follower, Johann Georg Hamann, has made irony and humor essential categories for apprehending Christianity. Shaftesbury considered Christianity a witty and good-humored religion, best apprehended in a corresponding frame of mind.

Erasmus recovered Socrates' traditional role as defender of foolishness against the world's wisdom, pitting this image against one which many Enlightenment writers favor, that of Socrates as a supreme rationalist. Erasmus transforms the ugly Socrates into a forerunner of Christ. Although the image of Socrates as Silenus is a commonplace of Renaissance humanism, the image is made famous by Erasmus in adage 2201, *Sileni Alcibiadis*, where Socrates is deemed "the most extraordinary Silenus of all" (Erasmus 1991, 271). Moreover, Erasmus ends his *Convivium Religiosum*, in which he compares Socrates to St. Paul, by imagining that one could address him in these words: "Sancte Socrates, ora pro nobis" ("Holy Socrates, pray for us") (Erasmus 1703–6; reprint 1961, I, 683).[99]

Erasmus' treatment of the Silenus lays the groundwork for the development of Christian grotesquerie. There is beauty in a fallen, decrepit, sick, dying man. This paradoxical insight lies at the heart of Erasmian comedy, which so often blends the earthly and the heavenly in outlandish ways. In such an outlook, the serious can stand where the playful stood only an instant before. These opposites are a pair, or, as Plato suggests, "sisters"

(Plato, Letter VI 323d). The Christian application of this inversion in Erasmus sees Christ as foolish and ridiculous in the eyes of his enemies and wise in the light of heaven. Folly herself is lifted up and subsumed within eternal mystery.

Erasmus may be said to have given Europe the paradox of the Wise Fool. For although that personified oxymoron is at least as old as Socrates and Christ, and although its medieval ancestors and apologists are legion, the first modern, and most influential, appearance is as the figure of Stultitia in the *Moriae encomium* or *The Praise of Folly*.

There, for the first time, the implications of an ironic and paradoxical dramatization of Nicholas of Cusa's *docta ignorantia* are fully realized and, because of the book's popularity, given widespread currency. The mode of irony that informs the speech of Erasmus' wise fool may be described, with the same phrase that Nicholas de Cusa coins to describe the nature of learned ignorance, as a *coincidentia oppositorum*. Whether these opposites are jest and earnestness, praise and censure, or wisdom and folly, it is the *coincidentia*—the synthesis, the equipoise, the concord—that produce the quality of the irony. Walter Kaiser explains that the ability to perceive such a *coincidentia* requires a certain type of mind and a certain type of historical epoch. *Stultitia* "seems to sum up—or rather to synthesize into the Janus-head of paradox—all of the contradictory tendencies of her age" (Kaiser 1963, 24–25). By the end of the *Praise of Folly*, Erasmus sanctifies folly and unifies it with the spirit of Christianity. At first folly is the benighted agent of shortsighted worldliness, but he then transforms her into the "foolish" spirit from a worldly point of view of self-sacrifice and charity. Erasmus' book imbues comic folly with moral authority and thus sets a precedent for placing comedy on a respectable footing. Erasmus shows that comic folly can be rehabilitated and used to put life in proper perspective. He uses folly, for example, to criticize and ridicule the sinful pride of the Church.

This paradoxical turn of mind derives from the Pauline descriptions of Christian existence. Paul employs the comic technique of reversal as a weapon for Christian faith: "It pleased God by the foolishness of preaching to save them that believe"; "we live as chastened but not killed, as sorrowful yet always rejoicing, as poor yet enriching many, as having nothing, yet possessing all things" (1 Cor. 1:22; 2 Cor. 6: 9–10). The way to truth lies in that which conventional wisdom calls folly, which, according to Robert Polhemus, "is often an unstated premise in mirth and an implicit claim of comic form" (Polhemus 1980, 10). The paradox in the final analysis must be accepted through belief because human intelligence cannot lay hold of its full significance. Erasmus can only explain the phenomenon of unpleasant things made pleasant by recourse to the operation of grace. For Walter

Gordon, this leads to the more extensive understanding of the whole of life in terms of the ludic (Gordon 1990, 156–7).[100]

Kierkegaard's early view of humor as intrinsic to Christianity is also voiced in contemporary studies, and in the theological mainstream there has recently been a recurrent interest in levity.[101] This work has focused variously on laughter, fantasy, festivity, play, carnival, and the free play of difference, and it has operated within several theological genres.[102] Recent theology has conflated humor with play and even with joy, although comic laughter is not the same as laughter that simply expresses joyfulness.[103] Kathleen Sands argues that the root similarity and limitation of this literature lies in its interest in using the comic to establish a theological foothold above the tragic (1996).[104] Whether taken as a metaphysical resolution to tragedy or a substitute for metaphysical resolution, the comic affords theology what Nathan Scott terms "a narrow escape" from tragedy into faith (Scott 1966, 77–118; quoted in Sands 1966, 505). The result of this forced contest between the comic and the tragic is fixed in advance: The comic view is made to seem self-evidently superior and closer to, if not identical with, the perspective of faith. The comic, then, has been used to form a theodicy, the justification of God—in other words, the justification of power as ultimately coherent and good.

Humor can be put to different use in Christianity, however, as some feminist thinkers suggest,[105] and as Robert Roberts, followed by John Lippitt, attempt to do: With arguments based on the significance Kierkegaard gives to humor, they defend the importance of humor in Christianity (Roberts 1987; Lippitt 2000b, 2005).

Protestant theologians Reinhold Niebuhr and Roy Eckardt have endorsed the view that humor should be excluded from Christianity's holy holies—Kierkegaard's final view of the matter (Niebuhr 1969, 134–5; Eckardt 1995, 101). This has actually been the most widespread view of the relation of Christianity with humor or laughter, as evidenced by histories on the subject.[106] Sociologist Peter Berger aptly remarks that some religions are more humorous than others, and among the Abrahamic religions, Christianity is the farthest from laughter.[107] This view is echoed in philosopher John Morreall's important *Comedy, Tragedy, and Religion* (Berger 1997, 197–8; Morreall 1999).[108]

The Christians share with Egyptian priests, as well as with Greek and Jewish ascetics, the ideal of the perfect human who never laughs (Adkin 1985; Resnick 1987). Jerome, Basil, and John Chrysostom opposed laughter and jocularity, as did the Fathers in general. This was justified by the view that there is no account of Jesus laughing in the Gospels. Laughter is mentioned in Jesus' reported sayings, but it is to berate those who laugh in godless sinfulness and to announce that they will weep in the fullness of time, whilst those who weep now, are blessed and will laugh later (Luke 6: 25, 21). At the same time Aristotle's thesis that laughter is a distinctive human property—the idea of *homo ridens*, "man gifted with laughter"—appears in both the Latin and the medieval Christian Latin traditions.[109] A heated debate on laughter with far-reaching consequences arises in the Middle Ages. If Jesus, the great model of imitation for humanity, never laughs during his human life, then laughter must be alien to man, at least to Christian man. Conversely, if one posits that laughter is a distinctive feature of humankind, then laughing man will certainly feel himself more able to express his own nature. Both views are found in ecclesiastical authors.[110]

At the beginning of the Middle Ages, confronted with a phenomenon it considers dangerous and does not know how to control, the Church totally rejects laughter. There is a long list of grim theologians, and there are repeated negative comments on laughter, which is understood as an expression of worldliness, sinful insouciance, and lack of faith. Monastic rules proscribe laughter. The codification of laughter and its condemnation in monastic circles result partly at least from the view that laughter is a phenomenon expressed in and through the body.[111] Conversely, weeping over the wretchedness of this world is praised as a Christian virtue. Christian saints rarely laugh except in defiance of imminent martyrdom.[112] Around the twelfth century, the Church brings laughter under control by distinguishing good laughter from bad laughter—admissible ways of laughing from inadmissible. The Church reaches a codification of the practice of laughter, of which scholasticism assumes ownership.[113] The Church's relation with laughter has not evolved much since Thomas Aquinas' rehabilitation of the Aristotelian virtue of wit or *eutrapelia*; before the middle of the twentieth-century, only the Gnostics recognized Christ's laughter.[114]

It follows that Kierkegaard's original contribution to a study of the comic does not lie in his first view of the relationship of humor and Christianity, and certainly not with his final view—that Christianity is out of reach of the humorous.

3. Shaftesbury's writings as well as those of other British philosophers were not readily accessible to Danish readers, including Kierkegaard, because of Danish and British hostilities during the Napoleonic Wars (Popkin 1951). Kierkegaard's direct knowledge of Shaftesbury may have been obstructed by political circumstances, but Shaftesbury's immense influence on German Romanticism, and particularly on Kierkegaard's unacknowledged mentor, Ludwig Holberg (Allen 2009), may explain the presence of Shaftesburean ideas in Kierkegaard's journals and writings. We have also seen the role played by Johann Georg Hamann, Shaftesbury's translator

and follower, as an important link between Shaftesbury and Kierkegaard. The role of Johann Gottfried von Herder, himself a Hamann follower as is Kierkegaard (Ringleben 2006), should be emphasized as an additional important source of Shaftesburean influence: Kierkegaard owned Herder's writings and quoted from them, very much as the writings of Shaftesbury were Herder's constant companions from an early age. Herder's *Conversations on God*, the work in which he attempts to summarize his philosophical and speculative convictions, exhibits throughout the direct influence of Shaftesbury. Moreover, the later works of Herder, the *Adrastea* and the *Brife zur Beförderung der Humanität* (Letters for the Advancement of Humanity), return to the English philosopher again and again. They are meant as a vindication of Shaftesbury's idea of religion against the theological attacks launched against his so-called deism. Herder also admires Shaftesbury as a master of philosophical style; the reason he calls him "the beloved Plato of Europe" is because Herder considers Shaftesbury almost the only modern writer who has tolerably learned the art of the dialogue and knows how to employ it in a manner worthy of the Platonic model. But on the matter of putting truth to the test of ridicule, Herder sees in Shaftesbury a "philosophical scoffer."[115]

Apart from these general considerations on the relations among Kierkegaard, Herder, and Shaftesbury, the reference to Shaftesbury that introduces Kierkegaard's interest in the legitimacy of the comic in *Concluding Unscientific Postscript* alludes to "little research projects," which translators Walter Lowrie and Howard and Edna Hong interpret as being Herder's *Adrastea*, chapter 14 (*CUPL* 570, n. 23; *CUP2*, 264, n. 263): "In the previous century, a thesis propounded by Lord Shaftesbury that makes laughter the test of truth engendered several little research projects to find out whether it is so" (*CUP1*, 512). In "Shaftesbury, Spirit and Cheerfulness" ("Shaftesbury, Geist und Frohsinn") found in *Adrastea*, Herder eulogizes Shaftesbury and commends both his view and use of humor:

> The first work Shaftesbury published himself was a letter about enthusiasm . . . Shaftesbury also suggested [against enthusiasm] . . . cheerful reason and something of that merry mirth, which pleasantly solves the strained facial wrinkles as well as the old brain cramps, wit and humor . . . Shaftesbury wanted to contribute actively, not only in teaching, to chase away that clumsy, bad humor; his writings are full of wit and good humor . . . with the freedom of the mind and of the wit Shaftesbury presented his moralists, a composition almost worthy of Greek antiquity and almost superior to it in its content. It shall

become a form of soul for every young man able to comprehend the beautiful and noble, because this might be the best
metaphysics that has ever been thought. . . . in addition to that
written in the method of cheerfulness, which was our author's
own, serious thought form, his muse and grace. . . . And yet,
intelligent wit and cheerfulness, as Shaftesbury wants them, are
not only the salt of how society commerces and of reading books,
they rather are the spice and flower of life itself, indispensable
for the formation of each noble adolescent. (Herder 1877–1913,
Adrastea, vol. I, chap. 14; translation Patrick Neubauer)

But Herder rejects the literal interpretation of the Shaftesburean idea
of ridicule as the test of truth:

Only rawness of reason or persistence of disease could have
accused him of such irrational principles as "Ridicule is the test
of truth, in a state of laughter, the serious can be examined best"
etc. One should just read his own defense, the case about the
freedom of wit and mirth with a clear eye to make sure of his
opponents' air strikes . . . Folly, and only the incorrigible, fine
or coarse folly, deserves ridicule; what man of senses will apply
scorn, which is always close to contempt, against the holy, the
venerable, the truly great and beautiful? . . . Because laughter
and jokes, wit and humor are transitions and do not want to
be more than that, who would want to revoke or scorn such
happy messengers between truth and folly or foolishness? But
on the other hand, who would choose them to be the final,
highest judgments? (Herder 1877–1913, *Adrastea*, vol. I, chap.
14; translation Patrick Neubauer)

Many Shaftesburean ideas are easily recognized in Kierkegaard's journals and writings as Kierkegaard paraphrases Shaftesbury without naming
him (a common practice of his, I am told by the journals' translator, Brian
K. Söderquist). For example, we read in the journals, "He who does not
constantly dare to submit his earnestness to the test of jest is stupid and
comical" (*JP* 2, 1743/*Pap.* VI A 3, n. d.), where "the test of jest" replaces
Shaftesbury's "test of ridicule." Moreover, the following quotes from Shaftesbury's *Characteristics* could appear to be written by Kierkegaard despite the
difference in wording: "There is a great difference between seeking how to
raise a laugh from everything, and seeking in everything what justly may be
laughed at" (*CR* I, 85); "And if I have either laughed wrong, or been imper-

tinently serious, I can be content to be laughed at in my turn . . . For he who laughs and is himself ridiculous, bears a double share of ridicule . . . we become more ridiculous than the people we ridicule" (CR I, 98, 57, 59); "A mirth not out of the reach of wit is gravest . . . a gravity not abhorrent from the use of that other mirth . . ." (*Life*, 362); a public discourse that is not grave but "light" is quite probably the most serious discourse of all (CR I, 54); there is a difference between "genteel wit" or "true raillery," on the one hand, and mere "buffoonery" or "banter," on the other; "buffoonery, satire and the common wit" are examples of contemptible human pursuits (*Life*, 53); and contemporary satire is "scurrilous, buffooning, and without morals or instruction" (CR I, 173).

The association between Shaftesbury's and Kierkegaard's thought is significant insofar as the former anticipates some of the problems that the latter is usually credited with formulating, such as the difficulty of giving advice, the relationships between the author and the public and the importance of the author's disavowal of authority, the importance of the theater for philosophy and for inner dialogue, the dangers of religious enthusiasm and emotional excess, the necessity of fighting philosophical abstractions and barren academicism, and the urge for an edifying philosophy whose heart is moral education. Shaftesbury's anti-systematism finds an interesting parallel in Kierkegaard's anti-Hegelianism: The former's search for "a discursive practice distinct from that of the lecture or the sermon" is similar to the latter's views on indirect communication. Shaftesbury's concept of the "virtuoso" is echoed in the moral significance of music and art for Kierkegaard, in the same way that Shaftesbury's view of the "genius" can be found in Kierkegaard's differentiation between the "genius" and the "apostle," especially in *The Book on Adler*.

Moreover, Shaftesbury anticipates some of the solutions Kierkegaard has found to the problems they both identify. Humor is helpful in philosophic writing for setting the reader free, annulling the author's authority, and enabling an autonomous appropriation of the content, which is necessary for independent thought and moral self-education. Satire is effective in the criticism of the Church, academic thought, and all that is abstract and thus does not aim at edifying. The comic is a tool of reflection needed for curbing one's enthusiasm and fighting emotional excesses, and is founded on an incongruity or contradiction whose existence is real. And last, but not least, the comic entertains an essential relationship with the truth.

However, there is an important difference between the uses of the comic by these two thinkers: Shaftesbury lightens the plight of ridiculousness in order to encourage the use of it in conversation, that is, to promote the use of reason and liberate wit and humor from ethical, political, and religious constraints. Kierkegaard uses similar views to those of Shaftesbury's on ridicule in order to attack illegitimate uses of the comic and protect Christianity as the sole life-view that has overcome laughter.

In order to assess Kierkegaard's contribution to the study of the comic and humor, however, a more detailed comparison of their roles within his and Shaftesbury's views of the good life is in order. Such a comparison is not an easy task because these thinkers differ in their views of the world, God, human nature, the ideal individual, and the role of sociability and rationality in attaining to the ideal individual: Shaftesbury is a deist, Kierkegaard a Christian; the former lives in a harmonious, beautiful, and beneficent universe among good-natured human beings, the latter lives in fear and trembling in solitude among sinners; the former promotes joy and a moral character akin to a work of art that is attainable through philosophy as inner and outer rational dialogue and by one's own powers; while the latter, plagued by an incomplete self, struggles as a sinner praying for God's grace to enhance religious suffering in solitude through a movement that takes him past philosophy and ethics to the doorsteps of true worship where he rests transparently in the power that establishes him.

Yet, as different as their worldviews are, both Shaftesbury and Kierkegaard consider the comic an instrument of thought that is an invaluable aid in reaching their respective goals. To that end, they recommend its use in inner and in outward communication, both oral and written. Superficially, their goal seems the same: To build a moral character in oneself and another; for Kierkegaard, however, it is a moral-religious character that is the aim, a goal that makes additional claims on the individual who initiates the conversation or the writing.

In writing, humor serves the common goal of both Shaftesbury and Kierkegaard: To annul the writer's authority and enable the reader to do the work for himself. For Shaftesbury, the justification of such an endeavor is both moral, to help one become a moral agent by one's own power, and prudential, to overcome the resistance of receiving advice as to how to live. Kierkegaard justifies this kind of authorship both for the reader and the writer on religious grounds: The writer has no religious authority, he is a sinner himself, and it is Christ that does the work both for himself and the reader.

The use of humor in conversation serves the same goal as in writing for Kierkegaard and is justified in the same way; yet another justification for humor's use in conversation is to protect the parties' interiority. For Shaftesbury, humor is important in conversation because it fosters rationality as criticism—a goal that is as foreign to Kierkegaard as the Shaftesburean practice of putting ideas to the test of ridicule in order to foster together the *sensus communis* is alien to Kierkegaard's individualistic philosophy. Truth is not the outcome of shared discussion for Kierkegaard, but has to be found in one's inwardness.

In inner conversation (Shaftesburean "soliloquy" or Kierkegaardian "inwardness") the role Kierkegaard gives to the comic follows the role his predecessor has prescribed, to serve truth by curbing enthusiasm and counterbalancing the emotions. The comic purifies the moods and counterbalances pathos, and thus stabilizes the inner equilibrium in order to help create the conditions for choosing the leap towards a higher level of tragic.

But Kierkegaard extends the role of the comic, I suggest, by making it a criterion of advancement on the negative Kierkegaardian theological ladder and the main positive indicator of the individual's relation to the truth. Kierkegaard maintains that by examining the content of our laughter can we know the sort of person we are. Jest is the attitude towards that which has been overcome, very much as for Hegel the comic destroys that which has been historically overcome and is therefore linked to the subject, who is certain to possess truth and be beyond contradiction (Hegel 1975, 1199–200). For lack of an external criterion for inward advancement, which is the sole progress Kierkegaard recognizes, the comic is the main tool of examination, correction, and evaluation an individual possesses for reflecting on himself and his personal experiences. The ethics of the comic enable the individual to situate himself in the spheres of living according to the content of the comic he is enjoying. Moreover, by encouraging the right laughter, one that corresponds to that which is really inferior, the individual advances through the stages along life's path because through laughter new norms are established. The penalty for violating the ethics of the comic is ridicule, a sanction found in Shaftesbury but made threatening enough by Kierkegaard to spur the learning of his ethics. Kierkegaard thus views the comic as both sword and shield whose mastery is crucial for inner progress from lower to higher stages of existence; the comic is philosophy's primary tool once it steps into the new existential role Kierkegaard designs for it, which is to lead the individual towards worshiping the true God.

The epistemological role attributed to good humor as a means for apprehending truth in Shaftesbury's philosophy has no parallel in Kierkegaard's thought; but humor fulfills an epistemological role in relation to the truth of Christianity for the young Kierkegaard through the intermediary of Hamann's Shaftesburean views on the matter; humor helps apprehend the truth for Hamann and young Kierkegaard because truth—the Incarnation—is paradoxical. Moreover, the later Kierkegaardian view is similar to the Shaftesburean view that truth will not withstand ridicule. Shaftesbury grounds this view in a vision of the universe as harmoniously beautiful and of the comic as false because it portrays the beautiful as ugly, whereas Kierkegaard grounds his view in a vision of the human being as a synthesis of contradictions, and truth as the domination of the highest contradiction: truth is protected by the comic from the comic because if something is true, it has conquered the comical as lower than itself. Thus, ridicule as the test of truth, in the sense that truth is immune to ridicule and whoever does not see that is ridiculous himself, is the key to Kierkegaard's ethics of the comic: the Kierkegaardian truth is approximated by using the "test of jest" Kierkegaard refers to in his journals in much the same way Shaftesbury proposes to use his "test of ridicule."

For both thinkers, the comic is an objective incongruity, which enables it to be a test for truth; but as Kierkegaard also requires that the incongruity be resolved on a higher level, this divergence yields a different concept of the comic. Not only is the view of the comic different for these philosophers, but so is their use of other related concepts as well: in Shaftesbury we find laughter, ridicule, wit, humor, and good humor; in Kierkegaard, the comic, irony, humor, and occasionally ridicule. Much more elaborate and subtle in Kierkegaard's thought, these terms bear the mark of Kierkegaard's contemporaries, as well as of an ethical-religious worldview that redefines the comic and Christianizes humor. Shaftesbury, in contrast, is a pioneer of the modern use of benign humor, who struggles to delineate the difference among humor, good humor, ridicule, wit, and laughter.

Finally, Kierkegaard and Shaftesbury are both Socratics who use the serio-comic as a tool for moral or moral-religious education much like the ancient followers of Socrates, such as the Cynics and the Stoics. Moreover, Shaftesbury's ideal character is a "middle genius, partaking neither of hearty mirth nor seriousness" (*Life*, 194–5), a mixture of "jest" and "earnest" that Shaftesbury calls "soft irony" because "a mirth not out of the reach of wit is gravest" and "a gravity not abhorrent from the use of that other mirth" is ideal (*Life*, 362). This is retained both in Kierkegaard's ideal of true earnestness as a mixture of jest and earnestness, and in his characterization of the humorist, with suffering and pathos substituting earnestness and counterbalancing the comic in the concept of humor. Both philosophers promote an ideal of a serio-comic individual, at least as far as the humorist goes in Kierkegaard's teleology, heir to Socrates and Diogenes the Cynic. Yet they are also differentiated by their vision of the highest individual, who is characterized by the presence of humor for Shaftesbury and by its absence unless as a mask for Kierkegaard.

Kierkegaard's originality does not lie in suggesting a relation between the truth and the comic. Nor does it lie in the two additional philosophic traditions in which it is inscribed, one, beginning with Plato, which criticizes common uses of the comic and offers an alternative view of it that reflects moral concerns, and the other, common to philosophy and literature, which uses the comic as a means to moral amendment.[116] Rather, it lies in the kind of Christian justification he gives to both the serio-comic and the comic's relation to the truth, and in the device of an ethics of the comic that guarantees this relationship.

To conclude the assessment of Kierkegaard's contribution, Kierkegaard does not innovate in his use of the serio-comic, or in a Christian justification of it, as Erasmus justifies his *Sultitia* or folly in Christian terms; rather, Kierkegaard is original in the kind of Christian justification he provides and in his argument for the serio-comic as an embodied philosophy, as a life style (the ironist and the humorist) and not only a literary form. As Kierkegaard explains in his doctrine of true earnestness (a mixture of jest and earnestness), the serio-comic is always necessary because it is first and foremost an existential requirement that is ultimately justified on religious grounds (*UDVS*, 96–97): Everything that is religiously important in the world is *also*, that is, *at the same time*, a jest, since no finite act can capture the infinite. The serio-comic is necessary to the Kierkegaardian task of "simultaneously to relate oneself absolutely to the absolute *telos* (end, goal) and relatively to relative ends" (*CUP1*, 525), because the comic reflects and expresses the relative attitude toward relative ends. Thus, by teaching people how to laugh, Kierkegaard teaches them how to live, because the comic devices he uses necessitate the incorporation of new existential norms: the comic teaches a sense of proportion because it indicates what is important and what is not, what pertains to eternity and what to temporality, what is worthy of an absolute relation and what of a relative relation, and how to maintain both relations simultaneously.

Kierkegaard is not original in finding a relationship between the comic and the truth, as Shaftesbury and Hamann precede him, but he innovates in the justification he gives to this relationship and in embedding it in an ethics of the comic that guarantees that in teaching how to laugh he teaches how to live. Kierkegaard's endeavor provides a criterion that distinguishes true ridicule from false ridicule, a criterion Shaftesbury assumes, but does not provide. Kierkegaard's ethics of the comic, which mirror the hierarchy of the life stages, supply "the test of the jest" that replaces Shaftesbury's "test of ridicule." The ethics of the comic guarantees that the relationship of superiority existing de facto between the laugher and the butt of the laugh matches the hierarchy Kierkegaard establishes between individuals whose lives embody different worldviews. In order to accomplish this, Kierkegaard uses the comic as a tool of reflection and ultimately of truth. Thus, in teaching how to laugh, Kierkegaard teaches how to live.

The importance of the last statement for understanding Kierkegaard's thought lies in Kierkegaard's avoidance of teaching how to live. As we have seen above in the discussion of the ironic Kierkegaard, whether Kierkegaard teaches how to live and whether his religiousness directs the whole production of his writings is still controversial. Accepting the idea that in teaching how to laugh Kierkegaard teaches how to live indicates a possible resolution of these controversies: Taking Kierkegaard's teachings on the comic seriously provides a key to understanding the rest of his writings.

However, Kierkegaard's views of the comic, irony, and humor are imbued with a specific metaphysics and philosophical anthropology. The comic involves suffering and infinity, making it an ethical-religious category. Kierkegaard's thoughts on humor and its relationship with suffering are profound and interesting, but the notions of guilt and eternity as well as the idea of God involved in Kierkegaardian humor may be at odds with the non-religious persons' view of humor, with different views of religion held by religious persons, and with different views of the relation between religion and humor. Given that Kierkegaard's edifying discourse of the comic is intended to lead us to a certain form of Christian living, the question of whether we should let Kierkegaard teach us how to laugh is disputable. In the next chapter, I propose a role for humor in the good life in which the views on humor and the good life are independent of religious presuppositions.

CHAPTER 3

HUMOR AND
THE GOOD LIFE

Peace of mind follows the suspension of judgment like its shadow.

—Diogenes Laertius on Pyrrho (*Lives of Eminent Philosophers*)

Humor needs not function within the confines of religious philosophies, as suggested by the views of the only modern philosophers to assign humor an important role in the good life—Shaftesbury, Hamann, and Kierkegaard. The role of humor in the good life proposed in this chapter is independent from religious presuppositions and is compatible with recent humor research. To fill the gap between the nineteenth and twenty-first centuries, however, I examine the views on humor, and if necessary for its understanding, on the comic, of Schopenhauer, Hegel, and his followers, Carlyle, Jean Paul, Santayana, Bergson, and Freud.

Arthur Schopenhauer, according to Terry Eagleton, is "a thinker so unremittingly gloomy that his work, quite unintentionally, represents one of the great comic masterpieces of Western thought" (Eagleton 2007, 82). Eagleton adds, however, that if Schopenhauer is still well worth reading, "it is not only because he confronts the possibility more candidly and brutally than almost any other philosopher, that human existence may be pointless in the most squalid and farcical of ways. It is also because much of what he says is surely true" (96). In his study of Schopenhauer, the French contemporary philosopher, Clément Rosset, rightly considers Schopenhauer a philosopher of the absurd (Rosset 1967). Adopting the well-known Shakespearian characterization of life as "a tale told by an idiot, full of noise and fury, signifying nothing" (*Macbeth*, act V, scene

5), Schopenhauer maintains that "no one has the remotest idea why the whole tragic-comedy exists, for it has no spectators, and the actors end-lessly worry with little and merely negative enjoyment" (Schopenhauer 1969, II, 357). Given that the world is an objectification of an irratio-nal force called the Will, which uses its representations blindly without ever attaining satisfaction, there is something ridiculous for Schopenhauer about the pompous self-importance of creatures who, convinced of their supreme value, pursue some edifying end that will instantly turn to ashes in their mouths. There is no grandiose goal to this meaningless sound and fury, only "momentary gratification, feeling pleasure conditioned by wants, much and long suffering, constant struggle, *bellum omnium*, everything a hunter and everything hunted, pressure, want, need and anxiety, shrieking and howling, and this goes on *saecula saecolurom* or until once again the crust of the planet breaks" (354; see 360).

Seen as a whole and only when its most significant features are emphasized, every individual's life is a tragedy; seen in detail, however, an individual's life "has the character of a comedy. For the doings and worries of the day, the restless mockeries of the moment, the desires and fears of the week, the mishaps of the hour, are all brought about by chance that is bent on some mischievous trick; they are nothing but scenes from a comedy" (I, 322). These little incongruities are sources of misery presented as "fleeting" moments in a comedy, but actually reflect the underlying conflict between the demands of the species and the desires of the individual (II, 553–4). Comedy "brings out the inexhaustible material for laughter, with which life and even its very adversities are filled" and "hastens to drop the curtain at the moment of delight." Comedy serves as the continued affirmation of the will to live; but were we to "contemplate somewhat seriously that burlesque side of life," we would reach the conclusion that "what exhibits itself thus is something that really had not be" (438).

Tragedy is more important than comedy because it is tragedy that reveals the truth about reality, its purpose being "the description of the terrible side of life":

> The unspeakable pain, the wretchedness and misery of mankind, the triumph of wickedness, the scornful mastery of chance, and the irretrievable fall of the good and the innocent are all here presented to us; and here is to be found a significant hint as to the nature of the world and of existence. . . . The motives that were previously so powerful now lose their force, and instead of them the complete knowledge of the real nature of the world, acting as a quieter of the will, produces resignation, the giving

up not merely of life, but of the whole will-to-live itself. (I, 252–3)

Only the denial of the will leads to the Schopenhauerian road to salvation from this "mock existence" (358). Yet humor and laughter have no place in it, nor do they provide the momentary solace from the will's pressure that the aesthetic experience offers. Schopenhauer, however, takes his theory of laughter seriously, boasting that there is "no question that here, after so many fruitless attempts, the true theory of the ludicrous is given, and the problem propounded [the real significance of laughter] but given up by Cicero definitely solved" (II, 92). Laughter is a prerogative and characteristic of the human being; animals are incapable of laughter because they lack reason and as a result universal concepts, which are necessary for laughter. Indeed, Schopenhauer's theory of laughter is initially presented as part of his theory of concepts in the first volume of his *The World as Will and Representation* (1819):

In every case, laughter results from nothing but the suddenly perceived incongruity between a concept and the real object that had been thought through it in some relation; and laughter itself is just the expression of this incongruity. (I, 59)

Schopenhauer develops at greater length his theory of laughter in the second edition of his book (1969 [1844], vol. II, Supplementary Essay No. VIII):

. . . the origin of the ludicrous is always the paradoxical, and thus unexpected, submission of an object under a concept that is in all other respects heterogeneous to it. Accordingly, the phenomenon of laughter always signifies the sudden apprehension of an incongruity between such a concept and the real object thought through it, and hence between what is abstract and what is perceptive. (II, 91)

We laugh at an incongruity between a perceived object and a concept, and concepts are the work of the faculty of reason (I, 39). Thus, the appearance of laughter is closely related to that of joy because "it must be delightful for us to see this strict, untiring, and most troublesome governess, our faculty of reason, for once convinced of inadequacy" (II, 98). In a late essay on philosophy and natural science, Schopenhauer comments on the physiology of laughter (Schopenhauer 1974, II, 103–76); in doing so, he mentions laughter as a result of tickling. This is laughter "excited entirely physically" and is thus different from most instances of laughter, which have a mental cause (168) and with which Schopenhauer's theory of humorous laughter is concerned.[1]

In the extended essay on laughter in the second edition of his main book, Schopenhauer provides examples to illustrate his theory and draws numerous distinctions within the genre of the ludicrous, such as that between wit and folly, parody, and irony. Among these forms, humor is highly valued by Schopenhauer. He bemoans the corrupt habit of calling every clown a humorist, as "the word humour is borrowed from the English, in order to single out and denote a quite peculiar species of the ludicrous which . . . is even akin to the sublime" (II, 101). Humor depends on "a special kind of mood or frame of mind" that is "subjective and thus exists primarily for one's own self" (100). Notwithstanding this subjective side, humor entails a specific relation to the object, and here Schopenhauer gives us a profound insight:

> . . . humor depends on a subjective yet serious and sublime mood, involuntarily coming into conflict with a common external world very different from it. It cannot avoid or abandon itself to this world; hence, for reconciliation, it attempts to think its own view and this external world through the same concepts, which in this way take on a double incongruity, now on one side, now on the other, with the real thing thought through them. In this way the impression of the intentionally ludicrous, and thus of the joke, arises, yet behind this the deepest seriousness is concealed and shines through. (II, 100)

Because humor is the result of a conflict between the self and an external object, the humorist speaks a truth about himself in his relation to the other or the object, and this truth can be expressive of a sublime and contemplative mood. Both the sublime and humor involve reflexivity or self-awareness, foreign to the consoling experience of beauty. Yet it is the humorous mood that is the source of the art of comedy and expressed in it, as "every poetical or artistic presentation of the comic, or even a farcical scene, through which a serious thought yet gleams as its concealed background, is a product of humour, and thus is humorous" (100f.). Humor always conceals seriousness in the joke and is thus the opposite of irony, whose seriousness conceals a joke: Humor is "the double counterpoint of irony" and is representative of the moderns in much the same way that irony is representative of the ancients (100–01).

Schopenhauer's contemporary, Georg W. F. Hegel, prefers humor to irony as well; his comments on humor can be fully appreciated when preceded by his view of the comic, whose importance within the body of his thought is rarely noticed. According to the prevalent interpretation of Hegel, "the tragic does not cease to sustain Hegelian thought: it accompanies the genesis of the dialectic, it marks the seriousness of action and the essence of history, in places it even comes to be confused with the absolute itself" (Beistegui 2000, 33). Hegelian dialectic is another name for the tragic and overcoming the tragic; dialectic is structurally tragic, and tragedy correspondingly dialectic. Moreover, the thinkers who hold that the tragic occupies a central place in Hegel's philosophy such as Jean Hippolyte and Peter Szondi also have been led to accord tragedy an apparently incontestable ascent over comedy (Hippolyte 1972, 19; Szondi 1978, I, 167–8; 172–3).

Most philosophers have favored tragedy, yet among classical philosophers, Hegel values comedy and the comic spirit the most highly, both in *The Phenomenology of Spirit* and in the *Aesthetics* (see Gashé 2000). In the former work, Hegel considers comedy to be the most accomplished spiritual work of art, the final stage of drama before it gives way to religion. Having destroyed serious drama, comedy finally turns its mockery on itself and vanishes. Whereas tragedy is universal truth victorious over the subjective individual, comedy is the victory of the individual over the system. Tragedy shows individuals bringing themselves to destruction, whereas comedy shows individuals dissolving everything into laughter and celebrating the victory. Hegel calls it the hale condition of the soul, but is clearly much more interested in tragedy, although tragedy gives way to comedy in Hegel's classification of the various poetic genres. Despite the crudeness of its expression and the buffoonery of its situation, comedy reveals a consciousness more developed than tragic consciousness. In a way, comedy is the completion of tragedy and the comic form continues that of the tragic: The masks fall away, plasticity gives way to irony and the objective equilibrium of the ethical substances cedes to subjectivity, which, through its laughter, masters everything.

In the *Aesthetics*, Hegel offers a general perspective on the place of the comic between subjectivity and objectivity. The problem of reconciliation between objectivity and subjectivity is not absent, and it is noteworthy that for Hegel reconciliation is possible through both tragedy and comedy. There is a difference, however. In tragedy the subject is finally resigned and renounces its individuality. In comedy, on the other hand, the subjectivity of the self-assured individual persists: "The general ground for comedy is therefore a world in which man as subject or person has made himself completely master of everything that counts to him otherwise as the essence of what he wills and accomplishes, a world whose aims are therefore self-destructive because they are unsubstantial" (Hegel 1975, II, 1199).

At this point Hegel differentiates between that which is merely ridiculous, harmless, and without consequences and that which is comic in general (1199–200). Laughter, in the former case, is only an expression of a self-complacent wit, while the comic destroys that which has no intrinsic value and that which is false and contradictory. The comic destroys that which has been historically overcome, and is therefore linked to the subject, who is certain to possess truth and to be beyond contradiction. By negating a given value, the comic leaves open the possibility of alternatives.

A consequence of this theory is that we can laugh at the past, but not at the present. This consideration applies also to the individual subject who can laugh at former weaknesses or mistakes—in short, at himself: "The comical as such implies an infinite light-heartedness and confidence felt by someone raised altogether above his own inner contradiction and not bitter or miserable in it at all: this is the bliss and ease of a man who, being sure of himself, can bear the frustration of his aims and achievements" (1200).

Hegel also differentiates between two sorts of humor—subjective and objective. The former, as exemplified by the humorist Jean Paul, is a form of humor to which he pays tribute yet criticizes, in a manner reminiscent of his criticism of Romantic irony, for being subjective and arbitrary (Hegel 1975, I, 295ff). However, Hegel claims that works of "true humor," such as Laurence Sterne's *Tristram Shandy* (1759), succeed in making "what is substantial emerge out of contingency." Their "triviality [thus] affords precisely the supreme idea of depth" (602). Objective humor occupies an important role in Hegel's thought. Humor remains for Hegel "the necessary head of a development immanent to the principle of the Romantic art form" although he rejects it at first together with Schlegelian irony as "the absolutization of the one abstract moment of subjectivity." Objective humor, thus, is not only instrumental in bringing about the passage from art to philosophical thinking, it is also, as Wolfgang Preisendanz demonstrates, the formal principle of art after art, of an art that, within its own medium, goes beyond itself as art (Preisendanz 1963, 121ff).

Preisendanz showed how complex and nuanced Hegel's concept of humor is, but the post-Hegelians Friedrich Theodor Vischer, Kuno Fisher, Karl Rosenkranz, Moriz Carriere, or Adolf Zeising are basically uniform in defining humor as a sense of reconciliation that is nonetheless aware of still unresolved tensions in reality; humor is tolerant of human foibles and inadequacies, for it views them *sub specie aeternitatis*. The post-Hegelian elevation of humour also can be seen among later German humanists, whose orientation is not in any literal way Hegelian, for example, Eduard von Hartmann, Theodor Lipps, Johannes Immanuel Volkelt, Hermann Cohen, and Arthur Kutscher.[2] From the twenty-five or thirty definitions of humor of the nineteenth century, this much of common agreement can be extracted: There is "an absence of scorn in humor, a presence of emotion, and . . . humor is an excellent thing" (Eastman 1972, 169). Thomas Carlyle's view, describing the humorist and aesthetician Jean Paul, is characteristic: "True humor springs not more from the head than from the heart; it is not contempt, its essence is love; it issues not in laughter, but in still smiles which lie far deeper. It is a sort of inverse sublimity, exalting, as it were, into our affection what is below us, while sublimity draws down into our affections what is above us." The bloom and perfume of a deep, fine, and loving nature, which is in harmony with itself, humor has its essence in sensibility, in "warm, tender, fellow-feeling with all forms of existence" (Carlyle 1827, 169).[3]

Jean Paul (pseudonym of Johann Paul Friedrich Richter), whom Carlyle eulogizes, distinguishes in his *School for Aesthetics* between harsh irony and a sympathetic humor characterized by four central features: Its totality, its use of the annihilating or infinite idea, its subjectivity, and its sensuousness. Humor is total, Richter argues, because its object is not a single specific folly, but universal folly. It is therefore mild and tolerant of individuals. Humor is annihilating or infinite because from its perspective of detachment and perfect vision, it sees all the contradictions of real and ideal, finite and infinite, and thereby annihilates all. Humor is subjective because it sides with the individual, not with the universal. And finally, humor is sensuous because it is grounded in material existence.

Referring to humor as "a kind of psychic vertigo" and comparing it to the feast of fools in the Middle Ages when "an inner spiritual masquerade innocent of any impure purpose reversed the worldly and the spiritual," Jean Paul complains that the present age is far too corrupt to allow such humor to reappear. The humorist introduces his personal circumstances upon the comic stage, although he does so only to annihilate it poetically. The humorist is both his own court jester and quartet of masked Italian comedians and at the same time their prince and director.

Opposed to the infinitely great, which evokes admiration, there must be something as infinitely insignificant, which evokes the opposite feeling.

The former is the sublime and the latter the ridiculous. Seen as a relation to the ridiculous and as a modus of the comical, humor is based on the division between the I and the world, which is connected to Christianity and thereby based on the suffering of the finite as an unsublatable feature of human existence. As an expression of this situation and the possibility of aesthetically mastering it, humor is defined through the whole of the relation to the world: "Humor as the reversed sublime destroys not the individual but the finite by contrasting it with the idea" (Preisendanz 1974, col. 1233).

Jean Paul influences the history of humor by understanding it as the "reversed sublime," as an attempt to mediate the infinite and the finite under the historical conditions of Christianity. In this attempt, the humorist surveys the infinite by means of the finite, experiencing the deficiency of not only this or that finite thing, but of the finite in general, without forgetting his own finiteness. Jean Paul's impressive image of the humorist, who points to a salvation hidden to himself, is the mythical bird Merops, which flies upside-down in the sky, always looking down to earth (Richter 1966 [1841], Part I, vol. 5, 129).[4]

An equally elevated view of humor can be found in the German philosopher and psychologist, Moritz Lazarus, who makes humor a religion of the mind:

> For the mind in humor is related to the Idea and to Reality exactly as the whole feeling of man in religion is related to God and the World. . . . The humorous mind sees itself and its actual life far from the Idea, powerless to attain its goal and its desire, and therefore tamed and broken in its pride, and oft even condemned to the despondent fierce laughter of self-contempt, and yet on the other hand elevated and purified through the consciousness that in spite of all, it possesses the Idea and the Infinite within itself, and in its even so imperfect works it reveals them and lives them forth, and is itself most inwardly at one with them, if only through the painful recognition they bring of its own imperfection. (quoted in Eastman 1972, 174)

Humor is raised on the wings of German philosophy almost to the height of devotion. The praise of humor is characteristic of the nineteenth century, but the sympathetic view of humor does not lose its popularity in the twentieth century, as evidenced by J. C. Gregory (1924), Stephen Leacock, who grants humor a philosophic depth by suggesting that it arises from the perception of the "incongruous contrast between the eager fret of our life and its final nothingness" (Leacock 1935, 219–20), and the Spanish-American philosopher, George Santayana, whose views deserve a more thorough examination.

"The young man who has not wept is a savage, and the old man who will not laugh is a fool," Santayana famously writes (Santayana 1950, F-57, 93). He is one of the rare philosophers who deem everything in nature comic in its existence, but also "lyrical in its ideal essence, tragic in its fate" (Santayana 1955, 305; 1922, 144). He entrusts laughter with an important role in his philosophy and on humor he has these few comments: Humor combines modesty with laughter; we identify our attitude as humorous when the situation is made contradictory by our being satirical and friendly at the same time; when humor is distant from satire, however, comedy does not seem amusing anymore, and humor passes out of the sphere of the comic altogether (Santayana 1922, 259; 1896, 158–9). Whether it is in the way of ingenuity, oddity, or drollery, the humorous person must have an absurd side, or be placed in an absurd position. Yet this comic aspect, at which we ought to wince, seems to endear the character all the more. This is a parallel case to that of tragedy, which elicits a complex emotion, "an element of pain overbalanced by an element of pleasure" (Santayana 1896, 141). In Santayana's later philosophy, humor is singled out as the means to maintaining convention while disclosing the masks that cover reality. The importance of humor lies in letting us cling to our illusions, for we cannot live without them (Santayana 1922, 66). Humor brings the reconciliation absent from other forms of the comic, which makes it an excellent tool for inevitable predicaments.

Henri Bergson is the sole philosopher to have written a book on laughter (1900). Renowned for his theory of laughter and his investigation of the techniques of the comic, *Laughter: An Essay on the Meaning of the Comic* offers comments on humor that have influenced an entire generation of French thinkers such as Vladimir Jankélévitch, Gilles Deleuze, and Clément Rosset.[5] Humor and irony differ in the manner in which they relate to the opposition between the ideal and the real, what should be and what actually is. Humor describes with scrupulous minuteness that which is done, and pretends to believe that this is what should be done. Jean Paul and other humor theorists have noticed that humor delights in concrete terms, technical details, and definite facts: Far from being an accidental trait of humor, it is its very essence. For Bergson, a humorist is a moralist disguised as a scientist (Bergson 1999, 143).

Bergson condemns as unscientific Freud's *Jokes and Their Relation to the Unconscious* (1905) in the appended critical bibliography of *Laughter's* second edition. Freud considers humor "one of the highest psychic functions, enjoying the special favor of thinkers" (1960 [1905], 56). He emphasizes its benign nature in an article published much later (1928 [1927]) than *Jokes*, which was composed contemporaneously with *Three Essays on the Theory of Sexuality* early in his career, but at a time when such important advances as the ego–id–superego triad and the connected dyad of the pleasure principle and the reality principle remained only latent in his thinking.

Jokes, the comic, and humor are linked through the pleasure principle (although Freud does not use the term in *Jokes*) and its recreation of the mood of childhood's inhibited pleasure. Freud retains the same distinctions and connections between jokes, humor, and the comic when extending these theories in his paper *Der Humor* of 1927. Humor is based on an economy of emotion coupled with the kind of elevation above vicissitudes outlined in chapter 7 of *Jokes*, but it is rendered more sophisticated via Freud's new category of the superego.

Humor demeans the ego's self-absorption as an adult trivializes a child's preoccupation. As the agency allowing this split attitude, the superego represents that internalization of parental authority and attitudes contained in all mature personalities: "The superego tries, by means of humour, to console the ego and protect it from suffering" (Freud 1928, 166). Thus, humor now mirrors the joke in that it represents the contribution of the superego to the comic while the joke represents the contribution of the id. It offers less pleasure than the comic and jokes, which explains why it never finds release in hearty laughter; "but (without rightly knowing why) we regard this less intense pleasure as having a character of very high value" (166).

Humor is healthy, comforting, liberating and elevating, even though serving an illusion, "the illusion that the travails of life are not travails at all" (Parkin 1997, 79). Its capability of deflecting suffering places it among the great methods that the human mind has constructed in order to evade the compulsion to suffer (Freud 1928, 163). The humorist economizes on his own self-concern or self-pity and thus converts the energy saved into positive pleasure. It has the infectious quality of pre-empting the need for pity on our part when responding to it. So humor can spread to an audience although it is independent of it: Unlike jokes, it needs no audience, and unlike the comic, it needs no victim.

Not everyone is capable of engendering or responding to humorous pleasure: It is "a rare and precious gift" to be able to reduce the world to a children's game, and thus by implication humor occurs much more rarely than other forms of the comic (Freud 1928, 166). Humor also functions differently from these in helping one rise above human vicissitudes, such as disease, death, and war. Vicissitudes of this kind inhibit the comic, but they can be a spur to humor, as the one enduring them can laugh at himself and with salutary effect, encouraging indifference to his circumstances. Such indifference reduces the plight of the victim to trivial proportions.[6]

This short historical survey illustrates the importance of humor in the nineteenth and twentieth centuries, and its independence from religious presuppositions: Humor need not function within religious borders to be deemed significant, as evidenced by Schopenhauer, Hegel, and his followers, Carlyle, Jean Paul, Santayana, and Freud. Yet despite the elevation of humor found in these views, it forms no part of the good life for Schopenhauer and Hegel, nor evidently for thinkers like Carlyle, Jean Paul, and Freud, whose works do not provide a full account of the good life.

A few prominent philosophers of the nineteenth and twentieth centuries interested in the subject single out *laughter* rather than humor, however: Henri Bergson in *Laughter: An Essay on the Meaning of the Comic* (1900) defends a vision of laughter that fits his metaphysics, but falls short of fulfilling a role in the individual's good life; Nietzsche and Santayana entrust laughter rather than humor with an important role in their respective views of the good life, but the choice of terms is not random for these accomplished aestheticians. To respect the terms used by these philosophers, the thought of Nietzsche, Bergson, and Santayana are examined apart, in a study on the role of *laughter* in the good life that goes beyond the scope of this book.[7] The present study seeks to provide a missing component in scholarly research—a much-needed supplement to the religious philosophies of Shaftesbury, Hamann, and Kierkegaard, one that offers an account of humor and its contribution to the good life within a philosophical framework compatible with recent research and independent of religious presuppositions.

Understanding the role humor can play in the good life begins with acknowledging the tragic sense of life. A vision that wanders wild without the cathexis provided by the aesthetic form in which it originated, the tragic sense of life requires the therapy that humor is able to provide. By construing tragic intrapsychic conflicts as comical incongruities, a conflict is simultaneously sensed as tragic and perceived as comical, leading thus to a humorous mood that reflects the ambiguity of life and the ambivalence of humankind. A humorous mood is helpful for becoming aware of conflicts, for deliberating over them, and for leaving unresolved the basic human predicament defined by the tension between one's desires and one's capacity for fulfilling them on the instinctual, emotional, and intellectual levels. It is important not to resolve this tension, I suggest in contradistinction to redemptive theories both religious and otherwise and to philosophical theories aiming at peace of mind, because such resolutions come at a price: They either renounce one's desires, or one's reason, or both. Although living with unresolved conflict is difficult, humor can play an important role in relieving the tension it creates.

Nevertheless, the humorous mood is transitory, and when it dissolves, there emerges the ridicule of repeatedly transmuting tragic oppositions into comical incongruities with an increasing capacity for suffering the former and no steady results from the latter. The resultant awareness is the view of human beings as ridiculous or *Homo risibilis*.

Ridicule dissolves, however, if we adhere to the view that we are ridiculous only to the extent that we ignore ourselves. The resolution that obtains mirrors both the resolution of the comedy plot, where the true identity of the hero changes everything, and the process of two-staged theories of humor, which require a higher level of resolution of the initial incongruity in order for a situation to be humorous. This resolution stands out because it does not require renouncing our desires, or reason, or both; thus, it allows the radical change we denied ourselves before acknowledging our riducule.

Through a multistage process involving a systematic use of humor that disciplines our taste to find pleasure in incongruities that are not immediately funny to us, a ladder of perfection can be climbed that leads to a state rivaling the highest philosophic and religious ideals. This achievement is gradual and is based on changing visions about oneself, others, and the world according to one's capacity to transmute suffering into joy through the alchemy of humor.

The lucidity we gain frees us from the comic as well as the tragic, at least from that part of the tragic that has been transmuted into the comic and has thus become constitutive of the tragic-comic protagonist that describes each of us. The freedom that results from the newfound harmony with oneself, others, and the world is characterized by joy and serenity.

Apart from the Hellenistic and Roman skeptical Pyrrhonists who graphically compare the peace of mind that follows the suspension of judgment to a shadow following the body, the proposal below is the only skeptical worldview I know of that aims at such an ideal and the only one to use humor to reach it.[8]

THE COMIC AND THE TRAGIC

The tragic sense of life originated in tragedy, but disengaged itself from the literary form in the nineteenth century, and now wanders freely without the much-needed cathexis that the aesthetic form gave it. The comic may provide a personal therapy for the tragic sense of life, inasmuch as the comic aestheticizes the tragic vision and enables us to find pleasure in it. The comic thus secures the knowledge of the human condition that the tragic sense of life reveals without the maddening pain and incessant brooding that accompanies it.

THE TRAGIC

Tragedy refers to a literary form, and in general lay usage, to an unfortunate event disrupting the existence of the individual or an entire people and crushing the possibility of disposing of one's life or destiny freely.[9] The *tragic* refers to both of the above meanings of tragedy, and also expresses a certain tonality of experience and thought, or manner of relating oneself to the experience of being, and a way of understanding this experience, of thinking about it and communicating it (Chirpaz 1998, 4). This use of "the tragic" or "the tragic vision" is far more restrictive than the general lay usage of "tragedy" or "the tragic," which can be synonymous with catastrophe and the sorrowful. Murray Krieger explains how the tragic vision differs from tragedy as a literary form:

> "Tragedy" refers to an object's literary form, "the tragic vision" to a subject's psychology, his view and version of reality. . . . The tragic vision was born inside tragedy, as a part of it: as a possession of the tragic, the vision was a reflection in the realm of thematics of the fully fashioned revelation of aesthetic totality which was tragedy. (Krieger 1963, 131)

In his essay on the tragic, Peter Szondi reminds us of a distinction worth repeating. He states that we have had a poetics of tragedy since Aristotle, but "only since Schelling has there been a philosophy of the tragic" (Szondi 2002, 1). Indeed, philosophic speculation on tragedy and the tragic did not develop until the period of German idealism. Since the nineteenth century "the tragic sense of life" has been with us as a modern, indeed a neo-Christian invention, with Nietzsche as its chief prophet and preacher (Galle 1993, 39, 34). Modern consciousness has separated the tragic sense of life from its aesthetic origins:

> Fearful and even demoniac in its revelations, the [tragic] vision needed the ultimate soothing power of the aesthetic form which contained it—of tragedy itself—in order to preserve for the world a sanity which the vision itself denied. . . . But what if we should find the Dionysian without the Apollonian? Here

we would have life unalleviated, endlessly and unendurably dangerous, finally destructive and self-destructive—in short, the demonical. In effect it would be like tragedy without that moment in which the play comes round and the cosmos is saved and returned to us intact. It would be, in other words, the tragic vision wandering free of its capacious home in tragedy. (Krieger 1963, 137)

The consequence of the liberation of "the tragic" from "tragedy" is that the former is disengaged from the therapy provided by the latter's aesthetic form:

The therapy produced by catharsis, which allowed the subversive elements to be healthily exposed and aesthetically overcome, would no longer be available. And the alienated members, now unchallenged, would be free to turn inward upon themselves to nourish their indignation in the dark underground. (137)

The greatest challenge the tragic view of life presents, I believe, is to produce a cathexis or therapy that does not deny its contents.

The tragic designates a tonality of thought that does not concentrate on exploring the world, but on explicating the reality of the human condition. Nor is the tragic vision a systematic view of life: It admits a wide range of variation and degrees; it is a sum of insights, intuitions, and feelings, to which the words "vision" or "view" or "sense of life," however inadequate, are more readily applicable. For Miguel de Unamuno, the tragic sense of life is a subphilosophy or a prephilosophy, more or less formulated and conscious, reaching deep down into temperament, not so much flowing from ideas as determining them (Unamuno 1972, 5).

Most writers on the tragic sense of life agree on its contents, however, it is the sense of ancient evil, of the mystery of human suffering, of the gulf between aspiration and achievement. Schopenhauer writes of "the unspeakable pain, the wretchedness and misery of humanity, the triumph of wickedness, the scornful mastery of chance, and the irretrievable fall of the just and the innocent" (Schopenhauer 1969, I, 252–3). Nietzsche too emphasizes suffering as the outcome of the constant struggle between the irrational, absurd, and ecstatic, on the one hand (the Dionysian), and the rational, intelligible, and harmonious, on the other (the Apollonian) (1966a). Nietzsche's follower, Clément Rosset, describes Being as tragic, and thus illogical, amoral, and contradictory; tragic in a tragic world, the human being is "solitary, that is, without love, base, thus without value, and mortal, therefore, without life." He is not responsible for the tension that defines the tragic; it is a mystery he can notice, but to which he cannot reconcile himself (Rosset 1991, 90, 22, 19; my translation). Rosset repeats Nietzsche's view of the human predicament as that of the human being who has ventured into the recognition of a truth that he is incapable of facing. This is the truth about his contradictory and tragic destiny—tragic, in the sense that Vladimir Jankélévitch understands it, as "the alliance of the necessary and the impossible" (Jankélévitch 1998, 313).

Similarly, for Richard Sewall the tragic vision is in its first phase primal, or primitive, in that it calls up out of the depths the first (and last) of all questions, the question of existence: What does it mean to exist? The tragic vision recalls the original terror, harking back to a world that antedates the conception of philosophy, the consolation of the later religions, and whatever constructions the human mind has devised to persuade itself that the universe is secure. It recalls the original un-reason, the terror of the irrational. It sees the human being as questioner, naked, unaccommodated, alone, facing mysterious, demonic forces in his own nature and outside, and the irreducible facts of suffering and death (Sewall 1965, 37).

Moreover, as Oscar Mandel maintains in "Tragic Reality," the human situation that lies at the root of tragic art is not simply that human effort fails, but that "failure lies implicit in the effort" (Mandel 1963, 60). He considers death, with its inevitable victory over effort, as the first tragic fact. The second tragic fact is sociopsychological: The very act of living in the society of others brings with it—unavoidably and "naturally"—friction, hate, and misery. The desire or need to live among one's kind is tragic because of the misalliance between human beings. "Thus the very act of birth is tragic not only because it is simultaneously the condemnation to death," Mandel explains, "but also because it fastens on the child the inevitability of suffering among his own species" (61).

We meet with tragic fact at every level; Mandel notes the intricacy of folly in wisdom, doom in success, flaw in every social reform, a phenomenon that Henry Alonzon Myers deems the ambivalence of tragedy and that Larry Slade, a protagonist of Eugene O'Neill's *The Iceman Cometh*, calls "the two sides of everything" (Myers 1956, 98–109): Attraction and repulsion, love and hate, illusion and disillusion, reform and reaction, utopian hope and end-of-an-age despair; these are the well-known materials of modern tragedies, which must end, if the artist fails to see the justice in "the two sides of everything," on a note of futility and hopelessness (101).

Finally, Conrad Hyers sums up "the tragic paradigm" as a view of life that sees existence individually or collectively as structured in terms of polarities, oppositions, contradictions, and their collisions. The tragic opposition may be seen within the individual, between persons or groups, in the very nature of things, or all three. At the individual level, we have a predilection for reading the psyche as an internal struggle between contending forces. The heart of the tragic is the divided personality, and the theme of the inner torment of the tragic psyche has had a long history, from Sophocles' King Oedipus, through Plato, Paul, the Middle Ages, Shakespeare, the Romantics, Dostoevsky, till Freud.

Sophocles' King Oedipus is a tortured soul confronted with the twin revelations of having killed his father and married his mother. For Paul it is the "wretched man that I am" of Romans 7 who laments: "I delight in the law of God, in my inmost self, but I see in my members another law at war with the law of my mind and making me captive to the law of sin" (22–4). In the Middle Ages this interior struggle is represented in many morality plays as a contest between the Seven Virtues and the Seven Deadly Sins, as an angel and a demon whispering their contrary bits of advice. Shakespeare's tragic outlook can be repeatedly seen in "equivalence," exemplified in the two-sided nature of human feelings, whereby the source of our pleasure and joy is also inevitably the source of anxiety and grief: The human being, in accordance with his capacity for feeling, which is always the same for joy as it is for sorrow, is fated to enjoy and suffer in equal measures (Myers 1956, 100). The romanticists of the eighteenth and nineteenth centuries envision the human being wrestling with irreconcilable passions that tear the psyche asunder, or hounded by the disparity between the ideal (imagined or professed) and the real. For Dostoevsky, the center of the conflict is between faith and doubt, a dilemma experienced by many of the characters from Crime and Punishment to The Brothers Karamazov (Hyers 1996, 24–25).

It is in literature that the tragic has found the par excellence form of its expression, as evidenced by so many literary works since the epoch of the Greeks.

Examples of the exploration of the tragic paradigm in the literature and drama of the nineteenth and twentieth century abound. The tragic sense of life has been portrayed in Conrad's The Heart of Darkness, Maxwell Anderson's Winterset, Faulkner's Absalom, Absalom, O'Neil's Long Day's Journey into Night, Camus' The Stranger, Sartre's Nausea and No Exit, Melville's Moby Dick, to name a fraction. Miguel de Unamuno's The Tragic Sense of Life has been very much a part of our modern sensibility.

Philosophy is almost averse to the tragic sense of life. Echoing Nietzsche's claims, Bernard Williams asserts that "moral philosophy is typically attached to the project of giving us 'good news' about our condition—whether in the form of the grand Hegelian narratives of progress or of Leibnizian theodicy. Even the bare Kantian fact of the good will is itself a kind of good news" (Williams 1996). For William Desmond, while tragedy reveals one of the ultimate forms of being at loss, philosophy strives to overcome loss, to place reason where tragedy faces rupture, to construct meaning where tragedy undergoes suffering (Desmond 1993). Clément Rosset suggests that philosophers generally resist admitting that tragic thought can ever be developed into a philosophy. Philosophy willingly admits that there is some tragic element in existence, literature, and art; yet it refuses to admit that a philosophy can be tragic in itself. Rosset adds an unacknowledged reason to his argument: A "tragic philosophy" would be inadmissible because it would mean the previous negation of all other philosophies. Thus, philosophers choose to leave the tragic to art and literature. This explains the difference one often finds between the philosophical and literary productions in the same civilization and at the same epoch, the latter basking in tragic brilliance and the former ignoring the tragic altogether (Rosset 1993b, 12).

This attitude toward the tragic explains why few philosophers can be deemed tragic, and why the philosophical status of those considered tragic is openly disputed. Rosset mentions Montaigne, Pascal, and Kierkegaard; Schopenhauer too is dismissed as a mere miserable man (Rosset 1991, 13). Moreover, the prominent tragic philosophers, Pascal, Kierkegaard, Shestov, and even Unamuno, to whom we owe the expression "the tragic sense of life," only partly deserve this characterization because they search for consolation in the "good news" religion offers, which can hardly deserve the epithet "tragic."[10] Indeed, in *The Death of Tragedy*, George Steiner sees the current demise of true tragedy as a byproduct of Christianity, whose promise of salvation for all sinners who repent has broken the back of the tragic assumption, the "unfaltering bias toward inhumanity and destruction in the drift of the world." For Steiner tragedy is founded on the assumption that there are in nature and in the psyche occult, uncontrollable forces able to madden and destroy the mind, and that beyond the tragic, there lies no "happy ending" in some other spatial and temporal dimension. The wounds are not healed and the broken spirit is not mended. In the norm of tragedy, there can be no compensation. Similarly, Karl Jaspers defends the position that the Christian promise of salvation stands in direct opposition to the unredeemed, unredeemable fatality of the Greek tragic vision: "The chance of being saved destroys the tragic sense of being trapped without chance of escape." To the same effect I. A. Richards considers tragedy to be possible only to a mind that is for the moment agnostic or Manichean, as "the least touch of any theology which has a compensating Heaven to offer the tragic hero is fatal" (Kerr 1967, 45, 37).

To the short and otherwise problematic list of tragic philosophers, we may add Schopenhauer, who sees the eternal strife of will against will as the ultimate nature of things, his follower Nietzsche, who considers himself the first tragic philosopher (Nietzsche 1979, III, BT, sec. 3; 1968, sec. 1029), a few French philosophers, such as Georges Bataille, Cioran,[11] and especially Rosset, who deems himself the sole follower of Nietzsche as a tragic philosopher (Rosset 1983, 34; 1993a, "Notes on Nietzsche").

Each age suffers from different tensions and terrors, but they open on the same abyss: Direction and focus may change, but the tragic vision is constant (Sewall 1965, 39). A tragic thought is a thought that is attentive to the constitutive contradiction of the human condition, which recognizes "the inevitability of paradox, of unresolved tensions and ambiguities, of opposites in precarious balance" (Sewall 1963, 120). Different authors have described this constitutive contradiction in a variety of disciplines and also within philosophy.

Sigmund Freud sees the constitutive contradiction of the human condition as a split between *id* and *superego*, and between the individual and society. The tragedy of childhood fate that points to the difficulty of becoming adult, the tragedy of the lifelong "repetition" of childhood scenarios, the tragedy of libidinal contradictions reflecting the wandering nature of human desire and thus the difficulty of loving, and the tragedy of the superego, pointing to the difficulty of self-knowledge and honestly judging oneself, all make conflict inescapable in human interaction. In his discussion of the tragic Freud, Paul Ricoeur emphasizes both the irresolvable situation in which desires can be neither suppressed nor satisfied and the ensuing narcissistic humiliation that even the lucid awareness of the necessary character of conflicts cannot diminish (Ricoeur 1974, 155–9).

Emile Durkheim finds that the constitutive contradiction is expressed in the opposition between the human being as an organism and an individual created by society; similarly, Peter Berger and Thomas Luckman see a dialectical process between the biological organism and the social self, and Claude Lévi-Strauss and more recently Agnes Heller point to the conflict between nature and culture.[12]

In philosophy, the most widespread view of a constitutive contradiction is between body and soul or mind. For Plato, the soul is dragged down and clouded by the dense and imperfect world of matter, haunted by a dim recollection of the pure realm from which it has fallen and torn apart by desires that move in opposite directions (*Phaedrus; Republic*). Pascal's well-known depiction of the human being as a "thinking reed" summarizes the contradictions that characterize humankind: "What a Chimera is man! What a novelty, a monster, a chaos, a contradiction, a prodigy! Judge of all things, an imbecile worm; depository of truth, and sewer of error and doubt; the glory and refuse of the universe. Who shall unravel this confusion?" (Pascal, *Pensées*, VI, 347–8; VII, 434).

Can we infer a tragic mode of thought from dramatic tragedies? Various humor theorists, such as Arthur Berger (1993), Conrad Hyers (1996), and John Morreall (1998, 1999) think it is possible. They compare this tragic vision, moreover, to a comic mode of thought derived from comedies. For example, John Morreall can compare the comic and the tragic visions of life, which he understands to be contrasting features of tragedy and comedy, because "the patterns we have discussed in tragedy and comedy are not just dramatic conventions for writing successful plays; they embody beliefs and attitudes concerning human life" (Morreall 1999, 339). He lists the following traits as representative of the tragic outlook: Simple conceptual schemes, low tolerance for disorder and ambiguity, avoidance of the unfamiliar, convergent thinking, noncritical thinking, emotional engagement, stubbornness, idealism, finality, denigration of the body, and seriousness. In contrast, the comic outlook is characterized as complex conceptual schemes, high tolerance for disorder and ambiguity, the search for the unfamiliar, divergent thinking, critical thinking, emotional disengagement, willingness to change one's mind, pragmatism, a second chance, celebration of the body, and playfulness. Socially, the comic and the tragic visions represent respectively anti-heroism versus heroism, pacifism versus militarism, forgiveness versus vengeance, social equality versus inequality, questioning versus acceptance of authority and tradition, situation ethics versus duty ethics, and social integration versus social isolation (Morreall 1998, 1999).

Although descriptions of the respective cognitive psychologies of the tragic and the comic are relevant to the tragic sense of life and the comic outlook superimposed on it, their respective social outlooks are not. But Morreall uses the differences between the tragic and comic visions to justify his preference for the comic over the tragic in order to "experience life as funny and fun" (Morreall 1999, 334). Here I differ from John Morreall. Because I consider the tragic sense of life epistemologically valuable, I am looking for a way to sustain its vision. The humorous state of mind I am first proposing incorporates both visions, the tragic and the comic, and derives its significance partly from the viability of the tragic it enables. The more radical vision I further advance, *homo risibilis*, not only refuses to reject the tragic sense of life, but fully accepts it; and the last step of embracing one's ridicule disengages the individual from both the tragic *and* the comic.

There are, furthermore, various theories that attempt to assess tragedy's nature, but these will not be examined here because the concern of this chapter is the *tragic sense* of life.[13] The tragic sense of life is a vision of life that may be revealed in tragedies, but it is different from tragedy in that there is no aesthetic form to give it meaning. It is a vision that wanders wild without the cathexis provided by the aesthetic form in which it originated. It is this lack of meaning and therefore of therapy that makes the tragic sense of life so tragic, and at the same time receptive to the therapy that humor is able to provide. I invoke tragedy, nevertheless, in order to confirm that the formula to which I will be reducing the tragic corresponds to it as well.

In *The Fragility of Goodness: Luck and Ethics in Greek Tragedy and Philosophy*, Martha Nussbaum differentiates between three different themes in tragedies. The first is evaluated as an ordinary fact of human life whose occurrence no one would deny: "The Greek tragedy shows good people being ruined because of things that just happen to them, things they do not control." The second theme is "something more deeply disturbing," but some cases "are mitigated by the presence of direct physical constraint or excusable ignorance": Tragedy "shows good people doing bad things, things otherwise repugnant to their ethical character and commitments, because of circumstances whose origin do not lie with them." Finally, the third theme is a more intractable sort of case—one which has come to be called, as a result, the situation of "tragic conflict." It is a case in which "we see a wrong action committed without any direct physical compulsion and in full knowledge of its nature, by a person whose ethical character or commitments would otherwise dispose him to reject the act. The constraint comes from the presence of circumstances that prevent the adequate fulfillment of two valid ethical claims" (Nussbaum 2001b, 25).

Nussbaum's indebtedness to Hegel's view of the tragic as the ethical conflict of two rights is evident (Szondi 1978, 165–74):

> We have been considering situations, then, in which a person must choose not to do (have) either one thing or another. Because of the way the world has arranged things, he or she cannot do (have) both. . . . He wants, however, to do (have) both . . . we have, then, a wide spectrum of cases in which there is something like a conflict of desires . . . : the agent wants (has reason to pursue) x and he or she wants (has reason to pursue) y; but he cannot, because of contingencies of circumstances to pursue both. (Nussbaum 2001b, 27)

She mentions a case in which the reason for pursuing X is not a desire, but issues from a moral claim that, as Bernard Williams has argued, cannot be avoided by eliminating the desire (Williams 1973).

Hegel's view has been criticized as a moral reading of tragedy, whose intent is to rescue free will; whereas the tragic resists moral interpretation (Ricoeur 1969, 217). In her characterization of tragedy, Nussbaum also empties the religious content of tragedy, which is a "questioning and an enacted testing of theodicy" (Steiner 1996, 136). Both Nussbaum's vision of the tragic as found in tragedies and critics who emphasize the a-morality and religiosity of tragedy can now be added to the descriptions of the tragic given above and taken into account in the formula of the human predicament I want to propose.

Transcribing the various descriptions of the tragic into a formula depicted in the most general terms and the minimum of metaphysical assumptions may make the tragic more palatable. I suggest that the experience common to most human beings is a tyranny of desires, needs, and wishes seeking satisfaction on the instinctual, emotional, and intellectual levels. This yearning is frustrated by reason because the knowledge of the possibility of satisfying desires is brought about by reason. To satisfy these desires, needs, and wishes is very difficult, sometimes impossible especially without paying a price that reason may refuse to pay. This formula is compatible with theories that consider rational thinking an emotional process. Because rational thinking is still in competition with other emotion-driven processes, this leaves us with a dichotomy between cognition and the passions (Hurley et al. 2011, 84). This formula is also compatible with theories that consider emotions rational, because the conflict between emotions and rationality still exist (Fridja 2004, 82).

The validity of this description of the human predicament can also be assessed through three well-known philosophic theories of the relations we entertain with the world, with others, and with ourselves. First, in his renowned *The Myth of Sisyphus* (1959 [1942]), Albert Camus maintains that the "absurd" arises because the world fails to meet our demands for meaning. I suggest that we consider the gap that exists between the individual and the world, which Camus calls the "absurd," as a gap between our need for value and meaning, on the one hand, and the impossibility of fulfilling that need in the world, on the other.

The absurdity of our situation derives from a collision within us rather than a collision between our expectations and the world, and can be described as a case of desires frustrated by the awareness of the impossibility of fulfilling them. Camus' claim that the world fails to meet our demands for meaning suggests that the world might satisfy these demands if it were different. But Thomas Nagel rightly remarks that what makes doubt inescapable with regard to the limited aims of individual life also makes it inescapable with regard to any larger purpose that encourages the sense that life is meaningful. Once the fundamental doubt has begun, it cannot be laid to rest. This is not the case that the world might satisfy these demands if it were different. There does not appear to be any conceivable world (containing us) in which irresolvable doubts could not arise. Consequently, the absurdity of our situation derives not from a collision between our expectations and the world, but from a collision within ourselves (Nagel 1987, 54).

A second well known theory that bears on the validity of the description of the human predicament proposed above is Jean-Paul Sartre's description of the clash between me and the other, between the individual and the group (Sartre 1957 [1943]). This clash can be construed as a tension between, on the one hand, my desires and, on the other hand, my awareness of the existence of other persons whom I ought to take into consideration and whose desires clash with mine.

Finally, Immanuel Kant views metaphysical questions as necessarily arising from the nature of reason, yet transcending reason's power of answering them: "Human reason has this particular fate that it is burdened by questions which, as prescribed by the very nature of reason itself, it is not able to ignore, but which, as transcending all its powers, it is also not able to answer" (Kant 1929, xviii). In *Dreams of a Spirit-Seer*, Kant speaks of "Metaphysics, with which, as fate would have it, I have fallen in love but from which I can boast of only a few favors" (Kant 1992–, Ak. 367). In *The Critique of Pure Reason*, he maintains that no matter how unsuccessful our metaphysical efforts may be "we shall return to metaphysics as to an estranged beloved" (Kant 1929, A850/B878). Kant holds that reason has a proper aim and an internal drive to reach it; because this drive is necessarily frustrated, the internal tension Kant describes will always arise between the necessary quest for metaphysical answers and the awareness of the impossibility of providing for this need.[14]

These three examples provided by Camus, Sartre, and Kant can be generalized to depict the core of human tension and dissatisfaction as a clash between expectations and the perception of reality. The yearning is frustrated by the awareness of the impossibility of fulfilling it. This fundamental clash arises sometimes from practical reasons, and sometimes from principled reasons, that is, from reasons that are inherent in the nature of desires, cognition, or the clash between them.

Some thinkers deem the tragic an essential element of the universe (Scheler 1963, 27), or a pervasive aspect of it (Santayana 1922, 144), making it thus available to all. Others see the tragic as accessible to only a few: Max Scheler believes that some people are blind or nearly blind to the tragic (Scheler 1963, 27), and Richard Sewall emphasizes that this is an attitude toward life with which some individuals seem to be endowed to a high degree, others less so, but which is latent in every person and may be evoked by experience (Sewall 1965, 37). Miguel de Unamuno finds the variability of the tragic sense of life characteristic of nations rather than individuals (Unamuno 1972). Americans are considered to be averse to the tragic sense of life, perhaps as a consequence of their vision of the "indefinite perfectibility of man" that Tocqueville noted as early as 1835. For example, Stanley Edgar Hyman describes the American psychoanalysts' reconstruction of Freud's views along the lines that are less "gloomy, stoic, and essentially tragic" than his "applied" psychoanalysis, whose effect "has been to re-repress whatever distasteful or tragic truths Freud dug out of his own unconscious or his patients' and to convert the familiar device of resistance into revisionist theory" (Hyman 1965, 278, 292).

The controversy over the accessibility of the tragic is related to a further debate on whether the tragic sense of life can be taught. Lionel Abel believes that only by undergoing tragedy one arrives at the tragic sense of life: "One does not acquire or develop the tragic sense," he maintains; therefore, "it is not realized, but imposed; one never possesses it, one has to be possessed by it" (Abel 1967, 178). For Schopenhauer, experiencing the sufferings of life is only one way, albeit the more common, to arrive at a tragic sense of life, but knowledge is another way to it (Schopenhauer 1969, II, 638).

Another controversy bears on whether the tragic sense of life should be developed. A few authors believe the tragic sense of life should be fostered (Krieger 1963; Muller 1956), especially since there is "a perhaps unconscious but forceful onslaught on our sense of the tragic that threaten[s] to destroy it utterly" (Krieger 1960, viii). Others, such as the humor theorists Arthur Berger, Conrad Hyers and John Morreall, contrast the paradigms they deem "the comic" and "the tragic" in order to defend the comic outlook (Berger 1993; Hyers 1996; Morreall 1998, 1999). I believe the knowledge of the human condition brought about by the tragic view of life is worth preserving, but without the tonality accompanying it, the maddening pain, and the constant brooding over it. The comic, I suggest, may prove helpful for disengaging the content of the tragic from its pain.

THE COMIC

The history of tragedy and comedy, various theories of humor, and the affinity of humor with sadness and suffering point to the possibility of construing contradictions as comical incongruities that were originally perceived as tragic. A considerable amount of information has been accumulated that bears on the important role that humor can play in the alleviation of conflicts, as well as on its other physiologic, psychological, and social benefits. I suggest that humor may alleviate intrapersonal conflicts as well. Various philosophers have praised self-referential humor but this form of humor has not been sufficiently investigated.

TRAGEDY AND COMEDY

The histories of the dramatic genres and scholarly views on the relation between tragedy and comedy indicate that there is a basic connection between the two.[15] Walter Kerr maintains, "the doorway to comedy is truly a back door through tragedy" (Kerr 1967, 17). In a chapter entitled "the tragic source of comedy," Kerr describes comedy as an epi-phenomenon of tragedy:

> Comedy, it seems, is never the gaiety of things; it is the groan made gay. Laughter is not man's first impulse; he cries first. Comedy always comes second, late after the fact and in spite of it or because of it. Comedy is really the underside of things, after the rock of our hearts has been lifted, with effort and only temporarily. It appears in the absence of something and as the absence of something. Man's primary concern is with the rock, with his heart, with tragedy. (19)

Comedy at its most penetrating derives from what we normally regard as tragic, Kerr believes. Comedy adds the last necessary ounce of truth to tragedy; it is not a relief, but "the rest of the bitter truth, a holy impropriety. The relief we find in it comes from its having finished the sentence . . ." (17).

The forms of tragedy and comedy are inseparable, for Kerr, one incomplete without the other. Tragedy is the forward, upward thrust; comedy is the drag or reminder. In early Greek arrangement of plays, the two are balanced in just this way, with the satyr child being born directly of its tragic mother. In the medieval rediscovery of drama, the two-faced pattern is repeated. Thus, "the first highly developed comic notes are developed not apart from, but out of, what has been presented as, most terrifying" (26). We have very good evidence, then, to show that comedy, in its fullness, comes after seriousness, after tragedy or its equivalent. And on somewhat lesser but nonetheless extremely provocative evidence, it seems likely that comedy comes *from* tragedy. If this is so, the two faces the theater shows us are in actuality the same face "worn by the same man, reporting the same event" (31). Northop Frye voices similar ideas in *The Argument of Comedy*: "Tragedy is really implicit or uncompleted comedy," he writes, and "comedy contains a potential tragedy within itself" (Frye 1964, 455). At the end of Plato's *Symposium*, Socrates insists to his friends, Aristophanes and Agathon, that "the genius of comedy is the same as the genius of tragedy, and that the writer of tragedy ought to be a writer of comedy also" (223 c–d). Beyond the literal sense that every writer should be able to do both, what Socrates seems to have had in mind is the undeniable truth that the highest comedy gains its power from its sense of tragic possibility and that the profoundest tragedy presents a full if fleeting vision through its temporary disorder of an ordered universe, to which comedy is witness. Without a sense of the tragic, comedy loses heart," Richard Sewall maintains, "it becomes brittle, it has animation, but not life. Without a recognition of the truths of comedy, tragedy becomes bleak and intolerable" (Sewall 1965, 34).

Moreover, both the tragic and the comic involve opposition and conflict. We have seen the kind of oppositions on which the tragic sense of life broods, but scholars who study comedy also emphasize that the comic always involves an encounter of two different, often directly opposed, levels or experiences, such as high–low, soul–body, mind–matter, artificial–natural, spirit–letter, human–animal, divine–human, ideals–reality, spontaneity–habit, culture–vulgarity, high aims–low needs. Bergson adds to the series above yet another oppositional pair, living–mechanical or life–automatism, which he attempts to establish as the core of all others (Bergson 1999).[16] Thus, the history of the genres and the constitutive part that oppositions play in both comedy and tragedy point to the possibility of transposing tragic oppositions into comical oppositions.

THEORIES OF HUMOR

Theories of humor may shed light on the transformation of tragic oppositions into comical incongruities. The theory of the comical attaches two distinct meanings to the term *humor*: broad and narrow. *Humor* is understood broadly when it is used interchangeably with the term *comical*. Some theorists apply the term *humor* to all kinds of comical works (see Dziemidok 1993, 101, n. 39). In this case, humor often is taken to mean the subjective aspect of the comical (both the capacity to experience the comical and the experience itself), as exemplified, for example, by R. J. Corsini's definition in *The Dictionary of Psychology*: Humor is "the capacity to perceive or express the amusing aspects of situations" (1999). Similarly, in the expression "sense of humor," "humor" is often semantically equivalent to "the comical." What is meant by "sense of humor" is the aesthetic sensitivity to the stimuli that evoke the experience of the comical: A *sense of humor* is the capacity to perceive the amusing aspects of a situation or to construe it as such. Humor, then, is the contemporary umbrella term we use to refer to the comic and its cognates.

Many authors make use of the narrow meaning of the term *humor* to specify a particular form of the comical (see Dziemidok 1993, 101, n. 41). Moreover, humor is associated with a specific axiological attitude and a view of the world together with the form of humorous writing expressing them, whose important component is the comical. In these last two related meanings, humor, because of its permissiveness, tolerance, and reflective character, is contrasted with militant and uncompromising satire, on the one hand, and the primitive forms of the comical connected with farce and vaudeville, on the other.

Unless otherwise indicated, *humor* is used here in its broad meaning, as interchangeable with the *comical*. The various theories that attempt to define, characterize or explain *the comical* or *humor* as an umbrella term for the comic and its cognates are usually divided into superiority theories, incongruity theories (which include ambivalence theories), and release and relief theories, although a richer taxonomy exists. For example, Patricia Keith-Speigel offers an analysis of eight primary categories, and Matthew Hurley et al. update the three categories of humor theories with an analysis of more recent work, adding biological theories, play theories, surprise theories, and Bergson's mechanical humor theory (Keith-Speigel 1972; Hurley et al. 2011, 37–55).

The most widespread contemporary view of the comical (humor) is as incongruity alone, or together with its resolution. There are various theories of incongruity, but they all present cognitions involving disjointed ideas, ill-suited pairings of ideas or situations, and/or their presentations in ways that diverge from habitual or expected customs (Flugel 1954, 722). The conflict-resolution theory is a variant of incongruity theory. Rod Martin reports on a long debate among cognitively oriented humor theorists as to whether incongruity alone is a necessary and sufficient condition for humor or whether it needs resolution as well. Some information-processing analysts, who have added to incongruity theory a component of conflict-resolution, as well as others, have a two-stage process in common: First, the perception of some complexity, incongruity, discrepancy, ambiguity, or novelty in the humor stimulus; second, the resolution (i.e., cognitive integration or understanding) of the stimulus (Martin 1998, 26).[17]

Oscillation, conflict-mixture and simultaneously experienced incompatible emotions or feelings characterize the ambivalence theories of the comical (humor) (Monro 1951). The difference between the incongruity and the ambivalence theories of humor lies in their emphasis: The former emphasize cognition and the latter emphasize feelings. As the comical/ humor has both cognitive and affective components, I use both theories, as well as the release and relief theories. The common basis of the theories pertaining to the latter group is their view that humor provides relief or release from too much tension.[18]

The notion of incongruity explains the relevance of humor to conflict or opposition. We can consider incongruity as a conflict or clash between ideas, emotions, desires, or among them. Conversely, we also can consider conflict an incongruity, and by using the incongruity and ambivalence theories, we can construe this conflict as comical. The humor thus created enables us to tolerate the tension generated by this opposition. This last point is clarified by the third group of theories, which views humor as a relief or release of too much tension. Within the framework of these theories, it is possible to assume that some situations construed as tragic also may be experienced as comical, thereby making the situation bearable.

ENJOYING INCONGRUITIES

Some comical situations are independent of any underlying tragic incongruity. More importantly, the person who is in the midst of experiencing a tragic incongruity may not perceive it as comical. Our reaction to incongruity may be negative emotions, puzzlement, or humorous amusement (Morreall 1989b). According to such disparate sources as Freud, Bergson, and Morreall, however, as soon as a humorous reaction to incongruity has been established, emotions cannot arise (Freud 1928; Bergson 1999; Morreall 1983a, 1983b). Freud adds that the emotion should be nascent or in its very beginning for humor to be able to replace it. However, based on Freud's view of pleasure as a byproduct of humor, I suggest that even later, especially if a more detached view of the current situation is required to act, humor, more than philosophical theory, has a better chance of asserting itself. As Freud explains, "we can only say that if someone succeeds, for instance, in disregarding a painful affect by reflecting on the greatness of the interests of the world as compared with his own smallness, we do not regard this as an achievement of humour but of philosophical thought, and if we put ourselves into this train of thought, we obtain no yield of pleasure" (Freud 1960, 289). Humor in Freudian terminology or a comic apprehension in mine can be induced by the incongruity created by the thought of the possibility of a more objective-reasonable view than the subjective-emotional situation one is experiencing; being even slightly pleasurable, this comical incongruity helps to set up a more detached view of the situation at hand.

"In the laughter with which we observe and greet the foibles of others," Reinhold Niebuhr notes "a nice mixture of mercy and judgment, of censure and forbearance" (Niebuhr 1969, 137); this is even more so in self-referential laughter, as Shaftesbury has shown through the device of soliloquy as a means for self-correction. If Michael Gelven and Agnes Heller are right in arguing respectively that "laughter is the most curious manifestation of reflexive reason" and "the instinct of reason" (Gelven 2000, 1; Heller 2005, 29), then it is reason through laughter that communicates with the emotions. Sooner or later, it is necessary to establish some distance from one's emotions in order to continue living. Gentle laughter at the folly of believing that the heart will get its way, that desires will be fulfilled, that mortals will not die, and that "this will not happen to me" is the first step toward bridging the gap between that which one desires and that which reason knows.

It may well be that philosophers cannot say much to themselves or to others who have lost a loved one, or an arm, or the ability to see. But, as Robert Solomon reminds us, we all meet or read about the rare sages who have suffered the most profound misfortunes and have retained a sense of acceptance, graciousness, and even humor about their lives (Solomon 1999, 115). Moreover, sadness, suffering, and humor may be intimately connected. This can be inferred from theories of humor that emphasize its survival value (Koller 1988, 26), or that view the comic as the sense and vital rhythm of life, celebrating a fertility god that is a symbol of perpetual rebirth and eternal life (Langer 1964, 498, 502, 503, 510). This connection also has been noted by suffering philosophers, such as Kierkegaard, who maintains that "the melancholy have the best sense of the comic," and Nietzsche, who asserts that "the deeply wounded have Olympian laughter; one has only what one needs to have," and "the most suffering animal on earth invented for itself—laughter" (Kierkegaard *EO1*, 20; also *JP* 1,700; Nietzsche 1968, sec. 1040; 990).[19]

If a tragic incongruity cannot always be perceived as comical by the person who is in the midst of experiencing it, most intrapersonal tragic conflicts, I believe, have the potential to transform themselves into comical incongruities, as theories of humor imply, histories of the dramatic genres and relations between the tragic and the comic illustrate, the association between sadness, suffering and humor indicates, and sheer survival recommends.

A considerable amount of information has been accumulated that bears on the important role that humor can play in the alleviation of social conflicts. Indeed, it is often said that humor is social; at least laughter is shared and is notoriously contagious. Humor itself is a universal, an ever-present phenomenon of every known society, a recognizable feature of every cultural inventory. Sociologists have pointed to consensus as the social glue that keeps diverse and sometimes-conflicting elements in human societies, groups, and associations together. Humor is one of the major means to achieving consensus because it signals to individuals that they share common experiences, ideas, themes, or values. It also functions as a mode of indirect communication that relieves stress and strain and enables the discussion of serious matters in a non-threatening way. It is an effective expression of aggression and hostility, as well as an expression of its contrary, a form of self-devaluation or self-humiliation that replaces hostility and indignation directed at others. It is a constant participant in the celebration of the significant arrival of major events in the lives of individuals or in the lives of an entire society. Humor also functions to correct human errors, voice social criticism, and disclose human sham or the posturing involved in deceit, pretense, and trickery. Humor can both reinforce and undermine stereotypes. One of its major functions is to provoke thought, and it is good in countering pain.

Finally, sociologists have documented the presence of both conflict and control among human groups. Humor is operative in terms of these concerns: It can be a devastating weapon of attack, and also can be used to manage group members by shoring up group morale (see Koller 1988, chap. 2). Although humor plays a significant role in social conflicts, it is important to note that sociological theories of humor diverge in their emphasis on this role: The functionalist approach emphasizes humor's ability to vent or expel hostility and thereby avoid or reduce social conflict; the conflict approach, in contradistinction, sees humor as a weapon, a form of attack, a means of defense, and an expression or correlate of social conflict (Speier 1998). Sociologist Giselinde Kuipers explains that conflict theories of humor have been used especially in the analysis of ethnic and political humor (Kuipers 2008, 368); they are exemplified in the case studies Marjolein 't Hart and Dennis Boss relate in *Humor and Social Protest* (2007).

Humor need not be social, however: Kierkegaard considers the humorist a socially alienated isolato who takes an unconciliatory stance toward the world, and who "like a beast of prey, always walks alone" (*JP* 2, 1719/ *Pap.* II A 694, January 13, 1838); Schopenhauer, as we have seen above, emphasizes the individualistic stance of the humorist; and Carlyle sees the humorist as solitary as well (Carlyle 1827, 14). Unlike a joke, Freud considers humor something that can be enjoyed by someone without the need to communicate it, and to which "another person's participation adds nothing new." Thus, "humour completes its course within a single person," and this is why "humour is the most easily satisfied among the species of the comic" (Freud 1960, 284). More recently Dineh Davis has argued, "humor begins within and may remain entirely within the individual (such as in self-talk or self-discovery), and as such can be dealt with within the disciplines of philosophy or psychology" (Davis 2008, 549). However, Willibald Ruch notes that in psychology and other disciplines, the scope of most theories of humor is limited to an analysis of jokes and cartoons (Ruch 2008, 28). This means that the analysis of individual, intrapersonal and noncommunicated self-referential humor that follows has been developed independently for the simple reason that heretofore research in this area has seldom been conducted and little or no data is available.

Nevertheless, there is much information about the role humor can play to ease personal conflicts. Today, the physiological and psychological benefits of humor are numerous and well documented, although the findings are less clear-cut than most people think. A sense of humor and the ability to laugh have long been viewed as important sources of both physical and psychological health. Since medieval times, a number of physicians and philosophers have suggested that laughter has important health benefits such as improving blood circulation, restoring energy, counteracting depression, and enhancing the functioning of various organs of the body (see Goldstein 1982; Moody 1978). In recent years, several of the physical health claims that have been made for humor come from the research of William Fry and colleagues.[20] In the past century, various psychologists and psychotherapists such as Sigmund Freud (1928), Abraham Maslow (1954), and Rollo May (1953) also have discussed the importance of a benign sense of humor for mental health.[21]

Belief in the positive health benefits of humor and laughter has become increasingly popular in recent years. A burgeoning "humor and health movement" has developed as well as organizations such as the Association for Applied and Therapeutic Humor. In recent years, the growth of the "laughter club movement," whose adherents promote laughter as a form of yogic exercise, has further added to the chorus of claims for the beneficial effects of even nonhumorous laughter on physical, mental, and spiritual health, as well as its potential for resolving conflicts at both the personal and international levels.

Humor may influence psychological health through the positive emotion of mirth associated with it. Like other positive emotions, mirth may enhance feelings of well-being and counteract negative emotions such as depression and anxiety. Consequently, individuals who frequently engage in humor may be less prone to various forms of emotional disturbance. Like other emotions, mirth is associated with a variety of biochemical processes in the brain and other parts of the body (Ruch 1993). Such emotion-related biochemical changes may have beneficial effects on physical health, such as increasing pain tolerance, enhancing immunity, or undoing the cardiovascular consequences of negative emotions. According to this model, overt laughter may not be necessary for health benefits to occur because humor and amusement may induce the positive emotion of mirth without the need for laughter. A healthy sense of humor would involve a generally cheerful temperament characterized by mirth, happiness, joy, optimism, and a playful approach to life (Ruch and Kohler 1998).

Humor may benefit psychological health through cognitive mechanisms. By shifting perspective and avoiding overly serious responses to situations, individuals who maintain a humorous outlook on life are less likely to become stuck in the cognitive distortion that gives rise to anxiety and depression. The humorous perspective may also be an important way of coping with stress. There is a large body of research pointing to the adverse effects stressful life experiences can have on various aspects of physical and psychological well-being. Thus, a humorous outlook on life and the ability to see the funny side of one's problems may enable individuals to cope more effectively with pressure and anxiety by allowing them to gain perspective and to distance themselves from stressful situations, enhancing their feelings of mastery and well-being in the face of adversity (Martin and Lefcourt 1983).

Finally, humor may benefit physical and psychological health through the social mechanism of increasing one's level of support. Individuals who are able to use humor more effectively to reduce interpersonal conflicts and tensions and to enhance positive feelings in others may consequently enjoy more numerous and satisfying social relationships. In turn, the greater levels of social support resulting from these relationships may confer stress-buffering and health-enhancing benefits (Cohen and Wills 1985).

A word of caution is in order, however. Rod Martin argues that claims for the benefits of humor are often simplistic, exaggerated, and unsubstantiated (Martin 2008). With regard to physical health, he sums up the research by suggesting, "the strongest evidence supports the idea of humor-related increases in pain tolerance, although the mechanisms are still unclear, and there is evidence that similar effects can also be found with negative emotions." With regard to psychological health, there is some evidence that a sense of humor can play a beneficial role in coping with stress, enhancing interpersonal relationships, and contributing to general well-being, "although this research is also somewhat inconsistent" (509). Relationships between humor and laughter, on the one hand, and psychosocial and physiological health, on the other, are more complex than many people believe. More research is needed to disentangle these complex relationships, Martin argues. Although there is little doubt that humor and laughter can enhance positive feelings of mirth, we have only an incomplete understanding of the ways in which different aspects of styles of humor many contribute to broader dimensions of mental health and satisfying social relationships (511).

To conclude the discussion of the benefits of humor, I suggest that Michael Gelven's argument in his *Truth and the Comedic Art* about "the comedic" can be endorsed for "humor" as well:

> The praise of the comedic may itself be trivialized by the over-ready: laughter makes us feel good. . . . These psychological consequences are true benefits, and it would be churlish to deny them. To focus on them as the central explanation is rather like drinking a vintage Chateau Margaux merely to experience the gentle high that follows, and not to taste its wondrous, magnificent flavor. . . . It is likewise not the mere psychological benefits that endorse comedic laughter. What would it be, then? The truth, perhaps? Even if it is truth it is only that peculiarly self-revealing truth about ourselves, which may be the most important kind, but it is also the most elusive. What enables us to praise comedic laughter apparently runs more deeply than obvious psychological benefits . . . (Gelven 2000, 6)

Humor's import is not confined to its psychological and physiological benefits. Its significance lies elsewhere, I suggest: Humor is an invaluable aid in attaining to philosophic ideals such as self-knowledge, truth, rationality, and virtue as well as more ambitious ideals such as liberation, joy and tranquility, as we shall shortly see.

SELF-REFERENTIAL HUMOR

In what follows I address only intrapersonal, rather than interpersonal, conflict.[22] Intrapersonal conflict calls for self-referential humor. The opinions of philosophers on this kind of humor diverge: Self-referential humor is recommended by the laughing philosopher, Democritus: "Why did you criticize my laughter, Hippocrates? You people do not laugh at your own stupidity but each laughs at another's" (Hippocrates 1990, Letter 17, line 5), by Seneca, who asserts that "no one becomes a laughing-stock who laughs at himself" (*On Firmness*, 16.3–17.4), and by Montaigne, who writes that "our own specific property is to be equally laughable and able to laugh" (1965, Bk. I, chap. 50). Hobbes explicitly refers to laughter at one's own past foibles. He does not interpret it as sympathetic, however. Rather, it is a form of superiority that "put[s] the rest into jealousy and examination of themselves" (1840, IV, chap. 8, sec. 13). Shaftesbury has endorsed self-referential humor, which becomes fashionable in the nineteenth century, as we have seen at the beginning of this chapter. Nietzsche makes it his hallmark: regretting that philosophers lack self-laughter to mock the prejudices they baptize as "truth" (Nietzsche 1966b, sec. 5), Nietzsche chooses self-laughter as *The Gay Science*'s new motto (1886), and makes it the pinnacle of the artist's greatness and the highest virtue of the human ideal he proposes (Nietzsche 1967, III, sec. 3; 1954a, IV, 12, 18; 20). In the twentieth century, Roger Scruton asserts approvingly that "humor is not normally self-directed," whereas Daniel Dennett sees self-referential humor as the paradigm of all humor, and Avital Ronell, among others, considers it the mark of the philosopher (Scruton 1987, 169; Hurley et al. 2011, 131–3; Ronell 2003, 298–9).

Philosophers recommend self-referential humor for its ability to correct mistakes, improve morality, and foster the drive for self-perfection and self-transcendence. In their *Inside Jokes: Using Humor to Reverse-Engineer the Mind*, Matthew Hurley, Daniel Dennett and Reginald Adams Jr. make "the twinge of ridiculousness that you feel when you've made a mental blunder . . . the core of basic humor." The "first-person phenomenon" is the fundamental source of humor in their model: "The (first) person both makes the mistake and discovers it. Laughing at others is a more sophisticated development of the funny bone . . ." (Hurley et al. 2011, 132–3). Drawing on Nietzsche and Kierkegaard, John Lippitt proposes an existential laughter (1996) and argues that self-referential humor can be a tool in self-perfection (Lippitt 1999a, 2005). Influenced by Kierkegaard, Robert Roberts suggests that humor can be a tool for moral growth in virtue ethics and a form of wisdom: "A sense of humor about one's *foibles*," he writes, "is a capacity of character-transcendence; but character-transcendence is basic to the very concept of a moral virtue" (Roberts 1988, 127). Others have argued that humor and self-referential humor are virtues (Basu 1999a; Amir 2002). John Morreall has dedicated most of his academic career to foster philosophic interest in humor[23]; for Morreall, self-referential humor is the most basic and most important kind of humor (Morreall 2010, 20); it may foster both moral and intellectual virtues (Morreall 2009, 112–9). Finally, Simon Critchley views humor, which teaches us to laugh at ourselves rather than at others, as philosophy in action (Critchley 2002; see 2003; Morreall 1983a). Thus, the workings of self-referential humor in an intrapersonal conflict deserve closer scrutiny.

HUMOR

I consider an intrapersonal conflict as an incongruity between one's desires and their fulfillment. Once an intrapersonal conflict is construed as an incongruity, there is much that humor can do to foster awareness of the conflict and knowledge of its constituents, facilitate deliberation, and later, help one live consciously with unresolved conflict, or resolve the conflict on a higher level of understanding. In order to see how humor can accomplish this, we need a better knowledge of its constitution.

THE SENSE OF HUMOR

Rod Martin affirms that there is yet no standard conception of the construct of sense of humor (see Herzog and Bush 1994; Herzog and Karafa 1998); nor is there a theoretical framework on which investigators generally agree. Martin proposes a three-dimensional model of humor based on Hans Eysenck's tripartite framework (Eysenck 1942; Martin 1998, 58–59). Although Eysenck's model is originally meant to categorize the themes of jokes and cartoons, it might also be useful in conceptualizing the major dimensions of sense of humor in terms of cognitive, emotional, and conative (motivational) components. My view concurs with both models in viewing humor as a complex inner process or multidimentional construct involving simultaneous cognitive, emotive, and conative components; it differs from them, however, in the way I describe the emotional and conative components of humor.

From a cognitive point of view, humor enables the perception of the comic, that is, of the simultaneous duality or multiplicity of points of view. It enables "rapid cognitive-perceptual shifts" (Yovetich et al. 1990) between various conflicting points of views.[24] These points of view may contradict each other as well as clash with more serious aspects of the situation. Thus, the capacity to perceive a series of incongruities is party to the cognitive component of humor.

From a conative point of view, humor is indifferent to motivation, reducing desire and impeding action. As Wallace Chafe hypothesizes (1987,

2007, 23), humor's basic evolutionary and adaptive function is "disabling" (Fry 1992). A sense of humor is the safety valve preventing impulsive behavior that leads to counterproductive actions (Fry 1987). Chafe suggests that it is instructive to look at the main physiological and psychological manifestations of humor in light of his "disabling hypothesis": physiologically it incapacitates and psychologically, because it is pleasing, it diverts attention away from decisive action (Roeckelein 2002, 271).

From an emotional point of view, humor offers several major benefits. First, it desensitizes intolerance to ambivalence by converting the pain of ambivalence into pleasure. Second, humor moderates extreme feelings, such as fear, anger, or sorrow (Morreall 1983a, 1997). In contrast to the practical orientation of emotions, humor involves a more abstract and less purposeful activity. Unlike reason, emotion usually employs a limited and partial perspective—the personal perspective of an interested agent. In contrast, humor links different, apparently unrelated elements within a more general, broader perspective, thereby generating a disinterested experience (Morreall 1983b; Fridja 1986, sec. 2.5; Ben-Ze'ev 2000, 364–5). Humor's survival value consists, at least in part, in its functioning as a counterweight to the strong influence exerted by emotions and moods on our behavior. It draws attention away from the self and its desires, thereby enabling us to look at reality from a safe and somewhat different point of view than the emotional perspective (Ben-Ze'ev 2000, 63–64). This makes it possible for us to relax and cope better with reality. Rod Martin notes that there are several possible mechanisms by which humor may moderate or buffer stress (Martin 2000).[25] The function of humor as a moderator of stress paves the way to a third benefit: Humor provides release from the pressure of frustration generated by the conflict.

Fourth, by reducing shame and disgust, humor facilitates a confrontation with difficult aspects of the self and enables us to contemplate them more calmly. Michael Lewis explains that coping with shame essentially involves removing ourselves from the shaming situation, by confessing, denying (attributing the failure to an external source), and forgetting (reducing the weight of our flaw), as well as by using humor (Lewis 1992, 127–37). Humor is helpful because it provides us with a new perspective that transcends the current uncomfortable perspective. Adopting another perspective is contrary to the partial nature of emotions and is thus incompatible with an intense emotional state. Consequently, laughing at ourselves serves to distance us from the shaming situation as we join others (imagined or real) in taking a fresh perspective on it. The new vantage point humor provides thus helps to reduce the significance of the shaming situation (Ben-Ze'ev 2000, 515).

Humor also can reduce disgust. The move from shame to disgust tracks the move from public to private, from external to internal, from child to adult, from repulsive to repressive. In his *Anatomy of Disgust*, William Ian Miller argues that the comic and the disgusting share significant points of contact, and that there is an intimate connection between some styles of contempt, disgust, and the comic (Miller 1997, ix, 116). Much of the comic depends on a transgressive irreverence, a kind of feast of misrule in which, if not the violation, at least the mockery of certain norms is privileged. No sooner is an aspect of the disgust acquired than the very substance of that disgust becomes material for joking. Disgust usually can be indulged playfully for rather low scales. Miller explains, "there are ways within the rules of the repressive regime that disgust maintains to let the repressed return to see the sunlight. One way is via low comedies and dirty jokes, which allow some release but are not acceptable to people of taste" (173–4).

The experience of disgust can be more entertaining to us as is commonly the case in comedy when it is elicited by another's shamelessness or ineptitude. Through the distancing from ourselves that humor affords, our own inaptitude should also be a source of pleasure. I suggest that if the comic and the disgusting share significant points of contact, the comic may be actively used in self-referential humor to discharge disgust. Indeed, James Beattie has already argued for the association of laughter and distress (Beattie 1976). The role of fear or disgust in laughter is such that the fear or disgust stimulus retains this function even when promoted to laughter-stimulus; only fear or disgust is bisociated with a positive emotion. Beattie's view is corroborated by contemporary research on the Amerindian clowns that shows that in the clown the stimuli of fear and disgust are often indistinguishable from each other. In the light of the theory of bisociation, the very laughter itself is marked by ambivalence, the negative distressing affects of fear and disgust being neutralized by their exalted place in the ritual. Here, it suffices to note that this profound identity on the metaphysical and symbolic levels is reflected clearly on the psychological level in the stereotyped intermingling of hilarious laughter and fear/disgust that betrays the presence of the ritual clown. Rather than a mere intermingling, the fear/disgust may be seen as necessary components of the bisociative laughter. The problem then becomes one of determining the factors that contribute to the component of positive affect toward such comic figures, which by neutralizing the fear and disgust generates our laughter. Howard Pollio and John Edgerly explain this balance, especially in the clown-priest, as a result of the clown's simultaneous roles as butt and aggressor, which already suggests that he is the focus of a bisociative perception, one operational field he calls up (one role) being exploded by a contrasting field (the aggressor role) (Pollio and Edgerly 1996, 222).

Fifth, by gradually replacing feelings of anger, fear, sorrow, shame, and disgust with sympathy (Freud 1905; 1928) and compassion (Eisenberg and Strayer 1987), humor encourages self-acceptance, tolerance "of self and others," and "a sense of identification with humanity" (Martin 1998, 99). The sympathetic aspect of humor is noted in most dictionaries and encyclopedias where humor is contrasted with wit and irony. For example, in its entry on wit, Webster writes of humor: "Often suggesting a generalness or greater kindliness or sympathy with human failings than does wit" (1993); "humor implies an ability to perceive the ludicrous, the comical, and the absurd in human life and to express these usually with keen insight and sympathetic understanding and without bitterness" (*Webster's Dictionary of Synonyms and Antonyms* 1992, 439, "wit"). In the *Dictionary of Philosophy and Psychology*, J. M. Baldwin defines humorous and humor as "a complex feeling composed of an element of the comic and an element of sympathy" (1901–1905, 488). In *A Dictionary of Psychology*, J. Drever defines humor as the "character of a complex situation exciting joyful, and in the main quiet, laughter, either directly, through sympathy, or (indirectly) through empathy" (1973). Studies of comedians concur with these theories: Comedians are sympathetic to "our failings, our perceptions, and our emotions" (Barnett 1987, 155). Both in their consciously enunciated values and in their projective fantasies, they seem to have a preoccupation with morality and a sense of obligation to do good: "When they encounter the tragic, comedians are highly motivated to negate it and transmute it into something pleasant and funny. Furthermore, the humor of comedians may be seen as a strategy for soothing people and for denying the threats found in life" (Fisher and Fisher 1983).

Studies on empathy may teach us something about humor, especially because both concepts seem to be elements of wisdom (Orwoll and Perlmutter 1990). Although one cannot explain empathy "any more than one can explain memory, or imagination, one can investigate its parameters" (Wispé 1987, 34). It seems that in the construct of empathy itself, the interaction of cognitive and affective components is essential (Barnett 1987, 154). Empathy is obstructed by projecting the parts of ourselves we reject unto others (Kramer 1990, 292). Freud is aware of empathy and uses it in his discussions of humor (1960) and social psychology (1921). In his early discussion of humor, Freud uses empathy to mean that "we take the producing person's psychical state into consideration, put ourselves into it and try to understand it by comparing it with our own" (1960, 186). In his later work on humor (1928), he develops a sympathetic view of humor: The super-ego protects the ego, which is an exception to the common relations they entertain.

Through our distancing from intense emotions like fear or anger, and difficult feelings like shame and disgust, we experience these feelings as if they are someone else's, yet with sympathy. Instead of impeding compassion by projecting the rejected parts of the self unto others, this sympathetic distancing from self brings one closer to others. Along the same lines, Agnes Heller has argued that "comic works change my sense of distance and identification, or the relation between what is called rational thinking and emotional thinking, or egocentric thinking and other-oriented thinking" (Heller 2005, 212).

The cognitive, emotive, and motivational components of humor work in conjunction. Once intrapersonal tragic conflicts also are perceived as comical incongruities, humor's work on these conflicts can be described, so that the importance of the transposition from the tragic to the comic may be fully appreciated.

Construing tragic oppositions as comical generally results in a humorous mood or state of mind that retains both the tragic and the comical aspects of a conflict. The benefits of this kind of self-referential humor are fourfold. Humor may

1. facilitate self-knowledge through awareness of conflict and familiarity with its components;

2. enable deliberation;

3. help to cope with irresolvable conflict; or

4. advance the resolution of the conflict.

The latter benefit is explained in the section on ridicule, the former are explained here.

SELF-KNOWLEDGE, CONFLICT AWARENESS, AND DELIBERATION

An important component of self-knowledge is awareness of internal conflict as well as familiarity with the conflict's components. Many of the obstacles that prevent us from living a good life are defects in our character, and through self-knowledge we may become aware of them. Socrates, Plato, Aristotle, Augustine, Aquinas, Descartes, Spinoza, Shaftesbury, and Hume were as interested in self-knowledge as we are. According to John Kekes, self-knowledge is a mode of reflection, involving judgment, whose aim is to make our character less fortuitous and more deliberate. This is the same process as that of increasing control, for what moves our character in the desired direction is that we control it so as to approximate more closely than before our conception of a good life. This desirable transformation proceeds through the evaluation of our desires, capacities, opportunities, values, and actions with a view of forming out of them such enduring patterns as we regard conducive to living a good life (Kekes 1995, 127–8).[26] Similarly, self-knowledge, in the sense of knowing one's heart, true desires and leading passions, is needed as a first step for attaining to the ideal of authenticity or "being yourself" (Guignon 2005, 14).

Self-knowledge is a prerequisite of effective deliberation, which, in turn, is imperative for deciding whether and how to solve a conflict. Humor facilitates self-knowledge by creating the distance necessary to observe one's self with the calmness that characterizes aesthetic contemplation. Within this safe inward environment made so by suspending blinding emotions, silencing shame and disgust, and incapacitating rash action, hidden aspects of the self are encouraged to emerge under the impartiality of the humorous gaze.

Self-knowledge assumes the inner dialogue we are all familiar with and which has been explored by philosophers, anthropologists, and psychologists.[27] There are two main models of inner dialogue, the reflexive model and the social model, and humor fits within both models. The former interpretation takes speech to be the manifestation of reflection, that is, of the act by which I am able to think about some content within my consciousness. I may, for example, possess a moral intuition of the virtue of justice, and live according to its principles; but in reflecting on it, I examine this content from some higher or more abstract perspective. Where the original level is merely "lived" and relatively unexamined, the higher level is evaluative and critical. Because this evaluation requires conceptual analysis, I talk to myself when I reflect. I may compare the abstract perspective with the lived one, finding room for humor if we believe Schopenhauer on the discrepancy between concept and perception (Schopenhauer 1969, I, 59). This procedure is common in character building. If we follow Spinoza, who is exemplary here, we evaluate ourselves according to a correct principle of living that we apply constantly to the particular cases frequently encountered in life (*Ethics*, V, P10Schol). To fully accept the gap between the ideal and reality, humor is needed in order to help us cope effectively with shame and disgust, among other emotions.

Other accounts of inner speech invoke a more overtly dialogical structure. Among these is the idea that my inner conversation takes place among different personae; I might adopt a role such as "parent," "child," "teacher," or "victim" in relation to another such role within my self. My self might in fact be taken largely as a set of such roles, determined to a significant extent by my social relationships. This model allows for humorous interactions between these inner parts that mirror the important role humor plays in social conflicts. A familiar model for Freudian (and later) psychotherapy has the rational, conscious, articulating ego confronting its powerlessness in the face of the emotional, unconscious, and nonverbal id. The role of humor here is to encourage hidden aspects of the personality to emerge as a consequence of the promise of impartiality and tolerance associated with humor.

An important component of self-knowledge is awareness of internal conflict as well as familiarity with the conflict's components. One notable outcome of this process is the acknowledgment of ambivalence that is necessary for understanding oneself, others, and human relations in general. Its importance justifies a lengthy explanation of the workings and pervasiveness of ambivalence in our lives. The state of simultaneous conflicting feelings, ambivalence is experienced in thoughts and emotions of both positive and negative valence toward someone or something. Its opposite is a rigid intolerance for ambiguity, nuance, and paradox. A common example of ambivalence is feelings of both love and hate for a person. The term also refers to situations in which "mixed feelings" of a more general sort are experienced, or when a person experiences uncertainty or indecisiveness concerning something. Because both positive and negative aspects of a subject are present in a person's mind at the same time, ambivalence is a psychologically unpleasant state that often leads to avoidance and procrastination, or to deliberate attempts to resolve the ambivalence. Ever since the Swiss psychiatrist Eugen Bleuler introduced the term early in the twentieth century (Bleuler 1911), the ambivalence of human attitudes has been continually investigated, especially by psychologists. Bleuler identifies three types of ambivalence: the emotional (or affective) type in which the same object arouses both positive and negative feelings, as in parent–child relations; the voluntary (or conative) type in which conflicting wishes make it difficult or impossible to decide how to act; and the intellectual (or cognitive) type, in which persons hold contradictory ideas.

Long before the term was coined, the experience of ambivalence—being pulled in psychologically opposed directions—had been noted. In seventeenth-century France, the writings of Montaigne, La Rochefoucauld,

La Bruyère, and Pascal are the source for many *pensées* and maxims dealing with a wide range of ambivalent experiences. In his treatment of the emotions in Part III of the *Ethics*, Spinoza makes much of ambivalence, which he terms fluctuation or vacillation; it is the result of a transfer of emotions that he calls imitation (*imitatio*) (PP17 and 27). Spinoza also focuses on various other sorts of cases of ambivalence. In general, no observer of the human condition can fail to note the existence of mixed feelings, mingled beliefs, and contradictory actions.

Psychoanalysis has made ambivalence famous, as most persons think of ambivalence in connection with some complex and debatable claims of psychoanalytic theory. A few years before Bleuler's coinage, Freud notes the alternation of love and hate for the same person, with the early separation of the two sentiments usually leading to the repression of hate (Jones 1955, II, 47; see Winnicott 1949). In "The Rat Man" (1909) Freud indicates that the opposition between love and hate for the object could explain the particular features of obsessive thought (doubt, compulsion). In *Totem and Taboo* (1912–1913), he adopts the term *ambivalence* proposed by Bleuler in the text of his conference published in 1911 in the *Zentralblatt*. For Freud the term, in its most general sense, designates the presence in a subject of a pair of opposed impulses of the same intensity; most frequently this involves the opposition between love and hate, which is often expressed in obsessional neuroses and melancholy. In the metapsychological writings of 1915, he adds that it is the loss of the love object that through regression causes the conflict of ambivalence to appear.

Later, Freud integrates Karl Abraham's contributions to ambivalence in the thirty-second of his *New Introductory Lectures on Psycho-analysis* (Freud 1933). Within the oedipal conflict ambivalence is resolved as a neurotic symptom, either through a reaction formation or through displacement (Freud 1926). Reformulated in the second theory of instincts, ambivalence becomes part of the fundamental instinctual dualism between life instinct and death instinct. It has since become the mark of the Freudian theory of psychoanalysis: All paradigms found central to Freud (creation through catastrophe, family romance and transference) are marked with ambivalence, as they all mix love and hate, attraction and repulsion (Bloom 1983, 57–58).

In 1920, Karl Abraham emphasizes the intensity of the sadistic fantasy associated with urinary and digestive functions. In 1924, he extends and transforms the Freudian schema of the evolution of the libido into a complete picture of the development of the relation to the object along two lines: The partial or total nature of the investment in the object, and ambivalence. The precocious oral stage of sucking is preambivalent, neither love nor hate are felt toward the object. There follow four ambivalent phases: The late oral stage, which is cannibalistic and seeks the total incorporation of the object, the precocious anal-sadistic stage, which seeks the expulsion and destruction of the object, the late anal-sadistic stage, which seeks its conservation and domination, and finally the precocious-phallic genital stage. The final genital phase of love toward a complete object is post-ambivalent (Abraham 1927 [1924]).

Psychoanalysis has associated the awareness of ambivalence mainly with pathology. Also more recent psychoanalytical theories have associated ambivalence with psychological disorders, especially depression (Klein 1975; Racamier 1976), but contemporary therapists who have elaborated on Freud's first intimations on ambivalence and the oedipal conflict have emphasized the importance of ambivalence in human relationships (Mann 2002, 169; Valerio 2002, 264; see Winnicott 1949).[28]

Ambivalence has been recognized before and after psychoanalysis, however, as descriptive of our normal emotional make-up, indeed, as the mark of our emotions and attachments. In her *Upheavals of Thought*, Martha Nussbaum notes, "emotions seem to be characterized by ambivalence toward their objects. In the very nature of our early object relations . . . there lurks a morally subversive combination of love and resentment, which springs directly from the thought that we need others to survive and flourish, but do not control their movements" (Nussbaum 2001a, 13). In *The Subtlety of Emotions*, Aaron Ben-Ze'ev considers ambivalence to be typical of romantic love, as well as constitutive of the structure of various emotions, such as pity and envy (Ben-Ze'ev 2000, 439, 441, 449). The latter emotion, for example, involves both a positive evaluation of the other's achievements and a negative evaluation of the other's good fortune, creating an ambivalent reaction that entails both admiration and dislike of social targets (Smith 2008, 133–4). In "Ambivalence and the Logic of Emotion," Patricia Greenspan argues that ambivalence, understood as simultaneous "mixed feelings" or contrary emotions rather than the continuous changing of one's mind, is much more common than generally assumed. Ambivalence is possible without an abnormal breakdown of reasoning, as the "logic" of emotion allows for ambivalence (Greenspan 1980, 225).

A key concept in normal psychology, ambivalence also is embedded in social functions and professions. Indeed, one major source of psychological ambivalence is sociological ambivalence, which refers to the social structure, not to the personality. In its most extended sense, it refers to incompatible normative expectations of attitudes, beliefs, and behavior assigned to a status (i.e., a social position) or to a set of statuses in a society. In its most restrictive sense, it refers to incompatible normative expectations incorporated in a single role of a single social status. In both the most extended and the most restricted sense, the ambivalence is located in the social definition of roles and statuses, not in the feeling-state of one or another type of personality. Robert Merton believes that individuals in a status or status-set that has a large measure of incompatibility in its social definition will tend to develop personal tendencies toward contradictory feelings, beliefs, and behavior (Merton 1976, 7).[29]

Ambivalence has been identified as a characteristic of modern societies, which through internalization has become a personal problem threatening our sense of identity. In his study of ambivalence and modernity, Zygmunt Bauman suggests that the ambivalence of societal powers is transformed into the nagging fear of one's own inadequacy. The modern world is a world of conflict that has been interiorized; in becoming an inner conflict, it has turned into a state of personal ambivalence and contingency (Bauman 1991, 176). The outcomes of such a situation are depicted in William Ian Miller's *Faking It* (2005), which places problems of personal identity at the core of our modern existence.

Not surprisingly, anthropologists and sociologists interested in humor stress its role in situations plagued by ambivalence. A major theme recurring in anthropological humor theories, according to Mahadev L. Apte, is that expressions of humor are the result of attempts to resolve ambivalence in social situations, roles, statuses, cultural values, and ideologies. For example, ambivalence may occur because of a conflict between social obligations and self-interest; the use of humor may provide a relief from such ambivalence (Apte 1983, 194). Similarly, according to sociologist Christie Davies, ambiguous and contradictory situations and values play an important role in the creation of jokes (Davies 1990, 307–8).

This makes the recognition of ambivalence imperative. Although knowing one's feelings may seem simple, many ignore or try to sedate strong emotions like anger, sadness, and fear, and eschew ambivalence as threatening. But our ability to handle conflict depends on being connected to these feelings and on tolerating ambivalence enough in order to let it emerge. Paola Valerio suggests that acknowledging hateful feelings in ourselves as well as in others is necessary for truly loving (Valerio 2002, 264). Tolerating, if not enjoying, ambivalence is important, moreover, in order to minimize the violence of the one-sided perspective, which may often be at the origin of a tragic conflict, at least according to Hegel's view of tragedy (Hegel 1975, II, 1196).

If the ambivalence theory of humor, which states that oscillation, conflict-mixture and simultaneously experienced incompatible emotions or feelings create humor, is true, one of its possible consequences is that it desensitizes intolerance to ambivalence by converting pain into pleasure. Humor brings forth ambivalence, because in the humorous mode of thinking a thing can be both X and not-X at the same time (Mulkay 1988). Some variation of Arthur Koestler's idea that humor involves the activation of two normally incompatible frames of reference continues to form the basis of most humor theories today (Koestler 1964; Martin 2007, 72). In Koestler's original view, the "bisociation" or ongoing incongruity is that which creates the humorous effect, rather than its removal, as in the incongruity resolution model. Michael Apter uses the notion of synergy to describe this cognitive process, in which two contradictory images or conceptions of the same object are held in one's mind at the same time. This produces the pleasurable sensation of having one's thoughts oscillate back and forth between two incompatible interpretations of a concept. Thus, in humor, we playfully manipulate ideas and activities so that they are simultaneously perceived in opposite ways, such as real and not real, important and trivial, threatening and safe (Apter 1982).

The pleasure we derive from ambivalence through humor enables us to acquire the ability to feel simultaneous contradictory emotions about the same idea, event or person. It is the most fundamental skill required for handling both internal and interpersonal conflict. The alternative is often violence, one of the principle outcomes of our misguided belief in single-mindedness, which assumes that for one side of the argument to be absolutely true, the other side must be erased by all means possible.

Unfortunately, throughout history we have tended to interpret conflict, whether internal or interpersonal, as traumatic, as something that cannot be tolerated and must be avoided or stopped, rather than as a coping challenge. Likewise, we regard those who in any way contribute to conflict, even when they are nonviolent, as villains deserving censure, punishment or even retaliation. Yet ambiguity and ambivalence exists in everything human because we are capable of perceiving things in multiple and even contradictory dimensions. We can simultaneously hold in the mind's eye several layers of possibility. The simplest way of expressing it is that we can simultaneously do things, watch ourselves do them, comment on what we are doing, even criticize it, and at the same time imagine doing it in other ways. That complexity of perception is the principle trait that makes us what and who we are; and ambivalence is the key skill necessary for the creative management of this remarkable gift of multilayered comprehension. Enjoying ambivalence is also a prerequisite of ethical behavior. By allowing the conflict between the awareness of my needs and the perception of others' needs, while controlling the conflict's behavioral effect, humor enables a strong commitment to someone else's interests without losing sight of my own.

After acknowledging the existence of conflict and encouraging the emergence of the conflict's components, humor also may help in deliberating a solution by siding with the intellect, and mediating between the various components of the conflict. By keeping desire in check, and reducing sadness, fear, anger, shame, and disgust, humor effects "a momentary anesthesia of the heart" (Bergson 1999, 11) that is conducive to calm deliberation. Humor induces pleasurable rapid cognitive-perceptual shifts between various conflicting points of views, and governed by an impartiality that is sympathetic to all points of view, encourages diverse points of view to engage in dialogue. This characteristic of humor is also helpful in the process of endorsement and rejection of some, among the variety of, thoughts and desires that occur to a person. By this process a person comes to identify with some desires and thoughts, while rejecting others; by these acts of ordering and rejection, of integration and separation, one "create[s] a self out of the raw materials of life," as Harry Frankfurt and Heinz Kohut suggest, and forms one's character, as Joel Kupperman maintains (Frankfurt 1987, 38; Kohut 1977, 177; Kupperman 1991, 51).

Humor would be detrimental to deliberation if it were antagonistic to interest and seriousness. Various authors comment on humor's seriousness, not least, Schopenhauer: "Humor depends upon a subjective, yet serious and sublime mood," he explains. "Behind [the intentionally ludicrous] . . . the deepest seriousness is concealed and shines through" (Schopenhauer 1969, II, 100). Robert C. Roberts echoes this view in arguing that for all its power to distance us from ourselves, humor is as parasitic on serious interest as it is upon normal congruity: "An ultimate orienting seriousness about life gives one's sense of humor a depth and integrity and scope that it will not otherwise have" (Roberts 1987, 169–70). Thomas Veatch makes the violation of some affective expectation the core of humor. Humor cannot initially arise if we are not somewhat emotionally invested in the situations that give raise to it (Veatch 1998). Thus deliberation is served not only by the pleasure derived from humor, but also by humor's ability to maintain interest and seriousness.

LIVING WITH IRRESOLVABLE CONFLICT

After deliberation, the reduction of tension involved in a humorous state of mind enables us to live with an unresolved and perhaps irresolvable conflict, a situation exemplified by Joseph Agassi and Ian Jarvie's comment on the effect of a good joke: "though unable to resolve the conflict, it makes life a jot less unbearable" (Agassi and Jarvie 2008, 57). But the reduction of tension also may help to opt for deliberately leaving the conflict unresolved, an option that is less viable for those who do not use humor to relieve the tension created by the conflict. We may want to leave the conflict unresolved when the price of resolving it requires relinquishing either our rational or cognitive powers, or renouncing the desires we identify as characterizing us no less than our reason, or both.

Metaphysical and religious theories that propose redemption or peace of mind attempt to resolve the human predicament as it has been defined here. Redemption is a promise to the individual, the community or mankind as a whole. It can be realized in the course of human life; or, it may stand out as a hope to be fulfilled in a much wider perspective transcending the life of the individual, in an afterlife, in a messianic state or in a general cosmic context (Scholem 1968). No necessary connection exists between religion and redemption because the source of the need for redemption, such as death, evil, human suffering, and ignorance, can be answered in religious as well as nonreligious terms (Schär 1950). Whereas the notion of redemption, or salvation, is generally used within a religious framework, thinkers with no commitment to organized religion have borrowed the concept to propose new ways to be redeemed in this world and within the human lifespan. Some have addressed the individual, others, the community or humankind as a whole.[30] Spinoza, Schopenhauer, Nietzsche, and Santayana, for example, have replaced the redemption offered by organized religions with their respective philosophic personal redemptions.[31]

Both religious and nonreligious redemptions are radical responses to dissatisfaction with the human condition. According to the formula presented in this chapter, this dissatisfaction can be characterized as a clash between human desires and the impossibility of satisfying them on instinctual, emotional, and intellectual levels for either principled or practical reasons. This clash or the human predicament is the problem that a particular redemption attempts to resolve. Some philosophical theories prior to Christianity, such as Hellenistic Stoicism, Epicureanism, and Skeptical Pyrrhonism, do not hold "redemption" as their ideal, but rather *ataraxia*, tranquility or peace of mind, though their goal is similar to naturalistic philosophic personal redemptions.[32]

I suggest that most religious and philosophical solutions to the basic human predicament require renouncing one or more aspects of our humanity as we know it. These solutions come at a cost and should be evaluated accordingly. Theories of redemption, or peace of mind, either Eastern or Western, religious or nonreligious, can be divided into general types, the first type negating desire, the second making light of reason's limitations, and the third denigrating both desire and reason. A more thorough examination of these theories will enable me to substantiate these claims.

1. The first type of theories urges us to renounce our desires. It includes, among others, the Buddhist and Hindu views of release, Schopenhauer's theory of redemption, which is influenced by them, the Hellenistic schools of Epicureanism and Pyrrhonism, and even the outlook on emancipation of such a reasonable philosopher as Bertrand Russell.

In "A Free Man's Worship," Russell writes: "To renounce the struggle for personal happiness, to reject any wish for temporal lust, this is emancipation" (Russell 1917, 55). In *The Conquest of Happiness* (1930), Russell seems to endorse a less demanding way of living based on John Locke's program in *Some Thoughts Concerning Education* (Russell 1987, 440–1). However, Kenneth Blackwell has convincingly argued that Russell holds a Spinozistic ethics (Blackwell 1985): Although Blackwell emphasizes the positive outcomes of this ethics, such as nobility and impersonal love, I believe Russell's ethics is still predicated on the renouncement enunciated in "A Free Man's Worship."

Some religions originating in India share the common belief that freedom or release cannot be reached without the removal of worldly desires and passions: Desire leads to delusion and suffering, to the cycle of births and deaths. Hinduism includes a variety of views, however, Indian tantrism uses worldly desire to reach release, and the *Vedas* do not criticize desires. According to the Advaita Vedanta philosophy of Sankara (which is probably the most dominant philosophical school in modern-day Hinduism) release lies in detaching oneself from the false self and uniting with a nonmaterial self that is the true self and at the same time *brahman*—the "Absolute." This "Absolute" may be accessible to contemplative vision, but not to conceptualization. Although "Hinduism" is tolerant of various lifestyles, the road to final liberation often requires the renunciation of desires.

In Buddhism, desire and ignorance lie at the root of suffering. By desire, Buddhists refer to craving pleasure, material goods, and immortality, all of which are wants that can never be satisfied; as a result, desiring them can only bring suffering. Ignorance relates to seeing the world other than as it is. Liberation, in comparison, is obtained through understanding that leads to renunciation of our desires. The liberated state is called "nirvana," that is, extinction (of the desires).

Schopenhauer is heir to both Hinduism and Buddhism; he believes his philosophy captures not only the essence of Eastern mysticism, but also of Western mysticism as exemplified by early Christianity. He proposes accordingly an ethic of total renunciation, a denial of the will to live, as the sole road to redemption.[33]

0

HUMOR AND THE GOOD LIFE IN MODERN PHILOSOPHY

The Hellenistic and Roman school of Epicureanism urges us to renounce desires; it allows, however, for desires that are both "natural and necessary." Unnecessary desires for rich food, sex, status, power and the like, whose satisfaction does not serve to liberate us from pain and terror, are not "a bad thing in themselves," but they tend to "bring troubles many times greater than the pleasures" attributed to them and should therefore be avoided, or kept within severe limits. The "goal of living" is "health of the body and the freedom of the soul from disturbance (*ataraxía*)" (Inwood and Gerson 1988, 24, 26ff). Contrary to their reputation as unruly hedonists, Epicureans tend to live as secular monks.

The Hellenistic and Roman school of Pyrrhonism urges us to suspend all judgments because of the skeptical doubts that undermine all dogmatic claims to knowledge. We achieve tranquility as a result of suspending judgment, without intending to do so (Sextus 2000, 1.25–30): tranquility follows the suspension of judgment—in technical terms *ataraxía* follows *epochē*—like a "shadow following the body" (Laertius 1925, 9.107; see Sextus Empiricus 2000, 1.29). The Skeptics are frank about the radical alteration in lifestyle they ask of us. Pyrrho talks of "altogether divesting ourselves of the human being," and Sextus describes the Skeptic as a eunuch with respect to rational desires (Nussbaum 1994, 312). This is so because suspension of judgment frees us from the burden of worrying about what is true and right; it liberates also from the belief in a view of what is good—a belief that adds to the torment when the thing deemed bad is present; and it releases as well from all the evils that come from the intense pursuits of any special practical goal "with eager conviction." These evils prominently include emotion: Joy when the good is present, fear lest it vanishes; desire for the good before it is present; grief if it is absent and even fantasized guilt—being punished for something we have done. These emotions are based on ethical belief, and Sextus suggests that only the complete extirpation of belief gets rid of them.[34]

2. To the second type of theories, which promises a partial or full satisfaction of desires while disparaging reason's limits, belong all answers to metaphysical questions, religious theories, and various philosophies that encourage the satisfaction of our desires at the expense of others, whose similar right is brought to us by reason, for example, the Nietzschean philosophy of the liberated individual.

Nietzsche encourages self-affirmation with an ethic of power that emphasizes egoism and self-regard. Pity and altruism are criticized, and the strong individual is the one who enhances his instincts and is a law unto himself, unpredictable and unmanageable, as morality is the herd instinct in the individual. To be an individual is to be autonomous, to be supra-moral: "This is what *I am*; this is what *I want*—you can go to hell!" (Nietzsche 1968, sec. 349). However, this individualism is not egalitarian, as Nietzsche assumes a fundamental inequality among men. The heroic task, open only to the few, is to become a sovereign individual, and this higher morality necessitates immorality according to the herd standards. Nobility is inborn and uses its environment to grow. The aristocratic individual serves as the measure for all men, and his instincts sublimated in a philosophy or a morality may swamp a multitude of following moral "slaves" (see Thiele 1990, chaps. 2, 4). Egoism, however, is defeated by the existence of others, I suggest, whose similar right to the satisfaction of their desires is brought to us by reason.

To this type of theories, which promises a partial or full satisfaction of desires while disparaging reason's limits, belong also religious and metaphysical theories because metaphysics and religions overstep reason's capacity. Keith Ward characterizes religions as "belief-systems which articulate, with different degrees of systematization, competing theories about the meaning of human life" (Ward 2001, 11). That life is meaningful is religion's basic posit, Huston Smith explains, and the claim can be elucidated both subjectively and objectively, the difference being whether we are thinking primarily of life's meaning for us or, alternatively, trying to determine its meaning in the total scheme of things (Smith 2001, 255). Smith explains that objectively there is no way to decide that question:

> There are things to be said in favor of life's meaning, the chief being that it is the seasoned answer to the question, the one that has presided over every known human collectivity, but it is not enough to insure its truth. The hermeneutics of suspicion is always waiting in the wings, ready to challenge the existence of religion's "other world" by claiming that it is only wishful thinking—a projection of the human mind to compensate for the world's lack. "There is no other world," Malinowski intoned, and neither reason nor experience can prove him wrong. (261–2)

Irredeemably ambiguous to public gaze, life and the world come to us untagged, and serious doubts rightly arise about the validity of the meaning we ascribe to them. At the beginning of *The Wisdom to Doubt*, John L. Schellenberg simply states: "Reason requires us to be religious skeptics" (Schellenberg 2007, 1). Secular doubts call into question all religious views about the human condition that assume the existence of a supernatural realm. The arguments for and against belief in such a realm are familiar and endlessly debated.[35] Thus, there is no need to repeat them here.

Along with Plato, Shaftesbury, and Robert Burton in *The Anatomy of Melancholy*, Kant claims that the three areas where enthusiasm is most commonly found are unrequited love, religion, and metaphysics because all three are characterized by a powerful longing for an object that can never in principle be possessed.[36] The longing can be so intense, the frustration so painful, that the sufferer may delude himself into thinking his desire will be fulfilled. This is the essence of enthusiasm, a problem yet to be addressed today as testified to by the contemporary appeal of religion, various forms of mysticism, and uncritical theories of the New Age movement.[37]

The skepticism Smith points to is also relevant for the endeavor of metaphysics to provide knowledge of the world's constitution and our place in it. The long history of metaphysics is accompanied by a no less long history of its criticism. There may be a difference between metaphysics and science with regard to skepticism, but I do not wish to elaborate on this here.[38] Whether or not skepticism is based on Kant's criticism of metaphysics or on other grounds, a skeptical attitude toward metaphysics undermines the possibility of adhering à la lettre to the otherwise inspiring ethical prescriptions that follow from the particular metaphysical assumptions most philosophies adopt.

3. The third type of theories, which denigrates both desire and reason, is exemplified by Taoism and some forms of Western mysticism, but also by those philosophies that overstep reason's power while denigrating desires such as Stoicism and Kant's view of the good life as a life lived according to the categorical imperative.

In Taoism, the goal is to realize oneness with the cosmos seen as an unconceptualizable, ineffable realm, one that is "mysterious," and that, according to Chuang Tzu, does not permit discrimination or description. The adept approaches his goal in a purified condition, cleansed of emotions, desires and evaluations, and freed of all thought after fasting and years of silent meditation (Kohn 2001, 27, 34, 38).

Attempts to define mystical experience have been as diversified and as conflicting as attempts to interpret and assess its significance. Ronald Hepburn offers a useful definition:

> Mystical experience is religious experience, in a broad but meaningful sense of religious. It is sensed as revealing something about the totality of things, something of immense human importance at all times and places, and something upon which one's ultimate well-being and or salvation wholly depends. . . . There must be a unifying vision, a sense that somehow all things are one and share a holy, divine, and single life, or that one's indi-

vidual being merges into a "Universal Self," to be identified with god or the mystical One. Mystical experience then typically involves the intense and joyous realization of oneness with, or in, the divine, the sense that this divine One is comprehensive, all-embracing, in its being. (Hepburn 1967, 429)

The language used to express and describe mystical experience is richly paradoxical, figurative, and poetic. Whereas ineffability is descriptive of many mystical traditions, asceticism is descriptive of some mystical experiences that occur only at the end of a lengthy, arduous religious discipline, an austere and abstinent path. Neo-Platonism and Catholicism in the West have developed mystical paths of this kind. Mystics to whom these double characterizations correspond are denigrators of both desire and reason.

The Hellenistic and Roman school of Stoicism is the most extreme Western doctrine with regard to desires and passions. These should not only be renounced but also eradicated. The extermination of desires and passions is necessary in order to fit the determined order of a universe akin to a rational organism in which passions are illnesses. Eradication of desires and passions is the key to the sage's apathy or tranquility: He is happy while on the rack. Yet the belief in the rationality of the universe and in the necessary causal relation that determines all things oversteps reason's power.

A final example is Kant's ethical theory, which requires us to renounce inclinations and desires in order to live the good life according to the categorical imperative. This is undoubtedly a worthy ideal, whose grounding metaphysics is unfortunately difficult to establish within reason's limits.[39]

We may hesitate to choose any of the solutions that make light of reason's limits, or denigrate both desires and reason, but we should also be wary of those solutions that urge us to renounce our desires, lest we be dehumanized by a solution that purports to do away with that which makes us human. If there exists a problem and all the solutions to that problem prove to be unacceptable, then, there remains one possibility—to abstain from resolving the problem. Because our humanity depends on a balance between our desires and our reason, when a solution requires a negation of one or the other, or both, a non-solution is the better policy. A non-solution has positive content as well: It presupposes a careful perception of human nature as an amalgam of rationality and irrationality, assumes a lucid awareness of human possibilities and limitations, and gives value to life in prioritizing the everlasting struggle with the predicament that lies at the core of human existence.

Humor enables us to live with the basic human predicament without solving it because it provides relief from its tension. It enables us to maintain an open consciousness receptive to life's ambiguities and congenial to the doubts necessary for a tragic view of life. This is evocative of Kant, as Kant's criticism of enthusiasm points to a desire to maintain what Eric Voegelin calls "the balance of consciousness" (Voegelin 1990). Thomas Prufer has described this balance as the task of maintaining "the polarity or tension between openness to the plenitude of being, on the one hand, and situatedness in the phenomenality of finite beings, on the other hand" (Prufer 1962, 591). The philosophical *eros* Kant shares with the enthusiasts is what Prufer refers to as "openness to the plenitude of being." Kant's concern with the labor of articulating metaphysical insights in conceptual terms, his concerns with making metaphysics speak the language of common human reason and remain in touch with the *sensus communis*, and his populist emphasis on the primacy of practical reason or moral knowledge—all of these reflect his desire to balance his erotic openness to the plenitude of being with situatedness in the phenomenality of finite beings: "The philosophical act breaks down when either pole, openness to plenitude or situatedness in phenomenality, become exclusive of the other" (591). When openness to the plenitude of being uproots itself from situatedness in finite beings, then one has what Kant calls *Schwärmerei*. We know from Shaftesbury and Kant that humor is an antidote to such enthusiasm: "One will have to let enthusiasm run its course and laugh about it with Shaftesbury," Kant writes in a note.[40] But he seems to recommend humor as a tolerant attitude toward the enthusiasm of others while counseling Kantian critique rather than humor to combat inner enthusiasm.

The tragic view of life is not suitable for those who cannot live with unresolved doubts, whose bent of mind would reduce the fact of evil into something else or reconcile it into some larger whole. Although no one is exempt from moments of tragic doubt or insight, "the vision of life peculiar to the mystic, the pious, the propagandist, the confirmed optimist or pessimist—or the confirmed anything—is not tragic" (Sewall 1965, 37). The ambivalence we experience and the ambiguity we encounter are best explored, encouraged, thought out, and communicated with humor. Inasmuch as ambiguous means "open to more than one interpretation," thus, "doubtful or uncertain," humorous communication is inherently ambiguous; this is why humor is the best tool to convey ambivalence and ambiguity, and to testify to the elusiveness of truth in human affairs.

Humor provides an effective alternative to the urge for radical change, which usually involves giving up important aspects of our personality and human experience. It can do so by providing relief from the basic human tension between our desires on the instinctual, emotional, and intellectual levels, and between our awareness of the impossibility of fulfilling them, for practical as well as principled reasons. The special capacity of humor is its ability to help us reduce the tension created by this clash between expectations and reality because it can construe the clash as an incongruity. Enjoyment of the incongruous in a situation that otherwise would be construed as tragic amounts to transmuting through humor suffering into joy.

RIDICULE

If we accept that humans are doomed to an everlasting clash between desires and their satisfaction, the human condition lends itself to a double and contradictory evaluation as both comic and tragic. The possibility of characterizing the human condition as both tragic and comic is insufficient for favoring the comic interpretation over the tragic. An additional argument is required: I suggest that something that is both tragic and comic, or that has the potential to be either tragic or comic, cannot in the last account, be solely tragic. The tragic lacks the capacity of uniting contradictions that the comic possesses. This is referred to as "comic inclusivism, in contrast to the exclusivism of the tragic view" (Hyers 1996, 40). Similarly, John Crossan maintains that "tragedy is swallowed up in comedy" because the fact that "the same world can be interpreted in these opposite ways is itself comical" (Crossan 1976, 21).

A comical vision of sorts is the sole vision, I suggest, that enables us to view the human condition simultaneously as comic and tragic. If Kerr is right in asserting that "there is no act in life that is not, when seen as a whole, both tragic and comic at once" (Kerr 1967, 28), the vision that obtains by incorporating the comic and the tragic aspects of life is desirable because it is richer as well as more faithful to life's manifold aspects.

How can we characterize the new level of comic awareness that incorporates both the comic and the tragic in a steady vision? The humorous mood brought about by transposing tragic oppositions into comical incongruities is transitory. When it dissolves, the individual finds himself emotionally humiliated and conceptually amused by the awareness of repeatedly transmuting tragic oppositions into comical incongruities, with an ever new capacity for suffering the former and no steady results from the latter. Nevertheless, repetition is the bread of comedy. The awareness that takes place, I suggest, is a higher-level comic awareness, which I refer to as "ridiculousness," the view of human beings as ridiculous or *Homo risibilis*.[41] I use the term *ridicule* or *ridiculousness*, although ridicule is a harsher word in English than in French, and may even be considered offensive in the former language. Yet it is a common term in French philosophy also used by contemporary continental philosophers. As I am referring to French writers who use *ridicule*, I retain the term.

The view that the human being is inherently ridiculous (*homo risibilis*) originates with an eleventh-century monk's commentary on Aristotle's *Categories*. Aristotle enters the history of laughter with the assertion that humans are the only animals that laugh (*On the Parts of Animals*, III, 10, 673a, 8, 28). Following Aristotle, many, including Boethius, Alcuin, Rabelais, Voltaire, and Baudelaire, have characterized the human being as *homo ridens* or the laughing species. Few, however, have characterized him as *homo risibilis* or the laughable animal. Although this characteristic of the human does not escape Plato's keen eye in his discussion of laughter in the *Philebus* (48–50), Plato does not apply it to all persons, but only to those who are lacking in both self-knowledge and power. It is the eleventh-century monk, Notker Labeo, who innovates with his claim that the human being is not only the sole creature capable of laughter, but also the sole laughable creature: We laugh only at that which is human or that which reminds us of the human (*quia quidquid risibile est, homo est*) (Labeo 1972–1996).

Montaigne revives this view by maintaining that we are both *homo ridens* and *homo risibilis* as "our own specific property is to be equally laughable and able to laugh" (1965, Bk. I, chap. 50). Bergson draws attention to this defining characteristic at the very beginning of his book on laughter: "Several have defined man as 'an animal which laughs.' They might equally well have defined him as an animal which is laughed at" (Bergson 1999, 9). Recently, Simon Critchley has reprised both characterizations:

> *Homo sapiens* is therefore not so much *homo ludens* as Johan Huizinga famously argued, where humanity would be identified with the capacity to play. Rather, we are *homo ridens*, laughing beings, or indeed, *homo risibilis*, which suggests both "the risible or ridiculous being," and "the being gifted with laughter." (Critchley 2002, 41)

Bergson's view of the human being as an animal to be laughed at has also been echoed in Maurice Charney's observation that "to be human is to be inherently comic" (quoted in Gutwirth 1993, 116). Bergson rightly wonders why "so important a fact, and such a simple one too, has not attracted to a greater degree the attention of philosophers" (Bergson 1999, 9).

The view that we are laughable beings does not necessarily imply that we laugh at ourselves. Because Bergson considers laughter a social corrective, he emphasizes laughter aimed at others rather than at oneself. Prioritizing the self-mocking ridicule found at the core of Freud's paper "Der Humor" (1928), Critchley takes the argument one step further by viewing

humor as essentially self-mocking ridicule: "In humour I find myself ridiculous and I acknowledge this in laughter or simply in a smile" (Critchley
2002, 94). Helmut Plessner advances a view that is similar to *homo risibilis*
by characterizing the human being as the eccentric animal and laughter as
the confirmation of humankind's eccentric position in the world of nature
(Plessner 1982, 1970). Plessner's thesis is that the life of animals is centered,
that is, the animal simply lives and experiences. By contrast, the human
being has a reflective attitude toward its experiences and toward itself. This
is why humans are eccentric; they live beyond the limits set for them by
nature by distancing themselves from their immediate experience. Because
human beings live outside themselves, their reflective activity achieves a
break with nature. Indeed, Plessner goes further and claims that the human
is this break, this hiatus, this gap between the physical and the psychical. The working out of the consequences of the eccentric position of the
human is the main task of a philosophical anthropology, which is why
laughter has such an absolutely central role in Plessner's work.

    Apart from Labeo, Montaigne, Critchley, and Plessner, the view that
humans are ridiculous has rarely been advanced, and even less so to promote
self-mocking ridicule. However, other terminologies have been employed to
the same effect. For example, Santayana uses "absurd" for "ridiculous" and
"despise" for "self-mocking ridicule": In a letter he suggests that "perhaps
the only true dignity of man is his capacity to despise himself," although
"everybody is a *coward* about his own humanity. We do not consent to be
absurd, though absurd we are. We have no fundamental humility. . . . For
that reason we don't like Dickens, and don't like comedy, and don't like
the truth" (Santayana 1920, 230; 1922, 68–69).

    We also may associate the view of human ridicule with the more
ancient view of human foolishness. Beginning with St. Paul's doctrine of
the foolishness of Christianity and Tertullian's maxim *credo quia absurdum
est*, the wisdom of the Fool takes on philosophical shape in the *Learned
Ignorance* of Nicholas de Cusa and the Christian Pyrrhonism of Montaigne
and receives its classic formulation in Erasmus' *The Praise of Folly* (see
Davis 2011). Hume gives this tradition a twist of his own. The Humean
laughter of the true philosopher is directed at himself, for he is in the
highly reflective but ridiculous position of believing and at the same time
knowing that he cannot justify the belief to himself. The true philosopher
has come to see that the heroic moment of philosophical reflection is a
joke at his own expense. He refers to this "whimsical condition of mankind,
who must act and reason and believe; though they are not able, by their
most diligent inquiry to satisfy themselves concerning the foundations of

these operations, or to remove the objections which may be raised against them" (Hume 1975, 160). In his *Treatise on Human Nature* Hume describes this post-theoretic posture of the true philosopher as that of the Fool: "If I must be a fool, as all those who reason or believe any thing *certainly* are, my follies shall at least be natural and agreeable" (Hume 1978, 270). The Humean philosopher identifies with the "rabble" through the mediation of true philosophy, and embraces thus the ancient wisdom of the Fool. Unlike ordinary folly, philosophical folly is an attitude arising from the philosophical act that has arrived at a true understanding of its own nature. It is a joyful affirmation of common life in the face of contingency and despair following the failure of the philosophical act in its heroic forms. Hume calls it "the gaiety of MONTAIGNE" (Hume 1986, 179n; see Livingston 1998, 39–40).

Inscribing myself in these traditions, I suggest that *homo risibilis* is a fitting description of humankind because of the necessary seriousness and ensuing suffering with which we take ourselves and our endeavors in conjunction with the view that in the large scale of things we and our endeavors seem to be futile.[42] For lack of proof of the contrary, we may assume the latter view. This is tantamount to experiencing reality first as tragic (reality is serious and brings suffering) and construing it as comical (reality is futile). This acceptance of human ridicule is aided by the love of truth, unpleasant as truth may be, a love exemplified ideally by philosophers. The contemporary French philosopher, André Comte-Sponville, following a long tradition of philosophers that have made the love of truth the mark of the philosopher, reminds us that we may hope that truth will be happy, yet the philosopher will always choose truth over happiness (Comte-Sponville 1993, 199).

The view of human ridicule, however, is worthless without appropriating it as a vision of oneself. Understanding the ridiculous condition of humankind should lead to accepting one's own ridicule and finding comfort in it: The more ridiculous I am, the more I exemplify the human condition, the better I am as a human being. In *The Tragic Sense of Life*, Miguel de Unamuno voices a similar thought inspired by Don Quixote: "One must know how to make oneself appear ridiculous, and not only in the eyes of others but also in one's own eyes" (Unamuno 1972, 322). Similarly, Kierkegaard suggests, "humor wants to be a fool in the world" (*JP* 2, 1690/ *Pap.* II A 102), and Georges Bataille maintains that it is necessary for the human being "to want to be comical, for he is so, to the extent that he is a man (it is no longer a question of characters who are emissaries of comedy)—without a way out" (Bataille 1988, 169). Moreover, Avital Ronell makes the capacity to see oneself as ridiculous the mark of the philosopher:

Knowing one is being ridiculous nails you as a philosopher or
at least targets the philosophical component of your *Dasein*.
Being ridiculous already involves a philosophical insert, because
it implies the act of laughing at oneself. In "l'Essence du rire"
Baudelaire defines this ability to laugh at oneself falling (on
one's ass, back into childhood, forward into old age) as the
moment constitutive of philosophical consciousness. What de
Man interprets as irony—the philosopher splits in two, accel-
erating time while collapsing on the self—is set up by the fall
designating a split between the dumb buddy, on the one hand,
and the one who ridiculizes the faltered ego, on the other hand.
When the philosopher [Thales] falls, prompting the opening act
in the ur-scene of philosophical consciousness, this produces the
double effects of ironic consciousness. . . . The subject laughs
at himself falling; indeed, the fall announces the moment the
subject becomes a philosopher by means, precisely, of laughing at
himself, making himself ridiculous, *sich lacherlich machen*, thus in
falling making himself performatively. Affected by the laughter
of the other, as this other, the philosophical consciousness makes
itself happen by passing through the constituting moment of
making itself ridiculous. The laugh-along distinguishes the philosopher from the non-philosopher to the extent that a position
is taken outside the self, beyond which the self, detached, can
be observed. The moment savagely accelerates the history of the
self and its fall: to laugh at oneself is to laugh at oneself dying
from an improbable position beyond or on the other side of a
life that has disjoined by dint of the sudden slip into consciousness. (Ronell 2003, 298–9)

Nonphilosophers laugh at others, whereas the person who understands
that this other is himself and laughs accordingly becomes a philosopher.
The necessary distance from oneself that philosophy requires divides the
philosopher's consciousness, making him both laugher and butt. I would add
to Ronell's argument that the immaturity of the non-philosophical aspects
of the self are a source of perpetual amusement to the philosopher's cool
and sobering awareness, just as immaturity is the stuff from which comedy
is made.

Modern thinkers who advance the view that we are ridiculous usually
consider our ridicule tragic. For example, Simon Critchley suggests that "the
pretended tragical sublimity of the human collapses into a comic ridiculousness which is perhaps even more tragic" (Critchley 2002, 43). Critchley's

assertion echoes the view of Schopenhauer, deemed the philosopher of the absurd (Rosset 1967), and the view of the playwrights of the theatre of the absurd such as Samuel Beckett and Eugène Ionesco. Schopenhauer writes: "Thus, as if fate wished to add mockery to the misery of our existence, our life must contain all the woes of tragedy, and yet we cannot even assert the dignity of tragic characters, but, in the broad detail of life, are inevitably the foolish characters of a comedy" (Schopenhauer 1969, I, 322). Commenting on the ambiguity found in Samuel Beckett's plays, Alfred Simon tells us that "not only are human misery and comicality inseparable, they also are each other's paroxysm" (Simon, Le Monde, 27 Dec. 1989; my translation). Referring to The Chairs as a "tragic farce," Eugène Ionesco says that the "human drama is as absurd as it is painful. It all comes to the same thing, anyway; comic and tragic are merely two aspects of the same situation. . . . There are no alternatives; if man is not tragic, he is ridiculous and painful, 'comic' in fact, and by revealing his absurdity one can achieve a sort of tragedy."[43]

In her Immortal Comedy, Agnes Heller argues that although terming existential comedies "tragicomedies" is a misnomer, it still points to the specificity of existential comedy: "Whereas paradoxes are dissolved in a joke, and this is why it is a joke, they remain unresolved in the existential comic novel or drama. Whatever is ridiculed is also mourned; the thing which has been lost is mocked, but the loss still hurts" (Heller 2005, 97). It is interesting to note, moreover, that philosophers of the absurd have no sense of humor: Sartre has been deemed "among contemporary philosophers the most obvious candidate for the title 'Least Humorous'" (Davenport 1976, 170). He identifies both the serious man and the ironist as one of the figures of his analysis of bad faith (Sartre 1957, 580; 1965, 154). The Flies depicts the ironic temper as a flimsy, escapist disposition while exalting its natural antagonist's passionate, existential commitment (1955). On laughter Sartre has this sole comment: "Laughter is properly human because the human being is the only animal that takes itself seriously: hilarity denounces false seriousness in the name of true-seriousness" (Sartre 1971, 821; my translation). Camus reaffirms the value of irony in State of Siege (Camus 1958, 171) and complains in a personal conversation related by Clément Rosset that his sense of humor is overlooked by readers and critics alike (Polac and Rosset 2003, 80). There is hardly any humor in other existential philosophers as well, including Heidegger and Jaspers; despite their counting themselves among Nietzsche's followers, not only is their philosophical thought closer to tragedy than comedy (Heller 2005, 3), but it is also far from the Nietzschean association of tragedy with joy and laughter.

But if human ridicule is thought to reveal human tragedy, it does so because we take ourselves too seriously even when acknowledging our ridicule. In Dostoevsky's *The Brothers Karamazov*, the visitor in Ivan's nightmare insists: "Yet men, with all their indisputable intelligence, do take the farce of existence as something serious, and this is their tragedy" (quoted in Kallen 1968, 379–80). The contemporary American theologian, Reinhold Niebhur, concurs:

> What is funny about us is precisely that we take ourselves too seriously. We are rather insignificant little bundles of energy and vitality in a vast organization of life. But we pretend that we are the very center of this organization. This pretension is ludicrous; and its absurdity increases with our lack of awareness of it. The less we are able to laugh at ourselves the more it becomes necessary and inevitable that others laugh at us. (Niebuhr 1969, 140–1)

Because we are so serious about ourselves we see life as tragic in the first place; we are ridiculous because we take ourselves seriously and even more ridiculous when considering our ridicule a tragedy.

If it is true that works of existential comedy have expanded the phenomenon of the comic to territories from which they have been formerly excluded because "they sharpened our perception for a broader sense of the comic" (Heller 2005, 95–96), they did not expand it enough. I differ from those whose view is tragic-comic, including the playwrights of the absurd, in suggesting that as soon as we acknowledge the ridiculousness of our situation, the comedy is over: We cease to be comical, and with this, we cease to be tragic. We are beyond the tragic and the comic. There are two ways to explain the process of resolution by ridicule acknowledgment that I propose. One explanation stresses the similarities between this resolution and the comic plot resolution, which is based on the revelation of the hero's true identity. The second borrows the two-stage process of certain incongruity theories of humor, in which the incongruity is resolved on a higher level of understanding.

NEW IDENTITY RESOLUTION

Resolution through revelation of the hero's true identity is the basic plot of comedy, according to Christopher Booker. This kind of resolution has developed through several stages of comedy, beginning with Aristophanes

(Booker 2004, 107–52). At the heart of Aristophanes' comedy lies an *agon* or conflict between two characters or groups of characters. One is dominated by a dark, rigid, life-denying obsession; the other represents life, liberation, and truth. The issue is ultimately decided in favor of the latter. The eventual happy outcome hinges on a crucial turning point: The moment when the dark characters, obsessed with their divisive desire to make war, judge, or kill, are suddenly forced to recognize something so important about themselves that it completely changes their attitude, paving the way to reconciliation and celebration. Aristotle calls this *anagnorisis* or "recognition," the moment when something previously not recognized or known suddenly becomes clear. "Recognition," Aristotle explains, "means the change from ignorance to knowledge." Something is discovered that transforms the situation. Booker maintains that this transition from ignorance to knowledge remains at the heart of the comic plot, and provides the clue to the thematic intent of the story.

In the New Comedy, two new elements appear. First, comedy becomes a love story with the happy ending a union between hero and heroine in a way that symbolizes completion, the end of division, and the renewal of life. Apart from the addition of the love element, the story is still about the resolution of a conflict: Some state of darkness and confusion giving way, through "recognition" and a change of heart, to reconciliation and light. The second crucially important element concerns the nature of the recognition on which the resolution of the story turns: the nature of what it is to be discovered or made clear before a change of heart can pave the way to a happy ending. One of the main sources of confusion in the story and a chief obstacle to unity between the characters is that they are in some way unaware of each other's true identity, or indeed their own. This element of ignorance and the need to establish true identity is a prelude to resolution. Only when everyone's real identity has been sorted out can the way be made clear to the final union. This kind of resolution, then, centers on a process of "recognition" that ultimately leads to the revelation that someone's identity is different from what it seems.

In a fully developed comedy (Shakespeare's, for instance), recognition may involve four interrelated components, all working together. The first component, which is the only one that interests us here, is that characters trapped in a hard, divisive, unloving state—anger, jealousy, shrewishness, disloyalty, self-righteousness—must be softened and liberated by some act of self-recognition and a change of heart. They must in effect become a "new" or different person ("come to themselves"), and if they do not change in his way, they are destined to be punished or become the objects of general derision, so they can no longer harm others.

In Molière's plays the road to resolution lies through "inferior" figures in the story. This is by no means new as again and again since Aristophanes' comedies, characters are separated by an unspoken, invisible dividing line. The characters above the line represent the established order, an upper social level, the authority of men over women, father over children; those below the line, where the shadows fall, include servants, people of inferior class, wives, and the rising generation. The chief source of darkness in the story, in opposition to the life-giving forces, is the upper level, whereas the road to liberation passes through the inferior level. Through these examples from the history of the genre, Booker explains how "the essence of Comedy is always that some redeeming truth has to be brought out of the shadows into the light" (123).

I suggest that Booker's observation applies as well to the revelation of the human being's new identity, that is, the innate ridiculousness that constitutes the pervasive characteristic of humankind. Acknowledging our ridiculousness as a new identity is a redeeming truth, I believe, provided we adhere to the view that we are ridiculous only to the extent that we ignore ourselves. This view of ridicule, maintained by Baudelaire and Bergson, is intimated by Plato when he identifies to "know not thyself" as the source of ridicule (Baudelaire 1968, 378; Bergson 1999, 9; Plato, *Philebus*, 48). According to this view, the comic presupposes the butt's self-ignorance; inadvertently comical, the butt ceases to be so at the moment he realizes his ridiculousness.

Both Nietzsche and Carl Jung envision an ideal of the self in a union of opposites (Huskinson 2004, 165). In *Ecce Homo* and *Thus Spoke Zarathustra*, Nietzsche, as well as Jung (Jung 1951, par. 53), describe the experience of becoming *übermenschlich* or individuated (capable of harnessing the opposites and enduring the dangerous affects that the experience of wholeness occasions) in terms of a sudden conversion or "redemption" of the personality. This idea is not new: The tension of opposites as the primal life force goes back to the pre-Socratic philosopher, Heraclitus, in the West, and pairs of opposites are the basis of Chinese philosophy. The tension of opposites that characterizes *Homo risibilis* includes the union of rational and irrational tendencies, which translates into the union of objective futility and subjective seriousness. The self as a union of opposites brought about by a full acceptance of oneself as made up of incongruous oppositions changes the self's attitude toward all oppositions, including seriousness and futility. In the *Laws*, Plato emphasizes the importance of opposites, and of foolishness for wisdom, claiming that human affairs are not very serious although they must be taken seriously (816 d–e). Thomas Nagel has recently endorsed a view of the absurd that leaves us necessarily serious in our endeavor yet ironic once we notice our futility *sub species aeternitatis*, but he allows that this kind of tension may generate something new (Nagel 1987, 58–59; 1986, 4).

In contradistinction to these views and to the humorous mood's status quo about the tragic and the comic, or seriousness and levity, the attitude that obtains from accepting one's ridicule differs from previous experience. The view proposed here suggests that fully accepting our ridiculousness amounts to a complete liberation from it. Acknowledging ourselves as ridiculous and accepting ourselves without shame or self-blame enables us to transcend our ridiculous humanity. We regain our dignity, and have no need of the hermeneutics of the tragic or of the kind of comic that is parasitic on the tragic because the pain of the initial contradiction between our desires and the possibility of fulfilling them is eased. By accepting our ridicule, we have accepted this contradiction and have no more need of interpretations that attempt to make sense of it or alleviate its sting.

To use the language of redemption, we redeem ourselves by loving ourselves in our ridiculousness, in accordance to Nietzsche's insightful appeal: "Love yourself as an act of clemency—then you will no longer have any need of your god, and the whole drama of Fall and Redemption will be played out to the end in you yourselves!" (Nietzsche 1982, I, sec. 79).[44] By fully accepting ourselves as ridiculous, we transcend ridicule: we cease being comical. *Finita la comedia*, however, does not leave us in the grip of the initial tragic sense of life, I suggest, because the tragic and the comic are so inextricably linked now, that by transcending ridicule we have also transcended the tragic. Once we have transcended ridicule, we are not taken back to the original tragic situation with which we began because the comic has already taken away the tragic's agony, disarmed it, and sweetened its sting.

Moreover, after acknowledging ridicule, the tragic that remains is not only inseparable from the comic, but also determined by it. A protagonist becomes truly tragic-comic when his tragic destiny has been determined by the comicality of his personality or appearance, his situation, his existential perspectives, and his attempts to realize his dreams and ideals. This may be our situation after the comic modulates the tragic, and that which is achieved in the awareness of ridicule that perceives the situation in inclusive comical eyes. Now that our comicality as ridicule defines us, our comical features account for the tragic elements that remain in us. "If Don Quixote lost his comical features he would no longer be tragic," says the Bulgarian aesthetician Isaac Passy (Passy 1963, 71; quoted in Dziemidok 1993, 132–3). Don Quixote can be taken as representative of humanity because, as David Miller has noted, "the don exhibits all the absurdities of the human situation. . . . He is a fool, to be sure, but in being a fool, he is Everyman, and by being himself he is everybody" (Miller 1969, 91–92).[45]

Having transcended the comic (by acknowledging our comicality we gain lucidity and sober up), we transcend the tragic that inheres in ridiculousness (it is tragic to be ridiculous, but we have ceased to be ridiculous; hence we are tragic no more). This claim, despite its innovation, can be substantiated by philosophers who point to the possibility of *comedy* transcending *tragedy* such as Hegel and Friedrich Schiller. As we have seen previously, in Hegel's classification of the genres, tragedy gives way to comedy and reveals a consciousness more developed than tragic consciousness. Comedy is the completion of tragedy and the comic form continues that of the tragic. Having destroyed serious drama, comedy finally turns its mockery on itself and vanishes (Hegel 1975, II, 1199). A libertarian writer of tragedies, Schiller contends that the end of comedy is higher than that of tragedy; that where the end is attained, tragedy becomes superfluous. Comedy frees the human spirit from passion and enables the human being to envision himself and his world clearly and serenely, to recognize that chance is more influential than destiny, and to laugh at life's inconsequentialities rather than to rage or weep at its wickedness:

> Comedy aims at a more important end [than tragedy]; and if this end could be actually attained it would make all tragedy not only unnecessary, but impossible. The aim that comedy has in view is the same as that of the highest destiny of man, and this consists in liberating himself from the influence of violent passions, and taking a calm and lucid survey of all that surrounds him, and also of his own being, and of seeing everywhere occurrence rather than fate or hazard, and ultimately rather smiling at the absurdities than shedding tears and feeling anger at the sight of the wickedness of man. (Schiller 1964, 311)

"Such seeing is man's supreme goal," explains Horace Kallen, "It is the authentic happy ending," for to Schiller "tragedy was the human condition; comedy, man's self-liberation from this condition" (Kallen 1968, 347, 361). In contrast, Kerr is skeptical about the capacity of *comedy* to transcend itself:

> But the pain of comedy is possibly more protracted and more frustrating than that of tragedy, because it does not know how to expel itself. Tragedy's pain is productive; it comes of the abrasiveness of moving forward toward transformation. Comedy,

making capital of the absurdity of seeking transformation, must forever contain its pain. By denying freedom it denies release. Tragedy *uses* suffering; comedy can only live with it. Comedy can only live with it, that is to say, against the possible day when tragedy, in an ultimate successful transformation, frees them both. Comedy, hugging the fox to its breast, stays close to tragedy against that possible, eternally doubted, day. *Only the tragic absurdity is capable of transcending itself.*

What a good man the clown is, to endure so much, to survive so relentlessly, to keep us company in all weathers, to provide us with a way of looking at the worst that enables us to take a temporary joy in the worst! For that is what he does: he stands horror on its head to keep us tolerably happy against the day *when tragedy will look horror straight in the eye and stare it down.* (Kerr 1967, 340; emphasis added)

According to Kerr, only tragedy can transcend itself by staring the tragic down. Kerr may be correct within the limitations of the genres and of the tragic and the comic views outlined at the beginning of the chapter; but with regard to the view of human ridicule, I suggest that, if embraced, this higher-level comic can transcend both itself and the tragic. The proposal still may follow Kerr's suggestion that "tragedy will look horror straight in the eye and stare it down." This is so because of ridicule's affinity with the tragic, on which authors who adhere to our tragic-comic situation have commented. They consider our situation more tragic because of our ridicule. Only a comic of sorts can embrace both tragedy and ridicule, however, because only a higher form of the comic can incorporate both comic and tragic elements, as previously argued. Ridicule and the tragic feeling that accompanies it must be a form of the comic if we are interested in maintaining them both. Kerr is right, however, in asserting that horror needs to be stared down: We must stare down our ridicule in order to embrace it.

A full acknowledgment of our comicality that lies in the tragic liberates us from the tragic, but also enables us to transcend the comic. Like the Buddhist's raft used for passing the river, or the Wittgensteinian ladder, or again the Taoist's fish trap dispensed with when unnecessary, the comic disappears as soon as the tragic disappears.[46] This does not necessarily mean that humor disappears altogether: There are other forms of humor than the comic that evolves out of the tragic.

Insofar as one is defined by ridicule, a resolution of the basic human conflict is obtained by acknowledging oneself as ridiculous. This mirrors resolutions in the comic plot when the revelation of the hero's hidden identity changes everything. Embracing our ridicule saves us from ridicule, for one can be ridiculous only if one is unaware of being ridiculous. By acknowledging our ridicule, we transcend the tragic as well, for it is our ridicule that now determines our tragedy. By accepting the human condi- tion as ridiculous and embracing ridicule as the defining characteristic of humanity at its best, we transcend ourselves because full self-acceptance is alien to human beings, as Nietzsche and Freud have explained: Nietzsche resorted to the overman to overcome our human, all-too-human incapacity for *amor fati*, and Freud deemed us all neurotics because of our necessary flight from ourselves (Nietzsche 1954a; Freud 1926). Thus, humor, which is called on to renounce the urge to redemption, reveals itself as redemptive in bringing about a liberated state capable of rivaling the highest ideals of religion and philosophy.

COGNITIVE INTEGRATION RESOLUTION

There is another way of explaining the resolution I propose. Some of the tension generated by the basic human predicament may be relieved through a humorous state of mind, but the humorous mood is only transi- tory (MacHovec 1988, 8). When it dissolves, the problem at hand may be resolved on a higher level (Basu 1999a). According to the theory of conflict-resolution, which we mentioned earlier as part of the incongru- ity theory of humor, that which may seem incompatible now will seem compatible under a different form of thought (Roeckelein 2002, 172–4; Mulkay 1988, 22–23). Such cognitive humor has the following two-stage process: the perception of a complexity, incongruity, discrepancy, ambiguity, or novelty in the humor stimulus; and the resolution, that is, the cognitive integration or understanding, of the stimulus.

In order to explain the second stage of cognitive humor, it is impor- tant to understand the possible outcomes to a conflict, exemplified by an epistemic conflict, that is, a conflict between beliefs. In unresolved conflicts, we find ourselves confused and both pieces of information are stored with the conflict between them noted. In uncooperative resolution, one of the beliefs will survive while the other is destroyed. In cooperative resolution we may find a way to accept the truth of both beliefs through a creative insight and dissolve an apparent contradiction into compatibility. Whereas the humorous state of mind helps to sort unresolved conflicts and avoid the uncooperative resolution of the conflict that defines the human being, as we have seen, the second stage of cognitive humor helps to attain to a cooperative resolution in the following way.

An inward conflict is incongruous only when it is assumed that human beings are congruous, that is, that I am a congruous being. But were I to realize that both points of view that clash in the conflict are valid and that giving up one of them is simplifying and reducing the complex being I am, these opposing views would not be incongruous anymore. Both would be necessary for doing justice to the being I am. The repetition of the conflicting situation would encourage me to adjust my conception of self to accommodate this view. The higher level that obtains is a view that sees conflicts as normal because they are constitutive of the complex being I am and the complicated relations with and in a world I do not fully understand. The incongruity that gives rise to the tragic and the comic is not perceived as an incongruity anymore. Rather, this view echoes Heraclitus' phrase: "They do not understand that in being at variance with itself that it coheres with itself: a backward stretching harmony, as of a bow or a lyre" (Diels and Kranz 1972, Heraclitus, B51, 80). It also amounts to a harmonious congruence with myself, others, and the world, a situation that all philosophies seek to establish, as David Cooper argues in his introduction to his impressive *World Philosophies*:

> Hegel, and following him, Marx saw philosophy as the endeavor to overcome what they called the problem of "alienation" or "estrangement." By these terms, they meant the sense which many human beings—all of them, perhaps, at times—have of being "strangers," of not being "at home," in the world. Reading philosophers from all times and climes, I am struck by the accuracy of this perception of the central inspiration behind philosophical speculation, by the constant recurrence—from the earliest Indian thinkers recorded to twentieth-century existentialists—of the theme of alienation. (Cooper 1995, 5)

Cooper cites Wordsworth's poignant description of the tension latent in conflicting emotions which is the spur to philosophical thought: "The groundwork of all true philosophy is the difference between . . . that intuition . . . of ourselves, as one with the whole . . . and that [of] ourselves as separated beings, [which] places nature in antithesis to us" (5). At any rate, many of the world philosophies, Cooper argues, can fruitfully be regarded as attempts to resolve this difference or tension by offering accounts of human beings that do justice to the uniqueness of the species, yet without, so to speak, rendering its members freaks, outsiders, or strangers in the world. "What hardly any philosopher of the first rank has done is to ignore, or remain sanguine about the tension," he adds:

> Those, like Kant, who confessed to their failure to resolve it, did so with palpable disappointment, even despair. After all,

if the German poet Hölderlin was right and it is both "divine
and good" to be "at one" with the world, then the failure to
resolve the tension is not simply an intellectual débâcle, but a
human tragedy. (6)

If Cooper is right about the initial philosophical spur, the view proposed
here inserts itself in the history of philosophical attempts to overcome
alienation.

The cognitive aspect of the resolution—acknowledging our ridicule—
would be impotent in real life situations, however, if I could not accept
its contents emotionally, that is, if I could not embrace it. That which
enables me to accept it emotionally is no foreign element, but the emotional component of humor itself: The sympathetic and benevolent way
in which one treats oneself in humor (Freud 1928). Bohdan Dziemidok
differentiates between comical protagonists whom we like even though we
laugh at them and those whom we like because they are laughable. Many
theorists of the comic defend the thesis that one and the same object may
both evoke the experience of the comical and the feeling of friendship and
sympathy (Dziemidok 1993, 99–101). We have to pertain to this latter sort
of comical protagonists in order to accept our ridicule emotionally.

The full acceptance of oneself facilitated by humor is a complex
mechanism that draws its support from a certain view of humankind as
ridiculous. But both the view of humankind as ridiculous and the process
of its acceptance are not alien to humor; rather they are suggested to the
individual through the enticing pleasure humor generates from the ridiculous being one happens to be.

THE GOOD LIFE

Transmuting suffering into joy, the alchemy of humor reveals itself as
redemptive in bringing about a harmonious state and a serene joy that rivals
the highest philosophic and religious ideals. Before assessing the viability
and desirability of the good life obtained through a liberation from the
tragic by purposeful and systematic use of humor, it is helpful to differentiate
the ideas presented so far from the philosophical views on humor investigated in previous chapters as well as other views sympathetic to humor.

The proposal at hand follows Shaftesbury's use of soliloquy in that it
uses humor inwardly as a tool for self-discipline, for curbing exalted enthusiasm, and for systematically educating our sense of proportion. Like Shaftesbury, I see in humor a method for challenging all forms of irrationality and

a liberating tool that frees us from patterns of action and thought that are ultimately life-destroying. Like Shaftesbury, moreover, I suggest that humor has a habilitating function with regard to the truth. The difference lies in our respective views of the truth: For Shaftesbury humor denotes a fundamental capacity for the apprehension of the beautiful and the good, whereas I consider humor especially apt for perceiving the ambiguity of life and the ambivalence of human beings, that is, the muddiness of truth and goodness.

The basic human predicament described here differs from the Kierkegaardian human contradiction in that it does not assume any metaphysical presuppositions about the nature of the self. Moreover, contrary to Kierkegaard's view of the self in need of God to make it whole, the present proposal suggests a way to complete the self through a systematic use of humor. In its incorporation of both comic and tragic elements, the view of humor I propose is consistent with Kierkegaard's view of humor. It differs, however, from his view of the comic as subsumable under the tragic; I suggest, rather, that the mixture of pleasure and pain found in the "humorous mood" resolves into pleasure,[47] and that what is both tragic and comic is comical on a higher level. The final stage that obtains is different from Kierkegaard in that it is not inferior to religion and, unlike the Kierkegaardian view of humor, it is free from notions of guilt and God.

I do not refer to the higher state that obtains in terms of irony, as a number of authors have done in their attempt to point to a higher stage of the comic—"irony" (Morreall 1997), "comical irony" (Goldsmith 1991), "Pyrrhonist irony" (Gurewitch 1994), or "humorous irony" (Jankélévitch 1964). I use *humor* even when addressing human ridicule because the higher comical stage is characterized by a leveling sympathy and compassion, which are necessarily involved in humor, but alien to irony.[48] This is no semantic divergence: Without the sympathy and compassion necessary for embracing one's and another's ridicule, the resolution would not be possible.

That we may find the world acceptable, not through tragedy but through an essentially human laughter, however, has not eluded contemporary philosophers. In his recent *Jokes*, Ted Cohen describes the laughter of acceptance, which confirms, "we may dwell with the incomprehensible without dying from fear or going mad. That may be a religious thought, but I found it in thinking about the human response to jokes, in the laughter that is absolutely, characteristically, essentially human":

> . . . a human response to absurdity is laughter. It is not just jokes, but indeed it is also the world itself and its various inhabitants that are sometimes absurd to human contemplation. When we laugh at a true absurdity, we simultaneously confess that we can-

not make sense of it and that we accept it. Thus this laughter is an expression of our humanity, our finite capacity, our ability to live with what we cannot understand or subdue. (Cohen 1999, 41)

Simon Critchley voices similar thoughts about our aptitude for accepting our finitude. He suggests that a certain kind of laughter opens up this ungraspable and ever-weakening relation to finitude, which is based on acknowledging weakness and limitation rather than tragically attempting to affirm them (Critchley 1999, 222; see 2002, 119, n. 12).

In his *Laughing at Nothing: Humor As a Response to Nihilism*, John Marmysz gives his own definition of nihilism as essentially thwarted idealism in a way that is reminiscent of the basic incongruity considered as the human predicament in this chapter: "The full impact of the problem of nihilism strikes only when an individual passionately desires ultimate meaning, value, and purpose, but believes those things to be out of reach" (Marmysz 2003, 84–85). There are thus two elements to a nihilistic worldview: An idealized desire for a better world coupled with a belief that this can never be realized—"the real world is denigrated in comparison to the ideal, and the ideal is believed to be hopelessly out of reach" (85). This, for Marmysz, is the basis of a "nihilistic incongruity" on which his solution is founded. Marmysz, too, finds it in humor; through an analysis of jokes and the application of different theories about humor, Marmysz demonstrates that the "solution" to nihilism is to learn to laugh at it: "Humor allows us to confront incongruities and, instead of being overwhelmed by them, to understand them in an unusual and original fashion" (152). For this reason, humor creates "the capacity to *make* incongruities unthreatening and to interpret them in a manner that produces amusement" (153).

But the proposal advanced in this chapter is more radical than the views of Cohen, Critchley, and Marmysz on laughter's philosophic benefits. I suggest that the situation that obtains on this proposal is a celebration of humanity, an acceptance of one's finitude, a gracing of our folly, a therapy for the hubris and self-centeredness of the tragic view of life. The freedom that results from the newfound harmony with oneself, others, and the world is characterized by a serene joy that enables the affirmation of life and brings along moral and epistemological benefits. In the remainder of the chapter, I assess the viability and the desirability of the *Homo risibilis* proposal.

1. *The viability of Homo risibilis.* I begin assessing the viability of the proposal by addressing arguments on the limitations of self-laughter. Granted that one can recognize oneself as ridiculous, I address the viability of the joyful outcome of such a bleak perspective.

In his remarkable *Truth and the Comedic Art*, Michael Gelven argues that comedy graces our folly:

> The existential coherence of being comedic judges of our own comedic folly enables a truth that is so fundamental to what and who we are as foolish and hence rational persons, that, in its absence we cannot be complete, much less think about being complete. Fun enables us to be complete. This completeness has already been identified as the joyous recognition of our own self-reflective judging of our graced foolishness. (Gelven 2000, 149)

Although fun enables us to be complete, Gelven seems to restrict its salvific quality to comedy: "Unless we are able to participate in the comedic celebration we cannot, in any other way, reflect on our folly with fondness to the extent that it discloses fundamental truth," he writes. The rare, existential coherence of being comedic judges of our own comedic folly—which is being fun at its highest level—exists nowhere outside of art" (Gelven 2000, 148). In contradistinction to Gelven, I suggest that those who can recognize themselves as ridiculous can grace their own folly as well as the folly of others. If I have ever laughed in a comedy, I should laugh at myself outside a comedy. To do so, I have only to recognize that all laughter is self-laughter: It is at myself that I laugh. Not recognizing this fact makes me ever so ridiculous, which is yet another good reason to laugh at myself. As we have noted in the discussion of *homo risibilis*, the laughing philosopher Democritus already finds ridiculous our capacity to laugh at others instead of at ourselves. Indeed, nothing is less critical than excepting oneself from the human condition: Every laughter, argues Critchley, is self-laughter because "the object of laughter is the subject who laughs (Critchley 2002, 14). Recognizing oneself as laughable may be the defining characteristic of the philosophic consciousness, as Ronell has argued. If this is so, this recognition occurs independently of the performance of the conventional theater; it occurs in the theater of the mind where the philosophic comedy takes place.

Moreover, if I have ever laughed at myself while revisiting past experiences, I should laugh now, in *media res*. The spirit of humor, Stephen Leacock explains, "views life, even life now, in as soft a light as we view the past" (Leacock 1938, 216). Humor means looking at the present with the (kind) eyes of the future as if it were the past. A repeated claim about humor, however, is that it is impossible to use it in the present as one would in the future; some incongruous situations are just too heavy with practical consequences for most people to find funny while they are in these situations, yet "in retrospect they may seem funny" (Morreall 1983, 105–6, 109–10). Karl Marx begins his essay *Der 18te Brumaire des Louis Napoleon* (*The Eighteenth Brumaire of Louis Napoleon,* 1852), thus: "Hegel notes somewhere, that all great world-historical facts and personages, so to say, repeat themselves, he forgot to add: First as tragedy, then as farce." Marcella Goldsmith extends the meaning of his statement and generalizes it to include psychological phenomena; this is possible because "with time the subject detaches himself for whatever event may have caused his suffering and is able to view that event with serenity" (Goldsmith 1991, 118). Similarly, Hegel, as observed earlier, maintains that we can enjoy the comic only in retrospect, once we have sublated it; and this idea is preserved in Kierkegaard's thought on the comic, which, he asserts, needs a way out of the contradiction in order to be legitimate. Along the same lines, Jean Paul stresses the impossibility of someone finding oneself ridiculous while engaged "in his actions" (Jean Paul 1964, 317–18).

Philosophers who explain why ridicule applies to others or the comic to the past may be right, I suggest, when spontaneous laughter is involved. Indeed, these provisos are mostly advanced as part of the explanation of what (spontaneous) laughter is about. However, finding oneself ridiculous in the present while looking at others may involve no spontaneous laughter; one does not have to find it funny nor particularly enjoyable. To recognize one's ridiculousness and to acknowledge it is sufficient: If the other is ridiculous, so am I, and if I will recognize it in the future, I can recognize it now—otherwise, I am being ridiculous in my insistence that only the others are ridiculous and that only in the future can I consider this experience laughable. The enduring incongruity that lies at the basis of ridicule is indifferent to who is being ridiculous and to when it is easier to recognize it. It has nevertheless to be acknowledged independently from any pleasure it may bring. This supposes developing a taste for incongruity. With Kierkegaard and Nietzsche, I suggest that laughter can and should be learned. A discipline of laughter is important not just in order to enjoy oneself, but mainly because through laughter new norms can be adopted that eventually change one's attitude toward oneself, others, and the world.

The change of attitude that follows the acceptance of one's ridicule leads to a newly found harmony with oneself, others, and the world that results in freedom and is characterized by joy. Tragic philosophies that associate the tragic with joy may help us understand this apparent paradox. Even in a disharmonious world, a newfound harmony is joyful for Nietzsche and Rosset. Nietzsche conveys his relief thus: "The fatality of essence is not to be disentangled from the fatality of all that has been and will be. . . . One is necessary, one is a piece of fatefulness, one belongs to the whole, one is in the whole . . . that alone is the great liberation" (Nietzsche 1954b, VI, sec. 8). Rosset attests to a similar liberation during the performance of a tragedy:

> What can we do with the world . . . if it does not know the tragic? Alone with our tragic, in an anti-tragic world. . . . It is from this anxiety that the tragic drunkenness delivers us forever in affirming without hope of contestation: the world is tragic, the world is *the tragic*. . . . That is, destiny is at the measure of our destiny, the latter's value is not exceptional, but to the contrary a "sign" of the tragic reality. We are *tragic* in a *tragic world*: doesn't one see what marvelous accord fills us with joy? . . .
>
> We discover, in reality, a world with which we can establish a contact: it knows us, we know it, we agree with it on a fundamental point: nothing exists, nothing—*except* the tragic. (Rosset 1991, 90; my translation)

To be tragic in a tragic world is still a marvelous accord that fills us with joy. Adam Potkay's analysis of the emotion in his *The Story of Joy*, may help us understand how this can be so. Joy is "the mind's delight," because it is "the experience of reunion or fulfillment, of desire at least temporarily laid to rest. Joy is what we feel, and as self-reflective beings know we feel, in situation, real or imaginary, in which what was lost is found; what was missed restored; want constrained is lifted; what we desire arrives; or what arrives satisfies a desire we hadn't know we'd had" (Potkay 2007, vii). Joy's paradox involves the nexus of loss and restoration, self-dispersion, and perfect concentration. It is a passion for primacy, for recurrence; it arrives with restored life or with access to more life, and is the point and proof of one's insertion into a unified order of nature (16, 235, 96). From Spinoza and Shaftesbury onwards, joy arises from recognizing the self as part of God, Nature, and the rational structure of the universe, Potkay maintains (171). Were we to conceive of Nature as irrational and we as part of it, joy would still be the outcome of this recognition of the self as part of Nature, I suggest, on condition we could accept their irrationality. The benefits of *Homo risibilis* are predicated on this acceptance, but it is also a worldview that can only be reached through a gradual acceptance of irrationality and a practice that teaches us to enjoy it.

2. *The desirability of Homo risibilis.* I characterize the joy that results from embracing one's ridicule as a constant, serene, and affirmative joy, otherwise empty of content. I address the appeal of other philosophies that exempt us from acknowledging our ridicule, such as Nietzsche's and

Rosset's, by criticizing the feasibility and desirability of the joy they associate with the tragic. Finally, I spell the moral and epistemologic benefits of *Homo risibilis*.

Heinz Kohut observes that "joy relates to experiences of the total self"; it is both "cause" and "effect" of a process of self-development, and is related, in particular, to the self's journey toward an openness that would make it whole (Kohut 1977, 45). This is the joy that arises from the whole human being that Spinoza deems *hilaritas*, and which has been translated into English as "cheerfulness" or gaiety (*Ethics*, III, P11Schol.). It springs from oneself as a cause, from imagining one's own power of acting, and is therefore a constant joy and not a transient one. Spinoza, here, follows the Stoics' differentiation between kinds of joy: Joy as a passion or emotion that should be eradicated, on the one hand, and as a rational joy that is the outcome of a successful Stoic living, on the other (Nussbaum 1994, 399–400). Roman Stoics reserve *gaudium* for the latter to designate an equable state of mind, and *laetitia* to designate either irrational joy or, less negatively, the physical aspect of *gaudium* (Cicero 1945, 4.6.12–13; 340–1).

In contradistinction to the joy arising out of the humorous mood, which is transitory, the joy that follows from embracing one's ridicule is constant. It is heir to the Stoic and Spinozistic joy, because it follows from a newfound harmony with the world, regardless of its nature.

An interesting characteristic of joy is its freedom from desire. Martha Nussbaum notes, "Joy may inspire no desire, or simply the desire to act in some way expressive of joy . . ." (Nussbaum 2001a, 135). For Robert Solomon as well, joy tends to seek out and form intimate bonds with itself; it has no desire, except to share the mood. Its object is everything, but nothing in particular. The power and strategy associated with emotions are in joy's case "none necessary," and the question of the status involved in emotions "doesn't even arise" (Solomon 1976, 276):

> Joy is that happy passion that renders our world not only satisfactory but "wonderful." Like contentment, it formulates its values and expectations to conform with the world. As such, it has no ideology (except the *laissez faire* of the status quo or utter indifference to change), no concrete ideals or values. (275)

Because joy has no desire in particular, it is conducive to any action. Joy is so ethereal, however, that it is extremely difficult to describe "without slipping into the mush that such moods freely supply" (275).

Once joy is attained as a permanent state one's relation to life changes, for joy enables the affirmation of everything—an attitude recommended by proponents of tragic philosophies such as Nietzsche and Rosset. Neither, however, can point to a warranted way of getting there. Nietzsche combines his own keen sense of the tragic life with an uncontained joy although, as Robert Solomon rightly points out, "he is not always convincing" (Solomon 1999, 144). Nietzsche opens the fourth book of *The Gay Science* with a resolution for the New Year: "Some day I wish to be only a Yes-sayer," and urges us in *Twilight of the Idols* as well as in other writings "*to realize in oneself* the eternal joy of becoming—that joy which also encompasses *joy in destruction*" (Nietzsche 1974, sec. 276; 1954b, X, sec. 5). The joyful Dionysian affirmation is reached through self-overcoming, Nietzsche maintains, yet there is a gap between the destructive-lionesque stage and the creative and affirming-childlike state described in *Thus Spoke Zarathustra* (Part I, "On the Three Metamorphoses") and exemplified in other Nietzschean writings.[49]

True, Nietzsche explains that once you say yes to a single joy, you say yes to all woe, because joy and woe are connected (1954a, IV, "The Drunken Song"). Joy and woe may be connected, but one generally does not intend to embrace woe when affirming joy. After joy is present, woe may be joyful too. One does not, however, gain a clear indication of how to reach tragic joy, the joy that affirms everything. Moreover, one can doubt that tragic joy exists; tragic joy is found in Richard Wagner's *Art and Revolution* (1896, 40) and *Tristan and Isolde*, in the writings of his one-time disciple Nietzsche, and in William Butler Yeats' late Nietzschean poems; there is no trace of it in previous understandings of the tragic, especially not in Aristotle, whose theory of tragedy does not refer to joy (see Potkay 2007, chap. 8). Finally, even if such a joy is possible, one can doubt its desirability: Being also "a joy in destruction," it is predicated on cruelty toward others and toward oneself, as expressed in such passages as "what constitutes the painful voluptuousness of tragedy is cruelty," or "to see the failure of tragic natures and to laugh, that is divine" (Nietzsche 1966b, sec. 229; 1938, II, 380).

Rosset, the sole faithful disciple of Nietzsche's tragic philosophy, openly acknowledges the mysterious origin and advent of joy: He deems the love of life a graced joy, a Pascalian gift, which cannot be attained by a determined path, yet is absolutely necessary for affirming life. Indeed, our highest and most difficult task is to accept the real, to find satisfaction in the sensual and perishable world (1993a, "The Cruelty Principle," 83). Accepting the real, however, presupposes a consciousness that would be capable of both knowing the worst and not being affected by this knowledge of the worst. The faculty of knowing without suffering mortal damage, Rosset believes, is situated absolutely out of reach of human faculties:

This wisdom is not evident and supposes, in order to be effi-cacious, the extra-help of an extraordinary force, not to say supernatural, which I call the joy of living, the only resource that enables us to fulfill the wish expressed by Rimbaud in the last line of his *Season in Hell*: "to possess truth in body and soul." In other terms: to reach finally an accord between the faculty of knowing and the faculty of living. (Rosset 2001, 85; my translation)

Joy is the necessary condition, if not of life in general, at least of life lived consciously and in full awareness. The simple fact of taking reality into consideration, the simple exercise of reflection suffices here to discour-age all effort—unless joy somehow comes to one's assistance, a joy that, like that of the Pascalian God, steps in when all forces are failing and brings about, *in extremis* and against all odds, the triumph of the weakest cause. In the final apology of the second of the *Provincial Letters*, Pascal defines this act of sustaining precisely as an "extraordinary intervention." The intervention of joy is forever mysterious, impenetrable even for those who feel its beneficent effects:

In the final analysis, nothing has changed for them, and they understand no more than before. They have no new argument to invoke in favor of existence and they are still perfectly inca-pable of saying why or for what they are living. And yet from this moment forth they value life as indisputable and eternally desirable. This is the mystery inherent in the zest for life. (19)

This extraordinary and mysterious assistance, that which Pascal calls grace and Rosset calls joy, is necessary for life conceived as knowledge of reality, but it cannot be attained by a determined path akin to that of climbing a ladder of perfection.[50]

If indeed a clear path to joyfulness is indicated through a systematic use of humor, it answers the paradox of tragic philosophies—that which is most needed, joy, does not lie within the scope of our will (Rosset); or, although the will is the only way to attain to what is most needed, there is no assured path leading to it (Nietzsche). I believe with Rosset and Nietzsche that because we are joyful, we can affirm life—an impossible task if we try to affirm it without joy in our arsenal.

A serene joyfulness may be good in itself, but may also have beneficial moral consequences if we believe Spinoza, Nietzsche, and contemporary research regarding the effect of well-being and induced positive moods on altruism (Argyle 1987, 216–7). Because we are in a state of constant joy or happiness, we can be virtuous Spinoza maintains in contrast to most moralists. Virtue and blessedness are equally valuable and fundamental for Spinoza, for they prove in the end to be identical. Thus Spinoza asserts in his *Ethics*: "Virtue itself [is] happiness itself, and the greatest freedom" (II, P49Schol.). And he adds in the last proposition of the same book: "Blessedness is not the reward of virtue but is virtue itself; nor do we delight in blessedness because we restrain our lusts, but, on the contrary, because we delight in it, therefore we restrain our lusts" (V, P42). Blessedness is not the prize of self-control, as most moralists and religious thinkers have led us to believe: We can be virtuous because we are happy, and happiness is virtue itself.

Similarly, Nietzsche affirms that because we are joyful we can be generous. Nietzsche maintains that the happiness of the individual with strong, healthy instincts has its benefits for his neighbors. His love of self translates into an affirmation of the world. His sense of freedom and power allows magnanimity toward others. On the other hand, the unordered soul is spiteful and dangerous. Its viciousness amounts to a discontentedness with itself and a condemnation of life. For virtue, generally beneficial to one's neighbors, is that which follows happiness; it is a byproduct of a fulfilled life.[51] Leslie Paul Thiele notes that Nietzsche attributes this thesis to Goethe, who writes, "joyfulness is the mother of all virtue" (Thiele 1990, 75n).

Virtue is easier for the happy and generosity comes naturally to the joyful. Other paths that lead to joyfulness may achieve as much. However, there is a special characteristic of the life lived in full acknowledgment of one's ridicule: One's personal dignity and self-esteem do not arise from comparison with others. If Robert Solomon is right in asserting that "every emotion is a subjective strategy for the maximization of personal dignity and self-esteem," more concerned with our own security and esteem than they are with accuracy or fairness (Solomon 1976, 222, 209), and Aaron Ben-Ze'ev is correct in assuming that every emotion is based on comparison (Ben-Ze'ev 2000, 18), then ridiculous man finds no use for envy, jealousy, anger, and other comparative emotions. There is no one to serve as comparison, as ridicule equalizes, and the only self-esteem available to us stems from our sense of truthfulness, which, if made our supreme maxim, is, at least according to Kant, "the maximum of inner worth (of human dignity)" (Kant 2006, 195). It is an ethic of compassion, however, that follows most naturally from the egalitarianism of *Homo risibilis*. Similar to the Christian and Buddhist ethics, whose egalitarian vision lies at the heart of their shared concern for suffering (be it from sin or ignorance), but without need of their metaphysical presuppositions, such an ethics can be derived without unwarranted assumptions from the vision afforded by Homo risibilis.

The epistemologlical benefits of Homo risibilis are significant as well. First, its egalitarian view of our weaknesses can ground a much-needed view of human fallibility. An equivalent of humility without religious overtones, it is conducive to a greater openness to criticism, which, according to critical rationalists, is the sole content of rationality.

Second, the joy this worldview affords grants the capacity to withstand the truth about the human condition. John Kekes states in his Moral Wisdom and Good Lives that "the variety of inappropriate attitudes to the human condition is great. Discussing them would take a very long—and very depressing—book" (Kekes 1995, 176). He identifies and criticizes four frequent and most typical kinds of inappropriate attitudes he calls disengagement, denial, romanticism, and resignation. In disengagement, we deliberately turn away from the interests of humanity; alternatively, but equally wrongly, we deny or overreact to our understanding of permanent adversities; or we are lured by resignation (180–1). A right attitude to the human condition, one that involves no disengagement, denial, romanticism, and resignation offers greater realism. It leads to the acknowledgment of the pervasive forces of contingency, conflict, and evil, and it motivates us to mitigate their destructive consequences undaunted by the knowledge of possible failure. Realism is acquired after having chastened, reduced, purified, and strengthened hope by resisting the temptation to pursue facile solace: By distancing ourselves from our condition, by denying the facts, by romantic self-aggrandizement or world-weariness, or by succumbing to resignation. It is a life lived without expectation of cosmic justice, but also without bitterness in the knowledge that the world is not more hospitable to us.

Third, it is a serene life that is reached without renouncing one's reason or desires. By enabling us to accept our necessary failure, it grants us serenity while liberating us for action. Serenity is a goal of Eastern philosophies and religions such as Hinduism, Buddhism, and Taoism, as well as Western philosophies and religions such as all Hellenistic philosophies, Neo-Platonism, and the philosophies of Spinoza and Santayana. Religions that aim at redemption also aim at serenity.[52] I have criticized these philosophies and religions for the means that lead to that goal but I believe their goal is both worthy and within reach. The sort of humor described in this chapter can be developed and does not require special comedic skills (see Ruch 2008, 69–71). Its benefits are in proportion to its use, and the serenity it offers is gradual. The tragic sense of life that it assumes is common enough to make it serviceable to most, if not all, who wish to use it.

Finally, it is a skeptical and secular worldview that avoids unwarranted metaphysical and religious assumptions. It brings to mind the Skeptical Pyrrhonists who graphically declared that peace of mind follows the sus-pension of judgment like a shadow following the body: We suspend all judgments because of the skeptical doubts that undermine all dogmatic claims to knowledge, and tranquility follows the suspension of judgment—in technical terms *ataraxía* follows *epochē*—like a "shadow following the body" (Laertius 1925, 9.107; see Sextus Empiricus 2000, 1.29). This means that we achieve tranquility as a result of suspending judgment without intending to do so (Sextus 2000, 1.25–30). The proposal outlined here does not partake in the sort of skepticism endorsed by this school. It is nonetheless a skeptical worldview that shares the Pyrrhonists' dislike of unwarranted assumptions as well as their ideal of tranquility. Apart from this Hellenistic and Roman philosophy, the proposal outlined here is the only skeptical worldview I know of that aims at such an ideal and the only one to use humor to reach it.[53] The worldview proposed in this chapter naturally clashes with Shaftesbury's religious faith as well as with Hamann's and Kierkegaard's Christianity. Its significance derives partly from its con-troversy with them: Nonreligious persons need not despair of finding a role for humor in the good life, as humor is not only congenial to a skeptical worldview but discloses perhaps more fully its potency within an intellectual environment of this sort.

I have described a multistage process involving a systematic use of humor for disciplining our taste so that we can find pleasure in incongrui-ties not immediately funny to us: Beginning with the tragic, it traces the course leading from the comic to humor and on to ridicule, maps ridicule's banishment and with it the comic and the tragic, and culminates in an account of a liberated state of being characterized by joy and serenity. Through this process a ladder of perfection can be climbed that leads to a state rivaling the highest philosophic and religious ideals. This achieve-ment is gradual and based on changing visions of oneself, others, and the world that correspond to the human capacity to transmute suffering into joy through the alchemy of humor.

NOTES

INTRODUCTION

1. For the notion of "humor," see Nilsen 1993a, 302–6; Nilsen and Nilsen 2000, 57, 59, 293, 324.

2. For the relation of philosophy to the comic prior to the eighteenth century, see Amir 2013b.

3. Kierkegaard and Shaftesbury are connected also through Johann G. von Herder, Shaftesbury's admirer and Hamann's follower (Sparling 2011), whose influence on Søren Kierkegaard is significant.

4. For Gilles Deleuze's view of humor in the good life, as well as George Bataille's and Clément Rosset's views of laughter in the good life, see *Nietzsche's French Laughing Followers* (work in progress).

5. For Frederick Nietzsche's and George Santayana's views of laughter in the good life, and Henri Bergson's view of laughter *tout court*, see *Laughter and the Good Life* (work in progress).

6. For a thorough criticism of the conventional account of philosophy's attitude toward humor, see Amir 2014.

CHAPTER 1: SHAFTESBURY—RIDICULE AS THE TEST OF TRUTH

1. The references to Shaftesbury's works correspond to the abbreviations listed at the beginning of the book. The abbreviated names of works are followed by numbers: capital Roman numerals indicate books, lower case Roman numerals indicate parts or volumes, Arabic numbers indicate sections. *An Inquiry Concerning Virtue or Merit* is divided into books, parts, and sections (i.e., *Inquiry*, I, i, 1); *Miscellaneous Reflections on the Preceding Treatises, and other Critical Subjects* is divided into books and chapters (*Misc.*, I, i); the *Sensus Communis, an Essay on the Freedom of Wit and Humour* (*Essay*), *Soliloquy, or Advice to an Author* (*Soliloquy*), and *The Moralists, a Philosophical Rhapsody* (*Moralists*) are divided into parts and sections

(i.e., *Essay*, I, 1); finally, *A Letter Concerning Enthusiasm to My Lord* is divided into sections (i.e., *Letter*, 1). Often book references are followed by a reference to *Characteristics of Men, Manners, Opinions, Times, etc.*, indicated by CR (ed. John M. Robertson 1963 [1900], two vols.), followed by the volume number in capitalized Roman numerals and an Arabic number indicating the page. For example: CR II, 14, stands for *Characteristics*, vol. II, page 14. On the rare occasions that a reference is made to the three volume edition of *Characteristics of Men, Manners, Opinions, Times, etc.*, (1837, 6th edition, 3 vols.), it is indicated by CR3, followed by the number of the volume. References to *The Life, Unpublished Letters, and Philosophical Regimen of Anthony, Earl of Shaftesbury* (ed. Benjamin Rand, 1900), appear as abbreviation and page (i.e. *Life*, 1), and to the remainder of the material in the Shaftesbury Papers in the Public Record Office at Kew, Surrey, as the abbreviation P.R.O followed by references to arrangements there. For example, "Pathologia sive Explicatio Affectum Humanorum" is located at P.R.O 30/24/26/7/I, "Design of a Socratick History" at P.R.O 30/24/27/14, and "Askêmata" at P.R.O 30/24/27/10. These references, as well as references to other material found in the Shaftesbury Papers in the Public Record Office, are followed by an Arabic number indicating pages (i.e., P.R.O 30/24/27/14, 6).

2. The first earl encountered John Locke for the first time in the 1660s while in need of Locke's medical expertise. However, in subsequent years, the relation took on other dimensions as well. Most famously, Locke advised Shaftesbury on political matters and developed sophisticated arguments in support of the Whig cause (Klein 1994, 15, n. 31). Locke also was close to the Shaftesbury household and was in charge of educating the first earl's grandchildren. Although Locke's social and intellectual ties with the Shaftesbury household were closest during the 1670s, the third earl of Shaftesbury maintained contacts with Locke after the death of the first earl in 1683 and indeed to the end of Locke's life in 1704. Philosophical discussion was not a staple of that relationship. However, a number of letters between them dating to the early 1690s do broach philosophic subjects. Indeed, Locke encouraged his correspondent to convey his reflections, but Shaftesbury seemed to have felt a mixture of respect and intimidation, complicated by a sense of being misunderstood by Locke, who appeared to be an unsympathetic reader: after a few stabs at a philosophic exchange, the younger man developed an embarrassed and self-effacing discomfort mixed with rebellious impatience (Locke 1976, III, 709–10; IV, 248–95, 666–71; V, 650–66, 123–5). Substantive discussion disappeared from this correspondence after 1694 or so. Establishing a philosophic identity distinct from Locke and from the sort of philosophizing Locke represented became a theme in Shaftesbury's career. Locke's personal proximity to the young future third earl helps explain the emotional intensity that later informed Shaftesbury's search for a philosophical identity—his attack on Lockean positions involved attacking someone with whom he had a personal connection.

3. Shaftesbury knew Pierre Bayle (1647–1706), a French Protestant scholar and philosopher, who after the revocation of the Edict of Nantes settled in Holland. Bayle was renowned for his *Dictionary* (1734), and a skepticism targeting Christian orthodoxies in particular. Shaftesbury met with Bayle during his stays in Rotterdam

and praised him in a letter to John Darby, publisher of the *Characteristics* (dated 2 February 1708, P.R.O. 30/24/22/4 f., 63; in *Life*, 385–6). John Robertson maintains that through Bayle Shaftesbury was influenced by Spinoza's philosophy. In his introduction to Shaftesbury's *Characteristics*, Robertson refers to Spinoza as Shaftesbury's "chief forerunner" and notes that "his critics and commentators in general have rather oddly overlooked the fact that his philosophy, as regards its bases, is drawn more or less directly from Spinoza" (Robertson 1963, xxxi). Referring to the *Inquiry Concerning Virtue or Merit*, Robertson doubts Shaftesbury's capacity at the age of eighteen to have produced from his own meditations "a finished and formal philosophical treatise, of which the theses were capable of influencing European thought for a century," and calls it "an extravagant assumption." Furthermore, he claims that "it is morally certain that his main ideas were given him; and as a matter of fact they are nearly all explicit or implicit in Spinoza, whose teaching Shaftesbury was sure to hear of in his one-year sojourn in Holland in 1698, if he had not studied it before. . . ." (Robertson 1963, xxxi). Eric Weil, who sees Shaftesbury as an atheist mystic, notes the influence of Spinoza on Shaftesbury's version of pantheism, if only through the chapter dedicated to it in Bayle's *Dictionary* (Bayle 1734; Weil 1967, 172; see Larthomas 1986, 365). Stanley Grean notes the resemblance of the overall tendency between Spinoza's and Shaftesbury's philosophies, but does not infer a direct influence: "Shaftesbury's philosophy is part of a broad movement—not always connected—which manifested itself in seventeenth- and eighteenth-century Europe in such diverse quarters as Spinozism, Hasidism, and Cambridge Platonism, a movement to recover the joy in religion" (Grean 1967, 31).

    4. Shaftesbury introduced the term *moral sense* to philosophy, but did not make much of it. He also was the first to liken moral sense to a sense of harmony in music and proportion in architecture and art. Shaftesbury maintains that we are disposed to act virtuously by our affection for virtue. Francis Hutcheson and David Hume, his philosophical heirs, call this affection for virtue "moral sense."

    5. Even as a moralist, Shaftesbury is not considered to be speculative enough (see Klein 1994, 48–51; Grean 1967, 8). The lack of recognition of Shaftesbury in the history of philosophy may be due to his view of philosophy that was different from the view accepted in English and American universities at the end of the nineteenth and twentieth centuries (see Kuklick 1977; Rajchman 1985, ix–xxx).

    6. Shaftesbury's influence on Hutcheson's early work is impossible to miss; see Gill 2006, chap. 10. For Hutcheson on laughter, see Telfer 1995. Commenting on criticism of Shaftesbury's views, Stanley Grean remarks that "the power of Shaftesbury's thought . . . is seen in the very strength and virulence of the attacks made on his philosophy in the eighteenth century, a notable example being Berkeley's *Alciphron; or, The Minute Philosopher* (1732), wherein Shaftesbury is so unfairly represented" (Grean 1967, x). George Berkeley attacked Shaftesbury's Deism in the name of polite Christianity. So did Joseph Butler, an Anglican minister who became bishop of Durham in 1750, in his *Analogy of Religion, Natural and Revealed* (1736). In the name of egoism, Bernard Mandeville attacked the Shaftesburean account of natural sociability in *The Fable of the Bees* (1705).

7. After reading Shaftesbury's *The Moralists*, Leibniz wrote: "I found in it almost all of my *Theodicy* before it saw the light of day. . . . If I had seen this work before my *Theodicy* was published, I should have profited as I ought and should have borrowed its great passages" (Leibniz 1956, II, 103). The *Theodicy* was published in 1710 and *The Moralists* in 1709.

8. Herder, Letter 33 (1794), in *Sämmtliche Werke*, 1877–1913, VVII, 158 (my translation).

9. See Tave 1960, vii–ix. For the Latitudinarian Divines Isaac Barrow and John Hacket, and for the journalists of the *Tatler* and the *Spectator*, see there 1960, 4–8, and 8–15, respectively.

10. Willey 1986, 58; Robertson 1963, 8.

11. Shaftesbury's follower, Francis Hutcheson, has been credited with providing a clear definition of humor as incongruity and with rebutting Hobbes' theory of humor as superiority (Hutcheson 1750). However, he only reformulated and systematized Shaftesbury's views on humor.

12. In 1699 John Toland published without Shaftesbury's permission his precocious *Inquiry Concerning Virtue or Merit*, in some respects his best book. In *The Moralists*, he put forth his ethical doctrine afresh, with a lighter and more unsystematic touch. Later, he incorporated the *Inquiry* into the *Characteristics* (1711).

13. Many Britons came to think of Shaftesbury's grandfather, the first earl of Shaftesbury, not only as a failure but also as an object of scorn and an example of the worst kind of conniving, manipulative, opportunistic politician (see Voitle 1984, 8; Christie 1871). Shaftesbury must have been sharply affected by his grandfather's sullied reputation.

14. Locke 1824a, VIII, 272; quoted in Basu 1999b, 158.

15. The counsel Shaftesbury repeatedly stresses in the *Letter Concerning Enthusiasm* regards the use of ridicule as the proper regimen against "enthusiasm." Robertson notes, however, that "the very self-consciousness of the *Letter* might alone suggest the manner of its inception. It does not employ banter, but prescribes it: A man spontaneously given that way would have made the fun he recommended" (Robertson 1963, xxi). Moreover, Robertson notes that earlier that year, in the first of his *Letters to a Student*, dated February 24, 1706–1707, that Shaftesbury "is anything but good-humored about the 'enthusiasts'" (xxi). Yet even in the year in which he published his *Letter Concerning Enthusiasm* and his *Essay on Wit and Humour* we find him writing to his protégé with extraordinary heat against Lucian as "a wretch who was truly the most profane and impious" (Letter of January 28, 1708–1709), "a deliverance so surprising," according to Robertson, "as to make us feel afresh that the critic's leaning to humorous methods was a rather cultivated mood with him" (Robertson 1963, xxii).

16. To Coste, July 25, 1712 (*Life*, 504). The denunciation of Swift as a false wit follows the passage quoted. Shaftesbury had strong private qualifications regarding the way in which he had stated his public case for "ridicule." Peter Coste, his French translator, sent copies of Shaftesbury's works to Leibniz for comments. Leibniz was surprised to find many thoughts that accorded with his own principles

(Leibniz 1875–90, III, 381), but in the matter of ridicule he had reservations. He claimed that the best and most important things could be ridiculed falsely, and even when ridicule was on the side of truth, it was perhaps too dangerous to be allowed. The religious effect of using ridicule against superstition, he feared, could encourage impiety. The point at which Shaftesbury writes that the author seems to despise himself is at the beginning of the *Miscellaneous Reflections*, where, with light self-deprecation, he resumes a relaxed mode after the more severe and more rhapsodic *Inquiry Concerning Virtue and Merit* and *The Moralists*.

17. See Wolf 1993, for an analysis of the style of *The Adept Ladys*, and Wolf 1988 for the wit of *A Letter Concerning Enthusiasm*.

18. As one of the first attackers observes derisively, it is "good humour" which is "this Gentleman's fondling word"; his "most sovereign remedy" is "a certain mixture of ridicule and good-humour" (Fowler 1708, 2; see 1709, 21). According to Stuart Tave, John Brown, who wrote the most elaborate of the replies, came close to the truth when he said that Shaftesbury "sets out" with ridicule, and then "slides insensibly into mere encomiums on good-breeding, cheerfulness, urbanity, and free Enquiry; and then, from these premises, often draws Consequences in favour of ridicule, as if it were an equivalent term" (Brown 1751a, 71). But Charles Bulkeley, Shaftesbury's best defender, came even closer. Shaftesbury's method, Bulkeley said, is "no other than reasoning upon every subject in an easy, cheerful, good humoured way. . . . Nothing can be plainer than that his Lordship uses the word ridicule as synonymous to freedom, familiarity, good humour, and the like" (Bulkeley 1751, 19–20). In another reply to Brown he pointed out that the ridicule Shaftesbury recommended was always of "cheerfulness and good-humour," designed as a remedy for the gloom of superstition and the extravagance of enthusiasm (Bulkeley 1752, VI, 10–12). Shaftesbury's "innate disposition," according to John Toland, was to "*Socratic* Irony and innocent Raillery" (Toland 1721, viii), and these, Tave adds, "we know from Barrow and Addison, are virtual synonyms" (Tave 1960, 36).

19. For Leibniz's criticism of Shaftesbury, see Leibniz 1875–90, III, 407–17, 419, 423–31. When Peter Coste, Shaftesbury's French translator and the person who introduced him to Leibniz, relayed Leibniz's comments to him, Shaftesbury did not rebuke Leibniz's criticism in the letter he wrote to Coste (July 25, 1712; in *Life*, 504). This impressed Leibniz so much that after Shaftesbury's death he spoke of him as a man who recanted his views, who went from being a Lucian to being a Plato, which to Leibniz was a very extraordinary metamorphosis (Leibniz 1875–90, III, 381). It is doubtful, however, that Shaftesbury underwent such a remarkable transformation, and it is quite certain at any rate that he never was a Lucian. Rather, in his warm reaction against the Puritan tradition, he gave the appearance of having fallen into the opposite error of the rake. I believe his true path was the middle way of good humor.

20. Letter to Peter Coste, 25 Jul. 1712 (*Life*, 504).

21. Willey 1986, 35; Basil Willey documents these changes in chap. 2.

22. See *Moralists*, iii, 1; *Inquiry*, I, iii, 3.

23. *Inquiry*, I, i, 2; iii, 3; *Moralists*, i, 2–3; ii, 4; iii, 2; *Letter*, 4, 5.

24. *Inquiry*, I, ii, 2; *Moralists*, ii, 1; *Essay*, iii, 1.

25. For Shaftesbury's view of the affections, see Grean 1967, chap. 9.

26. *Inquiry*, I, iii, 3; *Moralists*, ii, 3; *Letter*, 5.

27. For Shaftesbury on miracles, see Willey 1986, 66–67. The Bible is not a book Shaftesbury would highly recommend, and we find him using disparaging irony in the Volterian style regarding certain Old Testament characters. The stories and characters of the Bible, he warns the potential author to whom he addresses his *Soliloquy, or Advice to an Author*, are not fit subjects for a "mere poet," because they are divinely inspired and thus beyond comprehension (*Soliloquy*, iii, 3; CR I, 229–31).

28. For Shaftesbury's view of immortality, see Grean 1967, 91–97.

29. *Inquiry*, I, iii, 3; *Moralists*, ii, 3; *Essay*, ii, 3, 4.

30. *Essay*, iii, 4; iv, 1; iv, 2; *Soliloquy*, iv, 3; *Moralists*, iii, 2.

31. In one of his papers on "Cheerfulness," Joseph Addison writes: "The Creation is a perpetual feast to the Mind of a good Man, every thing that he sees cheers and delights him; Providence has imprinted so many smiles on Nature, that it is impossible for a Mind which is not sunk in more gross and sensual Delights to take a survey of them without several secret Sensations of Pleasure. . . . Such an habitual Disposition of Mind consecrates every Field and Wood, turns an ordinary walk into a morning or evening Sacrifice, and will improve those transient Gleams of Joy, which naturally brighten up and refresh the Soul on such Occasions, into an inviolable and perpetual State of Bliss and Happiness" (Addison 1712).

32. For Shaftesbury's ridicule of Hobbes, see Willey 1986, 68–70. Richard Brett notes that Shaftesbury was a disciple of the Cambridge Platonists and, like them, detested the doctrines propounded by Hobbes. Although the latter belonged to an earlier generation, his influence still persisted in Shaftesbury's day (Brett 1951, 32).

33. Moral corruption results either from the excess of the self-directed affections or the social affections, or from the presence of any of the unnatural affections. Unnatural affections lead to neither the good of the individual nor the species, such as delight in witnessing suffering or destruction of others, a delight in disorder or sheer destructiveness, then malice or ill-will, and envy at the prosperity or happiness of another person that in no way interferes with one's own, then hatred of mankind and society, passions aroused by superstition and related customs, and finally, sexual perversions.

34. These instances of the use of "enthusiasm" are drawn from the *Oxford English Dictionary* entry and from Tucker 1972, 15.

35. John Dryden, for instance, used enthusiasm in a purely literary context in the preface to his translation of Juvenal's *Satires* in 1693. However, the change was particularly evident in the writings of John Dennis, whose project of rooting literary excellence in religion involved a favorable estimation of the uses of passion and enthusiasm in particular (1939).

36. CR3 I, 227; II 139–40, 293–4. The alignment of Locke with Hobbes comes in Shaftesbury's letter to Michael Ainsworth, June 3, 1709 (*Life*, 403). Shaftesbury's analogy of right and wrong in the spheres of music, architecture and painting appears in CR3 I, 214, 251–2; II, 129, 177; *Life*, 54.

37. Clarke 1969, sections 225–6, 230–2; Wollaston 1969, sections 274–90. Charles Taylor explains that "Samuel Clarke and William Wollaston spoke of certain acts being 'fitting'—e.g., the grateful return of favors for benefits conferred—as though this were something like a logical truth, whose contradictory would be senseless. Hugo Grotius seemed to be invoking principles of this kind in the introduction to *The Rights of War and Peace* (Grotius 1901, I, I, 10; I, I, 3). Some clung to this form of rationalism because it seemed the only way to defeat the extrinsic theory." By extrinsic theory Taylor means the view that good is distinguishable from bad, which nevertheless "depend[s] ultimately on self-love or self-interest, once we take into account the full consequences of our actions, including divine rewards and punishments" (Taylor 1989, 254, 259).

38. For a discussion of how Shaftesbury influenced eighteenth- and nineteenth- century German aesthetic thought, see Cassirer 1953, 198–202.

39. *Original Letters of Locke, Algernon Sidney, and Anthony Lord Shaftesbury,* ed. T. Forster, 1830, 271.

40. Chiefly through Henry of Bolinbroke, Shaftesbury's optimistic theory reached Alexander Pope, who described it in verse in his *Essay on Man* (1733–4).

41. Hippocrates, the fifth-century BC Greek physician, is usually credited with applying Humoralism to medicine. Humoralism as a medical theory retained its popularity for centuries largely through the influence of the writings of Galen of Pergamum, the prominent second-century AD Roman physician and philosopher, whose theories dominated Western medical science for well over a millennium. Through the neo-classical revival in Europe, humor theory dominated medical practice, and the theory of humoral types made periodic appearances in drama. In the Renaissance, Ficino associated melancholy with men of culture, and the theory that genius is associated with melancholy soon became fashionable. In 1858, Rudolf Virchow's *Cellularpathologie* decisively displaced humoralism.

42. See Joubert 1560, 1579. See the ancient Greek myth of Demeter, cured from melancholy by laughter (Gilhus 1997, chap. 2).

43. For a criticism of this argument, see Grean 1967, 79–80.

44. For Epictetus' influence on Shaftesbury, see Long 2001, 262.

45. For the Xenophonic Socrates, see Gera 2007. In his categorization of Socrates' followers, Shaftesbury works out of the doxographical tradition. According to Diogenes Laertius, Socrates' successors were Plato, Xenophon, and Antisthenes (Laertius, *Lives of Eminent Philosophers*, II, 47), and the latter's successor, Diogenes the Cynic (I, 15; VI, 2, 15, 21). According to Donald Dudley, however, Antisthenes has no direct relation to the Cynics (Dudley 1937, 1–16). Moreover, the epithetical characterization "manners" that Shaftesbury uses implies a distinctive way of conceiving philosophy: for Shaftesbury, there were no schools of thought in ancient philosophy, only philosophical "manners," where "manner" conflated two distinct ideas, a mode of inquiry and a manner of expression. This sort of categorization assigned weight not to particular ideas or doctrines, but to the form through which a particular philosophy could be recognized and situated.

46. Shaftesbury, *Design of a Socratick History*, P.R.O. 30/24/27/14, 53.

47. Shaftesbury, *Design of a Socratick History*, P.R.O. 30/24/27/14, 53. Irony appears to be synonymous with humor that designates educated laughter. Horace's

letters are also presented as a model, whose "concealment of order and method" is held to be "the chief beauty" (*Misc.*, I, iii; CR II, 168). Horace has a satiric program, which he describes in *Satires* 1.4. G.L. Hendrickson (1900), followed by many others, sees in this satire a clever adaptation and working model of Aristotle's theory of liberal jest as well as a guide to the free person's appropriate manner of jesting. Kirk Freudenburg (1993) argues that Horace draws his theoretical tenets about the comic from two irreconcilable camps, namely, the Peripatetic tradition followed by Cicero and the *Iambos* tradition, which Horace knew primarily from Lucilius as well as from Iambic poetry, Old Comedy, and Cynic moralizing. The result is a hybrid theory that, against all precedent, seeks to maintain the integrity of both traditions: "Horace wants it all: as a theorist, he combines the best features of two otherwise hostile traditions to create his own unique perception of satiric humor; and as an artist, he writes in the best traditions of ancient comedy, both Old and New" (Freudenburg 1993, 54). Horace proposes in the first lines of this satire to take up the topic of *libertas*, "freedom," a word the satirist applied to the Old Comic poets, and Lucilius to denote primarily freedom of speech in the context of humorous, censorial poetry. Another model for Horace's theory is the Roman orator, Cicero, who combines rhetoric with wisdom. He was heir to the Aristotelian liberal jest and refers to Socrates as the one who brought philosophy from the sky to earth, and takes him as his model. He does this since he aims to combine action and philosophy. For Cicero, see Klein 1994, 44–46. For Shaftesbury's view of Horace, see Wolf 1993.

48. Shaftesbury to Peter Coste, 1 Oct. 1706, P.R.O. 30/24/45/iii/48v; *Soliloquy*, CR3 I, 258, 328.

49. Shaftesbury, Letter dated Jan. 28, 1708/9, *Several Letters Written by a Noble Lord to a Young Man at the University* 1716, 24–25.

50. *Life*, 504. Because *A Letter Concerning Enthusiasm* was attributed to Swift, Shaftesbury seeks to disengage himself from him. The full quotation on Swift reads: "Witness the prevalence and first success of that detestable writing of that most detestable author of the *Tale of a Tub*, whose manners, life, and prostitute pen and tongue are indeed exactly answerable to the irregularity, obscenity, profaneness, and fulsomeness of his false wit and scurrilous style and humour. Yet you know how this extraordinary work please even our great philosophers themselves, and how few of those who disliked it dared declare against it" (To Coste, July 25, 1712; in *Life*, 504).

51. For Epictetus' facetiousness, see Epictetus, *Discourses*, 1926, II, 27, vii, 6.

52. To Le Clerc, Nov. 6, 1709, and "Philosophical Regimen," in *Life*, 412, 227, 197.

53. *Pathologia sive Explicatio Affectum Humanorum*, written in the winter of 1706–1707, is conserved in the Public Office of London under code P.R.O. 302 (P.R.O. 30/24/26/7).

54. Tave 1960, vii–ix. Stuart Tave describes the evolution of the idea of the amiable humorist in the eighteenth century and the role Shaftesbury played in it.

55. Benjamin Whichcote always had as his overriding goal his listeners' moral improvement. Indeed, it is the practical nature of Whichcote's sermons that Shaft-

esbury stresses in his preface to the sermons: He justifies their publication because of the salutary effect they can be expected to have on the character of the audience.

56. Shaftesbury's philosophy was part of a broader movement in the seventeenth and eighteenth centuries in Europe that endeavored to bring joy to religion. Others who shared this conviction were Spinoza, the Cambridge Platonists, and followers of Hasidism (Grean 1967, 31). These were joined by devoted humanists such as Francois de Sales in France, who promoted redemptive laughter, laughing Jesuits, and Pierre de Besse, who published in 1615 the Christian Democritus, a book referring to the legend of the laughing philosopher, Democritus. This movement was widespread throughout the Netherlands as well (Minois 2002, 342–52).

57. On laughter as a threat to social order and established institutions of the eighteenth century, see Redwood 1976, 183. For a different view, one that sees eighteenth-century discussions of laughter emerging from social stability and consensus in direct opposition to the perceived threat of laughter dominating the sixteenth and seventeenth centuries, see Anselment 1979, 3. On raillery and its relation to ridicule, and particularly its lack of an object, see Knox 1961, 187–221.

58. Richard Brett argues that the idea that ridicule is a test of truth is more than an aphorism or a passing thought for Shaftesbury. It is a thought Shaftesbury consistently maintains and firmly believes. Moreover, it makes sense in relation to his view of truth as congruence and falsehood as incongruity (Brett 1951, 171). Alfred Aldridge suggests that "the chief value of ridicule for Shaftesbury was its use as a test of demeanor or attitude, as a weapon against imposture" (Aldridge 1945, 154), an interpretation shared by Jean-Paul Larthomas (1986), Ernst Cassirer (1953, 183) and echoed in Konrad Lorenz's theory of humor (Lorenz 1966, 252–3). Stanley Grean suggests that the logical terminology "test" and "criterion," although misleading, have at least a figurative application: Ridicule has a kind "of proving power in that what cannot stand up under free and humorous examination, in Shaftesbury's opinion, is not well-grounded in reason and Nature" (Grean 1967, 124). Stuart Tave, however, dismisses ridicule altogether: Not only "Shaftesbury nowhere clearly says that it is a test," but "his true path was the middle way of good humor" (Tave 1960, 35, 39).

59. Benjamin Ibbott, A Course of Sermons (1727) delivered in 1713–1714, quoted in Aldridge 1951, 373.

60. Quoted in Casati 1934, 623; see Leibniz 1956, II, 1023.

61. Adam Smith, like Shaftesbury, emphasizes the malevolent nature of laughter (1759). A small vexation in another excites no sympathy, he says, because our sympathetic passions are not as strong as our original passions: "There is, besides, a malice in mankind, which not only prevents all sympathy with little uneasiness, but renders them in some measure diverting. Hence the delight which we all take in raillery" (quoted in Tave 1960, 204).

62. Herder, Letter 33 (1794), in Sämmtliche Werke, 1877–1913, VVII, 158 (my translation).

63. This passage also may account for Stuart Tave's conviction that Shaftesbury means good humor, not ridicule (Tave 1960, 39), and for Leibniz's observation that Shaftesbury has exchanged ridicule for humor and good humor, a remark

that Shaftesbury did not reject (see note 19). Shaftesbury insists that everything becomes serious during the process of inspecting the imagination. Reduction and inversion turn fantastic representations into a grave subject. This is the opposite of buffoonery, which turns serious subjects into burlesque (P.R.O 30/24/27/10, f.57, 129).

64. For Shaftesbury's views on tolerance, see Grean 1967, chap. 7.

65. Richard Brett justly remarks that before we dismiss Shaftesbury's theory too summarily we should bear in mind that in certain respects it agrees with more recent accounts of the nature of comedy (Brett 1951, 171). Henri Bergson, for instance, defines comedy as an attempt to impose a mechanical explanation upon a reality that cannot be explained that way. It springs from an endeavor to produce a harmony that, although internally consistent, is untrue when we take account of the nature of reality. Comedy is internally congruous, but compared with reality is fundamentally incongruous (Bergson 1999).

66. Laurent Jaffro remarks on the similitude between Shaftesbury's views and Lorenz's (Jaffro 1996). On militant enthusiasm, see Lorenz 1966, 223, 231–5, 242–8, 250–3; on laughter, see there, 152, 240, 253, 254.

67. The pamphlets attacking the *Letter* were written by Edward Fowler (1708, 1709) and Mary Astell (1709). The latter published under the pseudonym, "Mr. Wooton."

68. Shaftesbury's Whiggism is expressed in his support for tolerance and his attacks on Tory High Church loyalties. However, the material Shaftesbury uses against the ecclesiastical propensities of Toryism had already been used in the seventeenth century to combat rather different targets. The arguments against "priestcraft" had its origin in the Protestant attack on the powers of the Catholic Church while the argument against "enthusiasm" emerged in the Protestant attempt to subdue its own more extreme expressions. On "priestcraft" and "enthusiasm" in eighteenth-century religious discourse, see Manuel 1983, 34–51.

69. The meaning of *Enthusiasm*, a technical religious term applied both negatively and positively in the seventeenth century, expanded broadly and rapidly at the turn of the eighteenth century. By 1750, the term described philosophy, writing, the various arts, and even love. See note 34 for references.

70. See Katja Maria Vogt's forthcoming essay "Plato on Madness and the Good Life," in *Mental Disorders in Antiquity*, ed. W. Harris. Brill: Leiden.

71. For the difficulty in drawing a distinction between wit and humor in eighteenth-century practice, see Knox 1961, 189. For a different, albeit simplifying, view of the matter, see Billig 2005, 61–62: "Writers conventionally treated wit and humour as distinctly different phenomena. Wit involved playing with ideas or words, whereas humour occurred when the object of the laughter was a person. . . . Wit referred to clever verbal sayings, whereas 'humour' denoted a laughable character." For examples of the distinction between wit and humor and the confusing and contradictory uses of the terms, see Morris 1744, 13; Beattie 1776, 486; Campbell 1963, 19–20.

72. The notebooks are journals of self-examination. Organized topically, they offer an irregular record of Shaftesbury's inner life, mostly between 1698 and 1704.

They are tools for self-investigation and also for self-command, amounting to a kind of moral workbook. Shaftesbury wrote much of the material in the notebooks while immersed in deep intellectual engagement with the Roman Stoics Epictetus and Marcus Aurelius. In places, the notebooks are a commonplace book of Greek citations accompanied by Shaftesbury's commentary. Many entries are dated. A major shortcoming of the Benjamin Rand edition of the notebooks (1900) is the deletion of the dates. Additionally, it contains only a selection. For the notebooks see Klein 1994, 70–90. For Shaftesbury as Stoic, see Tiffany 1923.

    73. Epictetus, *Discourses*, 1926, III xii, 3–4, II 81–83; see also II xviii, 4–5, and III xxii, 13. Shaftesbury, P.R.O. 30/24/27/10, 366, 386.

    74. *Moralists*, i, 1; CR II, 5–6. On the rise of conversation as an arena for instruction in eighteenth-century Britain, see Burke 1993, 108–12. Laurence Klein suggests that the ideal situation for speech also provides a standard against which the sterility of distorted communicative patterns can be measured. These patterns correspond to the alternatives of unsociability and hyper-sociability. It seems appropriate to borrow the language of Jürgen Habermas here, because the ethics and politics of discourse are a pivotal part of his project, as they are for Shaftesbury as well. Habermas' early concern with defining the eighteenth-century public sphere in *The Structural Transformation of the Bourgeois Public Sphere* (1989) leads him, via a linguistic turn, to a theory of communicative action, in which an ideal speech situation—with parameters much like those of Shaftesbury—provides a model not only for the pursuit of truth but also for a just form of human life. See Klein 1994, 13–14, and Giddens 1985.

    75. This view of wit is in direct defiance of Locke's view that came to be much cited by the British writers on laughter in the eighteenth century. In his attempt to differentiate between "wit" and "judgment" Locke defines the former as a facility in putting together ideas that have some similarity, and "thereby to make up pleasant pictures and agreeable visions in the fancy" (Locke 1964, Bk. II, chap. xi, sec. 2). Judgment, which consists in the ability to distinguish carefully between ideas despite appearing congruous, is the superior faculty because clear thought depends on it: "Wit proceeds by way of Metaphor and allusion, wherein for the most part lies that entertainment and pleasantry of wit which strikes so lively on the fancy, and therefore so acceptable to all people; because its beauty appears at first sight, and there is required no labour of thought to examine what truth or reason there is in it" (Locke 1964, Bk. II, chap. xi, sec. 2). Locke concludes with the warning that these "agreeable visions" of wit fail to measure up to the "severe rules of reason." Locke's brief comparison between wit and judgment strongly favors the latter. Because wit and judgment are based on differing mental processes, Locke suggested that men "who have a great deal of wit, and prompt memories, have not always the clearest judgment or deepest reason" (Locke 1964, Bk. II, chap. xi, sec. 2).

    76. Lawrence Klein maintains, "Shaftesbury was the ideologist for a culture that would be both philosophical and gentlemanly, moral and conversable—in a word, polite" (Klein 1994, 119). Michael Prince concurs: Shaftesbury accommodates his texts for the modern reader, literate but uneducated, easily seduced

by powerful images, bored by perceptively administered knowledge (Prince 1996, 41).

77. Shaftesbury finds a correlation between current styles and the political history of taste grounded in common sense. With their liberty, the Romans lost also their style (*Soliloquy*, iii, 3; CR I, 219–20); the excess of buffoonery of the Italian theater reflects their lack of national liberty (*Essay*, iii, 1; CR I, 72), and the status of virtue in nations parallels the practice of humor (*Moralists*, iii, 1; CR I, 96). Also in the *Letter Concerning Design*, Shaftesbury points to a correlation between the political forms that common sense takes and taste (CR3 III, 402)

78. See Klein 2000, 89; on chatter, see Fenvers 1993, 1–27.

79. On the letter as a genre in Shaftesbury's writings, see *Misc.*, I, i; CR II, 157–9; II, iii; CR II, 225–6; II, ii; CR II, 207.

80. For the essay, see *Misc.*, I, i; CR II, 157–9; II, iii; CR II, 225–6; II, ii; CR II, 207.

81. Shaftesbury's *The Moralists*, which he preferred to the formal *Inquiry*, is populated with a range of voices in a range of combinations at a range of moments. Though not in a strict sense a dialogue, it is highly dialogic, a necessary condition for moral education. For *The Moralists*, see Prince 1996, 47–73. It is interesting to note that, not withstanding Shaftesbury's efforts to conceptualize and put in practice his views of writing, Shaftesbury's manner of writing was perceived by his early readers as confusing. His chief critic, John Brown, accused Shaftesbury of "frequently affecting a mixture of solemn praise and low buffoonery; not only in the same tract, but in the same paragraph":

> We have seen the noble Writer assuming the Character of a professed Dogmatist, the Reasoner in Form . . . [but] concerning Revealed Religion and Christianity, we shall find him chiefly affecting the *miscellaneous* Capacity; the Way of Chat, Raillery, Innuendo, or Story-telling: In a word, that very Species of the present modish Composition, which he so contemptuously ridicules [he also treats] as the Man in the Fable did his Pears; unconscious he should be ever afterwards reduced to diet on them himself. (Brown 1751a, 244–5; 242; quoted in Prince 1996, 38)

For Shaftesbury's view of philosophic writing, see Klein 1994, 102–19; Malherbe 2000.

82. P.R.O. 30/24/27/14; On the Socratic history Shaftesbury intended to write, see Klein 1994, 107–11.

83. On humor in Shaftesbury's thought, see Cassirer 1953, 170–86; Grean 1967 120–34; Jaffro, 1998, 93–101; Brugère 1999, 97–132, 331–41; Larthomas 1985, 488–96.

84. The title of *Inquiry into the Original of our Ideas of Beauty and Virtue*, Francis Hutcheson's first book, reads: "In which the principles of the Late Earl of Shaftesbury are explained and defended" (Hutcheson 1725, ii). In the preface to the second edition of his inquiry, Hutcheson emphasized his admiration for Shaftesbury's work: "To recommend the Lord Shaftesbury's Writings to the World," he

wrote, "is a very needless Attempt. They will be esteemed while any reflection remains among men" (Hutcheson 1745, xxi).

85. The *Essay on the Freedom of Wit and Humour*, published in 1709, was translated into French before 1713; Diderot, then in his first Deistic stage, published his adaptation of the *Inquiry Concerning Virtue and Merit* in 1745 (*Essai sur le mérite de la vertu*); Montesquieu panegyrized him; a complete French translation of his works and letters appeared in Geneva in 1769; and a complete German translation of the *Characteristics* in 1776–1779. By that time, Shaftesbury's account of optimism had even carried the day in Germany surpassing that of Leibniz (Lange 1925, 146–7), who had admitted its measure of congruity with his own; and there are clear traces of his influence in Kant's ethics as well as aesthetics.

86. For Ludwig Holberg as Kierkegaard's unacknowledged mentor, see Allen 2009.

87. For the controversy, see Aldridge 1945, 129–56; Brett 1951, 165–85. The extent of the controversy is evident in the dozens of references given in these studies, and they can be supplemented by material in Tave 1960, chap. 2–3, and 252, n. 28.

88. Hutcheson first contributed his *Reflections upon Laughter* (1750) as separate essays to *Hibernicus' Letters* (a periodical appearing in Dublin between 1725 and 1727).

89. See also two letters by Akenside, in the Appendix to Samuel Johnson's *Lives of the Most Eminent English Poets* (1854, III, 387–8). John Barrow recognizes facetiousness as one of the most effective devices to use against the skeptic who disavows the clear principles of reason that have already been approved by general consent and common sense.

90. Thomas Hobbes, "The Answer of Mr. Hobbes to Sir William Davenant's Preface before Gondibert," Paris, Jan. 10, 1650; reprinted in *Works* (1840, IV, 454f.).

91. The Hobbesian superiority view of laughter, to which Shaftesbury proposed an alternative, was definitely discarded in the eighteenth century with the help of Francis Hutcheson (1750), Abraham Tucker (1768–1778), George Campbell (1776), and James Beattie (1776). In the nineteenth century, the task was accomplished by William Greenfield's "On the Ludicrous" (1809), and Jean Paul Richter's *Vorschule der Aesthetik* (1813 [1804], sections 29–30; *Werke*, 1861–62, Part I, XI). For Thomas Carlyle, laughter becomes enormous, an explosive and deeply revealing release (1827). The incongruity theory also is suggested by Kant ("Laughter is an affection arising from the sudden transformation of a strained expectation into nothing" (Kant 1911, sec. 54), a view that is repeated by Friedrich Schelling but intelligibly altered and developed by Schopenhauer (Schopenhauer 1969, II, chap. 8). Kierkegaard also endorsed it. Today, the incongruity theory is so much in vogue that most scholarship on humor ranks past theorists of humor according to their intimations of it. See Morreall 1983a, 1987.

92. The references to Spinoza's *Ethics* are as follows: Roman numerals refer to books, "P" to "proposition," "Dem." to the short form of Demonstration, "Schol." to Scholium, and "Cor." to Corollary.

93. Spinoza's view of laughter as pure joy seems to contradict Descartes' view, which was influenced by Plato's view that laughter is a mixed joy (Plato, *Philebus*,

48). Joy is a significant notion for Spinoza, as it is "an affect by which the body's power of acting is increased or aided" (*Ethics*, IV, P41Dem.). However, the controversy is apparent when Descartes states that the philosopher prefers great joys, which are generally somber and serious whereas Spinoza says that "Cheerfulness cannot be excessive, but is always good; Melancholy, on the other hand, is always evil" (*Ethics*, IV, P42; Descartes 1955, 124).

94. See note 3. Robertson finds in Spinoza's *Ethics* or in his correspondence the main Shaftesburean doctrines: There can be nothing essentially evil in the universe as a whole, sin and evil are not positive, men cannot properly be said to sin against God; blessedness is not the reward of virtue but the state of virtue; acts done from fear of punishment are not virtuous; benevolence involves happiness; that things which are evil relatively to us are to be borne with tranquility, since nothing in the universe can be otherwise than it is; that angry passions constitute a state of misery (Robertson 1963, xxxi). See *The Ethics*, I, P17, Cor. and Schol.; P32 and Scholia; P36 and Appendix; II, P49Schol.; V, P42. Letters to Blyenbergh, Jan. and Feb. 1665 (esp. 32, 34, 36). See note 92 for references to Spinoza's *Ethics*.

95. The controversy about ridicule as the test of truth, namely, that which does not withstand ridicule is not true, does not exhaust the possible relations of humor with truth. Modern scholars of humor differentiate between the following possibilities: Is humor a lie, a non-*bona-fide* statement, or an expression of a deeper truth? Victor Raskin has dealt extensively on the topic of humor's relation to truth (Raskin 1992a, 1992b, 1992c, 1998).

96. Philosophers used laughter mainly as a tool for moral criticism: Criticism of ignorance (Plato); the tragic view of life (Plato, the Stoics); morality and religion (e.g., the pre-Socratic Xenophanes, the Cynics, the Peripatetic Theophrastus, the Hellenistic skeptical philosopher Timon of Phlius, the Platonic philosopher Lucius Apuleius, the Renaissance philosophers Erasmus and Thomas More, and the modern philosophers Pascal and Voltaire); and "academic" philosophy (e.g., the Cynics, Nietzsche, and Kierkegaard).

97. Kant, *Reflexion* 6050, Nachlass, *Kants gesammelte Schriften*, 1902–, XIII, 436, 1. 18–20. Kierkegaard, a severe judge of professors of philosophy, credits Kant with what he considers two exceptional qualities, a sense of humor and a rigorous honesty (Green 1992, 12, 75). According to Richard K. Simon, Kant makes humor important for philosophy by positing a fundamental incongruity between noumena and phenomena, and then by defining the comic as the perception of incongruity. This is fruitfully exploited by nineteenth-century thinkers who will posit humor, and especially irony, as thoughtful reactions to the perception of the world (Simon 1985, 108). As with Kant's theories of empirical knowledge and practical reason, his view of aesthetic judgment emerges from a long reflection on the work of his British and German predecessors. In particular, he assimilates many Shaftesburean ideas on aesthetics, notably Shaftesbury's view of the comic as incongruity and cheerfulness as not only temperamental but also the outcome of philosophic principles (Kant 2006, 131). Although he does not subscribe to the Shaftesburean idea that humor plays an epistemic role, he adopts Shaftesbury's view that humor chastens enthusiasm.

Kant views laughter as positive and affirms its therapeutic role. Significantly, he adds laughter to Voltaire's assertion in the seventh canto of the poem *Henriade* (1723) that hope and sleep are Heavens' gifts to counterbalance the multiples sorrows of life. Kant regrets, nonetheless, that it is so difficult to excite laughter in sensible people (Voltaire 1901c; Kant 1911, sec. 54). This eulogy of laughter is part of Kant's intense interest in his health and is part of the views about melancholy, hypochondria, medicine and the philosophical temper he advances in accordance with his own temperament (Johnson 2006; Sharfstein 1980, 210–30). Kant's cheerfulness is noted by R. B. Jachman, one of his friends and biographers, who writes, "Kant's disposition was by nature meant for cheerfulness. He saw the world with a glad look, apprehended its enjoyable external side and transferred his cheerfulness to external things" (sixth letter, in L. E. Borowski et al. 1912, 149); but Kant himself qualifies this cheerfulness as a hypochondriac's deceptive gaiety (Kant 2006, sec. 62; 1902, VII, 104).

In his *Critique of Judgement*, Kant labels his views on the comic a "remark," stating that "laughter is an affection arising from the sudden transformation of a strained expectation into nothing"; in other words, that which is originally perceived in one (often serious) sense is suddenly viewed from a totally different (usually implausible or ludicrous) perspective. Laughter follows from something absurd and "the jest must contain something that is capable of deceiving for a moment" (Kant 1911, sec. 54).

98. "And is the ridicule all gentlemen associate today with enthusiasm to be discounted? This ridicule is a powerful barrier against the extravagances of all the sectarians" (Voltaire 1989, 56; my translation.) This does not exhaust Voltaire's views on the comic, or Shaftesbury's influence on Voltaire, which lies in the latter's use of a pleasant form and tone in order to interest literate people and engage public opinion on difficult and abstract questions. In various writings, Voltaire mixes his most serious reflections with burlesque jokes and witticisms. This mixture of nobleness and triviality, of reason and fantasy, of the serious and the comical, is characteristic of his style.

Putting aside his early Jesuit education, François-Marie de Voltaire (1694–1778) wrote satirical anti-clerical essays that led to his exile in Holland in 1713 and imprisonment in the Bastille in 1717. He was the hero of the French satirists of his time, although he refused to accept this honor. In the two texts he wrote on satire, his attitude toward the genre was severe (*Mémoire sur la satire*, 1739, and *Epitre sur la calomnie*, 1756). From the age of 16, when he wrote somewhat satirical and therefore very condemnable verses, he imposed on himself a rule never to partake in that "detestable genre" (On the satirical Voltaire, see Quero 1995). Although he called himself a militant theist, Voltaire criticized what he saw as the anti-rationalistic obscurantism of Pascal. He found, however, Leibniz's theodicy—its attempt to reconcile the existence of evil with divine benevolence—equally repellent. His attack on Leibnizian optimism was most pointedly expressed in *Zadig* (1748), *Poème sur le désastre de Lisbonne* (1756), and *Candide* (1759).

In the entry "laughter" of his *Philosophical Dictionary*, he writes that those who seek the metaphysical causes of laughter are not mirthful. Laughter is not based on pride or superiority; rather he who laughs is joyful at the moment and prompted by no other cause (Voltaire 1901a). In his preface to *The Prodigal*, he repeats, "laughter always arises from a gaiety of disposition, absolutely incompatible with contempt and indignation" (Voltaire 1901d, 273). Violent peals of universal laughter seldom rise but from some mistake (273). He defines himself as an adept practitioner and a writer of "philosophical gaiety." In his poem, *Jean qui rit, Jean qui pleure*, any Heraclitus becomes Democritus when life circumstances are favorable (1772). His most memorable view on laughter is that laughter arises when theory is confronted with reality, as his novel *Candide* exemplifies (1901b).

99. See Christoph Wieland's letter to Zimmermann, 6 Oct. 1758, in Wieland 1963, I, 363; G. E. Lessing, X Letter on the New Literature, 25 Jan. 1759, in *Lessings Werke*, 1999, 50; see also Larthomas 1985.

100. For Romantic irony, see Alford 1984; Garber 1988; Behler 1990; Nilsen 1993c.

101. Karl Popper is known for his thesis that rationality equals critical dialogue and that critical thinking is the very essence of rationality. However, he adds that the purpose of critical discussion is the refutation of one's argument. Popper writes about critical rationalism in his works, *The Open Society and Its Enemies, Volume 2* (1962), and *Conjectures and Refutations* (1963). In *The Logic of Scientific Discovery*, Popper maintains that science does not, and cannot, verify its theories. Science makes progress by proposing bold conjectures in response to problems, which are then subjected to sustained attempted empirical refutation. This falsificationist conception of scientific method is then generalized to form Popper's conception of (critical) rationality, a general methodology for solving problems or making progress. As Popper puts it in *The Logic of Scientific Discovery*, "inter-subjective *testing* is merely a very important aspect of the more general idea of inter-subjective *criticism*, or in other words, of the idea of mutual rational control by critical discussion" (Popper 1959, 44, n. 1: see also Popper 1963, 193–200; 1972, 119, 243). In the introduction to *The Myth of the Framework*, he writes, "critical rationalism is a way of thinking and even a way of living. It's a faith in peace, in humanity, in tolerance, in modesty, in trying to learn from one's mistakes, and in the possibilities of critical discussion . . . [it is] an appeal to reason" (Popper 1994, xiii). In *The Open Society and Its Enemies* and *The Poverty of Historicism* (1961), Popper applies critical rationalism to problems of civilization.

INTERMEZZO: HAMANN—HUMOR AND IRONY AS CATEGORIES OF UNDERSTANDING

1. Tyll Eulenspiegel (c. 1290–1350) was a German peasant who performed clownish pranks and tricks. As a literary character, he was circulated in popular printed editions narrating the string of lightly connected episodes that outlined his picaresque career, primarily in Germany, the Low Countries, and France.

2. Hamann, *Biblical Reflections* (Smith 1960b, 121); *Socratic Memoirs* (179); for more references, see Hamann 1949–57, VI, 353.

3. Hamann's *Socrates' Memoirs* influenced Kierkegaard's magisterial thesis, *The Concept of Irony with Constant Reference to Socrates*. Hamann also inspired the young Goethe's projected plan for a drama on Socrates' life. See Goethe's letter to Herder from Frankfurt toward the end of 1771 (Goethe 1887, II, 11–13).

4. For Shaftesbury's influence on *Aesthetics in a Nutshell*, see German 1981, 21, and note 126; see also Wessel 1969.

5. See Goethe 1948, Bk. 12; quoted in Berlin 2000, 256n2.

6. For examples of *Stillbruch*, see O'Flaherty 1967, 78–79.

7. See Unger, 1911, I, 501ff. Hamann refers indirectly to his own sense of metaschematism following the model of the Apostle Paul (Hamann 1949–57, II, 150). See also the passage where he accuses the Enlighteners of engaging in metaschematism in their own way (III, 144).

8. For a helpful treatment of the subject of metaschematism, see Seils 1957, 73–74.

9. For more examples of Hamann's use of "metaschematism," see Alexander 1966, 154–5.

10. For the importance of Hamann, see Berlin 1994, Berlin 1999, 40–45, 48–49, and Sparling 2011. For an introduction to his life and philosophy, as well as excerpts from his writings, see Smith 1960b; for an analysis of the role of humor in his thought, see Alexander 1966, chaps. 7–8; for Shaftesbury's influence on Hamann, see Deupmann-Frohues 1999. Oswald Bayer's recently translated biography is also helpful for an understanding of Hamann's thought (Bayer 2011).

CHAPTER 2: KIERKEGAARD: HUMOR AS PHILOSOPHY AT ITS BEST

1. Translators Walter Lowrie and Howard and Edna Hong explain that in "little studies," Kierkegaard refers to vol. 14 of Johann G. von Herder's *Adrastea*, "Shaftesbury, Geist und Frohsinn" (*CUPL*, 570, n. 23; *CUP2*, 264, n. 263). See the end of the chapter for Kierkegaard's relationship with Herder and the next note for abbreviations of Kierkegaard's writings.

2. The references to the works of Kierkegaard and his pseudonyms are designated according to the abbreviations listed in the bibliography, with Arabic numbers referring to pages. For example, *CUP1*, 213 refers to *Concluding Unscientific Postscript*, page 213. Unless stated otherwise, all references are to the Howard V. Hong and Edna H. Hong edition. When the references are to the David F. Swenson and Walter Lowrie translation of *Postscript*, CUP is followed by an L (*CUPL*). References to *Søren Kierkegaards Samlede Værker* are written SV followed by volume and page number. When necessary a short title is used in the text, e.g., "*Postscript*." References to Kierkegaard's journals (*Søren Kierkegaards Papirer*. 1909–1938. P.A. Heiberg and V. Kuhr eds. 11 vols. in 19 parts. Copenhagen) is abbreviated *Pap.*, followed by Roman numerals that refer to volumes, sometimes followed by superscript numbers that refer to parts, then capital letters referring

to entries, and finally Arabic numbers that refer to pages (e.g., *Pap.* X[1] A 100). References to the *Papirer* in English are to volume and serial entry number in Kierkegaard's *Journals and Papers*. 1967–1978. Ed. and trans. by Howard V. Hong and Edna H. Hong. Bloomington and London: Indiana University Press. 7 vols. (e.g., *JP* 2, 1500).

     3. Various pseudonyms would admit to sharing the same ambition. Perceiving "with psychological interest how different the occasion of laughter is at every age," A, the pseudonymous author of the first volume of *Either/Or*, makes "the laughter of others and his own the object of observation" (*EO1*, 140). While sitting in Berlin's Konigstater Theatre, Constantine Constantius repeats and expands in *Repetition* Kierkegaard's notion of constructing a history of the human soul by discussing the way objects of laughter change at different stages of life: "Anyone wanting to make a psychological study of laughter at various social and temperamental levels ought not to neglect the opportunity offered by the performance of a farce" (*R*, 159). Richard Simon suggests that in this repetition of Kierkegaard Constantius makes the project of the pseudonymous authorship much clearer: The pseudonymous authorship is, if not exactly farce, then at least very similar to farce, the absolutely general acted out by talented comedians; and the effect on us, the audience, is to release our individual unique responses (Simon 1985, 105). For farce, see Davis 2003. For a thorough consideration of Kierkegaard's interest in acting, actors, and the theater, see Malantschuk 1971.

     4. *EO1*, 20; also *JP* 1,700/*Pap.* III A 112. Kierkegaard's nickname is well deserved: He confesses in his journals that his depression is his "most faithful mistress (*EO1*, 20; see *JP* 4, 5496/*Pap.* III A 114).

     5. *JP* 5, 5260/*Pap.* II A 662. In a journal entry, Kierkegaard confesses: "From a child I was under the sway of a prodigious melancholy, the depth of which finds its only adequate measure in the equally prodigious dexterity I possessed in hiding it under an apparent gaiety and *joie de vivre*" (quoted in Lowrie 1968b, 24).

     6. Also in the journals, Kierkegaard refers to himself as a genius (*Pap.* XI A 266; *PV*, 94; 95), "a poetic-dialectical genius, personally and religiously a penitent . . ." (*JP* 4, 6317/ *Pap.* XI A 56).

     7. For details on Kierkegaard's contemporaries such as Johan Ludvig Heiberg, Hans Lassen Martensen, and Bishop J. P. Mynster, see Stewart 2003b. For Kierkegaard's "insistent teasing" of prominent figures in Danish cultural life, see Kirmmse 1990, 240; Lippitt 2000b, 188.

     8. In a number of autobiographical confessions published in his lifetime, Kierkegaard claims that he provoked this ridicule deliberately, in order to confuse the public and make a reading of his serious works more difficult; to expose himself to that which is most feared by the public—ridicule—and thereby test himself; and to demonstrate to those who made the *Corsair* a publishing success that they really have no understanding of laughter, comedy, or irony. If these claims can be believed, then those who mocked him in 1846 did so in ignorance of the fact that he was both the object and the author of the mockery. His understanding is greater than their understanding, and future readers, who are privileged to read this confession, are let in on the secret. But, the opposite can also be true, and

several of Kierkegaard's biographers have argued that the elaborate justifications for the *Corsair* incident are fabrications made up, after the fact, to hide the depth of humiliation he suffered and the surprise he experienced that ridicule directed against him could have such powerful effects:

> I have never been a Diogenes, have never bordered on cynicism; . . . I have been able to crack jokes with an individual over my thin legs— but when it is the rabble, the utterly brutish humanity, the rowdies, silly women, school children, and apprentices who abuse me: that is the meanness and lack of character of a people directed against one who truly merits something from his people. The most tiresome aspect is that I am the only one who has the right to joke, but on those terms I cannot and will not joke. And yet I need the refreshment of laughter so often. But then, alas, that the one who is clearly the wittiest in a little country is the only one who is not witty—but the riffraff and the fools are all witty and ironic. (*JP* 6, 10–11)

9. On the holy fool, see Fedotov 1966, 316–43; Syrkin 1982. On the relationship of Kierkegaard to the holy fool tradition of the Orthodox Church, see Thulstrup 1978. Richard Simon suggests that "here, if anywhere, are the limits of Kierkegaard's appropriation of the comic and the clown—the holy fool does not include the profane fool. While the Christian Church tolerated both in the feast of fools tradition during the Middle Ages, Kierkegaard will not, or cannot" (Simon 1985, 96). Indeed, Kierkegaard's pseudonym, Vigilius, says that "in regard to earnestness he will know how not to tolerate any joking" (*CA*, 128). This is echoed in *Postscript* (*CUP1*, 483).

10. *AC*, 11, 23, 24. *AC*, 48, 215–6; *AC*, 48, 102–3; *AC*, 27, 60, 84, 85, 216. Kierkegaard also denounces "the play-Christianity of the priests" (*AC*, 80), deems the whole order of the clergy comical (24), considers Bishop Martensen's silence "Christianly . . . comical" (67), denigrates confirmation and the wedding Christian comedy (217–22), and so on. For the attack on Christendom, see Woronoff 2001.

11. McFadden 1982; Simon 1985. For the comic drama Kierkegaard created in Copenhagen, see Alastair Hannay's biography of Kierkegaard (2001).

12. *The Concept of Irony* is considered ironic as well as a parody of Hegel (Capel 1968, 385 n. 2); *Concluding Unscientific Postscript* is deemed a satire of Hegel's philosophy (Hannay 2001, 309), which "mimics" (one of the predicates in the work's subtitle), and which is often taken as parody (Allison 1972, 290); *The Concept of Anxiety* is deemed "the most ironic and certainly the most parodic of all the aesthetic works" (Poole 1998, 60).

13. A few scholars have described ways in which Kierkegaard is a trickster or humorist in his pseudonymous authorship (Malantschuk 1971, 90). Michael Weston pinpoints comedy as a key characteristic of Kierkegaard's entire pseudonymous authorship (Weston 1994, viii and *passim*). Josiah Thompson characterizes Kierkegaard as a "maieutic trickster" (Thompson 1973, 184), and Richard Simon as "a clown" in both his life and his work, adding "that clown, comedian, fool, is

the best way to understand the man who is also religious writer and philosophical poet" (Simon 1985, 124). When Kierkegaard's biographers examine his life from the standpoint of reality, they are led into medical diagnoses of illness and abnormality, but if they approached his life from the standpoint of the history of the comic, they would see harlequin. For Simon, Kierkegaard aspires to the role of a holy fool (96).

14. For an anthology of Kierkegaard's humor, see Oden 2004; Poole and Stangerup 1989.

15. For humor and irony in Kierkegaard, see Lippitt 1997, 2000a, and especially 2000b; Oden 2004, 1–42; Thulstrup and Thulstrup 1988; Perkins 1976; Evans 1983, chap. 10; another helpful treatment is found in Walsh 1994, chap. 7. For the comic, see Barrett 1990; Langston 1985; Otani 1980; Hong 1976. For humor, see Taylor 1980a; Cain 1980; Morris 1988; Hannay 2003, 9–23, 137–49; Olesen 2003. For irony, see McCarthy 1982; Schleifer 1984; Smyth 1986; Cross 1998; Strawser 1997; Rudd 1998; Golomb 2002; Garff 2002. For the reception of *Postscript*'s theory of the comic and for references to literature on the subject of humor and irony in Danish, see Olesen 2005.

16. The following is a list of some of Kierkegaard's pseudonyms: Victor Eremita (*Either/Or*, 1843), Johannes de Silencio (*Fear and Trembling*, 1943), Constantin Constantius (*Repetition*, 1943), Johannes Climacus (*Philosophical Fragments*, 1844; *Concluding Unscientific Postscript*, 1846), Vigilius Haufniensis (*The Concept of Anxiety*, 1844), Nicolaus Notabene (*Prefaces*, 1844), Hilarius Bookbinder (*Stages on Life's Way*, 1845), Anti-Climacus (*Sickness unto Death*, 1849; *Practice in Christianity*, 1850), Victor Eremita and Frater Taciturnus (three articles in *The Fatherland*), Frater Taciturnus writes to the *Corsair*.

17. In "Armed Neutrality," Kierkegaard explains why he has "to keep neutral" lest he himself be considered the ideal of Christianity (*PV*, 139).

18. The way salvation as a search for truth becomes a search for wholeness and unity is explored in Connell 1985. For an excellent analysis of Kierkegaard's diagnostic reflections on the self, in particular the diseases of "reflection," see Gouwens 1996, chap. 1.

19. On the development of a vocabulary of self-fulfillment in modernity and its conflicts with a "disengaged reason" of instrumentalism, see Taylor 1989.

20. W. Anz lists an entire set of categories that Kierkegaard obtained from Hegel: Existence, paradox, qualitative and quantitative dialectics, the reflection of anxiety, the moment, transition, leap, decision, synthesis, contradiction, recollection, idea, finite/infinite, possibility/actuality, self, spirit, personality, and history (Anz 1971).

21. The Danish man of letters J. L. Heiberg (1791–1860) introduced Hegelianism into Denmark, where it became the predominant school of thought during the 1830s and 1840s. Heiberg claimed that Hegel had freed him for the vocation of comic dramatist by refining his strong pantheistic bent to the extent that he could take seriously the finite and even farcical aspects of existence in their dialectical relation to the infinite. Other Danes adapted Hegelianism to different purposes. H. K. Martensen (1808–1884), for example, developed an influential Protestant

dogmatics. Such Hegelian interpretations of Christianity were the target of Kierkeg-aard's vigorous polemic against the Hegelianism of the 1840s and early 1850s, which was carefully developed in his *Concept of Anxiety* and *Concluding Unscientific Postscript*. See Bruce Kirmmse for a detailed discussion of Hegelianism and idealism in his contemporaries' views of theology and philosophy (Kirmmse 1990).

22. Immediacy and its cognates have several distinct usages in Kierkegaard's writings; these usages have in common the notion of something being unmediated, or directly given. In the first usage, one's immediate nature, or immediacy, can be defined as those features that are merely given to one's self: One's physical body and its characteristics, one's temporal position, one's socially determined identity, and so on. In the second usage, to be able to stand in immediate relation to something else depends on that relation being unmediated by critical reflection. (Examples of such immediate relations abound in the authorship: The pure sensuous immediacy of Don Giovanni, the child's unreflective trust in his parents and in the world, the individual's unreflective pursuit of desire-satisfaction, the ethical immediacy of the person who accepts and abides by the norms of his society without ever reflecting on them or calling their authority into question.) In the third usage, to live a life of immediacy is to take life as it comes, that is, to take life as a kind of happening in which one finds oneself, the nature of which is determined by various conditions that are also unreflectively accepted as just "the way things are." Climacus, the pseudonymous author of *Postscript*, explains that "the life-view of immediacy"—that which the immediate person's view of life centers around—"is good-fortune" (*CUP1* 433). The immediate person pursues that which he takes to be the good without reflecting on or calling into question its goodness; he lives a life whose content is determined by his given desires and ideals as well as by the norms of his society without considering in abstract reflection whether this conception of the good has any genuine merit, whether his desires and ideals should be transformed or modified, or whether his society's norms have any genuine authority over him.

23. For abstract thought's ability to transfer *ab esse ad posse*, see Law 1993, chap. 3.

24. Kierkegaard's proposal is not entirely without precedent: Augustine had proposed something similar to Kierkegaard's maieutics in Christianity. Climacus in *Postscript* explains that: "My main thought was that, because of the copious-ness of knowledge, people in our day have forgotten what it means *to exist*, and what *inwardness* is, and that the misunderstanding between speculative thought and Christianity could be explained by that. I now resolved to go back as far as possible in order not to arrive too soon at what it means to exist religiously, not to mention existing Christianly-religiously . . . If people had forgotten what it means to exist religiously, they had probably also forgotten what it means to exist humanly" (*CUP1*, 249). From the start Kierkegaard's motive in developing his theory of the stages of existence was to understand what it meant to be "a Christian in Christendom," a faithful disciple of Christ in the midst of self-satisfied religious-secularity under the auspices of the State Church. He takes as his point of departure certain psychological observations (dependency, despair, guilt, and a

sense of purpose or *telos*) and with these he provides a Christian interpretation of the nature and destiny of man.

25. Julia Watkin gives the following example: In *The Concept of Anxiety*, Kierkegaard's non-Christian pseudonym Vigilius Haufniensis speaks about the gate as the object of the ancient Greek's anxiety, but allows that only the Christian God, and not Greek fate, has independent existence. She argues that in this passage the voice of Kierkegaard himself is clearly heard (Watkin 2001, 7).

26. Johannes the Seducer is clearly indicated as an example of one living wrongly (i.e., one bound to come to a bad end) spiritually speaking. The aesthete A is an unhappy if talented man. Judge Williams is the picture of civic contentment. Even the struggling, suffering religious believer is on the right path; his or her sufferings in fact indicate that he or she is on the correct course.

27. Julia Watkin and Sylvia Walsh, among others, maintain that the important aspects of human existence explained by all the pseudonyms form a clear presentation of Kierkegaard's view of the nature and purpose of human life (Watkin 2001, 8–10; Walsh 1994). Roger Poole remarks, however, that this clear view is reached at the price of "reducing . . . the sheer incompatibility of the pseudonymous' views" (Poole 1998, 64). For a detailed exposition of the latter view, see Poole 1993.

28. For Kierkegaard's self-proclaimed irony, see Cross 1998; Garff 2002.

29. For competing schools of thought about Kierkegaard, see Gouwens 1996, 3–19; Poole 1998. Louis Mackey's opinion of Kierkegaard's writings is worth mentioning. Their "tone is just as ambivalent as their purpose is devious and their method duplicitous," he writes. "By virtue of his authorial self-restraint, his texts exhibit an almost complete abstention from determinate meaning and an almost perfect recalcitrance to interpretation. Like poetry, they 'resist the intelligence almost successfully'" (Mackey 1986, xxii–iii). This leads to a controversy regarding the correct tools of interpretation. Mackey maintains that "if Kierkegaard is to be understood as Kierkegaard, he must be studied not merely or principally with the instruments of philosophic or theological analysis, but also chiefly with the tools of literary criticism" (x). Walter Kaufmann could be understood as responding to this claim when he writes that "a writer who so persistently distinguished between what he called an aesthetic approach and what we might call an existential approach should not be approached and discussed on the aesthetic plane, as he usually is" (Kaufmann 1962, 18). Kaufmann astutely observes that Kierkegaard's "central aspirations [Christianity] are almost invariably ignored, and even those who notice them often give reasons why the things that mattered to him may be dismissed as really of no account" (11). Various schools of interpretation have different interests in the comic: theologians usually ignore it whereas postmodern commentators concentrate on the "how" of the comic instead of the "what," thereby overstating the irony and often using it to dismiss the very subjects most important to Kierkegaard.

30. Exactly how many stages exist is not altogether resolved in Kierkegaard's writings. On the number of stages, see Pojman 1984, 17, 157, n. 25. In continuity with earlier pseudonymous authors in the Kierkegaardian corpus, Johannes Climacus views personal existence as a development through three stages: first, the

aesthetic, which has its *telos* in immediate enjoyment through the satisfaction and refinement of natural drives, passions, moods, talents, mental capacities, and inclinations; second, the ethical, which has as its goal victory in the struggle to fulfill universal ethical requirements in the personal life of the existing individual; and third, the religious, which has its *telos* in eternal happiness, a fulfillment that is only anticipated in existence through a relation to God characterized by persistent inner suffering as the result of a consciousness of guilt and sin. But although Climacus retains the three-stage schema of the earlier pseudonymous works, the structure in *Postscript* corresponds to a view of the stages diagrammed as follows: Aesthetic, ethical-religious, Christian. The ethical optimism that accompanies the existential task of self-transformation into conformity with the ethical ideal flows progressively into a recognition of impotence in the existential pathos of immanent religiousness, or Religiousness A. Thus, these two stages in fact belong together. Within this schema, dialectical opposition, or either/or, occurs with respect to two factors, immediacy and immanence. In relation to immediacy, the dialectic decisively favors aestheticism, and the dialectical opposition may be diagrammed as aestheticism, the ethical-religious, and the Christian. Here Christianity stands in pathetic continuity with the ethical-religious inwardness over against aesthetic immediacy. In relation to immanence, however, the dialectic occurs primarily between Christianity and the ethical-religious, and the dialectical opposition is inverted: aestheticism and the ethical-religious, the Christian. In *CUP1*, 531n, however, Climacus mentions seven spheres: immediacy; finite common sense; irony; ethics with irony as incognito; humor; religiousness with humor as incognito; and then finally the Christian religiousness, recognizable by the paradoxical accentuation of existence. There are, nevertheless, "neutral men," who do not fit neatly in any sphere (*EO2*, 172).

31. Sylvia Walsh explains that defined in purely ideal terms, the Christian life, as Kierkegaard sees it, is an entirely positive existence, consisting of faith, hope, love, joy, forgiveness, consolation, new life, and blessedness. But these positive determinants are joined with and made recognizable through negative factors, such as the consciousness of sin, the possibility of offense, self-renunciation, and suffering. One does not come to have faith except through the consciousness of sin and the possibility of offense. Similarly, Christian love is expressed through self-renunciation, and joy is found in and through the strife of suffering in life (Walsh 1994, 227).

32. For Kierkegaard's change of attitude toward humor, see Collins 1983, 44–45, and 285–6, n. 10. Collins invites us to compare *Journals*, entry 121 with *Postscript*, 242–3; 400–4, and explains, "it is the contention of Pierre Mesnard, that, to the end of his life, Kierkegaard governed his personal relationship to Christianity under the sign of humor. This opinion confuses the attitude of humor with that of religious humility, which never claims to have already realized Christian principles but only to be engaged in trying to put them into practice. The distance between religious principle and practice leaves room for constant 'becoming' or improvement, but this is not the same as the uncommitted distance between the humorous mind and Christian truths" (Mesnard 1948, 462–3; see also Mesnard 1961; Collins 1983, 44).

33. On the forms of despair, see Nordentoft 1972, 240–322, Hannay 2003, 76–88; on the pathology of the self, see Hannay 1982, 157–204; on the relation of anxiety and despair, see Beabout 2002, 35–48; on the Anti-Climacus' writings, see Dunning 1985, 214–41.

34. Pojman 1984, 158, n. 10. The difference between Kierkegaard's and Hegel's use of negativity is that the former's fundamental orientation is Aristotelian whereas the latter's "negative" has a stronger dialectical role vis-à-vis "being." For a helpful discussion, see Stack 1976, especially chap. 2; and Taylor 1980b, chap. 5.

35. For the difference between adversity and religious suffering, see *ED* I 34–35; II 7–26, 67–87; III 7–35; see also Thulstrup 1980.

36. On truth, see Taylor 2002; Perkins 2002; Popkin 2002; Barrett 2002; and Westphal 2002.

37. Andrew Burgess finds that some aspects of the comic are recurrent within all of Kierkegaard's writings. First, the comic involves a contradiction or incongruity. Second, there needs to be an appropriate kind of feeling to go with the incongruity because, from *Stages* onward, there needs to be suffering. Third, another constant in Kierkegaard's writings is his ethical concern with the comic and its legitimate and illegitimate uses in conversation as well as in writing. See Burgess 1990, for a valuable chronological approach to the comic in all of Kierkegaard's authorship.

38. For examples of incongruities see *CUP1*, 516–7n; *JP* 2, 257; 2, 260; 2, 262; 2, 267. For Kierkegaard's view of incongruity, see Lippitt 2000b, 8–11.

39. See, for example, *SV*, IV 414; VI 259; VII 268, 291, 503, 613.

40. Marc Taylor maintains that Kierkegaard "decisively rejects the superiority theory" of humor (Taylor 1980a, 221); and because the relief theory of humor emerges after Kierkegaard's time, Taylor does not comment on this latter view of humor. Stephen Evans nevertheless attempts to envision Kierkegaard's reaction to the relief theory and finds its origins in Kierkegaard (Evans 1987).

41. James Beattie in *Essay on Laughter and Ludicrous Composition* is the first to subsume superiority under incongruity (Beattie 1776). In labeling all excessive behavior as incongruous, Beattie broadens the incongruity theory to encompass the superiority theory. Every comic vice represents a deviation from the golden mean, and all laughter asserts superiority over excessive behavior. According to Francis Buckley, Beattie simply redefines incongruity as superiority (Buckley 2003, 30). This move may well be grounded in the ethical project in which Beattie enrolled the comic, a project that is reminiscent of Shaftesbury's endeavor, as the following examples testify. In a letter explaining the purpose of his projected textbook, *Elements of Moral Science*, Beattie wrote: "I wish rather to form the taste, improve the manners, and establish the principles, of young men, than to make them profound metaphysicians; I wish, in a word, not to make Humes of them, or Leibnitzes, but rather, if that were possible, Addisons" (Beattie to William Creech, 28 March 1789; quoted in Sher 1990, 87). Beattie placed great weight on moral exhortation and instruction. In his lectures, he emphasized that philosophy was to be valued chiefly because "it regulate[d] human practice," and he made it clear that in his view the pursuit of knowledge was subservient to the cultivation of virtue. Beat-

tie's preoccupation with the inculcation of sound moral and religious values thus led him to renounce the anatomy of the mind for the graphic portrayal of virtue and piety, which included the use of humor. According to Beattie, "nothing is more interesting to human creatures than that which immediately concerns human passions, feelings and sentiments. And therefore it is an author's fault and not the fault of the subject, if every part of Moral Philosophy be not made extremely entertaining." As for those parts of the subject related to "our improvement in Virtue, and the regulation of the passions," Beattie claimed that they should be "not only entertaining but delivered with that simple and expressive eloquence which touches the heart, and disposes it to form good resolutions." Finally, Beattie asserted that in moral philosophy "the greatest exactness of method, accuracy of arrangement, and perspicuity of style are indispensable," and that "particular care should be taken to avoid ambiguity of language" (quoted in Wood 1990, 143–4). By implication, then, Beattie's own pedagogical style can best be understood as "entertaining" and "expressive," primarily designed to instill the principles of piety and virtue in the hearts of his pupils. Like Hume, Beattie believed that the roles of the metaphysician and the moralist were distinct, and he eagerly adopted the guise of the practical moralist. For Beattie as a moralist and for the role of humor in his teaching, see Sher 1990, Wood 1990.

42. For Christianity as the most humorous form of all religions, see *JP* 2, 252–3; 2, 255. For examples of how the comic relates to the stages of existence, see Oden 2004, 317–22.

43. T. F. Morris emphasizes Kierkegaard's assertion that humor "knows no way out" (*CUP1*, 520; Morris 1988, 311n). Humor shares this characteristic with the tragic, in contradistinction to the comic.

44. Many authors are sensitive to this tragic aspect of the human condition. Merold Westphal mentions Jean-Paul Sartre and Blaise Pascal (Westphal 1996, 69). For the tragic in Kierkegaard's thought, see Karsten Johansen, who analyzes mainly the small treatise in *Either/Or* entitled "The Ancient Tragic as reflected in the Modern" (Johansen 1976), and Pierre Mesnard, who doubts that the category of the tragic exists in Kierkegaard's life and thought (Mesnard 1961).

45. That Climacus intends an identification of the pathetic with the tragic here is an interpretation on my part inasmuch as he does not explicitly equate the two. This follows Sylvia Walsh's view of the matter (Walsh 1994, 199). In identifying the comic and the tragic in the subjective thinker, however, he implies an identification of the pathetic with the tragic, especially when he states that "the relative difference between the comic and the tragic within immediacy vanishes in double-reflection, where the difference becomes infinite and identity is thereby posited. Religiously, the comic expression of worship is therefore just as devout as its pathos-filled expression" (*CUP1*, 89). In other contexts, the term *the pathetic*, or *pathos*, is used more broadly to connote simply an intensified form of passion also characteristic of the subjective thinker.

46. In *Repetition, Stages on Life's Way*, and *Either/Or* certain stances are limited to the life-view of the pseudonymous authors. In many instances, Kierkegaard employs normal terms in special senses, always building on the usual sense but

unmistakably departing in order to add essential new content. This is the case in the use of all the key terms Vincent McCarthy studies, viz. irony, anxiety, melancholy, despair, and life-view. Thus, for example, irony for Kierkegaard does not merely refer to the tool of discourse but to a stance characterized by an attitude of passionate rebellion and rejection of the phenomenal world, after its illusory nature has been discovered. Anxiety revolves around "nothing" because around oneself and one's possibilities. Melancholy revolves around the religious nature of the personality, and despair has at least four senses: The choice of self, loss of hope, sinfulness, and the assumption of sin-consciousness (McCarthy 1978).

47. This final point of convergence is not radically new. On the contrary, Kierkegaard finally leads to an ancient view and ancient wisdom. In the end, Kierkegaard is Christian, and there is no escaping the Christian perspective that suffuses his work and marshals the direction of his analysis. Kierkegaard rediscovers ancient Christian truth for himself, and, according to his wish, for his readers. Vincent McCarthy suggests that his analysis may be summarized in the ancient dictum of Augustine, another psychologist of the soul, who said: "Our hearts are restless until they rest in Thee, [Lord]" (*Confessions*, I, ii; quoted in McCarthy 1978, 161).

48. The example given in *The Concept of Anxiety* is sin: "When sin is brought into esthetics, the mood becomes either light-minded or melancholy, for the category in which sin lies is that of contradiction, and this is either comic or tragic. The mood is therefore altered, because the mood that corresponds to sin is earnestness. The concept of sin is also altered, because, whether it becomes comic or tragic, it becomes in any case something that endures, or something nonessential that is annulled, whereas, according to its concept, sin is to be overcome" (CA, 14–5). The mood that corresponds to sin is earnestness "expressed in a courageous resistance" (CA, 15).

49. Apart from comedy and tragedy there is also a third genre for Hegel "of less striking importance." It is a harmonization of the tragic and the comic in which a serious individual exists in a comic environment, and thus there is a happy ending. But although Hegel is elsewhere enthusiastic about dialectical syntheses, in this discussion in *The Philosophy of Fine Art* he is not (Hegel 1975, II, 1202). Richard Simon suggests that the tragic-comic does not interest Hegel, in part because it ruins the neat symmetry of his argument about comedy (Simon 1985, 108).

50. See *SLW*, section 2, and passim. On the unity of the comic and the tragic, see Walsh 1994, 217, n. 19. On the unity of the tragic and the comic in *Either/Or* I and in *The Concept of Irony*, where romanticism is portrayed, see Glenn 1970.

51. Socrates is described by Climacus as "a solo dancer to the honor of the God" (*CUP1*, 89). Socrates may also be considered the model for the pseudonyms and their imaginary constructions who characterize themselves as dancers (see Walsh 1994, chap. 5; Howland 2006, 39–40). Like jesting, dancing may be understood as connoting earnestness in relation to the divine and not merely aesthetic frivolity.

52. For style as indirect communication, see *Pap*. VIII 1 A 33; *CUP1*, 64–65; 245n; *FSE*, 35–38. For an analysis of the style of the pseudonymous writings, see Mackey 1971. For Kierkegaard's reasons for using indirect communication, see Elrod

1981, 249–303; Pojman 1984, 148–54; Poole 1993; Olesen 2005. For an interesting study of Kierkegaard's theory of communication see Manheimer 1977, and for an illuminating yet brief overview of indirect communication, see Nordentoft 1978, 345–7. My discussion of indirect communication is deeply indebted to Pojman's discussion (1984).

53. The review is by Andreas Frederik Beck, *News Repertorium fur die theologosche Literatue und kirchlich Statistik* (Berlin, III, 1, April 30, 1845), 44–48.

54. The idea that only the earnest can understand the jest is emphasized in pseudonymous writings, by Climacus in *Postscript* (*CUP1*, 276–7, n. 422) and by Anti-Climacus in *Practice in Christianity* (both books edited by Kierkegaard), and by Kierkegaard himself in *My Point of View*. See also the journal entries under "Communication," including the extensive notes for a series of lectures on the subject, which Kierkegaard prepared but never delivered (*JP* 1, 617–8).

55. Louis Pojman's translation; quoted in Pojman 1984, 68. Adi Shmüeli notes that Kierkegaard has his pseudonymous authors undertake the same action that he himself undertook several times in writing his works (Shmüeli 1971, 136–7). The pseudonyms are either publishers (Victor Eremita in *Either/Or*) or binders of the book (Hilarius in *Stages on Life's Way*), who vanish, or characters, who retreat (Constantin Constantius in *Repetition*); some of the characters are editors, like Brother Taciturnus in *Stages*, who tells us that he has found the diary, "Guilty/Not Guilty," in a lake, and challenges the reader to discover the author's identity. Similarly, Kierkegaard does not introduce a single person in his works who says directly: "I am a believer, a Christian." To speak in this way would be utter nonsense. That is why his works always have two characters, one who describes the other as a believer. For example, in *Fear and Trembling* Johannes de Silencio tells us that Abraham is a believer, in *Repetition* Constantius declares that the young man has religious "sentiment," and the young man in turn refers to Job as a believer who has experienced repetition in his faith. Finally, Kierkegaard doubts whether he himself is a Christian and uses Anti-Climacus, the pseudonymous character in *The Sickness unto Death* and *Training in Christianity* as the model of the real Christian. However, Anti-Climacus speaks not of himself, but of Jesus. It is therefore always someone else who says that another is a believer. While pseudonymity, an essential element of the Kierkegaardian authorship, is a "doubly-reflected (indirect) communication," Kierkegaard, as he writes in "a First and Last Declaration" at the end of *Postscript*, does not use pseudonyms when publishing his edifying discourses because he wants to show that he is a religious writer even though he has published aesthetic works.

56. For a comparison of irony and Christian love, see Shmüeli 1971, 155. Any indirect communication supposes two disparate qualitative opposites, and Jesus is this as well. Furthermore, the teacher of indirect communication is always incognito, and this is so even with Jesus. Kierkegaard argues that Jesus as a man is the incognito who is God Himself, that is, in becoming a man, God is hidden in the human. The effect produced by Jesus as the embodiment of contradiction is similar to the sense of distance created by indirect communication. Initially His lowliness offends the learner. Nevertheless, there is a capital difference between

Jesus and any other indirect communication. The qualitative opposites established by the ironist and the humorist belong to the world of phenomena. Whether the matter in question is the union of the tragic and the comic, or unhappiness and happiness, the communication is always parasitic on a range of common things. Moreover, the designer of such a communication always keeps a distance from this world and is never the objective or disinterested witness of it. However, Jesus is different. In addition to the first type of indirect communication, Kierkegaard recognizes another form of indirect communication, one in which the communicator is a factor. Jesus is his own communication: He does not speak these things; he is these things. For additional essential differences between Jesus and other kinds of indirect communication, see Shmuëli 1971, chap. 9, 145–75.

57. For modern models of indirect communication, see Pattison 1992, 66–67.

58. Plutarch, 1967–84, Cato the Elder, Sayings of Romans, Moralia, III, 180–1.

59. Pap. II A 166; Hannay 2001, 94, 138.

60. For Erasmus' relationship to Menippean satire, see Benda 1979; Ball 1979.

61. On how the "indirect" moves from being a purely literary construct to one that involves the signifying activity of the "lived body," see Poole 1993, 74, n. 25.

62. For the fool, see Simon 1985, 94–95, Welsford 1968 and Willford 1969. Both Enid Welsford and William Willeford go great lengths to detail the characteristics of the fool—it is an inventory of personality that closely matches Kierkegaard's traits and behavior. There is the matter of the fool's dress, designed to call attention to itself, and the stick he carries as a scepter. Kierkegaard walks the streets of Copenhagen in old-fashioned clothes, carries an umbrella whether it is raining or not, and is lampooned for the uneven length of his trousers. There is the matter of the fool's orientation to the world, his failure to marry, and the confusion of his sexuality. The nature of Kierkegaard's sexuality has been rigorously debated among his biographers: Whereas he courted Regine Olsen, his fearful retreat from marriage is the event in his life that he wrote about most obsessively. There is the matter of the fool's introversion and his role on the boundaries of the normal. Kierkegaard protects his introversion and inwardness at all cost. Living on the boundaries of Copenhagen society, he watches as an eccentric outsider. There is the matter of the fool's purpose, his special ability to speak the truth with jest, to transvalue and invert, and thereby to bring an audience to a new understanding of the truth. This is the role Kierkegaard self-consciously adopts for himself. There is the matter of the fool's paradoxical speech, which alternates between jest and earnest, meaning and meaninglessness, the worthless and the valuable. This is the language of Kierkegaard's texts. Moreover, the fool's special interest in his own disguises, the ways in which he calls attention to his masks and asks us to see through the disguises is closely allied with the manner in which Kierkegaard presents his pseudonymous authorship to Copenhagen. Kierkegaard in the role of the fool lacks a partner, however. Most fools live in pairs, one as wit, one as butt, and without this other Kierkegaard is forced to improvise. He acts both parts himself, "master of irony and martyr of laughter" (JP 6, 119).

63. For example, Hegel, Sämtliche Werke, 1927, XIV, 534, 536, 559; XVIII, 87. For Hegel on comedy and tragedy, see the next chapter as well as Roche 1998

and Gashé 2000; for Kierkegaard's relationship to Hegel, see Mackey 1986; Taylor 1980b; Thulstrup 1980; and Stewart 2003a. However, it is to Danish Hegelians' view of the comic rather than to Hegel's that Kierkegaard objected. For J. L. Heiberg and H. L. Martensen's view of the comic, see Heiberg 1828; Martensen 1941a, 1841b.

64. This metaphor is applied explicitly to satire and the comic in the paragraph that ends *Postscript*'s footnote on the comic (*CUP1*, 459–62; cf. *JP* 2, 1746, sec. 13–15). Climacus suggests that a good training for would-be satirists, who want to be responsible for their comic powers, is to renounce laughing at what they despise and exercise their eye for the comical on items for which they have partiality and sympathy (*CUP1*, 462). Renouncing laughter at that which one despises and focusing on the comic in objects for which one is partial and sympathetic is Shaftesbury's advice to himself, as we have seen in the previous chapter. For the manner in which the concept of satire, which Kierkegaard considered treating when a student, bears on the relationship of comedy to tragedy, see Malantschuk 2002, 147. Humor also bears on these relationships, but satire's distinct nature in comparison to humor and irony, to the best of my knowledge, is not clarified in Kierkegaard's writings. Satire is used when something is "sad and ludicrous" and "comical and appalling" (*SUD* 43; 56); and while satire, much like irony, seems to exclude the jester, humor appears to be much more sympathetic and inclusive of the jester. Yet, Climacus classifies satire and caricature under humor rather than as a species of irony. On satire, see *JP* 1,140 /*Pap.* 11 A 571; *JP* 1, 189/*Pap.* X³ A 540; *JP* 2, 1800/*Pap.* XI² A 294; *JP* 4, 5262/*Pap.* II A 166; *JP* 4, 6282/*Pap.* IX A 432; *JP* 4, 6907/*Pap.* XI¹ A 497.

65. Kierkegaard chastises the playwrights Baron Holberg and Augustin Eugen Scribe, the former for presenting characters that are caught up in the grip of genuine suffering, and the latter as an example of a demoralizing writer who "wittily and entertainingly entertains the age—with the sins of the age" (*JP* 2, 1761). Frater Taciturnus (the character of *Stages on Life's Way* and the pseudonymous writer to the *Corsair*) directs allegation at the journal similar to those Kierkegaard directs at the playwright Scribe. Although many of his remarks of the ethical legitimacy of the comic precede his quarrel with the *Corsair*, the indication that Kierkegaard really believed that the hierarchy between the aesthetic, ethical, and religious stages reflects on the comic, can be found in his confrontation with the editor of this popular journal, Meir Goldschmidt. In an 1846 journal entry, Kierkegaard dismisses the *Corsair* as "contemptible," and criticizes its "misuse of the comic." The comic, he argues, "must have the resource of a consistent and well-grounded ethical view, a sacrificial unselfishness, a high-born nobility that renounces the moment; otherwise the medicine becomes infinitely and incomprehensibly worse than the sickness" (*COR*, xvii). The most difficult task, he writes, is "to maintain the conception of responsibility rooted in ethical and religious earnestness together with the delight of jest." The problem with the *Corsair* is that it performs only one part of this task, and never develops "the maturity that balances the two [earnestness and jest]," and as a result it "counterfeits and taints the comic and thereby silences the authentic comic" (178–9).

66. If philosophers are thought to be in dialogue with anyone at all, then it is with great names in the history of philosophy. These great thinkers are conceived to be involved in an ongoing dialogue in an ahistorical forum of ideas. Jon Stewart observes in *Kierkegaard's Relations to Hegel Reconsidered* that "it is thought that to be involved in seemingly petty polemics with little known Danish contemporaries would be unworthy of Kierkegaard's genius" (Stewart 2003a, 628).

67. The materialist philosopher Ludwig Feuerbach voices a similar criticism of Hegelianism. Absent-mindedness for Feuerbach designates the exotism of idealism conceived as a form of life. The "humoristico-philosophical" life characterized by the negligence of reality and the humor of an involuntary distance from life finds in the writer its professional incarnation (Feuerbach 1834, I, 341f). Shaftesbury, Marx, and Nietzsche launch the same criticism, preceded by the Renaissance Philosophers Erasmus and Montaigne, who ridicule the philosophers and theologians of the Middle Ages: Forgetting themselves in abstractions, they betray life, which is the true philosophical and theological concern. Following Erasmus and Feuerbach, Kierkegaard denounces Hegel's abstractions and the theologians' forgetfulness of the simple life of faith.

68. My discussion of the philosopher as fool is deeply indebted to Lippitt 2000b, chap. 2. See also Lippitt 1999b. Michael Weston argues that Kierkegaard's use of pseudonyms and the pervasiveness of comedy, irony, and humor in his critique of philosophy have their grounds in the ethical nature of this critique. Weston establishes this point in the case of pseudonymity (Weston 1994, 43). John Lippitt echoes the latter claim, namely, that the use of comedy, irony, and humor has an ethical-religious aim, to make us aware of a particular kind of illusion (Lippitt 2000b, chap. 2).

69. For Johannes' irony, see McCarthy 1978, 108–11.

70. Andrew Cross maintains that in one crucial respect Kierkegaard modifies his earlier conception of existential irony. The ironist not only dissociates himself from the others but also from himself—from the social, embodied person that he has been and now merely plays at being. This is the self's break from immediacy (Cross 1998, 126).

71. Niels Thulstrup explains that in *The Concept of Irony*, Kierkegaard had another and categorically different standard of irony than that of Hegel: "This is clearly stated in thesis 8, where he says that 'Irony, as an infinite and absolute negativity, is the lightest and weakest meaning of subjectivity,' which immediately suggests that subjectivity has other and higher possibilities than the ironic position" (Thulstrup 1980, 260). Robert Perkins suggests that Hegel and Kierkegaard both understand irony in terms of the development of subjectivity, but that Hegel expresses this in relation to objective history, whereas Kierkegaard thinks more of the concrete individual (Perkins 1970, 250–1).

72. Gregory Vlastos is convinced that Kierkegaard's treatment of Socratic irony is "hopelessly perplexed" by a "dazzling mystification," that is, by the "infinite absolute negativity" that Kierkegaard "fished out of Hegel," which seduces him into finding in the Platonic texts "the vagaries of a romantic novella" (Vlastos 1999, 43, n. 81).

73. For Kierkegaard on irony see McCarthy 1982, chap. 1; Cross 1998; Elrod 1975, 126–31. See also Schleifer 1984; Smyth 1986; Strawser 1997; Rudd 1998; Golomb 1992; Garff 2002.

74. How radical negation can culminate in the marvels of fulfillment provides interesting speculation in Louis Mackey's essay on *The Concept of Irony*: "Irony mastered remains unreconciled, and the actuality recuperated by mastered irony remains elusive" (Mackey 1986, 180). See also John Smyth's explanation, which is summarized in Morton Gurewitch (Smyth 1986, 201–2; Gurewitch 1994, 218, n. 38).

75. For explanations of the new poems and Martensen's view of the comic as it appears in the review, see the translator's notes to *The Concept of Irony* (Carpel 1966, 426–9, nn. 13–15).

76. For the relation of humor to irony in Kierkegaard's dissertation, see *CI*, 329; 178, n. 28. For the superiority of humor to irony, see Hannay 2001, 72–74; Pattison 1992, 53–55; Lippitt 2000b, 92–102.

77. See also essays in Conway and Gover 2002, especially by Garff, Golomb, and Emmanuel. Kierkegaard wrote about the *The Point of View*: "The book itself is true, and is, in my view, masterful, if a little bit is added in order to emphasize more strongly that I am a penitent, and a little more about my sin and my guilt, and a little more about my inner misery—then it is true" (*Pap.* X¹ A 78). "'The Point of View of My Life as an Author' must not be published. No! No!—And this is what is decisive . . . : I cannot present myself entirely truthfully. Even in the very first manuscript (which, however, I had written without any thought of publishing), I was not, however, able to emphasize what is the main thing for me: that I am a penitent, and that this fact is the deepest explanation of me. . . ." (62f.).

78. Alastair Hannay explains that if Kierkegaard were a subjective thinker, irony and humor would be his incognitos. In the pseudonyms the incognitos become "persons," or at least "figures" (Hannay 2001, 315).

79. Marc Taylor notes that of the eighty-four times Kierkegaard uses the word "humor" in his published writings, seventy-seven are in *Postscript*, as well as the eighteen of twenty-one occurrences of the "humorist" (Taylor 1980a, 221).

80. Kierkegaard owned Hamann's works and from the time of *The Concept of Irony* drew heavily on these texts while forming his views of irony. Christianity, as an offense to the Jews and foolishness to the Greeks, was Hamann's epitaph, which Kierkegaard adopted. Louis Pojman maintains that the decisive moment of turning toward Christianity as essentially anti-speculative, as that which does justice to the subjective aspect of human nature, appears to come through Kierkegaard's reading of Hamann in the fall of 1836 (Pojman 1984, 7–9). Kierkegaard, a young theology student, was first attracted by Hamann's comparison of speculative reason to the Mosaic law, which must be superseded by the Gospel. "Our reason is therefore exactly what Paul calls the Law—and the command of reason is holy, righteous, and good; but is it given to make us wise? Even so little as the Law of the Jews made them righteous, but it is given to lead us from the opposite, to show us how irrational our reason is, and that our errors through it should increase, as sin increased through the Law" (*Pap.* I A 237; quoted by Kierkegaard in German).

Reason is as inadequate for solving the ultimate problems of human life as the law is for solving the problem of sin. Knowledge is abrogated by grace through the Gospel, whose truth cannot be understood through reason. It is, continues Hamann, "*incredible sed verum*" (incredible but true).

Through Hamann, Kierkegaard discovers the category of humor, which comes to replace the category of irony as the deepest attitude toward existence (Pojman 1984, 7–9). Irony is the grim fate that inevitably wins out over man's finitude, causing all his projects to end in death. However humor is seen as divine freedom, which is disjunctive with irony's bleak necessity. It is positive and affirms that there is hope, although there is no reason for hope. Humor is the insight that God is wholly other. God's truth necessarily appears very different than our finite comprehension of what it should look like. That is, divine reason is fundamentally disjunctive with human reason. Consequently, it is bound to appear to man as absurd. Humor in the human being is the appropriate attitude toward Divine Folly. Only in the absurd does the possibility of seeing God arise.

The Hamannian theme continues to dominate Kierkegaard's thought throughout fall 1836. Reasoning, when brought to its ultimate conclusion, always ends in an absurdity, a *reductio ad absurdum*. In an entry, which adumbrates a discussion in the third chapter of *Philosophical Fragments*, Kierkegaard says that reason's goal is paradoxicality: "Just how much the Understanding can achieve in a speculative sense can be best seen in the fact that when it is carried out to its highest potential in explaining the Highest, it must be expressed as a contradictory statement" (*Pap*. I A 243, Sept. 19, 1836; see II A 239; III A 108). Pojman explains, "the significance of humor, then, is to show just how impoverished finite reason is, to laugh at all man's attempts by his understanding to scale the heavens. Secondly, it has a positive function of opening a person to accept the reality of paradoxical truth, and ultimately to acceptance of the highest paradox of the Incarnation. This humor is the road to salvation" (Pojman 1984, 8). It is only when Christianity ceases to be for Kierkegaard the most humorous worldview and humor is relegated to the last *terminus a quo* with regard to Christianity that Kierkegaard departs from Hamann. For Kierkegaard's relation to Hamann, see Smith 1964; Andersen 1982; Hay 2008. For the differences between the two thinkers, see Smith 1964, 193, n. 34.

81. Even as late as 1849 Kierkegaard writes, "Christendom is waiting for a comic poet à la Cervantes, who will create a counterpart to Don Quixote out of the essentially Christian" (*JP* 2, 1762). In *Judge for Yourself!* (written 1852–1854) he uses the lilies and the birds jestingly to teach the God-fearing worker the earnestness of God as a co-worker (*FSE*, 179, 183, 186). Kierkegaard's disengagement from Hamann's thought begins with a paragraph on the absurd nature of the Christian message. Apparently, Kierkegaard believed the quote to be Hamann's, but it came from the skeptical Hume. It is a prolepsis of what will appear in fully developed form in the *Postscript*:

The Christian religion not only was the first attended with miracles, but even at this day cannot be believed by any reasonable person

without one. Mere reason is insufficient to convince us of its verac-
ity. And whoever is moved by *faith* to assent to it is conscious of a
continued miracle in his own person which subverts all the principles
of his understanding and gives him a determination to believe what is
most contrary to custom and experience. (*Pap.* I A 100)

This quotation comes from sec. 10 of Hume's *Inquiry Concerning Human
Understanding*. What Hume stated tongue-in-cheek Kierkegaard took to be an
instance of the humorous and profound insight of Hamann. Miracle or "wonder"
stands in disjunctive relationship with human reason, and unexpectedly breaks with
the affairs and lives of men. The proper response to the wonderful is wonder, not
reason. Pojman explains, "wonder, in the sense of being awed by the supernatural,
is the appropriate response to the miracles in life, even as humor is the appropriate preparation for it" (Pojman 1984, 9). At this point, Kierkegaard returns to the
writings of Friedrich Schleiermacher, the theologian of wonder (*Pap.* II A 199,
December 7, 1837). In Schleiermacher, the two poles—abstract systematizing and
the personal subjective tendency—meet for Kierkegaard. Whereas Hamann is too
one sided and lacking in systematic comprehensiveness, Schleiermacher seems to
have balanced both tendencies, creating a personal philosophical theology. On
closer investigation, however, Schleiermacher turns out to be deficient regarding
the paradoxical, although his response to wonder is correct (*Pap.* I A 273).

82. On the last page of the *Concept of Irony* where the later project in
Postscript is anticipated, Kierkegaard refers the reader to Hans Lassen Martensen's
theological theory of humor (*CI*, 329). For Martensen's view of humor see Martensen 1841a, 1841b, sec. 56.

83. *CUP1*, 501; see also 617. In this passage, Climacus denies being a religious
individual, claiming to be solely a humorist, whereas in another passage he places
himself on the boundary of the religious within immanence seeking the Christian-
religious (*CUP1*, 451). In yet another passage, he identifies his position within the
borders of Religiousness A (*CUP1*, 557). Hence, it is never entirely clear where
Climacus fits within the various forms of religiousness.

84. The translation has been amended by Pojman 1984, 68.

85. In an appendix to *Postscript*, Climacus suggests that the whole work has
only been an experiment or imagery construction that is "about myself, solely and
simply about myself" (*CUP1*, 617). "Everything," he writes, "is to be understood in
such a way that it is revoked" (*CUP1*, 619). The revocation at the end of *Postscript*
has raised the contention that humorous revocation is a way of distancing oneself
existentially from the divine. Certainly it may be that, but Climacus' own revocation at the end of the book suggests another possibility, namely, that the existential
humorist may revoke his words in the interest of indirect communication. He
does not claim to be an authority on the subject of Christianity and has but one
opinion, namely, "that it must be the most difficult of all to become a Christian"
(*CUP1*, 619). He is thus qualified on the basis of his own self-reflection in the
book to be only an apprentice, or learner. For this purpose he seeks a "teacher of

the ambiguous art of thinking about existence and existing" who will allow him to ask questions and will go over everything until he has understood it, not simply learned by rote a paragraph a day (*CUP1*, 622–3). Having found no such teacher, Climacus is reluctant to assume the role of teacher himself, as if a learner in the art of existing could teach anyone else. Climacus thus leaves his readers free to master the art of existing for themselves just as he must do. Another possible interpretation of the revocation is that Climacus seeks to protect his own secret inwardness by cloaking his earnestness in jest. If that is the case, then his claim to be solely a humorist must be taken ironically—and humorously (Walsh 1994, 217). On Climacus' revocation, see also Lippitt 2000a.

86. Tonny Olesen finds the sources of these views about humor in Kierkegaard's contemporaries (Olesen 2003, 225–6, nn. 27–32). That humor entered the world with Christianity has been "likely introduced by Jean Paul," who designates humor as the Romantic-comic with "Romantic" meaning "Christian" (Richter 1813 [1804]; Olesen 2003, 225, n. 27). Moreover, the claim that humor gains its strength by bringing with it a category of totality seems to originate with Jean Paul, but is also found in H. L. Martensen (Martensen 1841b). The notion that humor is not a designation of the first immediacy but includes reflection is influenced by Gotthold Lessing's distinction between immediate and reflective humor in *Hamburgische Dramaturgie* (Lessing 1962, sec. 93). Jean Paul's view that "irony is added as the third modality within comedy" is appropriated by J. L. Heiberg, who subsequently redefines "humor" as the unity of "playfulness" (the immediate) and "irony" (reflection) (Richter 1813 [1804], programs VII and VIII; Heiberg 1828, column 4). Kierkegaard has excerpted the latter in Journal BB 1837. The idea that humor designates the unity of tragedy and comedy Olesen finds not in Jean Paul, who "only understands humor within comedy," but in Karl Solger, "who is most probably the first to do so" (1962 [1829], 215–20). The observation that humor designates a culminating standpoint is found in Hegel, who, in *Lectures on Aesthetics*, places humor just before the end of the Romantic form of art, and the notion that humor is melancholic [*vermodig*] likely derives from Solger as well (1962 [1829], 215–20). The literature contemporaneous with the writings of Kierkegaard is replete with discussions of humor as the counterpart to Greek irony. See, for example, Baur 1837 and Daub 1838, to whom Kierkegaard refers respectively in *Pap.* II A 186 and II A 79. Olesen does not mention eighteenth-century thinkers who influenced Kierkegaard on these matters, such as Hamann or Shaftesbury, or the sixteenth-century religious thinker, Erasmus.

87. On the role of humor, see Lippitt 2000b, chaps. 4–5, 60–103; Evans 1983, 195–210. Stephen Evans thinks of the existence spheres not in terms of a fixed schema but rather as "existential possibilities that can be helpfully reflected on with the help of certain defining categories" (Evans 1983, 199). Although it is helpful to relax the rigidity of the schema of the stages, or existence spheres, by thinking of them in this way, another solution is suggested by Sylvia Walsh, who argues that it may be possible to think of humor in terms of a gradation, or range, of humorous standpoints and as operative on the boundary between

immanent religiousness and Christianity as well as between the ethical and the religious (Walsh 1994, 212–17). Marc Taylor neglects the element of humor in Religiousness A. He views humor only as a boundary category within the ethical and Christian-religious stages, although he does place humor within immanent categories. Thus when Taylor discusses humor as the incognito of religious faith, he presumably means Christian faith, and not Religiousness A, as Evans and Walsh interpret it (Taylor 1980a).

88. What makes Religiousness B distinctive is the concept of God becoming human to make human salvation possible, as in when "the learner owes the teacher everything" (*PF* 38). For the difference between Religiousness A and B, see Deuser 1998. The centrality of *Postscript* in the corpus makes it easy to think that the richly developed contrast between Religiousness A and Religiousness B (the project initiated in *Philosophical Fragments* of comparing the modes of religious subjectivity embodied in Socratic and Christian faith) is the culmination of the authorship's presentation of the religious stage. However, this is not the case for Merold Westphal, who adds Religiousness C:

> Like Religiousness B, it is distinctly Christian, but whereas in Religiousness B Christ is the paradox to be believed, in Religiousness C he is also the Pattern of Paradigm to be imitated, most particularly in his compassion for the poor and the powerless . . . Religiousness C represents an ethic of radical compassion that welcomes the neighbor even across the class of ethically sanctioned marginalization. (Westphal 1998, 120–1)

Practice in Christianity is the most important text for Religiousness C, but *For Self-examination*, *Judge for Yourself*, and *Works of Love* are also important. For Religiousness C, see Westphal 1992; for Kierkegaard's Christian ethics, see Quinn 1998.

89. The characterization of religiousness in terms of hidden inwardness is something Kierkegaard later explicitly rejects in *Practice in Christianity* because it too easily becomes an excuse for the relaxation of rigorous striving in Christendom, where everyone is presumed to be a Christian in hidden awareness (*PC*, 215–32). In place of hidden inwardness Kierkegaard introduces the "inverted recognizability" of the Christian through external suffering brought about by opposition from the world (*PC*, 212, 215). But Christianity is still essentially inwardness for Kierkegaard, and he continues to speak of a true "concealed inwardness" in the form of "the suffering of real self-denial" on the part of true Christians (*PC*, 138–9).

90. Ideally, the religious individual would be so artful in disguising inwardness that not even the slightest hint of it would be apparent to others, but Climacus admits that "as long as the struggle and the suffering in inwardness continue he will not succeed in hiding his inwardness completely" (*CUP1*, 501). It is this element of imperfection that distinguishes the religious individual of whom Climacus speaks from the knight of faith in *Fear and Trembling*, for Climacus claims that the knight of faith is presented in an illusory state of completeness and thus in a false

medium, rather than in the medium of existence, where nothing is ever finished or complete (*CUP1*, 500–1).

91. Kierkegaard contrasts this view with the Hegelian view, which maintains, "in eternity a person will preserve a comic consciousness about the temporal" (*CA*, 207). For Vigilius Haufniensis, the pseudonymous author of *The Concept of Anxiety*, one of four attitudes toward eternity is comical—when eternity is conceived abstractly, that is, in metaphysical, aesthetic, and aesthetic-metaphysical perspectives. It is viewed negatively as the boundary of the temporal, or as imaginatively and dreamily present in poetry and art, or as comically preserving the temporal within itself. Vigilius primarily has in mind a statement by Poul Møller. The other intended target is Hans Martensen's Hegelian tendency to give superiority to the comic in an aesthetic-metaphysical viewpoint that swallows up the temporal in the eternal (*CA*, 154). Kierkegaard's own view of eternity is the basis of the somewhat bizarre conjecture he advances in his journals: "Granted that eternity is too earnest a place for laughter (something I have always been convinced of), it seems that there must be an intermediary state where a person is permitted to laugh outright . . . Socrates would be found in this intermediary state" (*JP* 2, 272).

92. In the last of the *Diapsalmata* of *Either/Or*, the young aesthete relates a tale in which he is granted one wish in front of all the gods in the assembly. He chooses "one thing, that [he] may always have the laugh on [his] side." Because the gods begin to laugh, he concludes that his wish has been granted (*EO1*, 41–42). But the gods laugh at him, for to have laughter always on one's side is to claim to transcend finitude, time, and history. The aesthete's existence is comical, because, as he notes, it is always comical "when subjectivity as mere form would assert itself," that is, when an individual "tries to be the absolute" (*EO1*, 140, 143).

93. Sotion and later his renown student, the Roman Stoic philosopher Seneca (4 BC–AD 65), presented laughter and crying as an alternative to anger (Stobaeus, *Florilegium* III, 20, 53; Seneca, *De Ira*, 2.10.5; 2.4.4–7; *Tranquilitate Anima*, 15.2–5).

94. On the *Corsair* affair, see Simon 1985; see the collection of material brought together as COR; Lowrie 1938, 347–63; Lowrie 1968b, 176–87; Perkins 1990; and Poole 1993, especially 188–99.

95. Buckley 2003, xiii, xii, 73, xi, 12. When relativism triumphs, the view that laughter signals inferiority becomes unpopular. Francis Buckley explains that the modern academy often is agnostic about norms and skeptical about truth. It prizes an irony in which perspective is all. Modernism is also strongly egalitarian and hostile to signals of inferiority. Buckley believes this may explain why superiority theories are out of fashion today. In addition to Buckley, who defends "a soft version of the Normative superiority thesis" (xii), Charles Gruner (1997) and Marcella Tarozzi Goldsmith (1991) may be the only scholars who defend the superiority theory today; they do so by subsuming the incongruity theory to it. In an agnostic and skeptical environment laughter cannot flourish, however. A comic relativism that asserts that one life plan is as good as another is wholly destructive of laughter, according to Buckley (Buckley 2003, 81).

96. According to Hobbes, we signal our superiority by laughter but the truly superior do not laugh. The most superior person scorns to tank himself against others. At the limit, he will seek to rise above all laughter. For Hobbes' theory of laughter, see Chapter 1, Concluding Remarks.

97. It follows that the example given by Merold Westphal is inadequate. Although the characterization of Climacus portraying "the existing thinker as having what we might call a metaphysical sense of humor" is accurate, the explanation of this sense of humor as "an appreciation of the inherent incongruities of being human" fails to provide an exact definition of human. Instead Westphal offers the following example: "Politicians who are able to laugh at themselves are somehow more human than those who take themselves with utter and unrelieved seriousness" (Westphal 1996, 72). This may be true, but it does not exemplify Kierkegaard's view and in this sense the example is inadequate. The metaphysical incongruities revealed by the Kierkegaardian sense of humor depend on a specific metaphysics and a particular view of what it means to be human, which may not be shared by those who are not religious or who do not endorse Kierkegaard's view of Christianity.

98. Among the great figures in Church history, Luther is the one with the most notable sense of humor. Peter Berger suggests that "the same robust sense of humor can even be detected in one of Luther's most famous statements, containing as it does the doctrine of justification by faith in a comic nutshell when he advises the over-scrupulous Melanchton 'to sin forcefully, but to believe even more forcefully' (pecca fortiter sed crede fortius)—a sentence that humorless Catholic critics have often used to discredit Lutherianism and equally humorless Lutherans have reinterpreted to make it inoffensive" (Berger 1999, 199). Luther's sense of humor permeates his correspondence and table talk and is emphasized in all his biographies. For Luther's humor, see Oberman 1989; Gritsch 1983; Zwart 1996.

99. Both Jerome and Augustine grasp the latent analogy between the Christ of the Gospels and the Socrates of the aporetic dialogues. Erasmus is a connoisseur of both, and it is no surprise that he elaborates on this thought in his *Praise of Folly*. Erasmus' attitude to Socrates' irony is important to recall in the context of his comparison with Christ and St. Paul. If references to Socrates' *ironia* in the Middle Ages are extremely rare, they become commonplace in the Renaissance; and from then on Socrates' *ironia*, writes Erasmus, become his *ironia familiaris* ("habitual irony") (Erasmus 1961, V, 844). For Socrates and the Early Church, see Edwards 2007; for Socrates and Kierkegaard, see Howland 2006.

100. For Erasmus and Kierkegaard, see Simon 1985; Jensen 2009. In Erasmus' *The Praise of Folly* (1971 [1509]), Folly (*Stultitia*) goes through three stages of existence: She is first comic, foolish, intoxicated, sexual, vain, in love with herself; she is then satiric, wise, critical of everything she has raised, angry at the world and its folly; finally she is the wise fool, religious, the simple Christian praised by Paul in 1 and 2 Corinthians. Richard Simon finds similarities between these stages and the three stages of Kierkegaard's pseudonymous authorship: Aesthetic, ethical, and religious (Simon 1985, 109). Appended to the *The Praise of Folly* is Erasmus'

"Letter to Martin Dorp," which explains that the mock encomium has been written "under a laughable persona" in order "to call the world back to true Christianity" (Erasmus 1971, 147, 156). Erasmus argues that it has the same serious purpose as his explicitly serious works but is nevertheless only a piece of foolishness that we do not have to take seriously. For the kinds of comedy found in Erasmus, see Gordon 1990, 6–7; for *The Praise of Folly*, see Kaiser 1963, 9–10; and for Erasmus as a laughing philosopher, see Kallen 1968, chap. 4.

101. See Scott 1966; Cox 1969; Kuschel 1994; Miller 1969; Crossan 1976; Taylor 1984; Wood 1988.

102. Some earlier works have been influenced by anthropologist Johann Huizinga's work on play (1955), or the theories of the classicist Francis Cornford (1961) and the Cambridge Ritual school, which understand Greek comedy as the dramatic expression of an older ritual cycle of death and resurrection (e.g., Wood 1988, 24; Crossan 1976, 22). By the mid-1970s, deconstructionist literary theory, as well as Mikhail Bakhtin's notion of "carnival" (1968), have also become significant for theological reflection on the comic. An enlightening analysis of the current interest of theology in humor can be found in Sands 1996.

103. In Reinhold Niebuhr's case, for example, the incongruities of humor, like those of faith, are theologically significant only because they point to a deeper level of congruity (Niebuhr 1969); John Crossan contends in a similar vein that parabolic paradoxes of the New Testament lead beyond language to the divine silence (Crossan 1976). Hugo Rahner and Karl-Joseph Kuschel construe Christian levity as an emulation of the detached laughter and unconditional freedom of God (Rahner 1972; Kuschel 1994). Conrad Hyers views comedy as "the playfulness which characterizes both Creator and creation alike" (Hyers 1987, 7; see Hyers 1981). Kathleen Sands justly remarks that when play, festivity, or carnival are affirmed as Christian, it is because they are made to represent an "endless" creativity, a radical, relativizing openness that cannot be contained in the purposive and conflicted aims of ordinary life (Sands 1996, 504).

104. Theology's interest has been confined to what Charles Baudelaire calls "the absolute comic," so described to contrast it with "the significative comic," which involves social criticism (Baudelaire 1956). For a recent thesis on the importance of the absolute comic, see Kern 1980. Kathleen Sands argues that the treatment of humor by some deconstructionists amounts to another variation on this theme, as when Candace Lang traces humor to the endlessly self-referential character of language (Lang 1988). In either case, Sands explains, the comic affords a certain victory over social constraint. She also mentions that for Edith Kern the victory can only be temporary and fantastic (Sands 1996, 504).

105. For alternative views, see Bell 1992; Sands 1994. Among religious feminists Mary Daly is due special credit for using humor to exorcise the God of patriarchy and for restoring the virtue of "Laughing Out Loud" to women (Daly and Caputi 1987; see also Sands 1996, 502).

106. See Sanders 1995; Minois 2000. For a good exposition of the relationship of Christianity and humor, see Lippitt 2000b, 169–74.

107. For humor in the Bible, see Lang 1962; in Judaism, see Radday and Brenner 1990; Murray 1993; Reines 1972; Morreall 2001; in Islam, see Rosenthal 1962.

108. Laughter plays a prominent role in Zen Buddhism and Taoism, and there is a positive attitude toward it in Hinduism, Buddhism and Confucianism. The different attitudes to laughter in Western in contrast to Eastern philosophies and religions may be due to the otherworldliness of Western religions and the Western view of the individual as an uneasy combination of body and mind, as well as of animal and godlike origins. For laughter in Hinduism, see Siegel 1987; in Buddhism, see Morreall 1999, 49–62; in Zen Buddhism, see Hyers 1974, 1989; Blyth 1959, 1969; Moore 1977; in ancient Chinese philosophy, see Harbsmeier 1989; in Taoism, see Hyers 1974, chap. 10; in Confucianism, see Chao-Chih 2001, chaps. 5–6. For humor and laughter in religions, see Morreall 1989a, 1999; Gilhus 1991, 1997; Sarazin 1991.

109. This view originates in Aristotle's remarks in a treatise on physiology: The human being is "the only one of the animals that laughs" (*De partibus animalium* III, 10, 673a, 8, and 28). For Aristotle's arguments on laughter, see Labarrière 2000; for the history of laughter as a human property since Aristotle, see Ménager 1995, 13–20.

110. For Jesus' laughter, see Le Goff 1992. The question of Jesus' laughter is encountered in sermons and homiletic literature. Moreover, it was not restricted to monastic or strictly ecclesiastical society, but was also very much alive in the University. In the thirteenth century, the University of Paris traditionally organized a yearly *quod libet* (a discussion on a chosen theme that is open to the general public) on precisely this subject. However, before the middle of the twentieth century, only the Gnostics had recognized Christ's laughter.

111. Although *risus monasticus* was illegitimate laughter, the monks managed to create written jokes, the *joca monacorum*, of which there are collections from the eighth century onward.

112. Christian behavior is more varied than Christian theoretical considerations. Mikhail Bakhtin has argued for the existence of a comic culture in the Middle Ages (1968). Although often frowned on by ecclesiastical authorities, such a culture is emphatically Christian in content. One should mention the Easter laughter (*risus paschalis*) as an important medieval practice: In the course of the Easter mass the congregation was encouraged by frequent obscene jokes and funny stories to engage in loud and prolonged laughter in order to celebrate the joy of the Resurrection. St. Francis of Assisi is a notable exception to the common view of laughter in Christianity. For laughter in the Middle Ages, see Le Goff 1997; Verdon 2001; Sanders 1995, 127–164; Minois 2000, 95–243. For laughter in the Renaissance, see Ménager 1995, 79–83.

113. Alexandre de Hales, the first great Franciscan doctor and lecturer at the University of Paris from 1220 to 1240, wrote one of the first scholastic texts on laughter. The important texts of Thomas Aquinas and Albertus Magnus also had an influence at the level of the practice of laughter. Thomas Aquinas revives

eutrapelia, the Aristotelian social virtue of wit as appropriate laughter for the free person (Aquinas 1972, II-II, quest. 168, art. 2). This plea for restrained laughter is followed by Pascal (Pascal 1941, *Provincial Letters*, no. 11). Employing his usual tripartite division, Aristotle claims that excess is buffoonery and deficiency is boorishness, but that there exists a true wittiness characteristic of an honorable and free person. Aristotle's views are further developed by Theophrastus and taken up by Cicero, who uses the Latin terms *liberalis* and *illiberalis* for the Greek "free person" and his opposite. The Stoic-peripatetic tradition, which can be found in Cicero's *De Officiis* and *De Oratore*, has a great historic influence (see note 47, Chapter 1). Aristotle's *eutrapelia* gains a negative connotation in Greek and Roman culture, however, which eventually reaches its peak with Christianity (Verdon 2001, 17). In his *Epistle to the Ephesians*, St. Paul counts *eutrapelia* among the vices to be avoided: "Neither filthiness, nor foolish talk, nor jesting, which are not convenient" (5: 4). Wit is condemned by Ignatius, Clement of Alexandria, Origen, and in literally dozens of passages, by Basil and John Chrysostom.

114. Jesus is laughing in the writings of ancient Coptic Gnostics. See the Apocalypse of Peter 81:11 and 83:1, translated in Robinson 1990, 377; and the Gospel of Judas 2.3–7, 3.6, 9.3, 14.12–14, translated in Pagels and King 2007, 109–10, 111, 115, 120.

115. On Shaftesbury as "the beloved Plato of Europe," see Herder's *Fragmente über die neurre deutsche Literatur*, *Sämmtliche Werke*, 1877–1913, I, 182, and *Eine Philosophie der Geschichte zur Bildung der Menschheit*, Erster Abschnitt, *Sämmtliche Werke*, 1877–1913, V, 499. On Shaftesbury as a "philosophical scoffer," see Herder's letter to Kant from 1768, in *Immanuel Kants Werke*, 1922–23, vol. IX, 64. On Herder and Shaftesbury, see Cassirer 1953, 199. On Kierkegaard and Herder, see Adamsen 2007. On Herder and Kierkegaard as Hamann's followers, see Ringleben 2006.

116. For a more comprehensive discussion of Kierkegaard's thought on the comic and its relation to the ancient comic traditions in philosophy mentioned in the introduction, see Amir's "Kierkegaard and the Traditions of the Comic" (2013a). These traditions, which survived throughout the Middle Ages and flourished in the Renaissance before being rediscovered in the Modern era, include the Ridiculous Philosopher (Thales), the Laughing Philosopher (Democritus), the Comical Philosopher (Socrates), Philosophy is Comedic (Plato, the Cynics), Wit is a Virtue (Aristotle), Laughter is the Mark of Humanity (Aristotle), the Laughless Philosopher (Pythagoras), the Mocking Philosopher (Gorgias), and modern and postmodern traditions of the comic such as Laughter is Epistemologically Valuable and the Comic is Ontologically Rooted.

CHAPTER 3: HUMOR AND THE GOOD LIFE

1. For criticism of Schopenhauer's view of laughter, see Lewis 2005; for Schopenhauer's various forms of the ludicrous, see Sprigge 1988. These articles

also provide good explanations of the role of laughter in Schopenhauer's vision of the world, on which little has been written.

2. See, for example, von Hartmann 1887, II, 391–425; Lipps 1898, 261–4; Volkelt 1905–1914, II, 529; Cohen 1912, II, 114–17; and Kutscher 1951, I, 158–61. Lipps has influenced both Freud's psychology and his view of humor.

3. For Carlyle on humor, see Ziolkowski 2011, chap. 5, 213–56.

4. For Jean Paul's humor, see Kleinert 2008. The comic is also praised as a philosophic capacity by Ralph Emerson in his 1843 essay of the same name: "The best of all jokes," he writes, "is the sympathetic contemplation of things by the understanding from the philosopher's point of view" (Emerson 1964 [1843], 379).

5. For these philosophers, see *Nietzsche's French Laughing Followers* (work in progress).

6. For Freud's view of humor and other forms of the comic, see Parkin 1997, chap. 2.

7. See *Laughter and the Good Life* (work in progress).

8. The argument presented in this chapter antedates the writing of the previous chapters of this book. Presentations in philosophy and humor conferences of earlier versions vary from 1984 to 2009 (Amir 1984, 1990, 1998, 2000, 2003, 2004a, 2004b, 2009a). I have benefited from my colleagues' comments in these conferences.

9. "Tragedy" refers to a literary form difficult to define. The motto of Paul Gordon's monograph on tragedy is as follows: ". . . It seems that there cannot be a true theory of tragedy, for underlying every theory of tragedy is the assumption that tragedy has a set of necessary and sufficient properties" (Weitz 1967, 160; quoted in Gordon 2001). Comedy follows in tragedy's footsteps; according to Robert Corrigan, it is "moving in the right direction in criticizing the 'formalistic fallacy' which assumes that a certain theme or structure can be identified which strings together all the varied beads of comedy" (Corrigan 1965a, 3; quoted in Hyers 1996, 9).

10. The Russian-French philosopher Leo Shestov generates his tragic philosophy in response to Shakespeare, Dostoevsky, and Nietzsche, and through his ongoing critique of Kant. In contrast to systematic philosophy, tragic philosophy is based on an acknowledgment of the actual horror and chaos of life. It is not meant to teach truth, but to probe and articulate the most personal, difficult, and paradoxical human experiences of the good and the true, and the first and final questions about the meaning and purpose of life. For Leo Shestov's philosophy, see Shestov 1969, Martin 1969, Philonenko 1998. Leo Shestov was Georges Bataille's teacher and influenced the latter's tragic philosophy. He has also influenced the early twentieth-century Russian existentialist school of philosophy: Nikolai Berdiaev, Aleksei Losev, and Merab Mamardashvili. For Shestov's followers, see Clowes 2007.

11. For the Romanian-French philosopher, Cioran, see Cioran 1973, 1990; Parfait 2001. For Georges Bataille, see Bataille 1943; Land 1900; Botting and Wilson 1998. For Nietzsche, Bataille, and Rosset, see notes 5 and 7.

12. See Durkheim 1964, 325–50; Berger and Luckman 1967, 180–3; Luckman 1971, 41–49; Lévi-Strauss 1963–1976, 1967, 1–47, 1969–1980; Heller 2005, 21.

13. See for example, Nussbaum 2001b and the updated bibliography there. There are anthologies on the substance and meaning of tragedy such as Abel 1967; Corrigan 1965a; Michel and Sewall 1963; manuscripts written in the wake of Nietzschean tragedy such as Witt 2007; Sallis 1991; and Gordon 2001; anthologies that examine the relation of philosophy to tragedy such as Kaufmann 1969; Georgopoulos 1993; Beistegui and Sparks 2000; and monographs on the tragic such as Myers 1956; Szondi 2002.

14. For Kant's view of reason's drives and aims, see Johnson 2006, 51–52; Yovel 1980, 15–19.

15. For the histories of tragedy, comedy, and the satyr play that follow early tragedies, see Cornford 1961; Gilhus 1997. For various views of the relationship between comedy and tragedy, see Koestler 1949, 371–80; Langer 1953, 326–66; Kerr 1967; Davenport 1976; Morreall 1997.

16. In her recent work on comedy, Alenka Zupančič suggests that Henri Bergson's gesture is more ambitious than simply adding yet another pairing—the living-mechanical (or life-automatism)—to the series of oppositions used in comedy. She thinks that he proposes this oppositional pair as the real core of all the others, and that a large part of his book on laughter is dedicated to the attempt to demonstrate the reducibility of different descriptions of the comical to this conceptual matrix. See Zupančič 2008, 111–12.

17. For incongruity as a necessary and sufficient condition for humor, see, for example, Nerhardt 1976; for incongruity together with its necessary resolution for humor, see Suls 1972. For information-processing analysts who add a component of conflict-resolution to incongruity theory, see Shultz 1972 and Suls 1983. For theorists who propose a two-stage process of humor, see, for example, Berlyne 1972 and Koestler 1964.

18. For incongruity theories, see Schopenhauer 1969; Kant 1911; Gerard 1759; Leacock 1935; for ambivalence theories, see Eastman 1972; Lund 1930; Menon 1931; Monro 1951; finally, for release and relief theories, see Spencer 1860; Lipps 1898; Kline 1907; Freud 1905; Rapp 1947.

19. For the relation of suffering and laughter in Nietzsche's thought, see 1966b, sec. 270; 1954a, IV, sec. 13, 15; 1982, sec. 386; 1979, II, sec. 4.

20. See Fry 1992b, 1994; Fry and Salameh 1987, 1993.

21. For humor and psychological well-being, see Morreall 2008 and Martin 2008. For contemporary uses of humor in psychological therapy, see Ellis 1977; Grossman 1977; Grotjhan 1970, 1971; Ventis 1987; Robinson 1977, 1983. For a bibliography of therapy and humor, see Nilsen 1993b, 11–15.

22. For the view that morality should solve both interpersonal conflicts and intrapersonal conflicts, see Wong 1984, 38. For differences between these conflicts, see McConnel 1988.

23. See, *inter alia*, Morreall 1983a, 1983b, 1987, 1989a, 1989b, 1997, 1998, 1999, 2009, 2010.

24. O'Connell 1976, Norrick 1986, and Minsky 1983 emphasize that humor enables switching between various conflicting points of views.

25. Vera Robinson explores the psychological and physiological functions of humor and the individual's ability to cope with internal stress (Robinson 1983,

116–9; 1977); humor serves as a moderator of stress for depressive (but not anxiety) symptomatology (Nezu et al. 1988); Rod Martin presents a theoretical model of stress and coping, and discusses the way in which nonhostile, self-accepting, realistic humor, and laughter represent a healthy broad-spectrum coping strategy (Martin 1988). See Jon Roeckelein for numerous references on humor and stress (Roeckelein 2002, 268–9).

26. For character, see Kupperman 1991, chap. 1. For the view that self-knowledge is necessary for moral wisdom, see Kekes 1995, chaps. 6–7. For limitations of our capacity to attain to self-knowledge by our own power without a dialogue with others, see Joplin 2000.

27. Inner dialogue has been explored by philosophers such as Plato (*Theaetetus* 189e–190a; *Sophist* 263a; *Philebus* 38cd), Augustine (*Confessions* 1991, Bk. VIII), Shaftesbury (*Soliloquy* [1711]; *Philosophical Regimen* [1992]), Hannah Arendt 1978, Gilbert Ryle 1979, Hans-Georg Gadamer 1989, Mikhail Bakhtin 1984, and Daniel Dennett 1991; anthropologists such as George Herbert Mead 1934, psychologists such as Jean Piaget 1959, Lev Semenovich Vygotsky 1962, Aleksandr Nikolaevich Sokolov 1972 and others. For a good survey of the variety of views of inner dialogue, see Blachowicz 1998 and 1999. See also Amir 2001, and Rowan and Cooper's *The Plural Self* 1999.

28. See also Charles Rycroft's *Critical Dictionary of Psychoanalysis* 1995 and Pinkus 2009 for a good survey of ambivalence. I am grateful to David Segal for his help in researching ambivalence in psychology.

29. For Robert Merton's typology of sociological ambivalence, see Merton 1976, 6–12.

30. A good survey of Western civilization from this perspective is found in John Passmore's *The Perfectibility of Man* 1970.

31. Spinoza asserts that his philosophy offers a road to salvation (*Ethics*, V, P36; P42 Schol.); so do Schopenhauer (1969, II, 638), and Nietzsche, although this aspect of the latter's thought is less often emphasized (1979, III, "Why I Write Such Excellent Books," sec. 8; 1967, II, sec. 24; 1954, "On redemption"; 1968, sec. 852; 1974, Preface, sec. 3). Philosophy contributes to the good life as Santayana conceives it, but it is also a road for "inward" or "philosophic salvation" (Santayana 1944, 428; 1980, 21, 192, 213).

32. For Hellenistic philosophies' view of *ataraxia*, or peace of mind, as a radical personal solution akin to personal philosophic redemption, see Nussbaum 1994. The messianic zeal of Epicureans was legendary, and Stoicism has been compared to a religion.

33. I am grateful to Itay Ehre for his help with Indian philosophies. For Hindu release, see Clooney and Nicholson 2001; for the Buddhist view of release, see Eckel and Thatamanil 2001; "The middle way," which has become synonymous with Buddhism is misleading: It is a middle way between extreme Hindu asceticism and a dissolute life of pleasures, but its attitudes toward desire is not mild and conciliatory (see Marinoff 2007, chap. 3).

34. For Schopenhauer's view of renouncing the will and its sources in Eastern thought, see Berger 2004. For desire in Epicureanism and Pyrrhonism, see Nussbaum 1994; Long 1986.

35. There are good reasons for rejecting the dream that the gods exist, and the number of books on this subject is great. I merely mention four recent works: Dennett 1993; Kekes 1995; Kitcher 2007; Wielenberg 2005.

36. See Plato, *Phaedrus*, and Burton 1989, 867. Burton discusses enthusiasm in love, religion, and philosophy in "Love-Melancholy," the Third Partition of his book. See also Shaftesbury (*Letter*, 2; CR I, 15–16); Kant, "Sickness of the Head," 1992– (Ak. 2: 267), 268; Johnson 2002, 79–80.

37. For the new age movement, see Amir 2009b.

38. See Karl Popper's work (e.g., 1959, 1963, 1994) and its critics.

39. For mysticism's attitude toward desire and reason, see Carmody 1996; Borchert 1994. For the Stoics' eradication of desires and emotions, see Sorabji 2000, 181–210, and for a criticism of the Kantian metaphysics of the categorical imperative, see Allison 1990.

40. Kant, *Reflexion* 6050, Nachlass, *Kants gesammelte Schriften*, 1902–, XIII, 436, 1. 18–20; translated by Patrick Neubaeur.

41. "Ridicule," says *Webster New World Dictionary*, "from the Latin *ridere*, to laugh. As a noun, it is 1. The act of making one the object of scornful laughter; or 2. Words or actions intended to produce such laughter. As a verb: to make fun of; deride; mock" (*Webster New World Dictionary*, 514). "Ridiculous: deserving ridicule; absurd" (515).

42. That we should take into consideration the view from nowhere is Nagel's contention (Nagel 1987, 1986). This is not embraced by other philosophers, such as Robert Solomon (1976, chap. 1) and John Kekes (1995, 175–8; 2010, 234–8). For both, the fact that this view makes our concerns futile is a good reason not to embrace it.

43. *The New York Times*, June 1, 1958, sec. II, 3; quoted in Esslin 1961, 101.

44. The literature on self-love's benefits is enormous. I recommend Liebman 1946, chap. 2.

45. Don Quixote opens the gallery of many figures such as the majority of Chaplin's Charlies from his mature period, and the main protagonist (by Vittorio de Sica) of Roberto Rossellini's *Il Generale della Rovere*. Concerning Charlie Chaplin, Conrad Hyers writes: "If ever there was a comic figure that approached universality it was Chaplin's Tramp . . . he was the arch-typical comic hero, grappling with universal human problems . . . In Charlie the whole of the human condition was represented symbolically . . . He touched the heart of the human predicament in a way that was as profoundly wise as it was delightfully humorous" (Hyers 1996, 4–6). Peter Berger too identifies Charlie Chaplin as the paradigm of the tragic-comic in the history of the film, but it is in prose literature that tragicomedy in everyday life is best caught. In European literature, Berger identifies Cervantes' Don Quixote as "the paradigmatic embodiment of the tragicomic hero" (Berger 1997, 119). There are more recent cases, however, such as Sholem Aleichem (1859–1916) and Isaac Bashevis Singer (1904–1991).

46. The "raft parable" occurs in The *Discourse on the Parable of the Water Snake* (*Alagaddūpama Sutta*) in the *Majjhima Nikāya* of the Pāli Canon, *The Middle Length Discourses of the Buddha* (1995). See also the parable in sec. 19 of *Chuang*

Tzu called "Mastering Life" (Wieger 1984) and Wittgenstein's parable of the ladder in the *Tractatus Logico-Philosophicus* (1963).

47. Plato has made laughter itself an ambivalent emotion (*Philebus* 48–50). Since Plato onward, the conflict-mixture theories attempt to explain this mixture of pain and pleasure (Eastman 1972, chap. 5).

48. For irony, see Mueke 1966; Booth 1974; Attardo 2000a, 2000b; Giora 1998.

49. The tension between Nietzsche's critical and positive philosophy is common knowledge in the secondary literature, and is sometimes solved by dividing Nietzsche's thought into periods. See, for example, Magnus and Higgins 1996.

50. For the difficulties inherent in Rosset's view of joy, see Tellez 2009, 135–48.

51. For Nietzsche's view of generosity, see Nietzsche 1954a, I, "On the Gift-Giving Virtue." According to Nietzsche, one can be moved to do things for other people out of a self-sufficient sense of having more than enough, a superabundance, of things. Nietzsche considers this kind of "noble" giving ethically superior to giving based on pity or a sense of obligation. See, among many other places, 1966b, sec. 260, and 1974, sec. 55, and Shapiro 1991.

52. On serenity in the West, see Sorabji 2002; Ballesteros 2000; Liebman 1946. For Eastern views of serenity, see the bibliography mentioned in previous notes.

53. There are many forms of skepticism; because the view presented here considers certainty unattainable, it is skeptical about the claims of metaphysics and religion insofar as they are considered certain. It claims, moreover, that relinquishing one's desires or reason, or both, for unwarranted claims is not necessary. Pyrrhonism is a much more radical and pervasive form of skepticism. For Pyrrhonian skepticism, see Sinnott-Armstrong 2004; for its practice, see Nussbaum 1994, 280–315; for other forms of skepticism, see Popkin 1996; for philosophy from a skeptical perspective that considers certainty unattainable, see Agassi and Meidan 2008.

BIBLIOGRAPHY

WORKS BY SHAFTESBURY

Shaftesbury, Anthony Ashley Cooper. 1981– . *Standard Edition, Complete Works, Selected Letters and Posthumous Writings, in English with German Translations.* Ed. and trans. Wolfram Benda, Gerd Hemmerich, Wolgang Lottes, Erwin Wolff, Friedrich A. Uehlein, Ulrich Schödlbauer. Stuttgart, Frommann-Holzboog. The first volume includes: *The Adept Ladys.* I, i, 376–431.
———. 1963 [1900]. *Characteristics of Men, Manners, Opinions, Times, etc.,* ed. John M. Robertson, two vols. Gloucerster, MA: Peter Smith.

Vol. 1 includes:
A Letter Concerning Enthusiasm to My Lord *****. 1708.
Sensus Communis, an Essay on the Freedom of Wit and Humour. 1709.
Soliloquy, or Advice to an Author. 1710.
An Inquiry Concerning Virtue or Merit. 1899; revised, 1711.

Vol. 2 includes:
The Moralists, a Philosophical Rhapsody. 1709.
Miscellaneous Reflections on the Preceding Treatises, and other Critical Subjects. 1711.

———. 1837. *Characteristics of Men, Manners, Opinions, Times, etc.,* 6th edition, 3 vols, corrected. London: James Purser.
———. 1997 [1751]. Preface. Benjamin Whichcote, *The Works,* vol. 3, i–xiii. Aberdeen: J. Chalmers. Reprinted, New York and London: Garland.
———. 1969 [1914]. *Second Characters or the Language of Forms by the Right Honourable Anthony, Earl of Shaftesbury,* ed. Benjamin Rand. Cambridge: Cambridge University Press. Reprinted New York: Greenwood Press. Includes:

A Letter concerning the Art, or Science of Design. 1732.
A Notion of the Historical Draught or Tablature of the Judgment of Hercules. 1712 French; 1713 English.
The Picture of Cebes, trans. from the Greek.
Plastics, uncompleted notes.

————. 1992 [1900]. *The Life, Unpublished Letters, and Philosophical Regimen of Anthony, Earl of Shaftesbury*, ed. Benjamin Rand. London: Swan Sonnenschein and New York: Macmillan. Reedited, London: Routledge/Thoemmes Press.

————. 1721. *Letters from the Right Honourable the Late Earl of Shaftesbury to Robert Molesworth, Esq.* Ed. John Toland. London.

The Shaftesbury Papers in the Public Record Office in London (P.R.O.) include, among others:

> Askêmata, two notebooks, P.R.O 30/24/27/10. 1698–1712.
> Design of a Socratick History. P.R.O 30/24/27/14. 1703–1707.
> Pathologia sive Explicatio Affectum Humanorum. P.R.O 30/24/26/7. 1706.

————. 1716. *Several Letters Written by a Noble Lord to a Young Man at the University.* London.

1830. *Original Letters of Locke, Algernon Sidney, and Anthony Lord Shaftesbury.* Ed. T. Forster. London.

WORKS BY HAMANN

Hamann, Johann Georg. 1949–1957. *Sämtliche Werke*, historisch-kritische Ausgabe. Vols. I–VI. Ed. Joseph Nadler. Vienna: Herder.

————. 1955–1979. *Briefwechsel.* Vols. I–VII. Eds. Walther Ziesemer and Arthur Henkel. Wiesbaden/Frankfurt: Insel Verlag.

————. 1967. *Hamann's Socratic Memorabilia.* Trans. with Commentary James C. O'Flaherty. Baltimore, MD: Johns Hopkins University Press.

————. 1968. *Sokratische Denkwurdigkeiten und Aesthetica in Nuce.* Stuttgart: Philipp Reclam.

WORKS BY KIERKEGAARD

Kierkegaard, Søren. 1962–1964. *Søren Kierkegaards Samlede Værker.* eds. A. B. Drachmann, J. L. Heiberg, and H. O. Lange, and Peter Rhode, 20 vols, third edition. Copenhagen: Gyldendal.

————. 1978–. *Kierkegaard's Writings*, ed. and trans. Howard V. and Edna H. Hong and others, 26 vols. Princeton, NJ: Princeton University Press.

————. 1909–1948. *Søren Kierkegaard's Papirer*, 1st edition, ed. P. A. Heiberg, V. Kuhr, and E. Torsting, 20 vols. I–XI.3. Copenhagen: Gyldendal. 2nd edition, ed. Niels Thulstrup, photo-offset with two supplemental volumes, I–XIII, 1968–1970.

————. 1967–1978. *Journals and Papers*, ed. and trans. Howard V. Hong and Edna H. Hong. Bloomington and London: Indiana University Press. 7 vols.

————. 1940. *Christian Discourses*, including also *The Lilies of the Field and the Birds of the Air* and *Three Discourses at the Communion on Fridays*. Trans. Walter Lowrie. London and New York: Oxford University Press.

————. 1941. *Concluding Unscientific Postscript*. Trans. David F. Swenson and Walter Lowrie. Princeton, NJ: Princeton University Press.

————. 1943–1946. *Edifying Discourses*. 4 vols. Trans. David F. Swenson and Lillian Marvin Swenson. Minneapolis, MN: Augsburg Publishing House.

————. 1944. *Training in Christianity*. Trans. Walter Lowrie. Princeton, NJ: Princeton University Press.

————. 1962. *The Present Age and of the Difference Between a Genius and an Apostle*. Trans. Alexander Dru. New York, NY: Harper Torchbooks.

————. 1962. *Works of Love*. Trans. Howard V. and Edna H. Hong. New York: Harper and Row.

————. 1966. *The Concept of Irony with Constant Reference to Socrates*. Trans. Lee M. Capel. London: William Collin Sons; Bloomington and London: Indiana University Press.

————. 1968. *For Self-Examination. Judge For Yourself!* Trans. David F. Swenson and Walter Lowrie. Princeton, NJ: Princeton University Press.

————. 1968. *Attack upon "Christendom."* Trans. and introduction by Walter Lowrie. Princeton, NJ: Princeton University Press.

————. 1980. *The Sickness unto Death*. Eds. and trans. Howard V. Hong and Edna H. Hong. Princeton, NJ: Princeton University Press.

————. 1980. *The Concept of Anxiety*. Trans. R. Thomte and Albert B. Anderson. Princeton, NJ: Princeton University Press.

————. 1981. *The Corsair Affair and Articles Related to the Writings*. Eds. and trans. Howard V. Hong and Edna H. Hong. Princeton, NJ: Princeton University Press.

————. 1985. *Fear and Trembling and Repetition*. Trans. Howard V. Hong and Edna H. Hong. Princeton, NJ: Princeton University Press.

————. 1985. *Philosophical Fragments and Johannes Climacus*. Trans. Howard V. Hong and Edna H. Hong. Princeton, NJ: Princeton University Press.

————. 1987. *Either/Or*. 2 vols. Eds. and trans. Howard V. Hong and Edna H. Hong. Princeton, NJ: Princeton University Press.

————. 1988. *Stages on Life's Way*. Trans. Howard V. Hong and Edna H. Hong. Princeton, NJ: Princeton University Press.

————. 1991. *Practice in Christianity*. Eds. and trans. Howard V. Hong and Edna H. Hong. Princeton, NJ: Princeton University Press.

————. 1992. *Concluding Unscientific Postscript*. Eds. and trans. Howard V. Hong and Edna H. Hong. Princeton, NJ: Princeton University Press.

————. 1998. *Armed Neutrality*, and *The Point of View for My Work as an Author*. In *The Point of View*. Eds. and trans. Howard V. Hong and Edna H. Hong. Princeton, NJ: Princeton University Press.

————. 2009. *Concluding Unscientific Postscript to the Philosophical Crumbs*. Ed. and trans. Alastair Hannay. Cambridge: Cambridge University Press.

REFERENCES

Abel, Lionel. 1967. Is There a Tragic Sense of Life? In *Moderns on Tragedy*, ed. with an introduction by Lionel Abel, 175–86. Greenwich, CT: Fawcett.

———, ed. 1967. *Moderns on Tragedy*, ed. with an introduction by Lionel Abel. Greenwich, CT: Fawcett.

Abraham, Karl. 1927 [1924]. A Short History of the Development of the Libido. In *Selected Papers of Karl Abraham*, trans. Douglas Bryan and Alix Strachey. London: Hogarth Press.

Adamsen, Johannes. 2007. Herder: A Silent Background and Reservoir. In *Kierkegaard and His German Contemporaries*, Tome I, *Philosophy*, ed. Jon Stewart, 167–77. Aldershort: Ashgate (*Kierkegaard's Research: Sources, Reception and Resources*, vol. 6).

Addison, Joseph. 1712. Cheerfulness. *Spectator* 393.

Adkin, Neil. 1985. The Fathers on Laughter. *Orpheus* 6/1: 149–52.

Agassi, Joseph, and Ian Jarvie. 2008. *A Critical Rationalist Aesthetics*. Amsterdam and New York: Rodopi.

———, and Abraham Meidan. 2008. *Philosophy from a Skeptical Perspective*. New York, NY: Cambridge University Press.

Akenside, Mark. 1744. *The Pleasures of Imagination*. London.

Aldridge, Alfred Owen. 1945. Shaftesbury and the Test of Truth. *Publications of the Modern Language Association* 60: 129–56.

———. 1951. Shaftesbury and the Deist Manifesto. *Transactions of the American Philosophical Society Held at Philadelphia for Promoting Useful Knowledge* 41: 297–385.

Alexander, William M. 1966. *Johann Georg Hamann: Philosophy and Faith*. The Hague: Martinus Nijhoff.

Alford, Steven E. 1984. *Irony and the Logic of the Romantic Imagination*. New York, NY: Peter Lang.

Allen, Julie K. 2009. Ludvig Holberg: Kierkegaard's Unacknowledged Mentor. In *Kierkegaard and the Renaissance and Modern Traditions*, Tome III, *Literature, Drama and Music*, ed. Jon Stewart, 77–92. Aldershot: Ashgate (*Kierkegaard's Research: Sources, Reception and Resources*, vol. 5).

Allison, Henri E. 1972. Christianity and Nonsense. In *Kierkegaard: A Collection of Critical Essays*, ed. Josiah Thompson, 289–322. Garden City, NY: Doubleday. (Reprinted from *The Review of Metaphysics* 20/3: 432–60).

——. 1990. *Kant's Theory of Freedom*. Cambridge: Cambridge University Press.

Amir, Lydia B. 1984. How to Be Saved from Salvations? Paper presented at the 4th Conference of the International Society for Humor Studies, Tel Aviv, Israel.

——. 1990. Humor, Humiliation and Humility. Paper presented at the 8th Conference of the International Society for Humor Studies, Sheffield, England.

——. 1998. Humor as a Virtue. Paper presented at the 4th International Congress on Philosophical Practice: The Role of Values in the Life of the Individual, Bensberg, Germany.

——. 2000. Humor as a Worldview—a Philosophy for Our Time. Paper presented at the 12th Conference of the International Society for Humor Studies, Osaka, Japan.

——. 2001. Don't Interrupt My Dialogue! In *Thinking through Dialogue*, ed. Trevor Curnow, 239–43. Oxted, Surney: Practical Philosophy Press.

——. 2002. Pride, Humiliation and Humility: Humor as a Virtue. *International Journal of Philosophical Practice* 1/3: 1–22.

——. 2003. Humor within a Philosophic Perspective: A New Approach. Paper presented at the 15th Conference of the International Society for Humor Studies, Chicago.

——. 2004a. Morality, Conflicts and Humor. Paper presented at the 2nd International Congress of Axiology, Wuhan, China.

——. 2004b. The Role of Humor in Self-Education: Handling Moral Conflicts with a Smile. Paper presented at the 7th International Congress of Philosophical Practice, Copenhagen, Denmark.

——. 2009a. Humor and Time. Paper presented at the Time, Transcendence, Performance Conference, Melbourne, Victoria, Australia.

——. 2009b. Rethinking Philosophers' Responsibility. In *Creating a Global Dialogue on Value Inquiry*, eds. Jinfen Yan and David Schrader, 21–56. Lewiston, NY: The Edwin Mellen Press.

——. 2013a. Kierkegaard and the Philosophical Traditions of the Comic. *Kierkegaard Studies Yearbook* 2013: 377–401.

——. 2013b. Philosophy's Attitude towards the Comic—A Reevaluation. *The European Journal of Humor Research* 1/1: 6–21.

——. 2014. Taking the History of Philosophy on Humor and Laughter Seriously. *The Israeli Journal of Humor Research: An International Journal* 5.

Andersen, Albert. 1982. Hamann. In *Kierkegaard's Teachers*, eds. Niels Thulstrup and Marie Mikulová Thulstrup. Copenhagen: C.A. Reitzels (*Bibliotheca Kierkegaardiana*, vol. 10).

Anselment, Raymond. 1979. *Betwixt Jest and Earnest: Marprelate, Milton, Marvell, Swift and the Decorum of Religious Ridicule*. Toronto: University of Toronto Press.

Anz, W. 1971. Philosophie und Glaube bei S. Kierkegaard: Uber die Bedeutung der Existenzdialektik fur die Theologie. In *Søren Kierkegaard*, ed. H. H. Schrey, 179–239. Darmstadt: Wissenschaftliche Buchgesellschaft.

Apte, Mahadev L. 1983. Humor Research, Methodology, and Theory in Anthropology. In *Handbook of Humor Research*, vol. 1: *Basic Issues*, eds. P. E. Mc Ghee and J. H. Goldstein, 183–212. New York, NY: Springer.

Apter, Michael. 1982. *The Experience of Motivation: The Theory of Psychological Reversals*. London: Academic Press.

Aquinas, Thomas. 1972. *Summa Theologiae*. Trans. Thomas Gilby. London: Backfriars.

Arendt, Hannah. 1978. *The Life of the Mind. Vol I: Thinking*. New York, NY: Harcourt, Brace, Jovanovich.

Argyle, Michael. 2001. *The Psychology of Happiness*. Hove, East Sussex: Routledge. 2nd edition.

Aristotle. 1970. *The Rhetoric of Aristotle*. Ed. John Edwin Sandys, commentary Edward Meredith Cope. Hildesheim: G. Olms.

———. 1973. *The Ethics of Aristotle*. Ed. with an introduction and notes by John Burnet. New York, NY: Arno Press.

———. 1987. *Poetics*. Trans. Richard Janko. Indianapolis, IN: Hackett.

———. 2001. *On the Parts of Animals I–IV*. Trans. with an introduction and commentary by James G. Lennox. Oxford and New York: Oxford University Press.

Astell, Mary. 1709. *Bart'lemy Fair, or an Enquiry after Wit*. London: Printed for R.W. Wilkin.

Attardo, Salvatore. 2000a. Irony as Relevant Inappropriateness. *Journal of Pragmatics* 32/6: 793–826.

———. 2000b. Irony Markers and Functions: Towards a Goal-Oriented Theory of Irony and its Processing. *Rask* 12: 3–20.

Augustine, Saint. 1991. *Confessions*. Trans. with an introduction and notes by Henry Chadwick. Oxford: Oxford University Press.

Badelon, Françoise. 2000. Enthousiasme, fanatisme et mélancholie. In *Shaftesbury: Philosophie and Politesse*, eds. Fabienne Brugère et Michel Malherbe, 13–30. Paris: Honoré Champion.

Bakhtin, Mikhail. 1968. *Rabelais and His World*. Trans. Hélène Iswolsky. Cambridge, MA: MIT Press.

———. 1984. *Problems of Dostoevsky's Poetics*. Minneapolis, MN: University of Minnesota Press.

Ball, Martha Chalene. 1979. *Menippean Satire in More's "Utopia" and Erasmus' "Praise of Folly."* Athens, GA: University of Georgia.

Ballesteros, Antonio. 2000. *Historia de la Serenidad: Un Recorrido Poético-Filosófico a Través del Concepto de la Serenidad en Occidente*. Madrid: Oberon.

Barnett, M. A. 1987. Empathy and Related Responses in Children. In *Empathy and its Development*, eds. N. Eisenberg and J. Strayer, 146–62. Cambridge: Cambridge University Press.

Barrett, Lee C. 1990. The Uses and Misuses of the Comic: Reflections on the Corsair Affair. In *International Kierkegaard Commentary: The Corsair Affair*, ed. Richard Perkins, 123–39. Macon, GA: Mercer University Press.

———. 2002. Subjectivity is (Un)truth: Climacus's Dialectically Sharpened Pathos. In *Epistemology and Psychology: Kierkegaard and the Recoil from Freedom*, eds. D. C. Conway and K. E. Gover, 22–34. London and New York: Routledge (*Søren Kierkegaard: Critical Assessment of Leading Philosophers*, vol. 2).

Basu, Samy. 1999a. Dialogic Ethics and the Virtue of Humor. *Journal of Political Philosophy* 7: 378–403.

———. 1999b. "Woe unto You That Laugh Now!" Humor and Toleration in Overton and Shaftesbury. In *Religious Toleration: "The Varieties of Rites" from Cyrus to Defoe*, ed. J. C. Laursen. New York, NY: St. Martin's.

Bataille, Georges. 1943/1973. *Oeuvres complètes*. Paris: Gallimard.

———. 1988. *Inner Experience*. Trans. and with an introduction by Leslie Anne Boldt. Albany, NY: SUNY Press.

Baudelaire, Charles. 1956. *On the Essence of Laughter in the Mirror of Art*. Trans. Jonathan Mayne. Garden City, NY: Doubleday.

———. 1968. De l'essence du rire, et généralement du comique dans les arts plastiques. In *Oeuvres complètes*. Paris: Seuil.

Bauman, Zygmunt. 1991. *Modernity and Ambivalence*. Cambridge, UK: Polity Press.

Baur, Ferdinand Christian. 1837. *Das Christliche des Platonismus oder Sokrates und Christus: Eine religions-philosophische Untersuchung*. Tübingen: Fues.

Bayer, Oswald. 2011. *A Contemporary in Dissent: Johann Georg Hamann as Radical Enlightener*. Trans. Roy A. Harrisville and Mark C. Mattes. Grand Rapids, MI: W. B. Eerdmans.

Bayle, Pierre. 1734. *Dictionaire historique et critique*. Amsterdam: Companie des Libraires.

Beabout, Gregory. 2002. Drawing out the Relationship between Anxiety and Despair in Kierkegaard's Writings. In *Epistemology and Psychology: Kierkegaard and the Recoil from Freedom*, eds. D. C. Conway and K. E. Gover, 35–48. London and New York: Routledge (*Søren Kierkegaard: Critical Assessment of Leading Philosophers*, vol. 2).

Beattie, James. 1776. On Laughter and Ludicrous Composition. In *Essays*, 583–706. Edinburgh: William Creech.

Beck, Andreas Frederik. 1845. *News Repertorium fur die theologosche Literature und kirchlich Statistik*, Berlin, III, 1, April 30, 44–48.

Behler, Ernst. 1990. *Irony and the Discourse of Modernity*. Seattle and London: University of Washington Press.

Beistegui, Miguel de. 2000. Hegel: or the Tragedy of Thinking. In *Philosophy and Tragedy*, eds. Miguel de Beistegui and Simon Sparks, 152–66. London and New York: Routledge.

———, and Simon Sparks, eds. 2000. *Philosophy and Tragedy*. London and New York: Routledge.

Bell, Catherine. 1992. *Ritual Theory/Ritual Practice*. New York, NY: Oxford University Press.

Benda, Frederick Joseph. 1979. *The Tradition of Menippean Satire in Varro, Lucian, Seneca and Erasmus*. Austin, TX: University of Texas Press.

Benda, W. 1982. *Der Philosoph als literarische Künstler: Esoterische und satirische Elementen bei Lord Shaftesbury*. Erlangen-Nürnberg.

Ben-Ze'ev, Aaron. 2000. *The Subtlety of Emotions*. Cambridge, MA: MIT Press.

Berger, Arthur A. 1993. *An Anatomy of Humor*. New Brunswick, NJ: Transaction Publishers.

Berger, Douglas L. 2004. *"The Veil of Māyā": Schopenhauer's System and Early Modern Thought*. Binghamton, NY: Global Academic Publishing.

Berger, Peter L. 1997. *Redeeming Laughter: The Comic Dimension of Human Experience*. Berlin: Walter de Gruyter.

———, and Thomas Luckman. 1967. *The Social Construction of Reality*. New York, NY: Doubleday

Bergson, Henri. 1999 [1911]. *Laughter: An Essay on the Meaning of the Comic*. Trans. C. Brereton and F. Rothwell. Kobenhavn and Los Angeles: Green Integer.

Berkeley, George. 1901 [1732]. *Alciphron; or, The Minute Philosopher*. In *The Works of George Berkeley*, ed. A. C. Fraser. Oxford.

Berlin, Isaiah. 1962. *The Age of Enlightenment: The Eighteenth Century Philosophers*. New York, NY: New American Library.

———. 1994. *The Magus of the North: J. G. Hamann and the Origins of Modern Irrationalism*. Ed. Henry Hardy. London: Fontana Press. Reprinted in Berlin, Isaiah, 2000, *Three Critics of the Enlightenment: Vico, Herder, Hamann*, ed. Henry Hardy, 243–564. Princeton, NJ: Princeton University Press.

———. 1999. *The Roots of Romanticism*. Princeton, NJ: Princeton University Press.

Berlyne, Daniel E. 1972. Humor and Its Kin. In *The Psychology of Humor: Theoretical Perspectives and Empirical Issues*, eds. Jeffrey H. Goldstein and Paul E. McGhee, 43–60. New York, NY: Academic Press.

Billig, Michael. 2005. *Laughter and Ridicule: Towards a Social Critique of Humour*. London: Sage.

Blachowicz, James. 1998. *Of Two Minds: The Nature of Inquiry*. Albany, NY: SUNY Press.

———. 1999. The Dialogue of the Soul with Itself. In *Models of the Self*, eds. Shaun Gallagher and Jonathan Shear, 176–200. Thoverton, Exeter: Imprint Academic.

Blackwell, Kenneth. 1985. *The Spinozistic Ethics of Bertrand Russell*. London and Boston: George Allen and Unwin.

Blanshard, Brand. 1980. Selections from *On Philosophical Style*. In *Philosophical Style: An Anthology about the Writing and Reading of Philosophy*, ed. Berel Lang, 123–43. Chicago, IL: Nelson-Hall.

Bleuler, Eugen. 1952 [1911]. *Dementia praecox*. Trans. Joseph Zinkin. New York, NY: International Universities Press.

Bloom, Harold. 1983. *The Breaking of the Vessels*. Chicago, IL: University of Chicago Press.

Blyth, R. H. 1959. *Oriental Humor*. Tokyo: Hokuseido Press.

————. 1969. Zen Humor. In *Holy Laughter*, ed. Conrad Hyers, 198–207. New York, NY: The Seabury Press.

Booker, Christopher. 2004. *The Seven Basic Plots: Why We Tell Stories*. London: Continuum.

Booth, Wayne C. 1974. *A Rhetoric of Irony*. Chicago, IL: University of Chicago Press.

Borchert, Bruno. 1994. *Mysticism: Its History and Challenge*. York Beach, ME: S. Weiser.

Borowski, L. E., R. B. Jachman and A. C. Wasianki. 1912. *Immanuel Kant: Sein Leben in Darstellungen von Zietgenossen*, ed. Felix Gross. Berlin: DeutscheBibliotek.

Botting, Fred, and Scott Wilson, eds. 1998. *Bataille: A Critical Reader*. Oxford and Malden, MA: Blackwell.

Brett, Richard L. 1951. *The Third Earl of Shaftesbury: A Study in Eighteenth-Century Literary Theory*. London: Hutchinson's University Library.

Brown, John. 1751a. On Ridicule, Considered as a Test of Truth. In *Essays on the Characteristics of the Earl of Shaftesbury*. London: C. Davis.

————. 1751b. An *Essay on Satire Occasioned by the Death of Mr. Pope*. London.

Brugère, Fabienne. 1999. Théorie de l'art et philosophie de la sociabilité selon Shaftesbury. Paris: Honoré Champion.

The Buddha. 1995. *The Middle Length Discourses of the Buddha: A Translation of the Majjhima Nikaya*. Trans. Bhikkhu Nanamoli and Bhikkhu Bodhi. Somerville, MA: Wisdom Publications.

Buckley, Francis H. 2003. *The Morality of Laughter*. Ann Harbor, MI: University of Michigan Press.

Bulkeley, Charles. 1751. *A Vindication of My Lord Shaftesbury: On the Subject of Ridicule*. London.

————. 1752. *Animadversions on Mr. Brown's Three Essays on the Characteristics*. London.

Burgess, Andrew J. 1990. A Word-Experiment on the Category of the Comic. In *International Kierkegaard Commentary: The Corsair Affair*, ed. Robert L. Perkins, 85–121. Macon, GA: Mercer University Press.

Burke, Peter. 1993. *The Art of Conversation*. Ithaca, NY: Cornell University Press.

Burton, Robert. 1989 [1621]. *The Anatomy of Melancholy*. Eds. Thomas C. Faulkner, Nicolas K. Kiessling, Rhonda L. Blair, introduction by J. B. Bamborough. Oxford: Clarendon Press.

Butler, Joseph. 1900. *Analogy of Religion, Natural and Revealed* (1736). In *The Works of Bishop Butler*, ed. J. H. Bernard. 2 vols. London: Macmillan.

Cain, David. 1980. Treasure in Earthen Vessels: Johannes Climacus on Humor and Faith. *Liber Academia Kierkegaardiensis* 7: 67–115.

Campbell, George. 1963 [1776]. *The Philosophy of Rhetoric*. Carbondale, IL: Southern Illinois University Press.

Camus, Albert. 1958. *State of Siege*, in *Caligula and Three Other Plays*. Trans. Stuart Gilbert. New York, NY: Knopf.

————. 1959 [1942]. *The Myth of Sisyphus and Other Essays*. Trans. Justin O'Brian. New York, NY: Vintage Book.

Capel, Lee M. 1968. Introduction. In Søren Kierkegaard, *The Concept of Irony with Constant Reference to* Socrates, trans. Lee M. Capel. Bloomington and London: Indiana University Press.

Carlyle, Thomas. 1827. *Critical and Miscellaneous Essays: Jean Paul Friedrich Richter.* London: Frazer.

Carmody, Denise Lardner, and John Tully Carmody. 1996. *Mysticism: Holiness East and West.* New York, NY: Oxford University Press.

Casati, Ennemond. 1934. Hérauts et Commentateurs de Shaftesbury en France. *Revue de Littérature Comparée* 14.

Cassirer, Ernst. 1953. *The Platonic Renaissance in England.* Trans. James P. Pettegrove. Edinburgh: Thomas Nelson and Sons.

Cazamien, Louis F. 1952. *The Development of English Humor.* Trans. René Guyonnet. Durham, NC: Duke University Press.

Chafe, Wallace. 1987. Humor as a Disabling Mechanism. *American Behavioral Scientist* 30: 16–26.

———. 2007. *The Importance of Not Being Earnest: The Feeling Behind Laughter and Humor.* Amsterdam: John Benjamins.

Chao-Chih, Liao. 2001. *Taiwanese Perceptions of Humor: A Sociolinguistic Perspective.* Taipei: Crane.

Chirpaz, François. 1998. *Le Tragique.* Paris: P.U.F. Que sais-je?

Christie, W. D. 1871. *Life of Anthony Ashley Cooper, First Earl of Shaftesbury.* 2 vols. London.

Cicero. 1945. *Tusculan Disputations.* Trans. J. E. King. Loeb Classical Library. Cambridge, MA: Harvard University Press,

———. 2001a. *On Obligations (De Officiis).* Trans. with introduction and notes by P. G. Walsh. Oxford: University Press.

———. 2001b. *On the Ideal Orator (De Oratore).* Trans. with introduction, notes, appendices, glossary, and indexes James M. May and Jakob Wisse. New York, NY: Oxford University Press.

Cioran. 1973. *De l'inconvénient d'être né.* Paris: Gallimard.

———. 1990. *Sur les cimes du désespoir.* Translated by André Vornic. Paris: L'Herne.

Clarke, Samuel. 1969. *Discourse of Natural Religion.* In *British Moralists 1650–1800,* ed. D. D. Raphael. Oxford: Oxford University Press.

Clooney, Francis X. S. J., and Hugh Nicholson. 2001. To Be Heard and Done, But Never Quite Seen: The Human Condition According to the Vivekacūdāmani. In *The Human Condition: A Volume in the Comparative Religious Ideas Project,* ed. Robert C. Neville, 73–99. Albany, NY: SUNY Press.

Clowes, Edith W. 2007. Groundlessness: Nietzsche and Russian Concepts of Tragic Philosophy. In *Nietzsche and the Rebirth of the Tragic,* ed. Mary Ann Frese Witt, 126–37. Madison, NJ: Fairleigh Dickenson University Press.

Cohen, Hermann. 1912. *Ästhetik des reinen Gefühls.* 2 vols. Berlin: Cassirer.

Cohen, Sheldon, and Thomas A. Wills 1985. Stress, Social Support, and the Buffering Hypothesis. *Psychological Bulletin* 98/2: 310–57.

Cohen, Ted. 1999. *Jokes: Philosophical Thoughts on Joking Matters.* Chicago, IL: University of Chicago Press.

Collins, Anthony. 1729. *Discourse Concerning Ridicule and Irony*. Berlin.

Collins, James. 1983. *The Mind of Kierkegaard*. Princeton, NJ: Princeton University Press.

Comte-Sponville, André. 1993. *Valeur et vérité*. Paris: P.U.F.

Connell, George. 1985. *To Be One Thing: Personal Unity in Kierkegaard's Thought*. Macon, GA: Mercer University Press.

Conway, Daniel C., and K. E. Gover, eds. 2002. *Authorship and Authenticity: Kierkegaard and His Pseudonyms*. London and New York: Routledge (*Søren Kierkegaard: Critical Assessment of Leading Philosophers*, vol. 1).

Cooper, David E. 1996. *World Philosophies: An Historical Introduction*. Oxford and Cambridge, MA: Blackwell.

Cornford, Francis M. 1961 [1914]. *The Origin of Attic Comedy*. Garden City, NY: Doubleday.

Corrigan, Robert W. 1965a. Aristophanic Comedy: The Conscience of a Conservative. In *Comedy: Meaning and Form*, ed. Robert W. Corrigan, 353–62. San Francisco, CA: Chandler Publishing Company.

———, ed. 1965b. *Tragedy: Vision and Form*. Scranton, PA: Chandler Publishing Company.

Corsini, R. J. 1999. *The Dictionary of Psychology*. Philadelphia, PA: Brunner/Mazel.

Cox, Harvey. 1969. *The Feast of Fools*. Cambridge, MA: Harvard University Press.

Critchley, Simon. 1999. Comedy and Finitude: Displacing the Tragic-Heroic Paradigm in Philosophy and Psychoanalysis. *Constellations* 6/1: 108–22.

———. 2002. *On Humour*. London and New York: Routledge.

———. 2003. Is Humor Human? In *Becoming Human: New Perspectives on the Inhuman Condition*, ed. Paul Sheehan, 43–52. Westport, CT and London: Praeger.

Cross, Andrew. 1998. Neither Either Nor Or: The Perils of Reflexive Irony. In *The Cambridge Companion to Kierkegaard*, eds. Alastair Hannay and Gordon D. Marino, 125–53. Cambridge and New York: Cambridge University Press.

Crossan, John Dominic. 1976. *Raid on the Inarticulate: Comic Eschatology in Jesus and Borges*. New York, NY: Harper and Row.

Daly, Mary, and Jane Caputi. 1987. *Webster's First New Intergalactic Wickedary of the English Language*. Boston, MA: Beacon Press.

Daub, Carl. 1838. *Vorlesungen über philosophische Anthropologie*. Berlin: Duncker and Humblut.

Davenport, Manuel M. 1976. Existential Philosophy of Humor. *Southwestern Journal of Philosophy* 7: 169–76.

Davies, Christie. 1990. *Ethnic Humor around the World*. Bloomington and Indianapolis, IN: Indiana University Press.

Davis, Dineh. 2008. Communication and Humor. In *The Primer of Humor Research*, ed. Victor Raskin, 543–69. Berlin and New York: Mouton de Gruyter.

Davis, Jessica Milner. 2003. *Farce*. New Brunswick, NJ: Transaction Publishers.

———. 2011. The Fool and the Path to Spiritual Insight. In *Humour and Religion: Challenges and Ambiguities*, eds. Hans Geybels and Walter van Herck, 218–47. London: Continuum.

Demetrius. 1932. *On Style*. Loeb Classical Library. London: W. Heinemann.

Dennett, Daniel C. 1991. *Consciousness Explained*. Boston, MA: Little, Brown and Company.

———. 1993. *Breaking the Spell: Religion as a Natural Phenomenon*. New York, NY: Viking Press.

Dennis, John. 1939. *The Critical Works of John Dennis*. Ed. Edward Niles Hooker. Baltimore, MD: The Johns Hopkins University Press.

Descartes, René. 1955. *Les Passions de l'Ame*. Introduction and notes by Geneviève Rodis-Lewis. Paris: Librairie philosophique J. Vrin.

Desmond, William. 1993. Being at Loss: Reflections on Philosophy and the Tragic. In *Tragedy and Philosophy*, ed. N. Georgopoulos, 154–86. New York, NY: St. Martin's Press.

Deupmann-Frohues, C. 1999. Komik und Methode. Zu Johann Georg Hamanns Shaftesbury-Rezeption. In *Johann Georg Hamann und England: Hamann und die englischsprachige Aufklärung, Acta des Siebten Internationalen Hamann-Kolloquiums*, ed. Bernhard Gajek, 205–28. Frankfort: Peter Lang.

Deuser, Hermann. 1998. Religious Dialectics and Christology. In *The Cambridge Companion to Kierkegaard*, eds. Alastair Hannay and Gordon D. Marino, 376–96. Cambridge: Cambridge University Press.

Diels, Hermann, and Walther Kranz. 1972. *Die Fragmente der Vorsokratiker*, 16th ed. Dublin and Zurich: Weidman.

Diem, Herman. 1959. *Kierkegaard's Dialectic of Existence*. Trans. Herman Knight. Edinburgh and London: Oliver and Boyd.

Drever, J. 1952/1973. *A Dictionary of Psychology*. Harmondsworth, UK: Penguin.

Dryden, John. 1693. Discourse concerning the Original and Progress of Satire. In *Satires Persius and Juvenal*. London.

———. 1926. *Essays of John Dryden*. Ed. W.P. Ker. 2 vols. Oxford: The Clarendon Press.

Dudley, Donald R. 1937. *A History of Cynicism*. London: Methuen and Company.

Dunning, N. Stephen. 1985. *Kierkegaard's Dialectic of Inwardness: A Structural Analysis of the Theory of Stages*. Princeton NJ: Princeton University Press.

Durkheim, Emile. 1964 [1914]. The Dualism of Human Nature and Its Social Conditions. In *Essays on Sociology and Philosophy*, 325–50. New York, NY: Harper and Row.

Dziemidok, Bohdan. 1993. *The Comical: A Philosophical Analysis*. Trans. Marek Janiak. Dordrecht, The Netherlands: Kluwer.

Eagleton, Terry. 2007. *The Meaning of Life*. Oxford and New York: Oxford University Press.

Eastman, Max. 1972 [1921]. *The Sense of Humor*. New York, NY: Octagon Books.

Eckel, Malcolm D., and John J. Thatamanil. 2001. Beginningless Ignorance: A Buddhist View of the Human Condition. In *The Human Condition: A Volume in the Comparative Religious Ideas Project*, ed. Robert C. Neville, 49–71. Albany, NY: SUNY Press.

Eckardt, Roy A. 1995. *How to Tell God from the Devil: On the Way to Comedy*. New Brunswick, NJ: Transaction Publishers.

Edwards, Mark. 2007. Socrates and the Early Church. In *Socrates from Antiquity to the Enlightenment*, ed. M. B. Trapp, 125–42. Aldershot: Ashgate.

Eisenberg, N., and J. Strayer, eds. 1987. *Empathy and Its Development*. Cambridge: Cambridge University Press.

Ellis, A. 1977. Fun as Psychotherapy. *Rational Living* 12: 2–6.

Elrod, W. John. 1975. *Being and Existence in Kierkegaard's Pseudonymous Works*. Princeton, NJ: Princeton University Press.

———. 1981. *Kierkegaard and Christendom*. Princeton, NJ: Princeton University Press.

Emerson, Ralph W. 1964 [1843]. The Comic. In *Theories of Comedy*, ed. with an introduction by Paul Lauter, 378–87. New York, NY: Doubleday Anchor.

Emmanuel, Steven M. 2002. Reading Kierkegaard. In *Authorship and Authenticity: Kierkegaard and His Pseudonyms*, eds. D. C. Conway and K. E. Gover, 51–70. London and New York: Routledge (*Søren Kierkegaard: Critical Assessment of Leading Philosophers*, vol. 1).

Epictetus. 1926. *The Discourses as Reported by Arrian, The Manual, and Fragments*. Trans. W. O. Oldfather. Loeb Classical Library. London: William Heinemann; New York: G. P. Putnam's Sons.

———. 1937. *The Golden Sayings of Epictetus*. Trans. and arranged by Hastings Crossly. The Harvard Classics, ed. Charles W. Elliot. New York, NY: P. F. Collier and Son.

Erasmus, Desiderius. 1961 [1703–06]. *Opera omnia*, ed. Jean Leclerc. Hildesheim: Georg Olms.

———. 1971. *Praise of Folly (1509)*. In *Praise of Folly and Letter to Martin Dorp 1515*, trans. Betty Radice, with introduction and notes by A. H. T. Levi. London: Penguin.

———. 1991. The Sileni of Alcibiades. In *The Collected Works of Erasmus*. Toronto: University of Toronto Press.

Esslin, Martin. 1961. *The Theatre of the Absurd*. Garden City, NY: Doubleday.

Evans, C. Stephen. 1983. *Kierkegaard's Fragments and Postscript: The Religious Philosophy of Johannes Climacus*. Atlantic Highlands, NJ: Humanities Press International.

———. 1987. Kierkegaard's View of Humor: Must Christians Always Be Solemn? *Faith and Philosophy* 4/2: 176–86.

Eysenck, H. J. 1942. The Appreciation of Humour: An Experimental and Theoretical Study. *British Journal of Psychology* 32: 295–309.

Fedotov, G. P. 1966. *The Russian Religious Mind*. 2 vols. Cambridge, MA: Harvard University Press.

Fenvers, Peter. 1993. *"Chatter": Language and History in Kierkegaard*. Stanford, CA: Stanford University Press.

Ferreira, M. Jamie. 1991. *Transforming Vision: Imagination and Will in Kierkegaardian Faith*. Oxford: Clarendon Press.

Feuerbach, Ludwig. 1834. *Der Schriftsteller und der Mensch*. In *Sämtliche Werke*, eds. Wilhelm Bolin and Friedrich Jodl, 195–6. Stuttgart: Frommann Verlag-G. Holzboog.

Fisher, Seymour, and Rhoda L. Fisher. 1983. Personality and Psychopathology in the Comic. In Handbook of Humor Research, eds. Paul E. McGhee and Jeffrey H. Goldstein, vol. 1, 41–60. New York, NY: Springer.

Fiske, George Converse. 1919. The Plain Style in the Scipionic Circle. Madison, WI: University of Wisconsin Studies in Language and Literature 3.

———. 1920. Lucilius and Horace: A Study in the Classical Theory of Imitation. Madison, WI: University of Wisconsin Studies in Language and Literature 7.

Flugel, J. C. 1954. Humor and Laughter. In Handbook of Social Psychology, ed. G. Lindsey, vol. 2, 709–34. Reading, MA: Addison-Wesley.

Fowler, Edward. 1708. Remarks upon a Letter by a Lord Concerning Enthusiasm. In A Letter to a Gentleman. Not Written in Raillery, Yet in Good Humour. London: W. D. John Wyat.

———. 1709. Reflections upon A Letter Concerning Enthusiasm, to Lord *****. In Another Letter to a Lord. London: H. Clements.

Frankfurt, Harry. 1987. Identification and Wholeheartedness. In Responsibility, Character, and the Emotions: New Essays in Moral Psychology, ed. Ferdinand Shoeman, 34–56. Cambridge: Cambridge University Press.

Freud, Sigmund. 1953–1974. The Standard Edition of the Complete Works of Sigmund Freud, 24 volumes, ed. by James. Strachey et al. London: The Hogart Press and the Institute of Psychoanalysis. [SE]

———. 1909. Notes upon a case of obsessional neurosis. SE, 10: 151–318.

———. 1912–1913. Totem and Taboo. SE, 13: 1–161.

———. 1915. Repression. SE, 14: 143–58.

———. 1921. Group Psychology and the Analysis of the Ego. SE, 18: 67–143.

———. 1926 [1925]. Inhibitions, symptoms, and anxiety. SE, 20: 75–172.

———. 1933 [1932]. New introductory lectures on psycho-analysis. SE, 22: 1–182.

———. 1928 [1927]. Humor. SE, 21: 159–66. International Journal of Psychoanalysis 9: 1–6.

———. 1960 [1905]. Jokes and Their Relation to the Unconscious. Trans. James Strachey. Harmondsworth, UK: Penguin [SE, 8: 8–236].

Freudenburg, Kirk. 1993. The Walking Muse: Horace on the Theory of Satire. Princeton, NJ: Princeton University Press.

Fridja, Nico H. 1986. The Emotions. Cambridge: Cambridge University Press.

———. 2004. The Psychologists' Point of View. In Handbook of Emotions, eds. Michael Lewis, Jeannette M. Haviland-Jones, and Lisa Feldman Barrett, 3rd edition, 68–87. New York, NY: Guilford Press.

Fry, William F. 1987. Humor and Paradox. American Behavioral Scientist 30: 42–71.

———. 1992a. Humor and Chaos. Humor: International Journal of Humor Research 5/3: 219–32.

———. 1992b. The Physiological Effects of Humor, Mirth, and Laughter. Journal of the American Medical Association 267: 1857–58.

———. 1994. The Biology of Humor. Humor: International Journal of Humor Research 7/2: 111–26.

———, and Waleed Salameh, eds. 1987. Handbook of Humor and Psychotherapy. Sarasota, FL: Professional Resource Exchange.

————, and Waleed Salameh, eds. 1993. *Advances in Humor and Psychotherapy.* Sarasota, FL: Professional Resource Exchange.

Frye, Northop. 1964. *The Argument of Comedy.* In *Theories of Comedy,* ed. with an introduction by Paul Lauter, 450–60. New York, NY: Doubleday Anchor.

Gadamer, Hans-Georg. 1989. *Truth and Method.* Second, revised edition. Translation revised by J. Weinsheimer and D. G. Marshall. London: Continuum.

Galle, Rolland. 1993. The Disjunction of the Tragic: Hegel and Nietzsche. In *Tragedy and Philosophy,* ed. N. Georgopoulos, 39–56. New York, NY: St. Martin's Press.

Garber, Frederick, ed. 1988. *Romantic Irony.* New York, NY: Harcourt.

Garff, Joakim. 2002. The Eyes of Argus: The Point of View and Points of View with Respect to Kierkegaard's Activity as an Author. In *Authorship and Authenticity: Kierkegaard and His Pseudonyms,* eds. D. C. Conway and K. E. Gover, 71–96. London and New York: Routledge (*Søren Kierkegaard: Critical Assessment of Leading Philosophers,* vol. 1).

Gashé, Rodolphe. 2000. Self-dissolving Seriousness: On the Comic in the Hegelian Concept of Tragedy. In *Philosophy and Tragedy,* eds. Miguel de Beistegui and Simon Sparks, 38–54. London and New York: Routledge.

Gelven, Michael. 2000. *Truth and the Comedic Art.* Albany, NY: SUNY Press.

Georgopoulos, N., ed. 1993. *Tragedy and Philosophy.* New York, NY: St. Martin's Press.

Gera, Deborah Levine. 2007. Xenophon's Socrateses. In *Socrates from Antiquity to the Enlightenment,* ed. Michael Trapp, 33–50. Aldershot: Ashgate.

Gerard, A. 1963 [1759]. *An Essay on Taste: Together with Observations Concerning the Imitative Nature of Poetry.* 3rd ed. with an introduction by Walter J. Hipple, Jr. Gainesville, Fla.: Scholars' Facsimiles and Reprints.

German, Terence J. 1981. *Hamann on Language and Religion.* Oxford: Oxford University Press.

Giddens, Anthony. 1985. Jürgen Habermas. In *The Return of Grand Theory in the Human Sciences,* ed. Quentin Skinner, 121–39. Cambridge: Cambridge University Press.

Gilhus, Ingvild Saelid. 1991. Religion, Laughter and the Ludicrous. *Religion* 21: 257–77.

————. 1997. *Laughing Gods, Weeping Virgins: Laughter in the History of Religion.* London: Routledge.

Gill, Michael B. 2006. *The British Moralists on Human Nature and the Birth of Secular Ethics.* Cambridge: Cambridge University Press.

Giora, Rachel. 1998. Irony. In *Handbook of Pragmatics,* eds. J. Verschueren, J-O Ostman, J. Blommaert, and C. Bulcaen, 1–21. Amsterdam, Netherlands: Benjamins.

Glenn, John D. 1970. Kierkegaard on the Unity of Comedy and Tragedy. *Tulane Studies in Philosophy* 19: 41–52.

Goethe, Johann Wolfgang von. 1848. *The Autobiography of Goethe.* Trans. John Oxenford. Vol. 1. London.

————. 1887. *Werke*. Sophienausgabe. Weimar.

Goldsmith, Marcella Tarozzi, 1991. *Nonrepresentational Forms of the Comic: Humor, Irony, and Jokes*. New York, NY: Peter Lang.

Goldsmith, Oliver. 1759. The Augustan Age of England. *The Bee* 8 (Nov. 24).

Goldstein, Jeffrey H. 1982. A Laugh a Day: Can Mirth Keep Disease at Bay? *The Sciences* 22/6: 21–5.

Golomb, Jacob. 2002. Kierkegaard's Ironic Ladder to Authentic Faith. In *Authorship and Authenticity: Kierkegaard and His Pseudonyms*, eds. D. C. Conway and K. E. Gover, 97–112. London and New York: Routledge (*Søren Kierkegaard: Critical Assessment of Leading Philosophers*, vol. 1).

Gordon, Paul. 2001. *Tragedy after Nietzsche: Rapturous Superabundance*. Chicago, IL: University of Illinois Press.

Gordon, Walter M. 1990. *Humanist Play and Belief: The Seriocomic Art of Desiderius Erasmus*. Toronto: University of Toronto Press.

Guignon, Charles B. 2005. *On Being Authentic*. London and New York: Routledge.

Gouwens, David J. 1996. *Kierkegaard as Religious Thinker*. Cambridge and New York: Cambridge University Press.

Grant, Mary A. 1924. *The Ancient Rhetorical Theories of the Laughable: The Greek Rhetoricians and Cicero*. Madison, WI: University of Wisconsin Studies in Language and Literature 21.

Grean, Stanley. 1967. *Shaftesbury's Philosophy of Religion and Ethics: A Study in Enthusiasm*. Athens, OH: Ohio University Press.

Green, Ronald M. 1992. *Kierkegaard and Kant: The Hidden Debt*. Albany, NY: SUNY Press.

Greenfield, William. 1809. *Essays on the Sources of the Pleasures Received from Literary Compositions*. London: J. Johnson.

Greenspan, Patricia S. 1980. A Case of Mixed Feelings: Ambivalence and the Logic of Emotion. In *Explaining Emotions*, ed. Amélie Rorty, 223–50. Berkeley, CA: University of California Press.

Gregory, J. C. 1924. *The Nature of Laughter*. London: Kegan Paul.

Gritsch, Eric. 1983. *Martin—God's Court Jester*. Philadelphia, PA: Fortress Press.

Grossman, S., 1977. The Use of Jokes in Psychotherapy. In *It's a Funny Thing, Humour*, eds. Antony J. Chapman and Hugh C. Foot. Oxford: Pergamon.

Grotius, Hugo. 1901. *The Rights of War and Peace, Including the Law of Nature and of Nations*. Trans., notes and illustrations from the Political and Legal Writers A.C. Campbell, introduction by David J. Hill. Washington: M. W. Dunne.

Grotjan, M. 1970. Laughter in Psychotherapy. In *Celebration of Laughter*, ed. W. Mendel. Los Angeles, CA: Mara.

————. 1971. Laughter in Psychotherapy. *International Journal of Group Psychotherapy* 21: 234–8.

Gruner, Charles R. 1997. *The Game of Humor: A Comprehensive Theory of Why We Laugh*. New Brunswick, NJ: Transaction.

Gurewitch, Morton. 1994. *The Ironic Temper and the Comic Imagination*. Detroit, MI: Wayne State University Press.

Gutwirth, Marcel. 1993. *Laughing Matter: An Essay on the Comic*. Ithaca, NY and London: Cornell University Press.

Habermas, Jürgen. 1989. *The Structural Transformation of the Bourgeois Public Sphere*. Trans. Thomas Burger. Cambridge, MA: MIT Press.

Hannay, Alastair. 1982. *Kierkegaard*. London: Routledge and Kegan Paul.

———. 2001. *Kierkegaard: A Biography*. Cambridge and New York: Cambridge University Press.

———. 2003. *Kierkegaard and Philosophy: Selected Essays*. London and New York: Routledge.

Harbsmeier, C. 1989. Humor in Ancient Chinese Philosophy. *Philosophy East and West* 39/3: 289–310.

't Hart, Marjolein, and Dennis Boss, eds. 2007. *Humor and Social Protest*. Special Issue of *The International Review of Social History* 52, supplement S15.

Hartmann, Eduard von. [1887]. *Asthetik*. 2 vols. Leipzig: Haake, n.d.

Haury, Auguste. 1955. *L' Ironie et l'humour chez Ciceron*. Leiden: E. J. Brill.

Hay, Sergia Karen. 2008. Hamann: Sharing Style and Thesis: Kierkegaard's Appropriation of Hamann's Work. In *Kierkegaard and His German Contemporaries*, Tome III, *Literature and Aesthetics*, ed. by Jon Stewart, 97–114. Aldershort: Ashgate (*Kierkegaard's Research: Sources, Reception and Resources*, vol. 6).

Hayman, John. 1968. Raillery in Restoration Satire. *Huntington Library Quarterly* 31/2: 107–22.

———. 1970. Shaftesbury and the Search for a Persona. *Studies in English Literature, 1500–1900*, 10/3: 491–504.

Hegel, Georg Wilhelm Friedrich. 1927. *Sämtliche Werke*. Jubiläumsausgabe in zwanzig Bänden auf Grund des Originaldrucks. Neu herausgegeben von Hermann Glockner. Stuttgart: Fr. Frommanns Verlag H. Kurtz.

———. 1975. *Aesthetics, Lectures on Fine Arts*. 2 vols. Trans. T. M. Knox. Oxford: Clarendon Press.

Heiberg, Johan Ludvig. 1828. *Kjøbenhavns flyvende Post*. Copenhagen.

Heller, Agnes. 2005. *Immortal Comedy: The Comic Phenomenon in Art, Literature, and Life*. Lanham, MD: Lexington Books.

Hendrickson, G. L. 1900. Horace Sermones 1.4: A Protest and a Program. *American Journal of Philology* 21: 121–42.

Hepburn, Ronald W. 1967. Mysticism, Nature and Assessment of. In *The Encyclopedia of Philosophy*, ed. Paul Edwards, vol. 5, 429–34. New York, NY: Macmillan and The Free Press.

Herder, Johann Gottfried von. 1877–1913. *Sämmtliche Werke*, ed. B. Suphan. Berlin: Weidman.

Herzog, T., and B. Bush. 1994. The Prediction of Preference for Sick Humor. *Humor: International Journal of Humor Research* 7/4: 323–40.

———. and J. Karafa. 1998. Preferences for Sick versus Nonsick Humor. *Humor: International Journal of Humor Research* 11/3: 291–312.

Hippocrates. 1990. *Pseudepigraphic Writings*. ed. and trans. Wesley D. Smith. E. J. Brill: Leiden.

Hippolyte, Jean. 1971. Le tragique et le rationel dans la philosophie de Hegel. In *Figures de la pensée philosophique*. Paris: P.U.F.

Hobbes, Thomas. 1839–1845. *English Works of Thomas Hobbes of Malmesbury*. Ed. Sir William Molesworth. London: John Bohn.

———. 1840. Human Nature. In *Works*. London: Molesworth.

Hong, Howard V. 1976. The Comic, Satire, Irony and Humor: Kierkegaardian Reflections. *Midwest Studies in Philosophy* 1: 98–105.

Horace. 1959. *The Satires and Epistles of Horace*. A Modern English verse translation by Smith Palmer Bovie. Chicago, IL: University of Chicago Press.

———. 1989. *Epistles. Book II and Epistles to the Pisones ("Ars poetica")*. Ed. Niall Rudd. New York, NY: Cambridge University Press.

Howland, Jacob. 2006. *Kierkegaard and Socrates*. Cambridge: Cambridge University Press.

Huizinga, Johann. 1955. *Homo Ludens: A Study of the Play-Element in Culture*. Boston, MA: Beacon.

Hume, David. 1975. *David Hume's Enquiries Concerning Human Understanding*. Ed. L.A. Selby-Bigge, 3rd. edition rev. P. H. Nidditch. Oxford: Clarendon Press.

———. 1978. *A Treatise of Human Nature*. Ed. L. A. Selby-Bigge. 2nd edition with text revised and variant readings by P. H. Nidditch. Oxford: Clarendon Press.

———. 1986. *Essays, Moral, Political, and Literary*. Ed. Eugene Miller. Indianapolis, IN: Liberty Classics.

Hurley, Matthew M., Daniel C. Dennett, Reginald B. Adams, Jr. 2011. *Inside Jokes: Using Humor to Reverse-Engineer the Mind*. Cambridge, MA: MIT Press.

Huskinson, Lucy. 2004. *Nietzsche and Jung: The Whole Self in the Union of Opposites*. Hove and New York: Brunner-Routledge.

Hutcheson, Francis. 1725, 1st ed., *Inquiry into the Original of our Ideas of Beauty and Virtue*.

———. 1745. 2nd ed. *Inquiry into the Original of our Ideas of Beauty and Virtue*.

———. 1750. *Reflections upon Laughter, and Remarks upon The Fable of the Bees*. Glasgow.

Hyers, M. Conrad. 1974. *The Laughing Buddha: Zen and the Comic Spirit*. Durando, CO: Longwood Academic.

———. 1981. *The Comic Vision and the Christian Faith: A Celebration of Life and Laughter*. New York, NY: Pilgrim Press.

———. 1987. *And God Created Laughter: The Bible as Divine Comedy*. Atlanta, GA: John Knox Press.

———. 1996. *The Spirituality of Comedy: Comic Heroism in a Tragic World*. New Brunswick, NJ: Transaction.

Hyman, Stanley Edgar. 1965. Psychoanalysis and Tragedy. In *Tragedy: Vision and Form*, ed. Robert W. Corrigan, 287–301. Scranton, PA: Chandler.

Ibbott, Benjamin. 1727. *A Course of Sermons*. London.

Inwood, B., and L. Gerson, eds. 1988. *Hellenistic Philosophy: Introductory Readings*. Indianapolis, IN: Hackett.

Jaffro, Laurent. 1996. Humour et libre pensée: Shaftesbury et le rire du daimôn. *Lumière et Vie* 230: 37–51.

REFERENCES

──────. 1998. *Éthique de la communication et art d'écrire: Shaftesbury et les Lumières anglaises*. Paris: P.U.F.

Jankélévitch, Vladimir. 1964. *L'ironie ou la bonne conscience*. Paris: Flammarion.

──────. 1998. *Philosophie Morale*. Paris: Flammarion.

Jensen, Finn Gredal. 2009. Erasmus of Rotterdam: Kierkegaard's Hints at a Christian Humanist. In *Kierkegaard and the Renaissance and Modern Traditions*, Tome II: *Theology*, ed. Jon Stewart, 111–28. Aldershot: Ashgate (*Kierkegaard Research: Sources, Reception and Resources*, vol. 5).

Johansen, Karsten Friis. 1976. Kierkegaard on "the Tragic." *Danish Yearbook of Philosophy* 13: 105–46.

Johnson, Gregory R. 2002. *Kant on Swedenborg: Dreams of a Spirit-Seer and Other Writings*. Trans. Gregory R. Johnson and Glenn Alexander Magee. West Chester, PA: Swedenborg Foundation.

──────. 2006. The Tree of Melancholy: Kant on Philosophy and Enthusiasm. In *Kant and the New Philosophy of Religion*, eds. Chris L. Firestone and Stephen R. Palmquist, 43–61. Bloomington and Indianapolis, IN: Indiana University Press.

Johnson, Samuel. 1854. *Lives of the Most Eminent English Poets*. London.

Jones, Ernest. 1955. *Sigmund Freud: Life and Work*. 3 vols. London: Hogarth Press.

Joplin, David A. 2000. *Self-Knowledge and the Self*. New York and London: Routledge.

Jørgensen, Sven-Aage. 1968. Postscript. In *Sokratische Denkwurdigkeiten und Aesthetica in Nuce* by J. G. Hamann. Stuttgart: Philipp Reclam.

Joubert, Laurens. 1579. *Cause Morale du Ris, de l'excellent et très renommé Démocrite, expliquée et témoignée par ce divin Hippocras en ses Epîtres*. Paris.

──────. 1560. *Traité du ris, contenant son essence et ses merveilleux effeis, curieusement recherchés, raisonés et observés*. Paris.

Jung, Carl, G. 1951. Aion: Researches into the Phenomenology of the Self. In *Collected Works*, eds. H. Read, M. Foedham, G. Adler and W. McGuire, trans. R. F. C. Hull, 20 vols. London: Routledge and Kegan Paul.

Kaiser, Walter. 1963. *Praisers of Folly: Erasmus, Rabelais, Shakespeare*. Cambridge, MA: Harvard University Press.

Kallen, Horace M. 1968. *Liberty, Laughter and Tears: Reflections on the Relations of Comedy and Tragedy to Human Freedom*. De Kalb, IL: Northern Illinois University Press.

Kames, Lord. 1762. *Elements of Criticism*. Edinburgh.

Kant, Immanuel. 1902–. *Kants gesammelte Schriften*. Berlin: Koniglischen Preussischen Akademie der Wissenschafte.

──────. 1911. *Critique of Aesthetic Judgement*. Trans. with seven introductory essays, notes, and analytical index by James Creed Meredith. Oxford: Clarendon Press.

──────. 1922–1923. *Immanuel Kants Werke*. Ed. Ernst Cassirer. Berlin.

──────. 1929 [1788]. *Critique of Pure Reason*. Trans. Norman Kemp Smith. New York, NY: St. Martin's Press.

──────. 1992–. *The Cambridge Edition of the Works of Immanuel Kant* (German Akademie (Ak) pagination provided in margins). Eds. Paul Guyer and Allen W. Wood. Cambridge: Cambridge University Press.

———. 2006. *Anthropology from a Pragmatic Point of View*. Trans. and ed. R.B. Louden, with an introduction by M. Kuehn. Cambridge: Cambridge University Press.

Kaufmann, Walter. 1962. Introduction. *The Present Age*, by Søren Kierkegaard. Trans. Alexander Dru. New York, NY: Harper and Row.

———. 1969. *Tragedy and Philosophy*. Garden City, NY: Doubleday and Company.

Keith-Speigel, Patricia. 1972. Early Conceptions of Humor: Varieties and Issues. In *The Psychology of Humor: Theoretical Perspectives and Empirical Issues*, eds. Jeffrey H. Goldstein and Paul E. McGhee, 81–100. New York, NY: Academic Press.

Kekes, John. 1995. *Moral Wisdom and Good Lives*. Ithaca, IL: Cornell University Press.

———. 2010. *The Human Condition*. Oxford: Clarendon Press.

Kern, Edith. 1980. *The Absolute Comic*. New York, NY: Columbia University Press.

Kerr, Walter. 1967. *Comedy and Tragedy*. New York, NY: Simon and Schuster.

Kirmmse, Bruce H. 1990. *Kierkegaard in Golden Age Denmark*. Bloomington and Indianapolis, IN: Indiana University Press.

Kitcher, Philip. 2007. *Living with Darwin*. New York, NY: Oxford University Press.

Klein, Lawrence E. 1994. *Shaftesbury and the Culture of Politics*. Cambridge: Cambridge University Press.

———. 1999. Introduction. In Shaftesbury, Anthony, *Characteristics of Men, Manners, Opinions, Times, etc.* Cambridge: Cambridge University Press.

———. 2000. Shaftesbury et l'identité de la philosophie. In *Shaftesbury: Philosophie et Politesse*, eds. Fabienne Brugère et Michel Malherbe, 79–92. Paris: Honoré Champion.

Klein, Melanie. 1975. The Oedipus Complex in the Light of Early Anxieties. In *The Writings of Melanie Klein*. London: Hogarth Press. (Reprinted from *International Journal of Psycho-Analysis*, 1945, 26: 11–33.)

Kleinert, Markus. 2008. Apparent and Hidden Relations between Kierkegaard and Jean-Paul. In *Kierkegaard and His German Contemporaries*, ed. Jon Stewart, Tome III, *Literature and Aesthetics*, 155–70. Aldershot: Ashgate (*Kierkegaard's Research: Sources, Reception and Resources*, vol. 6).

Kline, L.W. 1907. The Psychology of Humor. *American Journal of Psychology* 18: 421–41.

Knox, Norman. 1961. *The Word Irony and Its Context, 1500–1755*. Durham, NC: Duke University Press.

Koestler, Arthur. 1949. *Insight and Outlook*. Lincoln, NE: University of Nebraska Press.

———. 1964. *The Act of Creation*. London: Pan Books.

Kohn, Livia. 2001. The Chinese Religion. In *The Human Condition: A Volume in the Comparative Religious Ideas Project*, ed. Robert C. Neville, 21–46. Albany, NY: SUNY Press.

Koller, Marvin. 1988. *Humor and Society: Explorations in the Sociology of Humor*. Houston, TX: Cap and Gown Press.

Kramer, D. A. 1990. Conceptualizing Wisdom: The Primacy of Affect-Cognition Relations. In *Wisdom: Its Nature, Origin and Development*, ed. R. Sternberg, 317–32. Cambridge: Cambridge University Press.

Krieger, Murray. 1960. *The Tragic Vision*. New York, NY: Holt, Rinehart and Winston.

———. 1963. Tragedy and the Tragic Vision. In *Tragedy: Modern Essays in Criticism*, eds. Laurence Michel and Richard B. Sewall, 130–146. Englewood Cliffs, NJ: Prentice-Hall.

Kuipers, Giselinde. 2008. The Sociology of Humor. In *The Primer of Humor Research*, ed. Victor Raskin, 361–98. Berlin and New York: Mouton de Gruyter.

Kuklick, Bruce. 1977. *The Rise of American Philosophy: Cambridge, Massachusetts, 1860–1930*. New Haven and London: Yale University Press.

Kupperman, Joel. 1991. *Character*. New York, NY: Oxford University Press.

Kuschel, Karl-Josef. 1994. *Laughter: A Theological Reflection*. London: SCM Press.

Kutscher, Arthur. 1951. *Stilkunde der deutschen Dichtung*. 2 vols. Bremen-Horn: Dorn.

Labarrière, Jean-Louis. 2000. Comment et pourquoi la célèbre formule d'Aristotle: 'Le rire est le propre de l'homme,' se trouve-t-elle dans un traité de physiologie (*Partie des Animaux*, III, 10, 673 a 8)? In *Le rire des Grecs: Anthropologie du rire en Grèce ancienne*, ed. Marie-Laurence Desclos, 181–89. Grenoble: Jerome Millon.

Labeo, Notker. 1972–96. De partibus logicae. In *Die Werke Notker des Deutchen*, Neue Ausgabe, eds. Eduard H. Sert and Taylor Starck. Altdeutsche Textbibliothek.

Laertius, Diogenes. 1925. *Lives of Eminent Philosophers*. Trans. R. D. Hicks. Cambridge, MA: Harvard University Press.

Land, Nick. 1990. *The Thirst for Annihilation: Georges Bataille and Virulent Nihilism (an Essay in Atheistic Religion)*. London and New York: Routledge.

Lang, Candace D. 1988. *Irony/Humor: Critical Paradigms*. Baltimore, MD: Johns Hopkins University Press.

Lang, D. B. 1962. On the Biblical Comic. *Judaism* 11: 249–54.

Lange, Frederick Albert. 1925. *The History of Materialism and Critics of Its Present Importance*. 3rd ed. with introduction by Bertrand Russell. New York, NY: Humanities Press.

Langer, Susanne K. 1953. *Feeling and Form*. New York, NY: Scribner's.

———. 1964. The Great Dramatic Forms: The Comic Rhythm, from *Feeling and Form* (1953). In *Theories of Comedy*, ed. with an introduction by Paul Lauter, 497–522. New York, NY: Doubleday Anchor.

Langston, Douglas. 1985. The Comical Kierkegaard. *Journal of Religious Studies* 12/1: 35–45.

Larthomas, Jean-Paul. 1985. *De Shaftesbury a Kant*. Paris: Didier.

———. 1986. Humour et enthusiasme chez Lord Shaftesbury (1671–1713). *Archives de philosophie* 49: 355–73.

Law, David R. 1993. *Kierkegaard as Negative Theologian*. Oxford: Clarendon Press.

Le Goff, Jacques. 1992. Jesus a-t-il ri? *L'histoire* 158: 72–74.

———. 1997. Laughter in the Middle Ages. In *A Cultural History of Humour*, eds. Jan Bremmer and Herman Roodenburg, 40–53. Cambridge: Polity Press.

Leacock, Stephen. 1935. *Humor, Its Theory and Technique*. London: Lane.
———. 1938. *Humor and Humanity*. New York, NY: Henry Holt.
Liebman, Joshua Loth. 1946. *Peace of Mind*. London, Toronto: William Heinemann.
Leibniz, G. W. von. 1875–90. Remarks on the Characteristics. *Die Philosophischen Schriften*, ed. C.J. Gerhardt. Vol. 3. Berlin.
———. 1956. Remarks on the . . . *Characteristics*. In *Philosophical Papers and Letters*, ed. Leroy Loemker. Chicago, IL: University of Chicago Press.
Lessing, Gotthold Ephraim. 1962. *Hamburg Dramaturgy*. New York, NY: Dover Publications.
———. 1999. *Lessings Werke*. Darmstadt: Wissenschaftliche Buchgesellschaft.
Lévi-Strauss, Claude. 1963–1976. *Structural Anthropology*, vols. I–II. New York, NY: Basic Books.
———. 1967. The Story of Asdiwal. In *The Structural Study of Myth and Totemism*, ed. Edmund Leach, 1–47. London: Tavistok.
———. 1969–1980. *Introduction to a Science of Mythology*, vols. I–IV. New York, NY: Harper and Row.
Lewis, Michael. 1992. *Shame*. New York, NY: Free Press.
Lewis, Peter B. 2005. Schopenhauer's Laughter. *Monist* 88/1: 36–51.
Lippitt, John A. 1996. Existential Laughter. *Cogito* 10/1: 63–72.
———. 1997. A Funny Thing Happened to Me on the Way to Salvation: Climacus as Humorist in Kierkegaard's Concluding Unscientific Postscript. *Religious Studies: An International Journal for the Philosophy of Religion* 33/2: 181–202.
———. 1999a. Laughter: A Tool in Moral Perfectionism? In *Nietzsche's Futures*, ed. John A. Lippitt, 99–126. New York, NY: Macmillan/St Martin's.
———. 1999b. Illusion and Satire in Kierkegaard's *Postscript*. *Continental Philosophy Review* 32/4: 451–66.
———. 2000a. On Authority and Revocation: Climacus as Humorist. In *Anthropology and Authority: Essays on Søren Kierkegaard*, eds. Poul Houe, Gordon D. Marino, and Sven Rossel. Amsterdam, Netherlands: Rodopi.
———. 2000b. *Humor and Irony in Kierkegaard's Thought*. New York, NY: Macmillan.
———. 2005. "Is a Sense of Humour a Virtue?" *The Monist* 88: 72–92.
Lipps, Theodor. 1898. *Komic und Humor: Eine psychologish-äesthetische Untersuchung*. Hamburg/Leipzig: Verlag von Leopold Voss.
Livingston, Donald W. 1998. *Philosophical Melancholy and Delirium: Hume's Pathology of Philosophy*. Chicago, IL: The University of Chicago Press.
Locke, John. 1824a. Memoirs of the Life of Earl of Shaftesbury. In *The Works of John Locke*, vol. 8. London.
———. 1824b. *Some Thoughts Concerning Education*. In *The Works of John Locke*. London.
———. 1964 [1690]. *An Essay Concerning Human Understanding*. London: Sage Publications.
———. 1976. *The Correspondence of John Locke*. Ed. E.S. DeBeer. Oxford: Clarendon Press.

Long, Anthony A. 1986. *Hellenistic Philosophies: Stoics, Epicureans, Sceptics*. 2nd edition. Berkeley and Los Angeles, CA: University of California Press.
————. 1996. The Socratic Tradition: Diogenes, Crates, and Hellenistic Ethics. In *The Cynics: The Cynic Movement in Antiquity and Its Legacy*, eds. R. Bracht Branham and M.-O. Goulet-Cazé, 28–46. Berkeley, CA: University of California Press.
————. 2001. *Epictetus: A Stoic and Socratic Guide to Life*. New York, NY: Oxford University Press.
Lorenz, Konrad. 1966. *On Aggression: A Natural History of Evil*. Trans. Marjorie Latzke. London: Methuen.
Lowrie, Walter. 1938. *Kierkegaard*. London: Oxford University Press.
————. 1968a. Introduction to Søren Kierkegaard, *Attack upon "Christendom."* Princeton, NJ: Princeton University Press.
————. 1968b. *Short Life of Kierkegaard*. Princeton, NJ: Princeton University Press.
Luckman, Thomas. 1971. *The Invisible Religion*. New York, NY: The Macmillan Company.
Lund, F. H. 1930. Why Do We Weep? *Journal of Social Psychology* 1: 136–51.
MacHovec, Frank J. 1988. *Humor*. Springfield, IL: Charles C. Thomas.
Mackey, Louis. 1971. *Kierkegaard: A Kind of Poet*. Philadelphia, PA: University of Pennsylvania Press.
————. 1986. *Points of View: Readings of Kierkegaard*. Tallahassee, FL: Florida State University Press.
Magnus, Bernd, and Kathleen M. Higgins. 1996. Introduction. In *The Cambridge Companion to Nietzsche*. Cambridge: Cambridge University Press.
Malantschuk, Gregor. 1971. *Kierkegaard's Thought*. Eds. and trans. Howard V. Hong and Edna H. Hong. Princeton, NJ: Princeton University Press.
————. 2002. Kierkegaard's Dialectical Method. In *Authorship and Authenticity: Kierkegaard and His Pseudonyms*, eds. D. C. Conway and K. E. Gover, 117–65. London and New York: Routledge (*Søren Kierkegaard: Critical Assessment of Leading Philosophers*, vol. 1).
Malherbe, Michel. 2000. Shaftesbury: du style en philosophie. In *Shaftesbury: Philosophie et Politesse*, eds. Fabienne Brugère and Michel Malherbe, 118–34. Paris: Honoré Champion.
Mandel, Oscar. 1963. Tragic Reality. In *Tragedy: Modern Essays in Criticism*, eds. Laurence Michel and Richard B. Sewall, 60–5. Englewood Cliffs, NJ: Prentice-Hall.
Mandeville, Bernard. 1924 [1705]. *The Fable of the Bee, Or, Private Vices, Publick Benefits*. Ed. F.B. Kaye. 2 vols. Oxford: The Clarendon Press.
Manheimer, Ronald J. 1977. *Kierkegaard as Educator*. Berkeley, CA: University of California Press.
Mann, David. 2002. Misanthropy and the Broken Mirror of Narcissism. In *Love and Hate—Psychoanalytic Perspectives*, ed. David Mann, 164–85. Hove, East Sussex: Brunner-Routledge.
Manuel, Frank. 1983. *The Changing of Gods*. Hanover and London: University Press of New England.

Marinoff, Louis. 2007. *The Middle Way: Finding Happiness in a World of Extremes*. New York and London: Sterling.

Marmysz, John. 2003. *Laughing at Nothing: Humor as a Response to Nihilism*. Albany, NY: SUNY.

Marshall, David. 1986. *The Figure of Theatre: Shaftesbury, Defoe, Adam Smith, and George Elliot*. New York, NY: Columbia University Press.

Martensen, Hans Lassen. 1841a. *Fædrelandet*, January 10–12, 398–400: 3210–12.

———. 1841b. *Grundrids til Moral-philosophiens System*. Copenhagen: C.A. Reitzel.

Martin, Bernard. 1969. Introduction. In Lev Shestov, *Dostoevksy, Tolstoy and Nietzsche*. Ohio, OH: Ohio University Press.

Martin, Rod A. 1998. Approaches to the Sense of Humor: A Historical Review. In *The Sense of Humor: Explorations of a Personality Characteristic*, ed. Willibald Ruch, 15–60. Berlin: Mouton de Gruyter.

———. 2000. Humor and Laughter. In *Encyclopedia of Psychology*, ed. A. E. Kazdin, vol. 4. Washington, DC: American Psychological Association. New York, NY: Oxford University Press.

———. 2007. *The Psychology of Humor: An Integrative Approach*. Amsterdam: Elsevier.

———. 2008. Humor and Health. In *The Primer of Humor Research*, ed. Victor Raskin, 479–521. Berlin and New York: Mouton de Gruyter.

———, and Herbert M. Lefcourt. 1983. Sense of Humor as a Moderator of the Relation between Stressors and Moods. *Journal of Personality and Social Psychology* 45: 1313–24.

Maslow, Abraham. 1954. *Motivation and Personality*. New York, NY: Harper and Row.

Mattila, Antti. 2001. *"Seeing Things in a New Light": Reframing in Therapeutic Conversation*. Helsinki: Helsinki University Press.

May, Rollo. 1953. *Man's Search for Himself*. New York, NY: Random House.

McCarthy, Vincent A. 1978. *The Phenomenology of Moods in Kierkegaard*. The Hague/Boston: Martinus Nijhoff.

———. 1982. The Ethics of Irony in Kierkegaard. *Kierkegaardiana* 12: 57–68.

McConnel, T. C. 1988. Interpersonal Moral Conflicts. *American Philosophical Quarterly* 25: 25–35.

McFadden, George. 1982. *Discovering the Comic*. Princeton, NJ: Princeton University Press.

Mead, George Herbert. 1934. *Mind, Self and Society*. Chicago, IL: Chicago University Press.

Ménager, Daniel. 1995. *La Renaissance et le rire*. Paris: P.U.F.

Menon, V. K. 1931. *A Theory of Laughter*. London: G. Allen and Unwin.

Merton, Robert K., 1976. *Sociological Ambivalence and Other Essays*. New York, NY: The Free Press.

Mesnard, Pierre. 1948. *Le vrai visage de Kierkegaard*. Paris: Beauchesne.

———. 1961. Is the Category of the "Tragic" Absent from the Life and Thought of Kierkegaard? In *A Kierkegaard Critique*, eds. Howard A. Johnson and Niels Thulstrup, 103–15. Chicago, IL: Henri Regnery Company.

Michel, Laurence, and Richard B. Sewall. 1963. eds. *Tragedy: Modern Essays in Criticism.* Englewood Cliffs, NJ: Prentice-Hall.

Miller, David L. 1969. *Gods and Games: Toward a Theology of Play.* New York, NY: World Publishing Company.

Miller, William I. 1997. *The Anatomy of Disgust.* Cambridge, MA: Harvard University Press.

———. 2005. *Faking It.* Cambridge: Cambridge University Press.

Minois, Georges. 2000. *Histoire du rire et de la dérision.* Paris: Fayard.

Minsky, M. 1983. Jokes and the Logic of the Cognitive Unconscious. In *Methods and Heuristics,* eds. R. Groner, M. Groner and W. F. Bischof, 171–93. London: Erlbaum.

Monro, D. H. 1951. *Argument of Laughter.* Carlton, Victoria: Melbourne University Press.

Montaigne, Michel de. 1965. *Essais.* Eds. P. Villey and V. Saulnier. Paris: P.U.F.

Montesquieu, Baron de, Charles-Louis de Secondat. 1979. *Pensées diverses.* In *Oeuvres complètes.* 7 vols. Paris: Garnier.

Moody, Raymond A. 1978. *Laugh After Laugh: The Healing Power of Humor.* Jacksonville, FL: Headwaters Press.

Morreall, John. 1983a. *Taking Laughter Seriously.* Albany, NY: SUNY Press.

———. 1983b. Humor and Emotion. *American Philosophical Quarterly* 20: 297–304.

———, ed. 1987. *The Philosophy of Laughter and Humor.* Albany, NY: SUNY Press.

———. 1989a. The Rejection of Humor in Western Thought. *Philosophy East and West* 39/3: 243–66.

———. 1989b. Enjoying Incongruity. *Humor: International Journal of Humor Research* 2/1: 1–18.

———. 1997. *Humor Works.* Amherst, MA: Human Resource Development Press.

———. 1998. The Comic and Tragic Visions of Life. *Humor: International Journal of Humor Research* 11/4: 333–55.

———. 1999. *Tragedy, Comedy and Religion.* Albany, NY: SUNY Press.

———. 2001. Sarcasm, Irony, Wordplay, and Humor in the Hebrew Bible: A Response to Hershey Friedman. *Humor: International Journal of Humor Research* 14/3: 1–9.

———. 2008. Applications of Humor: Health, the Workplace, and Eduction. In *The Primer of Humor Research,* ed. Victor Raskin, 429–78. Berlin and New York: Mouton de Gruyter.

———. 2009. *Comic Relief: A Comprehensive Philosophy of Humor.* Malden, MA: Wiley-Blackwell.

———. 2010. Comic Vices and Comic Virtues. *Humor: International Journal of Humor Research* 23/1: 1–26.

Morris, Corbyn. 1744. *An Essay toward Fixing the True Standard of Wit, Humor, Raillery, Satire, and Ridicule.* London: J. Roberts.

Morris, T. F. 1988. "Humour" in the *Concluding Unscientific Postscript. Heythrop Journal* 29: 300–12.

Mueke, D. C. 1966. *The Compass of Irony.* London: Methuen.

Mulkay, M. 1988. *On Humour*. Cambridge: Polity Press.

Muller, Herbert J. 1956. *The Spirit of Tragedy*. New York, NY: Knopf.

Murray, Donald. 1993. Humour in the Bible? In *Humour and History*, ed. Cameron Keith, 21–40. Oxford: Intellect.

Myers, Henry Alonzon. 1956. *Tragedy: A View of Life*. Ithaca, NY: Cornell University Press.

Nagel, Thomas. 1986. *The View from Nowhere*. New York, NY: Oxford University Press.

———. 1987. The Absurd. In *Life and Meaning: A Reader*, ed. Oswald Hanfling, 49–59. Oxford and New York: Basil Blackwell.

Nerhardt, Goran. 1976. Incongruity and Funniness: Towards a New Descriptive Model. In *Humour and Laughter: Theory, Research, and Applications*, eds. Antony J. Chapman and Hugh C. Foot, 93–116. London: Wiley.

Nezu, A., C. Nezu, and S. Blisset. 1988. Sense of Humor as a Moderator of the Relation between Stressful Events and Psychological Distress: A Prospective Analysis. *Journal of Personality and Social Psychology* 54: 520–25.

Niebuhr, Reinhold. 1969. Humor and Faith. In *Holy Laughter: Essays on Religion in the Comic Perspective*, ed. Conrad Hyers, 134–49. New York, NY: The Seabury Press.

Nietzsche, Friedrich. 1938. *La Volonté de Puissance*. Texte établi par F. Wurzbach; trad. par G. Bianquis. Paris: Gallimard.

———. 1954a. *Thus Spoke Zarathustra*. In *The Portable Nietzsche*, trans. and ed. Walter Kauffman. New York, NY: The Viking Press.

———. 1954b. *Twilight of the Idols*. In *The Portable Nietzsche*, trans. and ed. Walter Kauffman. New York, NY: The Viking Press.

———. 1966a. *The Birth of Tragedy and The Case of Wagner*, trans. Walter Kaufmann. New York, NY: Vintage.

———. 1966b. *Beyond Good and Evil*. Trans. W. Kaufmann. New York, NY: Random House.

———. 1967. *The Genealogy of Morals*. Trans. W. Kaufmann and R. J. Hollingdale. New York, NY: Vintage.

———. 1968. *The Will to Power*. Trans. W. Kaufmann and R. J. Hollingdale. New York, NY: Vintage.

———. 1974. *The Gay Science*. Trans. W. Kaufmann. New York, NY: Random House.

———. 1979. *Ecce Homo: How One Becomes What One Is*. Trans. R. J. Hollingdale. London: Penguin Books.

———. 1982. *Daybreak: Thoughts on the Prejudice of Morality*. Trans. R. J. Hollingdale, intro. M. Tanner. Cambridge: Cambridge University Press.

Nilsen, Alleen Pace, and Don L. F. Nilsen. 2000. Humor and Philosophy. In *Encyclopedia of 20th Century American Humor*. Westport, CT: Greenwood Press.

Nilsen, Don L. F. 1993a. Humor, Aesthetics and Philosophy. In *Humor Scholarship: A Research Bibliography*. Westport, CT: Greenwood Press.

————. 1993b. Humor and Therapy. In *Humor Scholarship: A Research Bibliography*, 11–15. Westport, CT: Greenwood Press

————. 1993c. Irony. In *Humor Scholarship: A Research Bibliography*, 92–97. Westport, CT: Greenwood Press.

Nordentoft, Kresten. 1978. *Kierkegaard's Psychology*. Trans. Bruce H. Kirmmse. Pittsburg, PA: Duquesne University Press.

Norrick, N. R. 1986. A Frame-Theoretical Analysis of Verbal Humor: Bisociation as Schema Conflict. *Semiotica* 60/3–4: 225–45.

Nussbaum, Martha C. 1994. *The Therapy of Desire: Theory and Practice in Hellenistic Ethics*. Princeton, NJ: Princeton University Press.

————. 2001a. *Upheavals of Thoughts: A Theory of Emotions*. Cambridge: Cambridge University Press.

————. 2001b. *The Fragility of Goodness: Luck and Ethics in Greek Tragedy and Philosophy*, revised edition. Cambridge: Cambridge University Press.

O'Connell, W. E. 1976. Freudian Humor: The Eupsychia of Everyday Life. In *Humour and Laughter: Theory, Research, and Applications*, eds. Antony J. Chapman and Hugh C. Foot. London: Wiley.

O'Flaherty, James C. 1966. *Unity and Language: A Study in the Philosophy of Johann Georg Hamann*, with an introductory note by Walter Lowrie. New York, NY: AMS Press.

————. 1967. *Hamann's Socratic Memorabilia: A Translation and Commentary*. Baltimore, MD: Johns Hopkins University Press.

Oberman, Heiko. 1989. *Luther*. New Haven, CT: Yale University Press.

Oden, Thomas C., ed. 2004. *The Humor of Kierkegaard: An Anthology*. Princeton and Oxford: Princeton University Press.

Olesen, Tonny Aagaard. 2003. The Hermeneutics of Humor in the *Postscript*. In *Søren Kierkegaard and the Word(s): Essays on Hermeneutics and Communication*, eds. P. Hone and G. D. Marino, 215–27. Copenhagen: C.A. Reitzel.

————. 2005. The Painless Contradiction: A Note on the Reception of the Theory of the Comic in *Postscript*. *Kierkegaard Studies Yearbook* 2005: 339–50.

Orwoll, L., and M. Perlmutter. 1990. The Study of Wise Persons: Integrating a Personality Perspective. In *Wisdom: Its Nature, Origin and Development*, ed. R. Sternberg, 160–80. Cambridge: Cambridge University Press.

Otani, Masaru. 1980. The Comical. In *Concepts and Alternatives in Kierkegaard*, eds. Niels Thulstrup and Marie Mikulová Thulstrup, 229–35. Copenhagen: C.A. Reitzels (*Bibliotheca Kierkegaardiana*, vol. 3).

Pagels, Elaine, and Karel L. King. 2007. *Reading Judas: The Gospel of Judas and the Shaping of Christianity*. New York, NY: Penguin.

Parfait, Nicole. 2001. *Cioran ou le défi de l'être*. Paris: Desjonqueres.

Parkin, John. 1997. *Humour Theorists of the Twentieth Century*. Lewinston, NY: The Edwin Mellen Press.

Pascal, Blaise. 1941. *Pensées; The Provincial Letters*. "Pensées" translated by W. F. Trotter, "The Provincial Letters" translated by Thomas M'Crie. New York, NY: Modern Library.

Passmore, John. 1970. *The Perfectibility of Man*. London: Duckworth.

Passy, Isaak. 1963. *Tragichnoto*. Sofia.

Pattison, George. 1992. *Kierkegaard: The Aesthetic and the Religious*. London: Macmillan Press.

Perkins, Robert L. 1970. Hegel and Kierkegaard: Two Critics of Romantic Irony. In *Hegel in Comparative Literature*, ed. Frederick G. Weiss. Jamaica, NY: St. John's University Press.

———. 1976. The Categories of Humor and Philosophy. *Midwest Studies in Philosophy* 1: 105–8.

———. 2002. Kierkegaard, a Kind of Epistemologist. In *Epistemology and Psychology: Kierkegaard and the Recoil from Freedom*, eds. D. C. Conway and K. E. Gover, 224–36. London and New York: Routledge (*Søren Kierkegaard: Critical Assessment of Leading Philosophers*, vol. 2).

Philonenko, Alexis. 1998. *La Philosophie du Malheur*. Vol. 1: Chestov et les problèmes de la philosophie existentielle. Paris: J. Vrin.

Piaget, Jean. 1959. *The Language and Thought of the Child*. Trans. Marjorie and Ruth Gabain. New York, NY: Humanities Press.

Pico de la Mirandola, Giovanni. 1965. *On the Dignity of Man, on Being and the One, Heptaplus*. Intro. Paul J. W. Miller, trans. Charles Glenn Wallis, Paul J. W. Miller, Douglas Carmichael. Indianapolis, IN: Bobbs-Merrill Educational.

Pinkus, Karen. 2009. *Alchemical Mercury: A Theory of Ambivalence*. Palo Alto, CA: Stanford University Press.

Plato. 1966. *Works*. In 12 Volumes. Trans. Harold North Fowler, intro. W.R.M. Lamb. Cambridge, MA: Harvard University Press; London: William Heinemann.

Plessner, Helmut. 1970. *Laughing and Crying: A Study of the Limits of Human Behavior*. Trans. James Spencer Churchill and Marjorie Greene, forward by Marjorie Greene. Evanston, IL: Northwestern University Press.

———. 1982. Autobiografische Einfuhrung, Der Mensch als Lebewesen, Das Lacheln. In *Mit anderen Augen. Aspekte einer philosophischen Anthropologie*. Sttutgart: Reclam.

Plutarch. 1967–1984. *Moralia*. Vols. 1–16. Ed. Frank Cole Babitt and trans. Frank Cole Babitt, W. C. Helmbold, Phillip De Lacy, Benedict Einarson, Edwin LeRoy Minar, F. H. Sandbach, Harold North Fowler, and Harold F. Cherniss. Loeb Classical Library. Cambridge, MA: Harvard University Press.

Pojman, Louis P. 1984. *The Logic of Subjectivity: Kierkegaard's Philosophy of Religion*. Alabama, AL: The University of Alabama Press.

———. 1999. *Kierkegaard's Philosophy of Religion*. San Francisco, London and Bethesda: International Scholars Publication.

Polac, Michel, and Clément Rosset. 2003. *Franchise Postale*. Paris: P.U.F.

Polhemus, Robert M. 1980. *Comic Faith: The Great Tradition from Austen to Joyce*. Chicago, IL: University of Chicago Press.

Pollio, Howard R., and John W. Edgerly. 1996. Comedians and Comic Style. In *Humor and Laughter: Theory, Research, and Applications*, eds. Antony J. Chapman and Hugh C. Foot, 215–42. New Brunswick, NJ: Transaction Press.

Poole, Roger. 1993. *Kierkegaard: The Indirect Communication*. Charlottesville and London: University Press of Virginia.

———. 1998. The Unknown Kierkegaard: Twentieth-century Receptions. In *The Cambridge Companion to Kierkegaard*, eds. Alastair Hannay and Gordon D. Marino, 48–75. Cambridge: Cambridge University Press.

———, and Henrick Stangerup, eds. 1989. *The Laughter Is on My Side*. Princeton and Oxford: Princeton University Press.

Pope, Alexander. 1950. *An Essay on Man*. Ed. Maynard Mack. London: Methuen.

Popkin, Richard H. 1951. Kierkegaard and Hume. *The Journal of Religion* 31: 518–23.

———, ed. 1996. *Scepticism in the History of Philosophy*. Dordrecht: Kluwer Academic Publishers.

_____. 2002. Kierkegaard and Scepticism. In *Epistemology and Psychology: Kierkegaard and the Recoil from Freedom*, eds. D. C. Conway and K. E. Gover, 237–56. London and New York: Routledge (*Søren Kierkegaard: Critical Assessment of Leading Philosophers*, vol. 2).

Popper, Karl R. 1959. *The Logic of Scientific Discovery*. London: Hutchinson.

_____. 1961. *The Poverty of Historicism*. London: Routledge and Kegan Paul.

_____. 1962. *The Open Society and Its Enemies*. London: Routledge and Kegan Paul.

_____. 1963. *Conjectures and Refutations*. London: Routledge and Kegan Paul.

_____. 1972. *Objective Knowledge*. Oxford: Oxford University Press.

_____. 1994. *The Myth of the Framework*. London: Routledge.

Potkay, Adam. 2007. *The Story of Joy*. Cambridge: Cambridge University Press.

Preisendanz, Wolfgang. 1963. *Humor als dichterishe Einbildungskraft: Studien zur Erzajlkunt des poetischen Realismus*. Munich: Eidos Verlag.

_____. 1974. Humor. In *Historisches Wörterbuch der Philosophie*, vol. 3, ed. Joachim Ritter, Karlfried Gründer and Gottfried Gabriel. Basel and Stuttgart: Schwabe, columns 1232–34.

Preston, William. 1788. *Essay on Ridicule, Wit and Humour*. Dublin: Transactions of the Royal Irish Academy.

Prince, Michael. 1996. *Philosophical Dialogue in the British Enlightenment: Theology, Aesthetics, and the Novel*. Cambridge: Cambridge University Press.

Prufer, Thomas. 1962. The Philosophical Act. *International Philosophical Quarterly* 2.

Pyper, Hugh S. 1997. Beyond a Joke: Kierkegaard's *Concluding Unscientific Postscript* as a Comic Book. In *International Kierkegaard Commentary*, vol. 12: *Concluding Unscientific Postscript to "Philosophical Fragments,"* ed. Robert L. Perkins, 149–67. Macon, GA: Mercer University Press.

Quero, Dominique. 1995. *Momus philosophe: Recherches sur une figure littéraire du XVIIIe siècle*. Paris: Champion.

Quinn, Philip L. 1998. Kierkegaard's Christian Ethics. In *The Cambridge Companion to Kierkegaard*, eds. Alastair Hannay and Gordon D. Marino, 349–75. Cambridge: Cambridge University Press.

Racamier, Paul-Claude. 1976. L'interprétation psychanalytique des schizophrénies. In *Encyclopédie médico-chirurgicale*. Paris: EMC.

Radday, Y. T., and A. Brenner, eds. 1990. On Humour and the Comic in the Old Testament. Sheffield: JSOT Press.

Rahner, Hugo. 1972. Man at Play. New York, NY: Herder and Herder.

Rajchman, John. 1985. Philosophy in America. In Post-Analytic Philosophy, eds. John Rajchman and Cornel West, ix–xxx. New York, NY: Columbia University Press.

Ramsay, Allan. 1753. An Essay on Ridicule. London: A. Millar.

Rapp, Albert. 1947. Towards an Eclectic and Multilateral Theory of Laughter and Humor. Journal of General Psychology 36: 207–19.

Raskin, Victor. 1992a. Humor and Truth. The World and I (August): 670–2.

———. 1992b. Humor as a Non-bona-fide Mode of Communication. In Proceedings of 1992 Annual Meeting of the Deseret Language and Linguistic Society, ed. Elray L. Pedersen, 87–92. Provo, UT: Brigham Young University.

———. 1992c. Meaning, Truth, and the Sense of Humor. In Selected Proceedings of the Seminar on Humor and Communication. Annual Meeting of Speech Communication Association, eds. Alan Harris and Salvatore Attardo. Chicago, IL: SCA.

———. 1998. The Sense of Humor and the Truth. In The Sense of Humor: Explorations of Personality Characteristic, ed. Willibald Ruch, 95–108. Berlin and New York: Mouton de Gruyter.

Redwood, John. 1976. Reason, Ridicule and Religion: The Age of Enlightenment in England 1650–1750. Cambridge, MA: Harvard University Press.

Reid, Thomas. 1863. Essays on the Intellectual Powers of Man. In The Works of Thomas Reid, D. D., ed. Sir William Hamilton. Edinburgh: Maclachlan and Stewart.

Reines, H. W. 1972. Laughter in Biblical and Rabbinical Literature. Judaism 21: 176–83.

Resnick, I. M. 1987. "Risus monasticus": Laughter and Medieval Monastic Culture. Review Benedictine 97/1: 90–100.

Richter, Jean Paul. 1813. Vorschule der Aesthetik nebst einigen Vorlesungen in Leipzig uber die Parteien der Zeit, 2. verb. und vermehrte Aufl. Stuttgart: J. G. Cotta (1804).

———. 1841. Vorschule der Aesthetic. In Sämmtliche Werke. Berlin: G. Reimer.

———. 1861–62. Sämmtliche Werke. Vermehrte Aufl. Berlin: G. Reimer.

———. 1964. From Introduction to Aesthetics [1804]. In Theories of Comedy, ed. with an introduction by Paul Lauter, 307–14. New York, NY: Doubleday Anchor.

Ricoeur, Paul. 1969. The Symbolism of Evil. Trans. Emerson Buchanan. Boston, MA: Beacon Press.

———. 1974. The Conflict of Interpretations. Evanston, IL: Northwestern University Press.

Ringleben, Joachim. 2006. Søren Kierkegaard as a Reader of Hamann. Kierkegaard Studies Yearbook 2006: 207–18.

Roberts, Robert C. 1987. Smiling with God: Reflections on Christianity and the Psychology of Humor. Faith and Philosophy 4/2: 168–75.

————. 1988. Humor and the Virtues. *Inquiry: An Interdisciplinary Journal of Philosophy* 31: 127–49.

Robertson, John M. 1963. Introduction. In Anthony Shaftesbury, *Characteristics of Men, Manners, Opinions, Times, etc.* Gloucester, MA: Peter Smith.

Robinson, James M, ed. 1990. *The Nag Hamadi Library in English.* 3rd rev. ed., trans. Members of the Coptic Gnostic Literary Project. San Francisco, CA: HarperCollins.

Robinson, Vera. 1977. *Humor and the Health Professions.* Thorofare, NJ: Slack.

————. 1983. Humor and Health. In *Handbook of Humor Research*, eds. Paul E. McGhee and Jeffrey H. Goldstein, vol. 2, 109–28. New York, NY: Springer.

Roche, Mark William. 1998. *Tragedy and Comedy: A Systematic Study and a Critique of Hegel.* Albany, NY: SUNY Press.

Roeckelein, Jon E. 2002. *The Psychology of Humor: A Reference Guide and Annotated Bibliography.* Westport, CT: Greenwood Press.

Ronell, Avital. 2003. *Stupidity.* Urbana and Chicago, IL: University of Illinois Press.

Rosenthal, F. 1956. *Humour in Early Islam.* Philadelphia, PA: University of Pennsylvania Press.

Rosset, Clément. 1967. *Schopenhauer, philosophe de l'absurde.* Paris: P.U.F.

————. 1983. *La Force majeure.* Paris: Minuit.

————. 1991 [1960]. *La Philosophie tragique.* Paris: P.U.F., Quadrige.

————. 1993a. The Overwhelming Force; The Cruelty Principle; Notes on Nietzsche. In *Joyful Cruelty: Toward a Philosophy of the Real*, ed. and trans. David F. Bell. New York, NY: Oxford University Press.

————. 1993b [1971]. *Logique du pire.* Paris: P.U.F., Quadrige.

————. 2001. *Le Régime des passions et autres texts.* Paris: Minuit.

Rowan, John, and Mick Cooper. 1999. *The Plural Self: Multiplicity in Everyday Life.* London: Sage.

Ruch, Willibald. 1993. Exhilaration and Humor. In *The Handbook of Emotions*, eds. Michael Lewis and J. M. Haviland, 605–16. New York, NY: Guilford Publications.

————. 2008. The Psychology of Humor. In *The Primer of Humor Research*, ed. Victor Raskin, 17–100. Berlin and New York: Mouton de Gruyter.

————, ed. 1988. *The Sense of Humor: Explorations of Personality Characteristic.* Berlin and New York: Mouton de Gruyter.

————, and Gabriele Köhler. 1998. A Temperament Approach to Humor. In *The Sense of Humor: Explorations of a Personality Characteristic*, ed. Willibald Ruch, 203–28. Berlin and New York: Mouton de Gruyter.

Rudd, Anthony. 1998. Kierkegaard's Critique of Pure Irony. In *Kierkegaard: The Self in Society*, eds. George Pattison and Steven Shakespear, 82–96. London: Macmillan Press.

Russell, Bertrand. 1917. A Free Man's Worship. In *Mysticism and Logic*, 46–57. London: George Allen and Unwin.

————. 1930. *The Conquest of Happiness.* London: George Allen and Unwin.

————. 1987. *Autobiography.* London: Unwin.

Rycroft, Charles. 1995. *Critical Dictionary of Psychoanalysis.* London: Penguin Books.

Ryle, Gilbert. 1979. *On Thinking*. Totowa, NJ: Rowman and Littlefield.

Sallis, John. 1991. *Crossings: Nietzsche and the Space of Tragedy*. Chicago and London: The University of Chicago Press.

Sanders, Barry. 1995. *Sudden Glory: Laughter as Subversive History*. Boston, MA: Beacon Press.

Sands, Kathleen M. 1994. *Escape from Paradise: Evil and Tragedy in Feminist Theology*. Minneapolis, MN: Augsburg/Fortress Press.

———. 1996. Ifs, Ands, and Butts: Theological Reflections on Humor. *Journal of the American Academy of Religion* 64/3: 499–523.

Santayana, George. 1896. *The Sense of Beauty*. New York, NY: Scribner's.

———. 1920. *Little Essays, Drawn From the Writings of George Santayana by Logan Pearsall Smith, With the Collaboration of the Author*. New York, NY: Scribner's; London: Constable.

———. 1922. *Soliloquies in England and Later Soliloquies*. New York, NY: Scribner's; London: Constable.

———. 1940. *The Realm of Spirit*. New York, NY: Scribner's; London: Constable.

———. 1950. *Atoms of Though: An Anthology of Thoughts from George Santayana*. Selected and edited, with an introduction, by Ira D. Cardiff. New York, NY: Philosophical Library.

———. 1955. *The Letters of George Santayana*. Ed. Daniel Cory. New York, NY: Scribner's; London: Constable.

———. 1980. *Reason in Society*. New York, NY: Dover.

Sarazin, Bernard. 1991. *Le rire et le sacré*. Paris: Desclée de Brouwer.

Sartre, Jean-Paul. 1955. *The Flies*, in *No Exit and Three Other Plays*. Trans. Stuart Gilbert and Lionel Abel. New York, NY: Viking.

———. 1957 [1943]. *Being and Nothingness: An Essay on Phenomenological Ontology*. Translated and with an introduction by Hazel E. Barnes. London: Methuen.

———. 1965. *Existential Psychoanalysis*, trans. Hazel E. Barnes. Chicago, IL: Henry Regnery.

———. 1971. *L'Idiot de la famille: Gustave Flaubert de 1821 à 1857*. 3 tomes (1971– 1972), tome 1. Paris: Gallimard.

Schär, Hans. 1950. *Erlöslungsvortellungen und Ihre Psychologische Aspekte*. Berlin: Rascher.

Scheler, Max. 1963. On the Tragic. In *Tragedy: Modern Essays in Criticism*, eds. Laurence Michel and Richard B. Sewall, 27–44. Englewood Cliffs, NJ: Prentice-Hall.

Schellenberg, J. L. 2007. *The Wisdom to Doubt: Justification of Religious Skepticism*. Cornell, IT: Cornell University Press.

Schiller, Friedrich. 1964. From *On Simple and Sentimental Poetry* [1795]. In *Theories of Comedy*, ed. Paul Lauter, 307–13. New York, NY: Anchor.

Schleiermacher, Friedrich. 1907. *Vertraute Briefe über Friedrich Schlegels Lucinde*. Jena.

Schleifer, Ronald. 1984. Irony and the Literary Past: On *The Concept of Irony* and *The Mill on the Floss*. In *Kierkegaard and Literature: Irony, Repetition, and Criticism*, eds. Ronald Schleifer and Robert Markley, 183–216. Norman, OK: University of Oklahoma Press.

Scholem, Gershom. 1968. Opening Lecture. In *Types of Redemption; Contributions to the Theme of the Study-Conference Held at Jerusalem 14th to 19th July 1968*: (Studies in the History of Religions, XVIII), eds. R. J. Z. Werblowski and C. J. Bleeker, 5–12. Leiden: E. J. Brill.

Schopenhauer, Arthur. 1969. *The World as Will and Idea*. Trans. E. F. J. Payne. 2 vols. New York, NY: Dover.

———. 1974. *Parega and Paralipomena*. Trans. E. F. J. Payne. Oxford: Clarendon Press.

Scott, Nathan A. Jr. 1966. The Broken Center. In *Studies in the Theological Horizon of Modern Literature*. New Haven, CT: Yale University Press.

Scruton, R. 1987. Laughter. In *The Philosophy of Laughter and Humor*, ed. John Morreall, 156–71. Albany, NY: SUNY Press.

Seils, Martin. 1957. *Theologische Aspekte zur gegenwärtigen Hamman-Deutung*. Evangelische Verlagsanstalt.

Seneca, Lucius Annaeus. 1995. *Moral and Political Essays*. Eds. and trans. John M. Cooper and J. R. Procope. Cambridge: Cambridge University Press.

Sewall, Richard B. 1963. Tragic Form. In *Tragedy: Modern Essays in Criticism*, eds. Laurence Michel and Richard B. Sewall, 117–29. Englewood Cliffs, NJ: Prentice-Hall.

———. 1965. The Vision of Tragedy. In *Tragedy: Vision and Form*, ed. Robert W. Corrigan, 34–39. Scranton, PA: Chandler.

Sextus Empiricus. 2000. *Outline of Scepticism*. Eds. Julia Annas and Jonathan Barnes. Cambridge: Cambridge University Press.

Shapiro, Gary. 1991. *Alcyone: Nietzsche on Gifts, Noise and Women*. Albany: SUNY Press.

Sharfstein, Ben-Ami. 1980. *The Philosophers: Their Lives and the Nature of Their Thought*. New York, NY: Oxford University Press.

Sher, Richard B. 1990. Professors of Virtue: The Social History of the Edinburgh Moral Philosophy Chair in the Eighteenth Century. In *Studies in the Philosophy of the Scottish Enlightenment*, ed. M.A. Stewart, 87–126. Oxford: Clarendon Press.

Shestov, Lev. 1969. *Dostoevsky and Nietzsche: The Philosophy of Tragedy*. Trans. Spencer Roberts. In *Dostoevsky, Tolstoy and Nietzsche*, introduction by Bernard Martin. Ohio, OH: Ohio University Press.

Shmuëli, Adi. 1971. *Kierkegaard and Consciousness*. Princeton, NJ: Princeton University Press.

Shultz, T. 1972. The Role of Incongruity and Resolution in Children's Appreciation of Cartoon Humor. *Journal of Experimental Child Psychology* 13: 456–77.

Siegel, L. 1987. *Laughing Matters: Comic Tradition in India*. Chicago and London: University of Chicago Press.

Simon, Alfred. 1989. *Le Monde*, 27 December.

Simon, Richard Keller. 1985. *The Labyrinth of the Comic: Theory and Practice from Fielding to Freud*. Tallahassee, FL: Florida University Press.

Sinnott-Armstrong, Walter, ed. 2004. *Pyrrhonian Skepticism*. Oxford: Oxford University Press.

Smith, Adam. 1976 [1759]. *The Theory of Moral Sentiments*. Eds. D. D. Raphael and A. L. Macfie. Oxford: Oxford University Press.

Smith, Huston. 2001. The Meaning of Life in the World's Religions. In *The Meaning of Life in the World Religions*, eds. Joseph Runzo and Nancy M. Martin, 255–68. Oxford: Oneworld.

Smith, John. 1660. *Excellency and Nobleness of True Religion*. London.

Smith, Richard H. 2008. *Envy: Theory and Research*. Oxford: Oxford University Press.

Smith, Ronald Gregor. 1960a. The Hamann Renaissance. *The Christian Century* LXXVII 26, June 29: 768–60.

———. 1960b. *J. G. Hamann 1730–1788: A Study in Christian Existence, with Selections from His Writings*. London: St. James Place, Collins.

———. 1964. Hamann and Kierkegaard. In *Zeit und Geschiste. Dankesgabe an Rudolf Bultmann zu 80. Geburtstag*, ed. E. Dinzle. Tubingen: J. C. B. Mohr.

Smyth, John Vignaux. 1986. *A Question of Eros: Irony in Sterne, Kierkegaard and Barthes*. Tallahassee, FL: Florida State University Press.

Sokolov, Aleksandr Nikolaevich. 1972. *Inner Speech and Thought*. Trans. G. T. Onischenko, ed. D. B. Lindsley. New York, NY: Plenum.

Solger, Karl W. F. 1962 [1829]. *Vorlesungen über Äethetik*. Darmstadt: Wissenschaftliche Buchgesellschaft.

Solomon, Robert C. 1976. *The Passions: Emotions and the Meaning of Life*. New York, NY: Doubleday.

———. 1999. *The Joy of Philosophy: Thinking Thin versus the Passionate Life*. Oxford and New York: Oxford University Press.

Sorabji, Richard. 2002. *Emotion and Peace of Mind: From Stoic Agitation to Christian Temptation*. Oxford: Oxford University Press.

Sparling, Robert Alan. 2011. *Johann Georg Hamann and the Enlightenment Project*. Toronto: University of Toronto Press.

Speier, Hans. 1998. Wit and Politics: An Essay on Laughter and Power. *Amercian Journal of Sociology* 103/5: 1352–401.

Spencer, Herbert. 1860. *The Physiology of Laughter*. First published in *Macmillan's Magazine*, March 1860.

Spinoza, Benedict. 1951. *A Theologico-Political Treatise and a Political Treatise*. Trans. with an introduction R. H. M. Elwes. New York, NY: Dover.

———. 1985a. Ethics. *The Collected Works of Spinoza*, ed. and trans. Edwin Curley, vol. 1. Princeton, NJ: Princeton University Press.

———. 1985b. Short Treatise on God, Man, and His Well-Being. In *The Collected Works of Spinoza*, ed. and trans. Edwin Curley, vol. 1. Princeton, NJ: Princeton University Press.

Sprigge, T. L. S. 1988. Schopenhauer and Bergson on Laughter. *Comparative Criticism* 10: 39–65.

Stack, George J. 1976. *On Kierkegaard: Philosophical Fragments*. Atlantic Highlands, NJ: Humanities Press.

Stewart, Jon. 2003a. *Kierkegaard's Relations to Hegel Reconsidered*. Cambridge: Cambridge University Press.

———, ed. 2003b. *Kierkegaard and His Contemporaries: The Culture of Golden Age Denmark*. Berlin and New York: Walter de Gruyter.

Steiner, George. 1996. Absolute Tragedy. In *No Passion Spent: Essays, 1978–1996*, 136–37. London: Faber and Faber.

Stobaeus. 1824. *Ioannis Stobaei Florilegium*. Vol. 3. Ed. Thomas Gaisford.

Strabo. 1917–1932. *The Geography*. Trans. Horace Leonard Jones. Based in part upon the unfinished version of John Robert Sitlington Sterrett. Loeb Classical Library. London: W. Heinemann.

Strawser, Michael. 1997. *Both/And: Reading Kierkegaard from Irony to Edification*. New York, NY: Fordham University Press.

Suls, M. Jerry. 1972. A Two Stages Model for the Appreciation of Jokes and Cartoons. In *The Psychology of Humor*, eds. Jeffrey H. Goldstein and Paul F. McGhee, 81–100. New York and London: Academic Press.

———. 1983. Cognitive Processes in Humor Appreciation. In *Handbook of Humor Research*, eds. Paul E. McGhee and Jeffrey H. Goldstein, vol. 1, 39–57. New York, NY: Springer.

Syrkin, Alexander. 1982. On the Behavior of the "Fool for Christ's Sake." *History of Religions* 22/2: 150–71.

Szondi, Peter. 1978. *Schrifen*. Ed. Jean Bollack. Frankfurt am Main: Suhrkamp.

———. 2002. *An Essay on the Tragic*. Trans. Paul Fleming. Palo Alto, CA: Stanford University Press.

Tave, Stuart. 1960. *The Amiable Humorist: A Study in the Comic Theory and Criticism of the Eighteenth and Early Nineteenth Centuries*. Chicago, IL: Chicago University Press.

Taylor, Charles. 1989. *Sources of the Self: The Making of the Modern Identity*. Cambridge, MA: Harvard University Press.

Taylor, Mark C. 1980a. Humor and Humorist. In *Concepts and Alternatives in Kierkegaard*, eds. Niels Thulstrup and Marie Mikulová Thulstrup, 220–28. Copenhagen: C.A. Reitzel (*Bibliotheca Kierkegaardiana*, vol. 3).

———. 1980b. *Journeys to Selfhood: Hegel and Kierkegaard*. Berkeley, CA: University of California Press.

———. 1984. *Erring: A Postmodern A/theology*. Chicago, IL: University of Chicago Press.

———. 2002. The Strategy of the Authorship. In *Authorship and Authenticity: Kierkegaard and His Pseudonyms*, eds. D. C. Conway and K. E. Gover, 250–77. London and New York: Routledge (*Søren Kierkegaard: Critical Assessment of Leading Philosophers*, vol. 1).

Telfer, Elizabeth. 1995. Hutcheson's Reflections upon Laughter. *The Journal of Aesthetics and Art Criticism* 53/4: 361–9.

Tellez, Jean. 2009. *La joie et le tragique: Introduction à la pensée de Clément Rosset*. Paris: Germina.

Theophrastus. 2004. *Characters*. Ed. with introduction, trans. and commentary by James Diggle. Cambridge: Cambridge University Press.

Thiele, Leslie Paul. 1990. *Friedrich Nietzsche and the Politics of the Soul: A Study of Heroic Individualism*. Princeton, NJ: Princeton University Press.

Thompson, Josiah. 1967. *The Lonely Labyrinth: Kierkegaard's Pseudonymous Works.* Carbondale, IL: Southern Illinois Press.

———. 1972. *The Master of Irony.* In *Kierkegaard: A Collection of Critical Essays,* ed. Josiah Thompson. Garden City, NY: Doubleday.

———. 1973. *Kierkegaard.* New York, NY: Alfred A. Knopf.

Thulstrup, Marie Mikulová. 1978. Studies of Pietists, Mystics and Church Fathers. In *Kierkegaard's View of Christianity,* eds. Niels Thulstrup and Marie Mikulová Thulstrup, 61–67. Copenhagen: C.A. Reitzels (*Bibliotheca Kierkegaardiana,* vol. 1).

———. 1980. Suffering. In *Kierkegaard and Human Values,* eds. Niels Thulstrup and Marie Mikulová Thulstrup, 135–62. Copenhagen: C.A. Reitzels (*Bibliotheca Kierkegaardiana,* vol. 7).

Thulstrup, Niels. 1980. *Kierkegaard's Relation to Hegel.* Trans. G. L. Stengren. Princeton, NJ: Princeton University Press.

———, and Marie Mikulová Thulstrup, eds. 1988. *Irony and Humor in Søren Kierkegaard.* Copenhagen: C.A. Reitzels.

Tiffany, Esther. 1923. Shaftesbury as Stoic. *Publications of the Modern Language Association* XXXVIII: 641–84.

Toland, John. 1721. *The Late Earl of Shaftesbury's Letters to the Right Honourable the Lord Molesworth.* 3rd ed. London.

Tucker, Abraham. 1768–1778. *The Light of Nature Pursued.* 7 vols. London.

Tucker, Susie I. 1972. *Enthusiasm: A Study in Semantic Change.* Cambridge: Cambridge University Press.

Unamuno, Miguel de. 1972. *The Tragic Sense of Life in Men and Nations.* Trans. Anthony Kerrigan, introduction by Salvador de Madariaga, afterword by William Barrett. Princeton, NJ: Princeton University Press.

Unger, Rudolf. 1991. *Hamann und die Aufklärung.* 2 vols. Jena.

Valerio, Paola. 2002. Love and Hate: A Fusion of Opposites—A Window to the Soul. In *Love and Hate—Psychoanalytic Perspectives,* ed. David Mann, 251–64. Hove, East Sussex: Brunner-Routledge.

Veatch, Thomas C. 1998. A Theory of Humor. *Humor: International Journal of Humor Research* 11/2: 161–215.

Ventis, W. Larry. 1987. Humor and Laughter in Behavior Therapy. In *Handbook of Humor and Psychotherapy,* eds. William Fry and Waleed Salameh, 149–69. Sarasota, FL: Professional Resource Exchange.

Verdon, Jean. 2001. *Rire au Moyen Age.* Paris: Perrin.

Vlastos, Gregory. 1991. *Socrates: Ironist and Moral Philosopher.* Cambridge: Cambridge University Press.

Voegelin, Eric. 1990. Reason: The Classic Experience. In *Anamnesis,* ed. and trans. Gerhart Niemeyer. Columbia, MI: University of Missouri Press.

Vogt, Katja Maria. 2013. Plato on Madness and the Good Life. In *Mental Disorders in Antiquity,* ed. William Harris. Brill: Leiden, 177–92.

Voitle, Robert. 1984. *The Third Earl of Shaftesbury: 1671–1713.* Baton Rouge and London: Louisiana State University Press.

Volkelt, Johannes Immanuel. 1905–1914. *System der Ästhetik.* 3 vols. Munich: Beck.

Voltaire, François. 1820–22. *Oeuvres complètes*. Nouvelle édition. Paris: Carez, Thomine et Fortic.

———. 1901a. *Philosophical Dictionary*. In *The Works of Voltaire: A Contemporary Version*, a critique and biography by John Morley, notes by Tobias Smollett, trans. William F. Fleming, 42 vols., vol. 3, part 1. New York, NY: E. R. DuMont.

———. 1901b. *Candide*. In *The Works of Voltaire: A Contemporary Version*, a critique and biography by John Morley, notes by Tobias Smollett, trans. William F. Fleming, 42 vols., vol. 1. New York, NY: E. R. DuMont.

———. 1901c. The Henriade. In *The Works of Voltaire: A Contemporary Version*, a critique and biography by John Morley, notes by Tobias Smollett, trans. William F. Fleming, 5–160, 42 vols., vol. 38. New York, NY: E. R. DuMont.

———. 1901d. Preface to the Prodigal. In *The Works of Voltaire: A Contemporary Version*, a critique and biography by John Morley, notes by Tobias Smollett, trans. William F. Fleming, 42 vols., vol. 10. New York, NY: E. R. DuMont.

———. 1989. *Traité sur la tolérance*. Paris: GF-Flamarion.

Vygotsky, Lev Semenovich. 1962. *Thought and Language*. Ed. and trans. Eugenia Hanfmann and Gertrude Vakar. Cambridge: Cambridge University Press.

Wagner, Richard. 1896. Art and Revolution. In *Prose Works*, trans. William Ashton Ellis, 8 vols. vol. 1, 21–65. London: Routledge and Kegan Paul.

Walsh, Sylvia. 1994. *Living Poetically: Kierkegaard's Existential Aesthetics*. University Park, PA: Pennsylvania State University Press.

Warburton, William. 1811. *The Works of the Right Reverend William Warburton, DD*. Ed. Richard Hurd. London.

Ward, Keith. 2001. Religion and the Question of Meaning. In *The Meaning of Life in the World Religions*, eds. Joseph Runzo and Nancy M. Martin, 11–30. Oxford: Oneworld.

Watkin, Julia. 2001. *Historical Dictionary of Kierkegaard's Philosophy*. Lanham, MD: Scarecrow Press.

Weil, Eric. 1967. *Logique de la philosophie*. Paris: Vrin.

Weitz, Morris. 1967. Tragedy. In *The Encyclopedia of Philosophy*, ed. Paul Edwards, vol. 8, 154–61. New York, NY: Macmillan and The Free Press.

Welsford, Enid. 1968. *The Fool: His Social and Literary History*. London: Faber and Faber.

Wessel, Leonard P. 1969. Hamann's Philosophy of Aesthetics: Its Meaning for the Storm and Stress Period. *Journal of Aesthetics and Art Criticism* 27: 433–43.

Weston, Michael. 1994. *Kierkegaard and Modern Continental Philosophy*. London: Routledge.

Westphal, Merold. 1992. Kierkegaard's Teleological Suspension of Religiousness B. In *Foundations of Kierkegaard's Vision of Community*, eds. George B. Connell and C. Stephen Evans. Atlantic Highlands, NJ: Humanities Press International.

———. 1996. *Becoming a Self: A Reading of Kierkegaard's "Concluding Unscientific Postscript."* West Lafayette, IN: Purdue University Press.

———. 1998. Kierkegaard and Hegel. In *The Cambridge Companion to Kierkegaard*, eds. Alastair Hannay and Gordon D. Marino, 101–24. Cambridge: Cambridge University Press.

———. 2002. The Subjective Issue—Truth is Subjectivity. In *Epistemology and Psychology: Kierkegaard and the Recoil from Freedom*, eds. D.C. Conway and K. E. Gover, 295–311. London and New York: Routledge (*Søren Kierkegaard: Critical Assessment of Leading Philosophers*, vol. 2).

Wieger, Leon. 1984. Trans. *Wisdom of the Taoist Masters: The Works of Lao Zi (Lao Tzu), Lie Zie (Lieh Tzu), Zwang Zi (Chuang Tzu)*. Lampeter: Llanerch.

Wieland, Christoph Martin. 1963. *Wielands Briefwechsel*. Berlin: Akademie Verlag.

Wielenberg, Erik J. 2005. *Value and Virtue in a Godless Universe*. Cambridge: Cambridge University Press.

Willeford, William. 1969. *The Fool and His Scepter: A Study in Clowns and Jesters and Their Audience*. London: E. Arnold.

Willey, Basil. 1986. *The Eighteenth Century Background*. London and New York: Ark Edition.

Williams, Bernard. 1973. Ethical Consistency. In *Problems of the Self*, 166–86. Cambridge: Cambridge University Press.

———. 1996. The Women of Trachis: Fictions, Pessimism, Ethics. In *The Greeks and Us*, ed. R. B. Louden and P. Schollmeier, 43–53. Chicago, IL: University of Chicago Press.

Winnicott, D. W. 1949. Hate in the Counter-Transference. *International Journal of Psycho-Analysis* 30: 69–74.

Wispé, L. 1987. History of the Concept of Empathy. In *Empathy and Its Development*, eds. N. Eisenberg and S. Janet, 17–37. Cambridge: Cambridge University Press.

Witt, Mary Ann Frese. ed. 2007. *Nietzsche and the Rebirth of the Tragic*. Madison, NJ: Fairleigh Dickenson University Press.

Wittgenstein, Ludwig. 1963. *Tractatus Logico-Philosophicus*. Frankfurt am Main: Suhrkamp.

Wolf, Richard B. 1988. Shaftesbury's Wit in a *Letter Concerning Enthusiasm*. *Modern Philology* 86: 46–53.

———. 1993. Shaftesbury's Just Measure of Irony. *Studies in English Literature, 1500–1900* 33/3: 565–85.

Wollaston, William. 1969. *Religion of Nature Delineated*. In *British Moralists, 1650–1800*, ed. D. D. Raphael. Oxford: Oxford University Press.

Wong, D. 1984. *Moral Relativity*. Berkeley, CA: University of California Press.

Wood, P. B. 1990. Science and the Pursuit of Virtue in the Aberdeen Enlightenment. In *Studies in the Philosophy of the Scottish Enlightenment*, ed. M.A. Stewart, 127–49. Oxford: Clarendon Press.

Wood, Ralph C. 1988. *The Comedy of Redemption: Christian Faith and Comic Vision in Four American Novelists*. Notre Dame, IN: University of Notre Dame Press.

Woronoff, Jon. 2001. Forward. In Julia Watkin, *Historical Dictionary of Kierkegaard's Philosophy*. Lanham, MD: Scarecrow Press.

Xenophon. 1923. *Xenophon IV: Memorabilia, Oeconomicus, Symposium, Apology*. Trans. E. C. Marchant. Loeb Classical Library. Cambridge, MA: Harvard University Press,

Yovel, Yirmiyahu. 1980. *Kant and the Philosophy of History*. Princeton, NJ: Princeton University Press.

Yovetich, N., J. Dale, and M. Hudak. 1990. Benefits of Humor in Reduction of Threat-Induced Anxiety. *Psychological Reports* 66: 51–8.

Ziolkowski, Eric. 2011. *The Literary Kierkegaard*. Evanston, IL: Northwestern University Press.

Zupančič, Alenka. 2008. *The Odd One In: On Comedy*. Cambridge, MA: MIT Press.

Zwart, Hub. 1996. *Ethical Consensus and the Truth of Laughter: The Structure of Moral Transformations*. Kampen: Kok Pharos.

INDEX

Bayle, Pierre, 14
  acquaintance with Shaftesbury,
    288–89n3
  Dictionary, 288n3
  introducing Spinoza's thought to
    Shaftesbury, 289
  and Shaftesbury's thought, 14, 20, 51
Beabout, Gregory, 310n33
Beattie, James, 3, 244, 296n, 299n,
    310–11n41
  on the association of laughter and
    distress, 244
  discarding the superiority theory of
    humor, 299n91
  distinction between wit and humor,
    296n71
  Elements of Moral Science, 310n41
  *Essay on Laughter and Ludicrous
    Composition*, 310n41
  on the role of humor in moral edu-
    cation, 310–11n41
  and Shaftesbury, 310–11n41
  subsuming superiority under incon-
    gruity, 310n41
Beck, Andreas Frederik, 313n53
Beckett, Samuel, 288
Behler, Ernst, 302
Beistegui, Miguel de, 213, 328n13
Bell, Catherine, 324n105
Benda, Frederick Joseph, 314n60
Benda, W., 18
Ben-Ze'ev, Aaron, 243, 250, 284
  on ambivalence, 250
  on comparison, 284
  on shame and humor, 243
Berdiaev, Nikolai, 327n10
Berens, Christoph, 98
Berger, Arthur A., 227, 231
Berger, Douglas L., 329n34
Berger, Peter L., 226, 327n12
  on humor in Christianity, 199
  on Luther's humor, 323n98
  on the tragic-comic, 330n45
Bergson, Henri, 2, 3, 8, 209, 233, 234,
    235, 287n5, 328n16

  on Freud, 217
  on *homo risibilis*, 262
  on humor, 217, 253
  on irony, 217
  *Laughter: An Essay on the Meaning of
    the Comic*, 193, 217, 219
  positive and normative superiority
    thesis, 193
  on self-ignorance as comical, 149,
    269
  and Shaftesbury, 296n65
Berkeley, George, 3, 12
  Alciphron, or The Minute Philosopher,
    75, 289n6
  on ridicule as the test of truth, 75
Berlin, Isaiah, 303n5
  on Hamann, 89, 90, 303n10
Berlyne, Daniel E., 323n17
Besse, Pierre de, 295n56
Bible, the, 91, 92, 125, 292n27,
    325n107. *See also* the *Gospels*,
    New Testament, *Old Testament*
Billig, Michael, 296n71
Blachowicz, James, 329n27
Blackwell, Kenneth, 255
Blanshard, Brand, 81, 83
Bleuler, Eugen, 249
  on ambivalence, 248
  Zentralblatt, 249
Bloom, Harold, 249
Blyth, R. H., 325n108
Boethius, 262
Bolinbroke, Henri, 293n40
Booker, Christopher, 267–69
Booth, Wayne, 331n48
Borchert, Bruno, 330n39
Borowski, L. E., 301n97
Boss, Dennis, 237
Botting, Fred, 327n11
Brahman, 255
Brett, Richard L., 18, 19, 49, 69,
    292n32
  on the controversy about ridicule,
    13, 299n87
  on Shaftesbury's view of ridicule